FAVORITE AMERICAN PLAYS
of the Nineteenth Century

Favorite
American Plays

of the
Nineteenth Century

EDITED WITH AN INTRODUCTION BY

BARRETT H. CLARK

PRINCETON · NEW JERSEY
PRINCETON UNIVERSITY PRESS

1943

Requests for authorization of the use of any of the plays in this volume, on the stage, the screen, or for radio or television broadcasting, or for any purpose of reproduction, should be addressed as follows: for *Metamora*, to the University of Utah, Salt Lake City, Utah; for *The Heart of Maryland*, to the Century Play Company, 522 Fifth Avenue, New York City; for *My Partner*, to Robert Campbell, Actors Fund of America, 1619 Broadway, New York City; for *Monte Cristo*, to Richard J. Madden Play Co., 515 Madison Ave., New York; for *The Great Diamond Robbery*, to Samuel French, 25 W. 45th St., New York; and for the other plays, to Dramatists Play Service, 6 E. 39th St., New York.

CONTENTS

15249

INTRODUCTION

ERE in a single, compact, low-priced volume I have brought together nine preeminently popular and successful American plays, none of which was published until recently, and then only in the relatively limited units that comprised the twenty volumes of *America's Lost Plays*. To these I have added another, *The Mighty Dollar*, which has never before been printed or published anywhere. This celebrated comedy would have been a part of the *Lost Plays* series if I had been able to clear the publication rights in time, but it was only after plans were completed for the printing of the hundred plays in the series that I was lucky enough to find the present owner and secure from him his ready assent to publication.

In my general preface to the *Lost Plays* I wrote that it was the "result of the first sustained and coordinated effort to rescue a large and representative group of manuscript plays from the public collections of this country, and from the hands of private individuals. A constantly growing interest, not only in the history of the American theater but in its plays—stimulated in recent times largely by the pioneer work of Dr. Arthur Hobson Quinn and the late Montrose J. Moses—had proved to many of us that the study of our native theater revealed much more than exclusively theatrical data: it necessitated and fostered further investigations into our social and political history as a nation.

"We who have collected these hundred plays . . . have sought to bring together an exhibition not only, and perhaps not primarily, of samples of the playwright's craft, but of curious and illuminating criteria of public taste over a period extending from the Revolution down almost to the present day. . . . For the sake of those who would trace the history of native playwriting, or investigate the broader aspects of the cultural development of the American people, the most characteristic examples of our dramatic output are of unquestioned value and interest. That plays of native authorship, until fairly recent times, are not masterpieces . . . is entirely beside the point. If every aspect of the activity of man and its effects on his fellow men deserves our respect and attention, then indeed the American theater is, I believe, quite as important to us as any other characteristic function or activity.

"Our choice of 'lost' plays was determined largely by the importance of the writer himself (hence the occasional presence in these volumes of certain relatively unimportant plays by important writers), and the popularity of the individual play regardless of the author's distinction. It has been our intention in general to bring to light as many manuscripts as we could find that served to show us of today what plays of the past hundred and fifty years, as yet unpublished, were popular in their day, and to extend our knowledge of the work of such writers as were already known to a certain extent. As for the term 'American,' it is used in the broad sense of plays, regardless of authorship, using American themes; plays, regardless of theme, written by residents of the United States or enjoying wide popularity in America; as well as plays of various sorts written by native-born writers, whether actually produced in this country or not."

The editorial scheme I have adopted in preparing the present volume is restricted to one of the two policies followed in the preparation of the entire series. I have chosen only those plays that achieved widespread and lasting popularity, regardless of the author's reputation or significance. The word popularity when applied to the plays I am here reprinting is to be interpreted in a literal sense, and this statement will, I think, carry weight when I say that some of the less popular titles in this book were seen by more theatergoers during their theatrical lifetimes than either *Abie's Irish Rose* or *Tobacco Road*, while the most popular, *Metamora*, enjoyed an almost continuous stage life of nearly forty years, not counting occasional revivals that persisted several years after the death of the star for whom it was written.

The substance of my brief stage histories of the plays here offered I have taken from the prefaces of the *Lost Plays* volumes in which they first appeared, while for the material on *The Mighty Dollar* I am wholly responsible.

Before outlining the short stage histories of the plays in this book I should like to remind the reader that source materials on the American drama and theater are relatively meager, and in only a few cases have exhaustive inquiries been made that enable historians to speak with finality on matters of fact. The critical and historical work of writers on the subject is, until recent times, almost wholly unreliable, useful and entertaining though much of it is; even our latest investigators, trained as they are in the modern techniques of research, have been forced to rely to a considerable extent on such odds and ends of source material as can be got from the old newspapers that happen still to survive. There are important cities in this country where the theater flourished for over a century whose stage history has never been investigated or recorded. During the past twenty-five years, however, several of our colleges and universities have allowed, and in some cases actually encouraged, postgraduate research in American theatrical history. The results of this work have occasionally been published, but the greater part of it is buried in the shape of typed theses and dissertations, or printed in outline or fragmentary form in one of the learned journals. Dr. Quinn, of the University of Pennsylvania, author of our first real attempt to present a consistent account of native dramatic products (*A History of the American Drama From the Beginning to the Civil War*, and *A History of the American Drama From the Civil War to the Present Day*), has for over two decades stimulated his students and others to extend the field of his own inquiries and conquer new territory. To a large extent many of the relatively numerous recently published studies of the native theater are the result of the stimulus given by Dr. Quinn. Among these are Thomas Clark Pollock's *The Philadelphia Theater in the 18th Century*; Reese D. James's *Old Drury of Philadelphia*; and Arthur Herman Wilson's *A History of the Philadelphia Theater 1835 to 1855*, but a good deal of other valuable data on the subject is found in the more specialized work on types of drama and individual dramatists by H. W. Schoenberger, Sculley Bradley, B. W. McCullough, Ralph H. Ware, and John G. Hartman. Outside the sphere of Dr. Quinn's direct influence, and in some cases undertaken before that influence could be felt, are George C. D. Odell's monumental *Annals of the New York Stage*, still in course of publication; Eola Willis's *The Charleston Stage of the 18th Century*; William G. B. Carson's *The Theater of the Frontier*; Joseph S. Schick's *The Early Theater in Eastern Iowa*; Myrtle E. Henderson's *A History of the Theater in Salt Lake City From 1850 to 1870*; Melvin Schoberlin's *From Candles to Footlights*; George R. MacMinn's *The Theater of the Golden Era in California*; and the seventeen substantial volumes on the theater and drama of the West Coast already published under the editorial direction of Laurence Estavan of the Works Project Administration of California.

To this partial list of work accomplished (which could easily be extended) should be added a great deal of unpublished work of equal value and even greater extent.

Yet, as most of the editors of the individual volumes of *America's Lost Plays* readily admit, it has rarely been possible for them to determine the positive authenticity of play texts, or the dates of opening productions, or the length of run, or in some cases the authorship of important plays. The data I offer here, much of it based on the longer and more detailed studies of the editors, shares, therefore, the same occasional uncertainty. The work we have all done in bringing together and commenting on the plays published in our series is only one step in the long process of recording an important part of our national history.

METAMORA

Metamora; or, The Last of the Wampanoags was written by the actor-playwright John Augustus Stone for Edwin Forrest, who had advertised in 1828 that he would pay what was for that time the substantial sum of five hundred dollars for a five-act tragedy of which the "hero, or principal character, shall be an aboriginal of this country." Of the fourteen plays submitted Stone's was adjudged the best. It was first produced at the Park Theater, New York, December 15, 1829. The original cast, as published by Prof. Odell (*Annals of the New York Stage*, vol. iii), follows:

METAMORA	MR. FORREST
LORD FITZARNOLD	MR. RICHINGS
SIR ARTHUR VAUGHAN	MR. CHAPMAN
GUY OF GODALMIN	MR. WOODHULL
HORATIO	MR. BARRY
ERRINGTON	MR. LANGTON
CHURCH	MR. T. PLACIDE
WOLFE	MR. NEXSEN
TRAMP	MR. POVEY
HOLYOKE	MR. WHEATLEY
KANSHINE	MR. BLAKELEY
CHILD	MISS S. PARKER
OCEANA	MRS. HILSON
NAHMEOKEE	MRS. SHARPE

Metamora remained in Forrest's repertory, and was performed during almost every year of Forrest's long and successful career as an actor, a period of nearly forty years. As Eugene R. Page points out in his preface to *Metamora and Other Plays*, there were only two out of twenty-five consecutive seasons in Philadelphia during which the play was not seen there. After Forrest's death it was occasionally revived by other actors, and there is record of a performance as late as 1887. Its latest revival was a radio broadcast of the greater part of the text based on the MS which I found a few years ago. The radio version was played over Station WEAF in New York under the auspices of the National Broadcasting Co. in the summer of 1939, at which time I introduced the performance with a brief history of the recovery of the long-lost MS.

The text in the present volume is reprinted from Volume 14 of *America's Lost Plays*, edited by Eugene R. Page. The original MS I traced by writing to George D. Pyper, author of *The Romance of an Old Playhouse*, who mentioned certain old prompt-books he had found in the Salt Lake Theater. I then communicated with Miss Maud May Babcock, of the University of Utah, who had one of her students go through several old trunks of plays which Mr. Pyper had turned over to the University. During more than fifty years the search for *Metamora* had brought to light only the MS of the role of the leading character. The investigation begun at my suggestion by Miss Babcock's student was successful, and four of the five acts were found. These were copied, under the supervision of Prof. Wallace A. Goates of the State University, and with the help of the local photographers, Hatch and Hatch, a legible copy of the MS was made on microfilm. This MS, together with a copy of the MS of the role of Metamora preserved in the Forrest Home at Holmesburg, Pa., were brought together, analyzed by Mr. Page, and printed, with notes, in Mr. Page's volume. Part of the Forrest Home MS is printed in place of the missing Act IV of the Salt Lake City MS. These two constitute the MS which is reprinted in the present book. It is with the generous help and by permission of Mrs. Randolph S. (L. Ruth Murray) Klein that the Holmesburg MS has been used.

On the occasion of the first performance of *Metamora* in New York a Prologue and an Epilogue were provided. Since neither of these has been printed since they appeared in a privately-published pamphlet over fifty years ago, I am including them in this place. The pamphlet referred to is *Occasional Addresses*, edited by Laurence Hutton and William Carey, and printed in New York by the Dunlap Society in 1890.

PROLOGUE TO "METAMORA"

Dec. 15, 1829

Written by Mr. Prosper M. Wetmore. Spoken by Mrs. Barrett, New Park Theater, New-York.

Not from the records of Imperial Rome,
Or classic Greece—the muses' chosen home—
From no rich legends of the olden day
Our bard hath drawn the story of his play;
Led by the guiding hand of genius on,
He here hath painted Nature on her throne;
His eye hath pierced the forest's shadowy gloom,
And read strange lessons from a nation's tomb:
Brief are the annals of that blighted race—
These halls usurp a monarch's resting-place—
Traditions's mist-enshrouded page alone

Tells that an empire was—we know 'tis gone!
  From foreign climes full oft the muse has brought
Her glorious treasures of gigantic thought;
And here, beneath the witchery of her power,
The eye hath poured its tributary shower:
When modern pens have sought th'historic page,
To picture forth the deeds of former age—
O'er soft Virginia's sorrows ye have sighed,
And dropt a tear when spotless beauty died;
When Brutus "cast his cloud aside"; to stand
The guardian of the tyrant-trampled land—
When patriot Tell his clime from thraldom freed,
And bade th'avenging arrow do its deed,
Your bosoms answered with responsive swell,
For freedom triumphed when th'oppressors fell!
  These were the melodies of humbler lyres,
The lights of Genius, yet without his fires;
But when the master-spirit struck the chords,
And inspiration breathed her burning words—
When passion's self stalked living o'er the stage,
To plead with love, or rouse the soul to rage—
When Shakespeare led his bright creations forth,
And conjured up the mighty dead from earth—
Breathless—entranced—ye've listened to the line,
And felt the minstrel's power, all but divine!
  While thus your plaudits cheer the stranger lay,
Shall native pens in vain the field essay?
To-night we test the strength of native powers,
Subject, and bard, and actor, all are ours—
'Tis yours to judge, if worthy of a name,
And bid them live within the halls of fame!

Epilogue to "Metamora"

Dec. 15,   *Written by Mr. James Lawson. Spoken*
1829   *by Mrs. Hilson, New Park Theater,*
                 New-York.

Before this bar of beauty, taste, and wit,
This host of critics, too, who throng the pit,
A trembling bard has been this night arraigned;

And I am counsel in the cause retained.
Here come I, then, to plead with nature's art,
And speak, less to the law, than to the heart.
   A native bard—a native actor too,
Have drawn a native picture to your view;
In fancy, this bade Indian wrongs arise,
While that embodied all before your eyes;
Inspired by genius, and by judgment led,
Again the Wampanoag fought and bled;
Rich plants are both of our own fruitful land,
Your smiles the sun that made their leaves expand;
Yet, not that they are native do I plead,
'Tis for their worth alone I ask your meed.
How shall I ask ye? Singly? Then I will—
But should I fail? Fail! I must try my skill.
   Sir, I know you—I've often seen your face,
And always seated in that selfsame place;
Now, in my ear—what think you of our play?
That it has merit truly, he did say;
And that the hero, prop'd on genius' wing,
The Indian forest scoured, like Indian king!
   See that fair maid, the tear still in her eye,
And hark! hear not you now that gentle sigh?
Ah! these speak more than language could relate,
The woe-fraught heart o'er Nahmeokee's fate;
She scans us not by rigid rules of art,
Her test is feeling, and her judge the heart.
   What dost thou say, thou bushy-whiskered beau?
He nods approval—whiskers are the go.
   Who is he sits the fourth bench from the stage?
There; in the pit!—why he looks wondrous sage!
He seems displeased, his lip denotes a sneer—
O! he's a critic that looks so severe!
Why, in his face I see the attic salt—
A critic's merit is to find a fault.
What fault find you, sir? eh! or you, sir? None!
Then, if the critic's mute, my cause is won.
Yea, by that burst of loud heartfelt applause,

I feel that I have gained my client's cause.
Thanks, that our strong demerits you forgive,
And bid our bard and Metamora live.

FLYING SCUD

Flying Scud; Or, A Four-Legged Fortune, is the work of the celebrated and highly successful Dion Boucicault. It opened at the Holborn Theater, London, October 6, 1866, and the first American performance was at Wallack's Theater, New York, April 24, 1867. Following is the original cast as given in Brown's *A History of the New York Stage:*

TOM MEREDITH	FREDERIC ROBINSON
CAPT. GRINDLEY GOODGE	B. T. RINGGOLD
COLONEL MULLIGAN	W. H. NORTON
BOB BUCKSKIN	J. C. WILLIAMSON
FRED LANAGHAN	MISS TALFOURD
JULIA LATIMER	CLARA JENNINGS
LADY WOODBIE	MRS. JOHN SEFTON
SAM WOBBLER	JOSEPH CURRAN
MO DAVIS	CHARLES FISHER
NAT GOSLING	A. W. YOUNG
LORD WOODBIE	MARY BARRETT
QUAIL	G. F. BROWNE
CHOUSER	W. J. LEONARD
DORLING	MR. GRAHAM
TITTUMS	MR. WARD
JENKINS	W. H. POPE
BAILIFF	MR. ROBERTS
DICKY BRUSH	E. CASHIN
NEB COMPO	FANNY GREEN
HARRY STOFEL	MISS SCOTT
JIM TITLER	MISS DAY
HALL HOFFER	MRS. M. TIMONY
TOM BUTLER	MISS WILLIAMS
JACK LYLE	MISS CLARK
JOE HIRAM	MISS TIMONY
JERRY LEMON	MISS GRAHAM
TONY GRIMSHAW	MISS THOMAS
KATEY RIDEOUT	AGNES ELLIOTT

Both the London and the New York productions were highly successful. In the United States the play was constantly revived, and toured extensively throughout the country. Available records show that it was popular for at least twelve years after the first New York performance, and it remained on the active stock lists of several leasing agents until the end of the Century. It is also significant that before I saw the authentic MS I had read two other MSS bearing the same title but having little similarity to the Boucicault play. To Cyril Hogg, director of Samuel French, Ltd., of London, I am indebted for the MS which he found in the archives of his office; inasmuch as his firm published practically all the Boucicault plays that have ever been printed, the text he sent me is, he states, the actual author's MS or one that was approved by him. Its authenticity has been further established by Dr. Allardyce Nicoll who, with F. Theodore Cloak, first edited the play in Volume 1 of the *America's Lost Plays* series, under the title *Forbidden Fruit and Other Plays*.

The latest revival, to my knowledge, was a radio broadcast of the present MS which I arranged for and introduced over the air in the summer of 1939. This was over Station WEAF, National Broadcasting Co.

DAVY CROCKETT

Davy Crockett; Or, Be Sure You're Right, Then Go Ahead, was written by Frank Hitchcock Murdoch. At least he wrote the original MS, but after the unsuccessful opening production the actor Frank Mayo did a good deal of revision on it. Just what he did we have no means of determining, but we do know that as a rule starring actors who bought "vehicles" from playwrights, as well as many who did not buy them, often revised and rewrote their scripts, and went on doing so for years. I have seen three MSS of *Davy Crockett*, each varying considerably from the other. One of two such MSS I had decided would go into the *Lost Plays* series, when Dr. Quinn called my attention to a MS in his possession, which he had got from a member of the Mayo family. This, in Dr. Quinn's expert opinion, was a fuller and obviously better text than either of those I owned. By permission of Dr. Quinn, the editors, Dr. Isaac Goldberg and Prof. Hubert Heffner, were enabled to print this text in Volume 4 of *America's Lost Plays*, under the title *Davy Crockett and Other Plays*.

Davy Crockett opened at the Opera House in Rochester September 23, 1872. "This original production," according to Prof. Heffner, "was by no means a success, but Mayo believed in the play and continued to work over the script. From time to time he tried it out on other audiences as he toured from place to place. On February 24, 1873, Mayo brought the piece to the Park Theater in Brooklyn, and played it with the regular Park Theater company."

When at last *Davy Crockett* came to New York, Mayo was evidently satisfied with the text and the production. He, of course, played the leading role. It was first performed in New York at Wood's Museum June 2, 1873, with the following cast:

DAVY CROCKETT	MR. FRANK MAYO
ELEANOR VAUGHN	MISS ROSA RAND
MAJOR HECTOR ROYSTON	MR. T. W. KEENE
OSCAR CRAMPTON	MR. J. J. WALLACE
NEIL CRAMPTON	MR. HARRY STEWART
YONKERS ⎫	⎧ MR. CHARLES STURGES
BIG DAN ⎬ Hunters	⎨ MR. C. M. MANLEY
BRIGGS ⎭	⎩ MR. R. J. LEWIS
QUICKWITCH	MR. L. R. WILLARD
WATSON	MR. G. C. CHARLES
PARSON AINSWORTH	MR. WELSH EDWARDS
LITTLE BOB CROCKETT	MISS AGGIE KEENE
LITTLE SALLY	MISS MARY PAGE
DAME CROCKETT	MRS. D. B. VAN DEREN
LITTLE NELLY	LITTLE KITTIE

From that time onward the play toured the country, year after year, and was closely associated with the star actor who had "created" the part of Crockett. It was likewise seen in England when in 1879 Mayo played it, beginning in June of that year, in Liverpool. Until the day of Mayo's death in 1896, it was a popular favorite throughout the land.

MONTE CRISTO

The authorship of the so-called James O'Neill Version of *Monte Cristo* could, according to the standards of nineteenth century theater practice, with entire propriety be attributed solely to the famous actor who made the play his own in more senses than one. The history of the O'Neill *Monte Cristo* is long and interesting, and a good deal of it is related by Mr. J. B. Russak in his preface to Volume 16 of *America's Lost Plays*, entitled *Monte Cristo ...and Other Plays*. To Mr. Russak I am indebted for most of the material I am here summarizing. Alexandre Dumas' famous novel *The Count of*

Monte Cristo first appeared in Paris in 1845. It was turned into a play by the author under the title *Monte Cristo*, in 1848. The play was in 20 acts, 37 tableaux, and 221 (French) scenes. It failed in the theater. In 1868 Benjamin Webster secured the English rights of production in an adaptation made by the actor Charles Fechter. Performed the same year in London, this play likewise failed. Meantime another dramatization had been acted and published. As early as 1848 still another drama on the same subject had been produced, by Lester Wallack, in New York, where it had something of a run. About 1870 Fechter made further revisions in the version of the play acquired and produced by Webster, collaborating for that purpose with Arthur Leclercq. This version was first performed at the Globe Theater, Boston, in September of 1870. In 1873 the same verison (doubtless again revised) opened at the Grand Opera House, New York, where it had some success. Fechter continued to act in his version on tour, his last appearance being in December 1877.

In 1883, after Fechter's death, John Stetson, proprietor of the Globe Theater in Boston, got the rights to the Fechter MS, and in February of the same year the play opened under his auspices at Booth's Theater, New York, with James O'Neill playing Dantès. The critics were not cordial, one of them writing that "*Monte Cristo* will not last long." But the manager kept the play going. From that time on *Monte Cristo* grew in popular esteem, and O'Neill and *Monte Cristo*, until well into the present Century, were as closely associated in the public's mind as Jefferson and Rip Van Winkle.

In 1885 O'Neill purchased the Fechter version of the play from Stetson. "As O'Neill continued to play *Monte Cristo*," says Mr. Russak, "he made a number of changes in the script. The original 'Fechter version' is not extant in manuscript form." The copy used in the volume edited by Mr. Russak and here reproduced, is one furnished me by Eugene O'Neill, who certifies it as authentic. This was compared by Mr. Russak with another MS, now at the Museum of the City of New York. He states that "perhaps the script closest to" the Fechter version is the one just mentioned, and that the copy printed in the *Lost Plays* "appears to be a later version and reflects the changes which James O'Neill made in the script as it became a success."

Once more I acknowledge with thanks the friendly help given me by Eugene O'Neill, and his permission to reprint *Monte Cristo*.

Following is a copy of the original cast of the play as produced on February 12, 1883, at Booth's Theater, New York:

EDMUND DANTÈS	JAMES O'NEILL
NOIRTIER	HENRY LEE

ALBERT	HART CONWAY
VILLEFORT	H. BRADLEY
FERNAND	B. F. RINGGOLD
DANGLARS	GERALD EYRE
CADEROUSSE	J. W. SHANNON
ABBÉ FARIA	H. A. WEAVER
MOREL	J. A. HOWELL
OLD DANTÈS	JOS. A. WILKS
PENELON	R. F. RUNYON
FIRST POLICE AGENT	J. W. ARCHER
LE MARQUIS D'ARAMBURO	J. SWINBURNE
MASSINET	GEO. DEWEY
GERMAIN	C. LECOMPTON
GOVERNOR OF THE PRISON	H. FELLOWS
FIRST GAOLER	C. F. LOON
SECOND GAOLER	A. YOUNG
MAN	W. E. ABLE
BRIGADIER	W. A. BOYD
SECOND POLICE AGENT	J. R. SOLDENE
SIGNOR CIRRILLIO	S. D. HOVEY
M. BLANC JOUR	A. JACQUES
COM. OF POLICE	F. B. BOUDINOT
SENTINEL	W. C. MORTON
SERVANT	B. F. BERTON
FISHERMAN	W. J. MERRETT
MERCÉDÈS	KATHARINE ROGERS
CARCONTE	MRS. J. BRUTONE
MLLE. DANGLARS	CLARA BAKER
MME. LA MARQUISE D'ARAMBURO	ANNA BOUDINOT
MLLE. DE LISLE	LILLIAN LEWIS
MLLE. DE COURCEY	MISS R. QUINTON
FISHERWOMAN	KATE LEE

The O'Neill *Monte Cristo*, after serving its owner and star actor for years in full-length form, was reduced to tabloid dimensions and toward the end of the star's life played by him in vaudeville not very long before his death in the early 20's. It was likewise a stock favorite, was used more than once as the basis of motion pictures, and in the summer of 1939 was broadcast over Station WEAF, as part of a program that included eight other of the *Lost*

Plays. Since then it has occasionally been revived by nonprofessional University producing groups.

THE BANKER'S DAUGHTER

What was later to be known as *The Banker's Daughter* was first produced as *Lilian's Last Love* at Hooley's Theater, Chicago, September 4, 1873. In revised form, and under the title by which it was subsequently known, it opened at the Union Square Theater, New York, November 30, 1878, with the following cast:

JOHN STREBELOW	CHARLES R. THORNE, JR.
LAWRENCE WESTBROOK	JOHN PARSELLE
BABBAGE	J. H. STODDART
G. WASHINGTON PHIPPS	J. B. POLK
BROWN	W. J. LE MOYNE
COUNT DE CAROJAC	M. V. LINGHAM
HAROLD ROUTLEDGE	WALDEN RAMSAY
M. DE MONTVILLAIS	C. W. BOWSER
DR. WATSON	H. F. DALY
JERROLD	W. S. QUIGLEY
LILIAN WESTBROOK	SARA JEWETT
FLORENCE ST. VINCENT BROWN	MAUD HARRISON
MRS. FANNY HOLCOMB	MRS. E. J. PHILLIPS
LIZETTE	SARAH COWELL
NATALIE	{ LITTLE EFFIE BARRET { LITTLE LELIA GRANGER

The first New York production had a run of a hundred and thirty-seven performances. It was produced the following year in London under the title *The Old Love and the New.*

The text here reprinted is from Volume 10 of the *America's Lost Plays* series, edited by Professor Allan G. Halline. The text used by him is the privately-printed (but not published) edition of the play as copyrighted by Bronson Howard in 1878.

Professor Halline lists in his preface some of the subsequent productions of the play, including revivals, road tours, and stock performances. The last regular so-called "first class" production he records took place at the American Theater, New York, in 1901. It was, he adds, "reported playing in stock as late as 1914."

MY PARTNER

My Partner, described as "an original American play," was first produced at the Union Square Theater, New York, September 16, 1879, with the following cast:

JOE SAUNDERS	LOUIS ALDRICH
NED SINGLETON	HENRY CRISP
WING LEE	CHARLES T. PARSLOE
MAJOR HENRY CLAY BRITT	FRANK MORDAUNT
MATHEW BRANDON	HARRY EDWARDS
JOSIAH SCRAGGS	J. W. HAGUE
SAM BOWLER	I. H. BURNETT
WELLINGTON WIDGERY	CHARLES WEBSTER
JIM JOHNSON	JOHN DAILEY
MARY BRANDON	MAUDE GRANGER
GRACE BRANDON	MINNIE PALMER
MISS POSIE PENTLAND	ALICE GREY

The play ran in New York for a little over a month, and was then taken on tour, after certain changes were made in the cast. According to Dr. Wilt, soon after the opening performance "Campbell sold the rights . . . to Aldrich for the sum of ten dollars a performance—a fact Campbell bitterly regretted later. Aldrich then sold a small interest in the play to Parsloe, and from 1880 to 1884 Aldrich and Parsloe played in *My Partner* throughout the country. In 1884 the partnership was dissolved and Parsloe sold his interest back to Aldrich. After trying another play in which he failed, Aldrich returned to *My Partner*, playing in it until 1887 with various people in Parsloe's old part. After 1887 Aldrich leased the rights to other actors, and the play was frequently given until the end of the century. The last professional performance of which I have any record was at the People's Theater in Chicago, May 8-14, 1904." The play was also performed in London in 1884, and in Berlin (in a German adaptation) the year before.

My Partner survived as a stock favorite until comparatively recent times. It was made into a motion picture in 1909.

The MS was kindly provided by Mr. Robert Campbell, the author's son, and first published in Volume 19 of the *America's Lost Plays* series, edited by Dr. Napier Wilt under the title *The White Slave and Other Plays*. The alternate ending of Act II is based on a MS in the University of Chicago Library.

A TRIP TO CHINATOWN

A Trip to Chinatown; Or, an Idyl of San Francisco enjoyed the reputation for many years of holding the long-run record of consecutive performances in New York City, the total number being six hundred and fifty-seven. The play is further notable as having first introduced to the world the celebrated songs *Reuben, Reuben, I've Been Thinking, The Bowery,* and *After the Ball.*

It opened November 9, 1891, at Hoyt's Madison Square Theater, New York, with the following cast:

WELLAND STRONG	HARRY CONOR
BEN GAY	GEORGE A. BEANE
RASHLEIGH GAY	LLOYD WILSON
TONY GAY	LILLIAN BARR
WILDER DALY	
WILLIE GROW	BLANCHE ARKWRIGHT
NORMAN BLOOD	ARTHUR PACIE
NOAH HEAP	HARRY GILFOIL
HOFFMAN PRICE	FRANK E. MORSE
TURNER SWIFT	
SLAVIN PAYNE	HARRY GILFOIL
WAITERS	
ISABELLE DAME	GERALDINE MCCANN
CORA FAY	MAGGIE DALY
MAY WING	LUCY DALY
FLIRT	ALLIE ARCHMERE
MRS. GUYER	ANNA BOYD

The phenomenal success of the play in New York was repeated throughout the country, and until well into the new century it toured and became a standard favorite with the stock companies. With much of the original music, and in a condensed version, it was broadcast over Station WEAF in the summer of 1939.

As for the text here used, it is a reprint of that published in Volume 9 of the *America's Lost Plays* series under the title *Five Plays by Charles H. Hoyt,* edited by Douglas L. Hunt. Professor Hunt writes in his preface that the play is printed as "supplied to me in a copy . . . sent me by Mr. George W. Poultney of San Francisco . . . who appeared in at least one of the Hoyt companies playing on the Pacific coast. He assures me that it is the form of the play in which he acted. It differs radically from the copy in . . . New York [i.e., the copy bequeathed to the New York Public Library by the author], so much so, in fact, that I have printed the entire last act of both versions. . . . The music for the songs . . . was also supplied me through Mr. Poultney's kindness."

THE GREAT DIAMOND ROBBERY

The Great Diamond Robbery was first performed at the American Theater in New York September 4, 1895. Following is the cast:

DICK BRUMMAGE	W. H. THOMPSON
FRANK KENNET	ORRIN JOHNSON
SENATOR McSORKER	ODELL WILLIAMS
DR. LIVINGSTONE	JOSEPH E. WHITING
CLINTON BULFORD	GEORGE C. BONIFACE
MARIO MARINO	BYRON DOUGLAS
GRANDFATHER LAVELOT	JOSEPH WILKES
SHEENEY IKE	B. R. GRAHAM
COUNT GARBIADORFF	GEORGE MIDDLETON
JANE CLANCEY	C. B. HAWKINS
MICKEY BRANNIGAN	JAMES BEVINS
JIMMY McCLUNE	GUSTAVE FRANKEL
PHILIP	PRINCE LLOYD
FRAU ROSENBAUM	MADAME JANAUSCHEK
MRS. BULFORD	BLANCHE WALSH
MARY LAVELOT	KATHERINE GREY
MRS. O'GEOGAN	ANNIE YEAMANS
PEGGY DALY	FANNY COHEN
MADAME MERVANE	FLORENCE ROBINSON
MARY WATSON	RAY ROCKWELL

Though the play received what we now call "mixed notices" from the press, there was, says Mr. Garrett H. Leverton in his preface to the first printed edition of the text, "no doubt as to its success with audiences. In 1905—ten years after the New York opening—the play was still listed by theatrical journals as one of the most popular plays from coast to coast." It was also turned into a motion picture, and is still remembered as one of the best of the early examples of its type.

The text of *The Great Diamond Robbery* was furnished by Mr. Otis Alfriend, who is its present owner, and permission to publish it was granted by him and his agent Samuel French, Inc. It was first published in Volume 8 of the *America's Lost Plays* series, edited by Garrett H. Leverton.

THE HEART OF MARYLAND

The Heart of Maryland was produced for the first time at the Grand Opera House in Washington, October 9, 1895. Its first New York production was at the Herald Square Theater on October 22 of the same year, with the following cast:

GENERAL HUGH KENDRICK	FRANK MORDAUNT
COLONEL ALAN KENDRICK	MAURICE BARRYMORE
COLONEL FULTON THORPE	JOHN E. KELLERD
LIEUTENANT ROBERT TELFAIR	CYRIL SCOTT
PROVOST SERGEANT BLOUNT	ODELL WILLIAMS
TOM BOONE	HENRY WEAVER, JR.
LLOYD CALVERT	EDWARD J. MORGAN
THE SEXTON	JOHN W. JENNINGS
UNCLE DAN'L	SCOTT COOPER
CAPTAIN LEIGHTON	A. PEARSON
CAPTAIN BLAIR	A. C. MORA
AIDES-DE-CAMP OF GENERAL KENDRICK'S STAFF	{ WILLLIAM JOHNSON FRANK STANWICK ROBERT MC INTYRE
CORPORAL DAY	EDWIN MEYER
BLUDSOE	EDWIN F. MAYO
LITTLE TRUE BLUE	MASTER JOHNNY MC KEEVER
O'HARA	J. H. HAZLETON
RUGGLES	THOMAS MATLOCK
FORBES	JOSEPH MAXWELL
PHIL	JOSEPH A. WEBBER
SENTRY	E. J. BOYCE
SCOUT	C. H. ROBERTSON
MRS. CLAIBORNE GORDON	HELEN TRACY
CORPORAL	H. E. BOSTWICK
MARYLAND CALVERT	MRS. LESLIE CARTER
PHOEBE YANCEY	GEORGIA BUSBY
NANNY MACNAIR	ANGELA MC CAUL

The play ran in New York for 229 performances. Professor Glenn Hughes and Professor George Savage add this note to their record of its popularity: "After its successful run in New York the play was in demand throughout the country, and was sent on tour in October 1896, opening in Philadelphia ... and ending at ... New York in May 1897. The play's third season opened" in San Francisco in August of the same year and "included a transcontinental tour, ending at Hartford, Conn., in March 1898. At the close of this tour the company was sent to England, where the play opened at the Adelphi Theatre, London, on April 8, continuing until June 25."

It need hardly be added that *The Heart of Maryland* was for many years a stock favorite.

The play was first published in Volume 18 of the *America's Lost Plays* series, entitled *The Heart of Maryland and Other Plays*, edited by Glenn Hughes and George Savage. Shortly before her death Mrs. Leslie Carter, who owned all rights to the play, graciously gave me permission to publish it.

THE MIGHTY DOLLAR

Benjamin E. Woolf's immensely popular and successful play *The Mighty Dollar* is the only one in the present volume which has never before been published. Long before the *Lost Plays* series was ready for press I had found a MS of the Woolf play, intending to include it in one of the volumes, but it was not until most of the books had already appeared in print and the others were in press, that I established contact with the owner of such rights to it as may now exist. I am therefore indebted to Mr. S. J. Woolf, of New York City, for permission to use the play here. I asked Mr. Woolf for information on Benjamin Woolf and inquired whether he knew of the existence of any MSS left by the author of *The Mighty Dollar*. Unfortunately he had no material, and was even surprised that I had in my possession a text of the play. He referred me to the *Dictionary of American Biography*, where a short sketch of the life of Woolf appeared in 1936. To this I owe most of the biographical data below. He also added the following paragraph: "The family tradition is that the expression PDQ originated in *The Mighty Dollar*, and although OK was probably used before that play was produced I think that you will find that it was a favorite expression of Bardwell Slote."

Benjamin Edward Woolf was born in London February 16, 1836. At the age of three his family brought him to the United States. Both parents and (later) his brothers combined a variety of unusual talents: among them were composers, musical conductors, chemists, inventors, editors, and mathematicians. The youthful Benjamin was trained by his father to be a musician, and it is noteworthy that in spite of the many plays he wrote he is considered rather as a conductor and composer and music critic than dramatist. His opera *The Doctor of Alcantara*, of which he wrote only the libretto, achieved considerable success, while the operetta *Pounce & Co.*, for which he wrote the music as well, was a favorite with American audiences for some time. Most of his life was spent in Boston, where he followed a long career, on the *Globe*, the *Saturday Evening Gazette*, and the *Herald*, both as dramatic and music critic. His career as playwright (he wrote more than sixty plays) covered a period of well over thirty years. His last play, *Westward Ho*, was produced at the Boston Museum in 1894. He died February 7, 1901.

By all odds Woolf's most famous play is *The Mighty Dollar*. It was first produced at the Park Theater, New York, September 6, 1875, with the following cast:

Hon. Bardwell Slote	W. J. FLORENCE
Roland Vance	J. G. SAVILLE
Lord Cairngorm	W. J. FERGUSON
Colonel Tom Dart	J. C. PADGETT
Hon. George Saville	L. R. WILLARD
Charley Brood	CHARLES VILLERS
George Washington Skidmore	J. W. BRUTONE
Lafayette Berry	FRANK LANGLEY
Arthur Lemaitre	WALLACE GRANT
Mrs. General Gilflory	MRS. FLORENCE
Blanche Mossthorn	ANNIE EDMONSON
Clara Dart	MAUDE GRANGER
Libby Ray	EDITH OSMUND
Laura Seabright	PEARL EYTINGE

T. Allston Brown, in his *History of the New York Stage*, records that "despite an interruption on the eighth night of their engagement, through the closing of the house by the sheriff on an attachment against them, the Florences reaped the benefits of a run of one hundred and four nights." According to Dr. Odell (*Annals of the New York Stage*), "changes came into the cast . . . the character of Laura Seabright is not listed." I call particular attention to this last sentence, which will explain some of the discrepancies we find on comparing one program with another, and on comparing the text in my possession with the extant programs (and there are many) I have seen. Characters are listed in one program and not in another; the spelling of names, especially that of Cairngorm, is rarely uniform. It is probable that no one MS of *The Mighty Dollar*, as produced at any one time, is identical with any other.

The play did not meet with critical approval, but it was a popular hit. According to F. E. McKay and C. E. L. Wingate, who wrote a pleasant sketch on Mr. and Mrs. Florence in their book *Famous American Actors of*

Today, these players appeared in *The Mighty Dollar* more than two thousand five hundred times. The play toured the country time and again, and was current in the repertory of the Florences until shortly before Mr. Florence's death in 1891.

"It is related," write McKay and Wingate, "that the play came to be written in the following manner: Mrs. Florence while abroad was constantly amused at the French phrases which wealthy but uneducated American women would use. She thought that it would be a good idea to transfer one of these persons to the mimic stage. Mr. Florence had also in mind a character suited to himself; namely, that of a good-humored but not over-scrupulous Western lawyer. The Florences accordingly went to Ben Woolf, and had him write a play with these two characters as the prominent personages. The piece was originally called *The Almighty Dollar,* and was subsequently changed to *The Mighty Dollar,* in order to avoid criticism by religious people."

The text of the play I am here using is a relatively recent copy of what I assume to have been an authentic prompt script. The minor characters in it are not all listed in the program of the first production, and there are several variant spellings of those names that are there listed. Long search and considerable investigation on my part have failed to bring to light any other MS with which I might compare it. I have good reason to think that my MS is one of those widely-circulated MSS that was copied from that of some stage manager of one of the many travelling companies that played Chicago: indeed the MS comes from that city. I have during my investigations in connection with the *Lost Plays* sometimes had before me a copy of one of the so-called "bootleg" MSS of a certain play and another MS that I knew to be that of the author, and on evidence further furnished by a stage manager or actor who played in the play in question, found that the unauthorized version was a more accurate record of what was actually played than the authorized. Professor Hunt has made similar investigations in connection with several of the Hoyt plays, and has reached similar conclusions.

In preparing the MS of *The Mighty Dollar* for the press I have corrected minor errors of spelling and punctuation, and allowed the publisher to adopt certain simple typographical conventions which were followed in setting up the texts of the various volumes of the *Lost Plays* series.

I should like, once more, to make public acknowledgment of help and advice given me in connection with the whole project of which the present volume is an adjunct: to the editors of each of the twenty volumes so often referred to in these pages; to the editorial board (Robert Hamilton Ball,

Hoyt H. Hudson; Glenn Hughes, Garrett H. Leverton, E. C. Mabie, Allardyce Nicoll, Arthur Hobson Quinn, and Napier Wilt); to Ligon Johnson, the copyright attorney; and to Dr. David H. Stevens, Director of the Division of Humanities of the Rockefeller Foundation, to whom we are indebted for the subsidy which made it possible for the editorial work and the collection of material to be accomplished, and for his continued and enthusiastic co-operation. Finally, to Joseph A. Brandt, formerly director of the Princeton University Press, belongs the credit of actually undertaking the hazardous and difficult job of bringing to life, in the form of twenty beautiful volumes, the entire series, a job that involved courage and foresight and an immense amount of hard work. That he was ably assisted by an equally enthusiastic staff is only another way of saying that he communicated to others something of his genius for making the publishing business an exciting adventure.

BARRETT H. CLARK

METAMORA;
Or, THE LAST OF THE WAMPANOAGS

An Indian Tragedy in Five Acts
as played by Edwin Forrest

By John Augustus Stone

CAST OF CHARACTERS

INDIANS

METAMORA, *chief of the Wampanoags*	G. B. WALDRON
KANESHINE, *an Indian prophet*	J. R. CLAWSON
ANNAWANDAH, *the traitor*	J. M. SMITH
OTAH, *an Indian boy*	H. MAIBEN
INDIAN BOY, *child of Metamora*	(MISS E. CLAWSON)
NAHMEOKEE, *wife of Metamora*	MISS ADAMS
INDIANS, WARRIORS, ETC.	

ENGLISH

	(Costumes)	
LORD FITZARNOLD	*(rich shape, Charles II)*	N. S. LESLIE
SIR ARTHUR VAUGHAN	*(dark shape)*	E. G. WOOLEY
MORDAUNT	*(dark shape)*	J. S. LINDSAY
ERRINGTON, *chief of the council*	*(Puritan shape)*	D. E. MCKENSIE
WALTER, *an orphan*	*(plain shape)*	J. S. SIMMONS
CAPTAIN CHURCH	*(breast plate, trunks)*	THOMPSON
WOLFE	*(plain)*	J. C. GRAHAM
GOODENOUGH	*(do)*	KELLY
TRAMP	*(do)*	MCINTOSH
OCEANA, *Mordaunt's daughter*		MRS. LESLIE
SOLDIERS, SAILORS, PEASANTS, ETC.		

(The page above is, except for punctuation, a reproduction of the cast of characters, as they appeared in Salt Lake City, January 10, 1866, included in the manuscript itself, except for the name in parenthesis which has been copied from a playbill originally appearing in the *Deseret News Print*. The page from the original manuscript has been reproduced rather than the *Deseret News Print* playbill because of the descriptions of costumes contained in the former.)

ACT I.

SCENE 1: *Sunset. A wild, picturesque scene; high, craggy rocks in distance; dark pine trees, etc. Rocks cross stage, with platform cross behind. Steps, etc., at back. A rude tomb, flowers growing around it. Half dark. Mordaunt discovered leaning on tomb. Slow music.*

MOR. The sun has sunk behind yon craggy rocks; and day's last beams are fading from the clouds that fleet in hurrying masses through the sky, like tattered banners of a flying host! England, my home! When will thy parent arms again enfold me? Oh! When for me will dawn a day of hope? Will not sincere repentance from my scathed brow efface the brand of regicide?

TRAMP. [*Outside*] What ho! Good Master Mordaunt! [*Cannon*]

MOR. Ha! What mean those sounds? Now, your news? [*Enter Tramp*]

TRAMP. A gallant bark, urged by the favoring breeze, makes for the crowded shore.

MOR. From England! Ha!

TRAMP. St. George's banner floats from her high mast, and her long signal pennon gleams with green and gold.

MOR. 'Tis he—he comes and with him hope arrives. Go, hasten, fellow; seek my daughter; say the Lord Fitzarnold comes to greet her. [*Tramp crosses to R. behind*] Marshal my followers in their best array—away to the beach and let loud music welcome him ashore. [*Exit Tramp*] What mingled feelings crowd about my heart, blended so strange and wild? Sunned by his sovereign's smile, Fitzarnold comes to woo and wed my daughter. Born on the heaving deep, the child of storms, and reared in savage wilds, her worth and beauty well may grace the courtly halls of England. And yet, to force her gentle will, whose every thought has been to soothe my sorrows and relieve my cares! Yet must she wed Fitzarnold. His alliance can with oblivion shroud the past, clear from my scutcheon every rebel stain, and give my franchised spirit liberty. [*Exit. Slow music, four bars. Enter Oceana, looking around as if in search*]

OCEANA. Sure, 'twas my father's voice, and loud in converse. Father! Dear father! Not here? And yet I thought—[*Flute heard, distant*] Ha! whence that strain? So soft yet strange. Methinks some pious minstrel seeks the moonlight hour to breathe devotion forth in melody. [*Music changes*] Hark! It changes place and measure, too. Now deeper in the woods it warbles, now it seems aloft floating in plaintive tones through the air. This place—the hour—the day—heavens! 'tis my mother's birthday, and her grave undecked with flowers! O my mother, my dear mother! Perhaps her angel spirit hovers here o'er her lone daughter's steps, a guardian still. [*Kneels to tomb*] Ah, what flower is this? "Forgetmenot!" [*Music ceases*] My mother, look from thy seraph home upon thy child, and when for those thou lovest on earth thou breathest a prayer, oh, then forget me not. [*Places flower in bosom. Enter Walter*]

WALT. Oceana!

OCEANA. Walter, was thine the strain but now I heard?

WALT. 'Twas but an humble tribute to thy beauty, but could not match the sweetness of thy voice, whose every tone, attuned to dulcet sounds, can melt the soul to nature's harmony.

OCEANA. Walter, this from thee.

WALT. Nay, blame me not; although dependent on Sir Arthur Vaughan, nameless and poor, yet do I not despair, for in my heart a sacred treasure lies I would not barter for my patron's gold.

OCEANA. What means't thou, Walter?

WALT. Thine own sweet image, which naught on earth can banish or efface—a whispered hope I dare not speak aloud—a light thine own bright eyes have kindled up.

OCEANA. Nay, Walter, you ask not of the danger I escaped!

WALT. Danger! What danger? When?

OCEANA. 'Twas yestere'en, when I was lingering on the eastern beach, all heedless of the coming night, a panther growling from the thicket rushed and marked me for his prey. Powerless I stood—my blood stood still—I shrieked as I strove to fly, when at the instant, from a ready hand, swift as the lightning's flash, an arrow came and felled the monster as he crouched to spring.

WALT. Didst mark who sent it?

OCEANA. Full well I did. High on a craggy rock an Indian stood, with sinewy arm and eye that pierced the glen. His bowstring drawn to wing a second death, a robe of fur was o'er his shoulder thrown, and o'er his long, dark hair an eagle's plume waved in the breeze, a feathery diadem. Firmly he stood upon the jutting height, as if a sculptor's hand had carved him there. With awe I gazed as on the cliff he turned—the grandest model of a mighty man.

WALT. 'Twas Haups great chieftain, Metamora called; our people love him not, nor is it strange; he stands between them and extended sway, ready alike with words of power to urge, or gleaming weapon force his princely dues.

META. [*Outside*] Hah! Ha!

OCEANA. [*Going up*] Behold his dread encounter with a wolf. His vanquished foe with mighty arm he hurls down the steep height where mortal never trod.

META. Hah! Hah! [*Enters on rock, passes across and off*]

WALT. [*At Metamora's exit*] 'Tis Metamora, the noble sachem of a valiant race—the white man's dread, the Wampanoag's hope. [*Enter Metamora down R.*]

META. Ha, ha, ha! Turned on me—brave beast; he died like a red man.

OCEANA. Chief, you are hurt; this scarf will staunch the wound. [*Offers it*]

META. No! [*Rejects it*]

WALT. 'Tis Oceana—she whose life you saved.

META. Metamora will take the white maiden's gift. [*Oceana ties his arm with scarf*]

OCEANA. But yestere'en thou savedst my life, great chief; how can I pay thee for the generous deed?

META. Hearken, daughter of the pale face; Metamora forgives not a wrong and forgets not a kindness. In the days of his age, Massasoit, my father, was in the white man's dwelling; while there, the spirit of the grave touched him and he laid down to die. A soft hand was stretched out to save him; it was the hand of thy mother. She that healed him sleeps in yonder tomb; but why should Metamora let his arrows sleep in the quiver when her daughter's life was in danger and her limbs shook with fear? Metamora loves the mild-eyed and the kind, for such is Nahmeokee.

WALT. Such words, and more than all, such deeds, should win you, chief, the love of all our people. Would you were more among us. Why never seek our homes? Sir Arthur Vaughan's doors will open to the Indian chief.

OCEANA. My sire will thank thee for his daughter's life.

META. The red man's heart is on the hills where his father's shafts have flown in the chase. Ha! I have been upon the high mountain top where the grey mists were beneath my feet, and the Great Spirit passed by me in his wrath. He spake in anger and the old rocks crumbled beneath the flash of his spear. Then I was proud and smiled, for I had slain the great bird whose wing never tires, and whose eye never shrinks; and his feathers would adorn the long black hair of Nahmeokee, daughter of Miantonemo, the great hunter. The war and the chase are the red man's brother and sister. The storm cloud in its fury frights him not. Wrapt in the spoils he has won, he lays him down and no one comes near to steal. The Great Spirit hears his evening prayer, and he sleeps amidst the roar of a mighty cataract.

WALT. Were all thy nation mild and good like thee, how soon the fire of discord might be quenched.

META. Metamora has been the friend of the white man; yet if the flint be smitten too hard it will show that in its heart is fire. The Wampanoag will not wrong his white brother who comes from the land that is first touched by the rising sun; but he owns no master, save that One who holds the sun in his right hand, who rides on a dark storm, and who cannot die. [*Crosses to L.*]

WALT. That lofty bearing—that majestic mien—the regal impress sits upon his brow, and earth seems conscious of her proudest son. [*Conch shell heard sounding, R.*]

META. Ha! My young men return from their evening toil, and their hands are filled with the sweet fish of the lake. Come to my wigwam; ye shall eat of fish that the Great Spirit of the waters sends, and your hearts shall be made glad. [*Going R. but returns and takes from his head an eagle plume*] Maiden, take this; it means speed and safety; when the startling whoop is heard and the war hatchet gleams in the red blaze, let it be found in thy braided hair. Despise not the red man's gift; it will bring more good to you than the yellow earth the white man worships as his god. Take it— no Wampanoag's hand will e'er be raised against the head or hand that bears the eagle plume. [*Crosses to Walter*] Young man, be thou like the oak in its spreading power and let thy tough branches shelter the tender flower that springs up under them. Look to the maiden of the eagle plume, and—come to my wigwam. [*Exit*]

OCEANA. Teach him, Walter; make him like to us.

WALT. 'Twould cost him half his native virtues. Is justice goodly? Metamora's just. Is bravery virtue? Metamora's brave. If love of country, child and wife and home, be to deserve them all—he merits them.

OCEANA. Yet he is a heathen.

WALT. True, Oceana, but his worship though untaught and rude flows from his heart, and Heaven alone must judge of it. [*Enter Tramp*]

TRAMP. Your father, lady, requires your presence.

OCEANA. Say I come. [*A distant drum*]

WALT. What is that?

TRAMP. The drum that summons Lord Fitzarnold's escort. He comes a suitor for my lady's hand. [*Exit Tramp*]

WALT. Deny it, Oceana—say 'tis false!

OCEANA. It is—

WALT. Untrue?

OCEANA. Oh, most unwelcome.

WALT. Heavens! You tremble—and your cheek is pale—my Lord Fitzarnold, that most courtly gentleman, and must my hopes—

OCEANA. Walter, dost thou mean—

WALT. Obey thy sire. I cannot say farewell. But, oh, when highborn revelers carouse, and proud Fitzarnold lords it at the board, give one brief thought to me! That blessed thought shall soothe the fond complainings of my heart and hush them to repose. [*Exit Walter L. Oceana exit R.*]

SCENE 2: *Lights up. A room in Sir Arthur's house. Enter Sir Arthur and Walter.*

WALT. Yet hear me, sir.

SIR A. Forebear; thou art too hot.

WALT. 'Tis not the meanness of our state that galls us, but men's opinions. Poverty and toil and consciousness of lowly destiny sit lightly where no scorn is heaped upon them. But yesterday I was indeed content, for none despised, none had learned to scoff the son of charity, the wretched ship boy who could trace existence no further than the wreck from which you plucked him; but now 'tis changed, all suddenly begin to find me base.

SIR. A. Marry, go to! You wrong yourself and me. Have I not fostered you—like a father tutored you? In early life bereft of wife and child, wearied of discord and fierce civil strife, I left the haunts of wild and factious men, to woo contentment in this wilderness. My heart was vacant and received thee in. Do not by any rash, unworthy act forsake that heart. Who is it finds thee base?

WALT. All, since Fitzarnold is expected here.

SIR A. Fitzarnold! What a plague! There is naught talked of or thought of but Lord Fitzarnold! And yet this noble viscount, but for his coat and title were a man to look with scorn upon—a profligate and spendthrift as fame already has too truly shown him.

WALT. And 'tis for such a man that Master Mordaunt sets me aside—for such a man his daughter must cast me off.

SIR A. Tut! Master Mordaunt is too wise a man to give his daughter to this Lord Fitzarnold. Patience awhile, and watch the progress of this meteor. Patience, and trust to fortune. [*Exit*]

WALT. This lordly suitor comes to wake me from my cherished dreams, and crush the hopes which lately looked so fair. And shall I yield the glorious prize I deemed was wholly mine? Yield, and without a struggle? No, by heaven! Look to thyself, Fitzarnold. Let Oceana be but true, I heed not all thy power, thy wealth, thy titles, backed though they be by Mordaunt's selfish views. [*Exit*]

SCENE 3: *The harbor. Ships anchored in the distance. Military music. Mordaunt, Errington, Goodenough, Church, Soldiers, Citizens (male and female) discovered. A boat comes on from L., with Fitzarnold, Wolfe, and Sailors, who land. Shout.*

MOR.   Long live the king! Welcome Fitzarnold! Rest to the sea-worn! Joy to each and all!

FITZ.   I thank thee, Mordaunt! But I did not think to see such faces in the wilderness! Thy woody shores are bright with sparkling eyes, like Argonaut's adventurous sailors. But where's the golden boon we look for, sir? Fair Oceana—Mordaunt, where is she? [*Walter enters, L., and stands against wing*]

MOR.   So please you, my lord, at home, eager to pay your lordship's kindness back, and prove she can discern thy courtesy.

WALT.   [*Aside*]   Indeed! Dost say so, worldling?

MOR.   Pray thee, regard these gentlemen, my lord—our council's father, Errington—and this our army's leader; elders of the State. [*Introducing them severally; Fitzarnold salutes them, and at last approaching Walter, extends his hand; Walter bows coldly but does not take it. Music eight bars*]

FITZ.   How now, young sir? Mordaunt, who is this?

MOR.   My noble lord, I pray thee, heed him not! A wayward youth, somewhat o'er worn with study. [*Crosses to Walter*] Rash boy! Be wise and tempt me not; I can destroy—

WALT.   Thy daughter's peace and wed her there. [*Mordaunt gives Walter a look of hate and turns from him*]

MOR.   Forth to the hall—a strain of music there. [*Crosses to R.*]

FITZ.   Young sir, I shall desire some further converse with you.

WALT.   At injury's prompting, deeds, not words, were best. My lord, you shall find me. [*Touches his sword*]

FITZ.   Now for thy fair daughter, Mordaunt, come. [*Music. Exeunt all but Walter and Wolfe. Peasants and Soldiers exeunt, R.*]

WOLFE.   Thou goest not with them?

WALT.   No, nor before, nor follow after. But why dost thou ask?

WOLFE.   Because I know thee.

WALT. Then thou knowest one who will not take a lordling by the hand, because his fingers shine with hoops of gold—nor shun the beggar's grasp if it be honest. Thou knowest me?

WOLFE. Yes!

WALT. To know oneself was thought task enough in olden time. What dost thou know?

WOLFE. That thou wert wrecked and saved.

WALT. Aye, more's the pity! [*Aside*] Had I been drowned I had not lived to love and have no hope.

WOLFE. Thou art a good man's son.

WALT. A pity then, again. Were I a rascal's offspring, I might thrive. What more?

WOLFE. Thou shalt possess thy mistress.

WALT. Didst mark that lord?

WOLFE. He is my master.

WALT. Then I am dumb. Be faithful to him, and now farewell. [*Crosses to L.*]

WOLFE. Yet in good time I will say that you will bestow a blessing for.

WALT. Indeed! What mean you? [*Enter Tramp, L., with packet*]

TRAMP. News from the Indians. [*Shows packet*] 'Tis for the council by a horseman left, who bade me see it with all haste delivered. The Indian tribes conspire from east to west and faithful Sasamond has found his grave! This packet must be borne to Mordaunt.

WALT. Trust it with me.

TRAMP. That I will readily, so thou wilt bear it safely.

WALT. Aye, and quickly, too. [*Takes packet, crosses to R.*] Let me remember Metamora's words—"Look to the maiden of the eagle plume." [*Exit hastily, followed by Wolfe, and Tramp. Quick curtain*]

ACT II.

SCENE I: *Music. Interior of a wigwam; a skin rolled. Stage covered with skins, etc. Child on skin near R. entrance. Nahmeokee near it. Metamora at L., preparing for the chase.*

NAH. Thou wilt soon be back from the chase.

META. Yes, before the otter has tasted his midday food on the bank of the stream, his skin shall make a garment for Nahmeokee when the snow whitens the hunting grounds and the cold wind whistles through the trees. Nahmeokee, take our little one from his rest; he sleeps too much.

NAH. Oh, no! But thou, Metamora, sleepst too little. In the still hour of midnight when Wekolis has sung his song, and the great light has gone down behind the hills, when Nahmeokee's arms like the growing vine were round thee—as if some danger lay waiting in the thick wood—thou didst bid me bring thy tomahawk and the spear that Massasoit had borne when the war cry of the Wampanoags was loudest in the place of blood! Why is thy rest like the green lake when the sudden blast passes across its bosom?

META. Nahmeokee, the power of dreams has been on me, and the shadows of things that are to be have passed before me. My heart is big with a great thought. When I sleep I think the knife is red in my hand, and the scalp of the white man is streaming.

NAH. Metamora, is not the white man our brother? And does not the Great Spirit look on him as he does on us? Do not go towards his home today because thy wrath is kindled and it spreads like the flames which the white man makes in the dark bosom of the forest. Let Nahmeokee clasp her arms around thee; rest thy head upon her bosom, for it is hot and thy eye is red with the thoughts that burn! Our old men counsel peace, and the aim of the white man will spare.

META. Yes, when our fires are no longer red, on the high places of our fathers; when the bones of our kindred make fruitful the fields of the stranger, which he has planted amidst the ashes of our wigwams; when we are hunted back like the wounded elk far toward the going down of the sun, our hatchets broken, our bows unstrung and war whoop hushed; then will the stranger spare, for we will be too small for his eye to see. [*Trumpet; enter Otah*]

OTAH. O son of Massasoit, the power of the white man approaches, and he looks not like one who seeks the Wampanoag's friendship! Look where the bright weapons flash through the clouds of his track.

META. Ha! Let the paleface come with the calumet or with the knife, Metamora does not fear their power. Where is Annawandah, skilled in talk? Let him approach me. [*Exit Otah*]

NAH. Our child would not rest in the mid-hour of night for the hidden snake had bitten him as he lay stretched in the rays of the sun. I rose from my seat to get the dried leaves the Good Spirit has filled with power to heal; the moon was bright and a shadow passed me. It was Annawandah passed our wigwam; his step was like the course of the serpent and he paused and listened. My eye followed him to the seaside, and his light canoe shot like an arrow across the slumbering waters.

META. Humph! Was he alone?

NAH. Alone.

META. And he went with fear?

NAH. Like one who goes to steal. [*Trumpet. Enter Otah*]

OTAH. Look! The white warrior comes. [*Enter Church, Sir Arthur Vaughan, and Goodenough, with musqueteers (sic)*]

CHURCH. Although we come unbidden, chieftain, yet is our purpose friendly.

META. Why do you bring your fire weapons if you come to hold a talk of peace?

CHURCH. It is our custom.

META. Well, speak; my ears are open to hear.

SIR A. Philip, our mission is—

META. Philip! I am the Wampanoag chief, Metamora.

SIR A. We are directed by our council's head, for the times are filled with doubt, and to make *sure* our bond of peace and love to urge your presence at the council.

NAH. [*Aside*] Do not go.

META. Daughter of Miantinemo, peace! [*To them*] I will go.

CHURCH. Our troops shall form thy escort there.

META. I know the path.

SIR A. We must not go without thee, chief.

META. I have breasted the cold winds of forty winters and to those that spoke kindly to me in the words of love I have been pliant—aye, very yielding like the willow that droops over the stream, but till with a single arm you can move the mighty rock that mocks the lightning and the storm seek not to stir Metamora when his heart says no. I will come! [*Crosses to R.*]

CHURCH. We shall expect thee, chief.

META. Metamora cannot lie.

CHURCH. Stand to your arms. [*Trumpet. Exit Church, Goodenough, Otah and Soldiers*]

SIR A. Be thou not rash, but with thy tongue of manly truth dispel all charge that wrongs thy noble nature. Throw not the brand that kindles bloody war lest thou thyself should be the victim. [*Sir Arthur going, L.*]

META. My father's deeds shall be my counsellors, and the Great Spirit will hear the words of my mouth. [*Exit Sir Arthur*] Now, Nahmeokee, I will talk to thee. Dost thou not love this little one, Nahmeokee?

NAH. Oh, yes!

META. When first his little eyes unclosed, thou saidst they were like mine; and my people rejoiced with a mighty joy, that the grandson of Massasoit, the white man's friend, should rule in the high places of his kindred; and hoped that his days would be long and full of glory. Nahmeokee, by the blood of his warlike race, he shall not be the white man's slave.

NAH. Thy talk is strange, and fear creeps over me. Thy heart is beating at thy side, as if thy bosom could not hold it.

META. Because 'tis full of thee—and thee, my little one. Humph! Bring me the knife thy brother wore in battle—my hatchet—the spear that was thy father's when Uncas slew him for the white man's favor. Humph! These things thou gavest me with thyself; thinkest thou this arm can wield them in the fight?

NAH. Ah! Thy bravery will lose thee to me.

META. Let not thy heart be troubled. If I require assistance from my people, I will lift up a flame on the lofty hill that shall gleam afar through the thick darkness.

NAH. I shall remember thy words.

META. Take in thy babe; I am going. [*Crosses to L.*]

NAH. Metamora, dost thou go alone?

META. No; Manito is with me. [*Exit. Nahmeokee exit*]

SCENE 2: *A room in the house of Mordaunt. Enter Oceana.*

OCEANA. Free from Fitzarnold's gaze, I feel myself again. Why came he here? His looks appalled [me] yet my father smiled—ah! he comes. [*Enter Mordaunt*]

MOR. How now, my daughter; how is this? Why have you left his lordship thus?

OCEANA. I thought 'twas time.

MOR. It is not time to play the prude, when noble men confess thy charms and come fair suitors to thee. Fitzarnold loves thee and his alliance is so dear to me, I'll have no scruples of a timid girl to weigh against it. For long years I've nursed this fondness and I now command obedience.

OCEANA. That union must remain unblessed wherein the helpless hand is giving no heart to bear it company. O my father, how at the altar can I take that vow my heart now whispers never can be kept.

MOR. Hear me, rash girl, now that none o'erhear our converse. Learn thy father's destiny—the name I bear is not my own!

OCEANA. My father!

MOR. Thou didst not know my former life and deeds. Hardy adventure and the shock of arms, civil contention and a monarch's death make up the past, and poison all who come! 'Tis thou alone can clothe my future days with peace and shed one cheering ray o'er a dark scene of terror.

OCEANA. Art thou distraught?

MOR. Do not deny me, girl, and make me so! I am an outcast and a man forbid. Fitzarnold knows me and he asks my child—has power, and gaining thee preserves thy sire. Speak, Oceana! Thy resolve: what is it?

OCEANA. Thou canst not mean it, father! No, it cannot be!

MOR. Girl, it is as certain as our earthly doom. Decide, then, now between my honor and my instant death! For by thy mother's memory and by my soul, if my despair do find thee pitiless, my own right hand shall end a wretched life and leave thee nothing for a bridal dower but my curses and a blighted name. [*Crosses to R.*]

OCEANA. My throat is parched! I pray a moment's peace, a moment's pause. [*Business. Mordaunt paces the stage in great agitation, at last falls on his knee to Oceana. Walter enters, starts at seeing them and remains at back*]

MOR. Look at thy father, lowly begging life of thee. I will not swear, I will not rave, my child, but I'll implore thee! If thou hast ever loved me and dost so still, show that affection now! Let not thy father's name forever stand a mark for men to heap their curses on—relent, my child.

OCEANA. I can endure no more—rise, my father.

MOR. Dost thou promise?

OCEANA. All, all!

MOR. Swear, by truth! by honor! By the dead—

OCEANA. To wed Fitzarnold—

WALT. [*Comes up*] Hold! Hold, rash girl, forebear! Thou art ensnared and wouldst pronounce thy doom.

MOR. Lightning consume thee, meddling fool! What bringst thou here?

WALT. No pleasant duty, sir; a message which the council sends thee here. [*Gives packet to Mordaunt*] I am no spy, nor do I care to know secrets too dread for thine own heart to hold.

MOR. Beggar, begone! [*Strikes him with packet and crosses to L. Walter draws swords. Oceana interposes*]

OCEANA. It is my father, Walter, mine.

WALT. A blow.

OCEANA. Oh, thou wilt forgive him!

WALT. Never! I will forth, and ere he shall enforce thee where thou hast no joy, will rend the mask he cheats us with. [*Crosses to L.*]

OCEANA. And if thou dost, by heaven I'll ne'er be thine.

WALT. [*Sheathes sword*] Old man, an angel's bosom shelters thine. Instruct Fitzarnold in our quarrel's cause. No daughter bars my way to him. [*Exit. Enter Fitzarnold*]

FITZ. How now, you tremble; what has chanced?

MOR. A moody beggar who abused my love and I chastised him for it—that's all.

OCEANA. My father—

MOR. Go to thy chamber.

OCEANA. Would it were my grave. [*Exit*]

MOR. My noble lord, that moody stripling whom you saw last night—whether set on by Vaughan, his patron, or by the vainness of his own conceits, resolves to break my daughter's marriage.

FITZ. And wilt thou suffer this? What is the villain's state?

MOR. Dependence on Sir Arthur Vaughan; his wealth a goodly person and the [law?] love of schools. [*sic*] [*Bell tolls*] Hark! I am summoned to the council. Wilt thou along? [*Fitzarnold crosses to L.*]

FITZ. I trust he finds no favor with your daughter.

MOR. She shall be thine, my lord; thine with free will and full contentment. Now for the council. [*Exeunt*]

SCENE 3: *Flourish. The council chamber. Errington, Sir Arthur and Church on raised platform. Mordaunt and Fitzarnold seated at table, L. Elders, etc. Goodenough and Soldiers, R. Villagers, etc. Walter and Tramp.*

ERR. 'Tis news that asks from us most speedy action. Heaven has in sounds most audible and strange, in sights, too, that amazed the lookers-on, forewarned our people of their peril. 'Tis time to lift the arm so long supine, and with one blow cut off this heathen race, who spite of reason and the word revealed, continue hardened in their devious ways, and make the chosen tremble. Colleagues, your voices—speak—are you for peace or war?

SIR A. What is your proof your Indian neighbors mean not as fairly towards our settlements as did King Philip's father, Massasoit?

ERR. Sir, we have full proof that Philip is our foe. Sasamond, the faithful servant of our cause, has been dispatched by Philip's men, set on to murder him. One of his tribe confessed the horrid truth—and will, when time shall call, give horrid proof on't. I say this chieftain is a man of blood, and Heaven will bless the valiant arm that slays him. [*Metamora enters suddenly and remains at C. When Metamora enters, all start and grasp their swords. The soldiers prepare to fire. All are silent and confused*]

META. You sent for me and I am come. Humph! If you have nothing to say I will go back—if you fear to question, Metamora does not fear to answer.

ERR. Philip, 'tis thought you love us not, and all unmindful of our league of peace, plot with the Narragansetts, and contrive fatal disorder to our colony.

META. Do your fears counsel you? What is it makes your old men grave? And your young men grasp their fire weapons as if they awaited the onset of the foe? Brothers, what has Metamora done that doubt is in all your faces and your spirits seem troubled? The good man's heart is a stranger to fear, and his tongue is ready to speak the words of truth.

ERR. We are informed that thou gavest shelter to a banished man, whose deeds unchristian met our just reproof—one by our holy synod doomed—whom it is said you housed, and thereby hast incurred our church's censure—and given just cause to doubt thy honesty.

META. Why was that man sent away from the home of his joy? Because the Great Spirit did not speak to him as he had spoken to you? Did you not come across the great waters and leave the smoke of your fathers' hearth because the iron hand was held out against you, and your hearts were sorrowful in the high places of prayer. Why do you that have just plucked the red knife from your own wounded sides, strive to stab your brother?

ERR. Indian, this is no reply for us. Didst thou not know the sentence of the court on him whom thou didst shelter?

META. If my rarest enemy had crept unarmed into my wigwam and his heart was sore, I would not have driven him from my fire nor forbidden him to lie down upon my mat. Why then should the Wampanoag shut out the man of peace when he came with tears in his eyes and his limbs torn by the sharp thorns of the thicket? Your great book, you say, tells you to give good gifts to the stranger and deal kindly with him whose heart is sad; the Wampanoag needs no such counselor, for the Great Spirit has with his own fingers written it upon his heart.

MOR. Why dost thou put arms into thy people's hands, thereby engendering mischief towards us?

META. If my people do wrong, I am quick to punish. Do you not set a snare for them that they may fall, and make them mad with the fire water the Great Spirit gave you in his wrath? The red man sickens in the house of the palefaces, and the leaping stream of the mountains is made impure by the foul brooks that mingle with it.

SIR A. Chieftain, since these things are so, sell us thy lands and seek another biding place.

META. And if I did, would you not stretch out your hand to seize that also? No! White man, no! Never will Metamora forsake the home of his fathers, and let the plough of the strangers disturb the bones of his kindred.

CHURCH. These are bold words, chief.

META. They are true ones.

ERR. They give no token of thy love of peace. We would deal fairly with thee—nay, be generous.

META. Then would you pay back that which fifty snows ago you received from the hands of my father, Massasoit. Ye had been tossed about like small things upon the face of the great waters, and there was no earth for your feet to rest on; your backs were turned upon the land of your fathers. The red man took you as a little child* and opened the door of his wigwam. The keen blast of the north howled in the leafless wood, but the Indian covered you with his broad right hand and put it back. Your little ones smiled when they heard the loud voice of the storm, for our fires were warm and the Indian was the white man's friend.*

ERR. Such words are needless now.

META. I will speak no more; I am going.

MOR. Hold! A moment, Philip; we have yet to tell of the death of Sasamond, who fell in secret and by treachery.

META. So should the treacherous man fall, by the keen knife in the darkness and not ascend from the strife of battle to the bright haven where the dead warrior dwells in glory.

ERR. Didst thou contrive his murder?

META. I will not answer.

ERR. We have those can prove thou didst.

META. I have spoken.

ERR. Bring in the witness. [*Exit Goodenough*] We, too, long have stayed the arm of power from execution. Come, we parley with a serpent and his wiles are deep.

META. Injurious white man! Do not tread too hard upon the serpent's folds. His fangs are not taken out, nor has its venom lost the power to kill.

ERR. Approach! [*Goodenough returns with Annawandah*]

META. Annawandah!

ERR. Behold, deceitful man, thy deeds are known.

META. Let me see his eye. Art thou he whom I snatched from the war club of the Mohigan [*sic*], when thou hadst sung thy death song, and the lips of the foe were thirsty for thy blood? Has Metamora cherished thee in his wigwam and hast thou put a knife into the white man's hand to slay him! The foul spirit hath entered thee, and the pure blood of the Wampanoag has left thy veins. Thy heart is a lie, and thine eye cannot rest upon the face of truth, when like the great light it shines on thee in unclouded glory. Elders,

---

* Lines between asterisks are reprinted from the Forrest Home manuscript, because they are illegible in the University of Utah manuscript.

can he speak to you the words of truth, when he is false to his brother, his country and his god?

ERR. He was thy trusty agent, Philip, and conscience-smote revealed thy wickedness.

META. You believe his words?

ERR. We do, and will reward his honesty.

META. Wampanoag! No, I will not call thee so. Red man, say unto these people they have bought thy tongue, and thou hast uttered a lie!

ERR. He does not answer.

META. I am Metamora, thy father and thy king.

ERR. Philip o'erawes him—send the witness home.

META. I will do that! Slave of the white man, go follow Sasamond. [*Stabs Annawandah, who staggers off, R. All stand up, general movement*]

ERR. Seize and bind him. [*Soldiers make a forward movement*]

META. Come! My knife has drunk the blood of the false one, yet it is not satisfied! White man, beware! The mighty spirits of the Wampanoag race are hovering o'er your heads; they stretch out their shadowy arms to me and ask for vengeance; they shall have it. The wrath of the wronged Indian shall fall upon you like a cataract that dashes the uprooted oak down the mighty chasms. The war whoop shall start you from your dreams at night, and the red hatchet gleam in the blaze of your burning dwellings! From the east to the west, in the north and in the south shall cry of vengeance burst, till the lands you have stolen groan under your feet no more!

ERR. Secure him!

META. Thus do I smite your nation and defy your power.

ERR. Fire on him. [*Business. Metamora hurls hatchet into stage, and rushes out, C. Soldiers fire after him. Mordaunt, who has moved forward, receives a shot and falls in chair. Tableau. Drums, trumpets, and general confusion. Quick curtain*]

ACT III.

SCENE 1: *A chamber in Mordaunt's house. Enter Fitzarnold.*

FITZ. Mordaunt wounded, and perhaps to death, struck by a shot that was leveled at the chief; and the fierce storm of war at distance heard, which soon may burst tremendous o'er our heads! This is no place for me. She must be mine tonight! Aye, this night, for fear his death may snatch his gold and daughter from me. Within there, Wolfe! [*Enter Wolfe*] Go get a surgeon for this Mordaunt's wounds, a scribe and priest for me—wilt be silent?

WOLFE. I will observe! Does my lord wed tomorrow?

Fitz. No, this night; and with tomorrow's sun I spread my sail for England.

Wolfe. Ha!

Fitz. How now! What meanest thou? Wouldst thou to rival me?

Wolfe. My lord!

Fitz. Well, well; go see thy duty done. [*Exit*]

Wolfe. My lord, be sure on't. Now for young Walter. I will fulfill my duty but not to thee, my Lord Fitzarnold! Thou wilt not thank me for the priest I'll bring. [*Exit*]

Scene 2: *An Indian village, deep wood, set wigwam, R. Lights half down. Conch shell heard. Nahmeokee enters from wigwam.*

Nah. Sure 'twas the shell of Metamora, and spoke the strain it was wont when the old men were called to council, or when the scout returns from his long travel.

Meta. [*Outside*] Nahmeokee!

Nah. It is—it is Metamora. [*Enter Metamora*]

Meta. Is our little one well, Nahmeokee?

Nah. He is. How didst thou leave the white man with whom thou hast been to hold a talk?

Meta. Like the great stream of the mountain when the spirit of the storm passes furiously over its bosom. Where are my people?

Nah. Here in the deep woods where Kaweshine,* the aged priest, tells them the mighty deeds of their people, and interprets to them the will of the Great Spirit.

Meta. Otah! [*Otah enters*] Summon my warriors; bid them with speed to council. [*Exit Otah*] I have escaped the swift flight of the white man's bullets but like the bounding elk when the hunters who follow close upon his heels. [*Reenter Otah with Kaweshine and all the Indians. Indian march, eight bars. Indians form at L.*] Warriors, I took a prisoner from the uplifted weapon of the Mohigan, when the victor's limbs were bloody and the scalps at his belt had no number. He lived in my wigwam; I made him my brother. When the spirit of sleep was upon me, he crept like a guilty thing away, and put into the white man's hand a brand of fire to consume me, and drive my people far away where there are no hunting grounds and where the Wampanoag has no protecting Spirit.

Kawe. Annawandah?

Meta. Annawandah!

* From this point on, the manuscript reads *Kaweshine* instead of the original reading, *Kaneshine.*

KAWE. Where is he, chief of thy people, and where is the dog whose head the Great Spirit will smite with fire?

META. Where the ravenous bird of night may eat the flesh of his body. Here is the blood of the traitor's heart! [*Shows knife*] My people, shall I tell you the thoughts that fill me?

KAWE. Speak, Metamora, speak!

META. When the strangers came from afar off, they were like a little tree; but now they are grown up and their spreading branches threaten to keep the light from you. They ate of your corn and drank of your cup, and now they lift up their arms against you. O my people, the race of the red man has fallen away like the trees of the forest before the axes of the palefaces. The fair places of his father's triumphs hear no more the sound of his footsteps. He moves in the region his proud fathers bequeathed him, not like a lord of the soil, but like a wretch who comes for plunder and for prey. [*Distant thunder and lightning*]

KAWE. The chief has spoken truly and the stranger is worthy to die! But the fire of our warriors is burnt out and their hatchets have no edge. O son of Massasoit, thy words are to me like the warm blood of the foe, and I will drink till I am full! Speak again!

META. "Chief of the people," said a voice from the deep as I lay by the seaside in the eyes of the moon—"Chief of the people, wake from thy dream of peace, and make sharp the point of thy spear, for the destroyer's arm is made bare to smite. O son of my old age, arise like the tiger in great wrath and snatch thy people from the devourer's jaws!" My father spoke no more; a mist passed before me, and from the mist the Spirit bent his eyes imploringly on me. I started to my feet and shouted the shrill battle cry of the Wampanoags. The high hills sent back the echo, and rock, hill and ocean, earth and air opened their giant throats and cried with me, "Red man, arouse! Freedom! Revenge or death!" [*Thunder and lightning. All quail but Metamora*] Hark, warriors! The Great Spirit hears me and pours forth his mighty voice with mine. Let your voice in battle be like his, and the flash from your fire weapons as quick to kill. Nahmeokee, take this knife, carry it to the Narragansett, to thy brother; tell him the hatchet is dug from the grave where the grass is grown old above it; thy tongue will move him more than the voice of all our tribe in the loud talk of war.

NAH. Nahmeokee will not fail in her path; and her eyes will be quick to see where the stranger has set his snare.

META. Warriors! Your old and infirm must you send into the country of the Narragansett, that your hearts may not be made soft in the hour of battle.

NAH. Go you tonight, Metamora?

META. Tonight! I will not lay down in my wigwam till the foe has drawn himself together and comes in his height to destroy. Nahmeokee, I still will be the red man's father and his king, or the sacred rock whereon my father spoke so long the words of wisdom shall be made red with the blood of his race. [*Hurried music. Metamora and Indians exeunt. Nahmeokee goes in wigwam*]

SCENE 3: *A chamber in Mordaunt's house. Clock strikes twelve as scene opens. Thunder distant. Enter Oceana in plain attire.*

OCEANA. I know not how it is but every thunder peal seems to bear words portentous. The moaning blast has meaning in its sound and tells of distant horror—it is the hour when I bade Walter come! Can he have braved the tempest? Hark, I hear a step! [*Knock*] How my heart beats. [*Enter Fitzarnold*] It is—it is Fitzarnold!

FITZ. Fitzarnold, lady! Why this wonder? Is it fear? Can she whom thunder frights not shrink from me?

OCEANA. My lord, the hour is late; I feign would know who sent thee hither.

FITZ. Thy honored father.

OCEANA. Thy purpose?

FITZ. Read it there. [*Gives letter*]

OCEANA. Ha! Tonight! Be thine tonight?

FITZ. Aye, tonight. I have thy father's secret.

OCEANA. I know thou hast, and in that mean advantage wouldst mar his daughter's happiness forever—away! I blush that thus I parley words with thee—get thee gone. [*Crosses to L.*]

FITZ. Yes, when thou goest with me; not till then, lady. I will not waste the time that grows more precious every moment to me. [*Thunder*] What though the lightning flash and thunder roll—what though the tempest pours its fury down, Fitzarnold's soul does swell above the din! Nay more, dares brave the storm within thy breast, and shrinks not from the lightning of thine eye.

OCEANA. Would it could kill thee!

FITZ. It can do more—can conquer like the fiery serpent. It pierces, and as it pierces charms—Oceana!

OCEANA. Stand back! I will alarm my sire.

FITZ. And if thou dost, he will not aid thee. My treasures are embarked, aye, all but thee; thy father gives consent, the priest waits and ere morning, father, daughter, son, shall all be riding on the wave for England.

OCEANA. No, never!

FITZ. Convince thyself—[*Stamps his foot. Walter enters disguised as a priest*] Now, scornful lady, thy bridal hour has come; thy tauntings do but fan the flame that rages here.

OCEANA. Is there no refuge?

FITZ. None, but in these arms.

OCEANA. No hope—no rescue!

FITZ. None! None!

OCEANA. Walter, on thee I call—Walter, where art thou?

WALT. [*Throws off disguise*] Walter is here.

FITZ. Villain! Thy life or mine! [*Fitzarnold draws, Oceana throws herself between them*]

OCEANA. Forebear! No blood! [*To Walter*] Thou must come stainless to these arms.

WALT. Sayest thou? Wilt thou take me to them?

OCEANA. I will—I do. [*They embrace*]

FITZ. Thy father's blood be on thee; he is Fitzarnold's victim. [*Exit, R. Bell rings. Enter Tramp, L.*]

TRAMP. The savages approach! The Wampanoag chieftain and his crew, at distance, peal their startling yell of war! Haste, sir, to meet them.

WALT. Retire thee for a while, my Oceana—thou, sir, on the instant follow me—your sword! your sword! [*Exit, R. with Oceana, Tramp follows*]

SCENE 4: *A view of Mordaunt's house on the beach, R. Sea in distance, ship on fire. Garden and staircase leading down to the water. Lights down at opening of scene. Distant yells heard. Enter Fitzarnold hastily.*

FITZ. Almighty powers! Hemmed in on every side! No hope. [*War whoop*] Hark to their savage yells! No means are left for flight, for on the waves my precious vessel burns—by the fell savage mastered! No retreat! [*War whoops. Exit Fitzarnold hastily. Metamora and all the Indians enter up staircase entrances. Music hurried, forte till all are on.*]

META. [*Pointing to Fitzarnold*] Follow him! [*To others*] Go into the white man's dwelling and drag him to me that my eye can look upon his torture and his scalp may tell Metamora's triumph to his tribe—go. [*Otah and Kaweshine are about to enter the house when Oceana appears*]

OCEANA. Forebear, ye shall not enter.

META. Warriors, have I not spoken. [*Throws her around to L. Indians go in*]

OCEANA. Great chieftain! Dost thou not know me?

META. I am a Wampanoag in the home of mine enemy; I ride on my wrongs, and vengeance cries out for blood.

OCEANA. Wilt thou not hear me?

META. Talk to the rattling storm or melt the high rocks with tears; thou canst not move me. My foe! my foe! my foe!

OCEANA. Have mercy, Heaven! [*The Indians return dragging in Mordaunt and down R.*]

META. Hah!

MOR. Mercy! Mercy!

OCEANA. My father! Spare my father! [*Rushes to Mordaunt*]

META. He must die! Drag him away to the fire of the sacrifice that my ear may drink the music of his dying groans.

OCEANA. Fiends and murderers!

META. The white man has made us such. Prepare. [*Business*]

OCEANA. Then smite his heart through mine; our mangled breasts shall meet in death—one grave shall hold us. Metamora, dost thou remember this? [*Shows eagle plume*]

META. Yes.

OCEANA. It was thy father's. Chieftain, thou gavest it to me.

META. Say on.

OCEANA. Thou saidst it would prove a guardian to me when the conflict raged. Were thy words true when with thy father's tongue thou saidst, whatever being wore the gift, no Indian of thy tribe should do that being harm.

META. The Wampanoag cannot lie.

OCEANA. Then do I place it here. [*Places it on Mordaunt's bosom*]

META. Hah!

OCEANA. The Wampanoag cannot lie, and I can die for him who gave existence to me.

MOR. My child! My child! [*Red fire in house*]

META. Take them apart! [*Indians separate them*] Old man, I cannot let the tomahawk descend upon thy head, or bear thee to the place of sacrifice; but here is that shall appease the red man's wrath. [*Seizes Oceana; flames seen in house*] The fire is kindled in thy dwelling, and I will plunge her in the hot fury of the flames.

MOR. No, no, thou wilt not harm her.

OCEANA. Father, farewell! Thy nation, savage, will repent this act of thine.

META. If thou art just, it will not. Old man, take thy child. [*Throws her to him*] Metamora cannot forth with the maiden of the eagle plume; and he disdains a victim who has no color in his face nor fire in his eye. [*Bugle sounds*]

Mor. Gracious heavens!

Meta. Hark! The power of the white man comes! Launch your canoes! We have drunk blood enough. Spirit of my father, be at rest! Thou art obeyed, thy people are avenged. [*Exit hastily followed by the Indians. Drums and trumpet till curtain. Enter Walter, Goodenough, Church, Soldiers, Peasants, male and female, all from behind house. Soldiers are about to fire, when Walter throws himself before them and exclaims*]

Walt. Forebear! Forebear! [*Walter and Oceana embrace. Tableau. Curtain*]

ACT IV.

The fourth act of *Metamora* is missing from the University of Utah manuscript. Scene and property plots provided at the beginning of the manuscript, together with the Forrest Home manuscript, which includes Metamora's lines, cue lines, and a few stage directions, and clues from the rest of the play suggest the following summary:

The plot of Act IV is chiefly concerned with the capture of Nahmeokee by the white men, the capture of Walter (Horatio) by the Indians, and the demands and threats of the Indian chieftain, Metamora. There are three scenes: an oak chamber, a dark wood, and a landscape. The first scene, obviously located in one of the white men's houses—perhaps that of Errington, the head of the council—shows Nahmeokee a captive. Because Metamora does not appear in this scene, no part of it can be given here. Scene 2 introduces Walter (Horatio), captured by the Indians and about to be killed, until Metamora learns of the capture of Nahmeokee and decides to hold the youthful hero as a hostage. In the third scene Metamora, going to the rescue of his wife, meets the white men with Nahmeokee in the open country, and after several defiant speeches, accepts an offer of peace. Thereupon Nahmeokee is released and sent home to inform the Indians of the terms. (We later discover that Metamora keeps his agreement, but that an attempt to kill Nahmeokee is made by the white men.)

The following pages include the lines from the Forrest Home manuscript, together with a few parenthetical explanations and speculations. (See the introductory note to this play for acknowledgements and additional information concerning this manuscript.)

Scene 1: Missing from both the University of Utah manuscript and the Forrest Home manuscript.

SCENE 2: Cue lines of other speakers than Metamora will be indicated by dashes. *Metamora disc^d., regarding the scene.*

————Captive's blood. [*The report of a pistol his [sic] heard. Horatio enters, the Indians raise their tomahawks to strike him*]

META.   Forbear! Let the young man say why he has come into our country unbidden. Why does he tempt the ire of our warriors, when their weapons are red with the blood of the battle?

————white and red man, brothers. (Apparently this is Horatio's explanation of his hope to appease the opposing forces.)

META.   No, young man, the blood my warriors have tasted, has made their hearts glad, and their hands are thrust out for more. Let the white man fear. The arrow he has shot into the mountain has turned back and pierced his own side. What are the elders' words?

————raised no more. (Perhaps the elders demur.)

META.   Humph! And meanwhile he sharpens his bright weapons in secret and each day grows more numerous. When the mountain torrent first springs from the earth it is very weak, and I can stand up against its waters, but when the great rains descend it is swift and swollen, death dwells in its white bosom and it will not spare.

————avenge their countrymen. (The white men, it is feared, will come again in greater numbers.)

META.   Well, let 'em come. Our arms are as strong as the white man's, and the use of the fire weapon he has taught us—my ears are shut against thee.

————[*Without*]   Metamora!

META.   Hah!

————Nahmeokee!

META.   Dead?

————bore off the queen a captive.

META.   Nahmeokee is the white man's prisoner. [*To Horatio*] Where is thy horse?

————near yonder tree. (Obviously Horatio's lying. Horatio, it should be remembered, is the Walter of the preceding acts.)

META.   Unbind this captive. Young man, you must abide with the Wampanoag, until Nahmeokee return to her home. Woe come to you if the hard hand has been laid upon her. Bear these two to my wigwam.

————whose blood I bear. (Probably Horatio again.)

META.   If one drop fall from Nahmeokee's eye, one hair from her head, the axe shall hew your quivering limbs asunder, and the ashes of your bones be carried away on the rushing wind.

SCENE 3:

————Take her child from her. (Spoken by one of the white men in charge of Nahmeokee and her child.) [*Enter Metamora*]

META. Stand back, or the swift death shall take wing. [*Pause*] Which of you has lived too long? Let him lift up his arm against her.

————What comest thou for? (The same speaker as at the beginning.)

META. Boy! Thou art a child, there is no mark of the war upon thy brows. Send me thy elder, or thy chief, I will make my talk to him. [*Bugle. Enter Errington and Soldiers*]

————Philip a prisoner! (Probably spoken by Errington.)

META. No. He has arms in his hand and courage in his heart. He comes near you of his own will and when he has done his work he will go back to his wigwam.

————you answer boldly. (Probably Errington again.)

META. What is there I should fear?

————man of blood. (Errington continues.)

META. Does he love mercy, and is he the white man's prince?

————Yes.

META. How did Nahmeokee and her infant wrong you, that you hunted her through the thorny pathway of the glen, and scented her blood, like the fierce red wolf in his hunger?

————sue for peace. (Probably Errington.)

META. Not till the blood of twenty English captives be poured out in sacrifice. Beware! the knife is sharpened, the stake is fixed and the captives' limbs tremble under the gaze of the prophet of wrath. Woe come to them! When my people shall hear their king has been murdered by the palefaces or is bound in the dark place of doom.

————standing in the midst. (Perhaps several speeches here omitted.)

META. Which can easier escape the hunter's spear, the tiger that turns upon it in its wrath or the lamb that sinks down and trembles? Thou hast seen me look unmoved towards a torturing death—shall mine eye be turned downward when the white man frowns?

————regard his words. (One of the councilors speaks.)

META. Yes.

————Wilt yield compliance. (A peace offering is made, whereby, among other things, Nahmeokee's release will be pledged.)

META. I will; Nahmeokee shall bear to my people the tidings that the prisoners shall return to their home, and the war whoop shall not go forth on the evening gale.

————remember thy words. (Errington.)

META. Grieve not that [I?] linger in the dark place of the condemned, for the eye of the Great Spirit will rest on me there.

————Nahmeokee shall return. (Probably Errington.)

META. 'Tis very good. The horse stand under the brow of the hill. Speak no more. I read thy thought in thine eye, but the white man must not know it. It will do. Go Nahmeokee. I am ready to follow you.

————forth to prison. (Apparently some business omitted here. Part of this speech seems addressed privately to Nahmeokee. The following stage direction supports the conclusion that at this point the white men attempt to seize the Indians, despite the previous agreement.) [*Soldier attempts to take his gun*]

META. No. This shall be to me as my child, and I will talk with it till I go back to my people.

————could it but talk.

META. It can! When the land of my great forefathers is trampled on by the foot of the foe, or treachery lurks round the Wampanoag when he bides in the white man's home, then—it *can talk*.

ACT V.

SCENE 1: *Same as Act I, Scene 1. Lights down. Oceana discovered leaning against tomb. Slow music, four bars.*

OCEANA. Tomb of the silent dead, thou seemest my only refuge! O Walter, where art thou? Alas! the kindly promptings of thy noble heart have led thee to captivity, perhaps to death! Welcome the hour when these dark portals shall unfold again, and reunite parent and child in the long sleep of death. [*Enter Fitzarnold*] Ah! Fitzarnold here!

FITZ. I come with words of comfort to thee and feign would soothe thy sorrow.

OCEANA. I do not ask your sympathy, my lord.

FITZ. A sea of danger is around thee, lady, and I would be the skillful pilot to guide thy struggling bark to safety.

OCEANA. Nay, but let me rather perish in the waves than reach a haven to be shared with thee.

FITZ. Thou hast no choice; thy father willed thee mine, and with his latest breath bequeathed thee to me. Walter, my stripling rival in thy love, has left thee here defenseless and alone. I deem as nothing thy unnatural hate, and only see thy fair and lovely form; and though thy flashing eyes were armed with lightning, thus would my arms enfold thee.

OCEANA. [*Clings to tomb*] Now, if thou darest, approach me—now whilst with my mother's spirit hovering o'er me—whilst thus with tearful eyes and breaking heart I call on Heaven to blast the bold audacious wretch, who seeks a daughter's ruin o'er her parents' grave.

FITZ. Aye, despite of all.

META. [*In tomb*] Hold! Touch her not!

OCEANA. Hark to that voice! Kind Heaven has heard my prayers. [*The door of the tomb opens, and Metamora appears. Oceana faints and falls*]

FITZ. Philip here!

META. He is the great spirit [who?] has sent me;* the ghosts are awaiting for thee in the dark place of doom! Now thou must go. Tremble, for the loud cry is terrible and the blaze of their eyes, like the red fire of war, gleams awfully in the night.

FITZ. I have not wronged thee.

META. Not? Didst thou not contrive the death of Nahmeokee, when the treacherous white man thirsted for her blood? Did she not with bended knees, her eyes streaming with woes of the heart, catch hold of thy shining broad garment thinking it covered man? Was not thy hand upraised against her, and thy heart, like thy hand, flint that wounds the weary one who rests upon it.

FITZ. No! no!

META. I saw thee when my quick step was on the hills, and the joy of Metamora's eyes felt thy blows. I feel them now! "Revenge!" cried the shadow of my father as he looked on with me. I, too, cried revenge and now I have it! The blood of my heart grows hotter as I look on him who smote the red cheek of Nahmeokee.

FITZ. As reparation I will give thee gold.

META. No! Give me back the happy days, the fair hunting ground, and the dominion my great forefathers bequeathed me.

FITZ. I have not robbed thee of them.

META. Thou art a white man, and thy veins hold the blood of a robber! Hark! The spirits of the air howl for thee! Prepare—[*Throws him around to R.*]

FITZ. Thou shalt not conquer ere thou killest me. This sword a royal hand bestowed! This arm can wield it still. [*Draws; Metamora disarms and kills him*]

---

* This is the actual reading of the manuscript. A more plausible reading would probably be: "He is. The Great Spirit has sent me."

META. Metamora's arm has saved thee from a common death; who dies by me dies nobly! [*Turns to Oceana*] For thee, Metamora's home shall screen thee from the spreading fury of his nation's wrath. [*Hurry till change. Exit bearing Oceana*]

SCENE 2: *A chamber. Enter Sir Arthur, meeting Errington and Church.*

SIR A. I have news will startle you.

ERR. Is't of the chief?

SIR A. It is; he has escaped our power!

ERR. Escaped! Confusion! How?

SIR A. But now we sought his prison and found it tenantless.

ERR. But how escaped he? There was no egress thence, unless some treacherous hand unlocked the door.

SIR A. And so we thought, at first; but on minute search we found some stones displaced, which showed a narrow opening into a subterranean passage, dark and deep, through which we crept until, to our surprise, we reached the tomb of Mordaunt.

ERR. The tomb of Mordaunt?

SIR A. The ruined pile which now serves as our prison was, years since, when first he sought these shores, the residence of Mordaunt, and this secret passage, doubtless, was formed by him for concealment or escape in time of danger.

ERR. Indeed!

SIR A. Yes, and he had cause to be so guarded, for once, unseen by him, I heard that wretched man commune with Heaven, and sue for pardon for the heinous sin of Hammond of Harrington!

ERR. Hammond! The outlawed regicide?

SIR A. Even so; it was himself he prayed for, the guilty man who gave to death the king, his lord, the royal martyr Charles. As Mordaunt, he here sought refuge from the wrath of the rightful heir now seated on the throne.

ERR. Think you the chieftain knew this secret way?

SIR A. 'Tis likely that he did, or else by chance discovered it and thus has won his freedom and his life.

CHURCH. We must summon our men. Double the guard and have their range extended. [*Exeunt Church and Errington*]

WOLFE. [*Without*] Where is Sir Arthur Vaughan?

SIR A. Who calls? [*Enter Wolfe*] Now, who art thou?

WOLFE. A suppliant for pardon.

SIR A. Pardon—for what?

WOLFE. A grievous sin, I now would feign confess.

SIR A. Indeed! Go on! Declare it then; I will forgive thee!

WOLFE. Long years have passed since then, but you must still remember when at Naples with your wife and child.

SIR A. Ha! Dost thou mean—

WOLFE. The flames consumed thy dwelling and thou together with thy wife and boy, escaped almost by miracle.

SIR A. Ha!

WOLFE. I there looked on midst the assembled throng, a stranger mariner. Urged by the fiend, and aided by the wild confusion of the scene, I snatched your boy and through the noisy throng I bore him to my anchored bark, thinking his waiting parents soon would claim with gold their darling. Next day came on a tempest and the furious winds far from the city drove us and thy child.

SIR A. Heavens! Can this be true?

WOLFE. He grew up the sharer of my sea-born perils. One awful night our vessel stuck upon the rocks near these shores and the greedy ocean swelled over her shattered frame—thy son—

SIR A. Go on—go on—

WOLFE. Was by mysterious power preserved and guided to his unconscious father. Walter is thy son.

SIR A. Man! Why didst thou not tell me?

WOLFE. I feared thy just anger and the force of law. I became Fitzarnold's follower but to this hour has memory tortured me.

SIR A. And Walter is a hostage to the savage foe; perchance they have murdered him!

WOLFE. No! Oceana's kindness to the Indian queen has purchased his freedom and my own.

SIR A. Where is he?

WOLFE. Looking for her he loves, fair Oceana! Whom, 'tis said, a party of the foe carried off.

SIR A. Quick, let us arm and follow him. For thee, this act of justice pardons thee. [*Exeunt*]

SCENE 3: *Indian village. Groups of Indians. Kaweshine and Otah discovered. Kaweshine has been addressing them. His looks are gloomy and bewildered.*

META. [*Outside, at change of scene*] Where are my people?

KAWE. Ha! 'Tis our chief—I know the sound of his voice, and some quick danger follows him. [*Metamora enters, bearing Oceana. Nahmeokee enters from wigwam*]

META. Nahmeokee, take the white maiden in; I would speak to my people; go in and follow not the track of the warrior's band.

NAH. Come in, my mat is soft, and the juice of the sweet berry shall give joy to thy lips. Come in, thou art pale and yielding, like the lily, when it is borne down by the running waters. [*She leads Oceana into wigwam*]

META. Warriors, I have escaped from the hands of the white man, when the fire was kindled to devour me. Prepare for the approaching hour if ye love the high places your fathers trod in majesty and strength. Snatch your keen weapons and follow me! If ye love the silent spots where the bones of your kindred repose, sing the dread song of war and follow me! If you love the bright lakes which the Great Spirit gave you when the sun first blazed with the fires of his touch, shout the war song of the Wampanoag race, and on to the battle follow me! Look at the bright glory that is wrapped like a mantle around the slain in battle! Call on the happy spirits of the warriors dead, and cry, "Our lands! Our nation's freedom! Or the grave!"

KAWE. O chieftain, take my counsel and hold out to the palefaces the pipe of peace. Ayantic and the great Mohican join with our foes against us, and the power of our brother, the Narragansett is no more! List, o chieftain, to the words that I tell of the time to come.

META. Ha! Dost thou prophesy?

KAWE. In the deep wood, when the moon shone bright, my spirit was sad and I sought the ear of Manito in the sacred places; I heard the sound as of one in pain, and I beheld gasping under a hemlock, the lightning had sometime torn, a panther wounded and dying in his thick red gore. I thought of the tales of our forefathers who told us that such was an omen of coming evil. I spoke loudly the name of Metamora, and the monster's eyes closed instantly and he writhed no more. I turned and mourned, for I said, Manito loves no. more the Wampanoag and our foes will prevail.

META. Didst thou tell my people this?

KAWE. Chieftain, yes; my spirit was troubled.

META. Shame of the tribe, thou art no Wampanoag, thy blood is tainted —thou art half Mohigan, thy breath has sapped the courage of my warriors' hearts. Begone, old man, thy life is in danger.

KAWE. I have spoken the words of truth, and the Great Manito has heard them.

META. Liar and coward! Let him preserve thee now! [*About to stab him when Nahmeokee enters from wigwam and interposes*]

NAH. He is a poor old man—he healed the deep wound of our little one. [*Gets to L. of Metamora*]

META. Any breast but Nahmeokee's had felt the keen edge of my knife! Go, corrupted one, thy presence makes the air unwholesome round hope's high places. Begone!

KAWE. Metamora drives me from the wigwam before the lightning descends to set it on fire. Chieftain, beware the omen. [*Exit*]

NAH. [*Aside*] Will he not become the white man's friend and show him the secret path of our warriors? Manito guard the Wampanoag!

META. Men of Po-hon-e-ket, the palefaces come towards your dwellings and no warrior's hatchet is raised for vengeance. The war whoop is hushed in the camp and we hear no more the triumph of battle. Manito hates you, for you have fallen from the high path of your fathers and Metamora must alone avenge the Wampanoag's wrongs.

OMNES. Battle! Battle!

META. Ha! The flame springs up afresh in your bosoms; a woman's breath has brought back the lost treasure of your souls. [*Distant march, drums and trumpet heard*] Ha! they come! Go, warriors, and meet them, and remember the eye of a thousand ages looks upon you. [*Warriors exeunt silently*] Nahmeokee, should the palefaces o'ercome our strength, go thou with our infant to the sacred place of safety. My followers slain, there will the last of the Wampanoags pour out his heart's blood on the giant rock, his father's throne.

NAH. O Metamora!

META. Come not near me or thou wilt make my heart soft, when I would have it hard like the iron and gifted with many lives. Go in, Nahmeokee. [*Distant trumpets. Nahmeokee goes in wigwam. Metamora kneels*] The knee that never bent to man I bend to thee, Manito. As the arm was broken that was put out against Nahmeokee, so break thou the strength of the oppressor's nation, and hurl them down from the high hill of their pride and power, with the loud thunder of thy voice. Confound them—smite them with the lightning of thine eye—while thus I bare my red war arm—while thus I wait the onset of the foe—[*Loud alarm*] They come! Death! Death, or my nation's freedom! [*Rushes off. Loud shouts. Drums and trumpets till change*]

SCENE 4: *Rocky pass. Trumpet sounds retreat. Enter Errington and Church.*

ERR. They fly! They fly—the field is ours! This blow destroys them. Victory cheaply bought at twice our loss; the red man's power is broken now forever. [*Enter Walter*] Is Oceana slain?

WALT. No; the chieftain Metamora rescued her from the base passions of the Lord Fitzarnold whom Metamora slew to avenge the wrongs he offered to his wife, and Oceana by the chief was borne in safety to his lodge.

ERR. In safety?

WALT. Yes; from the hands of Nahmeokee I received her, just as some Indians maddened by defeat, prepared to offer her a sacrifice.

ERR. Away then, Walter. [*Walter crosses to R.*] Sir Arthur now seeks thee out to claim thee as his own [son?]. (Parenthetical word *sic.*)

WALT. My father! I fly to seek him. [*Exit*]

ERR. The victory is ours; yet while Philip lives we are in peril! Come, let us find this Indian prophet whom Metamora banished from his tribe. He may be bribed to show us the chieftain's place of safety. [*Exeunt. Change*]

SCENE 5: *Metamora's stronghold. Rocks, bridge and waterfall. Nahmeokee discovered listening. The child lays under a tree, R., covered with furs. Slow music, four bars.*

NAH. He comes not, yet the sound of the battle has died away like the last breath of a storm! Can he be slain? O cruel white man, this day will stain your name forever. [*Slow music, sixteen bars. Metamora enters on bridge. Crosses and enters L.*]

META. Nahmeokee, I am weary of the strife of blood. Where is our little one? Let me take him to my burning heart and he may quell its mighty torrent.

NAH. [*With broken utterance*] He is here! [*Lifts the furs and shows the child dead*]

META. Ha! Dead! Dead! Cold!

NAH. Nahmeokee could not cover him with her body, for the white men were around her and over her. I plunged into the stream and the unseen shafts of the fire weapons flew with a great noise over my head. One smote my babe and he sunk into the deep water; the foe shouted with a mighty shout, for he thought Nahmeokee and her babe had sunk to rise no more.

META. His little arms will never clasp thee more; his little lips will never press the pure bosom which nourished him so long! Well, is he not happy? Better to die by the stranger's hand than live his slave.

NAH. O Metamora! [*Falls on his neck*]

META. Nay, do not bow down thy head; let me kiss off the hot drops that are running down thy red cheeks. Thou wilt see him again in the peaceful land of spirits, and he will look smilingly as—as—as I do now, Nahmeokee.

NAH. Metamora, is our nation dead? Are we alone in the land of our fathers?

META. The palefaces are all around us, and they tread in blood. The blaze of our burning wigwams flashes awfully in the darkness of their path. We are destroyed—not vanquished; we are no more, yet we are forever—Nahmeokee!

NAH. What wouldst thou?

META. Dost thou not fear the power of the white man?

NAH. No.

META. He may come hither in his might and slay thee.

NAH. Thou art with me.

META. He may seize thee, and bear thee off to the far country, bind these arms that have so often clasped me in the dear embrace of love, scourge thy soft flesh in the hour of his wrath, and force thee to carry burdens like the beasts of the fields.

NAH. Thou wilt not let them.

META. We cannot fly, for the foe is all about us; we cannot fight, for this is the only weapon I have saved from the strife of blood.

NAH. It was my brother's—Coanchett's.

META. It has tasted the white man's blood, and reached the cold heart of the traitor; it has been our truest friend; it is our only treasure.

NAH. Thine eye tells me the thought of thy heart, and I rejoice at it. [*Sinks on his bosom*]

META. Nahmeokee, I look up through the long path of thin air, and I think I see our infant borne onward to the land of the happy, where the fair hunting grounds know no storms or snows, and where the immortal brave feast in the eyes of the giver of good. Look upwards, Nahmeokee, the spirit of thy murdered father beckons thee.

NAH. I will go to him.

META. Embrace me, Nahmeokee—'twas like the first you gave me in the days of our strength and joy—they are gone. [*Places his ear to the ground*] Hark! In the distant wood I faintly hear the cautious tread of men! They are upon us, Nahmeokee—the home of the happy is made ready for thee. [*Stabs her, she dies*] She felt no white man's bondage—free as the air she lived—pure as the snow she died! In smiles she died! Let me taste it, ere her lips are cold as the ice. [*Loud shouts. Roll of drums. Kaweshine leads Church and Soldiers on bridge, R.*]

CHURCH. He is found! Philip is our prisoner.

META. No! He lives—last of his race—but still your enemy—lives to defy you still. Though numbers overpower me and treachery surround me, though friends desert me, I defy you still! Come to me—come singly to me! And this true knife that has tasted the foul blood of your nation and now is red with the purest of mine, will feel a grasp as strong as when it flashed in the blaze of your burning dwellings, or was lifted terribly over the fallen in battle.

CHURCH. Fire upon him!

META. Do so, I am weary of the world for ye are dwellers in it; I would not turn upon my heel to save my life.

CHURCH. Your duty, soldiers. [*They fire. Metamora falls. Enter Walter, Oceana, Wolfe, Sir Arthur, Errington, Goodenough, Tramp and Peasants. Roll of drums and trumpet till all on*]

META. My curses on you, white men! May the Great Spirit curse you when he speaks in his war voice from the clouds! Murderers! The last of the Wampanoags' curse be on you! May your graves and the graves of your children be in the path the red man shall trace! And may the wolf and panther howl o'er your fleshless bones, fit banquet for the destroyers! Spirits of the grave, I come! But the curse of Metamora stays with the white man! I die! My wife! My queen! My Nahmeokee! [*Falls and dies; a tableau is formed. Drums and trumpet sound a retreat till curtain. Slow curtain*]

END

DAVY CROCKETT;
Or, BE SURE YOU'RE RIGHT, THEN GO AHEAD

By Frank Murdoch

PROPERTY PLOT

Act   I. Plenty of dry leaves to cover the stage—four guns to load—powder-stuffed squirrel—water pail, sidesaddle.

Act II. Four buffalo robes—Cot C.—bar to break—bundle of twigs for Davy —snow to blow in door—six pieces of wood—Scott's poem of Lochin-var—an axe.

Act III. Same as Act II.

Act IV. Large pictures on easel—pen and ink and document for lawyer—table L.2.E.

Act V. Lighted candle in window—rifle on wall—small book for Parson—legal papers for Crampton.

SCENE PLOT

Act   I. A clearing in the forest with cottage R.2.E.—Well, rope and bucket L.2.E.—Rustic bridge from R. to L.U.E.—Steps L.C.—Window in cottage—Dried leaves cover the stage—Bench in front of cottage facing audience.

Act II. Interior of Crockett's hut—Fireplace L.2.E.—Door opening down stage R.2.E.—Sockets for the bar to fasten it.

Act III. Same as Act II.

Act IV. Handsome C.D. Room.

Act V. Interior of Crockett's home—Door L.2.E.—Table C.—Window of C. flat.

CAST OF CHARACTERS

DAVY	BOB
OSCAR CRAMPTON	QUICKWITCH
NEIL	WATSON
MAJOR ROYSTON	PARSON
BIG DAN	ELEANOR
BRIGGS	DAME
YONKERS	LITTLE SAL

ACT I.

SCENE: *A clearing in the forest, with Dame Crockett's cottage, set R. Well L.*

CHORUS. [*Before rise of curtain*]
> When high o'er the mountain
> Field, valley and crag,
> The sun gilds the fountain
> We watch for the stag—
> Crack! Crack! 'mid the covers
> Our free rifles ring,
> Far flies the wild, wild plover
> The eagle takes wing.
> A thousand bold echoes
> Roll round at our hand,
> And the startled air owns us
> The Kings of the Land.

Discovered: Dame, at window.

HUNTERS. [*Without*] Hello!

DAME. Didn't I hear voices, singing and hollering? There again—my old ears ain't what they once was, but I reckon I can tell Big Dan's voice a good quarter of a mile or so yet.

HUNTERS. [*Without*] Hollo! Hollo!

DAME. Yes—there they come—as wild a set as any in the settlement, and as hungry, too, I'll be bound—for they never come this way without empty stomachs. [*Exit into house. Enter Hunters, Big Dan, Briggs and Yonkers*]

BIG DAN. Hollo, Crockett! Hollo—nobody's to home.

BRIGGS. What did I tell you?

BIG DAN. Hollo. Marm Crockett. Commissary, hollo—o—o—

YONK. Dan your lungs is in your stomach. You never yell that way except when vittles is wanting. [*Dame appears*]

BIG DAN. Ah—there she is. I know'd if she was anywhere in the settlement I'd fetch her.

DAME. Why, where's my Davy?—ain't he with you?—I allow'd he was.

YONK. Ain't seen him these two days.

DAME. He started for the ridge this morning 'fore daybreak! Well, boys —what luck?

YONK. Bad enough—here's three on us been out on a tramp arter a bear since sun-up and nary a squint of the varmint—and now look at us—tired out and as hungry as catamounts—so how about provender, mother?

DAME. Oh, plenty, boys and something worth eating this time.

OMNES. What, mother?

DAME. Well, don't ax—just wait till I get it ready. [*Exit*]

BIG DAN. There goes the biggest-hearted woman in these parts.

YONK. You are right there. [*Enter Little Bob*]

BOB. Hollo, Big Dan.

BIG DAN. Hollo, yerself, Bob.

BOB. Hey—Sal—here's Big Dan. [*Enter Little Sal and Tot*]

BIG DAN. Come here, Sal.

BOB. Go to your sweetheart, you Sal.

SAL. He ain't neither my sweetheart. Davy's my sweetheart.

BOB. Davy's your uncle—how can your uncle be your sweetheart?

BIG DAN. Oh, Davy's the man—we are square on that point. Say, Sal, what's for supper?

BOB. I know, she don't.

OMNES. What, Bob?

BOB. Broiled bear steaks.

BIG DAN. Briled bar steaks—do you hear that, boys? Bob, where did that bar come from?

BOB. Davy killed him last night.

OMNES. Last night! I'm an Injun if I don't think it's the same critter we have been arter. Say, Bobby, what did the varmint weigh?

BOB. It warn't a varmint, it were a bar.

OMNES. Ha—ha—

BIG DAN. Bob, kin you hit a squirrel yet?

BOB. I bet you I can, right in the eye, too.

YONK. Oh, Brag is a good dog, sonny.

BOB. Well, who said you weren't?

OMNES. Ha, ha!

BIG DAN. Oh, he—he can do it. I've seen him afore.

BOB. Hey—yonder's one now.

OMNES. Where?

BOB. Up there in the big chestnut tree, yonder. Give me a rest if you want to see me fetch him.

BIG DAN. Steady, Bob.

BOB. You steady your own self.

YONK. He can't do it.

BIG DAN. He can. I tell ye he can. [*Bob shoots and runs off*]

YONK. Hit, by thunder! [*Re-enter Bob*] Well, what's the matter? You fetched him, didn't you?

BOB. Yes, but it ain't in the eye. But I can do it, I can.

BIG DAN. Never mind. Maybe I moved a bit.

YONK. Yes, you moved—but it's a pretty enough shot as it stands. Ha, ha! These Crocketts do beat all creation.

DAVY. [*Without*] Hollo.

BOB. That's him. That's our Davy.

YONK. Yes, that's his voice—as clear as a bell and as sharp as the crack of a rifle—not another one like it in the settlement, and yonder he comes with a two-year-old buck over his shoulder—good for you, my boy! [*Music —quick and lively—Auld Lang Syne. Enter Davy*]

DAVY. There you are, Mother. Forty-two, how's that? Why, hollo, boys, how are you?

YONK. In luck again, eh?

DAVY. Yes, the red fools, they will come my way. Well, it's what they are made for, I spec—but for all that I never drew my knife across the throat of one of 'em without a shudder. Don't seem like a square fight, no-how. Well, boys, how are you, anyhow?

DAME. Hungry as you be, I spec', and supper just about ready.

OMNES. Ha! Ha! [*Exit*]

DAVY. [*To Bob*] Where are you going?

BOB. To get some supper.

DAVY. No siree. You and me waits.

BOB. I want some of that bar.

DAVY. You talk to me about bar in that way, I'll sew you up in the skins.

DAME. [*Appearing*] Come, Davy, there's a nice rib and slapjacks piping hot.

DAVY. Now, you go in with the boys—you know, I never eat except when I'm hungry—[*Sees Bob. Business*] What's the matter with you? What are you hiding behind the well for? Come right here to your uncle—what have you got behind you? What's that—a grey squirrel? Who killed it—you, did you? Well, what's the matter with you?—Oh, you don't mean to tell me you have missed the eye, eh? Let me look—now what kind of a shot do you call that? A good inch from the eye—and after all my teaching too! Is it all to be throw'd away on you like that? Here—I'm ashamed of you—I am indeed —I don't think you are a Crockett arter all. I reckon you must have been changed in the cradle.

Bob. Well, they ought to have watched it, then—I say, Davy, what did they do with the other one?

Davy. The other what?

Bob. The other baby, the one that was took out?

Davy. Young man—yer mind's wandering—go in and get some supper. [*Exit Bob*] Ha, Ha! Just like that boy. [*Enter Dame, with pail. Goes to well*] Hold on, Mother, that's my work. I say, Mother, I've got some news for you. Squire Vaughan's daughter's coming home.

Dame. What! Little Nell?

Davy. Well, Little Nell, as she used to be called. But I reckon it's Miss Eleanor Vaughn now. Mother, do you remember she was took across to for-ren parts to be eddicated by her father? You remember, don't you?

Dame. Yes, and he died then—poor old man.

Davy. Yes, died and left her an orphan to the care of a guardian. I think that's what you call it. Well, he's fetching her home now, and that's why they are fixing up the old house so nice of late.

Dame. Son, I wonder if she will remember the time when you and her were sweethearts, eh, boy?

Davy. Why, Mother, how you talk? Oh, dear—no—I reckon she's gone and forgot us by this time.

Dame. Well, I allow you're right. [*Goes to door, takes pail from him*] Ah, thank you, son, you're allus good to your old mother. [*Exit*]

Davy. [*Solus. Business*] What am I for if I shouldn't be good to you? Bless that dear old face—she's getting on in years, and by and by she'll need a son's hand to keep the wolf from the door.

Neil. [*Without*] Hollo.

Davy. Strange voices.

Maj. R. [*Without*] Hollo.

Neil. Can you hear us?

Davy. Yes, I reckon we can. Hollo, what's the matter? What do you want?

Neil. Assistance. We have met with a serious mishap. [*Hunters appear*]

Davy. Hold on, boys, I'll see what's wrong.

Briggs. Who can it be?

Yonk. Strangers here, sure.

Dame. [*Entering*] Tinkers or peddlers. Such folks is allus getting into some sort of fix or other—there they come—why, ther's a gal with 'em—a real lady! [*Enter Major Royston leaning on Davy*]

Maj. R. Is it much further to this place of yours?

DAVY. Oh, no—right here. [*Eleanor and Neil enter. Crossing bridge*] Take care—look out. [*Neil falls. Davy catches Eleanor*] That's slippery where you are.

NEIL. Yes, I perceived so as I fell.

EL. I'm very much obliged to you, but don't you think it would be just as well to put me down?

DAVY. Oh—yes.

EL. Thank you. [*Goes to Major Royston*]

MAJ. R. Take care.

DAVY. What's the matter? Sprain, I allow.

MAJ. R. To be sure—you see that just leaning my weight on that ankle sends a shoot of pain all through me. See that?

DAVY. Yes. But if I were you, I'd lean my weight on the other leg.

MAJ. R. Sir!

EL. Oh, be patient, guardy.

MAJ. R. Patient? Haven't I a right to stand on which leg I please—on my right leg or my left leg?—I'll stand on my head, if I like—then, sir, what do you say to that?

DAVY. Oh, that's good, if you like it.

MAJ. R. I don't know, sir, but you are right. My name is Royston, sir. Hector Royston, ex-major in the Continental army, at your service or anybody's.

DAVY. Well, my name is Crockett.

EL. What?

DAVY. Crockett, Miss—

EL. Not Davy Crockett—not my old friend, Davy Crockett?

DAVY. Well, Davy's the name, but as for the old friend—

EL. Ah—you have forgotten me, while I knew your face before your name recalled it. Don't you know me? Who am I, now?

DAVY. Why, Mother, look—it's Nellie Vaughn!

EL. Yes, the same saucy Nell as of old, and this is your good mother? Have you forgotten me, too?

DAME. A thousand welcomes *home*.

EL. Home—yes, it was home while my poor father lived, but now—

DAME. Oh, miss—I didn't mean—pray, forgive.

EL. For what?—For recalling him to me?—I rather thank you, for his memory is the one green spot in my lonely life—no, not lonely, for here is his worthy representative. [*Goes to her guardian*]

MAJ. R. Take care—

DAME. I beg pardon, sir, but did you say your foot was sprained?

MAJ. R. No, marm, I did not. I said it was turned—there's a difference between a sprain and a simple turn—it was all the fault of that accursed saddle.

EL. Oh, Guardy—

MAJ. R. Eh—wh—I beg your pardon, madam, for the expression, but it was all the fault of the lady's saddle—the girth broke—the saddle turned—she turned with it—I turned to save her, my foot turned under me and, confound it, we all turned topsy-turvy together.

EL. Oh, Guardy!

DAME. He'd better step indoors. A basin of cold water and a bandage will set that all right.

MAJ. R. I thank you, madam, and I will take your advice.

EL. Assist him, Neil. [*Neil comes to him. Major Royston limps toward door. The children stand in front of him*]

MAJ. R. Get out! [*Children laugh. Major Royston falls and gets up*] Why don't you come, some of you, and pick me up? [*All laugh*]

EL. Oh, how beautiful it all seems! I declare, the place has changed just as little as its inmates—and what little folks—are these all Crocketts?

DAVY. Yes, all!

BOB. All 'cept me.

DAVY. What?

BOB. I was changed in the cradle.

DAVY. Oh, clear out.

BOB. Well, Davy says I was.

EL. Not yours, Mr. Crockett?

DAVY. Good Lord, no!

EL. Of course not. Well, come, little folks, I am the visitor and you must show me the way. [*Exit with children*]

BIG DAN. Davy Coo-Coo—Ha! Ha!

YONK. Davy Coo-Coo—Ha! Ha!

BRIGGS. Davy Coo-Coo—Ha! Ha! [*They all scamper off. Chorus—music. Repeated outside*]

DAVY. Mighty, but she's pretty! I feel just as I did when a little boy no bigger than Bob. Dear me, I forgot them horses! They'll want a feed—and while I'm about it I'll fetch up that damaged sidesaddle. I reckon I can tinker it up a bit, and maybe I'll get another of them looks in pay—pay—great Lord, that gal could buy me out, body and soul, for next to nothing, and I ain't for sale generally. I ain't, neither. [*Exit. Re-enter Eleanor followed by Neil*]

NEIL. So you have known these people before, Eleanor?

EL. Yes, and I am proud to know them still. I love their honest simplicity, rugged though it be. It refreshes me like a draught of pure spring-water, or a breath from this fresh mountain air. Why do you smile?

NEIL. You will hardly expect me to share your enthusiasm.

EL. Certainly not. Our tastes are very dissimilar.

NEIL. I am very sorry if our engagement has become irksome to you. It was no fault of mine, when abroad I was well enough—but now—

EL. [*Rises, sits on bench in front of cottage*] I see you are determined to be ill-natured. I wish you would go and look after my saddle—you know it must be mended before I can remount.

NEIL.—Oh, yes—[*Goes up*] I declare I am quite turned about. Which way did we come?—I think this way.

EL. I think the other.

NEIL. Yes, I daresay you are right.

EL. Well, why don't you go?

NEIL. You won't be afraid?

EL. Afraid of what?

NEIL. Of being alone.

EL. Why, I was born in these forests. I am the daughter of a backwoods-man.

NEIL. Very well, I'll hurry back.

EL. You needn't.

NEIL. Eh?

EL. Oh, do go and look after my saddle.

NEIL. Yes, I will. [*Exit*]

EL. This marriage with Neil Crampton is a mistake—a fatal error—I do not love him—I cannot love him—and if I am to understand this letter I am not so much to blame. A strange, ambiguous letter.—It is from Mr. Dunforth, poor papa's solicitor—it puzzles and disturbs me.—Let me read it again for the hundredth time: "My dear Miss Vaughn: You start to-morrow for your old home in the west. As your father's old friend and your legal advisor I feel in duty bound to offer you a word of caution. I have reason to believe that measures are afoot to coerce you into what I believe to be a matrimonial speculation." [*Enter Davy*] "If you doubt me I will only suggest that you keep one eye on your guardian's movements, another on those of Mr. Oscar Crampton—." Oscar Crampton, a man I never liked from the beginning, and yet Guardy trusts him—I can comprehend nothing—absolutely nothing. [*Enter Davy with saddle. Eleanor mistaking him for Neil*] Now, what in the world has he brought that saddle here for?—I thought I told you not to hurry back—now, don't say I didn't—I told you so very distinctly—not that

your society is so distasteful to me as you imagine—but because—because—
Oh, do put it down! [*Davy drops saddle*] Umph—he obeys me like a dog—
well, what you brought it for at all I don't know, I don't want it—[*Davy is
taking it off*] Well, you need not trouble yourself to take it back—[*Pause*]—
My smelling salts. Now, don't say you haven't got them. I'm sure I gave them
to you this morning—Well, why don't you—? [*She turns and sees Davy*]
Oh! Oh!

DAVY. I'm afeared you got the wrong pig by the ear.

EL. Oh, sir, I didn't mean—I—I—did you bring my saddle?

DAVY. Yes, but I'd just as leave take it back if you don't want it.

EL. Oh, no, I like to have my saddle with me. No, I mean I thank you
very much.

DAVY. You're welcome, miss—I heard the old gentleman say the saddle
was a little bit damaged, so I thought I'd just fetch it up and tinker it up a
bit—that's all.

EL. How good!—I thank you—I—oh, dear, I don't know what to say.
What's the matter with it?

DAVY. The belly-band's busted.

EL. And do you think it ought to be mended?

DAVY. Well, if you are going to ride on it again I think it might as well.

EL. Do you mend saddles?

DAVY. Well, I don't do it for a steady living, but I do sometimes, just to
keep my hand in—

EL. I wonder if I could—

DAVY. I don't think it would be just a lady's work.

EL. Oh, I like to do odd things, and I think I could do this.

DAVY. Well, go ahead—let's see how you'd do it.

EL. Oh, there's no difficulty about that—the girth is broken.

DAVY. Eh—yes, busted off there.

EL. Well, then, I would get a piece of leather, a real strong piece of leather
—and a needle and some thread—some real strong thread—then I would
make some holes in the leather—then—then—I would sew it right on there
and then I am sure it would buckle just as well as ever. There—why he's
laughing at something—is it so *very* funny?

DAVY. No, it ain't funny at all. [*Laughs*]

EL. Isn't that right?

DAVY. Yes, that's first-rate. [*Laughs*]

EL. Is there another way?

DAVY. Yes, I'm afeared there is, miss.

EL. A better way?

DAVY. I don't know that it's a better way—but it's a shorter way.

EL. How would you do it?

DAVY. I'd just let it out a couple of inches on the other end.

EL. Why, to be sure—how stupid I am!

DAVY. Yes.

EL. Sir!

DAVY. No, miss, only a trifle green.

EL. Thank you, sir.

DAVY. Oh, it's quite natural, miss. You haven't been used to this kind of work, and that makes a great difference—[*The Dame appears at window*]

DAME. Miss, the old gentleman is coming out. Won't you come and help him?

EL. Certainly. I shall be back soon. [*Exit with Dame*]

DAVY. I didn't think you could get so much fun out of saddle-mending. [*Enter Oscar Crampton*]

OSCAR. Hollo.

DAVY. Hollo.

OSCAR. Well, sir, can't you come to me?

DAVY. No, I'm busy. You ain't, so you can come to me.

OSCAR. You are very independent. I only wished to—

MAJ. R. [*Within*] Take care.

OSCAR. Ah! I know all I want. I will trouble you no further. [*Retires back*]

DAVY. Well, there's a man I reckon don't say his prayers every night. [*Crosses L. to Neil. Enter Major Royston, Dame and Eleanor*]

MAJ. R. I declare, madam, your bandages have worked quite a miracle. The pain is quite gone.

EL. We cannot sufficiently thank you, madam.

DAME. Don't try, miss—better let me make you up a couple of beds—going to be a bad night—snow on the mountains, sure.

EL. Thank you, madam. Much as we thank you, we are compelled to decline—

MAJ. R. The fact is, marm, we are expected by a friend—

OSCAR. [*Advancing*] By a friend who has anticipated your arrival and has hastened to meet you.

MAJ. R. He, here? [*Eleanor shudders*]

OSCAR. Well, old friend, a thousand welcomes—Miss Eleanor, your blooming looks are the best vouchers for your health. I am rejoiced to see it, but where is Neil, my nephew? I long to embrace the dear boy. Well, old friend, everything goes to a wish.

MAJ. R. A word with you, my dear friend.

OSCAR. That's right. Call me your friend—your dear friend—[*They go up*]

DAVY. That's all counterfeit—the men are playing 'possum—but the gal is in earnest. I can see it in her eyes.

EL. [*Aside*] My guardian seems distressed at this meeting, but why—why—?

OSCAR. Everything is to a wish—the house is arranged as much to her taste as if she were in reality its mistress.

MAJ. R. As if she were its mistress?—do you dare—? [*Offers to strike him*]

OSCAR. [*Seizing his hand*] Be calm, my dear Royston—you were always so passionate—take my arm, I insist—I command—ha—ha—you see how impossible it is to resist me! [*They exit. Bob enters stealthily—watching*]

DAVY. Bob—come here—[*He gives him the saddle. Bob goes off with it*] There's a screw loose somewhere.

EL. Yes, there is some mystery here—my guardian's agitation, nay—positive terror—this warning letter. I begin to doubt. Oh, for some friend! [*Crosses L.*]

DAVY. [*Coming forward*] I beg pardon, miss, but I think you called my name.

EL. Can this be intuition? It is, and I will follow it—Mr. Crockett, Davy—

DAVY. Yes, that's it, call me Davy—that's my name.

EL. Yes, that's the name I once called you by—then we were children and playmates.

DAVY. Yes, little fellows—I remember.

EL. If the occasion offered, *could* you defend the woman as you once protected the girl?

DAVY. *Could* I?—just try me!

EL. I take you at your word, Davy Crockett.—Do you see this letter?— It concerns the happiness of my whole future life, and yet I cannot comprehend it—here, you read it—and advise me. No, do not hesitate. Your strong man's nature will make all clear. Read it, for I trust you, Davy Crockett.

DAVY. Well, miss, I'd like to do what you ask, but I'm afraid it's impossible.

EL. Oh, you refuse to befriend your old playmate?

DAVY. No, miss, it ain't that—I've looked into them eyes and I've seen thar what I never see in the eyes of a living woman before, and I'd lay my life down this minute—I would—as I'm a man—but take back your letter and find a better friend than Dave Crockett, for I'm a backwoodsman—and I cannot read—

EL. He cannot read—[*Re-enter Neil*]

NEIL. I cannot find your saddle in that direction. I must take the other path.

EL. Ha! Ha! I fear your chance has gone; someone has been before you—

NEIL. Eh, who?

EL. Who?—Why—Davy Crockett. [*Re-enter Major Royston and Crampton, Dame and children*]

MAJ. R. Madam, good-bye—we are to be neighbors and we will see more of each other. Good-bye, Mr. Crockett. Good-bye, Davy.

OSCAR. [*To Neil, who is about to offer arm to major*] No, no, my arm alone shall support our dear friend. Your arm where it is due—lean on me, my dear friend. [*Exit Major Royston and Crampton. Neil gives arm to Eleanor—they go up. Bob follows with side-saddle on shoulder*]

EL. Not a word—not a look—[*Exit. Music soft—"Annie Laurie." Davy is rushing after them*]

DAME. Good Lord, what's the matter with the boy?—Davy, there's a queer look in your eye—what's the matter, nothing wrong, is there?

DAVY. No, Mother.

DAME. Where are you going?

DAVY. I don't know, Mother.

DAME. When are you coming back?

DAVY. I couldn't exactly say.

DAME. Davy! [*Business*]

DAVY. What, Mother?

DAME. Do you remember the time when you were a little boy no bigger than Bob? You used to go out in the woods and set your traps for rabbits. Sometimes it was pitch dark—What allus kept you from being scared and brought you back to your mother's side? What was it, boy?

DAVY. The light in the window, Mother. [*Warning for curtain*]

DAME. Davy, that light is there for you still. It will always be there for you—remember that it will always be there for you—

DAVY. I know it, Mother. [*Business*]

DAME. Now, son, where are you going?

DAVY. I don't know, Mother.

DAME. And when are you coming back?

DAVY. Mother, what's allus been mine and Father's motto? Ain't it been "Be sure you're right, then go ahead"?

DAME. But are you sure—dead sartin sure you're right this time?

DAVY. By the Etarnal, Mother, I think I am—[*Ring down very quick curtain*]

DAME. Then go ahead! [*Swell music on curtain*]

ACT II.

SCENE: *Interior of Davy Crockett's hut. Enter Davy.*

DAVY. Lord, how it do snow! I'm a good mile ahead of them, and they have got to pass this way. I'll allow, they'll be pretty glad of a shelter. Now, there's comfort—just a handful of twigs and everything outside wet through with the snow. Davy Crockett, you're a careless varmint—just enough to start a blaze and little more. [*Enter Neil*]

NEIL. Help—help!

DAVY. Well, I declare! It's that man!—Where's the girl?

NEIL. Out there, fainting—freezing—

DAVY. Freezing? 'Tarnal death! [*Exit. Neil crawls to corner of stage*]

DAVY. [*Re-enters bearing in Eleanor in his arms*] Not dead—but—dear me, how cold she is! Miss, try and rouse yourself. What am I to do for more wood? Oh, here—it is the bar of the door, but no matter. [*Breaks it*] Thar's something big enough to barbecue an ox. Another minute I'd have been too late. Too late—the word sends a cold shiver all through me.

EL. Oh—Oh—!

DAVY. Did you speak, miss?

EL. Oh, my feet—

DAVY. Thunder and lightning, what am I going to do now? Well, it's got to be done, so here goes—[*About to take off shoes*]

EL. What are you doing?

DAVY. Nothing, miss, nothing.

EL. Oh, my head—

DAVY. Yes, miss, and them feet, too. Do try and rouse yourself, for them shoes got to come off somehow.

EL. Take them off, please.

DAVY. Who! Me?

EL. I'm so drowsy.

DAVY. Poor girl! If I get through this night, it will be a clear case of Heaven's mercy—

NEIL. [*Groans*] Oh, you're coming round now, just when you ain't wanted. What are you doing there?

Davy. Well, come and look. There, miss, just keep them feet wrapped up, and I'll get some more wood if it takes the roof off the house. [*Exit. Neil groans*]

El. Is that you, Neil? Are you safe, too?

Neil. Yes, but don't excite yourself.

El. I won't—I won't—but—

Neil. Calm yourself, the peril is over.

El. Peril! Oh, I remember, I insisted on going into the forest in search of holly berries. Guardy remonstrated. I would not heed him—the snow fell faster and faster, the path became blocked—the horses became restive—and then—and then, all is a dreadful blank.

Neil. Do try and calm yourself.

El. Yes, but what will Guardy say, and Mr. Crampton, too?

Neil. Never fear. They will hunt the forest through to find us. In the meantime, let us thank Heaven that we have been saved from death.

El. Saved, and by whom?

Neil. By that hunter—by that—Crockett fellow.

El. Tell me, Neil, was he not here just now?

Neil. Yes, he went out a moment since.

El. I knew it, those tender eyes, that gentle face, that bent over me—it was no dream, then—no dream. [*Re-enter Davy with armful of wood*]

Davy. There's some wood. Oh, miss, you're all right, aren't you?

El. Then it was you, really—you whom I have to thank for saving my life?

Davy. No, miss, he did his part as well as I did. He came in and told me you were out thar freezing. Say, I was a bit savage with you, and I ask your pardon.

Neil. I'm proud to take it.

Davy. Miss, he's burning up with the fever—he's a sick man and no wonder.

Neil. No, it's only a slight ringing in my head.

Davy. Yes, that's it—that's the fever. Here, let me see if I can't squeeze you out a drop of spirit.

Neil. No! No!

El. Do, Neil, to please me.

Davy. Open your head—thar, don't make up faces—it's good—[*Neil drinks*] Takes the roof off your mouth. Now snooze away.

Neil. If you require my assistance, you will awake me, won't you?

Davy. Yes, we couldn't get on without you. Now, snooze away, for you need it bad.

EL. How good you are, Mr. Crockett!

DAVY. Don't say that, miss, for what I did for you I'd have did for any living soul that came to my door in a storm like that. But you are safe, and I thank the Etarnal for that.

EL. How strange we meet again!

DAVY. Yes, 'tis kind of singular.

EL. Is this your hunting lodge?

DAVY. Yes, this is my crib. This is where I come and bunk when I'm out on a long stretch arter game. Miss, here's something belongs to you—[*Hands her book*] You left it at my mother's house—

EL. Oh, *Marmion!*—it's dear Sir Walter's book.

DAVY. Is it? I allowed it was yours.

EL. Yes—I mean—thank you very much.

DAVY. Oh, you're right welcome—what is that, sarmons?—No?—Law, maybe—No? Well, I allowed it was, 'cause that's what lawyer and parson needs.

EL. Yes, and very good reading it must be. But this is lighter.

DAVY. Is it? Yes, that's right, light—I've seen weightier books than that.

EL. No, I mean—this is more interesting.

DAVY. Yes, I allow it must be, if you say so.

EL. Shall I read you something and let you be the judge?

DAVY. Well, if you would, I'd like it right well.

EL. Is he asleep?

DAVY. I hope so. Yes, he's snoring like a bar in midwinter. Miss—are you right comfortable there where you are?

EL. Oh, it's delightfully cozy.

DAVY. Ain't that good to hear you say that!

EL. Now, what shall I read?

DAVY. I don't know. I've no choice.

EL. I know—cut and choose at hazard.

DAVY. Yes, read that—

EL. Ha, ha! Now listen: "Oh! Young Lochinvar," etc. [*Reads first verse of Scott's poem of "Lochinvar"*]

DAVY. Sounds pretty, don't it—goes on jest like music. My, but that's pretty!

EL. "He stayed not for bread—." [*Second verse of "Lochinvar"*]

DAVY. There's a gal in it. Well, it makes it all the prettier. [*Eleanor reads third verse*]

DAVY. [*Interrupting*] Say, miss, this ain't true—what you're reading, is it?

EL. Well, it might be, although such things are rare nowadays. [*Finishes verse*]

DAVY. Yes, I reckon they be—go on, miss—go on!

EL. "Then spoke the bride's father.
  Tread me a measure, said young Lochinvar."

DAVY. A nod's as good as a wink to a blind horse.

EL. Why, how excited you are! Does it please you? You see, we have brought our young knight errant to the test. Father, mother, brother, all the world against him, but the lady's hand is in his own.

DAVY. Well, what did he do?

EL. What would you have done?

DAVY. Me—I—well, go on, let's hear it out.

EL. "One touch to her hand," etc. [*Reads sixth verse*]

DAVY. True blue, and the gal's his—go it, you divil—oh, gal! Well, there's something in this rough breast of mine that leaps at the telling of a yarn like that. There's a fire—a smouldering fire that the breath of your voice has just kindled up into a blaze—a blaze that will sweep me down and leave my life a bed of ashes—of chilled and scattered ashes.

EL. Heavens, what have I done? Sir—Mr. Crockett—Davy—

DAVY. Oh, don't mind me. I ain't fit to breathe the same air with you. You are scholared and dainty, and what am I, nothing but an ignorant backwoodsman, fit only for the forests and the fields where I'm myself hand in hand with nature and her teachings, knowing no better?

EL. Oh, hear me—

DAVY. No, I heard too much of you already. I've seen too much—afore you came. Dod rot me—I've skeered you—Miss, I didn't mean to skeer you. I'm an unlicked cub, but my heart's in the right place, and if ever you want a friend—

EL. A friend, Davy—?

DAVY. Well, you've made a fool of me. You've just gone and forced pesky nonsense out of my mouth, but I only want you to believe that I'm your friend. I'm ready to work for you, to starve for you.—What's that?—

EL. I hear nothing.

DAVY. Don't you? Well, maybe I'm mistaken. [*One howl*] No, thar it is again.

EL. What is it?

DAVY. Keep still and listen. [*Howl again*]

EL. I hear a long, low cry as of some animal in distress.

DAVY. Ah, you hear it then? I was right, wasn't I? [*Howl*] Thar it is again.

EL. What is it?

DAVY. That's wolves.

EL. Wolves—! [*Screams*]

DAVY. Don't be skeered.

EL. But—is there no danger?

DAVY. Ain't I here?

EL. Yes, but they are so dreadfully near.

DAVY. Yes, they tracked you in the snow, and smell blood.

EL. Blood!

DAVY. Take it easy, girl. This door is built of oak, I built it—and—blazes, the bar's gone! [*Warning curtain*]

EL. Gone! [*Wolves howl all around cabin*]

DAVY. Yes, I split it up to warm you and your friend. Rouse him up. The pesky devils is all around the house.

EL. [*Goes to Neil*] Neil—help! [*Wolves throw themselves against door. Bark*]

DAVY. Quick, there, I can't hold the door agin 'em—

NEIL. I tell you, Uncle, if the girl says no, there's an end of it—

EL. My God—he is delirious!

DAVY. What!

EL. 'Tis true, nothing can save us!

DAVY. Yes, it can!

EL. What?

DAVY. The strong arm of a backwoodsman. [*Davy bars door with his arm. The wolves attack the house. Heads seen opening in the hut and under the door*]

TABLEAU

ACT III.

SCENE: *Same. Discovered: Crockett still at the door. Eleanor.*

DAVY. This is getting kind of monotonous, this business is—[*Wolf howls*] Yes, howl away, but you got to scatter at dawn. That dear, blessed girl, she's had a sleep—and that is just as good as rest to me to think she owes her life to me—that will be no more to her after this than the dog at her feet at home —not so much—for he will feel the pressure of her soft white hand in his shaggy coat, and I'll never see her after tonight, never again—I mustn't if I could.

EL. [*Starting up*] Who's there? Who called?

Davy. No one. You must have been dreaming.

El. And have I been sleeping? How selfish, and you have not left that door the livelong night?

Davy. Well, miss, if I had ventured away from this door they'd been among us like a falling hemlock.

El. But you must be dreadfully tired.

Davy. Oh, no, takes more than a handful of wolves to wipe a man out in these parts.

El. But your arm, your poor arms!

Davy. That's right swellish, I must say, as if some rising young blacksmith had been sledging on it all night.

El. Oh, Mr. Crockett—Davy—

Davy. Oh!—my name spoken like that, miss—you ain't crying for me, are you?

El. Yes, look at my tears—my soul is welling through my eyes. This night has shown me all your noble self—your loyalty, your unselfish devotion. I read your nature, as you cannot, for in the greatness of your heart, you depreciate those qualities which in my eyes raise you far above your kind, to where, rugged and simple but still preeminent, you stand a man. Fate seems to have linked our lives, but the world divides us. We must part here, and both must learn to forget.

Davy. Forget! Hold on, miss, I have listened to you as a man dying of thirst listens to the trickling of a stream of water that he can't reach—and though I know there's no hope for me, yet you might have stopped this side of that word forget. Do you think I could forget you? Do you think I could forget the touch of your hand in mine, the sight of your face? You called me a man, and as a man I couldn't forget you if I would, and I wouldn't if I could.

El. Well, at least you will not think me heartless?

Davy. Heartless? When I've seen you cry for me?

El. And since you must remember me, let it be as one who dreaming of what might have been, is aroused at the voice of duty to dream no more. Can you do this and not reproach the dreamer? Brave knight—true friend—may Heaven bless you as I do!

Maj. R. [*Without*] Hollo—

El. Guardy's voice! [*Two shots*]

Davy. Take care. Look out. [*Two shots*]

Oscar. [*Without*] Hollo—

Davy. There's the other one. [*Two shots*] Aim low, boys, but slew 'em— do you hear the critters scamper? How I'd like to be among 'em!

MAJ. R. Bravo, lads—they are found—stand by the horses—open the door.

DAVY. Hold on! The door's bolted!

MAJ. R. Why don't you open the door?

DAVY. The bolt is a trifle swelled.

MAJ. R. Confound it! Open the door.

DAVY. 'Tarnal death, hold on! There's a sartin amount of patience required about all these things. Oh, right here near this joint—there she comes, and not an inch to spare. [*Enter Major and Oscar. Davy falls on couch*]

OSCAR. Neil! [*Hears Davy groan*] What is that man doing here?

EL. Look at him and ask. Look at his pale face, his torn and mangled flesh, his brave life's blood freely drained, and for me! Look at all this and then question. Shall I tell you what he has done? He has saved me from a fate too terrible for thought—myself and yonder wretched man—saved us, defended us, stood the livelong night at that door—his strong arm our only salvation, a living barrier between us and death, signing a compact written in his own blood. And for me, for me!

OSCAR. We are losing ground here—[*Goes up*]

MAJ. R. Don't fret, girl. He is only faint from loss of blood.

DAVY. Who's faint? Davy Crockett? It's a—there, don't you worry—I'm worth a dozen dead men yet.

OSCAR. Neil, don't you know me? Why, the boy is seriously ill.

MAJ. R. Oh, Eleanor—

EL. Hush, Guardy—poor Neil!

OSCAR. You remain here and I will summon the servants—he must be removed at once.

MAJ. R. Remove him? Do you want to kill the lad? Let him remain where he is.

OSCAR. Here! Impossible.

DAVY. You're right, Squire. If that boy ventures out in a storm like this, it is more than his life is worth.

OSCAR. But—

DAVY. Well, I reckon I know, don't I? I was raised in these parts and I know the fever when I see it. There's only one thing to be done, and that's got to be done quick.

OMNES. What's that?

DAVY. Well, just cover him up with the skins, build up a blazing fire— pour a horn or two of that liquor down his throat, and wait till I come back.

OSCAR. Where would you go?

DAVY. To the nighest settlement. A short ten miles from here.

EL. For what?

DAVY. For help, for a man what's sick and needs it bad.

EL. Are you mad, to venture out in such a storm, and in your condition? You shall not go.

DAVY. I must, girl—it's duty—duty.

EL. But you could never find the path in such a storm.

DAVY. Oh, yes, I could. I could find the path if the snow stood breast high.

EL. But for my sake, think—it may be death.

DAVY. Well, let it come.

NEIL. Oh, Eleanor! Eleanor!

OSCAR. Do you hear him, girl? Have you no heart?

MAJ. R. Speak to him, Eleanor. It may save his life.

EL. No, no, I cannot.

DAVY. Go to him, girl. There's your place by his side. [*Music, "Annie Laurie"—very soft*] There's a new light dawning on us both. Our ways in life lie different—Yours and his is by the warmth of the firelight, but mine is out thar in the storm fighting for life and breath. It's hard, I know, but I must not shirk my part. Good-bye, girl, I'll never see you again.

EL. Never!

DAVY. How can I, when you belong to him? But don't say you'll forget. And when time has passed, you might waste one thought on Davy Crockett. It's all he asks—it's all he's worth. Good-bye, I'm going out of the Heaven of your life. I'm going out of your sight forever.

EL. No, Davy, you shall not go. [*Warn curtain*]

DAVY. Oh, girl, don't tempt me—don't you see that Satan is tugging at the strings of my wicked, sinful heart, saying Don't go, stay here, let him die?

EL. Die?

DAVY. For he will die afore morning, if I stay, and that will leave you free—free for me to love. That's what is ringing in my brain, and I'm trying to fight it down—I'm trying to do what's right.

EL. Forgive me, Davy. You are right.

DAVY. Then let me "go ahead." [*Exit Davy. Ring down. Music swells*]

TABLEAU

ACT IV.

SCENE: *Interior of Major Royston's mansion. Discovered: Oscar.*

WAT. [*Without*] Take the candles to the supper room. I'll attend to the evergreens myself. [*Enter from C.*]

Oscar. Ah, Watson, more decorations, eh?

Wat. Yes, for the supper room. The house begins to look like a bazaar or a Christmas fair.

Oscar. Or a gentleman's mansion decorated for a wedding.

Wat. Yes, sir. I suppose the wedding will follow?

Oscar. All in good time, my dear friend.

Wat. Well, they will make an uncommon pretty couple—a very pretty couple. [*Exit C.*]

Oscar. [*Solus*] A pretty couple, yes—and a golden couple—rich—rich— and here the instruments with which I have brought it all about: Royston's I.O.U. on every one of them. And here the master's key of all the forged notes —Ah, Royston, little did you dream twenty years ago the interest I would demand today. Fool, you have sown the wind; now reap the whirlwind! [*Enter Neil from C.*] Ah, the bridegroom-elect, and what a face! Are you to be married or to be hanged?

Neil. Spare me your—sarcasm—I am unhappy enough without it.

Oscar. Unhappy, my dear convalescent? Your fever has not quite left you.

Neil. [*C.*] Ah, it is from the time I contracted that fever that I date my present unhappiness—but my eyes have been opened since. Uncle, I love the girl—yes, love her still, but her heart is not mine—never can be mine. I have known it ever since that night in the forest, and I should be either a fool or a coward to wed with her. [*Enter Major Royston*]

Maj. R. Neil, have you seen Eleanor?

Neil. Not within the hour, sir.

Maj. R. Nor I—she keeps her room with a pertinacity more marked than commendable.

Oscar. Ah, Major, we have been young ourselves, let us remember that.

Maj. R. Hypocrite! [*Enter Watson from C.*]

Wat. Squire, the lawyer is below.

Maj. R. Very well, I will see him in my own room. Crampton, will you join me?

Oscar. You know, my dear Royston, what a poor head I have for figures, but when the mutual interest of those dear to us is considered—Neil, where are you going?

Neil. To my own room. Do not be afraid. I'll join you at the proper moment.

Maj. R. [*Goes up to him*] Come, Neil, rouse yourself. Your dejection will affect your bride.

Neil. The reproof is deserved, sir. I will try. [*Exit C.*]

Oscar. Love is a strange disease, my dear Royston.

MAJ. R. True, but shame and the bondage of shame is still stranger.

OSCAR. Why, your abstraction almost equals poor Neil's—but come, the lawyer and the settlements await—[*Exit L.*]

MAJ. R. Heaven forgive me! What a wedding night, and what sad hearts to grace it! [*Exit L. Enter Davy*]

DAVY. So this is her home, and this is her wedding night! I wonder if that man loves the girl as well as I do? I don't think he do—and I don't think he kin. [*Enter Eleanor from door R.*] It's the gal herself, how pretty she do look! Just like a statue done up in real frost. [*Hides behind portrait*]

EL. Robed for the ceremony that links my fate to his! Orange blossoms on the brow, but in the heart what they should have decked me in is black, not white. The flowers should have been dead roses woven in a wreath of cypress.

DAVY. Poor girl, thinking so deep, and she don't seem just happy in her looks, neither!

EL. Oh, Father, you see me here, wayward as of old, and heartsore. If you can see, pity your child and send some kind friend to save me from this bitterness worse than death.

DAVY. [*Coming from behind portrait*] Here, I'm here, heart and hand, ready to serve you.

EL. You, here!

DAVY. I've skeered you agin—but I didn't mean to, 'deed I didn't. My heart got into my throat, and it was them words of yours that put it there, too.

EL. Oh, why have you come, and at such a time? Don't you know this is my wedding night?

DAVY. Well, how could I help knowing it? And I declare to you I never thought to see you again—Ah, I meant every word I said, and I tried dreadful hard to keep my promise, but since I see you first, I haven't been myself at all. I seem to be chained right down to the place where you are, and I can't shake myself clear nohow. Why, miss, for days and days I've hung about here watching the bare walls that held you, and last night I stood under your window from sundown to dawn again, and when the light went out behind your curtain it seemed to me as if the light of my life had gone out with it, for I knew today would give you to another man. Yet I stayed just to get one more look at the sweet face, and then to go away forever.

EL. Where?

DAVY. Well, I don't know where, and I don't care much, for it's all one to me now—but just say one kind word afore I go, will you? Say you forgive me?

EL. Yes, but leave me.

DAVY. I'm going, miss, and I'll never set eyes on you again.

EL. Stay! Don't go! You think me cold, unwomanly—do you think a woman, young, ardent, imaginative, could look on a love like yours unmoved? A love that asks nothing save the privilege of dying at my feet? You think this, you who saved my life, you who—Oh, Heaven, never pausing to look deeper into my heart to read my nature by your own, to see there that I love you—I truly know you for what you are, my hero and my lord—but the confession which should have been my pride is now my shame, for I am bound by honor and duty to another! [*Turning away*]

DAVY. No—no—to me, and to me alone, and by the Etarnal, I'm going to have you!

EL. How can you think to win me?

DAVY. Well! I don't think nothing about it—it's settled down into a matter of the deadest certainty—Yet hold on; can you;—a girl like you—can you think to join hands with an ignorant, backwoodsman like me? I'm just wild to hope it.

EL. Stay! If you can save me from this marriage which fills me with disgust and loathing,—do it, I am yours.

DAVY. Oh, I'll do it! If Satan himself stood there, he shouldn't bar my way out.

EL. Oh, be prudent!

DAVY. Don't worry, I'm only dazed a bit—I'm just dazed with the happiness of this minute—to think that this dear hand I never thought to touch again, to think it belongs to me. Oh, if I go mad, it's your own fault—There, I've given my heart; now let's talk business.

EL. But what plan? What scheme? [*Looking to left door*]

DAVY. Well, I don't know, yet stay—I'll tell you what to do—let the ceremony go on as it's commenced, until the time comes.

EL. And when it comes?

DAVY. Oh, I'll be thar.

EL. May Heaven help you!

DAVY. Yes—but Heaven helps the man as helps himself—fair means or foul, I mean to have you now, and the man that comes between us—oh, say it again!

EL. I love you, Davy.

DAVY. Come here—the clouds have passed away and—someone's coming.

EL. Davy—only be sure you are right.

DAVY. And then go ahead. [*Exeunt. Enter Major Royston*]

MAJ. R. [*From L.*] The shame and humiliation of this accursed affair will prove to much for me—tortured by a villain who is ready, nay, eager to proclaim my dishonor to the world, should I dare to thwart him. No—no, I must go on to the end. [*Re-enter Davy*]

DAVY. Very well, I'll see the squire myself.

MAJ.R. He here! Crockett, I'm pleased to see you, but—

DAVY. I know you'd rather have my room than my company, 'cause this is the gal's wedding night.

MAJ.R. Well—

DAVY. Yes, I know—but—she ain't married just yet.

MAJ.R. Well, much as I owe you, much as we all owe you, I must confess your call is a little inopportune. Is your business so very pressing?

DAVY. Yes—Oh, yes!

MAJ.R. Because we might take some other time.

DAVY. No, I don't see how it could be put off—'cause it's got to be done tonight.

MAJ.R. Very well, my lad, speak out and quickly.

DAVY. To tell you the truth, Squire, you can do me a big kind of a service. They tell me you've got a horse yonder, a black stallion that you are willing to back agin anything in the settlement.

MAJ.R. And he deserves it. Devilskin deserves it.

DAVY. Yes, I've seen the horse and I allow I'm a judge of horseflesh—that's why I come to you.

MAJ.R. Well?

DAVY. Well, I've got a little job on a little matter of something I kind of set my heart on. Well, it ain't worth while going into detail, is it?

MAJ.R. No, no, certainly not.

DAVY. No, because you might not see my little game with the same eyes that I do, 'cause I don't mind telling you thar's a gal in it—a pair of eyes I took a fancy to.

MAJ.R. Ho, Ho! A love scrape—oh, you sly dog!

DAVY. Nothing more, Squire, honor bright.

MAJ.R. Oh, don't mistake me. I was young myself once—and not so very long ago.

DAVY. I am right glad to hear that, 'cause you ain't going to be hard on me, are you, Squire?

MAJ.R. No, I admire you all the more. But you're a cunning dog, Crockett—well?

DAVY. Well, Squire, the game I'm going to play is full of danger and full of dare. It may be one man agin a score, and it may be one horse agin the field, and now to make a long story short, I wish you'd lend me that horse, Devilskin. Thar now, it's out.

MAJ. R. The stallion is yours—[*Business*] not as a loan, but as a gift. You saved my Eleanor's life—

DAVY. No, Squire, I wouldn't take your horse as a gift.

MAJ. R. Come, come, I know you are proud, but you shall not refuse him —take the beast and may Heaven prosper you in all you do!

DAVY. Well, that's good of you, Squire, you've floored me.

MAJ. R. Pshaw! Lad, take the horse, and once on his back you may defy pursuit, for he's strung like steel and the wind alone can catch him.

DAVY. Well, Squire, I'll take the horse, but with this special understanding—if ever you have cause to change your mind about me or mine, the bargain is off, and the horse will stand in your stable next morning.

MAJ. R. Oh, no fear of that—no act of yours could ever change my esteem for you.

DAVY. Well, I wouldn't be too sure of that—for this is a rough-and-tumble world and things is putty apt to get mixed, especially when there's a gal—

MAJ. R. Oh, I'll risk it.

DAVY. Well, good night—and give my best wishes to the bride.

MAJ. R. And to the bridegroom-elect, eh?

DAVY. Oh, he'll take care of Number One, I reckon.

MAJ. R. Well, good night, and don't make a mess of it.

DAVY. No, I'll do my part. The rest lies with Devilskin.

MAJ. R. Oh, he'll not fail you. Remember he's strung like steel.

DAVY. Is he? Well, the horse and man are both alike, and the wind alone can catch us. [*Exit*]

MAJ. R. There's a lad of mettle. I wish Neil was a little more like him. Ah, well, we cannot pick and choose in these matters. If we only could— [*Wedding March. Enter Oscar*]

OSCAR. The wedding march—how my pulse keeps time to it, and my heart throbs as if it would burst with the exultant triumph of this moment! [*Enter guests and Eleanor, Neil and Quickwitch from door L.*]

MAJ. R. Welcome all—is everything prepared? [*Go down C.*]

OSCAR. You see, Neil? What think you now? There is your bride,—her fair hand only waiting for the ring.

NEIL. Her hand indeed! Ah, if I but knew her heart were in it!

OSCAR. You talk like a poet or a fool. Come, play the host amongst your guests—your guests and mine. [*Music soft, "Annie Laurie"*]

MAJ. R. Eleanor, you are abstracted. Remember who you are and where you are.

EL. He does not come! My courage begins to fail me.

QUICK. Your signature, sir. [*Neil crosses to table*]

OSCAR. You hear, by a stroke of the pen and she is yours.

NEIL. Look, Uncle, look at her face now.

OSCAR. Fool—ingrate! Have you lost your senses! My hopes, my fortunes all are centered here, fail me and—come, Nephew! [*He signs*] So all is over. Now, Eleanor.

MAJ. R. Come, Eleanor.

OSCAR. The pen, sweet Mistress Eleanor. Only a word—write here—a little word, your name—your signature is all we want. [*Enter Crockett*]

DAVY. Hold on! Stop!

OSCAR. Who said "Stop"?

DAVY. I said "Stop."

OSCAR. And who are you?

DAVY. Davy Crockett—you need not introduce yourself, because I know you and it would only be a waste of time.

MAJ. R. Crockett, why are you here, and what do you want?

DAVY. My bride.

OMNES. His bride?

DAVY. Thar she is, if you don't believe me. Look in her eyes.

OMNES. Eleanor!

DAVY. Come on, let's go on with the marriage—here's everything—here's a lawyer, he's got the document, here's the bride—but thar's a small mistake about the bridegroom—I'm the man, consequently you ain't. Squire, I told you thar was a gal in it, didn't I?

OSCAR. Is this a trick?

MAJ. R. Crockett, leave my house and depend upon it you shall answer to me for this public insult.

DAVY. All right, Squire, I'm your man.

NEIL. Sir!

DAVY. Or yours.

OSCAR. Ha! Ha!

DAVY. Or yours, particularly yours.

MAJ. R. Leave my house, sir, or the servants shall force you out.

DAVY. Force—say, Squire, I want to tell you a story. There was once a game young knight, I think that is what they called him. He was a scout—a trapper, a man who forded rivers in his buckskins with nary a friend but his horse and his rifle. Away he went, caring for nothing, stopping at nothing, until he reached the house that held the gal of his heart. "What do you want here?" says the dad—"I want my bride," says the knight—"Get out," says the dad—"Whoop," says the knight, "I'm Lochinvar. Who dares to follow?" [*Runs off with Eleanor*]

OMNES. Stop him! Stop him!

TABLEAU

ACT V.

SCENE: *Interior of Dame Crockett's home. Discovered: Parson and Dame.*

PAR. So, Dame, you've heard nothing from Davy?

DAME. Nothing, Parson, nothing. He's more of a rover than ever. It's a good month since I set eyes on the boy.

PAR. Kind-hearted boy, Dame, but rash, rash to a fault.

DAME. Yes, Parson, he takes arter his father, but such as he is, he is my only one, and my heart gets heavy without him.

PAR. Well, Dame, it's getting late, and I must be going. [*Enter Bob in nightdress*]

DAME. Mercy on us! What's the boy doing out of bed?

PAR. What is it, my little man?

BOB. Has our Davy come yet?

DAME. No, child, why?

BOB. 'Cause I heard him.

DAME. Heard who?

BOB. Heard our Davy a-hollowing just now.

DAME. Oh! Parson! If anything should have happened to our boy!

PAR. Never fear, Dame, he is in good hands, remember that. Go to bed, Bobbie, and if your Uncle Davy comes, you'll see him in the morning.

BOB. He's a-coming now, I tell you, he is—

DAME. How do you know?

BOB. Why, can't you hear him a-hollowing? [*Horse's hoofs*]

DAVY. [*Outside*] Hollo! Hollo!

DAME. I do believe the boy's right. [*At window*]

DAVY. [*Outside*] Hollo! Hollo!

DAME. Yes, that's my boy! [*Taking light. Enter Davy and Eleanor*]

DAME. Marcy on us, who's this?

DAVY. Mr. and Mrs. Davy Crockett.

DAME. Miss Eleanor here, and with you? It's the girl's wedding night!

DAVY. So it is, sure enough.

EL. Oh, madam, don't condemn me.

DAVY. Sit down, you must be pretty well tired out. Mother, I left you single-handed and alone, but I've brought you home a daughter, your son's wife.

DAME. Your wife?

PAR. Marcy preserve us!

DAVY. Leastways, if she ain't my wife just now, she's going to be in considerable less than five minutes. [*Omnes outside—Hello—Hello*]

DAME. What's that? What does it mean? [*Hoofs*]

DAVY. [*Bars door*] It means, Mother, that we're here just in time. Parson, you're a saving angel. Come out with your book and marry us off-hand.

PAR. Eh! What?

DAVY. I know it's a little unregular, but it's our only hope.

PAR. I—I—don't understand?

DAVY. I ain't the least bit particular you should understand, so long as we do! Come now, do it, will you?

PAR. *I certainly will not.*

DAVY. Parson, if you're the man I take you for, you'll show it now. This girl belongs to me, I won her fair, square and legal. I saved her life, when the wolves were howling around her. I took her from the arms of them that are coming to take her from me now, but if a foot dares to cross that threshold, and she's not my wife, you'll see bloodshed.

DAME and PAR. Bloodshed?

DAVY. Mother, give me my rifle!

PAR. *Davy! Davy!*

DAVY. Will you marry us? [*Horse's hoofs swell*]

PAR. I certainly will. [*Takes book out of pocket, amidst noise and confusion at door*] Do you take this man—? [*Noise and confusion stop*] Do you take this woman—? [*Noise still kept up*] notwithstanding the irregularity of the proceeding—[*Noise—confusion—crash, door broken open. Enter Neil, Royston, Crampton*]

DAVY. Mr. and Mrs. Davy Crockett at home until further notice.

CRAM. Scoundrel!

DAVY. Yes, I know your name. You needn't introduce yourself.

MAJ. R. Eleanor, in the name of all the furies, what has *induced* you to take a step like this?

EL. Be patient, Guardy.

MAJ. R. Patience, girl! We are disgraced, ruined!

DAVY. Ruined! Didn't I tell you we were fast married?

OMNES. Married? Impossible!

DAVY. Impossible? Ask Parson!

PAR. Not at all, gentlemen, but a fact. I performed the ceremony myself.

CRAM. Did you dare?

PAR. I did, and am willing to bide the consequences of the act. [*Placing hands in sparring attitude*]

DAVY. Oh, Parson!

PAR. Heaven forgive me!

MAJ. R. Eleanor, in your father's name, I command you to leave that man!

EL. Never!

MAJ. R. I am your guardian.

EL. *He* is my husband.

CRAM. If you be man, tear the girl from *him*.

DAVY. [*Presents rifle*] Eternity is a-yawning for you, if you dare to touch her!

DAME. Stop, son! He is dead and gone that taught you how to kill, but I'm here still to teach you when to spare.

DAVY. I reckon you're right, too, Mother.

CRAM. [*To Neil*] You hear this, and say nothing?

NEIL. Uncle, this violence is shameful, and I am not base enough to be a party to it. [*Crosses to Eleanor*] Eleanor, I have known the truth of this from the first, and had not a *will* stronger than mine compelled me, I should long since have released you from all troth to me. They may divorce you, but from me you have nothing to fear. [*Exit door L.*]

MAJ. R. Eleanor, my girl, this is childish folly. His reckless ardor has excited your fancy, and you believe you love him, but when you find yourself alone amidst ignorance and privation, think of that, my girl, think well of that!

DAVY. It's true, every word he says. 'Tain't too late, take time to think; look about you—this is all I've got to offer you, and you've been used to better.

EL. Used to what? Gaudy jewels that please the eye when the heart is empty? Oh, I have been so lonely amidst all these splendors.

DAVY. But can you give it up, and *all* for me?

EL. I *love* you, Davy.

DAVY. Squire, *hearts* are trumps.

CRAM. If persuasion fails, use force.

MAJ. R. I will use force, as you shall see.

DAVY. Will you? Come on, then! [*Pointing gun*]

DAME. Davy!

DAVY. All right, Mother, put it away.

MAJ. R. Eleanor, my girl, a villain, cold and cruel, for years has held my name and honor in his hands. I have feared him until now, but now I defy him.

CRAM. At last the mask is off. I thank you, Royston, it will make my revenge the more complete. He speaks the truth. Listen, all. This man has been the slave of my caprice, and why not? You and all the world believe him upright and honorable, I, his fate, his nemesis, can *blast* his honor and lay bare his crime. I do it with a breath—I strike the first blow now—here are the proofs of his guilt, read, read—[*Handing Crockett papers*] You will not? Then I pronounce that man a criminal and a forger. [*Davy seizes papers*] Robber, ruffian!

DAVY. Look here, do you know what we do with men like you in these parts, when a man wearing the image of the Almighty Maker shames nature and changes off with the wolf? We of the hills and mountains band ourselves together, and form a court of law where there's mighty little learning, maybe, but where there's a heap of justice, and where a judge sits that renders a sentence—strikes terror to the boldest heart. Do you know his name? It's Lynch—Judge Lynch.

CRAM. Why—what do you mean?

DAVY. I mean business, and damned little of that. Now, what's your game? You're dumb. Well, I allowed you'd be. Squire, hold up your head. We are neither your judges, nor your accusers, but your children and your neighbors. Can you lay any claim to these documents?

MAJ. R. No, they are lawfully his—he holds my notes for large amounts. I am irretrievably in his power.

DAVY. Well, then, they belong to him.

EL. No, no, give them to me.

DAVY. First be sure you're right—then go ahead.

EL. The nature of these notes is best known to you. Make out your claim in full, and my solicitor will cancel all obligation.

MAJ. R. No, Eleanor, no. I cannot consent to this sacrifice. Your fortune is sacred.

EL. My fortune is there. I ask no other.

CRAM. You settle matters very easily, Mrs. Crockett.

DAVY. Eh!

CRAM. There is another debt, one of vengeance. How will you settle that?

EL. That is for you to do—treat it as I do these. Burn it. [*Burns letters*]

DAVY. Now, I allow, that makes him right sick.

CRAM. Royston, we shall meet again—my revenge shall come!

DAVY. Look here, you're a marked man in these parts. Keep a watch over your tongue, for if you don't—

CRAM. Well, if I don't—?

DAVY. Well, private interests must give way to public weal.

CRAM. Ill luck and disappointment on you all!

DAVY. Thank you—same to you!

CRAM. Bah!

DAVY. Yes, that is what the sheep said. [*Bob puts head in door*] Come here, Bob. There she is—there's your new Aunt Crockett.

BOB. Say, Davy!

DAVY. Eh!

BOB. Is she the one what was took out of the cradle?

DAVY. Young man, your mind is wandering—go back to bed and sleep it out. [*Exit Bob*] Mother, that boy's getting a deal too pert. He'll have to be took down. [*Parson rises to go*] Parson, take a chair. Mother, the light in the window has brought me back to my old resting-place.

EL. And me to my new resting place—the heart and home of Davy Crockett. [*Music, "Home Sweet Home"*]

CURTAIN

JAMES O'NEILL'S VERSION OF "MONTE CRISTO"

By Charles Fechter

CAST OF CHARACTERS

Edmund Dantès	Faria
Morel	Governor
Danglars	Sentinel
Noirtier	First Gaoler
Caderousse	Second Gaoler
Fernand	Brigadier
Fisherman	Albert
Man	Sailor
Villefort	Mlle. Danglars
First Agent	Mercédès
Second Agent	Carconte
Servant	Woman

The manuscript bears the following notation:

"This manuscript is the only and original version of the famous play 'Monte Cristo as produced and acted by James O'Neill. It is duly entered at Washington and copyrighted under the copyright laws of the United States of America. Any and all infringements on this copyright will be taken action against.

"Darcy & Wolford, Sole Agents
"for Mr. O'Neill."

ACT I.

MAN. 'Tis she—'tis she!

WOMAN. I tell you 'tis not.

MAN. I tell you it is!

WOMAN. A ship in sight! [*Enter Morel and Carconte*]

MOREL. [*To crowd*] Friends, yonder comes a rich cargo, and all must to-day partake of my good fortune. [*Gives money and goes upstage*]

CARC. [*R.C.*] Is not my husband here? Did he not come out with you?

MOREL. No.

CARC. The drunken sot, he is in some low wineshop!

MOREL. [*Looking through telescope*] Here come the officers of health and customs along with my supercargo. Douglass, how is it that Edmund is not with them? The captain usually lets him land before getting into harbor.

FISHER. Look, Monsieur Morel, the flag is half-mast!

MOREL. Good heavens, it is! What can it mean? What can have happened on board?

FISHER. Some chief officer dead, no doubt.

MOREL. It can't be Edmund Dantès! Here is Danglars! We shall know all from him. [*Enter Danglars*] Speak, Danglars, what means the flag lowered?

DANG. I am sorry, sir, to be the bearer of bad news. The captain is dead.

MOREL. What, my dear old friend?

DANG. He died of brain fever that carried him off in a few hours after we left Naples. 'Tis unfortunate, Monsieur Morel, very unfortunate. Such a captain is not easily found to look properly after the interests of such a house as yours, it needs an old and experienced seaman.

MOREL. A man need not be an absolute veteran to understand his business. What did Edmund Dantès do in this emergency?

DANG. Dantès! [*Aside*] Now for him! [*Aloud*] Oh, Monsieur Morel, the captain was scarcely dead, he was scarcely at the bottom of the sea, when Dantès assumed the command and caused us to lose a day at Elba, instead of steering for Marseilles direct.

MOREL. To take command of the vessel was his duty as mate, but to lose a day at Elba, there he was wrong. [*Coldly*] I shall take the account from him and soon know the merits of the case.

DANG. Very good, Monsieur Morel. Edmund is young, but I believe in his honesty.

MOREL. And I am assured of it. I will go and meet him. [*Exit, L.U.E.*]

CARC. [*To Danglars, coming down*] Caught are ye? I'm not sorry to see you getting into hot water. You have been the bane of my husband. Edmund will avenge me. [*Going up*]

DANG. [*Crosses to R.*] Not so fast, they laugh best, who laugh last.

NOIR. [*Enters R.U.E., stopping at Carconte*] Your pardon. May I ask madame, is not that the ship "Pharaon"?

CARC. It is, sir, and I am going to see her come into the harbor.

NOIR. Can you inform me where to find the captain?

CARC. Go to the bay of Naples, and you will find him at the bottom. [*Exit R.*]

NOIR. Is the woman mad?

DANG. She spoke the truth, sir. We lost our captain on the voyage, and his body lies where Carconte told you.

NOIR. And after his death, who took charge of the ship?

DANG. The mate.

NOIR. His name?

DANG. Edmund Dantès.

NOIR. And is he alive?

DANG. [*Sighing*] Quite alive!

NOIR. Where could I find him?

DANG. On board at present. In an hour's time, at the Reserve Inn. Any matter that I can answer in his stead?

NOIR. [*Going*] I merely wished a little information about the vessel's course this voyage.

DANG. I can give you that.

NOIR. You?

DANG. I am the supercargo on board the "Pharaon." What do you wish to know?

NOIR. Only whether the ship made land on the voyage.

DANG. Yes. [*Looking mysteriously around*] On the Isle of Elba!

NOIR. Thank you. [*Walks away*]

DANG. Well—

NOIR. What?

DANG. Is that all?

Noir. That is all.

Dang. I thought you wanted—

Noir. Thank you. [*Exit, R.2.E.*]

Dang. Something not quite straight here! That man came looking for the letter that Edmund received at Elba from the hands of the exiled emperor. Let me only be sure, and then—

Cader. [*Looking out of inn*] Wife gone? Then, I may show myself.

Dang. Caderousse!

Cader. Danglars! Hurrah! We'll crack a bottle in honor of your safe return.

Dang. [*R.C.*] You're drunk.

Cader. [*L.C.*] Drunk, of course, I am—and proud of it! So much the worse for them that are afraid of wine, that is because they are afraid of speaking the truth. I'll engage you never get drunk. [*Ship works on from R.*]

Dang. Idiot!

Cader. Am I? You're afraid to let your heart—ain't I complimentary? I say "your heart!"—you're afraid to let it disclose its thoughts, but I, never! I drink so much as ever I like—as much as I can—and then I open the floodgates of truth and avow I love wine, hate work, and pray for widowhood! Come on, have a glass. You won't? Well, give me your arm. You see, my head is light, but my legs are like pillars of lead. You never feel that way for you drink water like a shark. [*Sings*] "The bottle for me, the pump for thee!"

Dang. [*Looking off*] Who is that pretty girl?

Cader. Don't you know Mercédès, our brave Edmund's betrothed? Here comes the "Pharaon" into port, look at her—isn't she pretty? [*Exit into tavern with Danglars; ship seen coming into port. Enter Mercédès and Fernand, R.2.E.*]

Fer. Mercédès, for the last time, will you answer me?

Merc. You are your own enemy to ask me again.

Fer. Answer me a hundred times more, that I may at last believe it. Tell me that you scorn my love—that my life, my death are nothing to you—that you reject my hand, my heart! Ah, Mercédès, what have I done that you should kill thus?

Merc. Blame me not, Fernand, blame yourself. From the very first, I told you, "Fernand, I love you as a brother, but ask not, hope not more, for my heart is given to another."—Did I say so, Fernand?

Fer. Yes, oh, yes. But, you know Mercédès, it is a sacred law amongst us Catalans, to intermarry.

Merc. Not a law, merely a custom, Fernand, that is all. Fernand, I will never be yours because I love another, and I am his! [*Crosses to R.*]

Fer. You?

Merc. His! Fernand, do you hear? His, in the sight of Heaven, and whilst I live I cannot be another's without guilt.

Fer. I will kill him!

Merc. You will not! Fernand, what would it profit you? To find my friendship turned to hate? To know that in killing him, you had killed me?

Fer. The sea has not your constancy, Mercédès—a sailor's is a dangerous trade, and the ocean a vast grave. The sea will do my business.

Merc. You have a bad heart, Fernand. I blush to be your relative and to bear your name, but even were I to lose him, I should know that he died loving me, and I would die loving him.

Fer. But, if he were to forget you?

Merc. Forget me?

Fer. Aye, the ship is in port, why is he not here?

Merc. Heavens!

Fer. Ah, at last you know what jealousy is! It is fearful is it not?

Merc. Fernand!

Fer. I am avenged, Mercédès, he has forgotten you. [Crosses R.]

Edmund. [Outside] Mercédès!

Merc. 'Tis false, Fernand, he is here! [Enter Edmund. She flies to him, Fernand half draws knife]

Fer. No, it would kill her!

Edmund. Mercédès, my beloved Mercédès! [Sees Fernand] Oh, I did not know you had a companion, who is this man?

Merc. My cousin, Fernand Mondego, the man whom after you, I love best in the world.

Edmund. [C.] Then he is my friend. Brother of Mercédès, here is my hand! [Advances offering hand. Fernand refuses it]

Merc. Fernand!

Fer. [R., approaching Mercédès] No, no, it is too much! I cannot! Adieu, Mercédès, adieu! [Rushes off]

Edmund. [Looking after him] Mercédès, that man will cause us misfortune.

Merc. Misfortune? No, Edmund, now reunited, no misfortune can befall us. But, thou knowest not how I have suffered in thy absence, the nights I have passed. How I have prayed when the seas—now so calm, so smiling on thy return—roared dashing on the rocks when thou were away. And hast thou no thought of me?

Edmund. Thought of thee? Oh, what should I have thought of! Art thou not my Providence, my guardian angel, my life itself? When the tempest howled, when the sea and wind were raging, thy prayers were to thy patron saint, beloved one. My prayers were to Mercédès, and my prayers were heard. The storm abated, the sea grew calm, and believed in thee! Ah, Monsieur Morel!

MOREL. [*Enters*]   Yes. Monsieur Morel, not quite welcome, eh? He might have chosen his time better. Aye, aye, but there is little time to lose, happiness so rarely visits us here below, that when it passes by our portal we must seize it in its flight. But, I thought of you—everything is ready—I have had all the papers duly prepared. In the commerce of life there are so few honest debtors, Edmund, you are now in funds and must make prompt payment.

EDMUND.   Thanks, Monsieur Morel, for judging me so truly. Yes, I repay in ready coin the noble trust of my Mercédès. I place in her hand my present, my future, my life, my soul, they are thine, Mercédès, thine forever, my beloved wife! [*Enter Danglars and Caderousse*]

CADER. [*To Edmund*]   Well, my boy, have you forgotten your friends?

EDMUND.   Oh, how fares it, Caderousse? Bless you!

CADER.   And where are you going like that?

EDMUND.   Where happy people go, my friend, straight before them without caring what rises in the distance, or what lies behind them—au revoir! [*Exit with Mercédès*]

CADER.   There's a case of hearty love, if ever I saw one, but nothin' like love of the bottle! [*Exit*]

DANG.   Here are the ship's papers.

MOREL. [*Sits at table, L., looking at papers*]   All right, thanks. All complete and regular. I have only to sign the several returns.

DANG.   You have not spoken to Edmund Dantès, Monsieur Morel, I hope he gave you a satisfactory reason for anchoring at Elba?

MOREL.   I forgot all about that.

DANG.   Then he has given you the emperor's letter?

MOREL.   The emperor's letter?

DANG.   Yes, the letter he received at Elba from the emperor's own hand. His Majesty, Louis XVIII is not given to jesting with the friends of the ex-emperor, and I supposed the letter was for you.

MOREL.   For me?

DANG.   For whom can Edmund have brought it?

MOREL.   He never said a word to me about it.

DANG.   In that case, Monsieur Morel, say nothing to Edmund of what I have told you—I may have been mistaken. I should feel very sorry to get him into a mess.

MOREL. There are your papers and the entries signed—let this affair o Edmund's rest. He must have nothing to trouble him on his wedding day.

DANG. His wedding day?

MOREL. Let the crew of the "Pharaon" know of their captain's marriage

DANG. Edmund, the captain?

MOREL. Yes, that is my marriage present to him. [*Exit*]

DANG. Indeed? You have not got your captain's epaulettes yet, Edmund Dantès, nor will your next voyage be on board the "Pharaon." [*Enter Cader- ousse and Fernand, L.2.E.*]

CADER. [*C.*] Come along, my hearty, what's the odds? A woman lost and two bottles won! Come, have a glass—nothing makes one so thirsty as jeal- ousy. Come along!

FER. Let me alone, Caderousse, I won't drink.

DANG. Not drink, young man? 'Tis only whining lovers that don't drink.

CADER. Oh, he is one, and whining. He met his love in his rival's arms.

FER. He is not her husband yet. [*Crosses C.*]

DANG. He will be this evening.

FER. This evening?

DANG. The wedding is to take place at your house, Caderousse, at the Re- serve. I shall be there, we shall all be there. [*To Fernand*] You will be of the party, I presume?

FER. [*Furious*] I? I would rather see them both dead!

CADER. [*Knocks on table*] Waiter, some more wine!

DANG. If your rival could be got rid of without killing him, you would spare Mercédès's feelings—and Dantès need not die.

CADER. [*Drinking*] Why should Dantès die? I won't have Dantès die, he is a fine fellow. Here's to your health, Edmund!

FER. [*Angry*] Caderousse!

DANG. He's drunk; never mind him. Suppose you put between Edmund and Mercédès the walls of a prison—it would part them quite as effectively as a tombstone.

FER. Edmund in prison!

CADER. [*Drinking and following them dreamily*] Why? Why put Dantès in prison? I won't have Dantès in prison! I love Edmund, here's to your health, Edmund.

DANG. Hold your noise!

CADER. I shall drink his health if I like.

FER. But how to get him into prison?

CADER. [*Pushing away papers*] Take away all this rubbish, Danglars. It belongs to you, these are the weapons you're accustomed to. There is what

an kill a man more surely than lying in wait for him with a knife in some
dark corner.

DANG. The vagabond says true enough.

FER. How so?

CADER. I have a greater dread of a pen and an ink bottle, and a sheet of
paper, than I have of a sword and pistol and—a bottle of wine.

DANG. Do you understand?

FER. [*All sit at table, Caderousse singing*] No.

DANG. Fill his glass. [*Fernand fills Caderousse's glass*]

FER. Well?

DANG. Well, this drunkard has pointed out the way. If I bore a grudge
against Dantès, if I wanted to rid myself of him, I would take this sheet of
paper, I would dip this pen in the ink, and I would write thus—with the left
hand to disguise the writing—a piece of information in these words—[*Writes
with left hand*]

FER. [*Anxiously, reading over him*] "To the Procureur du Roi!"

DANG. [*Points to Caderousse*] Is he asleep?

FER. He sleeps—proceed.

DANG. [*Writes*] "The Procureur du Roi is informed that a man named
Edmund Dantès who arrived from Smyrna to-day, touched at the Isle of
Elba, where he was intrusted by the usurper Napoleon with a letter for the
Bonapartist Committee. The letter will be found either on his person, or in
his cabin on board the 'Pharaon.'—Signed, A Friend to the Throne and Religion."—The letter is placed in the hands of the Procureur du Roi, and the
business is done.

CADER. [*Who has awakened*] The business is done, but 'tis a rascally business!

DANG. [*Startled, but recovers*] For which I shall not make myself responsible. [*Crumples letter and throws it at Fernand's feet*] There, take it.
Danglars will not be the bearer.

FER. But I will! [*Picks it up and exit*]

CADER. Where's he off to in such a hurry?

DANG. To Mercédès's cottage, no doubt.

CADER. To Mercédès's cottage—do you think I am blind drunk? He is off
to the city. What does he want in the city?

DANG. How should I know?

CADER. [*Looking on ground*] And the letter—where's the letter?

DANG. What letter?

CADER. The letter. The letter informing against Dantès. The letter you
threw down there, where is it? I want that letter! I must have the letter!

[*Takes a glass which Danglars fills for him*] Ah, how well you know me—here's your health.

DANG. [*Looks off*] Just in time—here they come. [*Enter Edmund, Morel, and Crew of "Pharaon"*]

EDMUND. Monsieur Morel, all is prepared at the Reserve according to your orders. Caderousse, your wife wants you to arrange the table, supper will be ready in an hour. [*During the cheering Noirtier enters, and having Edmund pointed out to him by Danglars, touches his shoulder*]

NOIR. May I speak a word to you?

EDMUND. With me?

NOIR. You are the mate of the "Pharaon"?

EDMUND. [*Coming down*] I am, may I know your pleasure?

NOIR. I understand your ship cast anchor at the Isle of Elba?

EDMUND. She did.

NOIR. And you landed there?

EDMUND. I did.

NOIR. To execute a commission entrusted to your captain.

EDMUND. Who died on the voyage, yes.

NOIR. The emperor has made you the bearer of a letter.

EDMUND. How know you that?

NOIR. With orders to deliver it to a man unknown to you, who would accost you?

EDMUND. Yes.

NOIR. I am he.

EDMUND. The description corresponds exactly. Your name then, is—I have asked your name!

NOIR. It is for you to begin—and halve it.

EDMUND. True. N.o.i.r.—

NOIR. T.i.e.r.

EDMUND. Right.

NOIR. Now, give me the letter.

EDMUND. I thought it of too great importance to carry about me, and left it in my cabin on board.

NOIR. You can get it at once?

EDMUND. To go and return would take me altogether, an hour.

NOIR. Then go for an hour. I will await you here.

EDMUND. Would it be the same to you to come for it to the Reserve Inn?

NOIR. Why so?

EDMUND. Because I am going to be married there within an hour to the fair girl you see yonder, and I should be sorry to fail in attendance.

NOIR. I can understand.

EDMUND. At the Reserve, then?

NOIR. At the Reserve Inn.

EDMUND. In an hour from this. [*Goes up*]

NOIR. In an hour from this—pretty, very! [*Exit, R.*]

DANG. [*Who has overheard*] And my letter will be there in time! [*Sailors drink and cheer, as scene changes*]

SCENE 2: *Villefort's cabinet. A writing table heaped with papers near door at back. Villefort discovered at change. Germain and two Police enter.*

VILLE. First with you—what intelligence?

FIRST AGENT. The man we seek has been traced. He has been in the port, landed from a fishing boat, and shortly afterwards in the village of Catalans.

VILLE. Does he answer the description sent from the Prefecture in Paris?

FIRST AGENT. Assuredly. "About forty years of age, long black hair, combed back, black whiskers and moustache, meeting—wears a long sourtout buttoned up to his chin, and decorated with the Legion of Honor. Hat with a wide leaf."

VILLE. [*Looking over paper*] Just so! Is he in custody?

FIRST AGENT. Not yet, but he has been followed. We shall have him before night.

VILLE. Good. He is described as being a most dangerous conspirator, and a very likely person to be mixed up in this affair of Dantès, denounced to me in this anonymous letter. [*To other Agent*] What have you done in his case?

SECOND AGENT. Arrested him as he was getting into the "Pharaon's" boat to go on board.

VILLE. Was the letter found on him?

SECOND AGENT. No, sir. I have brought him here, whilst my comrades went to search his cabin.

VILLE. Bring him in. [*Exit Second Agent*] And see you to the immediate arrest of the other. [*Exit First Agent*] There is plainly some connection between these two affairs. [*Reads Danglar's letter*] "The Procureur du Roi is informed that a man named Edmund Dantès, who arrived from Smyrna to-day, touched at the Isle of Elba, where he was entrusted by the usurper, Napoleon, with a letter for the Bonapartist Committee. The letter will be found either on his person, or in his cabin on board the 'Pharaon'." [*Enter Second Agent with Edmund*]

SECOND AGENT. This is the Procureur du Roi.

EDMUND. The Procureur du Roi!

VILLE. Come forward. [*Edmund advances and bows to Agent*] Await my orders. [*Agent retires*]

EDMUND. What the deuce am I wanted for?

VILLE. Your name?

EDMUND. Edmund Dantès!

VILLE. Your occupation?

EDMUND. Mate of the ship "Pharaon."

VILLE. And you were arrested when going on board. How did you intend acting after visiting the "Pharaon"?

EDMUND. I intended returning as quickly as possible to the Reserve. I have been expected there this hour past.

VILLE. What for?

EDMUND. To get married—that's all.

VILLE. Go on.

EDMUND. To what purpose, may I ask? If justice will condescend to inform me in what matter she wants me to enlighten her, I will tell her all I know—only promising her I know very little.

VILLE. Your political opinions are said to be very violent.

EDMUND. My political opinions? Violent? Why, I'm almost ashamed to say I have no political opinions at all. My profession of faith is very concise; I love my father, I respect Monsieur Morel, I trust in Heaven, and I adore Mercédès—that is my political creed, Monsieur Procureur, it cannot be very interesting to justice.

VILLE. 'Tis strange.

EDMUND. What is?

VILLE. This accusation against you.

EDMUND. On account of my opinions?

VILLE. Even so.

EDMUND. Gracious me, how stupid! Oh, I beg pardon.

VILLE. Have you any great enemy to your knowledge? [*Looks at letter*] There must be someone who wishes you ill, very ill.

EDMUND. Well, possibly so. You know men better than I do, but if that "someone" be amongst those I love, I have no wish to know who he is, that I may not have to despise him.

VILLE. You appear to be such an honest-minded lad that in your case I will forego the ordinary cases. [*Hands him letter*] Read your denunciation— do you know the writing?

EDMUND. No, I do not know this writing. I see at once it is a counterfeit hand. I am indeed most unfortunate in having to deal with a man like yourself, for my accuser is a fearful enemy.

VILLE. How much truth is there in this paper?

EDMUND. There is truth, and no truth. There lies the guile, the venom of the charge.

VILLE. How is that?

EDMUND. It is true that I arrived from Smyrna, it is true that I cast anchor at Elba, it is true that I received a letter from the emperor's hand, but I was ignorant of any plot, and was totally unconscious of furthering any conspiracy.

VILLE. Yet, you went out of your course to touch at Elba; you therefore called there expressly of your own will, in the teeth of your owner's orders. This bears a very serious appearance.

EDMUND. I see too well it does, but it was not of my own doing and a very few words will explain it.

VILLE. Proceed. [*Sits, R.*]

EDMUND. Well then, on leaving Naples where I believe he had an interview with Murat, our captain fell ill of brain fever. He grew rapidly worse, and feeling himself dying and his senses about to desert him, he called me to his side. "Dantès," he said, "swear to me by your honor as a sailor, by your faith in Heaven, by your love for me, to discharge when I am gone, the mission I shall confide to you, and with which I was entrusted. Do not hesitate, Edmund, my body's rest, my soul's salvation, my honor are at stake!"—and the tears coursed down his bronzed and burning cheek. I could demur no longer. I swore. Then, with his ring, he gave me a packet, commanded me to steer for the Island of Elba. To land at Port Farrajo, to have the ring conveyed to the emperor and to place the packet in his own hands. In a few moments he was dead. I reached Elba. I had the ring conveyed to the emperor— I gave him the packet. He entrusted me with a letter which a stranger he described, would ask me for on landing at Marseilles. As soon as I arrived, the stranger presented himself, and I was on my way to get the letter, left in my cabin, when I was arrested. This is the truth, the whole truth, by my honor as a sailor, by my love for Mercédès, by my father's life!

VILLE. [*Rising*] Yes, I believe you. You are surely innocent.

EDMUND. Thanks, monsieur, adieu, and thanks. [*Going*]

VILLE. Stay—where are you going?

EDMUND. I am going away.

VILLE. But you are not free yet.

EDMUND. You say I am innocent—how are the guilty treated?

VILLE. That is just what you and I are going to consider.

EDMUND. You and I?

VILLE. Yes.

EDMUND. I am very much afraid our views about justice are widely different.

VILLE. Let us try.

EDMUND. First of all, if I am to have a voice in the matter, I acquit myself as an innocent man.

VILLE. I agree.

EDMUND. And I give myself full discharge.

VILLE. Granted—on one condition.

EDMUND. I impose no conditions on myself.

VILLE. But, you are not the sole judge in the case.

EDMUND. Quite right.

VILLE. There are two of us.

EDMUND. Unfortunately.

VILLE. And we must be unanimous.

EDMUND. I have said that would be difficult. Your condition?

VILLE. You are not to speak to any person whatsoever of your interview with the emperor.

EDMUND. I agree.

VILLE. You are not to say a word of what has passed between ourselves.

EDMUND. Granted.

VILLE. Finally, you pledge your word of honor to present yourself at my first summons.

EDMUND. I swear it.

VILLE. You see I am not too hard.

EDMUND. I do not complain.

VILLE. Very kind. Were you to see that stranger again?

EDMUND. Yes, at the Reserve.

VILLE. Off with you, then, wait for him there—let him accost you.

EDMUND. But how about the letter he is coming to claim?

VILLE. My men will give it to him.

EDMUND. What? [*Bell off R.*]

VILLE. Silence! Someone comes.

GER. [*Enters*] A stranger, sir, wishes particularly to see you on business of the greatest importance.

VILLE. [*Writing at table*] Impossible, I am engaged! I can't see him. Let him demand an interview in writing. [*Exit Germain. Villefort hands Edmund a letter*] Go at once by that door. [*Inside*] On your way, leave this note at the guardhouse.

EDMUND. [*Aside*] Well, I'm on pretty good terms with justice. 'Tis well to have friends in every quarter. [*Exit*]

GER. [*Enters*] This man insists on seeing you. He says, sir, if you knew who he was—

NOIR. [*Enters*] It is I.

VILLE. My brother! [*To Germain*] Go! [*Germain exit*]

NOIR. It appears you did not expect me. Is it the custom among the present nobility for younger brothers to make their elder brothers wait in the ante-room?

VILLE. Good heavens!

NOIR. What is the matter with you?

VILLE. The very description!

NOIR. What description?

VILLE. [*In trouble*] The description of your person sent down from Paris, and which I myself have furnished here for the police.

NOIR. So, you have given my description to the police, eh? Not very kind on your part, my younger brother—but when a son of a general of the empire becomes Procureur du Roi of His Majesty, Louis the XVIII, his first act is naturally to disown his family. His first thought to disembarrass himself of them.

VILLE. You insult me!

NOIR. Truth then, is offensive to you?

VILLE. What is it you want of me?

NOIR. A few moments shelter from your own bloodhounds who are now on my track, thanks to the description you had the goodness to supply them.

VILLE. [*Sits, R.*] Did I know that it referred to you? Did I know that you were still conspiring?

NOIR. And what the devil would you have me do? Everyone is not blessed with your turncoat talent. That comes to you from your lady mother, whose name I thank you for adopting: since at least you do not disgrace that of our common father, who had made her his second wife. But, what am I about? I am accusing you, whilst you are the judge. I ask pardon, Monsieur le Procureur. You said that I was conspiring.

VILLE. I hold the proofs.

NOIR. Against whom do I conspire?

VILLE. Against the king.

NOIR. Correct to syllable! Allow me to congratulate you on your police. I never thought they were so sharp.

VILLE. [*Crosses L.*] But you cannot remain in this house.

NOIR. I have no desire to do so. I mean to depart directly.

VILLE. And whither do you think of going?

NOIR. That is my business.

VILLE. How will you get out?

NOIR. By the door, of course.

VILLE. In the daylight?

NOIR. In the daylight.

VILLE. And in the midst of the men who are dogging you?

NOIR. In the midst of them.

VILLE. But, they will arrest you.

NOIR. They will let me pass in peace. And they will also most respectfully salute me. [*Goes to bell*]

VILLE. [*R.*] What are you doing?

NOIR. Ringing for your servant. [*Rising. Germain enters*] What is your name, my man.

GER. Germain.

NOIR. Then Germain, take this Napoleon, [*Gives coin*] 'tis the picture of the usurper, and I fear lest its possession compromise me. Now, show me to your master's dressing room, and then go and spend that bit of gold as fast as ever you can. [*Germain looks dubious*]

VILLE. Do as the gentleman tells you. [*Exeunt Germain and Noirtier. Sinks in chair*] Great heavens, is the hateful past of my family to haunt me ever on my aspiring path? Is this elder brother, proud and contemptuous, to come everlastingly between me and the goal of my ambition? What were life and fortune had this occurred in Paris—had the prefect of police sent the notification to any other official than myself? Should the arrest be effected under my immediate order, I were disgraced forever! How shall I throw them off the scent? How contrive his escape?—Who is there? [*Enter First Agent*] What do you want?

FIRST AGENT. I ask your pardon Monsieur le Procureur, your instructions have been faithfully observed. We are certain that the fugitive is in the street and we have his escape quite cut off. I come for a warrant to search the houses all around.

NOIR. [*Enters, changed in appearance*] Give it, Villefort, prompt action against the king's enemies! [*Goes R.*]

VILLE. You?

NOIR. [*Aside*] Take care, you will betray yourself! [*To Agent*] So, my friend, you have lit on this fellow—at least you have recognized him?

FIRST AGENT. Yes, long, black hair and whiskers, wide-leaved hat, military surtout with the ribbon of the "Legion."

NOIR. It would be impossible to be deceived. There is nothing so handy as an accurate description. [*Enter Second Agent*] It positively rains police agents to-day!

SECOND AGENT. The letter found on board. [*Gives Villefort letter*]

VILLE. [*Aside*] For him—addressed to Noirtier—if any but I had read it. [*Aside to Noirtier*] Away—away! Quit Marseilles instantly or you will betray us both.

NOIR. Well, I'll intrude no longer. To work Villefort; search, arrest, imprison! I—I shall be off to dinner. [*Agents bow to him*] Did I not tell you so? Your servant, gentlemen. [*Exit*]

VILLE. And this Dantès knows his person—has seen this letter—knows his name. A word from him can ruin me. [*To Agents*] Go with a strong party to the Reserve Inn instantly. There you will find the young sailor you apprehended this afternoon.

FIRST AGENT. Edmund Dantès?

VILLE. Yes. Arrest him—let him be conveyed at once to the dungeons of the Château d'If and kept in strict and most careful detention. There is the order to the governor. [*Signs and gives paper. Agents exeunt. Tears up letter to Noirtier*] This letter destroyed, the mouth of the young sailor sealed, no trace remains of the pernicious secret. And now to work, Villefort to work. [*Exit into room. Change of scene*]

SCENE 3: *The Reserve Inn overlooking the sea. A long table laid out under an arbor of vines. Discovered at change, Morel, Mercédès, Danglars, Caderousse, Carconte, Fisherman and Sailors. Caderousse drinks from bottle as he puts it on table. Carconte superintending setting of table.*

CARC. An hour behind time—my dinner will be spoilt.

CADER. And the wine will be so warm it won't be drinkable.

MERC. What can have happened to him—what can have happened to him?

MOREL. Come, come, no tears, no lamentations. He has but gone to the ship to bring up doubtless some handsome presents he purchased at Smyrna for his bride.

CADER. [*Touching Danglars on shoulder*] Is this then, part of the trick you concerted with Fernand?

DANG. [*Uneasy*] What trick?

CADER. The letter this afternoon.

DANG. What letter! The one I tore up?

CADER. You didn't tear it up, you threw it into a corner, and then when Fernand left, it was gone.

DANG. You don't know what you are saying. You were drunk.

CADER. Maybe so, but this sobers me. 'Tis a piece of rascality and I'll tell all about it.

DANG. [*Catching his arm*] You had better keep quiet.

SAILOR. [*Shouts*] Here is the mate—here is Monsieur Edmund!

DANG. [*Aside*] What's this, released?

EDMUND. [*Enters*] Yes, my friends, here is the mate! I am sorry I am so late, but it really was not my fault. I was not absent willingly, believe me.

MERC. What was the matter? Whence come you?

EDMUND. From the office of the Procureur du Roi.

MERC. What were you doing there?

EDMUND. That, my love of a future wife, is precisely what I am forbidden to tell you. I am on the most friendly footing with justice, and should any of you ever be accused of swallowing his own ship, or running away with the Château d'If, I'll be answerable for his acquittal. [*Laugh*] But come, let us make up for lost time. Is all ready for the ceremony?

ALL. Yes, yes!

MOREL. Now, my friends, you join me in a cheer for the commander of the "Pharaon," Edmund Dantès, her captain!

ALL. Hurrah for our captain!

EDMUND. Captain?

MOREL. Here is your commission signed by me, which gives you the "Pharaon."

EDMUND. O Monsieur Morel—O Mercédès—oh, my father! See, the tears are in my eyes. Oh, dear wife, dear friends, speak my thanks to my benefactor —I cannot say them, I cannot speak!

ALL. Vive Monsieur Morel!

CADER. All is ready for the happy couple.

MOREL. Come on then.

EDMUND. [*Embraces Mercédès*] I would not give this hour of my life for all the riches of Peru. [*Enter Police Agent and Noirtier*]

AGENT. Stop. Which of you is named Edmund Dantès?

EDMUND. [*Coming forward*] I am he.

AGENT. In the name of the law, I arrest you.

EDMUND. Good heavens!

MERC. My Edmund!

NOIR. [*Aside*] The bearer of Napoleon's letter arrested? I did well to change my outward man!

EDMUND. Whither am I to be taken?

AGENT. To the Château d'If.

EDMUND. I am lost!

DANG. [*Aside*] You are indeed! [*Agents seize Dantès, Morel keeps back Sailors, Mercédès falls in Morel's arms*]

ACT II.

SCENE I: *Eighteen years have elapsed since preceding act. Apartment in the house of the Count de Morcerf. Ball music heard within. Enter at rise, Morel and Servant. Morel is much aged, and poorly dressed.*

SERV. Have the goodness to wait here, sir.

MOREL. I did not know there was company, or—[*Looking at dress*]

SERV. A ball to celebrate my master's return from Jamaica. [*Exit*]

MOREL. [*Looking at letter in his hand*] "General, the Count de Morcerf." So, the letter I received is signed, but I know no person by that name. [*Reads*] "Hearing that M. Morel is in Paris, a person with whom he was acquainted many years since, and whose hand I have the honor to solicit, entreats his advice, before forming her decision. In full reliance on his prudence and sincerity, I anxiously await his visit and commit my happiness to his hands. Signed, Count de Morcerf." Who is the Count de Morcerf? Who is the person he speaks of?

MERC. [*Enters*] It is I, dear Monsieur Morel! Do you not remember me?

MOREL. Your features are not unfamiliar to me, madame, but I cannot immediately—[*Struck by recollection*] No, no, it cannot be!

MERC. Your hand—your hand! It is I, indeed.

MOREL. Mercédès—Mercédès Mondego!

MERC. Yes, Mercédès the Catalan. Mercédès, the bride and widow of our poor Edmund who disappeared eighteen years ago. Eighteen years of mourning and tears!

MOREL. But, madame, this style of dress. In whose house am I?

MERC. In my cousin Fernand's.

MOREL. The Catalan?

MERC. Yes. The poor fisherman of former days.

MOREL. Can it be so?

MERC. All is fortune and misfortune in this world, dear Monsieur Morel. Fernand is now Count de Morcerf, and this evening is the celebration of his return and his elevation to the peerage.

MOREL. It was he then, that wrote to me? [*Shows letter*]

MERC. Yes.

MOREL. And it is you whom he seeks to marry?

MERC. Yes.

MOREL. And you wish to consult me?

MERC. Yes.

MOREL. Truly, madame, I cannot see wherein my opinion is necessary, nor do I believe I can possibly give an opinion.

MERC. Why?

MOREL. You said but now, "All is fortune and misfortune in this world." Eighteen years have passed since your bridegroom was torn from your arms as he led you to the altar. Our poor lamented Edmund, whose father perished of grief and misery. Eighteen years have passed since you, too, disappeared. I find you to-day, but him I never found—no, notwithstanding my daily search, my hourly prayers. He rots in an unhallowed ground—you preside at the fête given in honor of your future husband's return. You said well, "All is fortune and misfortune in this world!"

MERC. Monsieur Morel, when you have listened to me, you will bitterly regret the cruel words that have escaped you.

MOREL. Madame.

MERC. Call me Mercédès as in the old time—the name I have borne bravely and amid all my wretchedness have never dishonored. Were my Edmund living, were this instant standing beside us, he might proudly join his hand in mine and find no cause to blush. I wear these robes for the first time to-day, and when I have told you all, if you so counsel me, I will lay them aside without regret, and resume the Catalan rags I wore yesterday.

MOREL. What mean you?

MERC. That when Edmund was torn from my arms—as you thought to remind me, as if I ever could forget—I also disappeared. They had bereaved me at the foot of the altar of the father of my child. Aye, our marriage was not the union of two loving souls alone, it was the reparation of a fault. A son was born to me—none knew the place of my retreat but Fernand who discovered it. Yet, knowing my deep sorrow, and fearing to intrude on my privacy, he enlisted as a soldier and sent me in a farewell letter, the money paid to him for this generous transaction. The sum was sufficient for my son's early requirements. For me, I needed nothing but to find Edmund again. I went forth—but what have I done, what have I suffered, Heaven only knows! Not a prison, but I have visited it. Not a man in power but I have knelt before him. Onward from day to day, from town to town, wheresoever I deemed a sign, begging on the road to attain my aim!!

MOREL. Poor soul! And your child?

MERC. Fernand by that time had risen to be a captain—had placed my boy in a military college. The war of independence broke out in Greece—Fernand accepted service under the Pasha of Jamaica to discipline his troops. Fernand —his last defender—received from the expiring pasha a casket of priceless jewels, the foundation of his present fortunes, arrived but yesterday in Paris with the rank of general; he is now Count de Morcerf and peer of France. I am still, and if such is your advice I will ever remain, Mercédès the Catalan, the widow of Edmund Dantès, the poor sailor wrongfully imprisoned.

MOREL. What would you of me?

MERC. In a few months my son, Edmund's son, will leave St. Cyr a lieutenant. In a few months I will have to tell him, "thy name is Albert Mondego, the base-born," or "thou art Albert Mondego, Viscount de Morcerf," the title by which Fernand will recognize him on espousing me. But, mark me, nothing on earth should compel me to this marriage, were there a single ray of hope that Edmund could be found. Oh, say, do you believe that Edmund still lives?

MOREL. Alas!

MERC. Have you ascertained nothing?

MOREL. Nothing.

MERC. He never reappeared at Marseilles?

MOREL. Never.

MERC. Then you, no more than I, have discovered nothing?

MOREL. Absolutely nothing. And yet I went direct to Monsieur Villefort; when at my urgent entreaty he visited the Château d'If whither Edmund was taken at first, he learned that the prisoner had been transferred by superior orders.

MERC. Transferred?

MOREL. Yes, transferred. There is something mysterious and fearful in this dire affair.

MERC. Can Edmund be dead?

MOREL. Doubtless, my child, and now listen to me. Let not the lover's heart silence the mother's. Your son's future claims your care. He has been brought up under the name of Mondego which is Fernand's name as well as yours. He will remain ever ignorant of his birth—none will suspect it— every career is open to him, and if I may judge by the noble conduct Fernand has displayed, the Count de Morcerf will prove a father to your boy. [*Enter Fernand in uniform*]

FER. Well spoken, Monsieur Morel! Accept my thanks for your kindly and correct opinion of me. I have shown that, hoping for no reward. I look upon Albert Mondego as my son, and I now solicit the right of securing to him my fortune and my titles. In the name of your child, Mercédès, I ask your hand!

MERC. Fernand, you know that I respect and honor you—you know that I should be proud to endow my son with a name so honorably acquired, but—

FER. Hold, Mercédès! I am aware of your objection ere you utter it, and

I reverence it. So long as there is the faintest chance of your beholding Edmund Dantès again in life you shrink from wedding another—is it not so? You are right, I should despise you, did you otherwise, and could my love for you be greater than it is, I would love you all the more for the sacred refusal.

MERC. [*Kissing his hand*] You are generous and good!

MOREL. Count, suffer me to clasp your loyal hand! You have a generous heart.

FER. Nay, my worthy friend, I love! And I would prove I merit some small return. Let us now seek united, what you have singly sought in vain; Villefort, for whom I have obtained the nomination to the ministry of justice, can refuse me nothing. He is now in the house—he expects this evening a special officer of prisons whom he dispatched to examine all gaol registers, and search out the name of Dantès, so that we may hope to learn the poor captain's fate to-day. Here comes Villefort—withdraw, Mercédès, none should salute you in this mansion but as the Countess de Morcerf. Return to your apartments, we will rejoin you there as I learn the result of the inquiry.

MERC. You will come soon?

FER. Without delay. [*Exit Mercédès. Enter Villefort, aged and careworn*]

VILLE. Do I intrude?

FER. By no means, dear Villefort. On the contrary we were impatient to see you. This is the former master of the unfortunate Dantès—I longed to introduce him to you.

VILLE. Oh, we are old acquaintances. Monsieur Morel, if I mistake not.

MOREL. You remember me, sir?

VILLE. I could never have forgotten the object of your inquiries.

MOREL. Yes, to detect the wretch who procured the incarceration of an innocent, honest youth—blighting his felicity, and crushing out his life—and all through vile, secret schemes.

VILLE. Enough, enough.

FER. [*To Morel, who seems surprised at both*] Of course, good sir, we are all indignant at the cause, but it is the fact we have to grapple with. What has become of Dantès? That is the problem to be solved, deeds are now required, not words. Am I right, Villefort?

VILLE. Unquestionably, count. And I am ready to serve you to the utmost of my power.

MOREL. Oh, thanks! You will recover him and restore him to those who love him, who pined for him so many long years?

VILLE. If it be in my power, I swear to do so. [*Morel and Fernand retire a little, conversing*] Yes, if the inspector, on whom I can rely, shall report to me that Dantès is alive, I will set him free. [*Servant enters, speaks to Fernand*]

FER. [*Comes to Villefort*]   The inspector you commissioned is below. Not finding you at home, he has come on here to take your orders for to-morrow.

MOREL.   O sir, do not go by halves. See him at once and spare us another night of anxious sorrow.

VILLE.   Well, count, if you can let me have this room without interruption, and my man brought here without passing among the other guests—

FER.   I was about proposing so.

MOREL.   I am most grateful for your consideration.

FER. [*To Servant*]   Bring him by the garden stairs, and see that no one enters this room but by Monsieur de Villefort's orders. [*Servant exit*] Now, monsieur, you are home, we will leave you. Monsieur Morel and I will wait the result of your interview in another room. You will terminate our suspense as soon as possible.

VILLE.   Be assured I will. [*Fernand and Morel exeunt, door R. Servant enters, R. door in flat, introducing Noirtier disguised*] If Dantès live, and I release him, and this brother of mine turn not up before I am appointed minister, my conscience will be calm and my career secure.

SERV. [*To Noirtier*]   This way.

VILLE.   Come in, Fooyar. [*To Servant*] Leave us. [*Servant exit, Villefort locks door*] We are alone—well?

NOIR. [*Facing him*]   Well, good brother, how are you?

VILLE.   You—alive?

NOIR.   Does it inconvenience you?

VILLE.   Whence come you?

NOIR.   From a prison inspection in pursuance of orders issued by you. Am I not your humble servant?

VILLE.   That dress?

NOIR.   Was that of your worthy Fooyar. I see you recognize it—it is rather tight fitting I grant, your agents are so wretchedly fed—but under the present reign of repression we must accustom ourselves to a little squeezing. This is a fine trade you made me take to.

VILLE.   I?

NOIR.   Certainly. That fellow Fooyar had always a penchant for firing the second barrel when he was sent out for game. He came upon me on the road to Marseilles whither I was going to embark for Italy to superintend a Carbonari meeting which takes place in a fortnight. I saw directly that he knew me and was making for the police station, of course. I therefor arrested him.

VILLE. You?

NOIR. Assuredly. Would you have me allow him to arrest me? I am too careful of your position—too regardful of my own person to suffer myself to be collared and handed over to justice by a rascal of that kind. He raised his hand against me—I felled him to the ground with a single push. He fired his pistol—I killed him with a blow of my stick—so should such beggars die. I took his clothes and papers, saw your name, found the affair interesting, and proceeded on the mission your understrapper would have pursued, had I not shortened his career.

VILLE. And you have been inspecting prisons?

NOIR. Only one. I know you a little better than you know Fooyar. I went direct to the Château d'If.

VILLE. What?

NOIR. This grows interesting, does it not?

VILLE. Why did you go to the Château d'If?

NOIR. Because your main instructions to Fooyar were to ferret out whether a certain individual was alive or dead. One Edmund Dantès, apprehended in the year 1815, and I strongly suspect it was your handiwork—for I know you thoroughly.

VILLE. Speak lower—for mercy's sake, speak lower!

NOIR. Ah, we are within hearing, are we? Lower then, it shall be. I know how disagreeable it would be to have one's character known when such as yours. Come nearer then, and hearken. [*Villefort approaches trembling, Noirtier speaks commandingly*] Your conduct in this whole affair is infamous!

VILLE. Infamous?

NOIR. I repeat the word, infamous? That lad was innocent, but he had my secret, and the secret being fraught with ruin to your position, you sacrificed that man—and that man I will have free!

VILLE. He lives, then?

NOIR. Yes, he lives. He languishes in that horrid dungeon into which your selfishness thrust him—but again I say, I will have him free. I give you one month: in a month I shall have returned from Rome—in a month you will find me on the Marseilles road at the Inn of the Pont du Gard, in a disguise of which you shall have timely notice. You will come there, bringing to me Dantès liberated, likewise a passport authorizing us both to pass freely and without fear throughout France.

VILLE. But, this man now embittered by me, soon to be inspired by you —this man boiling over with revenge would be my ruin, my destruction!

NOIR. It is my will that he be set free.

VILLE. It would be my death!

NOIR. It is my will!

VILLE. An end then, to agony and torture! This shall come to a close. I will drag you down with me! You, Dantès and I shall be engulfed together. I shall deliver you up to justice!

NOIR. Me?

VILLE. Yes, you!

NOIR. Do it, and for once in your life you will evince a spark of courage. [*Crosses, R. Rings violently at bellrope, R.*]

VILLE. What are you about?

NOIR. Summoning your myrmidons. [*Doors heard opening*] Come, denounce me.

VILLE. No, no, stop! I agree to all, I obey your will.

NOIR. In a month?

VILLE. In a month.

NOIR. At the Inn of the Pont du Gard?

VILLE. At the Inn of the Pont du Gard. [*Servants enter one door, Fernand and Morel at other*]

FER. Anything the matter?

NOIR. Nothing. My master giving final orders. Monsieur de Villefort, I am your most respectful servant. [*Bows low, exit, Servant following*]

FER. Well, what news?

VILLE. News? [*Recovering himself gradually*] Alas, gentlemen, I have sorry tidings. [*Mercédès appears on threshold*]

MOREL. Of our poor prisoner?

VILLE. Of him?

MOREL. Speak! Better cruel certainty than this horrid doubt.

VILLE. Hope to see Edmund Dantès no more, his sufferings are over.

ALL. Dead? [*Fernand supports Mercédès as falling*]

FER. Be careful, think of your child.

MERC. [*Throwing herself in his arms*] Oh, Fernand, Fernand!

FER. Yes, yes, lean on this heart, which will never fail you.

MERC. Fear not, Fernand, I will be firm. From this day forth, I bid farewell to mourning and devote myself to my child. Fernand when you will, I am your wife.

VILLE. Count!

FER. Oh, I ask pardon. Allow me to present you the Countess de Morcerf. I hope shortly to introduce my son.

VILLE. Madame, I was in ignorance.

Fer.   Monsieur Morel, will you conduct the countess to her rooms? I will go bid my guests farewell and return shortly. [*Sees Mercédès and Morel exeunt at door, L.*]

Ville.   [*Aside*]   My brother must not reappear—Dantès must die! Tomorrow I'll start for the Château d'If.

Fer.   [*Returns*]   And now, Monsieur de Villefort, I am at your service.

Ville.   [*Taking his arm*]   And pray, how old is your son?

Fer.   Nearly eighteen.

Ville.   The countess is a charming woman. [*Exeunt both. Change of scene*]

Scene 2: *The Château d'If at night. The two cells of Faria and Edmund are separated by a thick wall, excavated in its thickness for their escape, opening by a hole into each cell. Above the cells, a rampart where the guards pace. Discovered at change, Edmund, in the opening of the wall, Faria kneeling near the hole leading to it. The Sentinel paces to and fro on the rampart, clock strikes 11.*

Faria.   Well? [*Whispers*]

Edmund.   Only the thickness of the flag between us and the sky! between us and liberty! I can hear the tread of the sentinel above.

Faria.   So that by detaching one or two stones—

Edmund.   [*Close to him*]   The flag falls! And if we can seize the precise moment when the sentinel passes, he falls with it, too, we gag him, bind him fast, both climb through the aperture, and before they are up to change the guard, we shall have swum the coast and be free. Where are the ropes and the gag?

Faria.   There, under my bed.

Edmund.   Liberty at last!

Faria.   Yes, at last! After eighteen years of struggle, of incessant toil. Never shall I forget the patience, the devotion you brought to this rough task, when my enfeebled limbs were powerless to assist you. From this day forth, Edmund, you are my son, my heir.

Edmund.   My father!

Faria.   Think not it is an idle word, the Abbé Faria has never lied. Not towards our deliverance alone have you labored with such ardor, but towards our fortune—a colossal, incalculable fortune!

Edmund.   [*Aside*]   Relapsed into his old delusion!

Faria.   Dantès, you are a noble-hearted man, you never laugh in my face as the rest do, but you say to yourself "This man is mad." Do not deny it, I read your thoughts. Is it true?

EDMUND. It is true.

FARIA. Good. I expected that reply from your frankness. What hour was that struck when you were there?

EDMUND. Eleven.

FARIA. At midnight the guard is relieved, and we shall then have two hours before us ere they can perceive your escape, if it succeed. We have yet an hour to wait. Attend to me now, and you shall be satisfied that the wealth I speak of is no phantom, that the Abbé Faria is not the maniac he is thought to be.

EDMUND. I am all attention.

FARIA. I have often in our conversation dwelt upon the history of the Borgias, have I not? You remember the poisons by whose agency they made themselves heirs of the cardinals who died around them. My ancestor, Cardinal Spada, of whom I am the last descendant, was one of their victims. But, knowing them of old, he had buried his treasure in a place unknown to that age, and of which he was the proprietor—the Island of Monte Cristo. Therefore when the hour of his death arrived, when the Borgias came to search out his immense and renowned treasure, nothing was found in his palace. No gold, no jewels, nothing but an old breviary, in which was written "to my heirs."

EDMUND. Well?

FARIA. Well, its trifling value rendered its sale worthless, this worn old breviary remained in our family, but nobody thought of searching out the meaning of the words "to my heirs" written by the cardinal on his deathbed. At last the book fell to me, and for years, Edmund, I used to turn over the pages again and again—convinced that the breviary contained the mystery of the missing treasure. Finally one evening, feeling that the book was driving me mad, I flung it into the fire. The page on which the words were written was its first page, and the flames which had already seized upon the remainder of the book, made it radiate to my eyes, some other characters appeared upon the surface. I snatched the page from the fire and read, written in a sympathetic ink which at once became visible on exposure to strong heat, these lines—"Fearing from my knowledge of the Borgias, that they hope by my poisoning to secure my fortune speedily, I hid all that I possess in ingots, coined money, jewels, diamonds and trinkets, in the secret grottos of my Island of Monte Cristo. This treasure will be found on raising the twentieth rock, counting in a straight line from the little creek, eastward, and I bequeath it to my heirs."

EDMUND. This is a fairy tale!

FARIA. Here is the page, Edmund, it is reality!

EDMUND. Ah, let me once be free, and thou shalt be happy then, Mercédès.

FARIA. Your bride? Are you quite sure to find her on your return, my son?

EDMUND. Dead? Do you believe she is dead?

FARIA. You have been a captive, Edmund, for eighteen years, and oblivion is a tomb as sure as clay.

EDMUND. She forget me? Mercédès unfaithful? Oh, my father, doubt of Heaven—doubt of Providence—doubt of your own being—but never doubt Mercédès. My faith, my life, my happiness are all her. Do I cling to liberty, do I cling to life? No—I cling to Mercédès. I would fain live, I would fain be free, but for her. To see her, to regain her, and then to die if die I must, upon her last kiss.

FARIA. So may it be! And now, Edmund, that the hour of freedom is about to strike, think of vengeance. I have satisfied your mind by a clear train of inference—from the details you gave me—that Danglars was the denouncer. That he wrote the fatal letter and that Fernand was the bearer. That the renegade Villefort entombed you alive because he had his position to preserve, and therefore he who could denounce his brother must be extinguished. Villefort, Fernand, Danglars—let those three names be engraved upon your memory.

EDMUND. Hush! I hear footsteps upon the rampart!

FARIA. The sentinel no doubt.

EDMUND. [*In a low voice*] Give me the ropes, it is time we have all ready. I will live, I will regain my liberty—for thee, Mercédès. [*Takes rope and goes into excavation. Enter above, Governor, Villefort and Sentinel*]

GOV. There you will find the prisoner Dantès.

EDMUND. [*To Faria*] They are speaking of me!

VILLE. Is he in No. 17?

EDMUND. I know that voice.

GOV. Yes, he was brought to us with written instructions enjoining most rigorous treatment.

VILLE. Yes, I know. [*Aside*] Mine! He must perish at any cost. But, how?

SENT. [*Stops them*] I ask your pardon, governor.

GOV. What is it?

SENT. We are on guard every other day, as you know.

GOV. Yes.

SENT. I went on guard forty-eight hours since.

GOV. Well?

SENT. I walked on my usual beat, but I never found it sound so hollow before.

Gov. Indeed?

VILLE. Where?

SENT. Here. [*Striking flagstone with butt of gun*]

EDMUND. Discovered!

VILLE. What cell is under this flag?

Gov. No. 17, the cell of the very man so specially commended.

EDMUND. We are lost!

VILLE. [*To Governor*] Let the sentinel be reinforced by two soldiers, let all three be on the alert. [*To soldiers*] You are not to interrupt the prisoner in his attempt, but as soon as he raises the flag and believing himself safe, fire on him without mercy! Let his release come by death of his own procuring.

EDMUND. I am accursed!

VILLE. Bear in mind what I have told you—go away now.

SENT. [*Looking at Governor*] But—

VILLE. Obey my orders! [*Exeunt Governor and Villefort*]

EDMUND. Villefort! I thought I knew that voice. [*Goes into Faria's cell*] Oh, my father—my father—

FARIA. [*Exit Sentinel*] I have heard all, my son. Do you now doubt my words? Villefort, Fernand and Danglars—those are the three wretches who have destroyed you.

EDMUND. And escape is now impossible!

FARIA. You are mistaken, Edmund. This last blow kills me, but it insures your liberty, your fortune—it makes you master of the tormentors!

EDMUND. What say you?

FARIA. Do you know how they bury him who dies here?

EDMUND. No.

FARIA. They enclose him in a sack, fasten a shot to his feet, and throw him into the sea.

EDMUND. Horrible!

FARIA. I am dying, Edmund, they will give me such a burial. Thanks to the communication between the cells, you can take my place.

EDMUND. No, no, no, no!

FARIA. Silence! Obey me, it is the last wish of a dying man. Raise my bed—there in the foot which I have hollowed out, you will find a knife. Take it; when thrown into the waves, you will cut open the sack in which you are wrapped and swim to shore. You will then be free, and the treasures of Monte Cristo will be yours. I give them to you. Ah—death is upon me!

EDMUND. No, no, you shall not die! I will save you!

FARIA. They are coming, go. [*Cries with pain. Edmund goes into his cell. Enter Governor and Gaoler*]

Gov. [*Examining Faria*] Well? Dead!

SECOND GAOLER. [*Enters*] What has happened here?

FIRST GAOLER. Yes, he is dead. Get a sack, I'll prepare the ball.

Gov. Come. [*Exeunt*]

EDMUND. [*In his cell*] You were right, noble Faria. I will take your place. I must live. I have the wicked to punish and the good to reward. Your will be done! [*The cell sinks, platform discovered, sea and rocks seen beneath a stormy sky. Thunder. Change of scene*]

SCENE 3: *Platform of the Château d'If. Steps cut in the rock, leading to a sort of jetty from the second floor. Door of secret dungeons on first floor. Enter two Gaolers carrying a sack enveloping a form.*

FIRST GAOLER. Are you ready?

SECOND GAOLER. Ready! [*They swing the sack into the sea down steps*]

FIRST GAOLER. An ugly night on the sea.

SECOND GAOLER. Aye, under, too. [*They recross stage, exeunt in prison. The moon breaks out, lighting up a projecting rock. Edmund rises from the sea, he is dripping, a knife in his hand, some shreds of sack adhering to it*]

EDMUND. [*On rock*] Saved! Mine, the treasures of Monte Cristo! The world is mine!

ACT III.

SCENE: *Interior of the Inn Pont du Gard. Staircase leading to gallery with doors. Caderousse, Carconte, Brigadier and Gendarmes drinking at a table.*

CADER. [*R. of table*] I tell you 'tis as I say!

CARC. [*Hands under apron, dress tattered. Before fire*] Hold your tongue, Caderousse, you'll never rest until you drag down more ill-luck upon us, just as you did with your mad talk about Dantès' arrest.

CADER. Poor fellow!

CARC. Will you hold your peace?

CADER. He was a brave lad I tell you, but what is the good of being honest? Would you think it, because I proclaimed too loudly that I would answer for his innocence, I saw my establishment of the Reserve closed by the police.

BRIG. Caderousse, don't talk politics. [*L. of table*]

CARC. You cursed chatterer, do you want to take the bread again out of our mouths? Do you want to have this inn shut up, too?

CADER. Oh, your inn is a fine one, a profitable inn indeed, this Pont du Gard! We cannot sell three bottles of six sous wine a day. However, there's an end to it now, we are to be sold out to-morrow because of the unpaid taxes.

BRIG. If the job that brought us to your inn succeeds—the arrest of a desperate character by order of Monsieur Villefort—and as you can assist us, if the arrest is effected this evening, you will not be sold out to-morrow.

CADER. Rather vague, but the promise is made. Is it true?

BRIG. On the honor of a gendarme. [*Noise without*] Some cavalier is arrived! [*Goes to door, C., looks out*]

CADER. A traveller, not likely he will stop here. He will pass on. It is fair time at Beaucaire.

CARC. [*Who has gone to door*] No, he stops, he ties up his horse.

BRIG. [*To Men*] Attention! [*Men rise*]

CARC. Why, there are two!

BRIG. On one horse, too?

CADER. [*Looking out*] So there are. A young officer, quite a boy—and a priest!

BRIG. A priest?

CARC. Aye, like the raven, he brings no good luck. [*Crosses to fire*]

CADER. Hold your tongue, woman. Here they are! [*Enter Edmund dressed as the abbé, and Albert de Morcerf in uniform, kepi in hand, giving precedence to Edmund*]

ALBERT. [*L.*] You were looking for the Inn of the Pont du Gard, we are at it, father, and I am delighted that I have been able to be of assistance to you on the road.

EDMUND. [*C.*] Thank you.

BRIG. [*To Edmund*] You were looking for this inn?

EDMUND. Yes.

BRIG. And you intend making a halt here?

EDMUND. [*Smiling*] If you have no objection.

BRIG. Your name.

EDMUND. The Abbé Busoni.

BRIG. Your papers? [*Edmund hesitates*]

ALBERT. [*With importance*] Here are mine!

BRIG. Unnecessary, you are an officer and—

ALBERT. And he is a priest—two professions each alike sufficient against an imputation of untruth. If you suspect one, you must suspect the other —take my papers!

BRIG. But—

ALBERT. My name is Albert, Viscount de Morcerf.

CADER. [*Aside*] Fernand's son!

ALBERT. I am on my way to Marseilles to embark for Algiers, to join my regiment under orders to take the field. Here is my route on the road, take it I say, and let pass the man of peace.

BRIG. Lieutenant, I ask pardon. [*Takes papers*] But, I have a serious duty on hand. Have either of you passed any other travellers on the road, coming in this direction?

ALBERT. There was a sort of hawker who assisted the abbé to get up behind me on my horse, and who asked for the Pont du Gard Inn.

CADER. Another coming? This is miraculous!

BRIG. A hawker?

ALBERT. Yes. A strolling jeweller, or something of that sort.

BRIG. A jeweller!

ALBERT. By what he told us, he was going to the fair at Beaucaire.

CADER. It is old Johannes. I had quite forgotten him. He stops here every year.

BRIG. [*Aside to Men*] It is our man more likely. This is the character we are to look for. We'll report to Monsieur Villefort. [*Salutes*] Lieutenant and company, I salute you.

ALBERT. [*Salutes comically*] Brigadier and gendarmes, I salute you. [*Exeunt Brigadier and Gendarmes*] Come, my veteran [*To Caderousse*], give my horse a rub-down and a feed of oats. And you my good lady [*To Carconte*], let us have a bottle of your best to drink the stirrup cup.

CARC. [*Gets bottle from sideboard*] Directly!

CADER. [*As he goes out*] Fernand's son a viscount and an officer? Fernand a general and a peer of France? What's the good of being virtuous. [*Exit*]

CARC. [*Puts bottle and glasses on table*] Here's the wine. [*Exit upstairs*]

ALBERT. Thank you. Your health, father, may I have the happiness of meeting you again on my return from the war.

EDMUND. [*R. of table*] Thanks, my son, and may your wish be accomplished. I shall rejoice greatly to see you safe and sound again. Why do you look at me thus?

ALBERT. Oh, pardon.

EDMUND. Make no excuse, I am unknown to you, so exercise your right of question.

ALBERT. Well then, I look at you and vainly try to recognize you.

EDMUND. Have we seen each other before?

ALBERT. No, I believe not.

EDMUND. What then?

ALBERT. Although my reason clearly tells me that we have met to-day for the first time, it seems to me as though we were acquainted before— before united—where I know not. But consider two formerly separated in past ages, meeting in future generations. I experience when near you, feelings akin to those their souls must experience. I love you! Yes, from the moment I met you on the way, I felt the necessity of hastening to your aid, of being some service to you. When as you rode behind, your arms entwined me, a strange emotion thrilled my heart, a tear of delight sprang to my eye. But, you will perhaps laugh at me, and it is in spite of myself, as forced from me by a divine power, that I give you this confidence, I love you more than I love my father, almost as I love my mother!

EDMUND. A sainted woman must she be, to have endowed you with a heart so true, with such noble candor. You ought, indeed to love her for thus rearing you.

ALBERT. Alas, she did not rear me. She was far away, doubtless with my father whom I saw myself but at rare and long intervals. It is only within the last year that they have both returned to France where my father holds a high rank—that it has been given to me to know my mother. But, we have redeemed the lost time. Let all the ills of humanity fall on me—let my heart cease to beat—let all on earth cease to live—but let her be rich, bright and happy, be it at the price of my life—aye, of my eternal peace!

EDMUND. [*Embracing him*] The first genial drops that have fallen from mine eyes in well nigh twenty years. They flow from my heart, refreshing and consoling it. Thou, to whom I owe them, child, I thank you.

CADER. [*Entering*] The viscount's horse is ready.

EDMUND. So soon? [*Carconte comes slowly downstairs*]

ALBERT. Are you not going to Marseilles? Shall we not be on the road together?

EDMUND. No, impossible. Your duty calls you at once on shipboard. Mine detains me here. Perhaps we shall never meet again.

ALBERT. Oh, do not say that!

EDMUND. 'Tis like all else in life, but if in this world's pilgrimage you chance to meet my brother—

ALBERT. Your brother?

EDMUND. Monte Cristo.

ALBERT. What a singular appellation!

EDMUND. Monte Cristo is a little desert island that you encounter on your way to Palermo.

ALBERT. Oh, yes, I remember.

EDMUND. It is infested with pirates and smugglers. My brother, immensely rich, purchased it from Tuscany, and of this mite of rock he is lord paramount. Both pirates and smugglers yield obedience to his decrees and term him King of the Isle. In Epris he is called Sinbad, the sailor—in Rome, Busoni—and he will shortly be known in France under the name of Monte Cristo.

ALBERT. I long to see him.

EDMUND. Have you a card?

ALBERT. Yes.

EDMUND. Give it to me.

ALBERT. Here. [*Gives it. Edmund tears it*] What is that for?

EDMUND. For a token of recognition.

ALBERT. Between your brother and me?

EDMUND. Yes. The presenter of the other half, will be the Count of Monte Cristo. Trust in him as you confide in me.

ALBERT. If he resembles you, he shall be well received.

EDMUND. [*Offers hand*] Farewell.

ALBERT. Nay, au revoir. [*Exit*]

CARC. [*Going to fire*] The kiss of the black coat is a Judas kiss; mind the one this priest has given you does not work you woe, young man.

EDMUND. [*To Caderousse*] And now a word with you.

CADER. You wish to speak to me?

EDMUND. Yes.

CARC. Take care how you answer.

EDMUND. Is your name Caderousse?

CADER. From my birth?

EDMUND. You lived in Marseilles?

CADER. For forty years.

EDMUND. And were innkeeper there?

CADER. Yes, as I now am here.

EDMUND. You knew there a young sailor named Dantès.

CARC. See, now!

CADER. See what? I don't shame to say that I knew Edmund, why should I be afraid? I am an honest man, I have done wrong to no one.

EDMUND. So much the better for you if it be so, for sooner or later believe me, the honest man will meet his reward and the wicked be punished.

CADER. It is part of your trade to say that. For my part, I don't see that Providence troubles itself much about my honesty.

EDMUND. You shall judge for yourself presently. Did you really love this Dantès?

CADER. Edmund—did I love him? 'Twas because I stood up for him after his arrest, that I find myself brought to this plight, and I would willingly lose a finger off my right hand to save him from prison or to hear tidings of him. Have you seen him?

EDMUND. Yes.

CADER. How is he? What is he doing? Is he happy?

EDMUND. He is dead.

CADER. Dead?

EDMUND. Edmund Dantès is dead.

CADER. Poor boy!

EDMUND. Wait! Providence may sometimes seem to slumber as regards the good—

CADER. And sleep sound methinks.

EDMUND. It is but to prove them, and its awakening is terrible to the guilty, believe me. As surely as they will be punished, you will be rewarded.

CADER. I should like a substantial proof.

EDMUND. [*Producing paper parcel*] Behold it!

CADER. What is that?

EDMUND. Look and see.

CADER. [*Opens parcel*] A stone!

EDMUND. A diamond!

CADER. Of such size?

CARC. A diamond? Impossible! A diamond of that size would be worth— . [*Goes back of table*]

EDMUND. Fifty thousand francs.

CADER. And this is worth?

EDMUND. Fifty thousand francs.

CADER. Really and truly?

EDMUND. On my solemn word.

CARC. From whom then did you have it?

EDMUND. From Dantès.

CADER. Our Edmund? And who was to have it?

EDMUND. You shall know presently. [*Takes it*]

CARC. Ah, you are taking it back.

EDMUND. Listen to me. In the hour of his eternal farewell in prison Dantès said to me, "I had three good friends and an affianced wife," whose name was—I cannot remember the name of his betrothed.

CADER. Mercédès—

EDMUND. Yes, that was it. Pray give me a glass of water!

CADER. Here. [*Gets it*]

EDMUND. [*Drinks*] Thanks—where was I?

CADER. At "three good friends and his betrothed"—whose name was Mercédès.

EDMUND. Right. "You will go to Marseilles"—you are to understand it is Dantès who speaks?

CADER. Exactly so.

EDMUND. You will divide the price of this diamond into five parts.

CADER. Five parts? You only mentioned four persons—three friends and his betrothed.

EDMUND. Because I ascertained at Nismes that the fifth was dead. The fifth was Dantès' father.

CADER. That is true, the poor man is dead.

EDMUND. Aye, dead! Without his child to close his eyes, without embracing his son or knowing his fate! He doubtless died of grief.

CADER. Of starvation!

EDMUND. Of starvation!

CARC. Be cautious.

CADER. I will speak! What more can they do, now that they have ruined me and killed Edmund, and caused his father's death. I tell you he died of starvation!

EDMUND. Oh, horrible, horrible!

CADER. After his son was arrested, Dantès took to his bed, which he never left. Monsieur Morel brought the first physician in Marseilles to see him; he left also on the table, showing it to me, a red silk purse full of gold so that the old man wanted for nothing. But, all the money in the purse went to the doctor's visits—the old man let it go and never ceased to smile. One day at length the smile left his face, but his eyes were clear and open, looking to the Heavens—he was dead.

EDMUND. [*Swallowing some water*] Thanks! [*Gives hands*] And this red silk purse that Morel left filled with money?

CADER. I only found a scrap of paper in it with two lines, "For Edmund if he lives—a memorial of Morel's kindness."

EDMUND. [*Aside*] I will remember the good my father, and I will not forget the bad. [*Aloud*] And you say it was Danglars, you say it was Fernand?

CADER. I never mentioned them.

EDMUND. Who threw the son into a dungeon, and drove the father to death, broken-hearted and starved.

CADER. I never said a word of the sort.

CARC. You see—you see—

EDMUND. Denial is useless, I know all. Caderousse, you were by him when one of those wretches wrote the letter denouncing Edmund to the Procureur du Roi!

CADER. You know? I—

EDMUND. He wrote that letter with his left hand, and Fernand himself took it to Marseilles.

CADER. True, true, but forgive me, father—and may Edmund from Heaven forgive me. I had been made drunk, and nearly lost all sense.

EDMUND. I know it, Edmund knew it and forgave you.

CADER. [On knees] And remorse has pursued me ever since, day and night.

EDMUND. Rise and answer me. What has become of Fernand, of Danglars.

CADER. Fernand is a general, a count—a peer of France.

EDMUND. Fernand Mondego?

CADER. The same.

EDMUND. By what means?

CADER. That, no one knows.

EDMUND. [Aside] I'll know it! [Aloud] And Danglars?

CADER. Danglars, after robbing Monsieur Morel of the cargo of two vessels that were not insured and that were empty as everyone believes, set up as a banker at Nismes, then at Lyons, finally at Paris, where he is king at present among the financial celebrities. His daughter is engaged to the son of Fernand and Mercédès.

EDMUND. Mercédès married? Mercédès married to Edmund's denouncer —uniting her son to the Danglars?

CADER. It is so. Sophie Danglars is to marry the young Viscount de Morcerf.

EDMUND. What! No, I am mistaken. Not the young man who was here just now?

CADER. Yes, the son of Fernand and Mercédès, now the Viscount de Morcerf.

EDMUND. [Aside] And I grasped his hand and pressed him to my heart! Oh, woe to him! His father must love him, may well be proud of him— it is through his child I will strike Fernand. I will kill his son! [Aloud] Take the diamond, it is yours.

CARC. All ours?

EDMUND. Yes, the heritage is yours, and may you be as upright in prosperity as you have been in adversity.

CADER. And are you leaving us?

EDMUND. Yes. I have need of air, of space, of liberty. [*Aside*] I'll go pray at my father's grave and regain strength to live—strength to reward and to punish. [*Aloud*] You shall see me soon again. I shall return to demand—

CADER. What, the diamond?

EDMUND. No. The little red purse which Morel gave to old Dantès, who bequeathed it to his son. Adieu! [*Exit*]

CADER. Carconte, are we dreaming?

CARC. No—I hold the diamond in my hand. But, what if it is a false one?

CADER. You are always so superstitious! Why should he have given us a false one?

CARC. To extract your information without paying for it, simpleton.

CADER. We shall soon see that.

CARC. How?

CADER. It is now the fair at Beaucaire. Old Johannes, the rich jeweller who stops here every year and makes such rich purchases there, shall value it—buy it, perhaps.

CARC. You think so?

CADER. I do, indeed.

CARC. But fifty thousand francs is money.

CADER. Nothing to him. He has always double that, at least, in his pockets. What makes your eyes sparkle so?

CARC. Nothing. I was only thinking that he often sleeps here on his way to Beaucaire.

CADER. Well?

CARC. And—oh, nothing you would understand.

CADER. I am only afraid I understand you too well. [*Knock at door*]

CARC. Be silent, there's a knock at the door.

CADER. No, 'tis the wind. [*Knock*]

CARC. Can't you hear it?

CADER. Yes.

CARC. It must be Johannes.

CADER. Now I say wife, no nonsense.

CARC. Pshaw! Go open the door. [*Enter Noirtier as Jew peddler*]

NOIR. Good evening, good people.

CADER. Thank heaven, it's not Johannes.

NOIR. Why thank heaven? Don't you like my good friend Johannes?

CADER. Oh, yes, but—

CARC. But we did not expect him so soon and his room is not ready.

NOIR. Then get it ready, for I am here in his stead.

CARC. You?

NOIR. Yes, I. I have bought his stock and I am on my way to the fair at Beaucaire with my merchandise. Oh, I have money to pay my way, look here —and here—and here! [*Shows gold and notes*] Without reckoning the trinkets and jewelry in my box. [*Aside*] And the millions of francs to start my journal. [*Aloud*] Come, good people, you won't lose by your change of customers. [*Goes to fire*]

CADER. [*To Carconte*] You see these gentry are always in funds, he will be able to buy our diamond.

CARC. Try him.

NOIR. [*At fire*] Well, are you making any arrangements about me?

CADER. Just what we were doing good monsieur—monsieur—

NOIR. [*Rising*] Solomon Van Gripp.

CADER. A pretty name?

NOIR. It inspires immediate confidence.

CARC. [*Going to cupboard*] Here is wine.

NOIR. Have you nothing to eat?

CARC. Not much, but we can give you—

CADER. [*Making signs to her*] No, no, no, he can't eat that.

CARC. Why?

CADER. His name is Solomon.

CARC. Oh, the devil!

NOIR. Well, what meat have you in the house?

CADER. Meat?

NOIR. Yes.

CADER. We have only cabbage.

NOIR. [*Sadly*] Oh!

CADER. And bacon.

NOIR. [*Brightening*] Ha!

CADER. But you said your name was Solomon—

NOIR. I see. Never mind, my fine fellow, when I take it from your hands it won't come from a hog. Ha, ha, ha! Clever, that, isn't it? [*Aside*] I am becoming as great an ass in this disguise as Johannes himself. [*Carconte lays table, Caderousse takes Noirtier light to show him diamond*]

CADER. What is your opinion of this?

NOIR. [*Opens paper, goes to table*] What is it, a diamond?

CARC. Is it a genuine diamond?

Noir. It is indeed. What a stone! Magnificent! Must be worth—

Carc. Fifty thousand francs.

Noir. At least.

Cader. [*To Carconte*] You see?

Carc. Will you buy it?

Noir. [*In a natural voice*] I—why should I?

Carc. How you spoke that! Without a trace of accent.

Noir. [*Aside*] Near betraying myself! [*Aloud*] I am never a Jew in business. Ha, ha, ha! Clever said, that, eh? [*Aside*] I must stick close to my part, or be discovered and undone. [*Aloud*] Yes, I will take it. I will give you—I am a plain, downright man of business—I never go from my word—I will give you forty thousand francs, ready money.

Cader. How, forty thousand?

Noir. Yes, I never haggle—never.

Carc. But you said fifty thousand.

Noir. I?

Carc. Yes, you.

Noir. Never.

Cader. You said it was worth fifty thousand francs.

Noir. Your wife said so.

Cader. And you added, "at least."

Noir. Then I did not say fifty thousand francs.

Cader. But you said more.

Noir. Then I will give you forty thousand.

Cader. Ah!

Noir. I never go from my word. I am a plain, downright man of business. I'll now have something to eat. [*Does so. Aside*] I think I have got myself pretty well out of this.

Cader. [*To Carconte*] Well, shall we let him have it?

Carc. It is worth more than that.

Cader. We'll keep it, then. I'll go to the fair and see some dealers.

Noir. Well, have you made up your minds?

Cader. Yes, to sell it to somebody else.

Noir. Just as you please, only you won't find somebody else so easy to deal with as me.

Carc. Oh, as to that—

Noir. [*Eats*] Somebody else will ask you where you got such a stone.

Carc. [*To Caderousse*] That is true.

Cader. [*Draws her into corner*] What do you say to it?

Carc. I say it's hard, but we must let him have it.

CADER. [*To Noirtier*] Come, it's settled, the jewel is yours.

NOIR. And here is your money. Count it. [*Gives notes*]

CARC. [*To Caderousse*] What are those rags?

CADER. Bank notes, to be sure.

CARC. Are they of value?

CADER. As good as gold, and more portable.

CARC. Be cautious.

CADER. Be quiet!

NOIR. Now my good people, will you get my room ready?

CARC. Take our room, Monsieur Solomon, the bed is better, and I wish you to sleep comfortably. [*Looks at Caderousse*]

NOIR. I must not say nay, for I am dropping with fatigue. [*Thunder and lightning*] Oh, what weather. [*Aside*] I don't wonder it makes Villefort late. [*Looks at watch*] Ten o'clock. If within two hours a gentleman does not come whom I am expecting, and who will give my name when he asks to see me, you will awaken me, for I shall have to go out to Marseilles to-night.

CARC. [*Who has lit candle*] What, take the road again tonight? And in such weather?

NOIR. I fear neither wind nor weather.

CADER. But robbers?

NOIR. [*Showing pistols*] Here are a pair of trusty dogs who bark and bite at the same instant—ready for those who may covet your diamond, Caderousse.

CARC. [*Aside*] Armed! [*Aloud*] Are you coming?

NOIR. I'll follow you. [*Goes upstairs to chamber, seen through*] Good night, Caderousse.

CADER. Good night. [*Noirtier exit after Carconte*] I am glad he is armed. Carconte made me shudder with her notions. She's a dreadful woman, her gloomy words strike into you one by one like the stab of a knife. I'm all of a shiver still. Luckily he's armed, so there's nothing to fear.

VILLE. [*Has entered dripping wet. Touches Caderousse on shoulder*] Are you alone?

CADER. Who is there?

VILLE. Silence, fellow.

CADER. Monsieur de Villefort?

VILLE. Silence!

CARC. [*Above*] Did you call?

CADER. I—no. [*Villefort signing silence*]

CARC. Who are you talking with?

CADER. Nobody. I am talking with myself.

CARC. Idiot!

VILLE. What is your wife doing up there?

CADER. She is taking a traveller to our room.

VILLE. Who is he?

CADER. A jeweller who came this evening.

VILLE. About nine o'clock was it not?

CADER. Thereabouts.

VILLE. Is it Johannes who is in the habit of stopping here?

CADER. No, not he.

VILLE. Then this one travels under the name of Solomon Van Gripp.

CADER. Is not that his name?

VILLE. Answer me!

CADER. That was the name he gave. He told us to wait up for a person who would come to inquire for him, and desired us to call him at midnight if the other did not come.

VILLE. Did he not offer you a bargain? Be careful.

CADER. I don't know what you mean.

VILLE. No lies! The gendarmes are on the watch, and at the slightest signal—

CADER. I see it all! This vagabond priest has informed against us just as Carconte thought. So, you want to arrest us for the affair of the diamond?

VILLE. [*Aside*] What is this?

CADER. Mercy, Monsieur le Procureur, if it was stolen I know nothing of it. It was given to me and I sold it for forty thousand francs to the Jew upstairs. But I'll give up the money. 'Tis very hard, don't harm us.

VILLE. You were given a diamond of that value? Speak lower.

CADER. Yes.

VILLE. By whom?

CADER. By a priest.

VILLE. What for?

CADER. For inquiries I answered him about Dantès.

VILLE. The prisoner Dantès?

CADER. Yes. Edmund, who is dead.

VILLE. Is he dead?

CADER. Yes.

VILLE. Who told you so?

CADER. The priest that brought me his legacy.

VILLE. Where, how did he die?

CADER. That he did not tell me. He only gave me the diamond as his representative, and that is all.

VILLE. You swear it?

CADER. I swear it.

VILLE. Are you to see this priest again?

CADER. He is to return for a purse I promised him.

VILLE. [*Aside*] I shall know who he is. [*Aloud*] You sold this diamond to the man who has gone to sleep there?

CADER. For forty thousand francs, yes. [*Carconte creeps down, Villefort sits, Caderousse before him*]

VILLE. This traveller is of a very confiding disposition.

CADER. How so?

VILLE. To go to bed here in a lonely inn, by the side of a canal, so convenient of hiding all traces of a crime. In fact, were you not an honest man—nobody saw him enter—nobody would see him go out—you would regain possession of the diamond, keeping at the same time the price you have received for it. You would let the sale of your own goods and furniture take place tomorrow as if you were reduced to your last sou. None would suspect you, and you would be richer by 90,000 francs.

CARC. [*Coming between them and putting elbows on table, chin on hands*] To say nothing about the money he has about him.

VILLE. You were here?

CARC. And have heard all, and I agree with you.

CADER. How?

CARC. You must be very honest—and that man very unsuspecting.

CADER. It would be nefarious!

CARC. Since the Procureur du Roi advises it.

VILLE. I?

CARC. Don't speak so loud. He has not gone to sleep yet and may hear you.

VILLE. [*In trepidation*] Oh, heavens!

CARC. [*To Villefort*] Listen to me, and let us treat as equal to equal, since we have the same object. [*Goes R.*]

VILLE. We!

CARC. Bah! Don't you suppose I see clearer than this idiot here. You have a motive—such as it is—and I do not care to know it—for wishing to dispose of this traveller.

VILLE. I!

CARC. In plain words, you want to have him murdered. But, say so plainly, that I may know there is nothing to be dreaded from the law afterwards.

VILLE. Is he armed?

CADER. He has pistols.

CARC. Can he see clearly in the dark? Stuff!

VILLE. But you will see no clearer.

CARC. As if we did not know our own room.

CADER. I won't have anything to do with it.

CARC. Then I will do it alone. And you will be no less my accomplice, and you will keep silent through fear.

CADER. I'll give him warning—I'll call him—[*As he is about going up-stairs, Carconte takes her handkerchief and gags him*]

CARC. Now, give him warning. Now, call him.

VILLE. Oh, great heavens, whither am I fallen?

CARC. Seize his hands, quick! We must tie him fast. [*Villefort does so, stupefied. Carconte ties Caderousse's hands with his neckcloth. A stir is heard in Noirtier's room. They stand alarmed*]

NOIR. [*In room*] Good night, good people, good night.

VILLE. His voice, 'tis his voice.

CARC. Goodnight. [*Light goes out above*] He's going to bed—now to work. [*They throw cloak over Caderousse and carry him into chimney corner. Carconte gets hatchet, she and Villefort regard each other a moment*] Do you promise me we shall never be brought to trouble? And we shall have all the money he has about him.

VILLE. [*Almost speechless with terror*] Yes!

CARC. And you will guarantee our escape hence?

VILLE. Yes, yes, but go, go!

CARC. Watch the door that none may enter. Do not come to me unless I call. [*Goes upstairs, listens*]

VILLE. Well? [*In a low voice*]

CARC. He sleeps. [*Opens door, slips in, chair heard to fall, noise of struggle in room*]

NOIR. [*In room*] Who is there? [*Villefort goes to table, snatches knife; shot in room. Carconte comes from room bleeding, falls on stairs, breaking out rail in her fall, her head hangs through*]

VILLE. She has failed—she has failed. [*Dashes forward with knife. Comes face to face with Noirtier who enters from room, has thrown off disguise*]

NOIR. [*Offering breast*] Strike then! See, I offer you my breast defenseless. Strike to my heart! [*Advancing, Villefort recoils*] Coward, thou hast not even the courage of a vulgar criminal. Thou need'st hire assassins and yet payest them not. What, must thy brother die that it may remain unknown he were of thy family? I am not so proud, and I shall deliver my good brother up to the executioner. [*Goes towards door*]

VILLE. Since you force me to it, then—[*Rushes at him. Is held back by Caderousse who has released himself*]

CADER. Not so!

NOIR. Wretch!

CADER. Help—help!

VILLE. Will you be silent? [*Breaks from him and rushes for Noirtier, but stops before Edmund, who enters*] I am lost!

NOIR. [*To Gendarmes who enter*] Seize that man!

VILLE. Not alive, at least! [*Stabs himself, falls dead*]

EDMUND. [*Behind him, pointing to body*] "One!"

ACT IV.

SCENE: *The Count de Morcerf's conservatory. Discovered at rise Fernand, Albert, Mercédès in evening dress; Fernand receiving guests. Caderousse in livery.*

MERC. [*To Albert*] Are you certain the Count of Monte Cristo is in Paris?

ALBERT. Yes, dear mother, he arrived this evening about the same time I did. He seems to have followed my steps.

MERC. Why then did he not accept your invitation to our family dinner? I should have wished to communicate with the preserver of my son's life.

ALBERT. A previous engagement compelled him to refuse, at least such was the answer he gave my servant, was it not, Gaspardo?

CADER. Yes, sir. The count regretted that he was unable to sit at General de Morcerf's tables, but would do himself the honor of offering his excuses in person this evening.

ALBERT. [*To Mercédès*] You hear?

MERC. I fear he will not come.

ALBERT. Oh, he will come, I will answer for that. We have his promise.

CADER. Any further commands, sir?

ALBERT. No. Remain in the salon and announce the count when he arrives.

MERC. [*To Caderousse, who bows as going*] You are not French?

CADER. I, madame?

MERC. You are not from Marseilles?

CADER. I am said to be a native of Naples, and was resident in Africa when I entered your son's service.

MERC. Your name is—?

CADER. Gaspardo.

MERC. Gaspardo what?

CADER. Simply Gaspardo, I am in Paris for the first time.

MERC. Very good. I must be mistaken. [*Caderousse bows. Enter Danglars and his daughter, conducted by Fernand*]

ALBERT. Danglars and his daughter!

CADER. [*Aside*] Danglars, the blackguard! Well, Edmund will have them all in his net. [*Exit*]

FER. [*To Mademoiselle Danglars*] What a charming dress! No one has such taste.

DANG. You should compliment me, I know what it cost.

MLLE. DANG. Don't deceive yourself, father, you don't even suspect it.

DANG. Capital!

MERC. [*To Mademoiselle Danglars*] Whom are you looking for?

ALBERT. I wager I can guess.

MLLE. DANG. [*Giving hand*] Oh, some new silliness, no doubt.

ALBERT. Not in the least. I am not in question.

MLLE. DANG. Well?

ALBERT. You were about to ask—

MLLE. DANG. What?

ALBERT. If it were true—

MLLE. DANG. Go on.

ALBERT. That the Count de Monte Cristo was coming.

MLLE. DANG. You have won your wager, you guess correctly.

ALBERT. He is coming.

MLLE. DANG. Bravo!

DANG. [*Coming down*] And it is already known who he is.

MERC. Indeed?

DANG. Yes. He is a Polish refugee who has served in the Egyptian army and also organized a pearl fishery in Ceylon. The king, enchanted, gave him I don't know how many purses, and the same year he finished up six million of pearls.

ALBERT. [*Laughing*] Excellent!

MLLE. DANG. That is not it at all. His name is Zaccone, he is a Maltese— he has served in India—he worked a silver mine in Thessaly—and he has now come to Paris to establish artificial sea-water baths in the Champs Elysées. [*All laugh*] It is true, I assure you.

ALBERT. In the name of wonder, who has told you all this?

MLLE. DANG. The prefect of police. Some unusual splendor awakened his attention, and the count must answer his inquiries this evening.

ALBERT. Poor Monte Cristo, threatened to be arrested for being a vagabond as well as being too rich!

DANG. Well, the train his princess sports—

MERC. What princess?

DANG. She was with him this evening at the opera.

ALBERT. Monte Cristo at the opera this evening?

DANG. Certainly.

MLLE. DANG. Opposite the prefect's box, where we were.

MERC. [*Aside*] And for such a trifling motive he refused our invitation—'tis strange!

FER. But who tells you this woman is a princess?

DANG. Why, everybody. But see, here is Noirtier, editor of the "Imperial." As a well-informed journalist, he can probably enlighten us.

NOIR. [*Enters and bows*] Madame la Comtesse—General—[*Shakes hands*] Albert, welcome back, my dear boy. Glad to see you safe and well. [*Music stops*]

ALBERT. Thanks, dear friend.

DANG. You come just in time.

NOIR. [*Looks at him*] So? Many persons ought not to come at all.

DANG. Do you say that for me?

NOIR. Decidedly.

DANG. 'Tis worth while indeed, to be a subscriber to your journal.

NOIR. [*C.*] You read my paper without understanding it—I report your speeches without listening to them.

DANG. Impertinent. [*Mademoiselle Danglars runs to him*]

MERC. Gentlemen!

NOIR. Oh, don't be alarmed, madame, this is quite allowable, such are the curiosities of the press literature nowadays. It is no longer necessary to write good French, to have talents and convictions. Be slanderous and coarse, and you will print off four hundred thousand copies—write slang and you will be elected deputy, and you will make your fortune in twelve months. Now, in what way can I serve you?

MLLE. DANG. [*L.*] We want to know from you—

NOIR. [*L.C.*] Sixty-seven.

MLLE. DANG. What sixty-seven?

NOIR. I mean you are the sixty-seventh person who has asked me the same question.

MLLE. DANG. But, you don't know yet what mine is.

NOIR. My dear young lady, you must have a very poor opinion of my understanding. You were going to ask me, whence comes, and what is the name of the fair Greek whom Monte Cristo accompanied this evening to the opera. Is it not so?

MLLE. DANG. It is. [*All surprised*]

Noir.   Well. [*Mysteriously. All gather round*] I absolutely know nothing about it!

All.   Ah!

Dang.   That is rather too strong.

Noir.   I was even ignorant of the count's arrival in Paris.

Dang.   Why, your own journal was the first to announce it!

Noir.   Do you believe that I read my journal? Thank you, it is quite enough to write it. All I know of the count is, he saved the life of this brave young man—and that I love him for having preserved to us a good soldier and an honorable man—a rarity in these money-hunting days.

Mlle. Dang.   It seems odd that a soldier should be saved by a civilian on the field of battle.

Noir.   Yes, and unusual, too.

Albert.   The count has peculiar notions. In place of making war on men, he makes it on wild beasts, and says their bites are less dangerous.

Noir.   A man that knows the world.

Albert.   In Africa he is called the tiger-slayer.

Dang. [*L.*]   A queer employment.

Noir.   Less easy work than jobbing in the funds, eh?

Mlle. Dang.   Don't interrupt.

Noir.   I am dumb. Proceed.

Albert.   One day on the razzia, ambitious to win my spurs in the field, I dashed in pursuit of a body of Arabs without perceiving I was separated from my men, who themselves were surrounded on all sides. I was surrounded, seized. [*R.C.*] You know the delightful religious notions of the Arab gentry —they believe that their good angels carry them off after death to Mahomet's Paradise by the tuft of hair they grow on their skull. So, to debar their enemies from that celestial trip, they neatly sever their heads from their bodies.

Mlle. Dang.   How shocking!

Albert.   An ugly prospect, I confess, and when I think of it I cannot help slightly shuddering. I already felt the fatal blade on my neck, and I commended my soul to Heaven—my last prayer to my mother—when a shot rang out behind us, and the man who held me dropped dead at my side. The circle opened as if by magic around my preserver. "The tiger-slayer!" they cried, and in a twinkling I was behind the stranger's saddle on his Arab steed which bore us like the wind from the murderous band. We soon heard the spahi bugles and I said to the cavalier, "There are my men, I am saved and I owe my life to you." "You owe me nothing," he replied. "You rode behind me as did my brother behind you on his road to Marseilles." Then, reaching me a torn card, the other half of which I had by me, he said "I am the Count de

Monte Cristo, we are quits, adieu." "Shall I not see you again?" said I, detaining him. "Yes, at the Hôtel de Morcerf, on your next leave." "But, should I be killed in the war?" "You will not die on the field," he replied with a strange smile, "and on the day of your death you will find me before you—adieu." The next minute my soldiers were around me, whilst he disappeared in a cloud of dust. [*Music*]

MLLE. DANG. A perfect romance.

MERC. [*Hanging on Albert*] It is like a dream.

DANG. Are you sure of him this evening?

ALBERT. Yes, for he promised me.

DANG. Promises are air—a traveller's word.

NOIR. As good as a stock jobber's.

DANG. I'll bet he won't come.

CADER. [*Enters and announces*] His excellency, the Count of Monte Cristo.

NOIR. You have lost, I wonder who will pay? [*Edmund enters, Mercédès watches him and shrinks back*]

MERC. Oh—how he has aged!

FER. Who?

MERC. Look! [*Points to Edmund*]

FER. The count—do you know him?

MERC. I—I—can't tell. I know not—[*Albert has gone to Edmund and offers hand*]

EDMUND. [*Not taking it*] Pray present me to the Countess de Morcerf.

ALBERT. [*Leading him to her*] My mother, this is he.

MERC. [*Mastering her emotion*] Sir, but for you I should be in tears and desolation—bless you! [*Aside, as Edmund bows*] Oh, yes, I was mistaken. He never could be so changed.

FER. Welcome amongst us, count, the preserver to this house of its only heir, has a right to our eternal gratitude. [*Edmund bows without replying*]

MERC. [*Looking after him*] Oh, that look.

EDMUND. You praise me too highly.

MERC. [*Aside*] His voice, too!

EDMUND. To spare a mother's sorrow by saving the "only heir" of whom her husband is so justly proud, is simply discharging an act of common humanity.

NOIR. Count, you utter noble sentiments. I read your aim in life?

EDMUND. Do you?

MERC. [*Aside*] No, 'tis impossible. It would be too fearful.

ALBERT. Allow me, count, to present you to Mademoiselle Danglars, my betrothed. [*He bows*]

DANG. My daughter.

EDMUND. And your name is—

DANG. Danglars is my name.

EDMUND. Aye, Danglars and Company.

DANG. Eh?

EDMUND. Is not that your firm?

DANG. [*Looking at Mademoiselle Danglars*]   As banker it is—but—

EDMUND. Oh, I have only to do with the banker, and I am glad, that I may hand you this letter of credit.

DANG. From the house of Franch and Rossi at Rome. I will see you to-morrow on the subject.

MERC. [*Aside*] No, that tone, that bearing—no, it is a freak of my imagination. But, why did he refuse to sit at our table? Oh, I shall know if it is a determination.

DANG. [*Has read letter*] 'Tis impossible—'tis downright madness.

ALL. What? [*Music stops*]

DANG. The contents of this letter.

EDMUND. What is there so extraordinary in that letter?

DANG. It gives the Count of Monte Cristo unlimited credit in my house.

ALL. Well?

DANG. Don't you understand, unlimited.

EDMUND. Is the phrase good French?

DANG. [*Sneeringly*] Oh, quite correct as regards grammar, but not as regards competency.

EDMUND. Is not the house of Franch and Rossi safe?

DANG. I say nothing of them.

EDMUND. On the contrary pray tell me, are they in a bad state? I have some millions in their hands and—

DANG. Their bank is of the highest standing, but—

EDMUND. But—?

DANG. But their letter is so vague!

EDMUND. Well?

DANG. That seems absurd!

EDMUND. Meaning to say, you will not honor it.

DANG. "Decline where there is any doubt," say the wise. And as I doubt, I decline.

EDMUND. Through wisdom or insolvency?

DANG. Sir!

EDMUND. Sir?

DANG. My capital has never yet been questioned by any man.

EDMUND. Then I will be the first to do so.

DANG. You?

EDMUND. I!

DANG. You know nothing of business.

EDMUND. That is a question. [*Crosses to others*] Pray excuse this ridicu-
ous scene which I unwillingly introduce, but my self-respect requires that
his single hesitation should be explained.

DANG. [*Aside*] Can he know my position?

EDMUND. You lost five million francs yesterday by the fall, ten on the
Spanish loan. You must find fifty for the newly announced railway—add to
that forty you must have for current transactions, and it gives a total of one
hundred and five million francs. You see, I do not reckon badly for a man
who knows nothing of business.

DANG. [*Aside*] He knows all!

EDMUND. Do these few petty millions engaged prevent your opening
credit with me?

DANG. [*Aside*] If I hesitate, I am lost!

EDMUND. Well?

DANG. I will prove to you the contrary, sir. Fix the sum you wish to draw,
and even were you to require a million francs—

EDMUND. A million! And what use do you think a million would be to
me? If I wanted a measly million, I should open no account at all. I always
carry a million in treasury bonds in some corner of my pocket-book—see?
Showing them] Oh, no, how can I tell what whims may seize me, and what
sums I may require? Be prepared for ten or fifteen millions at first sight.
Goes up]

DANG. [*Aside*] I am ruined!

NOIR. [*In a low tone*] Ask him for the diamonds of his Greek companion
as guarantee.

EDMUND. What are you saying?

NOIR. The deuce! You have sharp ears!

EDMUND. I can read the eye—when Haidee is spoken of.

FER. Haidee!

EDMUND. Yes, my slave.

FER. Your slave?

EDMUND. Certainly, since I have bought her.

FER. Danglars gave her out to be a princess.

EDMUND. She is one in reality, general. Hers is a sad and terrible history.

FER. [*Aside*] Oh, heavens!

EDMUND. [*All gather round him*] Great and powerful was the vizier he father—so powerful and great that the Sultan's self grew jealous of him an decreed his death. But the palace guard was entrusted to a French office whom the vizier had loaded with kindness, and he slept in peace, relying o the gratitude and loyalty of the very man who sold him to his foes! And o a dark and fearful night, the assassins were introduced into a lower roo beneath the kiosk, and when Haidee's father awoke at the untimely noise, dull explosion was heard, and the boards under his feet flew in slivers aroun his head. Not daring to confront the lion face to face, the traitor had kille him through the flooring—and in a whirlwind of flames, as if Hell itse opened beneath his feet, fell Ali Tebelin, Haidee's father—Pasha of Janina

MERC. [*R.*] Janina? Why, that is—

FER. [*Aside to her*] Not a word, silence, or you will undo me!

MERC. [*Aside*] O saints above—could he be the man?

FER. And do you know the name of the trai—of the man who sold th pasha to his murderers?

EDMUND. I know—I know that he received as the price of his treacher a vast fortune and his master's daughter, whom he doubtless lacked the cou age to kill, for he sold her to the slave merchant from whom I bought her . Constantinople.

ALBERT. But this villain, this wretched coward, this traitor, was he n punished?

EDMUND. Not yet.

ALBERT. No?

EDMUND. Rest satisfied, he will be!

NOIR. And if I can assist in so doing, you can depend on me.

EDMUND. [*Taking his hand*] Thanks.

FER. [*Aside*] Is the hour of retribution come?

CADER. [*Announces*] His excellency, the Greek Ambassador.

FER. [*Aside*] He, too!

EDMUND. [*Aside*] He has kept his promise.

MERC. Go, receive him, Fernand, I wish to speak to the count.

FER. You?

MERC. Go! Albert—[*Fernand exit, Albert crosses to Mercédès*] I have a ways warned you against new acquaintances, do you know who this Mon Cristo is?

ALBERT. A perfect gentleman, as you can see for yourself.

MERC. Has the count ever clasped your hand?

ALBERT. Never.

MERC. Has he ever called you friend?

ALBERT. No.

MERC. And he has refused to sit at the same table with you?

ALBERT. Mother!

MERC. Leave us—take off Danglars and his daughter with you. I wish to be alone with this man. [*Albert goes to Danglars and Mademoiselle Danglars, Edmund talking to Noirtier*] If it be not Edmund, can it be his avenging angel. But, I am not guilty—O Heaven, protect my son, watch over my child.

MLLE. DANG. [*To Albert*] And is the ambassador in costume?

ALBERT. From head to foot.

MLLE. DANG. Will you present me to him?

ALBERT. Yes, and your father, too.

DANG. [*L.*] Come along then, quick.

MLLE. DANG. Give me your arm. [*Exeunt Mademoiselle Danglars, Albert and Danglars*]

MERC. Monsieur Noirtier—

NOIR. Madame—[*To Edmund*] Excuse me. [*Crosses to her*]

EDMUND. [*To Caderousse*] Well?

CADER. The newspaper is on the card table where Danglars is sure to find it.

EDMUND. Good.

CADER. And shall be put into Albert's hand at the fitting time.

EDMUND. You will take the "Etoile" to Danglars when I tell you.

CADER. [*Touches pocket*] I have it here.

EDMUND. Silence, we are observed.

NOIR. [*Bowing to Mercédès*] I obey, madame.

MERC. I shall know what to depend on.

EDMUND. You have not gone to receive the Greek Ambassador, madame; his wonderful accounts of Esperus and the reign of Ali Tebelin would interest you, I am certain. May I take you to the salon?

MERC. No, the heat is oppressive—I feel weak already—my head swims— [*Leans on Edmund, silent a moment*]

EDMUND. The powerful scent those flowers exhale is dangerous—go in.

MERC. No, thanks. I feel better. There is a touching Arabian custom which you must know, and of which I was recently reminding my son—

EDMUND. [*Aside*] Fernand's son!

MERC. It makes eternal friends of those who partake of the same meal; shall we share together? You still refuse?

EDMUND. We are in France, madame, not in Arabia. Here one can by paying for them, find bread and salt perhaps, but eternal friendship is an unknown feast.

MERC. You refuse?

EDMUND. I refuse. [*Mercédès lets hand fall*] Madame—

MERC. What has steeled your heart to act thus? What motive impels you?

EDMUND. [*Coldly*] I cannot tell.

MERC. [*Wildly*] I will then—you seek revenge.

EDMUND. I?

MERC. Yes, for an enforced deed—for an act of which you know not the motive, and which you tax with guilt. You seek revenge on a woman.

EDMUND. No, no, not on her. If she has the fortitude to be happy, may she be so. It is he that I would reach!

MERC. He?

EDMUND. Yes, the traitor who stepped between her and me. Oh, fear nothing, I will not touch him—Providence will strike him when the hour comes.

MERC. By ruining his fortune, is it not?

EDMUND. [*With irony*] No.

MERC. By degrading him in the army?

EDMUND. No.

MERC. By accusing him loudly before the chamber of peers, of treason and murder?

EDMUND. No, no, a thousand times no. That but touches his honor, and what is that to such a man? 'Tis at his heart I shall aim—'tis in his heart he shall be struck?

MERC. [*With a low cry*] Unhappy man, I understand you—you would kill my son.

EDMUND. [*In a rage*] Yours—and his!

MERC. O madman! This son, this child, my beloved Albert, is—

ALBERT. [*Enters with paper in hand*] Mother!

MERC. [*To Edmund*] Not a word before him! [*Edmund goes up*]

ALBERT. Mother, the count is looking for you, he wishes you to join him in detaining Danglars, who wants rudely to take away his daughter.

MERC. [*Embracing Albert*] Love him, too—respect him above all others and if any quarrel should arise between you, be thou silent. Do thou submit and come—come to me and tell me all.

EDMUND. Madame!

MERC. [*Seizing his arm*] I rely upon your honor, no provocation from you? This night you shall know all. Fear no longer. [*Goes into salon, leaving them face to face*]

ALBERT. Count—

EDMUND. What is it?

ALBERT. I have a great service to ask at your hands.

EDMUND. At mine?

ALBERT. Yes. Oh, don't refuse me, I feel that you would bring me harm.

EDMUND. What is it?

ALBERT. I am about to fight a duel.

EDMUND. You?

ALBERT. I.

EDMUND. A serious one?

ALBERT. A mortal one.

EDMUND. With whom?

ALBERT. With Noirtier.

EDMUND. This is madness. He might be your father—he is a most respected politician, a man whose honor and integrity—

ALBERT. It is not a question of his honor, but mine. The name I bear—

EDMUND. And does Noirtier attack that honor?

ALBERT. In his journal of to-day—here is a copy.

EDMUND. And what does he say in his journal?

ALBERT. It is horrible. [*Reads*] "From a correspondent at Janina—" [*Stops, unable to proceed*]

EDMUND. [*Aside*] The journal put in Danglars' way by Caderousse! [*Aloud*] What says the correspondent at Janina?

ALBERT. I cannot—read for yourself—it is too frightful. [*Sits, R.*]

EDMUND. [*Reads*] "From a correspondent at Janina it is now ascertained as a fact that the brave Ali Tebelin who was massacred in his castle was betrayed and given up to his enemies by the French officer whose fortune he had made, and whose name was Fernand." What of that?

ALBERT. Now do you understand? [*Rises*]

EDMUND. I understand your agitation, but still I do not see what there is to challenge Noirtier.

ALBERT. I required of him to retract his calumny.

EDMUND. And he refused?

ALBERT. No.

EDMUND. Well?

ALBERT. But he added a condition.

EDMUND. What was it?

ALBERT. Of his being first convinced that the statement was false.

EDMUND. And then you challenge him?

ALBERT. And he will either retract this odious lie, or I will kill him. [*Going, L.*]

EDMUND. Now, what would you ask of me?

ALBERT. First, that you would receive Noirtier's answer.

EDMUND. I will do so.

ALBERT. Then—and this is the service I ask you not to refuse—to be my second in case of a duel.

EDMUND. Be it so.

ALBERT. Ah, count, you said truly to me when you saved my life, "you will not perish in a battle, boy, and on the day of your death you will find me before you."—You keep your word.

EDMUND. I always do.

ALBERT. [*Looking off*] My father and Danglars—let them know nothing.

EDMUND. Rest satisfied. [*Exit, bowing to Fernand and Danglars, who enter*]

FER. Now, sir, we are alone—alone with my son, who is as much interested as I am—who has an equal right with me to call you to account for the scandal created by your refusal.

DANG. I have nothing to do with the scandal—I was leaving quietly with my daughter—you set the countess on us, we were detained. You force me to explain, and I simply say read the "Imperial" of to-day. It will be less unpleasant for you, and make it easier for me.

ALBERT. Have your read the "Imperial"?

FER. What is it all about, Albert, what does he allude to?

ALBERT. To a vile slander, father. They say, father, they dare to say that you, whose loyal services are so well known, whose bravery and valor have been so highly recompensed by the king, they say—oh, pardon me for repeating such infamies!—they say to enrich yourself, in a word, for a price, like the lowest traitors, you sold and assassinated your benefactor.

FER. Oh! Who said so?

ALBERT. [*Gives papers*] See here, and as for you who have hawked this lie—

DANG. It is my fault if the journal gives the name of the Count de Morcerf in full?

ALBERT. Thou liest! They do not give his name. [*Takes paper*] Look!

DANG. The "Imperial" does not, but the "Etoile" does. [*Enter Caderousse with paper*]

ALBERT. 'Tis false!

CADER. [*To Danglars*]   Here, sir, is the number of the "Etoile" you asked
or.

DANG.   Ah, here it is! [*Tears off cover, Albert snatches paper*]

ALBERT. [*Reads excitedly*]   "The French officer alluded to in the Janina
orrespondence of the 'Imperial' and mentioned under the name of Fernand,
ow bears the title of Count de Morcerf, and is a member of the chamber of
eers."

FER. [*Crosses L.*]   And who sends the journals in such good time?

DANG.   How do I know? Here is the cover.

FER. [*Reads*]   "The Count de Monte Cristo."

ALBERT.   He? Oh, this will drive me mad. [*Enter Edmund and Noirtier*]
Here they are at last.

NOIR.   Albert, my child, be calm.

ALBERT.   Do you retract, Noirtier, do you defend my father?

NOIR.   I regret to say that I cannot without forfeiting honor. I have acquired the sad proof of the allegation.

ALBERT.   From whom have you the proofs?

NOIR.   From the Ambassador of Greece himself. [*Fernand staggers against
he wall*]

ALBERT.   Furnished before witnesses no doubt.

NOIR.   Albert!

ALBERT. [*Draws off glove*]   Answer!

NOIR.   Before the Count of Monte Cristo, who represented you.

ALBERT. [*With mockery*]   Who represented me? Indeed, and what reply
did that noble friend make to this accusation?

NOIR.   That he could not doubt it, as he himself had it from Haidee.
Mercédès appears]

ALBERT.   Ah, the wretched coward! [*With uplifted glove to Edmund*]

EDMUND. [*Seizes his wrist and glove, turns to Fernand*]   Revenge is mine,
Fernand—I hold thy heart in my hand.

ALBERT. [*With dignity*]   You have a firm wrist, sir; to-morrow we shall
ee if you have as firm a heart.

EDMUND.   To-morrow I will return your glove from a pistol, wrapped
round a bullet.

MERC. [*Aside to Edmund*]   You will not do so, Edmund.

EDMUND. [*Looking at Fernand*]   I will!

MERC.   You will not harm a hair of his head!

EDMUND.   I will kill him!

MERC.   You will not even fight him.

EDMUND. I will kill him.

MERC. Try—he is your son!

ACT V.

SCENE: *The forest of Vincennes. Woodcutter's hut, door to front stage.*

EDMUND. [*Enters, followed by Noirtier with swords and Danglars with pistols. C.*] Are we arrived?

DANG. Yes.

EDMUND. This is the spot fixed for the duel between Albert and me?

NOIR. This is the spot. [*R.*]

DANG. But, thanks to your haste, we are considerably before the time mentioned.

EDMUND. I expect someone here whom I must see before I die.

NOIR. Die?

EDMUND. Is not this a duel to the death?

NOIR. But you are acknowledged to be the best swordsman, the first shot of the day. Your reputation makes the best duellist tremble, and—

EDMUND. And I could kill Albert at my pleasure—is it not so?

NOIR. Assuredly.

EDMUND. Well, Albert will leave the ground uninjured—and you will have, my good friend, to carry me off to my last home.

NOIR. Look you now, I have followed you throughout the ball last night, watched you throughout the challenge, and comprehended that you had a great act to accomplish, and I feel convinced that you act in justice.

EDMUND. Yes, I thought so, too.

NOIR. Why then, speak of death?

EDMUND. It is not time to answer your questions. Before I cross swords with Albert, or confront him, you shall know all.

NOIR. Let it be so. [*Crosses up to Danglars*]

EDMUND. [*Alone, resting on fallen tree*] It is all over now, the edifice built so slowly, reared with such trouble and labor falls at a blow—at a woman's breath—at a child's mere name. [*Looks upwards*] Oh, Thou art great and powerful, and I recall under Thy mighty hand, and submit to Thy eternal justice. How Thou dost lower us all to our level, when we proudly essay to soar into Thy Kingdom. I aspired to be Thy avenger, and Thou hast shown me by Villefort's dreadful end how Thy time has come. Thou knowest how to punish. Led by a mean and selfish jealousy, I sought to strike Fernand cruelly to the heart by slaying his son, and it is my heart Thou strikest, and before my weapon Thou placest mine own child. 'Tis justice, and I shall fall beneath that same weapon with which I meant to slay. I am prepared to die.

DANG. Someone approaches.

EDMUND. Can it be Albert already?

NOIR. No, it is his new servant.

EDMUND. [*Aside*] Caderousse at last! [*Caderousse enters*]

NOIR. How did you leave him?

CADER. Alas, full of rage and spite—he spent the whole night practising with a pistol, shooting at a mark.

NOIR. You have the choice of weapons, count, and must take—

EDMUND. The pistol, Noirtier, and give the boy a fair chance.

NOIR. 'Tis madness!

EDMUND. No, 'tis resignation, and you'll approve of it when you know all.

NOIR. We'll see. [*Exit with Danglars*]

EDMUND. [*To Caderousse*] Now, we are alone.

CADER. I have seen her.

EDMUND. You have?

CADER. Yes.

EDMUND. And you have told her?

CADER. All. How you were betrayed—Danglars' letter—Fernand's perfidy —even my involuntary share in the infamous plot.

EDMUND. And she has forgiven me my hateful project of revenge—does she not despise me?

CADER. She reveres and loves you.

EDMUND. Oh, say not that, courage will fail me, I should lack the strength to die.

CADER. She has abjured the base hypocrite Fernand, who for twenty years has defrauded her of her esteem and respect, as he robbed his benefactor of wealth and life. She rose, pale but firm and noble. From a secluded chest she drew her long-abandoned Catalan dress, and in those garments, unpurchased by the wages of treachery and murder, she will leave Fernand's mansion.

EDMUND. What?

CADER. "Tell Edmund this," did she add, "and while he lives—whose tainted name I and my son bear, let the secret I confided to Edmund concerning Albert remain sacred—I trust his honor"—and she handed me this medal, snatched from your neck in the last embrace when the felon's deed dragged you to prison.

EDMUND. [*Embracing him*] Ah, Mercédès, we are both condemned in this world!

CADER. Master!

EDMUND. Enough of this, listen. You will go to Marseilles—you will bear my last wishes—

CADER. Your last?

EDMUND. Keep silence and mark me. Here is a letter for Morel. It informs him of the spot where he will find the red silk purse which he left filled with gold for the wants of my poor old father. Its present contents will save Morel from bankruptcy. In a few days a new "Pharaon" which I have built, and which old Penelon himself has laden with the treasures of Monte Cristo, will bravely enter the port of Marseilles. She holds millons—their fortune—that of Morel, and the future fortune of Albert and Mercédès when they come; take the letter and go.

CADER. Here is Albert.

EDMUND. Go, he must not see you. [*Exit Caderousse*] And now let the dead reenter his tomb! The spectre fade away in the shade of night. [*Enter Albert and Danglars and Noirtier*]

DANG. [*Looking at watch*] You are late, viscount.

ALBERT. [*Salutes*] I ask pardon, gentlemen, for causing you to wait. An interview with my mother detained me, and I beg of you to accept her excuses and mine.

NOIR. But I do not see your seconds, Albert.

ALBERT. They are needless, my esteemed friend. My arrival alone suffices for what must pass between the count and myself. [*Noirtier and Danglars go up*] Remain, Noirtier. The presence of one man of honor is necessary at our conversation.

DANG. Sir?

NOIR. [*Staying him*] Your pardon, you are not spoken of. [*Danglars goes up*]

ALBERT. [*To Edmund*] Count, I harshly challenged you last night. I thought it my duty to repress a calumny. To-day, that which I thought to be a slander, has become a terrible truth. The Count de Morcerf is struck off the roll of peers, and the General Fernand is degraded. But, it is not the treachery of the officer Mondego toward the Pasha that makes me ready to excuse you—it is the foulness of the fisherman Fernand towards you that bows me with shame. It is for your eighteen years of incarceration that I humbly ask your pardon! [*Kneels to Edmund*]

EDMUND. Albert—sir—

ALBERT. Yes, I proclaim it publicly. You were justified in revenging yourself on my father, and I, the son of Mercédès, I thank you for having sought revenge on him. [*Kneels again*]

EDMUND. [*Aside*] Ah, your heart is there, Mercédès. [*Fernand appears at back*]

ALBERT. An angel from Heaven alone could have saved us from death. That angel came in my mother's form, if not to make us friends—that is impossible—at least to make two men of honor who esteem each other, regard their conscience more dearly than their vanity.

DANG. Ah, all ends with an apology, does it?

ALBERT. [*To Danglars*] And if anyone should doubt the motive which urges me, I shall speedily correct his opinion.

FER. [*Confronting him*] Even mine, Viscount de Morcerf?

ALBERT. My father!

ALL. Morcerf!

FER. [*To Noirtier and Danglars*] I have not to do with you, but with this man. [*To Edmund*] To this public insulter, who knows everyone and whom no one knows. Who then, are you, demon? You, who have clothed me in shame and contempt. You, who have by the light of Hell, read every page in my past life?

ALBERT. [*Covers face with hands*] Ah, Heaven!

FER. Come, who are you? Yesterday you called yourself Monte Cristo—in Italy, Busoni. In Epirus—I know not—I can't recollect. But of these hundred names you give yourself, which is your real one? That I may spit it in your face while I plunge my sword in your heart, or send a bullet crashing through your skull. Have you a name you dare avow?

EDMUND. [*Calm*] Fernand, of the hundred names you mention, you have forgotten one. I have but to pronounce it to strike you to my feet. Fernand, look me well in the eye. We have met but once—but look at me.

FER. Oh! 'Tis impossible.

EDMUND. You guessed at once, because Heaven at this moment lights them with a spark of its own fire.

FER. You alive, and knowing all?

EDMUND. All!

FER. And you did not kill me?

EDMUND. No. But, I have told Mercédès all.

FER. Ah, wretch, defend yourself! [*Throws pistols*]

EDMUND. [*Pushes pistol away with foot*] Fernand, you can murder me, but I shall not fight you.

FER. If you will have it, then—[*Cocks pistol, Mercédès rushes between them and stops him*]

MERC. Assassin!

FER. Ah—she? I am accursed! [*Runs into hut, shot heard within. Mercédès and Albert run to hut*]

ALBERT. [*Supports Mercédès*] Mother!

MERC. Dead!

EDMUND. "Two!" [*To Danglars, taking sword*] Your turn, now, defend yourself!

NOIR. Hold!

EDMUND. Back, Noirtier, I can kill this man, and this man shall die!

MERC. Edmund—

DANG. Edmund Dantès! [*Springs for sword*]

EDMUND. Ha, you know me now. Noirtier, be witness that I grant the honor of a duel to that viper whom I have the right to crush beneath my heel. It was that serpent who crawled beneath all those villainies, his venom that has poisoned all those lives! Danglars, your time has come! You are going to die. [*As he is rolling up sleeve, Danglars makes thrust at him. Noirtier throws it off with cane*]

NOIR. Coward! Go in, Edmund, and kill the villain. I will act as umpire!

DANG. You forget my secret thrust.

EDMUND. No, for Heaven fights on my side and nerves my arm! I tell you, Danglars, you are going to die.

NOIR. En garde!

EDMUND. En garde! [*They cross swords*]

MERC. [*To Albert*] On your knees, child, and pray for him. Albert, Albert —pray. Soon you shall know your birth—soon I can tell you all.

DANG. [*Making pass*] Hit!

EDMUND. Nothing. Your foul stroke is known! Now, Danglars, you are a dead man.

DANG. Have at thee! [*Lunging at him*]

EDMUND. Die! [*Runs him through*]

DANG. Ha! [*Dies and rolls at his feet*]

EDMUND. "Three!"

MERC. Your prayers have saved your father's life, Albert—you are his son!

CURTAIN

FLYING SCUD;
Or, A FOUR-LEGGED FORTUNE

By Dion Boucicault

CAST OF CHARACTERS

Tom Meredith

Nat Gosling

Lord Cecil Woodbie

Captain Grindley Goodge

Colonel Mulligan

Mo Davis

Chousir

Bob Buckskin

Ned Compo

Jerry

Mr. Quail

Jackson

A Servant

Katey Rideout

Julia Latimer

Lady Woodbie

Stable Boys, Bailiffs, Tenants, Policemen, A Waiter, Thimble Riggers, Negro Minstrels, Venders, Supers.

SYNOPSIS OF SCENES

ACT I.

SCENE 1: *Love Lane, near Doncaster. Nat's cottage embowered in shrubbery R. A pump L.C. Cottage R. Railings, etc. Enter Jerry and Lord Woodbie L.U.E.*

JERRY. Well, my lord, we shall be very sorry to lose you, I'm sure, nobody will be sorrier than the boys in our stable.

WOOD. I've been here now much longer than I intended; I should have gone before, but I thought I might as well wait till after the reading of the will—not that it's got anything to do with me—but the Squire was always a decent sort, and I am rather curious to know how he has left his money.

JERRY. The reading of the will has been fixed for three o'clock; notices have been sent to several of the principal tenants on the estate to attend. Poor Squire, I'm sorry he's dead; he might have lived till after the Derby. I know he had great hopes of one day pulling off the big race, but now he's dead and gone. Bless him, he was a right down good sort.

WOOD. Yes, I've always heard him spoken of as a steadfast friend, and where once he took a liking he was never known to change his mind. Have you seen Miss Latimer this morning?

JERRY. No, my lord, I don't think she's come out of the grounds yet. I saw her last night with her uncle, Colonel Mulligan.

WOOD. Oh, all right. I dare say I shall see them presently.

JERRY. I'm just going to look after the stable lads; they've got the horses out for an airing. If I should see Miss Latimer shall I tell her that you were asking after her?

WOOD. Yes—no—I mean, don't trouble; I dare say I shall see her myself.

JERRY. No trouble, if I happen to see her I'll mention it. Good morning, my lord.

WOOD. Good morning. [*Exit Jerry L.U.E.*]

WOOD. Oh, Julia, Julia, you've much to answer for. Here's another night I've passed without a wink of sleep. I never knew what it was to be in love before; it's a most awful complaint and I've got it very badly. I don't know what mama will say when she knows all about it. I'm afraid she's got higher notions for me, but I know she'll give her consent when she knows how much I love her. [*Laugh outside*] Good gracious, what's that? [*Enter Bob Buckskin L.U.E. smothered in blankets and speaking off*]

BOB. Yes, you may laugh, ye unfeeling monsters, you may laugh. You're a set as would laugh if you saw an omnibus run over your mother-in-law; necessity knows no law and I'm bound to do it. Here goes for another lap. [*Starts running around stage*]

WOOD. Good gracious! My good fellow, what are you doing?

BOB. Beg pardon, I didn't see you, my lord. I've just got off another three ounces. I'm bound to do it, there's no help for it. I'm making too much fat and this is the only way I can keep it down. While the stable boys have got their horses out for their exercise, I'm taking mine; I've done twelve miles this morning, had two doses of salts and senna, and three pints of boiling water. Oh, it's a splendid thing. I'll soon be as thin as the living skeleton who was being shown for a penny at the shop in High Street.

WOOD. You will kill yourself if you go on like this.

BOB. Not a bit of it. I'm bound to do it to keep myself in condition.

WOOD. You must have a good constitution to stand it.

BOB. Yes, my lord, my constitution has been a curse to me; everything I take turns to fat, everything I eat or drink agrees with me. It's all my constitution. If I lived on fat bacon for a fortnight, I shouldn't be able to get my clothes on or off. Milk I ain't allowed to touch; taters, I daren't look 'em in the face; every bit of bread I eat has to be toasted to a cinder; and as for beer, oh lor, beer. [*Grimaces*]

WOOD. Well, don't let me stop you; go on with your exercise.

BOB. Just what I was thinking. I'm getting cool here and the perspiration must be kept up. My lord, you might time me thirty times round the haystack over yonder. I'll back myself to do it in fourteen minutes.

WOOD. Come on then, we'll see.

BOB. This is my form. Watch. [*Runs twice round stage and exits R.U.E. Lord Woodbie follows laughing. If horses are used, all enter L.U.E. with Jerry and stable lads and all exit R.U.E. followed by Katey in riding habit. She looks round as if followed, then exits behind cottage. Music. Enter Goodge hastily L. He looks round*]

GOODGE. Where is she? Surely I have not mistaken the road? No, she disappeared round that corner and dived into this lane. Ha! A cottage hiding under the rose bushes. [*Looks over the paling*] The very nest for such a bird; I must waylay one of the servants and find out who and what she is. [*Enter Nat R. with a bucket and smoking a pipe*] Here is one.

NAT. [*Sings*]   In '44 I won the Hoaks
      And then they put me up
      To ride Sir Tatton's little mare
      As took the Chester Cup. [*Pumps water into bucket*]

GOODGE. The very fellow for my purpose.

NAT. [*Sings*] But, oh my, oh cry, it was just then d'ye see,
    The pootyest gal in Doncaster, she fell in love with me.

GOODGE. I say, my man.

NAT. Sir to you, sir. [*Sings*]
    She said she would be mine, ven I was growed a little bigger.
    She didn't know I dussn't put no meat upon my figger.
    Oh my, oh cry, vot is a chap to do
    Ven he's in love and got to ride,
    Vell under six stun two.
    [*Spoken*] Saddle and bridle included, mind you.

GOODGE. Do you live in that cottage?

NAT. Ess. [*Is going in with bucket*]

GOODGE. [*Holding up a sovereign*] D'ye see that?

NAT. [*R.*] Ess, how much do you want for it?

GOODGE. A very lovely girl rode down this lane a few minutes ago, on a
bay horse with black points.

NAT. [*Sings*] Oh, yes, she's as beautiful as a butterfly.

GOODGE. Confound the fellow, he's as bad as a barrel organ! Does she
live in that cottage, and can you tell me all about her?

NAT. Ess, her name is Katey Rideout, and she do live yonder.

GOODGE. Alone?

NAT. Nay, but wi' her auld grandfather.

GOODGE. What's his name?

NAT. He be called Nathaniel Gosling, but more often old Nat, hereabouts.

GOODGE. Then he is grandfather to an angel.

NAT. Yes, a thoroughbred 'un, and sich a temper, she's as sweet as milk,
as fine as silk, and as soft as a dooey morning.

GOODGE. Poetical. [*Hands him money*]

NAT. And all included in the sovrin. [*Pockets it*]

GOODGE. Does old squeezebags keep a sharp eye on the girl?

NAT. Lord love ye, I can get over him.

GOODGE. Egad! then I have hit on the right man to do my business for me.

NAT. You may bet your last shirt button on it.

GOODGE. I'll pay you handsomely if I win the girl.

NAT. I allus takes my tip for sporting information. [*Takes up the bucket*]

GOODGE. Then tell her that I am Captain Goodge, Grindley Goodge, of
Nobbley Hall. [*Going R.*] Stay, what is your name, my man?

NAT. Well, I be called Nathaniel Gosling, but more often old Nat hereabouts.

Goodge. The grandfather himself! I have been done.

Nat. [*Enthusiastic*] Yes, you have been done brown. I've got the sovereign, no money returned. [*Exit R.*]

Goodge. And here I stood, I, Grindley Goodge, to be reckoned up and turned into cash by a yokel like that. Can this old cub be the grandfather of such a lovely being as that girl? [*Enter Tom Meredith L.*]

Tom. I beg your pardon, sir, for addressing you, but I saw you in the lane and I hoped you would pardon my intrusion.

Goodge. Speak out, my man. Who are you, one of my tenants, eh?

Tom. Yes, sir, my name is Meredith, Thomas Meredith. I farm the low meadows.

Goodge. I know nothing about the estate except that I shall come into possession of it some day. What do you want?

Tom. I have received notice this morning, sir, to quit my place. I have no lease. Your uncle, before he died, said I would never be dispossessed.

Goodge. Then why did he not give you a lease?

Tom. He said I should never want one while he lived nor afterwards.

Goodge. Nor afterwards?

Tom. These were his very words.

Goodge. What a pity those words were not in black and white.

Tom. There never was a scratch of a pen between us. You seé, sir, my father, Colonel Meredith, owned this estate. He was a great racing man. Your uncle was his groom. But when my father was ruined and sold up, your uncle stepped into Nobbley Hall and became the squire. Perhaps when he found me his poor tenant, he remembered how good and generous my father had been to him, for though close-fisted to all the world, he was ever open-handed to me.

Goodge. It's more than he ever was to me, the old screw. I'm sorry I can't oblige you, but I must have all my meadow land for my racing stock.

Tom. I'll take in all your stud, sir. I trained for your uncle. There's a two-year old in the stable now, that never had any hand but mine over him.

Goodge. Thanks, but I have my own trainer. [*Going, crosses R.*]

Tom. See, Captain Goodge, I—I can't take no for your answer; it will just be ruin to me to quit the low meadows. I—I am in hopes of being married, sir. Now if you deny me I shall have no home to offer my young wife, for every penny I have is dug into your land or spent on the house I hoped that she would one day share with me. Don't turn me out like a dog, sir. Come, sir, let her add her persuasions to mine. She lives yonder.

Goodge. In that cottage? Are you then the accepted lover of that beautiful girl?

Tom. I can't say that she has out and out said yes, but I know that she likes me better than anyone else.

Goodge. How are you sure of that?

Tom. I've often told her that if I caught any fellow fooling round her, I'd break his neck, and she didn't object.

Goodge. I can't stop to see the lady; I am rather in a hurry. [*Crosses L.*]

Tom. But you will renew my lease, sir?

Goodge. No, I want the land. You've had your answer, go. [*Aside*] And I want the girl, so I must clear this fellow out of the estate. [*Exit L.1E.*]

Tom. There he goes, the thoroughbred heartless sporting character. He's all there with his napless drab hat, his drab face where all the wrinkles he is up to keep watch round his eyes; he looks clean shaved all over, and covered in air, tight from the choker to his boots; as much as to say, I don't think there is anything about me you can catch hold of, and there is so little anybody would care to take. [*Enter Katey Rideout R.*]

Katey. Well, Tom, what's the matter?

Tom. I am ruined, that's all. All I have worked for is to be swept away into the pocket of yonder eelskin, and I am left homeless.

Katey. A man who loves and is loved again, however poor he may be, is never homeless. Home is not built with bricks and mortar, Tom, but with flesh and blood.

Tom. But is there such a thing as home for me? am I loved again? Nobody can answer that but you. [*Nat appears and looks over paling*]

Katey. When you were in luck and I could have had you any day, I did not know my own mind, but now you are ruined, I feel jealous and exasperated.

Tom. What does that mean?

Katey. It means, Tom, that when you are turned out by the world I shall say, "Come home." [*They embrace*]

Tom. Ah, what a comfort that is to a fellow in his misfortune. [*Nat's business with rose plant*]

Nat. [*C. At back*] They ort to have their picters took jest so. What a hinterest even for their children.

Katey. [*R.*] Do you feel ruined now, Tom?

Tom. [*L.*] I feel reconciled to it, dear.

Katey. Well, I don't. We are as poor as mice. If you lose the farm, what are we to live on? We are not going to sponge on my old grandfather.

Tom. No, I'd never be a burden to the old man. Never! Never! Never!

Nat. Hear! Hear! Hear! [*Retires behind cottage*]

KATEY.   Then you must have that lease. [*Crosses R.*] Leave the captain to me; I can move his heart.

TOM.   How?

KATEY.   Never mind how, that is my business. [*R.*] The lease you shall have. Never ask me how I obtained it. Good-bye, Tom. [*At the door*] Have you not forgotten something?

TOM.   Ah! [*Runs to kiss her, she shuts the door in his face*] Bless her, what a treasure she is. [*Crosses. Enter Nat*]

NAT.   Don't rely on her to make your fortune. A man as reckons on a woman to make his way in the world ain't no better than a child.

TOM.   I tell you, Nat, I have not a hundred pounds in the world.

NAT.   And I tell you, lad, I have ten thousand. Hist!

TOM.   Ten thousand pounds?

NAT.   Every blessed copper on 'em.

TOM.   Where?

NAT.   In the stables at Nobbley Hall. That 'ere capital is stowed away in the loose box No. 14, in the form of the two-year colt.

TOM.   Flying Scud?

NAT.   Hist! I tell you, d'ye want to ruin me? Speak low. Yes, Flying Scud. For two years the Squire has been keeping that colt dark, and as month after month he grew under your training, we sor the bit of stuff coming an' comin' out as sure and clear as the ye'rly mornin' and then we kept it darker. Last June he was entered for the Criterion Stakes and then we slipped him in for the blue ribbin at Epsom. Nobody took no notice, while I got him on at 100 to 1. I swore I'd never back anything as wore hoofs, except to lose, but I've backed him to win and he will, he will. I've been a jockey, man and boy, for fifty-nine year, and never saw his match. Slip your money on him, Tom. Pitch it. Melt down your best breeches and put your last teaspoon in the pot, for as sure as we stand here, you and me has bred and trained a Derby winner. [*Crosses to L.*]

TOM.   You take my breath away!

NAT.   That's what I reckon Flying Scud will do to bigger men than you and me, when ahead of his horses he shows the field his plates. [*Whispering*] Ooraw! Ooraw! Ooraw!

TOM.   I'll back him, Nat, I'll back him.

NAT.   'Old 'ard, lad, the colt belongs to Goodge. That is, he will belong to him, for this afternoon the lawyer comes from London with the old Squire's will, which he will read at the 'all. Then Flying Scud with all his engagements will become the property of Captain Grindley Goodge.

TOM.   Well?

NAT. Well, when our beauty wins the Criterion Stakes, he'll be at evens for the Derby before Christmas.

TOM. I won't edge a penny, Nat, I'll stand or fall by him. [*Crosses L.*]

NAT. Then you'll fall, lad, for then Goodge will lay against him for the Derby, and he'll be run to lose. That's always the game them sort play.

TOM. What can we do?

NAT. Keep dark, lad, and let me work the oracle. There's three men, pals of hisn, now on a visit at the 'all. Mo Davis, Colonel Mulligan, and Chousir. Them three and Goodge are known as the quadruped.

TOM. The quadruped?

NAT. Ay, the four legs. And the heap of money they've run away with! Afore they've found out what's in Flying Scud's skin, you get your money on with all of 'em. Let 'em smell your money, they'll make it easy for you; then we'll let the light in upon them, and when Goodge finds he has got a flyer in his stable, a Derby crack, he'll give you the lease or whatever you ask him, for fear you should blow the secret and spoil the odds.

TOM. But I would not betray my employer.

NAT. I know it, lad, but he don't believe in honesty except what's paid for ad valorum, and that's where three sharp 'uns get licked. Leave it to me, boy. Off with you to the stable, I'll follow you.

TOM. Success, Nat, I feel success. Oh, my bright and bonny colt, when you've rubbed your nose against my cheek and looked so kind at me out of your dark eyes, did you know that you were going to win for me, not the Derby, but a greater prize than ever was contended for on the English turf, Katey Rideout, the girl I love better than my life, the prettiest girl in Yorkshire? [*Exit L.1E.*]

NAT. There goes a square, honest, good bit of stuff. His character is as sweet as new mown hay; free from dirt, of a fine nose, and jest such as any woman or friend may thrive on. [*Exit R.*]

SCENE 2: *The garden at Nobbley Hall. Front Cloth. Enter Goodge followed by servant.*

GOODGE. Has Joe gone down to the station to meet Mr. Quail with the dog-cart?

SERV. Yes, sir.

GOODGE. Let lunch be ready in the library at three o'clock. Have the principal tenants been notified to attend?

SERV. Yes, Sir.

GOODGE. Very good. [*Exit servant L.1E.*] I wish to enter into possession in style. Today will make me master of Nobbley Hall, and it comes not a day too soon, for my creditors began to look cloudy. Here comes two of them. They stick to me like leeches. Ah, my very dear friends, when can I afford to kick you out! Won't I pick my heaviest pair of boots for the festive occasion—in the meanwhile— [*Enter Mo Davis and Mulligan L.1E.*] Ah, Mulligan, how are you enjoying yourself? Eh, Davis?

MO. Ve have been taking stock of the place. Beautiful, ain't it, Mulligan?

GOODGE. It's good for the thousand I owe you, Mo, and for the seven hundred I am in your debt, eh? What do you think, my rollickers?

MO. A thousand was it? Vell I never think of it, Grindley, s'elp me, it never crossed my mind.

MULL. Don't mention it, old fellow.

GOODGE. Well, I won't. Have you any news from Lord Woodbie's trainer? How are the horses we sold him?

MO. Vulcan has broken down, and Tripod has been and justified his name, and goes on three legs. He says the stable looks like a coffin lid, it's full of screws. You couldn't paint von of them to look like a horse.

GOODGE. Where's the young lord now?

MULL. Playing billiards.

MO. His Lordship is a comfortable annooity to me, and Mulligan makes a settled income out of him at billiards.

GOODGE. While you and I manage his stable and advise him how to lay his money out.

MO. Ah, he's a young mine of wealth, as ve've discovered, and ve've all shares in him.

GOODGE. And a pretty sharp lookout we've kept upon each other to see that we shared alike.

MO. Oh, honor, ve couldn't get on nohow unless we had some principle; I say, Mulligan, go and keep an eye on young Lord Woodbie.

MULL. All right, I'll see to him. [*Exit. Enter servant L.1E.*]

SERV. Miss Rideout, sir, wishes to see you. She has just rode into the strawyard.

GOODGE. Miss Rideout, are you sure?

SERV. Yes, sir. [*Speaks apart to Goodge*]

MO. Vy, here comes Mr. Quail, the lawyer.

GOODGE. I must leave you, Mo, to receive him, for the prettiest girl in Yorkshire is waiting for me yonder. [*Exit with servant L.1E. Enter Quail R.1E.*]

MO. Ah, Quail, welcome to Nobbley Hall. You bring de vill, eh?

QUAIL. I see that Captain Goodge has taken possession already.

Mo. Vy not, ain't he a right to it; ain't he the heir?

QUAIL. You are an old and valued client, Mr. Davis. Ahem! Goodge owes you a thousand pounds.

Mo. Vell, vell, he will pay me when he fingers the old Squire's spondoolicks.

QUAIL. Don't make too sure that he will ever touch a penny of them.

Mo. Vot, vot, I thay, no jokin'! You don't mean to tell me the Squire has cut him off?

QUAIL. I have no right to say so much, but as you are an old client—

Mo. Oo, Oo, jumpin' Moses! I'm in a hole! Oo, Oo, it's ruin. A thousand pound! What's to be done?

QUAIL. Six months ago you instructed us to sue Goodge for this debt.

Mo. No, no, you was sent on by a third party. I didn't vant to quarrel vid him.

QUAIL. We obtained judgment. I issued execution yesterday. The officer is waiting at the village inn. Now the rest is your business, but take my advice. Put the screw on while Goodge is in feather. Let him borrow the money or get security now, for by tonight there may not be a feather left upon him. [*Exit L.1E.*]

Mo. Jumpin' Moses! Here's a pretty kettle of fish. There's no trustin' nobody. Even ven a fellow's dead and buried, he's down on you in his will. Poor Goodge, I pities him, s'elp me, he's out of luck. Vat's to be done? If I put the screw on, dere's young Lord Woodbie vill never let him be arrested; he'll pay it or go security. I'll offer to jine in a bill. I'll give the bums an 'int; I've not got an hour to act in. Poor Goodge! Vell, vell! I wouldn't 'urt 'im, but it's for his own good, 'cause ven he's down in the vorld agin I can lend him a fiver; I'll put the screw on. I wouldn't do it, but it's for his own good. [*Exit L.1E. Enter Julia Latimer L.1E.*]

JULIA. Did he see my signal? I waved my handkerchief to him through the billiard room window. Yes, he's coming. [*Enter Lord Woodbie L.1E.*]

WOOD. You wished me to join your ramble?

JULIA. I am afraid I interrupted your game.

WOOD. Oh, it is all right. I was playing with your uncle, Colonel Mulligan, but when I saw you beckon to me, I threw up the game and paid my stakes.

JULIA. I do not wish you to play billiards with my uncle.

WOOD. Why not? I can beat him, I can give him ten points in fifty.

JULIA. [*Aside*] Poor fellow. [*Aloud*] I know you can, but my uncle cannot afford to lose his money.

Wood. Then I am so glad he has won somehow of me a few hundreds by flukes. I never saw such a fellow to fluke.

Julia. He is almost as lucky as Mr. Chousir.

Wood. By Jove! Chousir is the worst hand at ecarté I ever did see. The blunders he makes!

Julia. But I thought he rose up a winner last night?

Wood. So he did, to his great amusement and surprise. But the beginners always have such extraordinary luck.

Julia. [*Aside*] Poor boy. [*Aloud*] Can you find no occupation more pleasing than cards or billiards?

Wood. Well, yes, I prefer to walk with you. I say, Miss Latimer.

Julia. Well, my lord?

Wood. I wish you would call me Cecil. I—I wish you'd tell me what to do to please you, because, I—I want to awfully. Do tell me something.

Julia. Don't bet, you lose your money; don't drink, you can't stand it; don't smoke, you don't like it.

Wood. Oh! By Jove! I can't get up in the morning till I've had a cigar, and positively I could not get over the afternoon without a pick-me-up at two and a stiff tod before dinner.

Julia. Well, I don't like it, and if you wish to please me—

Wood. Wish to please you. Oh, by Jove, if you only knew, 'pon my soul—

Julia. Don't swear.

Wood. Oh, I say, you're awfully hard on a fellow.

Julia. You are an only child, Lord Woodbie.

Wood. Yes.

Julia. The only child of a widowed mother?

Wood. Solitary chicken of the old bird.

Julia. Don't speak so of your mother; you don't feel it. When you are at Naseby Castle do you smoke in bed of a morning?

Wood. Well, the old lady will come and wake me, just as she did when I was a kid; it's an awful bore.

Julia. Do you take pick-me-ups and your tods there?

Wood. No, because she's always kissing me, and the infernal things smell so.

Julia. Do you swear in her presence?

Wood. [*After a pause*] No!

Julia. Lord Woodbie, do not affect vices for which you have no taste, nor mimic manners of which you are really ashamed. Smoking makes you sick, I have seen you grow pale at your second cigar.

Wood. Me?

JULIA. You abhor brandy, yet you drink it neat, just to show off. Tobacco and spirits offend your mouth, and you wince when you swear.

WOOD. I will do anything you tell me, you know I will, because—because—you won't be offended?

JULIA. Because?

WOOD. I love you. Oh, I do indeed, Julia. I never said so before, but you must know it. Don't you, don't you?

JULIA. Hush! Yes!

WOOD. Oh, Julia, if you knew how I go on about you when I am alone; I've laid for hours outside your door, and kissed the boots you had left there; I've been the most infernal idiot to go on so, but I can't help it.

JULIA. No, no, you must not love me.

WOOD. I shall have seventeen thousand a year when I become of age, and when my granduncle dies I'll be a duke. I'll marry you at once.

JULIA. I am not fit to hold the rank of your wife.

WOOD. You are fit to be a queen.

JULIA. What I am is best known to myself, but I will not impose on your heart.

WOOD. I see what it is. You look on me as a child, to be pitied and to chide, not to be loved.

JULIA. Think what you please, but believe me, what you ask is impossible.

WOOD. It is all over then? You turn away from me; very well, you love someone else; I hope he loves you, 'cause then you—you won't feel as I do now. Oh, what shall I do! What shall I do!

JULIA. Cecil, forgive me. [*She takes his hand*] Won't you speak to me?

WOOD. No! [*Throws her hand away and runs off L.1E. Enter Mulligan with billiard cue in his hand*]

MULL. [*R.*] What is the matter?

JULIA. [*L.*] Lord Woodbie has proposed to me.

MULL. That's elegant.

JULIA. I have refused him.

MULL. Refused, refused an earrul! Refused seventeen thousand a year?

JULIA. The boy does not know I am an adventuress.

MULL. A what? You, my sister's child, wid the blood of the Mulligan in you, an adventuress? Show me the man who will say it to my face.

JULIA. No, but I will show you fifty that will say it every day behind your back. They say that I have been employed by you and your companions to dazzle and blind such victims as that young lord, while you pick their pockets.

MULL. Are you mad or dhraming?

JULIA. No, I am wide awake; I wish I had been so three years ago when I left school to partake of your home and to become what I am, your accomplice.

MULL. Is this the gratitude for the education I've wasted on you?

JULIA. Marry me to a rich man; take your price, pay yourself; I am ready to be sold, but let it be to one I am not expected to love.

MULL. Do my sinses decave me? Do you mean to tell me that you love this slip of a boy?

JULIA. Yes, I do, and that is why I have refused him; [*goes R.*] I cannot cheat him in love as you do in play; I will not enter his family like a thief. [*Exit R.1E.*]

MULL. Once in, who cares how you get there? Refuse seventeen thousand pounds a year! There's no counting on a woman. When you've won the game for her, she'll revoke and play the divil wid your finest combination. [*Exit L.1E.*]

SCENE 3: *The Stable. Door R. in F. Door L. in F. with No. 14 painted on it. Hayloft R. with ladder up to it. Stable boys take two horses out through D.F. for airing. Jerry and stable helps discovered.*

JERRY. Bob not yet in? He's been out for some exercise, he wants a lot of flesh taken off him; in fact he wants regularly pulling through a sieve.

BOB. [*Outside*] Hallo, Jerry!

JERRY. Ah, here he is. [*Enter Bob, dressed up in wraps and looking very fat*]

BOB. Give us a peel, lads.

JERRY. Take 'em off very cautiously; don't let the wind come on him too suddenly. [*Business*] My eyes, ain't he drawed fine?

BOB. I've had an eight-mile bust, I was twenty-nine ounces over weight this morning, let's see if I've left them on the road. [*Jumps into scale*]

JERRY. [*Counting in weights*] Nine fourteen and a half and three pounds. Nine stun ten.

BOB. That vos my mornin's averdoopise. Take out a pound. Ooraw! I'm flying still; take out another. Ah, I'm comin' to that. Eight stun eight and a pinch of snuff. [*Jumps out*] There's a waste. Now I'll take a feed; wot's the bill of fare?

JERRY. Here you are. [*Points to a paper on the wall*]

BOB. [*Reads*] Cold tea, sop biscuit, stale toast and a mug of water. Oh, Lord! [*Enter Nat D.F.R.*]

NAT. Ah, my little pips, here we are, eh?

ALL. It's Nat! it's Nat!

JERRY. Blow'd if it ain't "Old Boots" hisself.

ALL. Ooray!

NAT. How are ye, boys? It does my witals good to see you.

JERRY. Sit down. Why, what form he is in, boys; he is jockey all over still, ain't he? Now, Bob, go and get him a drop of beer.

BOB. All right, give us the jug.

JERRY. You will find one on the table. [*Exit Bob D.F.*] Ah, Nat, when I look at you I always thinks of the glorious old times when it was reckoned the greatest honor a man could have, to hold the blue ribbon of the turf.

NAT. Ah, them was days and no mistake.

JERRY. You was well thought of, and your friends ought to have been proud of you.

NAT. I believe they was. I was laid down right as a boy, lads; I'd a father as wouldn't stand no fat, and he skinned me close before I could walk. He brought me up in the weight I should go and when I was old I didn't depart from it.

JERRY. Have you saved much?

NAT. Well, I might have saved more if I hadn't spent so much, but I suppose I mustn't grumble. You see I does pretty well even now; I gets all the information from the boys in the stables, I advertises in the "Pink un," and I sells tips, straight tips too, not like some on 'em. I can truly say that I've never done anything yet that I'm ashamed of, and I can look back on the past with the knowledge that I have never wronged man, woman, or child.

JERRY. If all had been like you, Nat, the turf would stand much better than it does.

NAT. Of course there are black legs in every calling, and the turf is no more free from them than anything else.

JERRY. I was talking to a jockey the other day, Nat, who said he could always ride better after having a glass of champagne. What's your opinion of that? [*Re-enter Bob with a pewter pot of beer*]

NAT. Rot, utter rot! No man ever did anything better through being under the influence of drink; and my advice to every jockey would be, never touch a drop of liquor till after the race. You've heard of the time when I rode Skyrocket for the Great Metropolitan Stakes.

JERRY. Yes, when Scaramouth won by two lengths.

NAT. Not a bit of it, Scaramouth won by two glasses of champagne.

JERRY. Two glasses of champagne? Why, how was that, Nat?

NAT. Well, I'll tell you. It wants a clear head to ride a race; there's no excitement in the world equal to it. I hadn't had much to eat on the morning of the race, and although it's bad to eat too much, still it's bad to ride on an empty stomach. I was feeling rather faint, and just when I was on my horse, my backer says, "Have a glass of champagne, Nat; it will do you good"; so I took it. It was beautiful and cool, had been standing in ice, and tasted to my parched throat like nectar. I looked longingly at the bottle and he generously offered me another glass. I took it and sure enough I did feel the better for it. "I'll win," says I, and off I started. I headed them all the first hundred strides. I dug my spurs into my horse, and he answered to it and I felt it was a sure thing. The champagne seemed to bubble all over me, and I felt as light as a feather. We sprung up the rise like a whirlwind. The roar of the people, the swarming of the carriages, the bright colors on the grandstand all flashed across my eyes like a dream. It was just then I felt the horse flag in his pace; my head began to swim and I seemed to lose my presence of mind as I heard the second horse close behind me. I lost my grip and control, and my blood seemed to turn to liquid fire; my brain seemed to be a blaze and my head felt like bursting. I could feel the second horse behind me, but my sight seemed to get blurred; my own horse seemed to slip out of my grasp, and I couldn't regain my hold. It was my fault. I had given him too much to do at first, and he couldn't keep it up. The second horse came abreast of me; I could see the jockey; we glared into each other's eyes as we went along neck and neck, stride for stride, until we came within a hundred yards of the winning post. Then the other jockey lifted his horse, yes, fairly lifted it, past me and won by two lengths. But he didn't, he won by two glasses of champagne. I had the best horse, but my horse hadn't got the best rider. Then I took a sacred oath never to touch a drop of intoxicating liquor on the day of a race, and I've never broken my word; and I advise you chaps to always do the same.

BOB. Well, that puts me in mind of what happened to me when I rode Blue Bell in the Ladies Plate; only I lost mine through the mare, Vixen, and not through having anything to drink.

NAT. Oh, that's an old story, and has got about, and been told over and over again.

BOB. Well, never mind who's been telling it, it really happened to me.

JERRY. What was it, Bob?

NAT. You've heard it before, Jerry, scores of times.

JERRY. Never mind, a good thing is never the worse for telling over again.

BOB. Well, I had a spell of very bad luck; hadn't won a race for the whole season, when I got a chance with Blue Bell for the Ladies Plate.

There was only two in it as far as the race was concerned, Blue Bell and Vixen—you know, the squinny-eyed mare. I rode Blue Bell, and Tommy Comfit rode Vixen. Tommy was always a bit nasty with me, and never lost a chance of queering me; and as for Vixen, we were never friendly. The betting was five to four on Blue Bell; the mare was in grand form, and I felt something inside me which seemed to say I had a sure win. When Vixen came out of the stables she seemed to look out of the side of her squinny eye in a vicious, nasty, spiteful way—something like this. [*Business*]

NAT. Don't go on like that, Bob, or you will be struck with a squint.

JERRY. Well, if ever I saw a mare look like that, I should think there was sommat up.

BOB. And so there was sommat up. Vixen had made up her mind that Blue Bell shouldn't win.

JERRY. 'Ow did she prevent it?

BOB. That's what I'm coming to. The starting bell was rang, and off we went.

NAT. Where was you, Bob?

BOB. Mounted on Blue Bell, to be sure.

NAT. Oh! I thought you said you fell off.

BOB. Now that just shows what attention you were paying to my story.

NAT. But I've heard it before.

BOB. Well, you've got to hear it again. Off we went. Blue Bell took the lead and kept it till the end of the race. Vixen kept coming slowly but surely on, till she got alongside Blue Bell, and there she stuck. Tommy Comfit was so close to me that I could smell his breath; I remember it distinctly, for he had been eating onions at the time.

NAT. P'raps he wasn't so close to you as you thought; the flavor of onions may be carried a long way.

BOB. I dug my spurs in Blue Bell's flanks, and tried to lift her forward; Tommy did the same thing with Vixen. I lashed Blue Bell; Tommy quilted Vixen, and there we kept side by side—nothing to choose between us. The other horses all fell behind, but on we went till the winning post came in sight. Then came the last grand struggle. I lashed at Blue Bell, and Tommy laid on to Vixen. The shouts on the course roared like thunder in our ears. On we went, foot to foot, muscle to muscle, head to head, neck to neck, nose to nose; and then Vixen gave such a look as never came out of a horse's eyes before, and put out her tongue and won. Won by a tongue. [*Enter boy with jug of beer*]

NAT. Bob, my son, what's all this here? You told me as you wos on a regiment! Oh, this won't do! This must all come off! D'ye drink beer?

Bob. A drop or so.

Nat. You look it. And you eat butter; I see it in yer. And cheese! What d'ye expect to come to with a constitootion and a career like wot you have?

Bob. I don't know what to do with myself.

Nat. Tomorrow, lad, you'll breakfast on a pint and a half of warm water, and you'll put that in it. [*Gives him packet*] Hepsom salts! So called 'cause they prepares the body for training. Then you'll put yourself on dry toast, stale bread, and arf a pint o' tea a day, no milk in it, mind ye. Ye mustn't look at sugar, and if you dream of beer at night, take another dose of salts in the morning.

Bob. Very good, sir.

Nat. Fifty years ago, they knew how to breed jockeys, but, love ye, I'd split a pen, and make more of a jockey than half the boys that gets the crack mounts now. And Nat Goslin', though I say it, was the pink of the Pig Skin in those days. You heard how I took the Chester Cup in 'fifty-nine? Ah! I'll tell you about that adwenter.

Song. [*With chorus of boys*]

"THE OLD JOCKEY'S LAMENT"

In 'forty-four I von the Hoaks, and then they put me up
To ride Sir Tatten's little mare as took the Chester Cup.
But, oh, my! oh, cry! it vos just then d'ye see,
The pootyest gal in Doncaster, she fell in love with me.

[*Spoken*] She vos a prize gal, sech a chest, deep and full forard, and wel let down.

She said she would be mine ven I was growed a little bigger,
She didn't know I mustn't put no meat upon my figger.
Oh, my! oh, cry! vat is a chap to do,
Ven he's in love and got to ride vell under eight stun two.

[*Chorus of "Oh, my!, etc."*]

I vos in form to go to scale, but, Lord, so small a mite
I never shall forget the day when I was coortin' she.
She undertook vith all her veight to sit upon my knee.

[*Spoken*] Fourteen stun six, I thought the roof had fell in.

I've heard that girls in general, vos made of hoop and bustle.
This gal of mine, her crinoline vos made of bone and muscle.
Oh, my! oh, cry!, etc.

[*Chorus of "Oh, my!, etc."*]

My little dear, ses she to me, I'd be afraid to take ye,
For if I'd give ye half a squeeze, it's two to one I'd break ye.
Next week as I was walking my five-miler on the downs,
I met her walking with a six-foot sergeant of Dragoons.

[*Spoken*] He'd got his arm 'round her vaist. "My lad," ses he,
"Take my advice. Next time you want to marry,
Jest handicap the gals, and see what weight you're fit to carry."
Oh, my! oh, cry!, etc.
[*Chorus of "Oh, my!, etc." After which the boys start into a jockey hornpipe,
general dance, solos: Nat, Bob, and Ned*]

I RIDE TO WIN
(Gentleman's Version)

The Queen of my heart is Rosie my own,
A trainer's fair daughter is she,
Her dad had to win a certain great race
Or ruined for life he would be.
He gave me the mount; that evening I met
My dear little Rosie, who cried,
'If you win the race, your wife I will be."
I kissed her and boldly replied,

[*Chorus*] Rosie, Rosie, to win I ride,
Rosie, Rosie, then you're my bride;
The mare's all right, and I'll make her spin,
For love and life, for wealth and fame, I ride to win.

The race day arrived, and there on the course,
A bookie crept up to my side,
And whispered, "A thousand if you will lose."
"No, never, you villain," I cried.
I saw the old man, his face full of care,

With Rosie close by all the while,
And then at the post, all eager to start,
I shouted to her with a smile. [*Chorus*]

The flag quickly fell; the lot got away,
But I kept the bonnie mare back;
Till swift as a dart, she worked through the crowd,
Got foremost of all on the track.
I touched her but once with whip and with spur,
Bent forward and gave her her head;
We shot past the judge—hurrah! we had won.
My cap proudly waving, I said. [*Chorus. After song and dance, Nat exclaims*]

NAT.   Ah, here comes Master Tom Meredith with Flying Scud from exercise. [*Enter Tom leading horse*]

TOM.   Soho! my beauty. There, that'll do! He is a shaving too heavy in the shoulder, Bob. Tomorrow morning at eight, you will give him a gentle pipe opener in his breast cloth.

BOB.   Yes, sir.

TOM.   Put him in his box. [*Business putting horse off*]

NAT.   Well, Tom, I don't know what you think, but I consider the horse in first-rate form.

TOM.   He's a picture. He looks as if he knew his own secret and revelled in it. Bob, I hope you never quit him.

BOB.   Quit him? I sleeps in his manger; me and the cat.

NAT.   Has any of the gentlemen down from the Hall been to look at him?

BOB.   They all come, and chucked an eye over him. One said he vos too slack; t'other said he'd got 'ocks like a cow, and axed me what I wallied him at, so much a pound.

NAT.   I'm agoin' to make your fortin, lad, for you're gettin' overweight for your business, and should lay by a trifle, for nobody knows the day when fat will come on him, and put him into private life.

BOB.   Please, sir, I've two pun ten saved up agin such an ewent.

NAT.   Then I'll put every shilling of it on the Scud for you, Bob. Now be off and take a constitutional four-miler, and get down some of that hextra.

BOB.   [*Downcast*].   I'm afraid it's bred in me, sir.

NAT.   No, Bob, 'tain't bread, it's beer. [*Exit Bob*] Now, Tom, you're going to meet these turfited, and don't be afeared.

TOM.   But how shall I begin?

NAT. Leave that to me. I'll cut out the running for you. It ain't the wally of the money only, but, oh, to see them four legs on the gridiron, and to see 'em getting it hot. Well, it will be a sight improvin' to youth, and gratifyin' to declining years. [*Enter Woodbie L.D. in F.*]

WOOD. Here I shall be alone. I cannot see those fellows with red and swollen eyes. [*Sees Nat and Tom*] Deuce take it. [*Turns away*]

TOM. That's one of them. [*Rain and thunder*]

NAT. [*Aside*] No, no.

WOOD. It's beginning to rain. [*Looks out*]

NAT. He's a gentleman all over; his money wouldn't have no flavor in it. Foller me; I'll point the covey. Pardon, sir. [*Exit passing Woodbie and followed by Tom L.D.*]

WOOD. What a fool I am. I will go back to Naseby and try to get over this feeling. [*Opens and reads letter*] "My darling boy: Let me entreat you to return to me, if only for a week. I hear you are wasting your youth and health sadly; and worse than all, you have formed an attachment for a worthless and designing woman, by whose arts you are retained amidst a bad set of men. I do not regret the money you have lost to these scheming persons, but I do regret that your affection should be shared between a heartless adventuress, and your attached mother, Cecillia Woodbie." This "designing adventuress" refused me; refused to be a countess because she could not love me. Hark, someone is coming here. [*Looks out*] 'Tis Goodge, and a lady. They are seeking shelter from the rain. I am not fit to be seen. [*Wipes his eyes*] I'll wait in the loft above until they are gone. [*Goes up ladder R. into loft. Enter Goodge D.F.*]

GOODGE. [*L.*] It is only a shower; this place will afford you shelter. [*Enter Katey D.F.*]

KATEY. [*R.*] I do not mind a ducking.

GOODGE. Nor I; provided I can choose my duck.

KATEY. I beg you to leave trifling, and consider my question. If you turn young Meredith out of the farm, there is not a tongue in the county that will not cry shame on you.

GOODGE. I care more for one word from your lips, than for what all the tongues in the kingdom can say.

KATEY. Then you will grant me a favor?

GOODGE. Will you grant me that word?

KATEY. You are jesting.

GOODGE. No, for I love you, and I am ready to make any sacrifice for your sake.

KATEY. I cannot listen to you. Let me go. [*Crosses R.*]

GOODGE. You must; you shall. You knew that I loved you, and you came here to avail yourself of that passion to obtain a favor from me, to bestow it on my rival, young Meredith.

KATEY. I came to plead to your good nature.

GOODGE. You cannot ask me to mend his fortune. [*Locks door L.*] Let me rather offer you a share in mine.

KATEY. Stand from before that door, if you please.

GOODGE. I cannot part with you. I love you. Well, there, I offer you my hand.

KATEY. Your case must indeed be desperate. [*Tom knocks at door D.F.*]

GOODGE. Nay, you shall not go. [*The door R. is tried*]

KATEY. Thank heaven, there is someone!

GOODGE. From the first hour I saw you, I marked you as mine, and mine you shall be.

KATEY. If you are a gentleman, sir, you will cease this importunity. [*Knocking at door*] Why do they not come in?

GOODGE. Because I have bolted the door.

KATEY. Bolted the door?

GOODGE. Hush! You must wait now till they have gone away.

KATEY. Oh, why did I come here?

TOM. [*Outside*] Hallo, Jack! Stephen! Who has locked the door?

KATEY. It is Tom's voice. Oh, sir, what can I say? How can I explain such a position?

GOODGE. You cannot, but you can pass out this way. Quick! [*Opens the R.H. door. She enters the stable of the Flying Scud. He locks her in, and then opens the R.F. door. Enter Tom, Chousir, Mulligan and Mo Davis R.*] Well, gentlemen, what do you want?

TOM. [*C.*] I beg your pardon, I did not know you were here.

MO. [*R.*] Ve have been accommodating this young gentleman vith the hods on the hanimal hinside there.

MULL. The odds to fifty pounds, Mr. Meredith.

TOM. I'll take them again.

MO. Done.

TOM. And again to you, sir.

GOODGE. [*R.*] I am sorry you should have backed Flying Scud, for it is my intention to withdraw him.

TOM. Withdraw him? Scratch Flying Scud?

GOODGE. I don't intend to run the horse, and therefore have no further need of your services. I'll trouble you for the key of these stables.

TOM. But, sir, the horse was engaged by your late uncle.

GOODGE. So were you. I discharge you both. Fetch me the keys. I'll show you who is master here.

MO. So, if you have dem monnies runnin' about doin' nothing, you may fetch dem as vell, and square up at once.

TOM. [*Aside*] If the Scud is scratched, I am ruined, and so is Nat. [*Exit L.*]

GOODGE. I must get rid of these fellows and release the girl. What a state she must be in! [*Enter two bailiffs L.1E.*]

1ST B. Captain Goodge?

GOODGE. Yes.

1ST B. We want you, if you please, sir, at the suit of Joel Lawrence.

MO. Vot is it? Why these vagobonds is hofficers.

MULL. The devil they are! [*Exit door L.*]

GOODGE. I am arrested.

MO. Vell! Dis is truly ridiculous. Vere is Lord Woodbie? He will go security. [*Enter Jerry door L.*]

JERRY. Mr. Quail, sir, sent me to say that he is waiting in the library to read the late Squire's will. [*Exit*]

MO. Vere is Woodbie? Dis vill never do; ve must take you out between us.

GOODGE. No, I'll attend the reading in custody. In half an hour I shall have my uncle's banking account at my mercy.

MO. No, Goodge, old fellow, let me and Woodbie pay this, just to show you ain't without friends as is friends. He von't let me put the young lord in. Ain't it selfish? [*Exit D.F. A pause. Katey knocks at door*]

KATEY. [*Inside*] Sir! Sir, are you there? For Heaven's sake, unlock the door. [*Enter Tom with keys R.D.*]

TOM. Here are the keys. Ho! nobody here? I suppose they are gone back to the house. [*Katey knocks*] What's that? [*She knocks again*] There is someone in there. [*He tries the door*] 'Tis locked. Hush! I hear sobs. It is a young woman. Ho! I understand why all the doors were locked; the captain had a girl with him, and we surprised their billing and cooing.

KATEY. [*Inside*] Sir, sir, Captain Goodge, do unlock the door.

TOM. That voice! It is—it is hers.

KATEY. They are all gone now, and I can get away unperceived.

TOM. 'Tis she! 'Tis Katey! She was concealed here. [*He buries his face in his hands*] She said she had an influence over him. I see what sort it was; and I was fool enough to think she loved me. [*Enter Nat D.E.R.*]

NAT. Tom, my lad, they are waiting for us in the library.

TOM. [*Aside*] If he knew!

NAT. You are as white as if you were all in a lather. What's up?

TOM. Come away, Nat, come away. We have no business here.

NAT. Why, what's the matter?

TOM. Don't speak to me; my heart is breaking. [*Hurries him away*]

CLOSE IN

SCENE 4: *Front exterior on the road to the Hall. Enter Bob L.1E.*

BOB. Well, they're agoing to read the old Squire's will up at the Hall, and I don't suppose there's much chance of him leaving me anything. People do say as how everything is a going to this Mister Grindley Goodge. He's a cove as I never did like; a sort of a domineering, overreaching, bullying, regular bad un. He's a regular hot un. His mother must have weaned him on pepper and mustard. Well, if he's going to be boss, it'll be the chuck out of all of us. If so, I think as how I shall get married and settle down. The awkward part of it is in making a selection of the proper party. My father used to say there was no depending on a woman. Oh, woman, woman, woman, woman! But there, I was allus susceptible of female loveliness.

> "If to their share some trifling errors fall
> Look in their faces, and you'll forget 'em all."
> —*Shakespeare*

There's one girl as would jump at me, the parlor maid at the Cat and Saucepan. True, she's got a glass eye, and a bit of a limp—something like this— but that's rather an advantage, for if I wanted to get out of her way, she couldn't very well run after me. And as for her glass eye, if ever I did anything wrong, and didn't want her to see me, I could get on the blind side of her. [*Exit. Enter Lady Woodbie with letter*]

LADY W. This letter which I have received puts it beyond all doubt that Cecil has formed an unfortunate attachment for a reckless adventuress, who is connected with a notorious gang of unprincipled scoundrels. Whatever happens, and at whatever cost, the affair must be broken off at once. [*Enter Mulligan and Mo Davis*]

MO. I tell ye, it's true. He's arrested and taken down to Nobbley Hall to hear the will read. Oh! Jumping Moses! If it's true what the lawyer hinted at, we shan't get enough to buy a return ticket to London.

MULL. Well, don't look at the worst side of things; let's get down to Nobbley Hall at once.

LADY W. I beg your pardon, gentlemen, did you say Nobbley Hall?

Mo. Yes, mum, ve vos just a-going there to hear the vill of the old Squire read.

LADY W. I am a stranger here, and have missed the road on which I was directed; can you point out the way to Nobbley Hall to me?

Mo. Allow me! Just over there, and turn to the right; then you'll come to a cross on the road, go over by the left, and take the second turning on the right, and there you are.

LADY W. Thanks. [*Exit L.*]

Mo. Who is the old party? Quite an aristocratic old geezer.

MULL. Why, don't you remember her?

Mo. Vell, I seem to have a kind of a glimmering kind of an indistinct notion as I've seen her somewhere afore, and yet I can't be quite certain where.

MULL. Well, I've seen her somewhere, I'm certain.

Mo. Oh, sender me! I remember now! Don't you remember Lord Woodbie a showin' us some portraits the other night, and among them was one of his mother?

MULL. His mother?

Mo. Yes, his mother! Now what's she down here about?

MULL. Why, can't you see? It's plain enough to me; she's got scent of what we're up to, and is going to queer our pitch with the young Lord Woodbie.

Mo. Oh, s'help me! It's like taking the bread out of honest people's mouths! We're in a hole! we're in a hole! What a blooming schermozzle. [*Enter Jerry R.*]

JERRY. Beg pardon, sir, but if you want to hear the will read, you had better come at once, as the lawyer said he's going to start sharp to time.

MULL. Well, come along, we might as well know the best or the worst.

Mo. Jumping Moses! There'll be no best about it, but all the worst.

MULL. Perhaps the old man may have revoked before he died; but in any case, whether we've lost in pot over Grindley Goodge or not, we must keep a tight hand over Lord Woodbie.

Mo. Tight hand; tight hand! These frisky young fools have got a nasty way of kicking over the traces and deserting their old friends. It's an old saying, but a true one, "Bring up a child in the way he should go, and when he's old, he'll do what he likes." [*Exeunt R.1E. Enter Lady Woodbie and Cecil L.1E.*]

LADY W. How strange that I should meet you, Cecil.

Wood. Yes, dear mother, I was on my way to Nobbley Hall, as I had been invited to attend the reading of the will, but changed my mind as I could have no interest in it, and preferred to take a meditative walk in the fields.

Lady W. Now, Cecil, look me straight in the face.

Wood. [*Aside*] Oh, Lord! What's coming?

Lady W. I believe you to be still the dear, loving-hearted boy that I have doted on from childhood, and incapable of a deceitful action. Believe me, that anything I have to say is for your own good. Now answer, is there any truth in that letter?

Wood. [*Hurriedly reading it*] Who could have written it? Yes, yes, dear mother, it is true. I do love her, love her devotedly.

Lady W. I was afraid you would say so. 'Tis a mad infatuation! You must learn to forget her.

Wood. Impossible! I can never forget, or cease to think of her. Believe me, mother, she's an angel.

Lady W. Yes, they're all angels before marriage, and I've often heard it said that's the reason husbands often wish their wives in Heaven soon afterwards.

Wood. If you only knew her, you wouldn't speak like that.

Lady W. Come now, Cecil, you are getting quite a man, but you don't know your own mind. You must give her up. Remember, it's only a couple of years since you thought you were in love with Sir Francis Reynold's niece.

Wood. But that was only a boyish fancy; I was not old enough to know my mind.

Lady W. And you are not old enough now to decide so serious a question. You must give up all thought of such a union. I am a woman of the world enough to tell you that more than half of the misery and unhappiness in this world is caused through ill-assorted marriages.

Wood. Mother, you are mistaken in your estimate of Julia. She is different from other women, different from any other woman I have ever met. But as I loved you in my childhood's happy days, so I love you now, and I promise you, my darling mother, that I will do nothing without your consent to my marriage with Julia. I will give her up, even if it should break my heart to do so.

Lady W. Spoken like my own true-hearted boy, Cecil. Cecil, you are still more than all the world to me, and, believe me, you shall never regret listening to the warning words prompted by a mother's love. [*Exeunt L.1E.*]

SCENE 5: *The library. Full stage. Door L. Window R. Quail at table R.C. arranging papers. Mulligan, Goodge, Mo Davis, and tenants discovered. Two policemen near door L. Enter Tom and Nat.*

QUAIL. [*C.*] Take a seat, Mr. Meredith.

GOODGE. [*L.*] Stop, sir; allow me to do the honors of my own house, if you please. [*To Tom*] You can stand there, my man. [*Gives chair to one of the tenants*]

NAT. [*L.C.*] No offense, sir. I say, Tom, we are the only upright men in the crowd.

QUAIL. [*Opens the will*] The will, gentlemen, I see is short and holograph.

Mo. Vat's that?

NAT. It's short for sweet, I hope.

Mo. But what does "holograph" mean?

QUAIL. Why everyone knows it means written entirely by one's own hand.

Mo. Ah! Some of my friends get writing other people's.

QUAIL. [*Reads*] "To Katherine Rideout, granddaughter of Nathaniel Gosling, I leave two hundred pounds in affectionate remembrance of the bunches of flowers she used to leave me."

NAT. Bless his heart, he didn't forget my dear Katey. Two hundred pounds in affectionate remembrance, Lord love him.

QUAIL. "To Dr. Dryden, who nearly caused my death by giving me enough physic to kill a whole stable of horses, I leave the—"

NAT. How much? The doctor is not here; I wonder what he'll think of his luck? Shall I go and fetch him?

QUAIL. Wait a minute. "I leave the empty pill-boxes and physic bottles, hoping they may never be refilled."

NAT. I shan't go and tell him; one of the others can go and let him know of his good luck.

QUAIL. "To Jeremiah Cobbler—"

NAT. Hallo, Jerry, it's your turn now.

QUAIL. "The sum of twenty-five pounds in consideration of his general good behavior."

JERRY. Twenty-five pounds? Then I'm going to have a holiday. Twenty-five pounds! I didn't expect twenty-five pence.

QUAIL. "To the proposed school for children of old jockeys who have never had a black mark against them, I leave the sum of five hundred pounds."

NAT. He couldn't have left it for a better purpose.

QUAIL. "To the hospital at Doncaster, I leave the sum of three hundred pounds."

NAT. Hear! Hear! Good again!

GOODGE. [*Aside*] Confound his generosity! All that will come out of what should be mine.

MULL. Cheer up, Goodge, those small legacies are merely flea-bites; merely flea-bites.

NAT. Order, gents, please! Order!

MULL. Yes; let's have a scotch and soda.

QUAIL. [*Sternly*] Eh?

MO. Jumping Moses! I forgot where I was.

QUAIL. "To the members of the Jockey Club, I leave fifty pounds to be spent in a good dinner to be eaten within twelve months from the time I go up aloft."

GOODGE. Or below; a mere matter of opinion.

MO. Above or below, I don't suppose it matters much. He's got friends in both places.

QUAIL. Silence, gentlemen!

MO. Yes, let's have a bit of silence, gentlemen, I am surprised at yer.

QUAIL. "To Robert Buckskin I leave the sum of twenty-five pounds, with a strong recommendation to spend it in Anti-Fat, as I believe he is naturally stout, and inclined to make flesh, and no amount of training will keep him a reasonable size."

NAT. Well, Bob, you and Jerry share and share alike.

BOB. I'm sure I didn't expect it any more than Jerry did. Twenty-five pounds! What'll I do with it?

MO. I'll bet you 250 to 25 that Kiddle-a-wink doesn't win the Esher Plate.

BOB. Right you are; book it a bet.

NAT. I'll stand in half with you.

BOB. Right you are.

QUAIL. Really, gentlemen, this is most unseemly. Silence! "To my legal advisers, Messrs. Quail and Fitter, I leave the sum of one hundred pounds each, and hereby appoint them trustees of this my last will and testament."

NAT. That's his will sure enough, but I don't see any testament.

BOB. P'raps it's one of them books on the table?

GOODGE. Proceed, sir, get on with the reading of the will.

NAT. I haven't heard your name yet, Tom. For your father's sake I should have thought he would have left you a few hundreds.

Tom. I respect his memory just the same, whether he has left me a thousand farthings or a thousand pounds.

Goodge. A thousand farthings is more like the figure than anything else.

Nat. Well, I'm not so sure about that.

Quail. No more am I. Listen to this, gentlemen: "Subject to the payment of all the before-mentioned legacies, I give and bequeath everything of which I die possessed to Thomas Meredith, the son of my old master. I wish to restore the property I made out of his father, and therefore I give and bequeath to him my estate at Nobbley Hall, together with all my property of every kind therein and thereon, on the following conditions: that whereas my bay colt, Flying Scud, by Hurricane, out of Sunshine, is entered at Newmarket and Epsom, the same Thomas Meredith shall run the horse on his fair merits for these races, and shall fulfil all the engagements previously made for the said Flying Scud."

Goodge. Then what is left to me?

Quail. Nothing. [*Stop music*] Your name is not mentioned in the document.

Mull. He hasn't even cut you off with a shilling.

Quail. Mr. Meredith, I congratulate you, sir.

Mo. Vell, you might knock me down with a fedder.

Nat. Ooraw! Ooraw! Three cheers, lads, for Thomas Meredith, the Colonel's son, the heir to Nobbley Hall.

All. Hurra! Hurra! Hurra!

Nat. What's the matter, Tom? The lad's stunned; he's knocked silly with his good fortune. Oh, lud! Where's my Katey? That's who he wants; my Katey, gents, that will be the lady of the manor, after all.

Tom. No, Nat. Katey and I can never be anything to each other now.

Nat. What d'ye mean? Oh, I see; you are rich. It's all off between ye; the girl is scratched; she won't suit your book no more.

Tom. [*Sternly*] Captain Goodge, I must beg you to hand me over the key of Flying Scud's stable.

Goodge. So that's where it bites him, is it? [*Goodge gives him the key after a pause*]

Tom. [*Handing it to Nat*] There, Nat, unlock Flying Scud's stable, and you will learn why your grand daughter can never be anything to me again. [*Nat is bewildered. Tom is surrounded by Mulligan, Chousir, Mo Davis and Quail, who congratulate him*]

Quail. I congratulate you, Mr. Meredith, you're a rich man now.

Tom. [*Losing self control*] Rich! I'd give every penny of my fortune if I could only think her the good and pure girl that won my heart's first love.

GOODGE. [*Aside L.*]   Jealous, eh! Then there may be a chance for me yet. [*Aloud to Tom*] Cheer up, Mr. Meredith, don't think so badly of her, perhaps she's no worse than many another girl.

TOM.   Don't you dare to speak of her. Quit the house at once!

GOODGE. [*Furiously*]   Quit the house?

TOM.   Yes, quit the house and never darken the threshold of it's doors again. Remember, *I* am now the master here.

TABLEAU

ACT II.

SCENE 1: *The club card room. Mulligan and Mo Davis discovered.*

MULL.   Here, Mo, aisy wid that champagne; pass a taist of it this way. [*Business. Enter Goodge C. from L.*] Here's Goodge! Well, Captain, wot's the state of the funds?

GOODGE. [*L.C., drinks*]   Well, gentlemen, we have got tied up in an infernal tangle. Money has become tight with us for some time. The bills we have forged and paid into the bank in Lord Cecil Woodbie's name, become due in two days after the Derby. I think our horse, Voltigeur, is sure to pull off, and if so, we are safe.

MO.   Vell, I never feel safe till we're out of danger.

GOODGE.   If you could only get Julia to extract a promise of marriage from Woodbie, we should be all right in any case, because his lordship would scarcely dare to prosecute us then for forging his name.

MULL.   I don't like the whole business, and I'm afraid Julia may kick over the traces.

MO.   Quite right. You can never rely on a woman, they're as bad as horses.

GOODGE.   Tom Meredith is coming here tonight, and has promised me my revenge for the large sum I lost to him the night before last. I don't propose to begin playing cards with him till he gets half drunk, and then I fancy I shall be able to turn him inside out.

MO.   Jumping Moses! he always seems to be inclined to turn us inside out.

GOODGE.   Curse him, I'll be even with him yet. He's never forgiven me that affair with his sweetheart, Katey Rideout.

MO.   And he's not likely to, either.

GOODGE.   Well, it's a sharp game between us, and we shall see who will win. He's flush of money lately, and if I only knew how to get a thousand or two cash tonight, I believe I could skin him out.

MULL. All the money we've got is out on the race, and I don't know which way to turn for more. If Voltigeur wins the Derby, we're all made men.

Mo. And if he loses, we shall have to make off somewhere else. All my bets are to be paid the day after the race, and if it goes against us, the day will be very useful to give me time to start off somewhere else, and set up business on the continent.

GOODGE. I must get a couple of thousand ready to meet Tom Meredith at cards tonight. You, Moses, can look over his hand, give me the tip what cards he holds, and losing is an impossibility.

Mo. That's all very well, but where are we to get the ready? I'm stoney broke.

MULL. Then what's to be done?

GOODGE. Something must be done; I cannot sit with Meredith tonight until this money is forthcoming. Have we no resource? Come, Mo, can't you make a raise?

Mo. Two thousand pounds! You might as well ask me for the crown of England.

GOODGE. That I shall win ten times this amount is sure.

MULL. It's a moral certainty. If any respectable married man could see you slip them cards, he'd advance the amount at once. Have you no plan yourself? [*To Goodge*]

GOODGE. I see only one hope now, Mulligan. You must invent some tale about Julia and tell it to Lord Woodbie, who has returned to London. [*They all start up*]

Mo. The bank is going to resume payment.

GOODGE. I met him in Rotten Row. He has just arrived from Vienna. The name of Julia brings the blood to his cheek; he is more in love with her than ever.

MULL. I know it. Ever since he has been abroad, he has written to her every week. She would not answer his letters, but she would sit up at night crying over them, and console herself by scrawling replies. Then she tore them up after relieving her feelings.

Mo. Just like me ven I was stone broke. I used to draw checks on the Bank of Elegance, and tear 'em up.

MULL. One day last week I found one of those letters on her desk, and, be jabers, sir, I posted it.

GOODGE. He has told me that he was coming to this club tonight. That letter has recalled him, Mulligan, you have saved us. [*Crosses to L.*]

Mo. He deserves the Victoria Cross.

MULL. Hush, here is Julia. [*Mo crosses behind table to C. Enter Julia C. from L.*]

JULIA. Uncle, I must say one word to you. Your pardon, gentlemen. [*Bows to Goodge*]

GOODGE. [*L.C.*] We were just going into the smoke room. [*Bows*] Good evening, Mull. Come, Mo. [*Crosses up C.*]

Mo. [*Aside*] I say, Goodge, she looks hagitated, don't she; out of sorts; her eyes is all staring, her features looks all ruffled up the wrong way.

GOODGE. Hush! Good evening, Miss Latimer. [*Exit C. and L.*]

MULL. Wait for me, Mo.

Mo. I'll smoke a cigar with you, just to show there's no narstymosity. [*Exit C.*]

JULIA. Lord Woodbie is in London, I have just seen him. He is following me; he did not know I saw him. I dare not trust myself to speak to him again. He must learn to forget me.

MULL. [*R.C.*] What has brought him back, I wonder?

JULIA. Uncle, I implore, do not ask me to receive him. Tell him I cannot, will not speak to him again. Say that my affections are engaged elsewhere. Hark! I hear his footsteps. [*Crossing R.*]

MULL. How do you know that?

JULIA. He followed me here from the park. [*Exit R. door. Enter Mo Davis from L.*]

Mo. He's come! [*Crossing down R.*] Lord Woodbie is here!

MULL. She won't see him. [*Enter Woodbie C. from L. Mulligan R.C.*] Ah, my lord, you are right welcome. [*Shakes hands. Aside to Mo*] Stick to me, I see a chance to get a rise for Goodge. [*Aloud*] Welcome, my lad, you've just got home in time for the Derby.

WOOD. [*L.C.*] You look rosier than ever, Mull. How do, Davis. I hope Miss Latimer is well?

MULL. Poor Julia! She is sadly changed, eh, Davis?

Mo. [*R.C.*] Ah, you might pass her off for somebody else.

MULL. I mane in spirit. [*Business. Kicks Mo*]

Mo. Vy did you not say so then? [*Kicks Mulligan*]

MULL. She lives a retired life, sees no one, especially since that unfortunate affair.

Mo. Ah, that was when she vos took worse. [*Aside*] Vot work is he hengergeneering now?

Wood. I trust that Julia—Miss Latimer has met with no—

Mull. It was a cousin, but he bore the name of Mulligan. That was nough!

Mo. She couldn't stand that. [*Aside*] Vere is he going to?

Mull. He was the manager of the Universal Bank; he was behind hand vith the accounts. Poor devil, it might happen to the best of us, but he was unlucky enough to get found out. He was in the hands of the police.

Mo. I didn't care so much for him, as I did for his young vife and fam- ly. [*Aside*] Vere the devil is he going to?

Mull. That's what touched Julia. The poor girl was distracted about it. She never told me a worrud, sir, of what she was going to do.

Mo. Not a syllable. [*Aside*] It's a hole; he's hexcavating a hole.

Mull. But she packed up every ornament she had; she took the rings off her fingers, the earrings out of her ears, even the ould diamond of the Mulli- gans that come down by female line from Mohelly Egan, the Prince of Gath-na-cush.

Mo. Every blessed Irish diamond in the family. [*Aside*] It's a hole.

Mull. And in the night she disappeared; pawned them, my lord, raised two thousand pounds; paid the dirty bank its claim; rescued the name of Mulligan from detection.

Mo. Two thousand pounds!

Wood. Noble girl! It was just like her.

Mo. Don't you see the blood of the Prince of Got-no-cash coming out strong in her?

Mull. She did not care for the loss of the jewels, not a bit; she never wore them.

Wood. Just what I was going to remark.

Mull. She enjoyed them in secret; she doted on the ould family associa- tions.

Mo. And besides, they wasn't set fashionable.

Wood. My dear Mulligan, I hope you will not be offended, but will you— will she allow me to restore these jewels? [*Takes out check book and goes up*]

Mull. Restore! What do you mean, my lord?

Wood. [*Writes at back*] Let me send at once to the place where they are deposited and release them. Nay, I will take no refusal.

Mull. She will never allow it.

Wood. Then do not mention my name in the matter. Here is a check for the money. [*Gives it*]

Mo. Beautiful! [*Crossing C. takes check*] I'll undertake the hopperation. [*Goes up C.*]

MULL. Give me your hand, Lord Woodbie; you have the heart of a lion.

Mo. [*Aside*] And the head of a goose. [*Exits C. and L.*]

Wood. Shall I not have the pleasure of seeing her this evening?

MULL. She's in the club. She came here with a message for me. I'll tell her that you are here; she will be astonished to hear it. [*Aside*] I'll have them together, and leave Master Cupid to do the rest. He's fairly caught. [*Exit C. and R.*]

Wood. Here is the dear little letter that brought me back. [*Reads*] "Dear, dear, dearest Cecil, I have been reading your dear letters, but they are sadly blotted with my tears. Ah, why are you not beside me to kiss them away? I have learned them all by heart. I sleep with them clasped to my heart; thus only can I rest. How I love you, Cecil, how I love you! Write no more to me, but come; I am weary of this resistance; come to your own Julia." When I read those burning whispers, I thought I had lost my senses, that I was dreaming. [*Enter Julia R.D. crosses to R.C.*] Ah, dearest Julia—

JULIA. Pardon me, my lord, I beg you not to address me in that manner.

Wood. Why are you so cold to me?

JULIA. Has not my uncle informed you that I am about to be married?

Wood. To be married?

JULIA. And as my feelings, my affections, are engaged elsewhere, I—I cannot listen to your expressions of attachment.

Wood. Am I dreaming? You are in love, and not, not with me?

JULIA. Ah, Lord Woodbie, why have you returned to inflict this needless pain on me and on yourself?

Wood. You ask me why I have come back? You who have learned my letters by heart?

JULIA. What do you mean?

Wood. Have you been trifling with me, or do you really sleep with them clasped to your breast? Is this the cry of your heart: "How I love you, Cecil, how I love you!", or is this a wicked forgery? [*Shows letter*]

JULIA. That letter! How came you by it?

Wood. It reached me in Vienna by post.

JULIA. [*Sinks in chair, head on table*] Betrayed, betrayed!

Wood. No, no, not betrayed, but confessed. Oh, Julia, how could you love me so, and rob me of so much happiness? Do not hide your eyes from me; you said you were weary of this existence.

JULIA. So I am! Be it for good or evil—I know—I know not how I have been betrayed. I have struggled honestly with my heart, but there are limits suffering, and I have reached them. [*Rises*] I love you, Cecil, I love you. Then I sent you from me—ah, may I never repent your return.

Wood. You never shall, Julia. We are both young maybe, but when a fellow is old enough to love as I do, he is as much a man as he ever will be. *Embrace. He leads off L.1E. Enter Bob and Nat*]

Nat. Bob, I want to see Mr. Meredith. [*Bob stamps L. and dances*] Hullo, Bob! What's a-swelling you out?

Bob. Please, sir, they've been at me, they have. Mr. Davis come an' hoffered me a tanner if I'd shut him in with Flying Scud in his box for ten minutes.

Nat. Kalkelation on Joovenile depravity! Well, Bob, you behaved like a honest boy, I hope.

Bob. Yes, sir, I took his tanner.

Nat. Eh!

Bob. And shut him in with the animal for ten minutes.

Nat. Wot!

Bob. Yes, sir, but I didn't mention that a policeman was there on dooty. Oh, sir, if you'd a seen Mo Davis' face arter he comed out.

Nat. He axed you to let him, and so you did. Good boy! Ah, them's the actions that when you come to my age o' life, you'll look upon with satisfaction to your innards. Go along and tell the lads at Leatherhead I shall be amongst them tonight at the Pigskin Club. And, Bob, how's your weight now?

Bob. Eight pounds over still, sir.

Nat. Put yourself in a double rug, and take a five-miler.

Bob. Oh, dear, I don't know where it comes from. Ain't it haggeravaitin'? I can't pass a brewery, but the very smell, I b'leeve, puts a hounce on me for hevery sniff. [*Exit up C.*]

Nat. That's a virtuous character in spite of his weight; but perfection can't be expected in this world. [*Loud laughter heard R.U.E.*]

Tom. [*Outside R.*] Wants to see me, eh? Well, here I am. [*Enter Tom, wildly laughing*]

Nat. Good evening, Master Tom.

Tom. Ah, good evening, Nat, how are you?

Nat. Pretty well, tank ye, sir, not so bad for an ould 'un. Sorry to say you're not looking so well. London air doesn't agree with you like the country. You don't look half so well as when you were in the training stable at Doncaster.

Tom. And I don't feel half so well. I daresay many envy me, but they little know what I think of myself. I was never intended for the so-called "fast life" in London. I'm getting pretty sick of it. Late hours and heavy drinking are enough to break the strongest constitution, and although I am regarded as the fortunate Tom Meredith, my money has no value for me. The smiles of lovely women make my heart ache. [*Down R.C.*] But what did you want to see me about, Nat, eh?

NAT. [*L.C.*] Well, sir, I've just come from Tattersall's. Our horse, Flying Scud, is steady at 5 to 4 on him. [*A little up L.C.*]

TOM. And you feel sure that he will win the Derby?

NAT. There ain't a hanimal in the list that the Scud couldn't give seven pounds to, and a licking—Voltigeur included. What did I tell you a year ago? Ain't he answered hevery particular?

TOM. You have doubled my fortune, Nat, and if I carry the Derby prize, I shall be a rich man. But I'd exchange place with my own stable boy if I could believe the story Katey told me.

NAT. I don't blame you for doubting it, and she don't blame you neither. It did look bad, and my poor girl don't see how she could get out of it.

TOM. Sometimes the conviction of her innocence comes over me, and then a hateful suspicion crawls back to my mind and drives me mad. [*Crossing L.*]

NAT. If Flying Scud could speak, he'd tell you what passed between her and Goodge, for he was the only human being present in the stable except theirselves. But speech is the only thing that can't be expected of him, bless his heart. Ah, if only horses could only speak, they'd have some strange stories to tell.

TOM. I don't mind confessing to you, Nat, that I love her still, most passionately.

NAT. D'ye think I don't know it? What takes you out to the Tottenham Club every night till arter daylight, gamblin'? What's druv you to drink, Tom? Why, your love for my gal. And I ses to her, "It's a heatin' into his constitution, and the only cure for him is just what he can't take, and your blessed self, my dear."

TOM. What is the use of a fortune that I can't share with her? Wine makes me forget her for a while, and when I gamble, it is with Goodge, for I'll ruin him, or he shall ruin me. [*Exit L.1E.*]

NAT. Goodge ruin you! Not while I'm on the green side of the turf he shan't. [*Exit L.1E. Enter Mo Davis with notes L.D., and Mulligan C. from R.*]

MO. I've got the check cashed; here's the spondoolicks. [*Enter Goodge C.*]

Goodge. Quick, Mo, have you got the flimsies? Here's Meredith coming alf drunk, mad for play, and ripe for plucking.

Mo. Here's the hoof. [*Business, Gag, one short, business*] Ain't he selfish? *Enter Tom, half tipsy, C., followed by Bob, waiter with brandy and water, Voodbie re-enter L.*]

Tom. Now, Goodge, I've come to give you your revenge. Bob, s'more randy. [*Waiter fills, Tom drinks, sits L. of table*] Five hundred on this ame. [*Cuts cards*]

Goodge. [*Deals*]   Five hundred, you say. [*Three cards each*]

Tom. [*Playing*]   Thousand, if you like. [*Goodge wins*]

Mo. [*Makes a sign to Goodge behind Tom's back*]   Oh, I'm backing Meredith, and Goodge winning all my money. [*Goodge cuts, Tom deals, lays again*]

Wood. [*L.C.*]   Is Goodge in luck? Then I'll back him for a hundred. *Puts notes on table*]

Tom. I cover it. [*Does so*] Goodge wins again! [*Mo, business*]

Goodge. [*Dealing again*]   Does the same bet stand? Five hundred again?

Tom. [*Playing*]   As I said just now, a thousand, if you like.

Wood. No, no, Meredith, you don't know what you're doing. It is not fair, Goodge, to let him go on.

Tom. [*Rising*]   What do you mean, my lord; do you 'sinuate that I can't play?

All. No, no, Meredith, sit down.

Goodge. A thousand it is.

Tom. If you can't afford the stake, who asked you to bet?

Wood. I never lay a stake on, sir, that I am not prepared to pay.

Tom. Then where is your stake? I don't see it. Where is it? [*Playing*]

Wood. There! [*Throws down notes. Goodge wins again*]

Tom. That is five hundred I owe you, my lord, there it is. [*Giving notes*]

Wood. Thanks, I—I—don't wish to take it. I am at liberty, I presume to consider the bet off?

Tom. No, sir, I allow no man to take such a liberty with me.

Wood. Then I decline the money because I have not won it.

Mo. Not won it!

Wood. No! I saw Mo Davis making signs behind Tom's back.

Mo. Me? Oh, jumping Moses, what a haccusation.

Mull. I hope you don't mean to insinuate, my lord, that there has been unfair play?

Wood. Yes, I do!

All. What!

Goodge. Are you mad, Woodbie?

Wood. I watched you, Captain Goodge, and I saw you signal the cards.

Goodge. You lie! [*Dashes cards in Woodbie's face, business; guests enter C. Glass crash, Mo business with Bob*]

Tom. Stick close to me, Lord Woodbie, I'll see you through. [*Tom, Bob, and Woodbie fight their way out C.*]

CLOSE IN

Scene 2: *Chamber in 1. Mulligan's lodgings. Enter Julia to begin, L.1E.*

Julia. My uncle and his companions have not yet returned from the club. What can detain them? Lord Woodbie begs me to go with him and see his mother at once, to add my entreaties to his to gain her consent to his marrying me. How can I ever expect to make her ladyship think that I should ever be worthy of him? Oh, Cecil, Cecil, why weren't you born without a name, and without a penny? Then I could show you how much I loved you. Ah, footsteps! My uncle returned, and Captain Goodge with him. The more I see of that man, the more I dislike him. They both look upset. What can have happened? I'll listen. [*Retires R. Enter Goodge and Mulligan L.1E.*]

Goodge. Now, Mulligan, what's to be done?

Mull. I am at my wit's end.

Goodge. Who could have foreseen such a result? We are ruined irretrievably. [*Knock L.*]

Mull. There's Mo Davis wid news of what happened after we left the club. Perhaps Woodbie will apologize. [*Enter Mo L.1E.*]

Goodge. Well?

Mo. Lord Woodbie repeats his haccusation. It was no use of me giving my word of honor; do all I could, nobody believed me.

Mull. [*R.*] Is the word of a boy like that to be taken against the protestations of three honorable gentlemen like us?

Goodge. Yes, when there is no doubt that he is a gentleman.

Mull. Do you mean to say that we are not?

Goodge. You're a fool!

Mull. Captain Goodge, I don't permit you to call me a fool! As the poet says, "The man that calls me a fool—"

Goodge. Tush, man! Tomorrow morning, the magistrate at Bow Street may call you a felon. Do you suppose that Meredith is going to pay one shilling of his losses?

Mo. Oh! Oh! Then how is all the paper I've given to be perwided for?

GOODGE. When this affair gets wind, all the creditors will come down on us like vultures.

MO. They are sure to. I shall be the first victim. Oh, vy didn't I stick to the cigar and cabbage leaf line? The swindle was small, but it was sure.

GOODGE. Where's Chousir?

MO. He's gone to enquire vot country there's no extradition treaty wid.

MULL. Do you mean to tell me, Captain Goodge, that you have placed me in the disgraceful position of being found out?

MO. Look at me; I shall be found out for passing those bills, but I'll swear I'm innocent party. Let us all be innocent, and leave Chousir in the hole.

MULL. That's an idea, and Chousir's only the son of a butcher, so he has no character to lose. Besides Julia can beg him off with Woodbie. We'll call the forgeries a slip of the pen. [Knock]

MO. There he is! I'll let him in. [Exit L.1E.]

GOODGE. I have no doubt you will, and let us all in if you could.

MULL. We must stand by one another, Goodge. This is a desperate business entirely. Is there no escape for us?

GOODGE. None that I can see. To obtain the money now is impossible; and Woodbie, after my insult to him, will be pitiless. [Crosses and looks off R. Enter Meredith L.1E.]

TOM. I beg your pardon, but as I entered, Mr. Davis left the house. He informed me that I should find Captain Goodge here. [Goodge turns and bows R.] I am commissioned by Lord Woodbie to deliver a message.

GOODGE. To what effect?

TOM. Are you prepared to avow the foul play practised by you and your confederates, and to tender him a full apology?

GOODGE. What if I decline?

TOM. In that case, I am directed to arrange a hostile meeting.

GOODGE. [Crossing] Ah! Will he fight? Will he fight?

TOM. You must feel that you cannot meet one who is little more than a boy.

GOODGE. Then why do you bring this message?

TOM. To ask you the favor he refused me; let me take his place. We have a long account to settle, Captain Goodge, and I am anxious to wipe off the score.

GOODGE. Oh, Katey Rideout's affair! You have taken a long time thinking it over; I thought you had forgotten all about that. Why didn't you settle up about her before?

TOM. Because I believed her guilty, but with my knowledge of your unscrupulous character has grown the conviction of her innocence. I did not believe that a man could behave as she accused you of doing, but you have taught me of what men such as you are capable. There is nothing too mean for you to attempt; you're a liar and a thief! a disgrace to manhood! And you ought to be expelled from every club in London, and warned off the turf.

MULL. You cannot stand that, Goodge.

GOODGE. [*To Mulligan*] One thing at a time, sir. [*To Tom*] When I have disposed of this young lord, I'll teach you what I'm capable of in another line, but I must give him a lesson before I attend to you. Here is my friend. [*Crosses R.*]

MULL. [*R.C.*] I think you might give Mr. Meredith the preference. Fight him first, and then settle with young Woodbie.

TOM. If he faces me first, the meeting with young Woodbie will never take place.

GOODGE. I know my own business best. Tonight, then, on the sands behind Calais Pier, at ten o'clock, after I have settled matters with you and your friend.

MULL. [*To Meredith*] Is that convaynient?

TOM. Perfectly.

MULL. [*To Goodge*] Pistols, I suppose? [*Goodge bows*]

TOM. Agreed! We shall be there.

MULL. At ten o'clock.

TOM. At ten o'clock. [*Bows and exits L.1E.*]

MULL. Good Heavens, Goodge, you don't mean to fight the boy. It will be infanticide.

GOODGE. I'll kill him, Mulligan. When he proposed this duel, I saw it at once, our only chance of escape. I am a dead shot, and Woodbie shall never return to dishonor the bills we have drawn in his name, and so expose us.

MULL. I never thought of that.

GOODGE. The frauds can never be traced to us without his evidence. As for Chousir, he will not betray us when he knows that he himself is out of danger. [*Crosses L.*]

MULL. I believe you are right.

GOODGE. I must practise for an hour or so, and get my hand in. I shall start for Dover by the early train. [*Exit L.1E.*]

MULL. [*Crossing L.*] I will meet you at the station. [*Enter Julia R.E.*]

JULIA. No you won't, uncle.

MULL. Julia!

JULIA. Goodge will kill him; he is a dead shot; and Woodbie will never return to prove your villainy and expose you.

MULL. Did you hear that? Then you know what hangs over me?

JULIA. I don't care what hangs over you; let the guilty suffer, not the innocent. I will go to Lord Woodbie and tell him all I have heard.

MULL. What, that Goodge is a dead shot, and that he may escape fighting this duel by accusing his adversary of felony? Do you know what such a spirit as his would do? He would pay the money, tear up the forged bill, and meet his man.

JULIA. And as you reckoned on his folly to bring him to ruin, you reckon on his honor to lead him to death; and I, I have brought him step by step to this.

MULL. What have you to do with this?

JULIA. [*Crossing L.*] You shall see.

MULL. [*Taking her wrists*] You are not going to betray me?

JULIA. I will not betray anyone, but, come what may, I will protect that poor boy from the consequences of his infatuation for me. [*Throws Mulligan off*] Go your way, I will go mine, and Heaven forgive you for what will be the result when we meet again. [*Exit L.1E.*]

MULL. What the devil is she going to do? [*Exit L.1E.*]

SCENE 3: *Hyde Park. In two. Enter Bob with black eye and letter.*

BOB. The Guvnor has given me this letter to be delivered to Lord Woodbie at once. Vot's in it, I wonder? Something seems to whisper to me there's summat up. I wos to be sure to give it into His Lordship's own hands, and wos to bring back an answer. [*Going R.*] After I've done it, I'm going to square up with Goodge's lad; I'm not going to have this black eye for nothing. [*Enter Julia L.1E.*]

JULIA. Stop, Boy! Lord Woodbie is going to fight a duel with Captain Goodge; your master is to be Lord Woodbie's second.

BOB. I ain't so sure about that.

JULIA. That letter is from your master to Lord Woodbie.

BOB. Well, yes, I was to be sure to give it to the young lord, and bring back an answer.

JULIA. I am going to Lord Woodbie's. Give me the letter. [*Bob hesitates*] Be assured that your master, Mr. Meredith, runs no risk from Captain Goodge. I know the gentleman's designs, and I am about to defeat them. [*Takes letter*]

BOB. She's on a lay! When she let Goodge's name out of her mouth, her eyes snapped like lucifers.

JULIA. [*Reads*] "Dear Lord Woodbie, I have seen Captain Goodge and his friend Colonel Mulligan. Our rendezvous is Calais Sands, behind the pier, at ten o'clock. T.M."

BOB. She has opened master's letter, and read it. Beg pardon, Missee, but this here won't do, you know.

JULIA. Hush! Be silent, and you will learn that I am your master's friend. [*Aside*] If this letter reached Cecil, no power on earth would prevent him keeping his appointment. It must not be delivered until it is too late for him to reach Calais this evening.

BOB. Hexcuse me, Miss, I'm very sorry for the young Lord Woodbie, but if he don't turn up when they've pitched the ropes, *my* master will have to go and pull his coat off. Now if this 'ere is a plant, and there's going to be any murder cropping out of the transaction, I'd as lief my master wasn't first come, first served.

JULIA. Your master shall be in no danger, I promise you, and Goodge shall find an antagonist who will inflict on him indelible disgrace. Go back and tell your master that Lord Woodbie will be there at Calais Pier tonight at ten o'clock.

BOB. Well, I believe, Miss, that you mean square, and I've no objection to serve his lordship, but I'm a-going with master this over the water business, and when I'm there, if I sees any sign of a cross, or my master getting in a hole, I'll split.

JULIA. Yes, you may do that. Farewell. [*Exit Bob*] Ah, Cecil, Cecil, how many times have I sworn to devote my life to you! Now he shall know how Julia keeps her word. [*Exit L.1E.; enter Katey and Nat R.*]

KATEY. Oh, Grandfather, Tom is in some great trouble; in the park there, he clenched his hand and bit his lip. I was watching him; I was watching him. [*Looking off*]

NAT. Of course you was; it's a lucky as heyes ain't got tooth, or you'd eat him.

KATEY. [*Looking R.*] I can see him still.

NAT. You are wuss than a cannibal; you live on that 'ere human bein'. Come, you'd best give him up.

KATEY. I can't! I can't! I love him more than ever.

NAT. Of course you do, now you can't get him.

KATEY. Oh, Grandfather, Grandfather! [*Hides her face on Nat's breast*]

NAT. Nay, I didn't mean to hurt ye. Don't cry. There. Why, to see thee married to that lad, I'd lay down in my own grave, and pull the turf over me. [*Katey sobs*] I would! There, deary, put up your tears; save 'em. Hush! yonder is Goodge.

KATEY. He has spoken to me already in the Row; I cannot escape from his pursuit. This conduct only confirms the scandal under which I am suffering.

NAT. And poor Tom is suffering as badly as you are.

KATEY. That's some comfort. What did he say of me?

NAT. "Sometimes," ses he, "my heart goes in for her, and then I feel as if I could take her in my arms again."

KATEY. Oh, why can't I pitch on one of those times.

NAT. "But arter that I gets skerry," ses he, "then I hates her, and I goes to the dogs."

KATEY. I'd go there too, with him, if he'd let me.

NAT. He is gamblin' away his fortune.

KATEY. So much the better. When he is poor he will come nearer to me.

NAT. He is making love to every girl he meets.

KATEY. I know it, but he has not settled down to one. Oh, dear, why can't he believe in me?

NAT. Ah, there now, if you had been a hoss, I could have given a warranty.

KATEY. If I could only make him believe me, I feel I could go down on my knees to him.

NAT. Ah! Hattitudes don't prove nothing.

KATEY. His heart must be as hard as iron, or my tears would have melted him.

NAT. Facts is waterproof, and on that 'ere occaision between you and Goodge, things didn't look sweet. Katey, when I heard on it, and then hopened that stable door, and saw you locked up there, well, it took all my faith in ye, and knowledge of your breed, to gie ye a clean bill o' health.

KATEY. There goes Goodge, the monster; oh, how I hate him. He has broken my life, ruined my happiness forever. [*She goes up a little L.*]

NAT. There she is, lamed for life, a confirmed case of nav'iclar in the heart. My poor gal, blisterin' won't do her no good. It is no use o' takin' such cases to the vet; she is nobbled, she is, scratched, and maybe will retire into private life in a paddock. [*Enter Bob L.1E.*] Hullo, Bob, what's up now?

BOB. Hullo, Nat. Haven't you heard? There's been a row.

NAT. Yes, you've got a notice in your peeper to that effect.

KATEY. Why, Bob, what have you been doing to your eye?

BOB. It wasn't me, Miss, it was Captain Goodge's lad. Him and me was at the club last night, waiting for our masters, and that's how we came to hear of it.

NAT. What?

Bob. Why, Goodge and his party set on my master last night, and sharped him at cards, but Lord Woodbie twigged and hexposed them, when up gets all four legs at master, and sets on him.

Katey. Oh, Tom!

Bob. "Come on," ses master to Goodge and Co., "I'll undertake to put you through the winding-up act," and before the spectators had time to take hodds, he set all four legs hexamining the carpet.

Nat. How do you know this?

Bob. I was there, and of course when me and Goodge's boy 'ad put up last night and littered down our horses, we had it out in our spare loose box; nine rounds comfortable and quiet, and Flying Scud a lookin' at us over the half door, amirin' that style of groomin'.

Katey. Was your master hurt?

Bob. Not he, Miss. When I accounted for wearing this cockade hon my heye, he larfed, tipped me a fiver to get it painted, a sov for Goodge's lad to square the doctor. Ah! I don't know why he ain't a royal dook, he have the heart of one. I suppose they'll settle the matter by what they call doolin', for I've got orders for the brougham to take master down to the Dover line, as it is there those ewents do come off, and I was carrying to Lord Woodbie a letter, but the young lady as the lord is sweet upon, took it. I shouldn't wonder but it is to ask him to hold the sponge.

Katey. What! My Tom going to fight a duel? They'll kill him! No, he shan't go! I'll cling to him; he may trample me under foot, but now I'll never leave him. Tom! Tom! [*Business with Nat. Exit L.1E.*]

Nat. You fat-headed bran mash, what did you tell her for? I've a good mind to put your other eye in mournin' for ye. [*Business, and exit Nat and Bob L.1E.*]

Scene 4: *Calais Sands. Enter Goodge, Moses and Mulligan R.U.E. or L.U.E.*

Mull. No sign of them yet. [*Looks around*]

Mo. Up to now he is invisible to the naked eye.

Goodge. They cannot have mistaken the place.

Mull. I'll look in this direction. [*Exit R.1E.*]

Mo. And I'll look in this. Jumping Moses, what's that?

Goodge. 'Tis your own shadow.

Mo. Oh, gracious goodness, to think I should ever live to be frightened by my own shadow. This is a dangerous business, Goodge. It puts my 'art in my mouth. [*Exit looking before him L.*]

GOODGE. After this affair, London will be too hot to hold me. I must disappear; after the Derby, I'll start for the gambling towns of Germany, and some new associates. [*Re-enter Mulligan R.1E. looks off R.*]

MULL. Here comes one of them at any rate. [*Re-enter Mo Davis*]

Mo. It isn't him; it isn't Lord Woodbie. [*Enter Tom and Bob with pistol case R.*]

TOM. I regret, gentlemen, that through some error, Lord Woodbie has failed to appear.

Mo. Then he will be posted as a coward through every club in London.

GOODGE. I presume he knew the hour and place?

TOM. I wrote to him, and he replied that he would meet me. [*To Bob*] You saw his lordship?

BOB. He said as how he'd attend to it.

Mo. A pretty way to attend to it by stopping away.

TOM. By some accident he has missed the departure of the boat.

BOB. [*Aside*] I'm the haccident.

MULL. On such an occaision he would take a special train.

Mo. Yes, he would have hordered a special train.

TOM. He may have done so, but he could not cross the Channel if he missed the steamer.

MULL. His own yacht lies at Dover; I saw it there.

Mo. And I saw it, too. I took particular notice of the crew, two men and a dog.

TOM. Well, gentlemen, I think it probable that he has been induced to decline this meeting. I confess I used every argument to make him do so.

GOODGE. On what ground, sir?

TOM. Firstly, because he is a foolish boy; and secondly, because he is not obliged to meet a blackleg, nor stand up to risk an honorable life before a professional assassin.

GOODGE. Professional assassin! How dare you apply such an expression to me!

TOM. Because it best expresses the man who would attempt to pay his debts by murdering his creditors.

GOODGE. Beware, Mr. Meredith, beware! I owe Lord Woodbie nothing.

TOM. You're a liar, and your friends there know it.

Mo. Jumping Moses! I know him to be a most honorable member of society. He wouldn't tell a lie on no account.

GOODGE. Why then do *you* wish to take his place?

TOM. Because you have stung the woman I love, and we believe in Yorkshire that the vermin rankles in the wound only as long as the vermin lives.

GOODGE. Your abuse shall not provoke me to meet you in his place. [*Julia on R.U.E.*] Nor does your bluster shield him from the brand of cowardice. [*Enter Julia dressed as Woodbie, comes down a little R.C.*]

TOM. Woodbie—

BOB. He has come to the post arter all.

MO. Wonders will never cease.

GOODGE. Come, gentlemen, we have lost enough time; measure the ground, Colonel.

MO. He vorks like a policeman, don't he? [*Bob crosses with pistol case to Goodge, Mulligan, passes from R.1E. to L.U.E. and places handkerchiefs*]

GOODGE. Your weapons are loaded, I presume?

TOM. I beg you, my lord, not to pursue this affair. This man is unworthy to meet you.

GOODGE. Lord Woodbie should have thought of that before he insulted me. I am here to meet his challenge; if he fails to meet me, I'll treat him as the boy you wish to make him out. I've brought my horsewhip.

JULIA. [*Imitating Woodbie's voice*] Proceed!

MULL. My man stands yonder; I have placed handkerchiefs at the distance. There is no choice of light, I think. Place your principal quickly, for look yonder, there is a movement on the pier, and we may be interrupted.

TOM. [*Having given pistol to Julia, places her L.U.E.*] I shall permit only one exchange of shots.

GOODGE. One will be enough. [*Takes place R.1E.*]

MULL. [*L.U.E.*] Is all ready? Will you give me the word?

TOM. No! [*Down 1E.*]

MULL. Then I will. On the word "three," gentlemen, you fire together.

MO. Hold hard; let me get out of the way. The bullet might go through him into me.

MULL. Now, gentlemen, are you ready? Now! One, two, three. [*Goodge fires*]

TOM. Woodbie has not fired. [*Runs up to Julia. Julia staggers to Tom's arms*]

BOB. He is falling!

GOODGE. He has it; he has it! [*Goes R.*]

MULL. Away wid you, quick. [*Exit Mulligan and Goodge R.1E., followed by Mo*]

TOM. Woodbie, speak! Where are you hurt? [*Enter Lord Woodbie L.*]

WOOD. [*Down R.C.*] Am I too late?

ALL. Woodbie! Who, then, is this? [*White Lime on*]

JULIA. [*Throws off hat*]   I am not hurt, Cecil, I—
ALL.   Julia!

QUICK ACT-DROP

ACT III.

SCENE 1: *Neat chamber in Nat Gosling's London lodgings. Julia discovered on sofa, Katey attending her. Nat with them. Table with physics, bottles, etc.*

KATEY.   Come, dear, just take this, and you'll be right in no time.

NAT.   It'll put you as right as a trivet.

JULIA.   Thanks, friends, thanks. I'm really not hurt, only this pain in my shoulder.

NAT.   The doctor said it was only a flesh wound.

KATEY.   Nothing serious! But, oh, how delightfully romantic, and all for the sake of the man you love. Oh, what wouldn't I give for a chance to be shot for Tom.

NAT.   For shame, Katey, for shame!

KATEY.   Grandfather, if it would do Tom any good, I'd have my arm shot off.

NAT.   What fond creatures these women are.

KATEY.   Perhaps he'd know that I loved him, then—and—and—

NAT.   And then p'raps he'd marry you.

KATEY.   Oh, Grandfather! [*Blushing*]

NAT.   And a nice thing it'd be to marry a one-armed wife. I wonder how the babbies 'ud get on when they wanted nursing.

KATEY.   Oh! Go along, do!

JULIA.   What has become of my uncle?

NAT.   After the duel, Goodge left before he discovered that it was you he had been firing at. You were brought over in the mail boat by Mr. Tom and Bob Buckskin, and brought here till it was decided what was to be done.

JULIA.   I hope that Mr. Meredith has done his best to hush the matter up; no good could come of its being made public.

KATEY.   Not a word has been said, or the newspapers might have made columns of it.

JULIA.   I wouldn't have it made known on any account. [*Bob knocks at door L.*]

BOB. [*Calls outside*]   Nat, are you at home?

NAT.   There's Bob Buckskin.

KATEY.   Come in, Bob. [*Opens door. Enter Bob*]

BOB. 'Um d'ye do, Miss. Hope you're better.

JULIA. Oh, it's nothing.

NAT. Calls a bullet in her shoulder nothing. Some of our bold militia would declare on for a pension for half as much.

BOB. She ain't got it there now, has she?

KATEY. No, no! The doctor extracted the bullet, and said that with perfect quiet, it was only a question of a few days before she'll be able to get about again.

JULIA. I'm so sorry I shan't be able to go to the Derby, I should so like to see it.

NAT. Yes, Flying Scud is going to win in a canter.

BOB. That's a moral; a dead certainty.

JULIA. I should like to send a message to my uncle that I'm comparatively unhurt.

NAT. Oh, he knows all about it; I sent him a message as soon as the doctor left. I knew your uncle very well, Miss, I saw him only yesterday on business, and have to see him again today about a horse.

JULIA. My uncle knew nothing of my taking Lord Woodbie's place, and had he done so, would have done everything possible to prevent it.

NAT. Well, he may be your uncle, Miss, but I'm afraid he ain't twenty-two carat.

KATEY. Hush, Grandfather! Hush!

BOB. Well, always speak of a man as you find him; and if he ain't a regular scorcher, I never met one.

KATEY. How rude of you, Bob.

JULIA. Believe me, friends, my uncle is not so bad as he appears to be. He has been led away by his companions, Captain Grindley Goodge and Mr. Davis.

NAT. Very likely, Miss, but you know the old adage, "Birds of a feather flock together."

BOB. Some of these days I'll let Mr. Jumping Moses have it, and if I get about him, he won't have many feathers left on him to flock with anybody.

NAT. Bob, if I have any more of such horrible sentiments, I'll have you bound down to keep the peace.

KATEY. [At window] Good gracious, there's a carriage drawn up to our door, and an old lady and a young gentleman have got out of it.

NAT. P'raps it's Mrs. Soursawkins, the greengrocery woman, calling with her son about a bottle of embrocation I promised for the boy's leg; he strained himself at football.

BOB. [At window] It ain't Mother Soursawkins, it's too much of a swell.

KATEY. Why I do believe it's young Lord Woodbie.

JULIA. [*Starting*] Lord Woodbie; Cecil here!

BOB. And the old lady is his mother, Lady Woodbie.

NAT. Quality visitors, by jingo! [*Loud knock and ring heard*]

JULIA. Can she be coming here to upbraid me?

NAT. Will you go to the door, Katey, or shall I?

KATEY. I'll go, Grandfather; you stay here. [*Exit L.*]

NAT. Now what can bring them here? [*Bob whispers to Nat*] Yes, I shouldn't be surprised a bit. [*Whispers to Bob*] D'ye think so? Well, that would be nuts to crack.

BOB. Well, you see if that ain't a very good guess at it.

NAT. I only hope that it may be so. [*Katey re-enters door*]

KATEY. Lady Woodbie and her son wish to see our visitor, Miss Julia.

NAT. All right, Katey, only remember the doctor's orders, she wasn't to be upset on no account. [*Enter Lady Woodbie, followed by Lord Woodbie D.L.*]

LADY W. You will excuse this unceremonious visit, I'm sure. [*To Nat*] Where is she?

NAT. [*Points to Julia*] Here she is, mum—leastways I suppose you're enquiring after Miss Julia?

LADY W. The generous girl who risked her life to save that of my son.

BOB. [*To Nat*] There, what did I tell you?

NAT. You're as good as a horicle.

LADY W. [*Goes up to sofa*] Miss Latimer, I have already wronged you; I did not know your truly noble disposition. I thought you a scheming woman, endeavoring to entrap my son's affections for the sake of his fortune. I humbly beg your pardon. Will you forgive me?

JULIA. Oh, Lady Woodbie, how can you ask me such a thing? I am afraid that for Cecil's—I beg pardon—Lord Woodbie's sake, you speak so to me.

WOOD. Dear Julia, my mother at last knows you for the dear good girl that you truly are, and it is by her own wish, and not by my solicitations, that she is here.

LADY W. I know all; I have heard everything. You knew of the projected duel, and for my son's sake, you kept the matter secret, and took his place on Calais Sands. You risked your life to save his mother from a lifelong misery. From my heart I thank you.

JULIA. I am grateful to you, my lady, for your kindness, which shall never be forgotten by me. All I hope is, that Lord Woodbie will not seek to meet Captain Goodge again.

LADY W. My son has now solemnly promised that he will not meet the man.

WOOD. Unless it be to tell him what I think of him—

LADY W. You must not be so impetuous, Cecil.

WOOD. All right, mother, I'll endeavor to bottle up my sentiments.

LADY W. And now, Miss Latimer, I have something of the greatest importance to say to you.

NAT. Shall we retire, mum?

BOB. Yes, shall we go outside on the mat?

LADY W. No, no, remain here, my good friends, for I should like you to hear what I am about to say. I have cruelly wronged this young lady by my suspicions of her, and I should like her and you to know that I am truly sorry for it.

JULIA. Do not again allude to it, my lady, I beg.

LADY W. My son, Cecil, knows what I am about to say. When he first spoke to me of marriage with you, I did all in my power to oppose it. Now I ask you to grace our family by becoming a member of it. I ask you to honor me by accepting my son's hand.

NAT. [*To Bob*] Well, hang me, if the old lady ain't been and popped the question. I wonder what sort of a Leap Year this comes in?

LADY W. Your answer, Julia?

JULIA. Oh, my lady, what answer can I make?

WOOD. Say that you will marry me by special license, and that you'll come with me to the Derby tomorrow and see Flying Scud win the blue ribbon of the turf.

JULIA. But the doctor?

NAT. Doctor "Cupid" is the best physician in the world.

SCENE 2: *Mulligan's rooms. Enter Mulligan and Mo Davis. Mulligan crosses back and forwards.*

MO. What's your caper?

MULL. Oh, man, the divil's luck, and the worst of it is on us.

MO. Vy, how's that?

MULL. Sure it wan't Woodbie at all we shot at Calais, but that poor girl of mine, who took his place.

MO. Vat! Julia dead!

MULL. No, praise be to Heaven, scarcely wounded. Goodge's bullet only scratched her arm, and she has hardly a mark. But, by the blood of the

Mulligans, it might have been worse. I have heard from Katey Rideout, that Julia is progressing favorably at Nat Gosling's lodgings.

Mo. Hush, here's Goodge. [*Enter Goodge L.1E*] Well, what's the state of the market?

Goodge. [*Throwing tissue*] There's the latest betting. How do you like it?

Mo. [*Reads tissue*] "5 to 4 on Flying Scud."

Mull. Oh, it's a misprint.

Mo. "7 to 2 against Voltigeur; 4 to 1 against Rasper; 4 to 1 against Locomotive," taken freely.

Goodge. Now, gentlemen, Woodbie having escaped my bullet through Julia's romantic folly, if Tom Meredith's horse wins the Derby, where shall we be?

Mull. Well, I should think in Australia within three months, feeding sheep.

Mo. I'll be sold for my weight in cat's meat.

Goodge. It's popular opinion that our horse, Voltigeur, isn't in it with Flying Scud, and Meredith's horse will win as sure as the sun shines. If so, every penny we have staked will be lost.

Mo. Oo! Vat'll become of me? Oo, jumpin' Moses, vy didn't the measles carry me off when I was young and innocent?

Mull. What's to be done?

Goodge. I'm for squaring the jockey. Who's the boy that gets the mount?

Mull. There's no dependin' on the honor o' thim boys; they'll be takin' your money and throw you over. I've been robbed fifty times that way.

Mo. Don't! O—o—o! I vos treated shameful dis mornin'. I'm all over from it.

Goodge. You don't know whom we have to deal with. After the affair on Calais Sands, Julia was taken to Nat Gosling's lodgings by Tom Meredith. I went there to make enquiries about her, and got into conversation with old Nat Gosling. He is feeling very sore about Tom Meredith's behavior to Katey, his granddaughter. Julia has escaped with a scratch on the shoulder; I saw the doctor, and he says she'll be out in a couple of days, more frightened than hurt.

Mo. Vell, if I got a bullet in me, I should die of fright.

Goodge. Don't I tell you it only skimmed her shoulder?

Mo. Vell, I think if it only skimmed me anywhere, it 'ud be more than enough. Oh, jumpin' Moses!

Mull. But what were you going to say about Flying Scud and Nat Gosling?

GOODGE. Well, I was going to say that he scarcely ever leaves the horse; that he almost lives in the stable. Last Christmas he got in six-months feed, and sleeps on it. The water the animal drinks is tested daily with litmus paper, and there's special police dotted round the park where Flying Scud takes his morning gallop.

Mo. It's worse than Sebastopol to get into.

GOODGE. So I thought to myself, why does old Nat stand by Meredith so strongly? When that snob found himself master of my fortune, he threw over Katey Rideout and broke off with her. Nat must want to serve him out for that, so I boldly proposed an offer; he hesitated; at last he consented to call on me here today. Now I propose that we run him with an offer of two thousand pounds, and knock him off his legs.

MULL. Two thousand pounds!

Mo. Say! Wouldn't he take something off for his revenge? He gets that in.

MULL. But where are we to get the money?

GOODGE. By one bold stroke for fortune. As Woodbie would not lend us the money, we have borrowed his name on account for the two thousand pounds.

Mo. On another bill. Lawyer Quail has advanced the money on it. He wants to get a slice of the young lord's ruin.

GOODGE. We shall be sure to take it up tomorrow after the race, so there's no risk of discovery.

MULL. Is there no fear of being found out?

Mo. No, no! Goodge is the best forger I know. Besides, as I said, it's sure to be taken up.

MULL. Yes, it's sure to be taken up.

Mo. So long as we aren't taken up, I don't mind.

GOODGE. I've just come from Quail's office, and asked him to accommodate us by cashing Lord Woodbie's acceptance. Of course he hadn't got the cash in the place, but promised to go and get it from the bank. You go round there and get the money; you'll be back in ten minutes.

Mo. There's a something about it that I don't like.

GOODGE. Nonsense! You'll get your share, won't you?

Mo. Vell, where is the forged document?

GOODGE. [Takes it from pocket-book] There it is.

Mo. The signature is beautiful; I can scarcely tell it from Lord Woodbie's own writing. Captain, you're a clever fellow, you deserve to be transported.

GOODGE. What?

Mo. I mean promoted with an award of merit. You write beautifully.
ou're a credit to the schoolboard. I say, suppose old Quail wants any receipt
r the money?

GOODGE. Oh, just endorse the bill, or give him any receipt he likes. Don't
e frightened, man—we shall be all one thing or the other after the race.
Ve've gone too far to think of sliding back now.

MULL. Come along, Davis, I'll go with you.

Mo. Yes, and you'll endorse the bill.

MULL. Oh, it won't do for Quail to see me in the matter. You're his client.

Mo. Oh—oh! Jumpin' Moses, if it's found out.

MULL. You didn't see our objections till just now.

Mo. I don't think I sees 'em now. I vos thinking of myself; I vosn't think-
ig of you. Ain't there no other way?

GOODGE. None! If we are to share the plunder, we must first divide the
sk; but there is no risk.

MULL. None at all. It will sure to be taken up.

Mo. That's what we shall all be if it ain't. [*Knock L.*]

GOODGE. Hallo, here's Nat. You go out the back way, both of you, while
admit him. Get back as quickly as you can.

MULL. We shan't be many minutes. [*Exit Mo and Mulligan R.1E.*]

NAT. [*Outside L.*] Does Captain Grindley Goodge live here?

GOODGE. Step this way, Mr. Gosling. [*Enter Nat*] I asked you to visit me
is morning, because I wish to explain to you how sorry I am that my little
ttentions to your granddaughter have injured her so much. But why will
ie not let me square the matter? Come, if she is a little fool, you are a
nsible fellow.

NAT. I am sir, uncommon; try me.

GOODGE. Although Meredith has jilted Katey, you stick to him and his
ortunes. Now this is not natural; so I said to myself, "I think I see Nat's
ttle game." Oh, you are a deep one.

NAT. Oh, ain't I, so deep that I can't see to the bottom of what you mean.
ist tell me what I've been a-doin' on.

GOODGE. You've been quietly betting against the Scud.

NAT. Oh!

GOODGE. You are going to sell the race tomorrow.

NAT. Ah!

GOODGE. And while you feather your own nest, you revenge yourself on
Ieredith.

NAT. Revenge is sweet, ain't it?

GOODGE. Have I guessed right?

NAT. What surprised me was that you didn't come before now, and make me comfortable, instead of trying it on with the stable boy. Wot's your offer?

GOODGE. I and my partner have laid heavily against your horse. We can afford to buy him off at two thousand pounds. My bets are nearly all with Meredith. If I win—I recover my estate, and then I promise you Katey shall be mistress of the old Hall—I will marry her, I'll make her my wife.

NAT. Two thousand pounds for me, and Katey to be made Mrs. Goodge.

GOODGE. Such a marriage will set matters right.

NAT. When can I have the money?

GOODGE. Immediately. Wait here, and I will go and bring my friends with it at once. [*Crosses L.*] May I say done?

NAT. Well, yes, I think you may.

GOODGE. [*Aside*] What a fool I've been to think he was not open to an offer. Moral: Never suspect a man of being honest. My fortune is safe now. Meredith, I have you under my heel. Where can Mo and Mulligan be? [*To Nat*] Just wait here a minute, Nat—I'll be back directly. [*Exit R.1E.*]

NAT. Two thousand pounds! Ah, it's a heap of money. Well, it's curious how horses do spile men—they're worse than women. There ain't in Nature a hanimal that's more nobler, more honest and hinnercent as an 'oss, but he's the cause of more meanness and dirt in the human 'eart, than all the female sex put together. [*Enter Goodge, Davis and Mulligan L.1E.*]

GOODGE. Well, Mr. Gosling, here we are, you see. These friends of mine would like to have your advice on the race tomorrow. They'll pay a good price for it.

NAT. Advice as is advice, means money. I am one of them as advertises to sell the names o' winning horses. Put a bushel of such winners in a sieve, ge 'em a shake, where are they? [*A pause*] Nowheres!

GOODGE. You sell the horses that lose, eh?

NAT. Ah! Them's my pick.

GOODGE. I've been hinting to my friends that you could sell us a safe loser for the Derby. Say Flying Scud, for instance; we'll give the price.

MULL. And he must be made safe.

MO. And we must see that he's comfortable.

NAT. Ah, I thought as you'd like to take the 'sponsibility on it off my hands.

GOODGE. Not that we doubt your honor.

MULL. and MO. Oh, no!

NAT. Werry good! Now here is the key of his loose box. You know the road to it well enough—you've been smelling round there long enough to count hevery 'air in his tail.

GOODGE. And here's the money. [*Takes notes from Mo and gives them to Nat*]

NAT. That's business.

GOODGE. How shall we get at the horse?

NAT. Just before daylight, the veterinary is a-comin' to fix his plates—now two on ye must get yourselves up to look like Jack Meadows and his man—I'll pass ye, and once you're inside, why if Flying Scud wins, it's your fault—ain't it?

Mo. If he wins after I've fixed him, I'll heat him, hoofs and all.

NAT. No cruelty, mind.

Mo. He'll catch nothing more than a slight cold that will make his coat stare, that's all.

NAT. Arter that, Meredith must win with him, if he can.

ALL. Aye; ha, ha! If he can!

NAT. I'll do my best, mind ye, and if ye get in a hole after all—

GOODGE. We'll forgive you.

NAT. That's your sort.

MULL. Our fortunes are made. [*Exit R.*]

GOODGE. [*Crossing L.*] And Meredith is broken, for tonight the favorite will be nobbled. [*Exit R.*]

Mo. Yes, he'll have a severe attack of the vishy washy villy vobbles. [*Exit R.*]

NAT. Will he? Well, I shouldn't be surprised if some of you will have an attack of the washy willy wobbles before you've done.

SCENE 3: *Front scene on road to stable. Enter Bob, Jerry and Ned Compo with stable lads L.1E.*

JERRY and OMNES. Tell us all about it, Bob.

BOB. Well, give a chap time to breathe.

NED. Ah, you've got too much flesh about you, Bob, to breathe comfortably.

BOB. Have I? Well, it ain't got nothing to do with you if I have.

JERRY. You ought to try Doctor Skinner's mixture, that 'ud bring you down.

BOB. I've had gallons of it.

NED. I fancy chloride of lime and Condy's Fluid mixed with a little benzoline and Mrs. Allan's Restorer would do him a world of good.

BOB. Yes, it might prepare me for another world.

JERRY. Bob, tell us about Nat Gosling, Mo Davis and the rest.

OMNES. Yes, tell us, tell us!

BOB. Well, first and foremost, there's a-going to be a fashionable wedding in high circles and society—Colonel Mulligan's niece, Julia Latimer, is a-going to marry young Lord Woodbie. I was present when the consent was given, and Katey and me is a-going to be one of the bridesmaids, and I'm going to be the best man.

JERRY. Well, if you're going to be the best man, some of the others must be rather rum 'uns.

BOB. If you insult me any more, Mr. Jeremiah Cobbler, I shall be under the painful necessity of giving you a smack in the jaw.

JERRY. What?

BOB. You heard what I said, a smack in the j-a-w.

JERRY. Oh, you will, will you. You'll have to go into training first.

BOB. [Threatening] What?

JERRY. [Squaring up] Eh? [Business]

NED. Come boys, don't quarrel.

JERRY. Well, what did he want to say he'd smack me in the jaw for?

NED. Now, Bob, tell us all about Nat and the shufflers.

BOB. Well, after the bit of a bother on Calais Sands, Miss Julia left her uncle's house, and came to Miss Katey at Nat Gosling's lodgings. Captain Grindley Goodge came there after her, and got talking matters over with Nat Gosling, and I believe there's a bit of business on. [Mysteriously]

NED. Business! What sort?

JERRY. I thought Nat Gosling wouldn't mix up with such a set.

BOB. Oh, leave Nat alone, he's got his head screwed on the right way. [Nat whistles outside]

JERRY. Hush, I hear Nat's whistle.

BOB. Then he can tell ye himself what's up. [Enter Nat L.1E.]

NAT. Well, Bob, have you told the boys?

BOB. Some of it, but not all.

NAT. Now lads, to make a long story short, I've sold the race tomorrow Goodge and his party have tipped me two thousand pounds to let them nobble Flying Scud, and I've got the money, and have promised them the key of the stables.

JERRY. Why Nat, all the stable is on the favorite.

NED. We all know, Nat, that Mister Meredith didn't behave fair and square to your granddaughter, Miss Katey, but we didn't think you'd take such a revenge as this. Howsomedever, I'm going to ride Flying Scud, and it'll be a fair race. I'll ride to win, and it wouldn't be twenty thousand pound

hat would stop me putting Scud first past the winning post if he's the best
horse in the field.

JERRY and REST. Bravo, Ned! Stick to that!

NAT. Ned Compo, I know'd a man as lived in Oundle in Northampton-
shire as made his fortune—and d'ye know how? by minding his own business. You mind yourn, and let Nat Gosling, the oldest man in the stable,
speak.

JERRY. Go on, Nat, let's hear the finish of it. What have you got to say?

NAT. Well, boys, as observed afore I was took up short, I've promised the
key of Flying Scud's stable, and two o' them will be here tonight to fix the
favorite.

JERRY. Nat, Nat, I couldn't have believed it of you.

NAT. Will ye shut up till I've done? I promised 'em the key of Flying
Scud's stable, but didn't promise the Scud should be in it when they came.
Now there's another horse, Voltigeur, a regular outsider, that's supposed to
make the running for Tom Flyer, that's been backed heavily by Captain
Goodge, Mulligan and Mo Davis. His stables are at the end of the yard.
Dick Purvis has had to go home, and there's the key of his box. Voltigeur
is the very image of Flying Scud—as like as two peas. You two [*pointing to
Jerry and Ned*] go and bring it down to our stables, change the horse cloths,
and let those chaps nobble their own fancy horse, instead of the pride of our
stables. What do you say to that, boys, eh?

JERRY. What! Let 'em nobble the wrong horse?

NAT. Precisely! And then put them in the hole they intended for us. And
as for the money I've got from 'em, it shall be fairly shared by every lad in
the stable.

JERRY and OMNES. Hurroy! "Old Boots" for ever!

NAT. [*Looking L.*] There they are at the end of the lane. You go and
meet 'em, Bob; don't bring 'em to the stable for about ten minutes or a
quarter of an hour. Tell 'em it ain't safe for 'em to come about till we're quite
ready for 'em.

BOB. All right, leave 'em to me. [*Exit L.*]

NAT. [*To Ned and Jerry*] You go and fetch Voltigeur; here's the key.

JERRY. Right you are, Nat. Come along, Ned. [*Exeunt L.*]

NAT. [*To rest*] You go to the yard and keep a sharp lookout. [*Stable
lads exit R.*] And now, Master Goodge and Co., I wonder how you'll like
being caught in your own trap. Tread Tom Meredith under your heel, will
yer? Not while Nat Gosling is on this side of the turf. Give Flying Scud an
attack of the wishy washy willy wabbles? Not if I know it, not if I know it.
[*Exit R.U.E. Re-enter Bob with Goodge, Mo Davis, disguised, L.*]

Bob. This is the way to the stables, gents, but you'd better wait in the lodge for about a quarter of an hour; some of the stable boys are about, and it 'ud be just as well to give 'em time to get out of the way.

Mo. Right you are. Goodge, you look spiffin; a regular business-like cut about your jib. I declare, your mother wouldn't know you.

Goodge. Stow your chaff, Davis, I'm in no humor for it. If we miss the game we have in hand, it will be rather serious, for I'm ruined.

Mo. So am I—so are we all—we're all ruined. But there ain't no chance of anything going wrong. Haven't we parted to two thousand quid? Only fancy, two thousand thich 'uns to be left alone with a gee-gee a couple of minutes.

Goodge. If Nat Gosling acts on the square, one minute will be quite enough for me.

Bob. Now, gentlemen, we'd better get inside the lodge and wait.

Mo. All right, my dear. It's rather cold; have a drop of this. [*Offers flask*]

Bob. No thank you, sir, no thank you. You may drug your horses, but you don't drug me.

Mo. Oh, jumpin' Moses! What a lot of suspicious people there are about.

Goodge. Well, come on, Mo, the sooner the job is over, the better I shall like it.

Mo. And the longer we are over it, the verser I shall like it. [*Business: Mo going to drink out of bottle. Goodge takes it from him and pockets it*]

Goodge. None of that just now.

Mo. Oh, ain't he selfish? Wants it all himself. [*Exeunt R.1E.*]

Scene 4: *Stable yard by night. Illuminated village in the distance, palings round loose boxes. Jackson discovered watching. Nat whistles outside.*

Jack. Hallo! Who's that? [*Whistles repeated*] Is that you, Nat Gosling? [*Enter Nat through gate*]

Nat. Yes, it's me. If I told ye it was somebody else, you wouldn't believe it.

Jack. I was expecting the farriers, and thought it might be one of 'em.

Nat. All right, you needn't wait now. Go and look if you see any signs of the farriers on the road.

Jack. Right you are, Nat. [*Exit through gate*]

Nat. I wonder whether Flying Scud's awake? [*Unlocks half door*] Ah, there he is—come over, my beauty. [*Business: with horse's head*] Thought to hocuss ye, did they? Well, we shall see, we shall see. Wants to give ye

a dose, do they? Well, what's good for Flying Scud can't be bad for Voltigeur. Talk about diamond cut diamond, or a Roland for an Allover!—why
it ain't in it. They'd give yer wishy washy willy wobbles, would they? I'll
wash 'em inside out before I've done with 'em. [*Jerry gives peculiar whistle
outside*] Hallo! There they are. [*Imitates whistle*] All right, my pippins, the
coast is clear. [*Enter Jerry and Ned leading the horse, Voltigeur, through
gate*]

JERRY.   Here ye are, Nat, this is Captain Goodge's horse, Voltigeur. We've
managed it. The stable boy is asleep. [*Village clock strikes in the distance*]

NAT.   Hark! Time's up! They'll be here in a quarter of an hour, or less.
Good evening, Voltigeur, sorry to put you to any inconvenience, but we
shall just trouble you to take Flying Scud's place in the stable for a few
minutes, and after your master's physicked you, you can go back to your
own stable.

JERRY.   Come along, Nat. Is Scud ready for the change?

NAT.   All serene, my beauty. [*Music. Nat brings Flying Scud out, and
Jerry with Nat change the two horse cloths on the two horses*] Now put
Voltigeur in Flying Scud's stable, and put the Scud in the spare box. Good,
good! Now we'll see who'll have an attack of the wishy washy willy wobbles.
Watch, boys, at the end of the lane, and when you see Goodge and Moses
disguised as farriers coming, give me the signal.

JERRY.   Right you are, Nat. Come on, Ned. [*Exeunt through gate*]

NAT.   Now they can come; I'm ready for them. [*Opens half of stable
door*] They thought to get at ye, did they? [*Repeat business with horse's
head*] They thought I'd sell you. I'd rather sell me life. See here now, and
listen to your ould nuss. The heye of all civilization is on ye this day, and
you know it. You're as vain as a peacock, and as pooty as paint. They'll
come to spile you, my dear; and arter their cookery, they'll expect to find
you strip tomorrow, and show a coat like a stubble field. Ay! but you will
come out like satin in the sunshine. I kin the faces they'll pull at that. Then,
my cock-a-wax, you'll pace among the admiring crowd, moving like suthin'
between a woman and a steam engine. That's when the ring will feel it. I
hear 'em at it now. The odds arisin', and bilin' over. Then you'll take your
gallop, my pippin, and when they sees your loopin' stride, they'll put settlin'
day afore their heyes in the biggest kind o' print. Now we're at the post.
Be quiet—no pullin'—steady! Down goes the flag—easy! Now ye knows
what's in ye. Wait on Rasper. Keep a heye on Locomotive. Round ye go,
shakin' off ruck, and takin' of it easy till the turn where I showed yer.
Then Ned will let yer go, and then go it. Locomotive is shook off like
a flea. Don't ye hear the outsiders saying, "Yalla! Yalla wins!" And the

edicated, a cryin', "Flying Scud!—The Scud ahead!" as ye go? My heart gets in my mouth. Rasper is close behind; ye may feel his pipes, as he puts on a spirt at the finish. He gains your quarter; Ned calls on ye; ye quit him like a bullet, and pass the post, held hard. Four lengths ahead; time—quickest on record. There's your programme! If ye falls short on it, never put your nose in my face again. [*Puts horse back. Enter Goodge and Mo Davis disguised R.1E.*] Show Mr. Meadows Flying Scud's box. He's come to 'just his plates.

Mo. [*Aside to Goodge*] That's the crib. I've been takin' stock of the lodgings, and know the jography.

GOODGE. All right. [*Enters the box R.*]

Mo. Here's my patent fixer—here it is. That will make his coat stare just for a day or two, eh? [*Exit into box*]

NAT. Ah! and it will make you stare for a year or two, or I'm mistook. Let's see what they're arter. [*Looks into their box*] Who is that at the head of the hoss? Oh, that's Davis. 'Tother one is going over his plates. Take keer; Voltigeur is 'andy with his heels—he'll ketch ye a wipe in a minute. The fust thing you'll know, you'll know nothin'. [*Re-enter Goodge and Mo Davis bringing on horse Voltigeur. They drug him on stage*]

GOODGE. There now, stand still!

Mo. 'Old ye head still, can't ye? There, that'll do ye a lot of good. Oh, jumpin' Moses! He's bit my finger.

GOODGE. He's got it! Our fortunes are made!

Mo. We've nobbled the horse. We've nobbled the favorite. [*Dancing with glee*]

NAT. [*Aside*] Yes, and I've nobbled you!

SCENE 5: *Front scene near Epsom Downs. Crowds of people, such as frequent races. Thimble riggers, Negro minstrels, vendors of race cards and dolls, vans, tents, drags, costermongers' carts, etc. Woodbie and Julia in a phaeton. Negro minstrel song is going on. Enter gipsy who tells Julia's fortune, while two cockneys are taken in by the thimble riggers. Enter policeman. The thimble riggers decamp. This scene should maintain several natural episodes in pantomime during the dialogue. A murmur outside. Enter Lord Woodbie and Julia accompanied by Lady Woodbie.*

LADY W. Come, my dear, this is the way to the course. We shall find our carriage just beside the stand.

JULIA. Lady Woodbie, I hope some day to be able to prove my gratitude.

Wood. Gratitude for what? For making me the happiest fellow alive? When the preliminaries are all settled, there will be nothing to delay our marriage.

Lady W. Ah, my dear boy, you are so impetuous.

Wood. Everything is prepared for our departure to the Continent, and won't we have a jolly honeymoon? [*Enter Jerry L.*]

Jerry. A word with you, my lord.

Lady W. Come, my dear, this way to our carriage. [*Exeunt R.*]

Wood. Ladies, I'll join you in a few minutes. Well, my lad, what is it?

Jerry. Mr. Meredith's compliments to you, sir, and he wants you to know that Captain Goodge's horse, Voltigeur, is took bad; can't run; in fact, scratched. He's anxious about you, as he's afraid you might be backing it, seeing as how you used to be so thick with the price.

Wood. Thanks! But I haven't backed it for a penny. All my bets are on the favorite, Flying Scud.

Jerry. And it's as sure to win as if it had already passed the post. [*Enter Captain Goodge*]

Goodge. Ah, good day, Lord Woodbie. Glad to see you looking so well.

Wood. You will oblige me, sir, by considering we are not on speaking terms.

Goodge. Oh, indeed! Not on speaking terms, eh?

Wood. I have promised my mother, Lady Woodbie, never to speak to you again.

Goodge. Quite right! Always do what your mammy tells you. Poor boy, you're not old enough to think for yourself. You ought to be ashamed of yourself.

Wood. I hope I shall never be ashamed of taking my mother's advice.

Goodge. Yes, you were always a favorite with the ladies. It isn't every fellow that can get a woman to go out and fight his battles for him. Thank goodness for the honor of old England, it isn't every *milksop* that can persuade a poor girl to dress herself in male attire and risk being shot to save her so-called lover's life.

Wood. Why you infernal scoundrel! Do you dare to insinuate that I knew anything of—

Goodge. Oh, of course you knew nothing about it. [*Changing tone*] It isn't likely. There isn't a man in the club but shall know all about it, and your cowardly behavior. Lord Woodbie, you knew perfectly well that Julia was going to take your place.

Wood. [*With suppressed passion*] Captain Goodge, you're a liar! [*Strikes him with glove in face*]

GOODGE. I'll horsewhip you on the course, in the presence of your friends
[*Enter Tom Meredith*]

TOM. Oh, no you won't! For if you try it on, I'll break your neck.

JERRY. And if he doesn't care to soil his hands by contaminating them
with your lavender water body, I'll see what I can do. [*Squares up*]

GOODGE. So, you cowardly cur, you've got your bullies close at hand to
protect you.

TOM. Come along, Lord Woodbie. Remember your promise to your
mother.

WOOD. Yes, but I—

TOM. Come, come! No more words! Follow me!

GOODGE. Yes, take him to his mother. Get his mother to mind him. Tie
him to her apron strings for safety—but that would be rather awkward—
perhaps the old lady doesn't wear aprons!

WOOD. Why, I'll— [*Business. Tom gets Lord Woodbie off*]

JERRY. [*To Goodge*] I'd give five pounds just to have you in our back
yard for ten minutes. [*Exit. More variety business introduced here. Enter
Mulligan L.*]

GOODGE. There's a report that there's something wrong in the crack's
stable. The betting is down to even, and three to two against him. [*A cheer
outside*]

MULL. What's the matter now? [*Enter Mo Davis L.U.E.*]

MO. Oh, dear! Oh, s'elp me! Oo—Oo!

GOODGE. What are you dancing about?

MO. There's been a mistake. I don't know! Eh! Voltigeur is scratched—
he's amiss!

GOODGE. Who cares?

MO. Yes, but Flying Scud is—is—

GOODGE. What, man? Speak! [*A cheer outside*]

MO. You hear? He is as clean as I am—cleaner—nothin' the matter with
him. We're done!

GOODGE. It is impossible! Damnation, man! You didn't give him the
physic, then?

MO. Yes, I did.

GOODGE. He didn't swallow it, then?

MO. Yes, he did.

GOODGE. Then it didn't work.

MO. I didn't go along vid it to see. [*Enter Tom Meredith with super
L.1E.*]

TOM. I'll bet three to one on Flying Scud! Three to one in hundreds.

SUPER. Done!

TOM. Done, and again.

GOODGE. No; enough on.

TOM. He's a picture! Thanks to old Nat, he never peeled in such form as
ιe does today. [*Cheers outside*] There! That's at him, again. The public
ould eat him up every bit.

MO. [*R.*] So could I. I'd bolt him whole if I vos along wid him.

GOODGE. [*Aside*] There has been some villainy here.

MO. We are the wictims! I'm a wictim!

GOODGE. We can't get at the horse, but we can get at the jockey. Ned
Compo is the lad. I'll fix the boy. Come with me. [*Exeunt Goodge and Mo
Davis L.1E. Variety business and introductions, five niggers ending with
hasing the welcher. Enter Nat L.U.E.*]

NAT. Now, sir, I've come for orders; how's the lad to ride?

TOM. Give him your own advice, Nat, I can't improve on it. I think we
ιave nothing to fear; let him ride as he may.

NAT. Nothin' is sure till it has happened.

TOM. Let him take the lead then, and keep it.

NAT. He can last, but won't give thirty shillings in change for a sovering.
Bell rings outside] There's the "clear the course." Ah, the old blood begins
ο tell inside me; my werry back gets lithsome, and I feel the old jockey
ιmovin' in me strong. [*Business. Enter Bob running L.U.E.*]

BOB. Where is he? Where's Nat?

NAT. Here I be. Wot's up?

BOB. Oh, lor'! Here's a go—oh, sir, Ned, sir, Ned Compo—

TOM. Well?

BOB. He's been and took bad, sir.

NAT. Took bad? How?

BOB. All over, sir. Down at the mouth. Here he is. [*Enter crowd with
Ned very pale*]

NED. Oh, Lord! Oh, dear!

NAT. Wot's up?

NED. 'Tain't what's up, it's what's down. I'm nobbled.

TOM. What d'ye mean?

NED. I jest took a small drain of brandy as a gent offered me—wery
kind he was—and a moment arter, I couldn't keep my saddle.

NAT. By jinks! They couldn't fix the horse, so they got at the jockey.

MO. [*Aside*] Grindley Goodge, for a thousand. [*Bell outside*]

NAT. Oh, dear—Oh, mussy me! The warmints; they've ruined ye, Tom;
and my beauty can't run.

ALL. Shame! Shame!

NAT. [*Suddenly*] Yes, he shall, by jinks! I'll double on 'em all yet. Peel the colors off that boy; gi' me his cap. [*Throws off his overcoat*] I ain't rode a race for five and twenty years. [*Enter Katey L.1E.*]

KATEY. Oh, Grandfather, what are you going to do?

NAT. Do, girl? I'm going to ride Flying Scud for the Derby. I'm four pounds overweight, but a pound or two won't count 'tween me and him. [*Re-enter Goodge and Mo Davis L.*]

GOODGE. The favorite can't win.

NAT. [*Dressed*] Can't he? But he will, though.

MO. Who will ride him?

NAT. I will! "Old Boots!"

CROWD. Hurray! Hurray! [*Exit Nat L.U.E.*]

MULL. The old man is crazy.

TOM. I am ruined—he can't have it in him at his age to pilot such a dare-devil animal. [*Cheers outside*]

GOODGE. [*R.*] How d'ye feel now, Meredith?

TOM. I feel like an honest man. How do you feel?

GOODGE. Rich as a pie!

WOOD. There they go! By Jove, the old fellow is in the saddle. [*Cheers*] The crowd recognize him—hark how they cheer. [*Cheers outside*]

KATEY. He's up and off; but will he ever be able to stick on?

CROWD. Now then, make way a little. Where are you shoving to? [*Bell. Cheers. A row and a fight, during which a tent is knocked down on one side and the carriages, etc., are moved off at the other so that the whole course and spectators, grandstand, etc., become visible. The police enter. Order is reestablished. Bell rings*]

CROWD. There they are. There, they are off. No, they ain't. Yes, I tell yer—see! Which is him in front—black and tan cap? That's Kettledrum colt. No—yes! Where's Nat? Where's the favorite?

GOODGE. He's nowhere! Look! He will be off in a minute.

MO. I vish he may break his neck. Oh, my inside is going it. Keep an eye on him.

MULL. Green and black is ahead. They'll never catch him. They're down in the hollow.

KATEY. Oh, Mr. Meredith, it is all Grandfather's fault, sir, if you are ruined.

TOM. Katey! If I could see into your heart, and know the truth! I'd rather win you than the Derby, but that is impossible.

KATEY. Alas! [*The crowd have turned and now watch the open course at the other side*]

ALL. Here they come! Here they come! Rasper is in front! Rasper! Rasper! No, Locomotive! [*The cloud of horses and jockeys appear*]

GOODGE. Locomotive and Rasper, neck and neck. Confederate, third. The favorite, a bad fourth.

TOM. Ay, but held—hard held. Now the old man is creeping on them. See! He catches Confederate, and passes.

CROWD. Rasper wins! Rasper wins! White and white!

TOM. The favorite for a thousand, even.

GOODGE. Done! Done!

TOM. Look! He collars Locomotive! Well done. Good race; good race! He's at Rasper's quarters! Now for it! Well done, Nat! Nat forever!

CROWD. Rasper! Flying Scud! Yalla wins! Rasper wins! Flying Scud! White! Flying Scud! Yalla, yalla! Hurray! Hurray! [*Immense tumult. The grandstand is seen to flutter with hats and handkerchiefs. The crowd surge and sway in the distance. A number is seen to go up in the distance on the post. Renewed cheers. The course is flooded with the crowd*]

TOM. No. 9! Flying Scud! [*Frantic cheers. Enter policemen surrounding Nat, who is mounted on Flying Scud and is on his way to the weighing room. Mo Davis appears very ill in one corner, Goodge, Mulligan and Chousir in another, stamping with vexation*]

TABLEAU

ACT IV.

SCENE 1: *Mulligan's lodgings. Goodge, Mo Davis and Mulligan discovered.*

MO. Oh, jumpin' Moses, what's to become of us? We're like the poor little "Babes in the Wood," only there's three of us.

MULL. By the blood of the Mulligans, we're cornered. Our creditors will swarm on us like bees on a treacle cask, and I shall be disgraced. *Me,* the descendant of the Prince of Gath-na-cush, in a direct line with the Mulligans of Castle Mulligan; our noble blood is disgraced forever.

GOODGE. Oh, damn your blood.

MO. Yes, damn your blood. Vot's the good of blood; it won't get us out of this schermozzle. Oh, dear! Oh, dear! I never vos in such a scrape before. Vot's to be done? Vot's you going to do?

GOODGE. Our only chance is immediate flight. We must get away from England at once.

Mo. Right you are! I'll go to the Argentine. I want to see my old friend Jabez, and if once I get over, they'll never bring me back again.

Goodge. Why, you fool, we haven't got enough money to get so far.

Mo. Then let me go on a steamer as a poor little stowaway, in among the coals and bilge water. Oh, why didn't my mother put me in a pail when I was born?

Mull. It's no use talking, gentlemen, we must proceed to action at once Julia has left me, and I have nothing now to live for. [*Weeps*]

Mo. Go on, crocodile, what are ye snivelling for? Look at the crocodile's tears running down the end of your nose.

Mull. Well, if they'd try to get down to the bottom of your nose, they couldn't.

Mo. Dat's right, dat's right, go on, abouse my nose now, just 'cos you can't pay your debts. Oh, this is an ungrateful world. I'm too good for it.

Goodge. Yes, you ought to have been an angel. Pity you haven't got a pair of wings.

Mo. And these are the men I once thought my friends. As Nebuchadnezzer said at the battle of Vaterloo, "And you, Brutus, go; never more be ossifer of mine."

Mull. What it comes to is this: how much money have we?

Goodge. Well, in the safe at our retreat at Lambeth Road, we've got about a hundred and twenty pounds.

Mo. Ve must divide it. Tell me how many times three times go into a hundred and twenty. Fifty—forty—thirty—seven. No, I vos never no good at figures. I'll have the hundred, and you shall have ten apiece; then I'll go to the Argentine, and throw myself on the mercy of the glorious republic; and when I'm settled down, I'll get up a subscription to send for you two to come over to me, and then we'll set up a branch establishment over there. D'ye see?

Goodge. We'll divide fairly, forty pounds apiece, and then take our chance. It must be done at once; tomorrow will be too late.

Mo. Yes, it's a hold saying, and a true one, "That a bush in the hand is worth two in the bird," and "Never put off till today, what you can do tomorrow."

Goodge. Chuck it, Mo Davis, and let us settle details with Mulligan.

Mo. Dat's a nice way to speak to me after all I have done for you.

Mull. Well, go on, what do you propose?

Goodge. Well, I think it would be best to— [*Knock heard at door*] Hush What's that?

Mo. P'raps it's the man called for the taxes.

MULL. [*Looking through keyhole*] It's Quail, the lawyer.

GOODGE. Open the door; we must brazen it out.

MULL. Come in, Mr. Quail, come in. [*Enter Quail, with him two clerks who remain at door*]

GOODGE. To what are we indebted for the honor of this visit?

QUAIL. I daresay you can guess.

GOODGE. I haven't the slightest idea.

MULL. Perhaps you have called to ask my instructions concerning the little bit of property I thought of buying in the borough.

Mo. Or perhaps to ask us to take some shares in the new company which is being floated to acquire the very prosperous walk stalls and oyster barrows in the borough, and amalgamate them with the lady's trotter baskets in Drury Lane. I'm told it's a sure certainty to pay twelve and a half per cent.

QUAIL. No, gentlemen, that is not my business. I have just heard that the bill I discounted for you bearing Lord Woodbie's name, is a forgery. I give you twelve hours to find the money, and provide for it.

Mo. [*Looking at watch*] Excuse me, Mr. Quail, I can't stop; I've got to see a man about a dog. I forgot all about it till just now.

QUAIL. Excuse me, Mr. Davis, but you mustn't leave the room.

Mo. I'm a hinnocent party, Mr. Quail. Upon my word and honor, I knew nothing about it. I hope you didn't think me capable of such a thing as having anything to do with a forged bill. I can scarcely write my own name, let alone anybody else's.

QUAIL. You forget, Mr. Davis, that I have been your confidential solicitor, and I know quite well what you are capable of. Gentlemen, I have no desire to proceed to extremities; all I want is my money. Your conviction would do me no good, and would not pay me back the cash I have advanced you, but I must protect myself. If the forged bill remains in my office twelve hours longer, I shall present it to Lord Woodbie, and you know what that means.

GOODGE. Yes. Seven years!

Mo. [*Fainting in Mulligan's arms*] Seven years!

GOODGE. Very well, Mr. Quail, since those are your terms, we'll try and find the money.

QUAIL. Then you confess the forgery?

GOODGE. As you seem to know all about it, I may as well do so. It was written in a moment of indiscretion. Mulligan suggested it, and I drew it up.

Mo. There, you hear him say I had nothing to do with it. [*Looks at watch*] If I don't go, that man will sell the dog to somebody else.

QUAIL. [*To Goodge*] Is this true?

GOODGE. Mo shared in everything with us. He came with Mulligan to your office to get the money.

Mo. Oh, hark at him! Where will he die when you go to?

QUAIL. Well, just step across to my chambers. And to prevent any possible difference of opinion hereafter, if I give you these twelve hours to find the money, you must give me the undertaking to do so in that time.

GOODGE. Come along, then. [*Aside to Mulligan*] In twelve hours we shall be out of the country. [*Going L.*]

Mo. Oh, I wish somebody would lend me the key of the Bank of England for ten minutes.

SCENE 2: *Front Street. Enter Nat and Lord Woodbie followed by Tom Meredith.*

TOM. I congratulate you, your lordship. I believe Miss Latimer to be one of the best girls that ever drew the breath of life.

WOOD. Thanks, Tom, thanks. I know I have your best wishes.

NAT. There was a time when Master Meredith thought the same of Katey, but all that's changed now.

TOM. No one more bitterly regrets it than I do, Nat.

NAT. Ah, I suppose that some day you'll be getting married to some fine lady of quality; then Katey will break her heart and die off like a flower, and I shall retire into private life until the Great Master of Life's course rings the saddling bell for me to weigh in and go up aloft.

TOM. Give me your hand, good, honest Nat, and believe me when I say that whatever Katey's feelings may be for me, mine towards her never change. Heaven knows that I love her as much as ever, but after what I saw with my own eyes, heard with my own ears, she could never become my wife; not that I shall ever marry another. I love her too dearly to ever think of such a thing.

NAT. Drat my old breeches if I can make it out. Human beings is funny things; I think I can understand hosses better.

WOOD. Here come Julia and Katey, accompanied by my mother. [*Looks at watch*] They are before their time. [*Enter Lady Woodbie L.U.E. with Julia on one arm, Katey on the other, followed by Bob. Bob crosses over to Nat after touching his hat to Meredith and Lord Woodbie*]

LADY W. Ah, Cecil, we are here rather earlier than I expected. I got my shopping at the stores done much quicker than anticipated. And while I was thus engaged, those two girls got comparing notes and talking over old times. Julia has told Katey something that you told her recently, Cecil, and if my ırmises are correct, the clouds may be lifted from Mr. Meredith's life, and ınshine will once more gladden his path.

NAT. Oh, my lady, what do you mean? A voice seems to whisper to me ıat it's something to do with my Katey.

LADY W. Quite right. It has a great deal to do with Miss Katherine.

WOOD. Why you don't think it possible that she was the young girl that ʼas locked up in the stable?

LADY W. But I do, though. She was telling Julia about her sad estrange-ıent with Mr. Meredith, and I have not the slightest doubt that when you ave told them the story you told us recently, all will be understood. Speak, ʼecil.

NAT. Oh, speak, sir, you're lifting me off a hoverflowing coal-sack on to feather bed.

WOOD. Well, I told my mother and Julia that some time ago at Don-aster, I came into Flying Scud's stable to escape a shower of rain, and to ide the tears that an interview with Julia had caused. That was when she efused to become my wife.

JULIA. Ah, but you didn't ask me properly, you know. [Coyly]

NAT. Go on—I remember meeting you as you came out.

TOM. I seem to have some recollection of it, too.

WOOD. I climbed up a ladder into the hayloft, and there overheard a owardly attempt on the part of Goodge to force his attention on a girl, who vidently wished to repel him. I was unable to get down without attracting heir attention, and was obliged to hear everything that took place. Hearing omebody coming, he told her she could get away by a side door, but instead ·f showing her the way out, he locked her up in Flying Scud's stable, and ʼas afterwards arrested for an unpaid tailor's bill before he had time to elease her. The bailiffs took him away with the key in his pocket. Since then ₁e has done everything to try to make her appear guilty, but, on my word ·f honor, she is innocent.

TOM. Katey! Katey, how I have wronged you. [Embrace]

NAT. Oo—raw! Oo—raw!

CECIL and JULIA. Julia! Cecil! [Embrace]

NAT. Oo—raw, again! Oh, I can't stand it. Bob, embrace me. [Business]

BOB. Here! 'Old 'ard! I ain't a lovely female.

NAT. I couldn't help it, Bob. It's too much for me.

BOB. Here comes old Quail, the solicitor. How would you like to em-·race him?

TOM. And you'll marry me now, Katey?

KATEY. Tom, Tom, I've loved you all the time.

NAT. Bless you, my chickabiddies, bless you!

LADY W. There'll be two weddings now, instead of one.

NAT. P'raps the clergyman will make a reduction in taking a quantity [*Enter Quail L.U.E.*]

QUAIL. Excuse me, Lord Woodbie, but my business is urgent and most important.

WOOD. Yes? What is it?

QUAIL. I don't know whether I ought to speak in the presence of this young lady. [*Indicating Julia*]

WOOD. My affianced wife. [*Introducing her*]

QUAIL. Yes, your mother has told me all, but Miss Latimer is the niec of one of the parties implicated in a most unpleasant business.

JULIA. My uncle? Colonel Mulligan?

QUAIL. The same, madame.

JULIA. I can almost guess what you're about to say. Please speak withou reservation.

QUAIL. [*Hands paper to Lord Woodbie*] That document is, I presume a forgery?

WOOD. [*After looking at it carefully*] I regret to say it is. The signatur is very like mine, but I never saw that bill before.

QUAIL. Written by Captain Goodge, accepted by Mo Davis, and en dorsed by Colonel Mulligan.

JULIA. If my uncle is guilty, and a forger, let him suffer for what he ha done. I have shielded him from the law too long already.

TOM. What is the amount?

QUAIL. Two thousand pounds.

TOM. Allow me to look at the bill. [*Does so*] You shall be paid, Mr Quail; please regard this debt as being purchased by me.

QUAIL. But the paper is not worth the stamp that's on it.

TOM. I'll buy it. I shan't miss it out of my winnings on the Derby.

QUAIL. Well, if you're willing to buy with your eyes open, I'll sell. [*Hand him bill*]

TOM. And now, Grindley Goodge, I'll show you no mercy. The law wil protect you against your racing debts, but with this proof of your forgery escape is impossible.

QUAIL. Escape! Ah, that's it! I gave them twelve hours to find the money but they have all three escaped, and I have put the police on their track.

TOM. We must go to the nearest magistrate, and obtain a warrant fo their apprehension.

QUAIL. I'll take you to one; there's no time to be lost. Your presence will
e necessary, my lord, so come. [*Exeunt L.*]

NAT. I feel twenty years younger.

BOB. And I feel two stone lighter.

NAT. Lord Woodbie is a trump.

BOB. And so is Meredith.

NAT. My Katey isn't to be scratched after all.

BOB. And Miss Julia has weighed in all right for the Matrimonial Stakes.

NAT. And what do you think of the old woman, Bob?

BOB. Why, she's another trump. Some of these high and mighty people
ave got their hearts in the right places after all.

NAT. This Captain Goodge put my darling Katey in a hole, but now
ve've got him in one, and before we let him out, he'll have to make a clean
reast of it.

BOB. Well, if he's going to make a clean breast of it, he'll want a main
drainage all to himself.

NAT. Follow me, Bob, let's be in at the finish. [*Exit R.*]

BOB. Well, this is a wind-up to a windy day. That Katey is a rare plucked
un; a girl that is a werry 'ard 'un to meet. Like a sound hoss; you don't
ee 'em every day. Marry her, I should think he ought to. He ought to
marry her once a month to his dying day. [*Exit L.*]

SCENE 3: *The garret. Table R.H., covered with a cloth; door L.H. Large safe.
Enter Mo Davis.*

Mo. Nobody saw me come in; vot an escape I've had. I'll lock the door
in'ards, and take the key out, so's there's no time to lose. Vere is my dupli-
ate keys? Here they are. There's Goodge's, and here's Mulligan's—now for
nine. Ah! [*He opens safe*] Here's the money. [*Takes it out*] All right; one
undred and twenty pounds. I'll start for Southampton by the next train, and
get aboard the first ship leavin' for anywhere. The police vill be alive tonight.
Bless me, what a sqveek I've had. [*Going. The door is tried*] Vot's that?
[*Recoils*] Bless me 'art, there's somebody—oo—whish—dey is talking. 'Tis
Goodge—oo—oo—here's a go! [*The door is violently shaken*] Oo—jumpin'
Moses, here's another hole! My life is a honeycomb. Vere can I hide till he
s gone? [*He creeps under the table. The door is burst open. Enter Goodge*]

GOODGE. I had no time for ceremony; in a few hours, the hunt will begin.
I must secure the money at once. Where is my key? I must force the other
ocks. What! [*Sees the safe open*] Damnation! Someone has been here. Yes,
the money is gone—not a penny left. Betrayed! Robbed by one of those

infernal associates of mine. Who could it be? Not Davis—he is safe in Quail's hands. It was Mulligan! There is another room yonder—he may be in there. [*Crosses R.D. Exits*]

Mo. He's gone—now's my time. [*Enter Mulligan with pistol case D.F.* Oh! [*Disappears under table again*]

MULL. If ever I come across that villain, Goodge, I'll pay him off. Poor Julia! And to think that I was accessory to such a thing. I can never show my face in Piccadilly again. A hansom cab would refuse me a fare. I'll borrow the few pounds here, and start for America. [*Turns and sees the safe* The divil! What's this? The safe open? The money gone! I've been robbed by one of them blackguards, friends of mine. [*Re-enter Goodge R.D.*] I could not have been Davis. It was Goodge!

GOODGE. [*Seeing Mulligan*] Ha!

MULL. [*Seeing Goodge*] Ha!

GOODGE. You Irish vagabond!

MULL. You cockney thief! [*Crosses to L.*] I left a hundred and twenty pounds in the safe. You have taken it out.

GOODGE. You vile perverter of the truth, it was you that took it. You mean thief! Give me half that money!

MULL. Disgorge your plunder, and share it like a gentleman. [*They seize each other*]

GOODGE. Stand back! [*Releases himself and runs to pistol case*] Stay! You pretend you have not on your person the contents of the safe. I know that you have.

MULL. And I am certain that they are safe in your pocket.

GOODGE. Take that revolver, then, and I will take this; let the survivor search the one who falls.

MULL. Done! I'll do society a service if I swing for it.

GOODGE. [*Standing behind table*] Are you ready?

MULL. [*R.H.*] One—two—three! [*They fire. The table begins to heave and roll about. Enter Nat, Woodbie, and Quail. Nat advances, and with Goodge lifts the table. Davis is discovered on his hands and knees, shot behind. They help him up*]

Mo. Oo—oo—I'm killed! [*They seat him in a chair; he springs out of it. Enter Tom with Bob, Jerry and detectives*]

TOM. Arrest these men!

GOODGE. You won't take me without a struggle for it. [*Business. Secured. Six supers, two to each*]

Mo. Mr. Meredith, you'll be sorry for this. I shall instruct my solicitor to commence an action against you for defamation of character.

GOODGE. I have yet to learn that a man can be treated like this for a few acing debts.

TOM. You're wanted on a charge of forgery, not only on this bill, which ou deluded Mr. Quail into discounting, but those which you paid into the ank, thinking to escape before they reached maturity.

GOODGE. So it seems more a matter of personal enmity.

TOM. It's clearing off old scores. You have tried to ruin me, and I see no eason to spare you now. The game is played out, and the victory is mine. *Enter Woodbie with Julia D.L.E.*]

MULL. Julia here! Forgive me, Lord Woodbie, I'm ashamed to look an onest man in the face.

NAT. [*D.L.*] How do you feel, Captain Goodge? Ain't you ashamed to ok an honest woman in the face?

GOODGE. Who do you mean? I've never said a word against Julia.

NAT. No, but you did against my Katey. [*Leading Katey over at door*] ook at her! Lord Woodbie has told all he overheard in the stables, and om Meredith is going to marry Katey after all.

GOODGE. I confess there's not a word of truth in anything I ever said gainst her. She was too good for me. If she had loved me, I might have een a different man.

JULIA. There you're wrong, Captain Goodge. A good woman may save weak man, but she can only share the fate of a bad one.

KATEY. Can't you let him go, Tom?

TOM. Yes, I'll let him go—to *transportation*.

MO. Oh, dear! Oh, dear! It's a good thing my mother's dead; dis dread-ul blow would have killed her. It's all through mixing with bad compan-ons. Vy didn't I join the "Band of Hope" ven I was young?

WOOD. I congratulate you, Tom. Flying Scud has turned out to be a our-legged fortune to you.

TOM. Yes, I shall make pots of money with him yet. Nat, we've entered cud for all the great races of the year.

NAT. Hush, you're telling them where to lay their money. You're giving ne away. You'll spoil my advertisements in *Sporting Life*. Let 'em apply to ne, "Old Boots." Oh, I forgot, they paid their tips as they came in. Well, I on't mind telling you, that our hoss is engaged to run over the course every ight this week. Take my advice, back him; and tell your friends they won't o far wrong if they put a bob or two on "Flying Scud."

CURTAIN AND FINIS

THE BANKER'S DAUGHTER

By Bronson Howard

CAST OF CHARACTERS

John Strebelow

Lawrence Westbrook

Babbage

G. Washington Phipps

Brown

Count de Carojac

Harold Routledge

M. de Montvillais

Dr. Watson

Footman

Lilian Westbrook

Florence St. Vincent Brown

Mrs. Fanny Holcomb

Lizette

Natalie

Time: 1869.

ACT I.

Set: *Handsome extension room in the house of Lawrence Westbrook, New York. Rich furniture, including handsome Japanese screen in L.U.C. At rise of curtain, enter Westbrook, R.U.D., followed by Footman.*

West. [*Crossing and sitting at L. table*] A poached egg, some anchovy toast, a little Chetna, some tea—in the meantime the papers and whatever mail there is. [*Sitting at table*] I feel a sort of shivering sensation; I seem to feel a draught; pull that screen around here. [*Footman does so*] That will do; what time is it?

Foot. Half past two, sir; the papers are on the table.

West. Very well! Get the mail.

Foot. Yes, sir. [*Exits R.U.D.*]

West. [*Yawning and shivering—opening Herald*] I think Babbage is right. I must be a fool to sit up listening to gossip of a society I really take no interest in; what the deuce is it to plain Lawrence Westbrook, banker and broker, who the best swordsman in Paris is, that he should sit up till five in the morning to hear it discussed? That Carojac must be a wizard though, if he performed half those feats; I suppose now that fellow would rather run a man through the body than inherit a fortune. He is about the only foreign nobleman that never asked me to cash a note for him. [*Enter Footman R.U.D.*] He says he has a greater favor than that to ask me.

Foot. [*At table*] The mail, sir.

West. [*Taking letters off salver*] Very well. [*Places letters on table*] See to my breakfast.

Foot. Yes, sir. [*Exits R.U.D.*]

West. [*Fixing on particular column in the Herald*] More failures! London catches it sometimes as well as New York. None of these can affect us, however; the gold balance at the Clearing House—two—four—twenty-nine—five. Hm! Hang it! I can't get up any interest in anything. [*Throws paper down*] Let me see these. [*Opens letters*] Babbage ought to have this. [*Takes up another*] The regular quarterly bill of Lilian's dressmaker. [*Takes up another*] From Strebelow! What can he write about? I saw him yesterday. [*Opens letter—reads*] Permission to address my daughter as a suitor. [*Looks pleased*] This is gratifying. I know few men that I respect more than John Strebelow. I'm sorry; it would not be May and December, but it would be

May and October. Strebelow must be forty—rich, honored, well-born, a man of unusual intellect. I wish he were but ten years younger. [*Looks at letter*] Will call for my answer this afternoon. He can have my permission; he'll never gain hers.

LILIAN. [*Heard laughing outside, R.L.D.*] Serious! Why, count! I can't be serious.

CAROJAC. [*Outside, speaking with French accent*] When will you be?

LIL. [*Bursting into room—riding habit, whip*] Whenever you are merry.

CARO. [*R., following in riding dress—whip*] But, mademoiselle, you always treat me the same way; you will never give me the answer. You parry all my attacks with a laugh.

LIL. [*C., laughing*] With so expert a chevalier, I must fence as best I may. No shield so safe against the point of a proposal as a lady's laugh, you know. That's your Balzac's aphorism. Do not look so sad; you seem like a Don Quixote, holding your whip as a small sword.

CARO. [*Vexed*] But—

LIL. Some other day, count, some other day.

CARO. I cannot wait; I must return to Paris.

LIL. [*Archly crossing to R.H.*] Good-by. Send me some gloves.

CARO. [*Bitterly*] You would not mock yourself of Mr. Routledge so.

LIL. Sir! You have no right—

CARO. I offend you—I beg your pardon; but I offer you—

LIL. [*Aside*] What I don't want.

CARO. The hand and title for a gentleman, and you will not give me an answer. But I will wait, and call tonight.

LIL. Tomorrow.

CARO. Tonight.

LIL. Indeed! I say now next week—next month—next year, if I wish. And, till then, Count de Carojac, *au revoir*. [*Exits laughing, snapping her whip, R.U.D.*]

CARO. She mocks herself of me. A week ago she was with Routledge when I call. She makes sport of me then, too, and he laugh; if I catch [*Clutching his whip*] M. Routledge in Paris, I may find a chance to make him smile wiz de oder side of him mouth. [*Going off R.L.D.*]

WEST. [*From behind screen, laughing*] Come here, count, come here. [*Rises, comes forward*] You must not be offended with Lilian; she is a spoiled child. But to be frank with you, I must tell you I am pretty certain you have no chance with her; with all her giddiness, if she at all entertained your proposal, she is naturally too true to so receive it.

CARO. Zen I will go back to Paris. I only wait here for her answer; when I hear her engagement with M. Routledge was what you call broke, I flatter myself I might—[*Enter Fanny R.L.D.*] Ah, Madame Halcomb! [*Bows*]

FANNY. [*R.*] I hope, count, you and Lilian had a pleasant ride.

CARO. [*C.*] Mlle. Westbrook enjoyed it vera much. She laughed all ze time [*Aside*] at my expense.

FANNY. A bad augury for you, count.

CARO. Oh, yes; I have my conje, and now will take me back to Paris. M. Westbrook, you will soon, I hope, geeve me an opportunity to repay there ze hospitality you tendayr me here.

WEST. [*L., shaking hands with Carojac*] I shall be only too happy, count, believe me.

CARO. [*Crossing to R.*] Zen, good-by.

WEST. A pleasant voyage.

FANNY. [*C.*] Good-by, count.

CARO. [*To Westbrook*] Much thanks. [*To Fanny, bowing and shaking hands*] Good-by. [*Exits R.L.D.*]

FANNY. So Lilian has refused the count.

WEST. [*Laughing*] She merely laughed at him; I had to do the refusing.

FANNY. [*Sitting on ottoman, C.*] Well, I'm glad it's over. She and Routledge fell out about him, and while he remained here it seemed impossible to know what might happen.

WEST. [*Laughing*] I certainly did not wish the count for a son-in-law; and I'm very glad my little girl had too much sense to be caught by his title. His character is not exactly what I like—ready to quarrel, a duelist!—and seeming to inherit but one ingredient of his ancestors' chivalry, its courage, and but one quality of their wit, its cynicism. A charming club acquaintance, but no son-in-law for me. Better Harold Routledge even.

FANNY. [*Approvingly*] Much better. [*Enter Footman R.U.E.*]

FOOT. Your breakfast is ready, sir.

WEST. Very well. [*Footman puts screen upstage. Exits R.H.*]

FANNY. [*Rising*] Your breakfast at three in the afternoon?

WEST. [*Crossing to R. and U.P.*] Yes, I was up late at the club; but I have a better husband for Lilian than either a French count or a poor artist.

FANNY. A better husband—who?

WEST. John Strebelow.

FANNY. A noble gentleman, but he is old; too old for a wife of eighteen.

WEST. Not forty yet!

FANNY. But I'm sure Lilian loves Harold Routledge.

WEST. Pshaw! I'll bet she has forgotten him already. Boys and girls of eighteen have whims, not love. You thought your heart would break when you married comfortable John Holcomb instead of romantic Alfred Harcourt. Yet you made a splendid wife, and a happy one.

FANNY. [*Dryly. Sits L.H.*] Did I? You judge by what you see, and all you see is the outside; where a woman is concerned, the blindest thing on earth is a man.

WEST. Well, well, sister, I'm not going to sell the girl. We'll talk of her again—after I've had my breakfast. [*Exits R.U.D.*]

FANNY. [*Solus*] Sell the girl! No, not so much a pound, I suppose, but like other fathers, you'll supply her a mentor where she wants a husband, and give her a stone where she asks for bread, on the plea that the stone is a diamond. [*Enter Lilian R.U.D.*]

LIL. [*Laughing*] Is the count gone? Good morning, aunt. [*Kisses Fanny*]

FANNY. Yes, pet. So you refused him?

LIL. Of course I did—courtship, castle, chivalry, and all. It was so very funny to see him. [*Laughs*]

FANNY. [*Looking at her steadily*] I thought you would.

LIL. You knew I would, when I laughed at him, which was from the door to Mount St. Vincent, and from Mount St. Vincent to the door again. He looked as if he'd like to call me out. [*Laughs*]

FANNY. This is the fourth offer you have refused in two weeks.

LIL. Is it? I don't want to marry. I'm as happy as a lark, and just as gay. I've done nothing but laugh all the morning. It was such fun. [*Laughs hysterically*]

FANNY. [*Rising and going to her, taking her by the waist*] Lilian, you are very miserable.

LIL. [*Looks up at Fanny; her hysterical laughter gradually becomes hysteric sobbing, and as she sinks on the chair, L.H., to which Fanny leads her, she bursts into tears*] My heart is breaking.

FANNY. [*Sighing*] I know, dear; I know! Harold Routledge sails for Europe tomorrow.

LIL. [*Sobbing*] I've tried so hard—so hard to forget him. I sent him back our engagement ring. I've done all I could to drive him from my mind. I stayed up half the night, reading all his letters before I—I b—burned them.

FANNY. My poor darling, listen to me; I lost my poor Alfred just in the same way! Don't repeat my mistake; write to Harold; tell him to come to you.

LIL. [*Rising and crossing to R. quickly*] Never! never! If my heart were to break a thousand times over, I would not do that. It is his place to write to me. He was in the wrong. [*Walks up and down the stage*]

FANNY. In the wrong?

LIL. He should have known me better than to fly at me about a mere flirtation with the Count de Carojac. He knew well enough it was all in fun; mere amusement.

FANNY. Well, well, dear, let me write to him. Let me tell him you have refused the count.

LIL. [*Demurely*] But, Aunt Fanny, he must not think I asked you to write.

FANNY. [*Smiling*] Certainly not. [*Crossing to R.*]

LIL. And you'll tell him I refused three other offers!

FANNY. [*Smiling*] Indeed I will.

LIL. And—ask him to—to call and see—and see you!

FANNY. Exactly.

LIL. [*Takes Fanny's head in her hands and kisses it*] Oh, you darling, good aunt!

FANNY. [*Kissing Lilian*] I am doing what I know your mother would do if she were alive to do it—what [*Sighing*] she would have done for me had I been wise enough to let her. I'll go to my room and write the letter.

LIL. You'll let me see it?

FANNY. Certainly not. It is none of your business, you know. [*Laughs*]

LIL. [*With frank, hearty laugh this time*] Ah—oh! Of course not—I forgot—I'm so happy.

FANNY. Heaven grant you may continue so, my darling. [*Exits R.U.D., R.2.E.*]

LIL. [*Solus*] Will he come? [*In affected doubt*] I rather think he will. I wonder how my eyes look—[*Goes to glass on mantel, L.H. Looks at herself; touches up her hair; turns from mirror*] I am pretty sure he will come. [*Enter Florence St. Vincent R.C.R.*]

FLOR. How de doo, Lilian?

LIL. [*Turning from glass*] Florence.

FLOR. [*Both sitting on ottoman, C.*] Riding with the Count de Carojac, eh? I saw you ride by our house. You to be a countess? Isn't the count magnificent? They say he's fought six duels, and he's a real nobleman, fresh from Paris, like the new spring bonnets just imported. I've been on the Boulevard driving with G. Washington Phipps, behind his new team—chestnuts—2:37. I suppose you've heard the news?

LIL. What news, dear?

FLOR. I'm going to be married.

LIL. [*Astonished*] Married! To whom?

FLOR. Mum! To old Mr. Brown, the millionaire.

LIL. To Mr. Brown! Why, he is nearly seventy!

FLOR. Exactly sixty-nine the twenty-eighth of last February. He says he's only fifty-nine, but I know better. I would not marry him if he were only fifty-nine; fifty-two years between us. There always ought to be some difference, you know.

LIL. Surely, Florence, you are not serious; your father cannot consent to such a sacrifice.

FLOR. My father is delighted! It is not every man that has a son-in-law old enough to be his father-in-law. My youngest son will be thirty-eight years old. When the minister pronounces me Mr. Brown's wife, I'll be a grandmother. [*Laughs*] One of my granddaughters is nearly as old as I am already. Brown is a millionaire three times over at least. Father is president of a life insurance company, and he knows about such things. He says the average life over seventy is about five years; allow five years more, for untoward accident; ten years, I'll be only twenty-nine. That's young, you know, for a rich widow.

LIL. Oh, Florence! Marriage is not a joke.

FLOR. Then I should like to know what it is. [*Laughs*] I haven't been able to keep my face straight five minutes at a time since I told old Brown I'd be his wife. [*Laughs. Enter Footman followed by Babbage R.L.D.*]

FOOT. I'll speak to Mr. Westbrook, sir. [*Exits R.U.D.*]

LIL. Oh, Mr. Babbage! [*Goes to him pleasantly as he moves downstage and gives him both her hands*]

FLOR. How do you do, Mr. Babbage?

BAB. [*With Lilian's hands in his, nods his head at Florence, then taps Lilian under the chin*] I su—I sue! Heigh-ho. [*Kisses Lilian*] Now run away both of you and play with your dolls. [*Florence and Lilian look at each other and laugh*] I have important business with your father, Lilian. [*Moves to L.H. Looks at papers in large pocketbook*]

LIL. [*Going*] Come, Florence.

FLOR. [*Aside to Lilian, as they go*] Brown is at least fifteen years older than he is. [*Laughs*]

LIL. Florence! [*Lilian and Florence exit C.U.D.*]

FLOR. [*Beyond the door, laughing*] It is such a joke on both of us. [*Her laugh is heard dying away in the distance*]

BAB. [*Solus, sitting R. of L. table*] Fifty thousand and a hundred and fifty—sixty-five—the registered bonds—Third National. [*Enter Westbrook, leisurely and yawning, R.U.D.*]

WEST. Ah, Babbage.

BAB. Just up? Three P.M.! Excuse my disturbing you so early in the morning.

WEST. [*Sits on ottoman, C.*] Right from the office, I suppose. For heaven's sake, don't talk business to me today, Babbage. I was out late last night, and I have a wretched headache.

BAB. You have a headache. Well, I've got something to cure your headache.

WEST. Eh!

BAB. Westbrook, you're a fool!

WEST. Thank you.

BAB. How much is this house worth?

WEST. Seventy-five thousand—why do you ask?

BAB. Is it free from incumbrance?

WEST. [*Embarrassed*] Y-e-s, that is—no—I put it in for a collateral yesterday—a private speculation of my own—a mere temporary matter.

BAB. How much?

WEST. Fifty thousand dollars.

BAB. Have you heard the news?

WEST. What news?

BAB. Do you want it sudden, or do you want it gradually? [*Pauses*] Westbrook, the firm of Babbage & Westbrook, Broad Street, will go into bankruptcy at three o'clock tomorrow afternoon. [*Rising—Westbrook is about to start to his feet, Babbage holds him down by the arm and resumes*] The firm of Traphagan & Traynor, London, went into bankruptcy this morning—news by cable. We hold their paper for three hundred and seventy-five thousand dollars. [*Westbrook falls back stunned in his chair*] How's your headache? [*Crossing to R.H.*]

WEST. My poor daughter!

BAB. Your own doing, Westbrook. The life of a quiet and respectable banker did not satisfy you; you must play the Rothschild, the merchant prince, live in imperial style, entertain foreign nobles, make your daughter—

WEST. Don't, Babbage—don't.

BAB. With your extravagance and private speculations, you've compelled the firm to run too near its capital, and now—

WEST. My poor daughter.

BAB. And mine! I have three daughters, four sons, and damn it, I've got a wife. Would to Heaven that were all. But our ruin involves others—you know what I mean.

WEST. Our depositors!

BAB. The earnings of the poor; of the legacy of the widow, the inheritance of an orphan.

West. My God! It is terrible! [*Rising, crossing to L. corner and back to L.C.*]

Bab. We need thirty thousand to fully meet our paper tomorrow. I've strained everything—everybody! We can't raise it. If this house were only free from incumbrance.

West. It is not, it is hopelessly involved. [*Sits R. of L.H. table; his hand falls on a letter*]

Bab. Then ruin must come to you and yours, to me and mine, to thousands of poor, honest, hard-working—

West. [*Rising in agitation*] There is a way.

Bab. A way!

West. [*Taking Strebelow's letter*] Here, read this—I can't.

Bab. [*After putting on spectacles, reads*] John Strebelow—Miss Westbrook's hand in marriage! I see—having pawned your house, you would pawn your child! Westbrook, you're a fool. [*Returns note to Westbrook*]

West. But—

Bab. [*In great agitation*] Damn me, but I'd rather see the firm of Babbage & Westbrook go to the devil, than see the happiness of that girl sacrificed to it. Besides, your daughter, like your house, is encumbered.

West. What do you mean?

Bab. I mean that Harold Routledge holds a mortgage on the property.

West. But Lilian and Mr. Routledge have had a serious disagreement. [*Rings bell*]

Bab. Of course they have. A woman never quarrels with a man she does not love, and damn it, never tires of quarrelling with the man she does love. You have been married—I am married, we both know it. [*Enter Footman R.U.D.*]

West. Let Miss Lilian know I wish to see her without delay.

Foot. Yes, sir. [*Exits R.U.D.*]

West. I take a different view of my daughter's happiness. I can hardly hope to avert the terrible calamity you announce through the wealth of Mr. Strebelow, though it may possibly so turn out. I certainly shall not ask him for a check convertible tomorrow in exchange for my daughter's hand; but with John Strebelow her future is safe, whatever comes to us. To give her to such a man is not to sacrifice, but to shield her from the storm. This is what I wish to do. If you care to hear the result, I will join you presently in the sitting room.

Bab. [*Going*] Yes, I'll wait. But if the credit of Babbage & Westbrook cannot be saved without the sacrifice of a young girl's heart, I'd rather see it crumpled to the dust, and act as assistant bookkeeper to a peanut stand for the rest of my natural life. [*Exits R. lower D.*]

WEST. [*Solus*] It is not for my sake, it is for her own. No girl could be the wife of a man like Strebelow and not learn to love him. She will be provided for; she will keep her rank in society. What father could do otherwise? [*Enter Lilian R.U.D.*]

LIL. You wish to see me, father?

WEST. [*Not looking at her*] Yes, I—I received this note a while ago. What answer shall I send, or rather give, for Mr. Strebelow will soon call?

LIL. Mr. Strebelow! [*Looks at letter*] Oh, papa!

WEST. [*His face still averted*] What shall I say to him?

LIL. It quite takes my breath away.

WEST. [*At the table, pretending to look at papers*] It is a grand offer.

LIL. Of course it is.

WEST. And you may well be proud of it.

LIL. Indeed I am proud, very proud.

WEST. [*Eagerly turning to her*] Then I may answer, yes.

LIL. Oh, no—no!

WEST. No, why?

LIL. I do not love Mr. Strebelow, papa. I esteem, revere him, like him very much; but I—I—I never thought of him in—in that way, you know.

WEST. You have broken off your engagement with Harold Routledge?

LIL. [*Agitated*] Yes, I—I have.

WEST. You would soon learn to love Mr. Strebelow; why, when you were but twelve years old, you know, you used to call him your sweetheart. Oh, your old liking for him will soon return, after you are married to him.

LIL. [*Starting*] After I am married to him. Why, papa!

WEST. [*Leading to ottoman, C.*] Listen, my child. I am ruined! In a few days I will have no home of my own, no roof to cover you.

LIL. [*Bewildered*] You, poor!

WEST. Worse than poor—bankrupt. I would see you sheltered from wants, from humiliations you have never yet known.

LIL. I'm not afraid, so long as I am with you. [*Kneeling at his feet*]

WEST. [*Putting her back on the ottoman, kissing her*] Brave girl! But it is not only poverty, it is shame, disgrace. It is not only ourselves, it is hundreds, thousands, will find their ruin in mine! Who will heap upon your father's head the curses of the poor, the wail of the widow, and the tears of the orphan. I cannot survive it. [*Rising, taking L. corner*]

LIL. [*Rising*] I see it! I see it! [*With forced calmness*] And this marriage would avert all this?

WEST. [*Back to L.C.*]   It would save us all. Thank God, your mother was spared this misery!

LIL.   Mother! Father, I—I will—I—

WEST.   Make the sacrifice—I mean—give your hand.

LIL.   My mother's last words to me were, "Do all you can to make your father's old age happy."

WEST. [*Averting his head again*]   One word will save it from infamy.

LIL.   Then I say it. Yes. [*Embrace*] But before you repeat that word to Mr. Strebelow, you must promise me one thing.

WEST.   Anything.

LIL.   It is this. You will tell Mr. Strebelow that I will be his—his wife. [*Pause*] That I accept him, if he will accept my hand without the heart I cannot now give him; and be satisfied with gratitude and respect instead of love. [*Crossing to L.H. Enter Footman, R. lower door, gives card to Westbrook*]

WEST.   Mr. Strebelow. Certainly, certainly. Show him in. [*Footman about to exit*]

LIL. [*To Footman*]   Stop—one moment. You [*To Westbrook*] will do what I asked?

WEST.   Yes.

LIL. [*To Footman*]   You can go. [*Exit Footman R.L.D.*] I could not trust myself to make such an explanation to Mr. Strebelow. I will leave you with him, father, and take with me your promise to be as frank with him as I have been with you. Then, if he will, he can take all I have left to give—my hand. [*Staggers*]

WEST. [*Leading her to a chair L.H.*]   But sit down, the suddenness of this has made you faint.

LIL.   Only a little; I—I don't think I will sit down—I might lack strength to rise again. [*Stands, leaning against chair. Enter Footman announcing Mr. Strebelow. Enter Strebelow R.L.D.*]

WEST. [*Going to meet him, they shake hands*]   My dear Strebelow, I'm delighted to see you, and to see you looking so well.

STREB.   Thanks. [*Crossing to Lilian, bowing*] Miss Westbrook. [*Goes toward her; she takes a feeble step to meet him; he holds out his hand, she places hers in it, her left hand clinging to the chair, L.H., for support*] May I hope my visit is equally welcome to you?

LIL. [*With calmness evidently voiced*]   So old a friend cannot be otherwise than welcome.

STREB.   I was in hopes your father had placed me in a more—I mean a different light than that of a mere friend.

LIL. My father has handed me your note, Mr. Strebelow. [*Stops short*]

STREB. Not, I trust, without the endorsement of his approval. [*Looking at Westbrook*]

WEST. I believe that Lilian can best tell you how much I approve of it.

STREB. [*To Lilian*] Let me hope to your father's approval, your own is added, and that—[*Seems embarrassed by Lilian's attitude*] and that I may expect an answer. [*Stops to take her hand*]

LIL. [*Giving her hand mechanically*] I must refer you to himself.

STREB. And after I have seen him, may I not see you?

LIL. [*Feebly*] Certainly. Father.

WEST. [*Crossing to Lilian, she takes his arm, lets go the chair, and walks to door R.U.E., turns, bows to Strebelow*] You will excuse Lilian and myself a moment. [*Exit, supporting Lilian, R.U.D.*]

STREB. [*Solus, crossing to L.C.*] Is my suit accepted under protest or is the strangeness of her manner the effect of mere timidity, a timidity probably increased by my formality? Still, there was an expression of suppressed emotion that may be either flattering or fatal to my affection. Those rumors, too, that I have heard upon the street. I will know the truth from Westbrook. I must in justice to her, in justice to myself. [*Enter Westbrook R.U.D.*]

WEST. [*Goes to Strebelow with outstretched hands*] John, I congratulate you.

STREB. Then I am accepted.

WEST. Why, certainly. Sit down.

STREB. [*Sits on ottoman, C.*] Westbrook, at such a moment frankness is a duty, and you will excuse it in a man to whom you entrust your daughter's happiness, and who trusts his own to her.

WEST. [*Embarrassed*] Certainly—certainly.

STREB. My proposal, though long contemplated by myself, must have appeared sudden to you—still more sudden to your daughter. Permission to address her as a suitor was all I expected. Her timid manner and her—

WEST. [*Trying to make light of it*] Tut! Tut! A girl of eighteen—besides she has been riding all the morning. Her nerves are out of order, and she is tired.

STREB. [*Watching him*] And she is yielding to no influence of yours?

WEST. [*Embarrassed*] Why should you think so?

STREB. Frankly then, because I have heard today that the firm of Babbage & Westbrook is likely to go to protest tomorrow.

WEST. [*Rising*] Mr. Strebelow!

STREB. Is it true?

WEST. We—we are—a little driven for ready money.

STREB.   How much will be necessary to make your paper good?

WEST.   Only thirty thousand dollars.

STREB. [*Rising*]   May I write here? [*Sits at L.H. table*]

WEST. [*Feigning astonishment*]   Why not?

STREB. [*Sits at table—writes*]   This is the seventeenth—[*Taking pocket check-book from pocket*]

WEST.   Of November—yes.

STREB.   I will meet your deficiencies, Mr. Westbrook.

WEST.   What! You?

STREB.   Yes. Here is the check for the amount you need. You can give me what security you please, and at your own convenience. Did your daughter know of your financial troubles?

WEST. [*With effort*]   She did not.

STREB.   Then I wronged you both. Calm and formal as I am, I have long loved your daughter. I was her knight, her champion in the old days. She used to say I would be her sweetheart. She would lay her head on my breast, and go to sleep there; the little thing would nestle there, and I believe she has never fairly grown out of it, and I—and I did not wish—but you are free now, and your free answer is—

WEST.   Yes.

STREB. [*Shaking hands with Westbrook*]   Pardon my frankness and accept my thanks. May I see her?

WEST. [*Crossing to L.H., rings bell on L.H. table*]   Of course.

STREB.   It will be the endeavor of my life to render her happy—a solitary man, she will have all my care, all my love, and if her father needs my aid, he has only to speak. [*Enter Footman R.U.D.*]

WEST.   Tell Miss Lilian Mr. Strebelow is waiting for her. [*Exit Footman R.U.D. Westbrook to Strebelow*]   There is not a man in the world to whom I would so confidently entrust her—and I know that in giving her to you, I do all a father can to insure her happiness—and it is in that belief I do what I am doing. [*Enter Lilian R.U.D.*]

LIL. [*Down R.*]   Mr. Strebelow!

STREB. [*Meeting her R.C.*]   Lilian! I may call you that now?

LIL.   My father has told you—

STREB.   Your father has told me all. [*He holds out his hand*]

LIL.   So be it then. [*Gives him her hand—he kisses it. Enter Aunt Fanny R.U.D.*]

FANNY.   Mr. Strebelow. [*Bows*]

STREB.   Mrs. Holcomb. [*Bows*]

FANNY.   Will you excuse me? I have a word to say to Lilian.

WEST. Mr. Strebelow, if you will accompany me to the sitting room, Mr.
Babbage and myself will explain how this sudden strain has arisen, owing to
failure of a firm in London whose papers we largely hold. [*They cross and
exit R.L.D., Strebelow bowing to the ladies*]

FANNY. He's come! I knew he would.

LIL. Harold!

FANNY. Yes. He's in the reception room. He kissed me for joy.

LIL. [*Wringing her hands*] Oh, what have I done? What have I done?
[*Crosses to R.*]

FANNY. I told him I would send you to him. He cannot sit still a moment
—not one moment.

LIL. See him—I will—I will. [*Goes toward door—at door rings bell*] But
now, heavens, I dare not. [*Enter Footman R.D.*] Tell Mr. Routledge that
Miss Westbrook cannot see him. [*Goes to Aunt Fanny*] I have concluded not
to see—never again to see Harold—Mr. Routledge!

FANNY. [*Surprised*] Why?

LIL. Because, [*Steadies herself*] Aunt Fanny, Mr. Strebelow is to be my
husband. Oh, Aunt Fanny, my heart is broken! [*Falls on ottoman. Quick
drop of curtain*]

ACT II.

*Salon. As curtain rises Lilian is discovered seated at piano L., Natalie stand-
ing by her side.*

NAT. Oh, no, no! I want you to sing some more.

LIL. But there is no more, dear.

NAT. [*Imperiously*] Then make some more.

LIL. My dear, I am not able to do that.

NAT. [*Laughs, throws her arms around her mother, kisses her*] Then sing
how much you love me. Oh, see, in the book [*Drags Lilian over to R., takes
volume of Moore's Irish Melodies off table R.H., holds it up to her. Opens it
haphazard*]

LIL. [*Taking book, sits R.C.*] This, this tells the story.

NAT. Oh, do sing.

LIL. [*Sings*]

> "I'd mourn the hopes that leave me,
>   If thy smile had left me, too.
> I'd weep when friends deceive me,

If thou wert, like them, untrue. [*Holding Natalie out be-fore her*]

"But while I've thee before me,
With heart so warm and eyes so bright,
No clouds can linger o'er me,
That smile turns them all to light." [*Catching Natalie in her arms and lifting her to her lap*] So it does, darling, so it does! [*She kisses child. Westbrook has entered, C.R., at the last line of the last verse and stops at threshold looking at mother and child*]

WEST. Thank Heaven! I wish Fanny Holcomb could see this falsification of her prophecies, this justification of my wisdom.

NAT. [*Sees him over her mother's shoulder*] Oh, mamma, a gentleman. Is this grandpapa?

WEST. [*Coming down as Lilian puts Natalie down*] Yes, grandpapa come at last. [*Opens his arms to her. Natalie rushes into them. Kisses her, etc.*]

LIL. Oh, father! [*They embrace*]

WEST. Natalie has almost forgotten me, eh?

NAT. Your hair has grown so white.

WEST. [*Patting Natalie's head*] It is a long time since it looked like yours. [*To Lilian*] But you seem surprised to see me. Did you not receive my telegram? [*Putting her down*]

LIL. No. Nothing but your letter announcing your departure by the *Europa*.

WEST. I wrote you from Liverpool, and telegraphed you from Dover. But how is John? [*Enter Strebelow, R.3.E., with letter and telegram in hand*]

STREB. [*As he enters*] A letter from your father, Lilian, dated Liverpool. He ought to be here.

WEST. He is here! [*Strebelow crosses to him*]

STREB. [*As they shake hands*] So you have come at last, after three years promising.

WEST. Business was such I could not get away.

STREB. And prosperity has waited on attention.

WEST. Yes. Thank Heaven, we have steered over all the breakers and stand on a firm shore at last.

STREB. And Babbage?

WEST. [*Smiling*] Just as happy and just as surly as he can be.

STREB. [*Laughs*] But what do you think of Natalie and Lilian?

WEST. As I look at both I think John Strebelow must be the happiest man on earth.

LIL.   Oh, father! [*Taking Natalie*] But I must go dress the child. I suppose you and Mr. Strebelow have a good deal to say to each other, so I'll leave you for a while. Come, dear.

NAT.   But can I come and see grandpapa again after I'm dressed?

LIL.   Certainly.

STREB. [*To Lilian*]   Why not let Lizette dress her, dear?

LIL. [*Hesitating*]   Yes—but—

NAT.   No, no. Mamma promised to dress me herself to see grandpapa. Come, mamma, come. So I can come back soon. [*Pulls Lilian out R.3.E.*]

LIL. [*Turning at door*]   Is she not lovely? [*Kisses her. Exit*]

WEST. [*Visibly affected, L.H.*]   I should like to thank you for the happiness you have conferred on me and mine. But I—I can't, my son—I can't.

STREB. [*R.H.*]   I've done my best to make her happy. I believe she is so. Though at times I cannot help noticing a sadness of look and tone that seldom leaves her save when with her child.

WEST.   They were both gay enough when I came in—laughing, singing, kissing.

STREB. [*Thoughtfully*]   Her whole heart is wrapped up in her child. If I were a younger husband, I might be jealous of the absorbing love she bears it.

WEST. [*Laughing*]   The law of nature! The husband is number one till baby comes. Then he becomes number two; and, after all, a husband may well content himself with the second place in his wife's heart, when he knows 'tis only a miniature of himself that fills the first. [*Gives him bundle of New York papers. Enter Lizette*]

LIZ. [*Announcing*]   Monsieur and Madame de Browne. [*Enter Florence C.D. from R. Lizette remains standing at door. Florence deep curtsy to Strebelow*]

FLOR. [*Down C.*]   How is the Duke de Strebelow this morning? Where is the duchess? Is Lilian well? Ah! The Marquis de Westbrook. So you have arrived at last. How de doo? How is everybody in New York?

WEST. [*Shakes hands with her*]   Delighted to see you looking so well.

STREB. [*Laughing*]   My dear Mrs. Brown, you lavish your titles with such princely generosity that we poor republicans—

FLOR.   "We republicans!" How I hate that word. Americans in Paris are at such a disadvantage in society! I am presented to Madame La Comtesse de Pompadilli, Cora Lacabella de Pontville, for instance, as plain Mrs. Brown. Mrs. B-r-o-w-n-e! I had to add the *e* myself. I want to keep in aristocratic practice. Browne is nearly seventy-six years old, you know. Perhaps I'll marry a duke some day or a Russian prince or an Italian nobleman, fresh from the almshouse.

STREB. [*Humoring her*] How is his highness—your royal consort—the Prince de Browne, this morning?

FLOR. The Prince de Browne is in his usual health; that is, he has the gout; he is coming upstairs now. Brown has the gout in its most aristocratic form. If he were a lineal descendant of William the Conqueror's entire army, he couldn't have it worse. [*Goes to the door, looks out*] Here comes the prince himself. [*Enter Brown, D.R., extremely senile. Hobbles on a cane. One leg bound up in bandages. He is richly, juvenilely dressed. Florence pats him*]

BROWN. He, eh, eh! My dear, [*Patting Florence under chin. Kisses her*] you got upstairs before me, didn't you? Strebelow, my dear fellow! Ah! Westbrook, [*Crosses to him*] got in at last, eh! Well? [*Shakes hands with Westbrook*]

WEST. Very well, thanks. But I'm sorry to see you so lame.

BROWN. Only a temporary attack, my dear boy. I'll be over it in six weeks. When such a thing attacks very old men they lack vitality to throw it off. [*To Strebelow*] But with a man of your age and mine, you know, [*Strebelow turns to hide a laugh as Florence nudges Westbrook*] the energy and elasticity of nature soon overcome its force. These premature attacks make some people think I'm old. It makes it appear as if there were some inappropriate difference, so to speak, between my wife's age and my own. [*Pats Florence under the chin*] We know better, don't we, my love? There isn't a better matched couple in the world. He, he! But time will fly, I suppose. Heigh-ho! Florence and I will soon be growing old together.

FLOR. Brown, my dear, you haven't had your afternoon nap yet. [*Goes to D.L.3.E.*]

BROWN. He, he, he! Yes, yes! During these temporary attacks I do like an afternoon nap, now and then. I'll go into the smoking-room and drop down on the lounge. I say, Westbrook, come with me and tell me all the news from New York, and put me to sleep. [*Moving up L.*] We regard this as Liberty Hall, Westbrook. Strebelow likes it. [*Strebelow courteously assents in dumb show*] Really I am getting as much attached to these afternoon naps as if I were a decrepit old man. If I don't get well soon, I dare say the habit will become so confirmed I'll keep up my nap for the next fifty years. [*Hobbles out L.3.E., followed by Westbrook*]

FLOR. [*In alarm down L.C.*] Fifty years! Strebelow, I'm really anxious about the prince.

STREB. No need to be anxious, my dear Mrs. Brown. I dare say he'll last for twenty years yet. He comes of a long and lingering family.

FLOR. [*With wry face*] That's comforting. [*Goes to easel*] But how do you like Lilian's portrait, now it is finally finished?

STREB. [*Going up L.C.*]   The expression is, I think, too sad.

FLOR.   You cannot blame the artist for that. I have not heard a hearty ᵤugh from Lilian since she has been married.

STREB.   That's very comforting.

FLOR.   Only tit for tat. You have invited M. Montvillais, the art critic, and ᵣe Count de Carojac to see the picture this afternoon.

STREB.   Yes, before it disappears forever from profane eyes in Lilian's ᵦoudoir.

FLOR.   By the way, I suppose you know the Count de Carojac has been ᵣaking desperate love to your wife lately?

STREB.   Has he?

FLOR.   Has he? Is that all you have to say about it? I expected—

STREB. [*Laughing*]   What?

FLOR.   That you would fly into a passion, tear your hair—seconds—pistols.

STREB. [*Laughing*]   I have no desire to face the most dangerous duelist in ᵖaris. Besides, de Carojac is a friend of mine, and as a French gentleman ᵣonsiders it his duty to prove his friendship by making love to my wife, in ᵣompliment to my taste.

FLOR.   And what do you consider your duty as an American husband?

STREB. [*Seriously*]   You forget I have an American wife.

FLOR.   I wonder if Brown has the same confidence in my nationality.

STREB. [*Laughing and going towards D.R.*]   I will inform the Duchesse ᵢe Strebelow that you are here. Speaking of female nationality in connection ᵥith the duties of a wife, I find it very hard to realize that Mrs. Brown is not ᵣ born Frenchwoman. [*Exits R.3.E.*]

FLOR. [*Sitting on piano stool, yawning*]   Strebelow is too phlegmatic for a ᵢight. [*Yawns*] I shall die of ennui. There is no getting a sensation out of ᵢnybody. If Carojac would make love to *me,* now. There might be some fun ᵢn that. But Brown has the gout, and he's too old for a row. It's very stupid.

LIZ. [*Entering C.R.*]   The Count de Carojac. [*Exits. Enter Carojac C. ᵣrom R.*]

FLOR.   Oh, so delighted to see you!

CARO. [*Down R.C.*]   Madame Brown, I am surprised.

FLOR.   And sorry to find me here. I know it.

CARO. [*Sardonically*]   I am too polite to contradict a lady.

FLOR. [*Going up L.C.*]   You are as polished as a razor, and just as sharp.

CARO.   Thank you.

FLOR.   Well, there's the picture. [*He crosses to easel*] I hope its beauty will console you for the loss of the original.

CARO.   I do not understand.

FLOR. Oh, yes, you do. She gave you the mitten.

CARO. The mitten. [*Coming down L.C.*] Zee gloves wizout fingers, wo is dat, eh?

FLOR. Mr. Routledge was too much for you in New York. Better mak good use of your time now, for he has just arrived in Paris, and may turi the joke against you once more.

CARO. [*Suppressing vexation*] M. Routledge eez een Paree, eh? [*Aside* If he zhoke weed me here, he may have to pay for zee zhoke. [*Goes t portrait*] Dayre is much melancholy in dee face.

FLOR. [*Watching him*] She's pondering over the past—the rides in th park, you know. [*Laughs*]

CARO. Zay mock zemselves of me altogether. Sac—

FLOR. [*Laughing still*] Now, don't be angry. Mrs. Strebelow will be her in a moment. Make love to her picture. I must go to the Prince de Brown and put a handkerchief over his old head or he will wake up sneezing. [*Run. off L.3.E. Reappears, watching Carojac*]

CARO. [*Before portrait*] The laugh is gone from the face now. I like i so much the better. I deed loof her. I think I loof her still. [*Enter Lilia R.3.E.*] She eez beauteeful! How lovely is the poise of the head, the outline of the face.

LIL. [*Coming forward*] I beg pardon, count.

CARO. Ah, madam, I was admiring.

FLOR. [*Peeping in and laughing*] The poise of the head, the outline o the face. [*Crosses to C. Lilian smiles*]

CARO. [*L.*] Zay laugh at me again.

FLOR. [*C.*] Better transfer your devotion to me, count.

CARO. I'll do any penance for my indiscretion, even that. [*Aside*] Zee she-devil!

LIZ. [*Announcing from C.R.*] M. de Montvillais! [*Exits as Montvillais enters*]

MONT. [*General bow*] Delighted, I am sure.

LIL. It is kind of you to come and give us the benefit of the acumen of so celebrated a critic.

MONT. [*Crossing to picture*] M-m-m! Ah, yes! Fine feeling! Le Rabiteau's usual precision of drawing—lacks tenderness in the flesh tints—richly toned, very.

FLOR. We know all about it now. [*Glancing at Carojac*] You French gentlemen are such excellent judges of pictures, eh, count?

CARO. [*Suppressing his vexation*] Yes, in art as in the politesse of life, zee French are the Greeks of our day.

STREB. [*Entering R.3.E.*] And the outer world barbarian, eh? [*Shakes ands with Montvillais and Carojac*]

MONT. Not exactly that, but—

STREB. Something very like it. But, Lilian, I forgot to tell you that your ld friend and playmate arrived in Paris yesterday on his way back to Rome. prevailed on him to stay over a day and give us at least one call.

LIL. Who?

STREB. Mr. Harold Routledge. I should think Mr. Routledge's success as n artist a fair reply to M. de Carojac's contempt of all art but French art.

LIL. [*At fireplace, R.H., with suppressed emotion*] Is Harold—is Mr. outledge here?

LIZ. [*Announcing C.R.*] M. Routledge. [*Exits C.R. Enter Harold C.R.*]

STREB. [*Moves to meet Harold, shakes hands*] This is kind of you, Mr. outledge.

FLOR. [*Going to him*] I am very glad to see you. [*Cordial shaking of ands*]

ROUT. Florence, Mrs. Brown, I should say. This is an unexpected pleasure. *Advancing*] Mrs. Streb—Mrs. Strebelow!

LIL. Mr. Routledge.

FLOR. [*Laughing*] Mrs. Strebelow, Mr. Routledge, why don't you shake ands? [*They shake hands*]

LIL. I am glad you did not pass through Paris without calling on us, Mr. outledge.

ROUT. You are very kind, madam. [*To Carojac*] Ah, Count de Carojac.

CARO. Mr. Routledge.

STREB. [*To Routledge*] M. de Montvillais. I beg your pardon, he is so elebrated a critic that I supposed you already knew him.

ROUT. [*Carojac sits on piano stool*] I had not the pleasure.

MONT. [*Condescendingly*] I know M. Routledge, by reputation. I had the onor to criticize his Dante and Beatrice, now in the Salon. In my private apacity I may say here in confidence it is a noble work, faultless. Of course, could not say that in public, you know.

ROUT. [*Smiling at Montvillais*] I shall respect your confidence, monsieur.

CARO. [*Meaningly*] I see zee picture, and like all Paree I recognize the original of the Beatrice. It must be unpleasant for Madame Strebelow. Veree unfortunate.

ROUT. [*As if stung, glances at Carojac, then at Lilian*] Really, sir—

STREB. [*Sitting on chair, L.C., looking at picture*] I have heard of the ikeness, and must go to the Salon and see your picture, Routledge.

ROUT. [*Seated L. of R. table*] The resemblance is purely accidental. Seeing Mrs. Strebelow now after six years, I must admit that it does exist. knew Mrs. Strebelow in our young days, and I dare say that memory uncon sciously took the place of inspiration.

CARO. Ah, zee memory must often be an annoyance to zee artist, eh Mixing the disappointments of zee past with zee hopes of the future.

ROUT. [*Quickly*] Not in this case, sir. The suggestion—

CARO. Oh, it is more than a suggestion. It really might be accepted as portrait of Madame Strebelow.

STREB. [*To Routledge*] Then you have been more successful than Le Rabi teau, here. [*Points to picture*] Completed but yesterday. Indeed, our little conclave today was to pass upon its merits. [*Rises*]

ROUT. [*Crossing to L.C.*] Rabiteau is an excellent artist.

STREB. Perhaps so. But in this case he has seemed inspired with a spirit o sadness.

CARO. [*At Routledge*] With him it could not have been memory.

MONT. [*Down C.*] I do not know about that. You recollect the scanda caused by his picture of the young Marquise de Pauliac?

FLOR. [*Quickly crossing to R.C.*] A scandal about a marquise. Oh, do tell it. [*Strebelow down L.C.*]

MONT. It is said that Rabiteau fell in love with her during her sittings, and she with him. But they very properly married her to a rich old nobleman instead of to a poor artist. Rabiteau had his revenge. He bestowed upon her face an expression that seemed to tell the story.

FLOR. [*Eagerly*] What story?

MONT. The story of a broken heart. Of a woman bearing in her bosom a secret that must not live, yet cannot die. A sadder story than that of the Spar- tan boy who let the cub eat his heart out ere he would reveal its guilty presence beneath his tunic. Some memory of this may have guided Rabiteau's pencil, suggested by a passing look on Mrs. Strebelow's face—a look of sorrow at the premature crushing of a new bonnet, perhaps, which memory ideal- ized. [*Florence goes to Lilian. Lilian holds Florence as if for support. Harold's eyes and hers meet. She turns away her head*]

STREB. [*Seeing all this*] And you think Mrs. Strebelow's face suggested his own experience?

MONT. Perhaps—as a child sees faces in the clouds. [*Going up C., talking to Florence*]

STREB. Tut, tut! Let us go to the smoking-room. [*To Lilian*] Mr. Rout- ledge will tell you the latest fashionable news from New York. Come, gentle- men. Carojac, come. [*Exit R.3.E. Carojac follows to the door and returns*]

FLOR. And I will return to Brown. [*Lilian tries to stop her. She looks knowingly from one to the other and crosses to L.H.*] I'm afraid the handkerchief has fallen off his dear old head. I'm a mother to Brown.

CARO. [*In low tone to Routledge*] An excellent opportunity to refresh your memory for future inspirations.

ROUT. I do not understand—

CARO. [*Bowing*] I shall be happy to give zee explanation when and where you will. [*Bows and exits R.3.E. To Lilian*] Madam!

LIL. Mr. Routledge.

ROUT. Madam.

LIL. My husband tells me you have just returned from the United States. But pray be seated. [*Harold brings forward chair L.C. Sits L. Lilian sits R.*]

ROUT. My first visit to America in seven years. During that time I scarcely ever left Rome.

LIL. The reputation you have acquired is proof of the good use you made of your time. [*Awkward pause. With the air of one who has made up her mind to do something she feared*] Mr. Routledge, I am glad to have this opportunity to refer to a subject, the—the delicacy of which, time has in—in some sort lessened.

ROUT. Really, madam, I am at a loss to understand what in the past can require an explanation between us. When you closed that past, you explained it.

LIL. No, sir! Nor could I then trust myself to do so. I feel now, have never ceased to feel, that the explanation is due to you.

ROUT. [*Rising*] I do not feel so, now.

LIL. [*Positively*] Then, sir, it is due to me. And in justice to me, I am sure you will hear it.

ROUT. [*Inclining his head*] Madam.

LIL. You and I were engaged to be married.

ROUT. [*Standing C.*] I thought so.

LIL. After our foolish quarrel I sent for you to return to me.

ROUT. So I understood the letter I received from Mrs. Holcomb. In obedience to that letter, I did return. I returned full of joy and happiness, and when my heart was at its fullest. I was discarded through the mouth of a lackey.

LIL. And you never knew why, never guessed why?

ROUT. [*Bitterly*] You are mistaken. I knew why the very next day. I knew why when I heard from Mrs. Holcomb that you had accepted the hand of Mr. John Strebelow, who is a very rich man.

LIL. But you did not know why I accepted him?

ROUT. [*Bitterly still*] Because he, as I said, is a very rich man.

LIL. Mr. Routledge, that is true. [*Rising*]

ROUT. You see, madam, no explanation was needed. [*Taking L. corner*]

LIL. No explanation I could then make. But Mr. Strebelow and myself have now been married and been happy together for seven years, and I can, I believe without injustice to him, explain why I did marry him for his money. I state it plainly and truly.

ROUT. I have no doubt the purity of your motives equalled the frankness of this confession.

LIL. Those motives I think it is just to you to state, due to myself to make clear. [*Invites him to sit R.C. She sits R.H.*] Ten minutes after, with my consent, Aunt Fanny wrote you to return, my father told me that he was ruined, that in his ruin was involved the ruin of hundreds of others who had trusted their all to him. He besought me to save him from infamy, spoke of the curses of the poor, drew so appalling a picture that in pity, in fear, scarce knowing what I did, I consented before I had even time to think of what I had done. Mr. Strebelow came and I accepted him. I had scarcely done so, when you called. I—I tried to go to you, Harold. I tried, I could not, and so—so—

ROUT. [*Rising*] Sent that message which condemned my heart to bitterness of isolation forever. [*Crosses to L. Sits*]

LIL. Can you forgive me?

ROUT. I have already done so. And you are happy?

LIL. I am content. [*Music*] And you, Harold?

ROUT. I suffered much, for I loved much. Had I loved less, the wound to my pride would have healed more quickly.

LIL. But you are happy now. Say you are. Say it.

ROUT. Lilian, I would not add to the burden you have borne, the weight of a single reproach, but I cannot say what you ask me. [*Up C.*] Work as I may, do what I will, the feeling of the past clings to me. It tinges my every thought, steals into my every canvas, makes the present wearisome, robs the future of every rainbow tint that makes work a consolation.

LIL. Oh, Harold, don't, don't!

ROUT. I should not say this to you, Lilian, but I have suffered so, cherishing a secret I dare not tell, and brooding over a love that would not die.

LIL. [*Weeping, goes to him*] Poor Harold!

ROUT. [*Puts one arm around her waist*] And you have not forgotten me, Lilian?

LIL. I have never ceased to sympathize with the sorrow I knew, I felt you were suffering. For I knew what it cost me to inflict it upon you.

ROUT. [*Madly rising*] And you—you love me still?

LIL. [*Starting back*] This is cruel of you. Unkind, Harold.

Rout. [*Catching her again*] I know not what I say, what I do. Let me
arry away with me some word of affection—some.

Lil. [*Breaks from him*] Leave with me untainted the respect I have al-
ays entertained for you, Harold. I was foolish thus to trust you—to trust
yself.

Rout. [*Following her*] You shall, you must.

Lil. I must remember what you seem to forget, that I am the wife of John
trebelow. One word more, and I ring. [*Hand over bell on table. Enter Caro-
c R.D.*]

Caro. [*Sardonically*] I thought so! You need not ring, madam. No scan-
al! [*Lilian screams, hangs her head*]

Rout. Sir!

Caro. [*To Lilian*] Mr. Routledge's memory of where he stands will calm
e ardor of his inspirations. [*Routledge bows. Count bows. Quick curtain*]

ACT III.

et: *Vestibule and stairway of the American Embassy at Paris. Guests com-
g up and going down stairs. Servant coming downstairs from L. off R.U.E.
trebelow and Carojac from cloakroom R.U.E. to C. French officer and lady
nter R.2.E., go off R.U.E. Servant from R.U.E. goes upstairs and off L.U.E.
ith card.*

Caro. Madame Strebelow is with you this evening, of course.

Streb. She will be down presently. You frequently honor our receptions
t the American Legation, M. le Comte.

Caro. Yes. The American ladies are so very beautiful.

Streb. And in the presence of female beauty, a French gentleman is never
lind; eh, M. le Comte? [*Laughs. Enter Florence R.U.E. downstairs*]

Flor. M. Strebelow, you are late. How is Lilian this evening? M. le
Comte. [*Nods*]

Caro. Madam.

Streb. [*R.H.*] Mrs. Strebelow was detained with her daughter.

Flor. [*C.*] Lilian is a slave to that child. [*Looking R.U.E.*] Why, here
omes the prince. I just left him on the sofa in the back hall room talking
ith Mrs. Gordon; I thought I'd got him fixed for two hours at least. [*French
fficer enters from cloakroom, goes upstairs and off L.U.E., then servant
omes from L.U.E. Exits into cloakroom. Enter Brown, L.U.E., hobbling with
ane downstairs from R.U.E.*]

BROWN. Ah, you are here, my dear—he, he! You lost me, didn't you? H
he, he! [*Patting her under chin*] I have been talking with young Mr
Gordon, my dear. You mustn't be jealous. I'm not a Don Juan, my love, I'r
not a Don Juan. [*Crosses to Strebelow. Laughs*] I say, Strebelow, old bo*
[*Apart to Strebelow, who has crossed to R.C. Florence talks with Carojac*
These young women are jealous creatures. [*Laughs*] They keep their eyes o
their husbands. [*Laughs*] It's fun to tease them now and then, [*Laughs*] isn
it? [*Poking Strebelow in the ribs*] Just for a little spice, you know! It
wicked, I know it's wicked, but [*Laughs*] I believe they love a man all th
more for a touch of—of deviltry—now and then—you know. [*Laugh
punches Strebelow. Gentleman enters R.D. Exits into cloakroom, after glan
ing at Brown and looking as if new to him*]

FLOR. [*To Carojac*] Wait till I get Brown fixed nice and comfortabl
somewhere. [*To Brown*] My dear, don't you want to come into the nex
room? There's a sofa and an easy chair. We'll have a nice visit, you and I, a
by ourselves. [*Gentleman and lady enter, R.D., are going toward cloakroon
Servant enters with salver from cloakroom, one card upon it; gentlema
places his card upon it. Servant goes up and off L.U.E. Gentleman and lad
into cloakroom*]

BROWN. [*Laughs*] Yes, my dear. I say, Strebelow, she's a little jealous, d
you see? She likes to be alone with me. Come, my love. [*Going with Flor
ence, looks back at Strebelow*] Try it Strebelow, try it with your wife. It work
to a charm—a little deviltry, you know. A trifle jealous, eh, Florence? Try i
Strebelow. Come, my love. I'm not a Don Juan, my dear, I'm not a Don Juar
[*Exits L.H.2.E.*]

FLOR. [*Finger to her lips*] Sh! I'll have the prince asleep upon the sofa i
less than five minutes. [*The Count bows and waves his hand. She returns i
Exits after Brown L.H. Enter Montvillais R.2.E. Austrian officer. They bou
to each other. Officer goes into cloakroom. French officer and lady com
down L. stairs, go up R. stairs*]

MONT. Good evening, gentlemen. Dropped in at the opera this evening
Ortalini's voice is splendid, but the chorus is execrable. Ah, a new bit o
bronze since the last reception—Hymen; rather too full about the torso
[*Enter G. Washington Phipps R.2.E. He is crossing the stage rapidly. Stop
suddenly. He is an energetic young American business man in manner an
appearance; dress suit*]

PHIPPS. Eh, Strebelow!

STREB. Mr. Phipps.

PHIPPS. [*Crossing to Strebelow*]   Glad to see you. Heard you were living
ere. How is your wife? [*Gentleman and lady enter from cloakroom, go up
nd off L.U.E. Servant comes down from L.U.E. and exits to cloakroom*]

STREB.   Well, thank you. When did you arrive in Paris?

PHIPPS.   This evening—half past seven train. Paris is a very pretty city.
treets well lighted. Magnificent opera house. The inside is particularly gor-
eous. Dropped into the Palais Royal on the way. The Comedie Fransaze is
onsiderably larger, but the Opera Comeek—

MONT. [*Suddenly*]   Pardon, monsieur—pardon!

PHIPPS. [*Looking at Montvillais, then at Strebelow*]   Friend of yours?

STREB.   Monsieur Montvillais, a fellow townsman—Mr. Phipps of New
York City.

PHIPPS.   G. Washington Phipps—dry goods.

MONT.   Dry—gudes?

PHIPPS.   Eighty-seven Church Street.

MONT.   Eighty-seven?

PHIPPS. [*To Strebelow, pointing back at Montvillais with his thumb*]
What line?

STREB.   Stationery.

PHIPPS.   Ah!

STREB.   The Count de Carojac, Mr. Phipps. [*The Count bows very low and
formally. Phipps crosses to Count, nods quickly. He sees the Count is still
bowing, and bows low himself*]

PHIPPS. [*L.C. to Strebelow*]   Same business?

STREB. [*R.C.*]   Cutlery and firearms.

PHIPPS.   Oh!

MONT. [*R.H.*]   Your pardon, Mr. Phipps. I owe you an apology for having
nterrupted your remarks. Pardon, but you have been to the Grand Opéra;
and to the Palais Royal, and the Comédie Français, and the Opéra Comique;
and you arrived in the city of Paris at half past seven this evening?

CARO. [*L.H.*]   You have seen considerable of the metropolis, Mr. Phipps,
during your comparatively short visit.

PHIPPS.   Not as much as I had hoped to see by this time. I have been in the
city of Paris *four* hours. Delayed at the Grand Hotel. It took me at least fifteen minutes, sir, to persuade the chambermaid who brought me candles that
I did not require her presence while I was changing my travelling suit for a
dress coat and black pantaloons. These French chambermaids are slow to
take a hint—in that direction. The Tuileries, by the way, presents rather an
imposing appearance in the snow and moonlight. I had the driver go round
by the way of the Tuileries and the Palace of the Louvre on the way to the

legation. The Ark dee Triumph is rather neat in its way. When we got to th Champs Elizas, I told the driver to take a half hour's turn to the Ark, and we came back by the way of the Foburg St. Honory and the Church dee Philipee. Tourists generally lose a great deal of time unnecessarily. I've go everything I want to see in Paris written down in my notebook. Bought a guide to Paris in London. [*Takes a small guidebook from pocket*] Pronuncia tion all spelt out in English. Carry a map of the city in my coat pocket. [*Take. map from one of his pockets and unfolds it. Enter English officer, and gentle man with lady from D. Exit into cloakroom*]

STREB. When did you leave New York, Mr. Phipps?

PHIPPS. November thirteen, two o'clock P.M. Arrived in Liverpool No-vember twenty-third, half past ten A.M. Exactly one week and a half ago Spent four days and a half in the city of London and vicinity. I saw London thoroughly.

MONT. Voilà l'Américain. He'll see all Paris in a fortnight.

PHIPPS. I shall be in Paris precisely three days. Detained till Friday on account of business—figured silks. I shall then run over to Switzerland. They tell me I can see Mont Blanc from the windows of the hotel in Switzerland. [*Enter Footman from cloakroom, English officer, gentleman, lady. Exit L.U.E. Gentleman and lady from L. stairs, to R. Footman comes down again and exits into cloakroom*]

CARO. Mon Dieu!

PHIPPS. That will save considerable time. Berlin, by the way is a very beau-tiful city—wide streets. Came from London by way of Berlin; remained there thirty-six hours. Missed a train; delayed five hours. Stopped over at Dresden on the route from Berlin, and at the Cologne Big Cathedral; bones of eleven thousand virgins in the church of St. Ursula. I didn't count 'em but my guide swore to the fact. He wouldn't let up on a single rib. Guides never lie in Europe.

MONT. You visited the Dresden Gallery, monsieur? You admire works of art?

PHIPPS. I like pictures. I spent nearly twenty minutes in the gallery at Dresden.

MONT. Diable! [*Servant starts downstairs to meet Phipps*]

PHIPPS. Oreveoar, gentlemen, as you Frenchmen say. See you again, Stre-below; my regards to your wife. [*Going up, hands card to attendant*] There's my card, sir—G. Washington Phipps, N.Y., U.S.A. [*Exits L. upstairs, pre-ceded by servant. Phipps bounds upstairs three steps at a time; is going off R.U.E. Servant calls, "This way, sir," pointing off L.U.E. Phipps says, "Oh! very well," bounds off L.U.E.*]

STREB. Whatever faults my countrymen may have, gentlemen, you will own that wasting time is not one of them.

CARO. Oui, mon ami, c'est vrai, c'est vrai. [*Moving to R.C.*]

MONT. Boom—whiz—z—chick! Mr. Phipps is a bullet. He is here and he s gone. [*Enter Lilian through arch R.U.E.*]

STREB. My wife. [*Goes to her*] But where's your father, dear?

LIL. Natalie insisted he should return to her. He said he felt too tired for a formal reception like this; but would, perhaps, call at a circle to see an old New York friend. In which case he will not be here till late. [*Seeing Montvillais*] Ah! M. Montvillais. [*They bow. She takes Strebelow's arm*] Come, let us make our bow upstairs, and return home. [*Going up C., they pass Carojac. Routledge is seen coming downstairs from L.U.E.*]

STREB. [*Up C.*] You overlook the Count de Carojac, my dear.

LIL. [*Laughing and turns, bowing slightly*] So I did. Pardon me, count! [*Count bows L.H. Routledge now on the steps, meets Strebelow and Lilian preparing to go upstairs. Awkward getting out of each other's way*]

ROUT. [*On steps L.C.*] I beg your pardon—

STREB. [*At foot of steps*] Ah, Routledge, glad to see you here.

LIL. [*Bowing formally*] Mr. Routledge.

ROUT. Mrs. Strebelow.

STREB. And you still persist in starting for Rome tomorrow?

ROUT. I must take the early train.

STREB. Then we must say good-by this evening.

ROUT. Yes, indeed. Good-by, sir. Madam, farewell. [*Bows. Strebelow and Lilian mount the first three steps. Strebelow, his wife on his arm, turns suddenly*]

STREB. Mr. Routledge.

ROUT. [*L.C., foot of steps*] Sir.

STREB. You must afford me an opportunity to bid for your Dante and Beatrice.

ROUT. Pardon me, but I do not intend to sell that picture.

STREB. Then at some future time. Good-by once more.

ROUT. Good-by. [*Exit upstairs Strebelow and Lilian. Routledge crosses to R. corner, turns and watches Mrs. Strebelow till off, then strolls off R.3.E.*]

MONT. [*Coming forward with Carojac*] But why?

CARO. Because I hate him. He made a laughingstock of me in New York. He came between me and—and—

MONT. But not here—not here in the legation.

CARO. Yes, here and now. He goes away tomorrow.

MONT. You will make a scandal. It will be said that Madame Strebelow is the cause of the fight. You have been dining. You are flushed.

CARO. [*Still more excited*] What do I care? Both he and she have always provoked me. I gave him his cue at Strebelow's house today. I will give him good cause to fight if he will face a sword. I'll teach him to laugh at Alphonse Carojac—

MONT. Well, but one moment. Come here where we can talk. [*Draws him off L.2.E. As they exit, Florence, who has been listening at the arch, L.U.E., enters*]

FLOR. [*Aside*] A sensation at last. A fight! Swords! The whole colony will be alive. I must tell Lilian. [*Runs to stairs, meets Phipps*]

PHIPPS. Mrs. Brown. [*They try to pass each other; finally she goes up, he comes down*]

FLOR. [*Up a few steps*] Don't stop me, I'm in a hurry.

PHIPPS. So am I. But I think I have something to say to you.

FLOR. What is it?

PHIPPS. Brown still alive?

FLOR. Yes.

PHIPPS. In good health?

FLOR. Nothing but the gout.

PHIPPS. Then I don't think I have anything to say. Good evening. [*Florence rushes upstairs and disappears. Coming down C., with back to audience*] Ah! Is this Hymen? [*Taking out notebook*] Knew him by his torch. Let me see? [*Writing*] That's the seventeenth statue of Hymen I've seen since I've landed in Liverpool—this one, I presume, is Diana. Diana comes under the D's. No, it can't be Diana. I have noticed Diana always wears the moon as a headdress. It must be Venus. I'll put it in the V's. [*Writes*] American Legation—Venus, number— I have seen ninety-seven Venuses since I landed in Liverpool. Venus is more popular than Hymen in Europe. American Legation—Venus number— [*Looks at statue again*] No, it can't be Venus either, too many clothes for Venus. Venus in full dress is not popular. In Europe I'll call it Juno. She goes under the J's. Patroness of marriage, the guidebook says. Juno, [*Writes*] number three. I'm short of Junos. Juno is not popular here as Venus. Let me see! [*Pulls out map*] I can instruct the driver to return to the hotel by way of the Maddyleen and the National Library. [*Holding map*] Perhaps we can dodge round by the way of the Cathedral of Noter-Dam. [*Goes up R., meets Routledge, who enters from cloakroom*]

ROUT. Ah, Phipps, I heard you were here. Are you in a particular hurry?

PHIPPS. No, I'm in a general hurry.

ROUT. Do you know the Count de Carojac?

PHIPPS. That black fellow in the cutlery and firearms line. Just been introduced. [*Looks at his watch*] Just nine minutes ago.

ROUT. He has been trying to provoke me—almost insulted me today.

PHIPPS. Punch his head.

ROUT. He insinuated a challenge to a duel.

PHIPPS. What for?

ROUT. Come into the anteroom. It is a very delicate matter; this place is
oo public. I would avoid it if I can honorably. [*As they go off, R.U.E.*] The
eputation of an American lady is involved in the— [*Exit, R.3.E., through
arch. Florence comes downstairs quickly*]

FLOR. I cannot find her anywhere. I've been through all the rooms. [*Enter
Lizette from R.U.E.*]

FLOR. Ah, have you seen Mrs. Strebelow?

LIZ. Not for a quarter of an hour.

FLOR. [*Gives her money*] You will find Mr. Brown asleep on the sofa in
he retiring room. Please go and sit by his side till he wakes up. [*Lizette, going*] Stop; when he does wake up, tell him—that's it, I'll go home with
Lilian—tell him his wife has gone, and say he must go right home. And
please help him on with his things. [*Lizette curtsies, and starts again*] And
please [*Lizette stops again*] see that his handkerchief is on his head, and if his
poor leg slips off the sofa, put it back, gently, so as not to disturb him. [*Lizette
curtsies again, and exits L.H.*]

FLOR. Poor old Brown. I have as much care of him as if he were a baby;
I have taken the place his mother occupied seventy-five years ago—but where
can Lilian be? She must know of this. I'm sure Carojac will do what he
threatened. It will be magnificent in all the papers. They will hear of it in
New York; the *Herald* will interview me as a friend of the lady whose name
was involved—what Mrs. Brown says—what Mrs. Brown thinks—description
of the combatants—Mrs. Brown, wife of the millionaire, now residing in Paris
—all in big type. I wonder what they'll think of it all on the Avenue? Mrs.
Brown—that horrid name! If it were only Livingston, or the Countess of
Brownatille. But where can Lilian be? I *must* find her. [*Goes upstairs quickly
—from L.H.2. Enter Carojac, Montvillais with him, from the R.H. arch.
Routledge, Phipps with him*]

PHIPPS. [*To Routledge*] You are right; the fellow must be a scoundrel.
For Strebelow's sake as well as for his wife's— [*Routledge and Phipps have

their hats in their hands. Routledge has cloak, Phipps coat on his arm. The are going off R.2.E.]

CARO. [*R.H., meaningly*] You are not running away, M. Routledge [*Music*]

ROUT. [*Stopping short*] Not from you, M. de Carojac.

CARO. I thought you would not, without giving me the opportunity to give you an explanation.

MONT. [*To Carojac*] Allons donc, Carojac.

CARO. [*Stopping Montvillais with gesture*] Laisse moi faire!

ROUT. [*Quietly*] I think, sir, I understand you without an explanation.

PHIPPS. [*To Routledge, aside*] The fellow has been drinking.

MONT. [*Coming to C.*] Permit me, M. Routledge, to offer the explanation. The count is a little irritated at the unfortunate resemblance to Mrs. Strebelow, which, in your Beatrice, is placed on exhibition.

ROUT. [*Quietly*] And why does the count concern himself about the matter, sir?

MONT. Oh, as a friend—an old and dear friend of Madame Strebelow.

CARO. [*Crossing to C.*] I think such things may be done in America—done in France they are an insolence which no French gentleman would be guilty of to a French lady. [*Enter Mrs. Brown and Lilian on stairs from L.U.E.*]

ROUT. [*A little more warmly*] If you seek a quarrel, sir, I beg you will find a cause unconnected with the name of any lady, American or French, and a place in which an American in accepting will not be forced to forget the respect due to the flag under whose protection you are speaking.

CARO. [*Insolently*] Zat is the first time I ever heard that a flag protected anything or anybody.

MONT. [*Expostulating*] Carojac, mon cher!

PHIPPS. [*To Routledge*] If you don't slap his face, I will.

ROUT. [*Waving Phipps aside*] That flag protects you now.

CARO. [*Still more insolently*] I beg your pardon. 'Tis you appeal to it. The Count de Carojac needs neither the American rag nor the American petticoat to protect him.

ROUT. [*Bursting out*] You are either drunk or a blackguard.

CARO. [*Rushing to Routledge*] Enfin! You are one liar—one coward! [*Throws his glove in Routledge's face*]

PHIPPS. [*Mad with excitement*] Knock him down! [*Routledge does so, when Carojac strikes him. Quick drop of curtain*]

ACT IV.

SCENE 1: THE DUEL. *The curtain rises on an empty stage. After a few seconds of silence, enter Routledge in circular cloak, followed by Phipps in overcoat from terrace.*

ROUT. [*Looking round on steps*] This *is* the spot.

PHIPPS. [*R.C., looking round*] Solemn, splendid, and icy. [*Pulls out notebook*] What do you call it?

ROUT. All that the Russian bullets left of a once royal château.

PHIPPS. [*Making note*] It makes me shiver.

ROUT. [*Thoughtfully*] How calmly the feverish city seems to sleep! Phipps, [*Phipps comes down R.C.*] I feel a strange sense of ominous awe— I feel as if I were destined never to leave this spot alive.

PHIPPS. [*Comes forward*] Nonsense! It's the first effect of the place— you'll soon shake that off.

ROUT. Maybe so, but this man is said to be the best swordsman in Europe.

PHIPPS. Do you know nothing of the smallsword?

ROUT. I am a pretty fair swordsman. I learned its use in the university in Germany and, in Europe, no artist's studio is complete without a pair of foils.

PHIPPS. I should fancy that fencing with foils for amusement is a very different thing from carrying on a serious discussion with buttonless swords.

ROUT. Not with me, I think. I am generally coolest in the moment of danger. But before they come, there is one thing I want you to promise me.

PHIPPS. What is it?

ROUT. That you will do all you can to prevent the real cause of this quarrel from being known. Remember, I fight to avenge an insult to our country simply. For Lilian's sake, for Strebelow's sake, let no suspicion get abroad of—

PHIPPS. You may depend upon me.

ROUT. Deliberately and persistently this man's jealousy and irritated vanity have forced this fight, and whatever way it ends, I would have his attempt to avenge himself for his rejection baffled as far as Lilian and her husband are concerned. You understand?

PHIPPS. I do. What you are doing, I would do, though practically I don't know a revolver from a jacknife, or a smallsword from a corkscrew. Hush! [*Listens*] They are coming. [*Pause. Enter Montvillais, Carojac, and Dr. Watson, R.1.E. They are all in overcoats. Montvillais carries three smallswords, the doctor, a box*]

MONT. [*To Routledge and Phipps*] Your servant, gentlemen. You will pardon the delay. The swords were at my apartments and we stopped on the

236 BRONSON HOWARD

way for Doctor Watson, [*Bows all round*] an old London friend of mine, who willingly agreed to offer his professional services to whosoever may need them.

DR. WATSON. [*To Routledge*] Pleased to make your acquaintance, sir. I shall be as happy, believe me, to attend you as to attend my friend's friend.

PHIPPS. Happy either way—strictly impartial.

ROUT. [*To Doctor*] I thank you, doctor. [*Doctor goes up*]

CARO. [*As if tired of the delay*] Allons, Montvillais. [*Montvillais advances C., presents the handles of the swords to Phipps, who takes them, looks at them—moves over to Routledge*]

PHIPPS. [*To Routledge*] I'm to take my choice, I believe.

ROUT. Certainly.

PHIPPS. [*Staring at each sword in turn, moving to C.*] About the same length apparently. [*Feels points with his finger, pricking it*] I never saw two bolts of black silk more like each other. I shouldn't have the least choice as to which of them was passed through my body. [*He reverses the swords, presenting the handles crossed to Montvillais. Montvillais takes one, places the point on ground, bends the blade each way several times. Phipps, watching him, imitates with the other sword*]

MONT. Are you satisfied, Mr. Phipps?

PHIPPS. Perfectly. [*Aside*] Mine seems to bend as much as his does. [*Routledge and Carojac take off their coats—stand in shirt sleeves. Phipps to Doctor*] Won't this be a trifle chilly?

DOC. They will be warm enough after their swords are crossed. The exercise will make them comfortable.

PHIPPS. [*Aside*] D——d comfortable. [*Montvillais holding up sword C., with point to front*]

MONT. Messieurs! [*Carojac and Routledge cross swords*] Allez! [*Carojac and Routledge fence—after some passes, Carojac springs suddenly back*]

CARO. [*Springing back*] Sacristi!

ROUT. [*Lowering his sword*] Pardon me! I believe you are wounded. [*The seconds cover their principals with overcoats*]

CARO. [*Holding his left hand*] Sanks, M. Routledge, for zee courtesy. A mere scratch. It will not detain us a moment, doctor! [*Doctor and Montvillais go to Carojac on side of stage. Routledge joins Phipps on other side of stage. Doctor wraps bandage round Carojac's arm*]

PHIPPS. [*To Routledge*] First hit for our side! Bravo!

ROUT. [*Shaking his head*] More luck than skill. His arm is made of steel and his wrist of India rubber.

CARO. [*To Montvillais*] It was his awkwardness, not his skill. I'll finish im in two passes now.

PHIPPS. [*To Routledge*] Are you cold?

ROUT. I'm hot as fire.

CARO. [*To Montvillais*] Finissons! [*They fence again. Enter Strebelow as Routledge is disarmed*]

STREB. [*On bridge*] Stop, gentlemen! [*Carojac runs his sword through Routledge as Strebelow cries "Stop"*]

ROUT. [*Falling into Phipps' arms*] Too late! I knew it! [*All turning round o look at Strebelow. Montvillais and Carojac exchange looks. The Doctor is uzzled*]

ALL. M. Strebelow!

STREB. [*Coming forward C., goes to Routledge*] Too late! Is there no doc- or here?

DOC. [*Coming forward*] I beg pardon. I— [*Goes to Routledge, kneeling ehind him*]

STREB. [*Dropping Routledge's hand*] Count de Carojac!

CARO. [*Resuming his coat*] M. Strebelow!

STREB. The cause of this quarrel?

PHIPPS. Of this murder, Strebelow!

MONT. Murder, sir.

PHIPPS. Ay, wilful, deliberate murder. The fellow forced the fight because ıe knew his superior skill. I call it murder.

CARO. Sir, you will answer to me for this.

STREB. [*Calmly*] Not till you have answered me. The cause of this quar- el? [*Phipps, Montvillais and Carojac look meaningly at each other*] Well, ount, are you ashamed to tell it? [*Enter Lilian, R.U.E., over terrace followed ›y Florence. Lilian in disordered dress. Rushes across to L.C., sees Routledge ying on the ground, the Doctor over him*]

LIL. Too late! Too late! Oh, Harold. Harold! My poor Harold! [*Throws ıerself beside Harold*]

ALL. Madame Strebelow!

DOC. Be careful, madam. You must not stir him.

LIL. Oh, Harold, speak! Speak to me.

STREB. [*In astonishment*] My wife!

LIL. Dying—dying—dying for me, who blighted his· heart! Harold! Har- ›ld! I've killed him, killed him.

CARO. [*To Strebelow, pointing to Lilian*] Well, M. Strebelow, do you un- lerstand the cause of the quarrel, now?

STREB. [*Raising Lilian, assisted by Florence*] I do not, sir.

CARO. He compromised your wife. He make her love for him public.
STREB. You lie, sir!
CARO. [*Smiling sardonically*]   Look for yourself. [*Indicating Lilian. Pause* *Strebelow draws Lilian to him—draws cloak round her fondly and carefully*]
STREB. [*Slowly*]   Gentlemen, this lady is my wife. For her truth, her faith and her honor, I pledge my life. Again I say, this man lies, and for this lie I will hold him accountable at the proper time and in the proper place. [*Quick drop of curtain*]

SCENE 2: "THE SEPARATION." *In the boudoir. At rise of curtain, enter Lizette L.C., followed by Strebelow, Lilian on his arm, then Mrs. Brown. Strebelow half leads, half supports Lilian to sofa, R.C., on which she sinks exhausted.*

STREB. [*To Mrs. Brown*]   Believe me, I am very grateful for your kind attention to Lilian. She seems better now. [*Crossing to Lizette*] Let the carriage wait. [*Exit Lizette L.3.E.*]
FLOR. [*Approaching Lilian*]   All she needs is a little rest—a little sleep. [*To Lilian*] You do feel better now?
LIL.   Yes, yes, much better, thank you. It was the shock—the shock. Is Harold—is Mr. Routledge dead?
STREB.   I trust not!
LIL.   For heaven's sake, send and see!
FLOR.   Dr. Watson promised to come here as soon as he had ascertained that Mr. Routledge had been safely moved.
LIL.   The suspense will kill me! [*Rises and walks across to L.H. During this scene, up to the entrance of the Doctor, Strebelow is intently watching Lilian*]
FLOR. [*Follows Lilian*]   Do calm yourself, Lilian. Do not look so wild. You frighten me. I'm sure we all share your horror.
LIL.   But who can share my feelings? Did you see the look of reproachful anguish his eyes cast upon me ere they closed—closed perhaps, forever? I shall go mad, mad, mad! [*Crossing back to sofa*]
STREB. [*Aside*]   "Reproachful anguish." [*Aloud*] I will send—there, there, dear! [*Rings bell on table L.H.*] Sword thrusts are not always fatal. Sit down, compose yourself. [*Sits at L.H. table and writes. Enter Lizette*] Send to this address, and inquire as to the condition of Mr. Routledge. Let the messenger take the carriage and return at once. [*Exit Lizette L.3.E. To Florence*] You must not be surprised at the extreme agitation of Lilian. Harold Routledge and she were old playmates; and the sensibility of—

FLOR. [*C.*] My dear Mr. Strebelow, I'm fairly astonished at being alive myself. The snow, the moonlight, the gray ruins of the historic château, the suddenness of the strife, the romantic aristocracy, and aristocratic romance of the affair made it all like a novel, till I saw Harold Routledge's blood on that man's sword. [*Lilian starts up from the sofa, crosses to L.H.*] Oh! Then I felt as badly, as horrified as Lilian herself. But [*To Lilian*] do calm yourself, dear.

LIL. Yes, yes, when the news comes I'll be calm—calm!

FLOR. I always liked Routledge; there was none of the plebeian about him. I recollect how glad I was when it was reported that you and he were engaged.

STREB. Engaged! Engaged to what?

LIL. [*Stops short, her back to audience and to Strebelow*] Engaged to be married.

FLOR. Why, Strebelow, you don't mean to say that you did not know Lilian Westbrook and Harold Routledge were once considered the Lucia and Edgardo of New York society? Why the match was—

LIL. [*Crosses to C., back to audience*] Please say no more about the—*Turns round, looks at Strebelow, at Florence, totters. Strebelow runs and catches her in his arms as she is about to fall, crosses with and places her on sofa R.C.*]

STREB. Take courage, take courage, I'm sure your old friend is safe.

LIL. [*Looking at Strebelow piteously*] It was never right. [*As Strebelow is bending over Lilian, his back to the door, enter Dr. Watson, seen only by Florence. Florence goes quickly to him, catches him by the wrist*]

FLOR. [*L.C. aside to Doctor*] Is he dead?

DOC. [*L.H. to Florence*] No, but he cannot live an hour.

FLOR. If you say that here, you'll kill Mrs. Strebelow. Be careful! [*Aloud*] Here is the doctor.

LIL. [*Springing to her feet*] At last! At last! [*Going toward Doctor*] Tell me the truth—the truth. Is Harold Routledge dead?

DOC. No, no! He is badly wounded—but not dead.

LIL. Is there any hope?

DOC. While there's life, science sees hope.

STREB. [*Encouragingly*] There, there! I told you so. [*Passing her over to sofa*]

LIL. Thank Heaven! [*Sinks on sofa R.H.*]

FLOR. [*Behind sofa*] Now, dear, you must rest. The doctor will take me home. I'm sure poor Brown must be in a dreadful state. I'll call early tomor-

row. Now go, and be sure you take a good sleep. Good-by! Good-by! Don'
rise!

STREB. [*Crossing to C.*] Good-by—and thank you.

DOC. Good-by, Mr. Strebelow; and if there is any change for either the
worse or the better, I will come and let you know. I'm going to him as soon
as I have left Mrs. Brown at home.

LIL. Do—do!

STREB. Good-by. [*Exit Florence and Doctor C.L. Strebelow closes C. doors
Strebelow and Lilian solus*] Well, Lilian! You had best retire.

LIL. 'Tis no use, John, I could not sleep.

STREB. Will you go to Natalie?

LIL. Not yet. Before I go to her, I must—

STREB. [*With forced calmness*] Speak to me? Better postpone it till tomor
row. You are exhausted. I can wait.

LIL. No, every moment of doubt, of anxiety, would but exhaust me more
I will hear you now.

STREB. Hear me? I thought it was *you* who wished to speak.

LIL. It is! It is! But I fear to begin.

STREB. Let me help you. You love Harold Routledge. Do you not?

LIL. I do not know. I did love him.

STREB. And were engaged to him?

LIL. [*Surprised*] Yes, certainly I was.

STREB. And he loved you?

LIL. Yes.

STREB. What broke the engagement?

LIL. A lover's quarrel.

STREB. And you have loved him ever since?

LIL. I do not know.

STREB. You do not know! Yet, except myself, everybody seemed to know
it. The painter saw it on your face and placed it on his canvas. The shallow
critic read it, and declared it, and I—I, your husband, living by your side
every day, every hour, for six years—I—I did not see it—did not feel it. [*Bit
terly*] Love is blind indeed! Oh fool! Fool!

LIL. But John, you knew?

STREB. I knew! Knew what? What I know now, what it has taken me six
years to know, is that the heart on which I reposed, in which I shrined a
man's truest love, has been veiled to me as a sanctuary to whose religion I
was a stranger. Yet I worshipped at it with the devotion of a saint; trusted it
with my man's faith, my all.

LIL. [*Drawing herself up with pride*] Nor has the trust been betrayed. My duty and your honor—

STREB. Duty! Honor! Who spoke of duty or of honor? I spoke and speak of love; of that love which in a wife is the sole invulnerable armor of a husband's honor; of that love without which honor is valueless, and life a blank; of the love in which honor dwells as unconsciously as flowers bloom and water flows. God help the husband whose honor is guarded by duty alone.

LIL. You should have said all this before.

STREB. Before! Before what?

LIL. Before we were married.

STREB. Believing that with your hand I received your heart, why should I have said it?

LIL. You knew I had been engaged to Harry Routledge; that but a few days before you proposed to my father for me, it was settled I was to be his wife.

STREB. [*Surprised*] How should I know it? You never mentioned him to me.

LIL. But my father told you.

STREB. Never! Never!

LIL. Then my father deceived me.

STREB. But why—why?

LIL. That I cannot tell, unless it was to—

STREB. To what?

LIL. Unless it was to avoid any delay in our marriage. Immediate ruin—

STREB. Immediate ruin. Then you knew of the threatening bankruptcy?

LIL. [*Astonished*] Certainly.

STREB. [*Staggered*] And—and you accepted me to avert it?

LIL. To save my father; yes.

STREB. Then your father deceived me—deceived us both!

LIL. [*Frightened*] Oh! Father! [*Sits on sofa R.C.*]

STREB. Then I did not marry you. I bought you. I became not your husband, but your owner. This marriage was not a union, but a sacrifice—a sacrifice not of one, not of two, but of three lives. O Heaven! what have we done? [*Falls into chair L.C.*]

LIL. [*Rises, goes to Strebelow*] Can you forgive me? [*Kneels*]

STREB. [*His face in his hands*] Wait! Wait! [*Pause. Lilian is kneeling by Strebelow's chair—both are weeping*] We must not forget our child.

LIL. [*Raises her head in alarm*] Natalie! But tell me you forgive me—for her sake—for her sake!

STREB. I have nothing to forgive but my blindness. I should have though
for both. I will do so now. Tell me, and tell me frankly—for frankness nov
alone can save us—do you still love Harold Routledge?

LIL. I don't know. [*Rising*]

STREB. [*Rising and following her*] Do you not know your own heart.
Don't sob so; be calm.

LIL. I did love Harold Routledge, I believe, with the love of a school-girl
We had a silly quarrel—broke our engagement. I wrote him to come back to
me the very day I accepted you. He came back, doubtless full of joy, of hope
of love—for he did love me. [*Sobs*]

STREB. [*Thoughtfully*] I recollect.

LIL. I refused to see him. [*Piteously*] What could I do? He went away
and we were married. Regret at the pain the sudden blow must have given
him remained with me long; but our Natalie was born—my heart turned to
her—to—

STREB. I understand.

LIL. I could not understand. I never did! Your kind love, your watchful
ness, your devotion won upon my mother's heart, but I feared to show it.
scarcely understood my own feelings, till—till he returned. But when I saw
him whose life I knew I had blighted, lying there dying, as I feared, remorse
shame took possession of me—possesses me still. I—[*Sits R.C. on sofa*]

STREB. Spoken and acted like the noble woman that you are.

LIL. And you do forgive me? [*Kneeling*]

STREB. Again I say, there is nothing to forgive but my own blindness, and
your father's folly.

LIL. And you will forget it all?

STREB. And continue our mutual sacrifice? That were to punish you—no
that!

LIL. What would you do?

STREB. Leave you, for a time maybe. Natalie—poor child of a loveles
union.

LIL. [*Screams*] Leave me, and—take Natalie?

STREB. [*Bitterly aside*] Oh, how little she knows me yet! [*Aloud*] No
poor mother! You shall keep your child. I would remain with you, too, wer
I a stronger man than I am. I can read clearly what is passing in your hear
but after seeing you sacrifice it to your father, I will not weakly tempt you to
sacrifice it again to your child.

LIL. [*Piteously*] And you will leave me?

STREB. With your father—

LIL. And when will you return?

STREB. When your heart calls me. When it calls the husband as well as the father.

LIL. Remain with me and trust me.

STREB. Near or far, 'tis not you I fear to trust, 'tis myself. To live beside you day by day, to hear you every hour, construing each heave of your bosom into a sigh for another, each moment of abstraction into a dream of him! No! No! I'm not strong enough for that.

LIL. Then be it as you will.

STREB. It must be so. Go to Natalie. [*Lilian goes to R., pauses, then exits R.1.E. Solus, sitting in armchair L.C.*] 'Tis all over. [*Before picture L.*] How plain its story seems now! That face, so long to me the sun of earthly beauty, the object of all my pride in the past, the prefiguration of all my hopes in the future, now tells me only the suffering victim carrying in her heart a secret that must not live. [*In agony*] A love that cannot die! [*Pause, while Strebelow looks at picture in silence. Enter Lizette*]

LIZ. A letter, sir. [*Strebelow still looking at picture, Lizette places letter in his hand, which rests on his knee. Exit Lizette L.3.E.*]

STREB. I will look at it no more. Let the face be veiled to me in the future, as the heart has been in the past. [*Draws curtain over picture, as he does so drops letter, picks it up, opens letter, continuing*] Harold Routledge dead! Dead! Leaving her a widow with a living husband, and leaving me a wifeless husband and a childless father! [*Drops into chair. Quick drop of curtain*]

ACT V.

Set the same as Act I. At rise of curtain, Babbage and Westbrook are discovered seated at table. Papers, etc.

BAB. The papers are all right, old boy. This one is mine, and that one ours. [*As he speaks spreads two written sheets of legal cap on table, pushing en toward Westbrook, who takes it and signs each, throws down pen and turns away*] Is that all the fuss you make about it, old fellow? It takes but single clip to cut the longest chain. [*Wipes his eyes*]

WEST. [*In evident emotion, shakes hands with Babbage*] Staunch friend and partner of thirty years, I—I—

BAB. That's all right, Westbrook, all right. Don't mind me. I'm a stupid old fool, I suppose. Here goes! [*Signs the papers in turn, hands one to Westbrook, putting the other in his pocket*]

WEST. And now—

BAB. And now the last papers are signed that dissolve the firm of Babbage & Westbrook after an existence of twenty-nine years, eleven months, and fifteen days. Well, are you satisfied? We retire with a little over two million and a half apiece, owing no man a dollar.

WEST. If figures never lie, we are two highly successful men.

BAB. Both our shares securely invested; government bonds, real estate. A number one, two copper-fastened, iron-bound, solid business men. Is that success?

WEST. If figures never lie?

BAB. Hm! Figures are the biggest liars in the world. Give a boy a one dollar bill and tell him to multiply the amount of happiness he can get out of it by two millions five hundred thousand. He will hardly believe that you and I envy him the happiness he extracts from the first ten cents he spends, knowing he has enough left for the circus and all the side shows. Heigh-ho! Westbrook, the bigger the figures, the bigger they lie.

WEST. [*Sighing*] Rather late to take that view of them now.

BAB. [*Rising*] Hm! Westbrook, there is one more document—I—I— [*Aside*] Some people would call me an old fool, I suppose, if they knew it. [*Aloud*] There is one more document I want to transfer. It isn't a very sharp financial operation. [*Takes paper out of his pocketbook, hands it to West-brook*] But it will ease my conscience a little.

WEST. [*Reading outside of paper*] A warrantee deed to Lilian West-brook Strebelow! [*Opens paper, glances over it*] Grand Street property! My dear Babbage, what do you mean? This property is worth over half a million. We allowed that much for it in the division of our assets.

BAB. It's only the odd half million, old boy. You and I own five millions of dollars between us. Take it, Larry. Forgive me for bringing it up. But—but it's been on *my* conscience for the last nine years. By rights, we owe it all to Lilian, poor girl! I know it isn't money she needs. She has enough of that. But an old brute like me has nothing but money to give her. It won't help *her* any, I know, but it may help to ease my conscience a little. It's only the odd half million, Larry.

WEST. [*Much affected*] Ah, old friend and wise partner, you seem better than I.

BAB. There, there, old fellow, forgive me for bringing it up. But how is she today?

WEST. Just as she was yesterday, as she was last week, last month, last year, as she has been every day since John Strebelow gave her back to me in Paris with the words: "Take back your daughter, Mr. Westbrook and be your task to soften to her memories of the past you made for her and me

You know how I brought her home; how John Strebelow made her practially mistress of the bulk of his fortune, now settled on their child; how since then he has resided in Rome. I do not believe he ever returned to Paris after his terrible duel with the Count de Carojac.

BAB. And he never writes to you?

WEST. Never. But I believe he corresponds regularly with Fanny Holcomb. Oh, Babbage, had I but heeded your warning on that dreadful day!

BAB. We should not be sharing five millions today, but I should feel a happier and a better man.

WEST. I'd give every penny of it to bring Harold Routledge back to life, to compensate John Strebelow.

BAB. The latter, at all events, is possible.

WEST. How?

BAB. Listen. Just as sure as John Strebelow loves your daughter, just as sure your daughter now loves him, and hungers for him today.

WEST. Would to heaven it were true.

BAB. It is true. Since we commenced winding up our business, I have been here every day. I have repeatedly seen Lilian and Natalie together. I never heard them talk that they did not talk of Natalie's father, that Lilian did not tell the child how great and good her father is. Natalie writes to him regularly; and Lilian oversees the correspondence.

WEST. [Eagerly] How do you know this?

BAB. About a month ago, the day that Illinois Central bounded up to ninety-two and tumbled back to eighty-seven, Natalie came to me with a curious little letter in her hand, the day Perkins & Johnson went under, you know, short on Erie and Wabash; Pacific Mail went clean out of sight. Natalie asked me to put a little picture, as she called the stamp, on her letter and drop it into the box that goes to Rome. The letter was addressed to John Strebelow. It is exactly five weeks ago. Take my word for it, Lilian is trying to woo her husband, and the child is writing the love letters.

WEST. Heaven grant it. But, Babbage—[Holding out paper]

BAB. Well?

WEST. This gift really I cannot—

BAB. Let me have my own way about that, old boy. It is a private speculation of my own. [Goes toward door] It's only the odd half million. [Reaches door, turns round] Here comes another who has retired from business too, only to resume an active partnership pretty soon, [Laughing] I think.

WEST. Who is it?

BAB. [Laughing] The relict of the late Mr. Brown. I hear her in the hall.

WEST. [*Going*] Then come this way [*To upper door*] to my room [*Westbrook leads off by upper door. Babbage turns to follow that way, going last, talking as he goes*]

BAB. I've kept the other two millions. What a heartless, grasping set we solid business men are. [*Going up R.*]

FLOR. [*Entering lower door*] Mr. Babbage! [*Crossing to L.H.*]

BAB. [*Turning back*] Mrs. Brown.

FLOR. How is Lilian today? [*Rings bell on L. table*]

BAB. [*Down R.C.*] The doctor was here half an hour ago.

FLOR. What did he say?

BAB. Nothing.

FLOR. Pshaw! If I were not a woman I could say that myself. [*Enter Lizette L.D.R.*] Excuse me one moment, Mr. Babbage. [*To Lizette*] Tell Mrs Holcomb I will run up to see her. I want to see her on business.

BAB. Business! [*Exit Lizette upper door R.*]

FLOR. [*To Babbage*] I was on my way down town to order some new cards. [*Takes out a card with a wide black margin*] I came in to ask Aun Fanny how wide I ought now to have the margin.

BAB. You call that business?

FLOR. Certainly. Aunt Fanny is a widow, like myself. What do *you* think Mr. Babbage? [*Hands Babbage card. He takes it, gravely looks at it through his spectacles*] The two years are up tomorrow.

BAB. [*R.H.*] Westbrook and I bought and sold stock for Mr. Brown fo upward of twenty years. Brown always liked a pretty wide margin himself [*Hands card back to Florence*] Always allowed a wide margin, too. One good margin deserves another.

FLOR. [*L.H.*] Poor dear old Brown! [*Runs her finger round card*] I'l keep it wide. Heigh-ho! How do you like my new dress, Mr. Babbage? Neat isn't it? Madame Raypangsay is so very artistic! It is a very delicate matte for a dressmaker to guide a young widow through the various stages of he affliction with good taste: absolute wretchedness, deep grief, profound melancholy, Christian resignation, sentimental sadness.

BAB. I trust your physician has hopes of yet pulling you through?

FLOR. The immediate danger is past. First, he prescribed retirement from the world. Severe as it was, I took the dose. Second he prescribed change of air

BAB. You took the dose at Saratoga?

FLOR. No, Saratoga was too gay. Heigh-ho! I retired to Newport. I an now a promising convalescent. The doctor told me he had one more pre scription. Really—I—

BAB. [*Dryly*] A second husband.

FLOR. Yes.

BAB. Will you take it?

FLOR. [*Laughing*] With all my heart!

BAB. You have something more *substantial* than that to offer your second husband.

FLOR. Thanks to my first, I have. Heigh-ho! [*Crosses to R.*] Don't you think there is a delicate suggestion of subdued grief in this corded trimming, Mr. Babbage? [*Without waiting for an answer, Florence looking at her dress, goes to lower door, looks at her train over her shoulder, at door kisses her hand to Babbage, and exits, lower door*]

BAB. [*Looking after her a moment*] Poor Brown! Always so anxious about his margin! There is nothing but a margin left of him now! Brown was one of us, a solid business man! [*Goes to upper door as he talks, exits, shaking his head*]

FANNY. [*Outside upper door as if meeting Babbage in the hall*] Ah, Mr. Babbage. Mr. Westbrook is upstairs.

BAB. Yes, I know. [*Enter Fanny, crossing to L.H.*]

FANNY. [*Looking round*] Not here.

LIL. [*Enters upper door*] Looking for me, aunt? I heard you come downstairs.

FANNY. [*Sits down L.C.*] Yes, dear, sit down. [*Lilian gets stool, sits by Fanny L.C.*] Have you thought of what I have said to you?

LIL. I have never ceased to think of it.

FANNY. You are growing more and more listless. Your health must give way at last.

LIL. [*Dejectedly*] I am so wretched, so miserable, have been all these years.

FANNY. I knew it all the time. Why do you not write to him?

LIL. I dare not.

FANNY. [*Coaxingly*] Why, dear?

LIL. Oh, aunt, if you had seen, had heard him, that terrible night, when he in his anger and disappointment, revealed to me the depth of his affection, the nobility of his manly nature—revealed to me what I would not confess to myself, that I did love, had long loved him, who I believed married me without a single thought of love—if you had seen that, heard that, you would understand why I dare not write to him now.

FANNY. Could he see what I have seen, heard what I have just heard, John Strebelow would be at your feet, the happiest of husbands, the proudest of fathers. Once more I tell you, child, you are repeating my mistake and your own. [*Enter Lizette U.D.*]

Liz. Mrs. Brown is waiting to see you in your own room, Mrs. Holcomb.

Fanny. Tell her I will be there in a moment. [*Exit Lizette U.D.*] I wish she had chosen some other time. [*Rising*] I would again, I do again urge you, for your own sake, for your child's sake, Lilian, above all for your husband's sake, to write to him. Unveil your heart, let him see himself there beside his child, and the past will be atoned for by a peaceful and happy future, believe me. [*Goes to upper door*]

Flor. [*Outside. Calls*] Mrs. Holcomb!

Fanny. I must go. I hear Florence.

Flor. [*Calls again*] Mrs. Holcomb!

Fanny. Coming. [*Louder*] I'm coming up, Mrs. Brown. [*Exits R.U.D.*]

Lil. [*Solus, rising*] No, I dare not write to him, I dare not ask him to return to me, though I know my heart will break if he remains away. [*Stops as if in thought. Calls*] Natalie!

Nat. [*Running in from U.D.*] Here I am, mamma! And here is dolly. We've been putting her house to rights.

Lil. [*Sits in chair used by Fanny, places Natalie on the stool she herself had used*] Tell me, dear, how long is it since you sent the letter to papa?

Nat. The one you spelt for me?

Lil. Yes.

Nat. [*Timidly*] I—I sent another since.

Lil. [*Astonished*] Another?

Nat. Yes, I asked Mr. Babbage to put the post office picture on for me and put it in the box. Was it naughty?

Lil. It is never naughty for you to write to dear papa. But you showed me all your other letters.

Nat. [*Assuming importance*] Oh, I wanted to say something important to papa.

Lil. You need never show me your letters to him unless you please. But how did you direct it?

Nat. Aunty Brown wrote on the envelope.

Lil. Would you like to write to papa today?

Nat. [*Clapping her hands*] Oh, yes, yes. [*Rising*]

Lil. And let me tell you what to write?

Nat. Oh, that'll make it so easy. [*Runs to drawer of secretary, C., gets paper, envelopes, takes them to table, L.H., Lilian puts hassock on chair and lifts Natalie to enable her to sit on it. Natalie takes pen*] Now, mamma, what am I to say?

Lil. "Dear papa."

Nat. [*Writing*] That's easy. Now?

LIL. "I do hope—" On the line below, dear.

NAT. [*Writing*] "Do ope."

LIL. *Hope*—that's it—"you will come back to America."

NAT. [*Spelling as she writes*] K-u-m, come.

LIL. Oh, dear, no! Let me guide your hand. [*Guides Natalie's hand, speaking the words as she causes the child to trace them*] Come back to America. [*With emotion*] Mamma wants you very much. [*Sobbing*] So very much she—will—die if you do not come. Come back to her, to me. [*Lilian, sobbing, falls on ottoman*]

NAT. Why, that's just what I wrote in the letter I did not show you.

LIL. [*Turning her face from child*] What you wrote?

NAT. [*Looking at letter*] Yes. I knew you wanted him to come back. I told him what Aunty Brown told me when she helped me to write.

LIL. [*Controlling herself*] What did she tell you?

NAT. [*Going to her*] That the doctor said you might go away if he did not come back soon, and then, you know, he could not find you at all.

LIL. [*Catching the child to her breast*] Oh, my darling! My darling! [*Kisses her*]

NAT. I put the picture of you that you gave me last Christmas into the letter for papa to see.

LIL. [*Turning away from Natalie as Lizette enters lower door*] Oh, John! John! If you but knew my heart today as well as you know my face! [*Sees Lizette*] Well?

LIZ. [*With letters on salver*] The mail, madam. Two letters from Mr. Westbrook and one for Miss Natalie. [*Natalie runs to Lizette, who gives her letter and then exits U.D.*]

NAT. [*Looking at letter*] Oh, what a dirty letter! That isn't from papa.

LIL. Let me read it for you. [*Takes letter, looks at it*] It is from papa. [*Stops*]

NAT. What makes it so ugly?

LIL. [*Looking at letter*] It is stained with sea water. Steamship *Hanover!* The steamer that was wrecked. Natalie, this letter was at the bottom of the big ocean.

NAT. And they got it out again?

LIL. Yes, and sent it on to you.

NAT. Oh, they knew it was from my papa. Do read it.

LIL. [*Opens letter; picture falls out*] What is that?

NAT. [*Picks it up, looks at it*] See, mamma, papa's picture?

LIL. [*Takes picture, looks at it in deep emotion*] His hair is almost white now—and in three years! [*Kisses picture*]

NAT. Read the letter!

LIL. [*Reads*] "My little darling, I will take the next steamer for America!" The next steamer for America.

NAT. I'm so glad, so glad! [*Clings to her mother's dress*]

LIL. [*Looks at date of letter*] August the eleventh. Natalie, Natalie, papa may be in America now. [*Enter Florence, upper door R.*]

FLOR. [*Stopping upstage*] Why, Lilian, what's the matter?

LIL. Florence! Natalie's father—my—Mr. Strebelow is coming home.

FLOR. Oh, he's found his senses at last, has he?

LIL. The news has excited me a little, and I must tell my father.

NAT. [*Pulling her mother upstage*] Yes, yes, we must tell grandpa and Uncle Babbage.

LIL. [*To Florence*] You'll excuse me a few minutes.

FLOR. Certainly. [*Lilian and Natalie exit upper door R. Solus*] Now, I am really glad of that. Lilian was breaking her heart. Poor thing! I don't wonder at it. What's the use of a husband two thousand miles away? [*Enter Phipps preceded by Lizette*] Phipps!

PHIPPS. Brown.

FLOR. Returned from Europe.

PHIPPS. Just off the steamer. [*To Lizette*] Give this card and this note to Mrs. Holcomb and tell her I am at her service. [*Lizette exits. To Florence*] Just reached the dock. Business tour in Europe this time. Wasted no time on sight-seeing as I did three years ago.

FLOR. What steamer did you come in?

PHIPPS. *Veal de Paree*—less than half an hour ago! Strebelow and I jumped into a carriage as soon as we touched the pier.

FLOR. John Strebelow?

PHIPPS. Left baggage to the curiosity of the officials of the Custom House; only a small valise, box or two of collars, a few neckties, half a dozen shirts.

FLOR. Mr. Phipps, please give my imagination some chance. But Mr. Strebelow?

PHIPPS. Is at his hotel! He was in such a hurry to see his child he could scarcely wait for the *Veal de Paree* to swing to. The note I brought was from him. He wants me to take Natalie to him in the carriage I have below. He's crazy to see the child.

FLOR. Indeed! and Lilian, his wife? Has he forgotten her?

PHIPPS. Thinks and talks to me of nothing else. Did all the voyage. I tried him on dry goods—no use! He took no more interest in the new styles of imported brocades—that reminds me! [*Takes out watch, then notebook*] I must not forget to—[*To Florence*] Excuse me, but I must get to the bank before three o'clock. Let me see. [*Reading notes*] Arnold, Matthison & Company, Axminster carpets, five and ten off. [*Enter Fanny U.D.*]

FANNY. [*R.*] Mr. Phipps.

PHIPPS. [*C.*] Ah, glad to see you—just back from Europe—get Strebelow's note?

FANNY. Thank you, yes; you will pardon me, but I came to tell you I sent the answer to Mr. Strebelow directly.

PHIPPS. And Natalie—is she ready?

FANNY. I have asked Mr. Strebelow to call here to see her.

PHIPPS. [*Nods*] Right. I understand—and Mrs. Strebelow?

FANNY. I am now going to tell her. You will excuse me?

PHIPPS. Certainly. [*Exit Fanny U.D.R.*] Mrs. Holcomb has what I call horse sense—most women have.

FLOR. [*Sits by fire*] You think so?

PHIPPS. [*Returning to his notes*] Yes—old women.

FLOR. Oh!

PHIPPS. [*At his notes*] Long Island Manufacturing Company. I wonder if I can run over to Greenpoint! It will do tomorrow. By the way, Mrs. Brown, while I think of it—Merrill, Cook & Company—half past—draft on London—must not forget that. [*To Florence*] You have now been a widow upward of two years, I believe.

FLOR. Two years tomorrow.

PHIPPS. [*At his notes*] Whitbeck, Oldhanger & Company, order filled per samples. [*Looks at his watch*] Half past two. [*To Florence*] Will you be my wife, Mrs. Brown? [*Looking at her as he closes his watch, puts it into pocket, and then returns to his notes*]

FLOR. [*Starting up*] Sir!

PHIPPS. Will—you—be—my—wife? [*At notes again*] Sorry I could not get those goods for Jones & Cunningham. [*To Florence*] I will drop in and see you this afternoon. [*Florence staggers; he catches her in his arms. Places her on ottoman. Pause. She jumps up quickly*]

FLOR. I have concluded not to faint, Mr. Phipps. Have you ever been struck by a cannon ball?

PHIPPS. No; I was hit by a baseball once.

FLOR. Then you cannot appreciate my feelings at the present moment. [*Surveys him*] I rather like you, Phipps. You're not handsome, but you interest me. The doctor has prescribed a second husband.

PHIPPS. Of course that is the only prescription that can cure a widow of her widowhood.

FLOR. I might as well take the dose in one form as another. I will swallow it with my eyes shut.

PHIPPS. I'm not a sugar-coated pill, madam—but—

FLOR. [*Laughs*] Phipps, there's my hand.

PHIPPS. [*Kisses her hand, returns to notebook*] September second—suppose we call it thirty days after date? [*Writes*]

FLOR. Thirty days from date?

PHIPPS. Yes—by the way, what is your middle name?

FLOR. Florence St. Vincent Brown. Have *you* a card about you? [*He gives her card*] Thank you. [*Reads card*] George Washington Phipps. [*Crosses to R.*] I shouldn't like to forget your name before the happy day.

PHIPPS. Easily remembered. Father of his country Phipps.

FLOR. Now, don't forget, Phipps—October second.

PHIPPS. October fifth!

FLOR. Eh?

PHIPPS. Three days' grace you know. [*Florence laughs. Phipps, writing in books*] October second and fifth; we shall both fall due on the same day— say half past three P.M.

FLOR. Half past three P.M.

PHIPPS. Sharp!

FLOR. Sharp! [*Laughs. Exits U.D.R.*]

PHIPPS. [*Solus, looks at his watch after Florence*] Hm! I can give her seventeen minutes more. [*Exits after Florence. Stage remains empty for a few seconds. Enter Lizette and Strebelow, R.H., lower door*]

STREB. I will wait. [*Exit Lizette R.U.D. Solus, looking around him*] The very room! Here, on this very spot, it was she gave me her hand. As I stand here, it seems but yesterday—yesterday it seemed an age! [*Enter Fanny R.U.D.*]

FANNY. [*R.*] Mr. Strebelow!

STREB. [*Turning to her*] Mrs. Holcomb! [*They go to each other and shake hands*]

FANNY. I am very, very glad to see you here—here in this house, once more, Mr. Strebelow.

STREB. I know you are—I understand, and thank you.

FANNY. Mr. Phipps brought me your request to send Natalie to you. In justice to Lilian I could not do that. I felt, as you must feel, that the proper place for you to see your child was where her mother is.

STREB. Tell me of her. How is Lilian?

FANNY. As well as she has been any day since she returned here. The news of your arrival has excited her a little. But you shall see her for yourself.

STREB. See her! See her!

FANNY. I will send her to you.

NAT. [*Running in*] Oh, Aunt Fanny, when will papa be here? [*Sees* *rebelow, catches hold of Fanny's dress; hides behind it, peeping out at* *rebelow*]

STREB. [*Holding his arms out to her*] Natalie, don't you know me?

NAT. [*Comes forward a little, looks at Strebelow, utters a cry, rushes to* *m*] Oh, papa! Papa!

STREB. [*Taking her in his arms*] Natalie, my child! My own darling! *Aunt Fanny steals silently to door*]

NAT. Oh, I'm so glad.

STREB. [*Sitting and holding the child out in front of him*] And you did *ot* know me?

NAT. Oh, yes, I did; but your hair is so white, just like your picture. Oh, *m* so glad—and mamma will be so happy.

STREB. [*Kisses her, then looking at her*] How you have grown—and your *air* is darker. How like her mother. [*Kisses her again. Fanny steals out upper* *oor*]

NAT. It was naughty of you to stay away so long. I knew you'd come *hen* I wrote you how much mamma wanted to have you here— And how *nhappy* she was without you. But what are you thinking about?

STREB. I came as soon as I received your last letter.

NAT. I knew you would.

STREB. [*Thoughtfully*] You wrote me a great many letters.

NAT. [*Proudly*] Didn't I? It was hard at first; but mamma told me wha* *ɔ* write, you know.

STREB. [*Eagerly*] Yes, yes. Mamma told you what to say to papa. And— *nd—and—*in the last letter, she told you to say how unhappy mamma was *vithout* papa? The words came from her—

NAT. Mamma did not know anything about the last letter. Aunty Brown *elped* me to write that, and Uncle Babbage put it in the box to Rome.

STREB. [*Rising and turning away from Natalie*] And—and your mamma *new* nothing about what was in it.

NAT. [*Proudly*] Not a word. I did it myself. [*Goes up for doll*]

STREB. [*To himself*] And I thought her hand had guided hers, and that *he* called the husband while the child called her father! [*Pause*] "Mamma *s* very unhappy without you." It was not she who said it—not she. Her heart *s* silent still! [*Rising, rings bell*]

NAT. [*Coming down to him*] What's the matter, papa? You're not going *o* cry; mamma cries, but papas never do, do they?

STREB. They often have most cause. [*Crossing to C. Enter Lizette*] Y(
may say to Mrs. Strebelow that I cannot wait at present. I have an engag
ment. I may call—I mean, I will return. [*Exit Lizette L.D.*] Good-by, Na
alie, [*Taking child in his arms*] good-by. [*Kisses her*]

NAT. Good-by?

STREB. Yes, papa must go now.

NAT. Why, papa, you've not seen mamma yet!

STREB. I know, dear—I know—but I must go now—I must. [*Places chil
on ground, goes toward lower door as Lilian enters upper door*]

LIL. [*At door*] John! [*Strebelow turns quickly*] Mr. Strebelow.

STREB. Lilian! [*Pause. Child looking at both in wonder*] Lilian, I am gla
to see you. [*Goes to meet her, extends hand to her frankly; she takes
timidly*]

LIL. You were going—without—without seeing me!

STREB. [*Embarrassed*] Believe me, I am—am—glad—more than glad t
see you. But I felt I had no right to bring about such a meeting without you
own express desire. When last we parted I pledged myself to that. I unde
stand your long—long silence perfectly, and so—so we meet only to pa
again.

LIL. Part again! [*Crossing to L.H. Aside*] I knew it!

NAT. [*Who, by her mother's side, has been wonderingly listening*] O
papa, don't go away.

STREB. [*Taking her up*] Papa must go—Good-by, Lilian. [*Holds out h
hand to Lilian. As Lilian steps to take it, her head averted, Natalie, who ha
one arm, tries to draw them together*]

NAT. Kiss mamma! [*Lilian and Strebelow, eyes meet. Her eyes are fu
of tears; they avert their heads from each other. Natalie looks from one to th
other. Pause*]

STREB. [*Mastering his emotions. Putting down Natalie*] There, there
Natalie, good-by. Farewell, Lilian, forever.

LIL. Forever!

STREB. For three years your heart has been silent; will it speak later
think you? [*Lilian is sobbing*]

NAT. Oh, papa, I forgot—my last letter. [*Runs to table, takes letter*] Her
it is [*Crosses to C.*] Mamma and I wrote it this morning; she held my hand
[*Gives him letter*]

STREB. [*Takes letter, about to put it in his pocket*] I'll answer it soon, dear

NAT. Oh, read it now, papa.

STREB. [*Reading*] "Dear papa—mamma wants you very much." [*Reads ter, stops, looks at Lilian*] Lilian! Lilian! Can you repeat these words with ur own lips?

LIL. With my whole heart. [*Throws herself into his arms as Fanny enters ealingly U.D.*]

STREB. [*Embracing*] My own wife—my wife! [*Enter U.D., Westbrook d Babbage following Fanny and Phipps; at L.D. follows Florence*]

FANNY. [*Demurely*] I beg your pardon. I was looking for Mrs. Brown.

FLOR. [*Same air*] I beg your pardon. I was looking for Mrs. Holcomb.

PHIPPS. Ah, Strebelow, let me present my future wife, Mrs. George ashington, the mother of her country, Phipps! [*Lilian goes to table, sits wn. Natalie runs over to H.*]

WEST. [*To Babbage*] My conscience is at rest at last!

BAB. Mine is more easy.

STREB. [*Goes to his wife, turns round, holds out his hand to Westbrook*] . the future before us, let us forgive and forget the past.

BAB. And retiring from business, speculate no more in human hearts.

CURTAIN

MY PARTNER

By Bartley Campbell

The main text of *My Partner* is based on a manuscript owned by Mr. Robert Campbell. The alternate ending of Act II is based on a manuscript in the University of Chicago Library.

CAST OF CHARACTERS

JOE SAUNDERS

NED SINGLETON

WING LEE

MAJOR HENRY CLAY BRITT

MATHEW BRANDON

JOSIAH SCRAGGS

SAM BOWLER

WELLINGTON WIDGERY

JIM JOHNSON

MARY BRANDON

GRACE BRANDON

POSIE PENTLAND

TIME: ACTS I AND II, MAY 1879. ACTS III AND IV, NOVEMBER 1879.
PLACE: SISKIYOU COUNTY, CALIF.

ACT I.

ENE: *Exterior of the Golden Gate Hotel, L.1.E. to 3. Northern California. istant view of Mount Shasta on drop in 5. Pathway over rocks, R. and scent over rocks into valley, L.3. Moon in C. Green medium. Music at rise curtain. Enter Posie from hotel, L.2., with a broom in hand.*

POSIE. [*Calling*] Wing Lee! Wing Lee! What on earth has become of at Chinaman? It's always the way! The more he's wanted the more he n't show up; talk about Chinese cheap labor, why when it comes to a nch, they ain't worth a bit a day. Wing Lee! Wing Lee!

WIDG. [*Coming down, R.H., from over the rocks, L.3.E.*] 'Ollerin' agin, ? Ain't ye afraid ye'll bust yer larynx?

POSIE. [*L. Saucily*] I don't know what that is, and I ain't afeerd of stin' it if I did.

WIDG. [*R.*] No h'occasion to exhibit h'indignation, Miss Posie—yer rynx is a wittle element connected with yer wind—[*Touching his throat*] w's the ball a-comin' on?

POSIE. You're a nice party, Mr. Widgery, to ask that question, going off Frisco and leavin' us up to our eyes in preparin' things, and comin' back e last minit.

WIDG. And I only came back the last minit to go the next. [*Sits on ump, R.C.*]

POSIE. [*In surprise*] Going to leave Mr. Brandon, who helped to bring u all the way from England? [*Sits on rustic bench by hotel, L.*]

WIDG. [*Reflectively*] Yes, 'tis 'ard; but I'm no use 'ere. I can't larn to mix ese H'american drinks, and clothes is clothes and wittles is wittles; poor randon! Hit's awful to see 'im situated like this—It's a h'awful pity!

POSIE. He's got the best hotel in Siskiyou County.

WIDG. But it's 'orrible to step from the 'ead of a London 'ouse in the ry goods way—Holborn, and a mill in Manchester—[*Sighs*] I've seen ronets in 'is 'ouse—when 'is father gave h'entertainments—genuwine gen- emen; not the sort o' folks h'axed to 'is 'ouse tonight. Ah! [*Sighs*] 'e 'as to o it now, clothes is clothes and wittles is wittles! [*Sighs*]

POSIE. I don't know nothin' 'bout yer titles, but there's just as good entlemen coming here tonight as ye kin find anywhere.

Widg. I'm a h'ignorant man, but I doesn't h'admire h'ignorance, an' doesn't call these h'unheducated miners like Joe Saunders, gentlemen?

Posie. If ye measure gentlemen by their manhood, there's enough Joe to make a dozen of yer coronet fellows, and if ye want education—the his partner, Ned Singleton—he's bin to college.

Widge. [Rises. Sagely] Yes, Ned, 'e's civilized, but still no match f Mary Brandon.

Posie. [L.] How do ye know it isn't Joe she cares most for?

Widg. Oh! I say! None of that. Might as well think of her fallin' love with old Scraggs, and her mother turned up her nose at 'im, ar nearly caused murder. [Commence to change, slowly, gradually to moo light]

Posie. [Amazed, rising and dropping broom] Did Mr. Scraggs lo Mary's mother? [Widgery closes one eye and nods] But she wouldn't ha him?

Widg. [Nods] H'it was presumption for 'im to think of h'it, but Josia Scraggs forgot 'imself, and it took a blow of a whip to bring him round hisself again—I suppose Brandon believes in bleedin' for 'igh fevers; anyho it cured Scraggs.

Posie. Do you mean that scar on his cheek?

Widg. Umph! [Nods]

Posie. I always thought that scar meant something. But they're goo friends now?

Widg. Gammon! He's very oily an' talks h'all right; but Mr. Brandon friend, oh, no! Take my word for it, Josiah Scraggs is a man wot nev forgives or forgets. I tried to 'int it to Mr. Brandon, but 'e is so honest hissel he never doubts h'others. [Crosses, L.]

Posie. [Crosses, R.] I always hated that Scraggs; now I despise him [Crosses to R.H.]

Widg. [L.] Don't say I told ye h'anything; it would hurt me and ne 'elp you.

Posie. [R.] Not a word.

Widg. [Aside] That is wery accommodating! [Aloud] Don't repeat wc I said, you know, for yer h'own sake! Always remember, clothes is clothe and wittles is wittles. [Exit into hotel, L.H.]

Posie. [Crossing, L.C., calling] You're perfectly right, Mr. Widgery Where is that Chinaman? Wing Lee! Wing Lee!

Scrag. [Entering over rocks, L.U.E. Crosses, R.] Hello, Miss Posie. Wha are you raisin' the devil for?

Posie. [L.H.] Didn't know as I was, but seein' I raised you—I suppose—

SCRAG. [*R.H.*] Oh, I'm the devil, am I?

POSIE. [*Retreating, L.H.*] Well, if you ain't—you're a pretty good imi-tion.

SCRAG. You think that smart, don't ye? Ye think that clever, but it ain't; s simply impudence.

POSIE. Shut up! I hate you!

SCRAG. And who are you, that you should hate me?

POSIE. Your betters, if you want to know!

SCRAG. [*With a grim smile*] Josiah Scraggs has fallen very low, when a chen wench is his betters; very low indeed! What next I wonder? [*Music*]

POSIE. [*Advancing angrily*] You want to know what next, do you? I'll you, sir—what next.

SCRAG. [*Grinning defiantly in her face*] You will, eh, Miss Posie?

POSIE. That's next, and that, and that! [*Striking at Scraggs with broom, o falls on stage, exit quickly into house, L.1.E., leaving broom on stage. ing Lee enters over rocks, L.U.E., carrying basket. Comes forward, puts wn basket and extends his hand sympathetically to assist Scraggs to rise*]

WING. [*L.*] Melican man fallee downee.

SCRAG. [*R. Rising*] Fall down! No, I was knocked down, kicked, and used.

WING. [*Business*] Me so sollee.

SCRAG. [*Sitting on stump, R.C.*] What good does your sorrow do? I don't nt anyone's pity. I'll make her sorry, which will be more to the purpose, ach more.

WING. You go to the ballee tonight?

SCRAG. Idiot! Do you want me to dance on one leg?

WING. Melican man no can dancee on one leggee? [*Business*]

SCRAG. Where is this dance?

WING. Here—hotel—sabee?

SCRAG. A dance, eh? Here at Brandon's?

WING. Humph! [*Nods*] Allee pretty gallee—allee nicee music, allee cee manee, squeeze allee samee nicee youngee ladee.

POSIE. [*Inside house, calling*] Wing Lee! Wing Lee!

WING. Comee allee timee—Bellee nicee music—nicee dancee. Bellee nicee anee squeeze pretty gallee!

POSIE. [*Inside house, calling*] Wing Lee! Wing Lee!

WING. Allee lightee! Me comee! [*Business and exit into house, L.1.E.*]

SCRAG. A ball at Brandon's, eh? He was always a soft fool, and these ung daughters are wrapping him around their fingers. Now that I've turned, he'll invite me, too! And he thinks that I have forgotten and forgiven him, he thinks me an idiot like himself, as if I could forget wit that livid scar blazing on my cheek. How I hate him, and his pretty brats The love I bore their mother has lain in my empty heart all these year until it has turned to poison, for she was the cause of all—she rejected m for him years and years ago—and he was rich then and I was poor. Bu since he has grown poorer and poorer, and I richer and richer, and whe I've broken his heart, and can lie down on his pauper grave and beat upo it with my bag of shining gold, then I'll feel my triumph is complete– complete. [*Is R.C. Rises*]

BRAN. [*L.C. Entering from hotel*] Where can Mary be? [*Sees Scraggs* Ah, Josiah, is that you?

SCRAG. [*R.H.*] All that's left of me.

BRAN. [*L.H. Shaking hands*] Your arrival is timely.

SCRAG. I'm glad to hear it.

BRAN. We are going to have a bit of a dance tonight, and to have you familiar face among us will revive the memory of the good old days whe we were both younger and happier men.

SCRAG. I suppose, from your jolly humor, you have raised the mone for me.

BRAN. [*L.H.*] Well, the fact is, not exactly! Business has been rathe dull, no water in the mines for months—and knowing you were no pinched—

SCRAG. [*Snappishly*] How did you know that?

BRAN. I read of your successful speculation in Frisco.

SCRAG. Because I have a glimmer of good luck, you imagine I don't wan my honest money, eh?

BRAN. [*Proudly*] I imagine nothing of the sort; you shall have you money, every penny, if it costs me the roof over my children's head.

SCRAG. [*L.*] Proud as ever.

BRAN. Do you doubt it?

SCRAG. [*L.*] If I ever did, do you think I would have trusted you?

BRAN. [*R.*] Did you not have good security, and do you not draw you interest regularly?

SCRAG. Of course, it's secure enough; but I loaned it for friendship, no for a beggarly interest, and to have you turn upon me in this way, I'd rathe lose it all. [*Meekly*]

BRAN. Perhaps I've been too hasty. I've a bad ugly temper—Josiah.

SCRAG. And a proud spirit, Mathew.

BRAN. Yes, and a proud spirit; and every reverse seems to make me more ːter; but you have been a true friend to me, Josiah, and I ask your pardon. ᵒffers hand]

SCRAG. If it were worth more, it would be yours more readily. [Shakes ·nd]

GRACE. [Calling inside hotel, L.2.E.] Papa! Where is papa! [Entering ᵐm hotel, L.2.E.] Oh, here you are, papa! Say, don't I look real nice! [Ad- ᵢring herself, down L.H.]

BRAN. [C.] Yes, a regular wild flower! Grace, don't you see Mr. Scraggs?

GRACE. [L.] Why so it is! But I was so busy looking at myself, I ːuldn't see anyone. [Shaking out her dress] Don't you think I look nice, ·raggs?

BRAN. [C. Reprovingly] Mr. Scraggs, my child.

GRACE. Well, Mr. Scraggs, then. Don't you think I look lovely?

SCRAG. [R.H.] Oh, yes, very pretty. [Going up, R.H.]

GRACE. Very pretty! Thank you, is that all you can say? There isn't a ᵗ of gallantry here in California. In the east young girls swim in flattery, ·ey say; here there isn't enough to wet one's shoes.

BRAN. [C.] Flattery is the tinsel of society—gallantry the golden warp ᵃt makes the whole fabric beautiful; there is a wide margin between ᵉm. [Going up, C. Comes down, L.]

GRACE. [L.] I don't understand you, but it sounds like sense.

SCRAG. [Down, R.C.] Your father means to say, flattery is but another ᵃme for insincerity.

GRACE. I don't care. I'd rather men were insincere than stupid. [Going ᵇ, C., and looking off for guests]

BRAN. [Crossing to L.H.] Not a bit like her mother, Josiah.

SCRAG. [R.C.] Not a bit! Not a bit!

BRAN. [L.] Nor like her sister! I sometimes regret having taken my ᵢildren away from the pleasure of a higher civilization, even for the chance ᵒf mending a broken fortune. A mining town is no place for a gentleman's ᵈaughter.

SCRAG. They seem to enjoy life.

BRAN. I do what I can to make them forget our altered condition—even ᵗis dance is a part of the daily deceit I practice.

SCRAG. [C.] Poverty teaches us humility.

BRAN. [L.] Don't say that! I hate the word! Humility is a beggarly bit ᵒf cant. As long as we are honest, sir, we can afford to be proud. [Exit into ᵒtel, L.2.E.]

SCRAG. [Crossing to and on steps of hotel] Good evening, Miss Grace.

Grace. [*Down R.C.*] Good evening, Scraggs. [*Scraggs exit into hot*
Oh, how I hate that man. [*Seated on stump, R.C.*] I wish he hadn't con
He seems to me like a great black snake, with soft velvet coils full of pois
And sister Mary says he was papa's rival once! Well, if mamma had marr.
that man I never would have forgiven her—never! [*Joe Saunders calls o*
side, "Hullo-o-o-o." R.U.E. Music. Going, L.H.] What's that? [*Going
and looking off, R.3.E.*] Why it's Joe Saunders coming down the mount.
path—for a wonder he's the first to get here and all fixed up, too. Oh, j
dressed to death! Why, Joe! Joe! [*Calling off*]

Joe. [*Enters over rocks, R.3.E. Comes down, C.*] Well, I just got h
kind o' early, I reck'n!

Grace. The first one.

Joe. I ain't too soon, am I? [*Music stops*] Why, hello, Grace, gal! Du
me—if you don't look nice enough to eat.

Grace. [*L.*] Do I, Joe?

Joe. [*R.*] Why you've got more fine fixings on than I've seen since I l
St. Joe in the good State of Missouri.

Grace. [*L.H.*] Were they stylish in St. Joe?

Joe. Stylish! Well, I should say so! They used to set the fashions for t
whole country.

Grace. [*In wonder*] They did?

Joe. Yes, indeed! Why, I've heard tell that when Sophie Higgins of
Joe went to Paris, there wasn't a woman there as dressed like her. And Pa
ain't no slouch of a place neither.

Grace. [*Strutting to L.H. corner, delighted*] Do I look like Sophie H
gins, Joe?

Joe. [*R.*] Well no, not exactly—she had a little difficulty with one eye
it always wanted to see what was going on round the corner, there! Wh
your eyes, Miss Grace, are as blue as the skies that bend over Shasta yond
and as straight as well—

Grace. [*Eagerly*] Well! Well!

Joe. Never mind—you'll do.

Grace. [*L.*] Will I, Joe?

Joe. You bet your boots. But where's your sister? Where's Mary?

Grace. I don't know. Do you want her?

Joe. Not particular! I'd like to see her—that's all.

Grace. [*Impressively*] Joe Saunders, do you love my sister?

Joe. Oh, go to glory.

Grace. But do you now, seriously?

Joe. Well, now, who don't love your sister Mary?

GRACE. But do you love her with all your heart?

JOE. Well, now, look here, Grace, gal—love your sister Mary—Don't u think I'd better tell her that?

GRACE. Yes, I do, Joe, and the sooner the better, or it may be too late. [*nter Sam over the rocks, L.U.E.*]

JOE. Too late! What do you mean! [*Business*] Why there isn't anyone e is there?

SAM. [*C. Coolly coming between, releasing Joe's grasp, puts Grace's arm in* ·] Yes, there is someone else, and a very particular person, too. [*Turns Grace*] I say, Grace, what does it mean? [*Joe goes R., goes upstage, busi- ss*]

GRACE. [*L. Going L.*]   What do you want to know for?

SAM. [*C. Crossing up. Drops his arm*] I've got some right to know. idn't I quit the circus for your sake? Didn't I take off the spangles and go diggin' for your sake?

GRACE. Did I ask you to?

SAM. No, but you looked as if you wanted me to, and that was enough r me. Besides, when I've been tired to death, didn't I come up here and rn cartwheels and handsprings and flip-flaps for you? [*Up, quarrelling ith Grace*]

JOE. [*Crossing to hotel side*] What's the use of my worrying, it's some her nonsense, I reckin. [*Ready, voices in laughter, L.U.E.*]

GRACE. [*Upstage. To Joe*]   Say, Joe, remember what I said.

JOE. Oh, you git out! [*Aside*] She may be right, though. I'll just have a lk with Mary this very night. [*Exit into hotel*]

GRACE. [*Sits on bench, L. corner, shaking her head sadly*] Poor Joe! It ay be too late already.

SAM. [*C.*]   Say, look h'yer! What does all this mean?

GRACE. [*Impatiently*]   All what?

SAM. This holding your hand, and mysterious remembers. If he's got the side track, tell me, and I'll leave the mines tomorrow, go back to the circus d break my neck from the trapeze.

GRACE. Don't be a fool. Joe don't care for me; it's sister Mary.

SAM. Where's his partner, Ned Singleton? I thought he was her particular ncy.

GRACE. It is hard to tell which she likes the best; the three are always gether. At first I thought it was Joe, then I thought it was Ned, then again thought it was Joe, and then I gave it up.

SAM. [*Reflectively*]   Joe's the best fellow.

GRACE. Yes, indeed.

SAM. But Singleton wears the best clothes, and you women are all alik and fine togs catches you every time. But she knew Joe first, didn't she?

GRACE. Since childhood; he carried her up from the stage office the nigl we came to the mountains.

SAM. If I get a chance I'm going to put in a good word for Joe. [*Crosse R.*]

GRACE. [*Rising, crossing to R.*] Hadn't you better attend to your ow affairs?

SAM. Oh, I'm all right! I haven't got any partner to steal your heart, an no one else dare. [*Distant voices. Music*]

GRACE. What's that?

SAM. [*Gazing over the precipice, L.3.E., and shading his eyes with h hand*] Major Britt and the rest of the boys coming to the dance.

GRACE. [*Clapping her hands*] Oh, ain't it nice? After all, there isn't an place like California, is there? [*Running up, L.C., and down, R.C.*]

SAM. [*Down, L.H.*] Except Heaven, and California up here in the mour tains is so close to it that none of us want to leave it. [*Laughter repeated mor forte outside, L.U.E. Enter Joe from hotel followed by Wing Lee, Brandor Scraggs*]

JOE. [*On platform, L.U.E.*] They're coming—they're coming every on on 'em. Come up, boys, come up everybody.

WING. [*Down by house. R. extreme*] Allee coming! Allee coming! Com lup, boys, come lup, gals, come lup, everybody. Come have dances.

BRAN. [*Crossing to Grace, R.H.*] Where is your sister? Where's Mary?

GRACE. I don't know, papa. [*Sam and Grace meet Miners, R.C., at back*

JOE. [*Aside. Down L.H.*] Well, it's kinder funny, I don't see Mary n whar, nor my partner Ned neither. [*Music forte until all on. Enter Jim John son and six or eight Miners with their Girls, L.3.E. Joe, L.*] Why, whar' the major?

BRITT. [*Enter over rocks, L.3.E., Oratorically*] Here is the major—here [*Start the moon*]

JOE. [*L. Shaking hands*] Well, major, you got here?

BRITT. [*C.*] Well, I should emphasize! Here we are landed at last on the top of Siskiyou, where the stars drink dew from the daisies and the singing of the Klamath comes mingled with the rustle of the pines.

OMNES. Hurrah! Hurrah! Hurrah!

WING. [*Coming down. Clapping hands*] Hullee! Hullee!

BRITT. [*C.*] Representative of an effete civilization, be quiet—Mongolian, subside. [*All laugh*]

JOE. [*R.C.*] Gentlemen, gentlemen! I move right here that Major Britt, as the representative of this yer district in the legislature, give us a speech.

OMNES. Speech! Speech! [*Enter Posie. Mr. Brandon and Sam assist Major to mount stump*]

BRITT. [*Business of mounting stump*] Gentlemen and ladies! Why, Miss Posie, how—standing here as one might say, among the misty curtains that drape the crystal walls of Heaven. [*To Brandon*] A drop of whiskey, if you please.

BRAN. [*R.C. To Wing Lee*] Wing Lee, bring the gentleman some of the best.

WING. Bestee blandy, for the Melican man dat talkee muchee.

JOE. Go fetch the brandy, yer yellow heathen—[*Points revolver at Wing Lee, who rushes hastily into hotel*]

BRITT. To resume, gentlemen—I—[*Business*] I—where was I?

JOE. Why, you were somewhere about the crystal walls of Heaven, major.

BRITT. Right! As I recently observed in the legislature, we, the people of this glorious commonwealth, blown from the four winds of the universe, are one family—the children of misfortune crowded out of the avenues of trade in the East, and founding a new destiny in the West, leaving behind us the luxuries of civilization, it is only on such occasions as this, when a generous hospitality bids us welcome to the festive board, that we feel—that we feel—[*Drops voice*] I can't get along if I don't get that liquor.

JOE. Whar that Chinaman? [*Looking off into hotel*] Hurry up that thar brandy.

WING. [*Reenters from house with decanter and glass. Handing glass and decanter to Britt*] Goodee landee! Don't drinkee too muchee.

BRITT. [*Pours out glass full*] Ah! [*Bows and drinks*]

WING. Oh, him takee schooner.

BRITT. [*Returning glass to Wing Lee*] Fellow citizens! Gentlemen! I am full—

WING. All leady—[*All laugh. Wing Lee exit into hotel*]

OMNES. [*Laughing and exclaiming*] Oh! Major!

JOE. [*Laughing*] Order! Order, for the major!

BRITT. I am full of admiration of this lovely scene—look about you—the moon like a beacon in motion, afloat upon a sea of azure; the dark pines whispering to each other, the river flashing like liquid silver, and singing as it flows, while the great dome of Shasta, clad in its mantle of eternal snow, shames by its purity and proportion the fabled fabrics of pagan Rome.

SAM. Bully for Shasta!

JIM. Bully for pagan Rome!

JOE. Order! Order! Go on, major!

BRITT. But, I will pass—

JOE. No! No! Major, don't pass—you never pass.

BRITT. It is our proud privilege to live among such scenes. Let us then rejoice and make the most of it. [*Steps down*]

JOE. Three cheers for Major Britt, and the State of California, where the trees are larger, and men's hearts bigger than anywhere else in all creation. [*All cheer*] Look here, gentlemen, I have got a little motion I would like to make—I move—

BRITT. [*With great dignity and crossing to stump*] Order! Order! [*Seats himself on stump*] The chair is ready for the question!

JOE. Well then, I move that we do now all adjourn to the bar of the Golden Gate, and thar liquor up.

BRITT. [*Rising*] As we say in the legislature, if there is no objection, it is carried.

JOE. You bet!

BRITT. Unanimously! [*All exeunt into hotel, followed by Sam and Grace. Business of Joe and Britt arm in arm. Bow to Grace, who exits into hotel*]

JOE. Ah! Ah! Would you, major! Always gallant, eh?

BRITT. [*At hotel steps*] Gallantry! That's my great point—just before an election. [*Exit with Joe into hotel, both laughing heartily*]

SCRAG. A noisy pack.

BRAN. [*Crossing to hotel*] But good-hearted. Won't you come in? [*On steps*]

SCRAG. No! I hate noisy crowds. I'll take a walk in the moonlight.

BRAN. You'll excuse me, Josiah?

SCRAG. Certainly, business is business. [*Brandon exit into hotel*] Yes, he' happy! So wrapt up in his daughters that as long as they are right, he can dine with pleasure on a crust. [*Starts*] But if harm should come to them. Ah! If I could only manage it! If I could only manage it! I must! I will [*Music. Exit, R.2.E. Noise in hotel. Enter Wing Lee hurriedly. Shouts in house and driven out by the crowd*]

WING. Me get a bouncee! Evlybody busee me, Miss Gracee scoldee me, Miss Posie slapee, cookee hitee, Bossee kickee; me no care, evlybody dancee me dancee, too, me must have fun, me must have fun. [*This speech can be gagged up. Music, reel inside house. Sam's voice heard calling figures*]

SAM. [*Inside*] 1st. Take your partners. 2nd. For'd two. 3rd. Ladies change 4th. Swing corners. 5th. Promenade all. [*During which Wing Lee indulge in dance with imaginary partner*]

BRAN. [*Calling inside*] Wing Lee! [*Wing Lee still dancing*]

VOICE. [*Inside, calling*] Wing Lee!

WING. [*Still dancing*] Help yourself.

BRAN. [*Appears at door*] Where is that Chinaman? [*Sees Wing Lee dancing*] Well, what the deuce are you doing now?

WING. [*Stopping suddenly, places hand on stomach*] Oh, me gottee clamps.

BRAN. I'll cramp you. [*Chases Wing Lee off behind house with broom, then exit into hotel. Music of dance inside of house ceases and music in orchestra begins and plays plaintive air until Mary Brandon enters over rocks, L.U.E., and well downstage*]

MARY. [*Impatiently*] Why don't he come? My eyes are weary watching, my heart is sore waiting. I've been down to the river's edge! The dark deep waters have a strange fascination for me, as they glide off in the mist and distance to the great ocean. [*Sits on stump, R.C. Takes off hat*] And I find myself wondering if it is the shortest way to rest after all. But do the guilty ever rest? Are there any waters cold enough to cool a feverish fear, deep enough to hide a wretched, sinful woman! [*Rises excitedly. Paces stage*] No! No! Ned is not so bad! He could not be so cruel, so base, so heartless! Oh! Why have I trusted so much, exacted so little? [*Going up*]

JOE. [*Entering hastily from hotel*] Now, whar is that Chinaman—you bet I'll find him. [*Business. Sees Mary*] Why, it's Mary! Now's my chance. They are all busy in there getting ready for another dance. So you bet, I'll pop right off. [*Aside*] Why—Mary. [*Aloud*] I mean Miss Mary! I've been looking for you everywhere.

MARY. [*Down R. Quietly*] For me, Joe?

JOE. Fact is, I wanted to ask you—[*Business*] to ask you—if—if—

MARY. Well!

JOE. If you'd seen my partner, Ned, anywhere. [*Aside*] That's the darndest lie I ever told.

MARY. No, is he not with you? [*Sits on stump, R.C.*]

JOE. [*Business*] No—you see I left him 'fore the glass making himself pretty, about two hours ago—to come to the ball, but it takes him so cussed long—still there's something to show for it. For I tell you, when that partner of mine gets all them store clothes on, he's a howler! [*Business*]

MARY. You love him dearly, don't you, Joe?

JOE. Love him! My partner—better than a brother; for brothers they quarrel sometimes, but Ned and I have worked together in the same claim, eat out of the same pan, slept under the same blanket. Why, he nursed me through fever, tender as a mother, when there warn't a woman within fifty miles.

MARY. And you saved his life at the risk of your own?

JOE. You mean the time that Jack Walker tried to stab him down in "Dead Man's Gulch"?

MARY. And you received the knife in your own shoulder?

JOE. Ah! That was a big day. [*Business*] Three men killed. Ah! There ain't no such good times in California any more. There were no women in the mines then.

MARY. Were you happier without women?

JOE. Lord bless you, no! Why, there ain't no happiness where there ain't no women. Why the night we heard your father was a-comin' with two gals —you just ought to seen the goings on. If an earthquake had shivered Shasta in splinters the excitement couldn't have been greater. There were more biled shirts around the stage-office that night than ever was seen there before. Every fellow was just smiling his broadest, and a-looking his prettiest, when the stage drove up, and thar war pistols drawn to see who'd open the stage door. Ha, ha, ha! But you should have seen how long their faces got when the two young ladies, as they expected, turned out to be but a pair of babies in pantalettes. [*Business*] I wasn't going to let them see my disappointment, so I just picked you up, little tot as you was, in my arms, and carried you up here to your new home. Do you know I felt better for a month after.

MARY. Indeed?

JOE. Yes, indeed. You see, I'd never had anything to love then, nor nothing to love me, and that's why I suppose my heart went right out to you.

MARY. [*Rises suddenly*] To me, Joe?

JOE. As it never went out to any human being afore. Not even to my partner. Why, I've seen your eyes in the glitter of the bright gold in the wash, in the stars that looked through the branches on the lonely mountain side, and the thought that you might some day be my own sang its song of hope in my heart as ye hear that river now singing to the willows that bend over it.

MARY. [*Retreating, amazed*] Why, Joe—how you talk!

JOE. [*Business*] It isn't me that's talking, it's my heart that's speaking. It's the pent-up flood of years breaking down the bars of silence. I—I—don't know what I'm saying exactly, but if ye can understand that I love ye better than myself—better than my partner—that I would willingly—ay—gladly, die for you, that's all I ask. [*Business*]

MARY. [*In distress, excitedly*] Oh! If I were only worthy of such devotion, I would give all the gold in the Sierras. [*Crosses to L.*]

JOE. [*Taking her hand*] And if all that gold were diamonds, I'd gladly give it all for this little hand I hold. [*Business*]

Mary. [*Turns, looks him steadily in the eye*] Joe Saunders, you have known me ever since I was a little child, have you not?

Joe. Longer than that.

Mary. [*Controlling her excitement*] Do you believe that I am a good, pure woman?

Joe. Do I believe it? Ask me if I believe that there's a God in Heaven!

Mary. [*Losing control of her feelings*] But suppose I should say that I have deceived you? That I have betrayed your blind faith, that I am—

Joe. [*Business*] Stop! I wouldn't believe you.

Mary. [*Turns upstage, covering her face with her hands*] Oh, that I could die! [*Sobbing*]

Joe. [*Business*] You're out of your mind, gal—why ye don't know what you're talking about—Oh, I see how it is, you've got the hysterics, ain't ye? Don't cry—don't cry.

Mary. Oh, let me cry! Tears are signs of penitence, at least, in a wretch like me. Think, if they but knew, if my father—[*Sinks in a faint on rustic bench by hotel. Music, polka*]

Joe. Mary! Mary! Look up, gal! She's fainted. They mustn't see her! What'll I do? Water, water! [*Goes to hotel door, stops*] I can't go in there, they're dancing. I know, there's water at the spring there, down in the canyon. I'll get the water there. [*Runs rapidly down over the rocks, L.U.E. and off. Enter Ned Singleton, slowly down the mountain path, R.2.E. Crosses to hotel door*]

Ned. Dancing, eh? Glad to see they are so jolly! [*Turns and sees Mary*] What's this? Mary lying out here in the moonlight! Mary! Mary! [*Arousing her. Music stops*]

Mary. [*Coming to, passing her hand over her eyes*] Yes, I hear, Joe—I— [*Looks up*] Ned! [*Rises, crosses to C.*]

Ned. Of course, it's Ned. Your own dear Ned. Why, what has happened? [*Polka inside of house ceases*]

Mary. [*Sinking on stump*] You've come at last. I had almost given you up.

Ned. Why, you knew I'd come sometime.

Mary. Sometime is a very long time to those whose hearts carry a secret as heavy as mine. [*Joe returns hurriedly up the mountain path, L.U.E., carrying his hat in his two hands as though it contained water; stops at back as he hears Mary and Ned in conversation; drops hat*]

Ned. Why, Mary, what are you saying? The fault is as much mine as yours. Besides, my dear girl, if you are guilty, am I innocent? [*Music*]

Joe. [*Aside, at back*] What's that, guilty! Heaven and earth!

MARY. But if you only knew what I suffer—the fear, the pain, the remorse! Through the long day I live a shameful lie, and gladly welcome the shadows of the coming night. But no night is dark enough to hide me from myself, and its silence only seems to mock the wild unrest that is always here. [*Strikes her breast, paces stage*] Here! Here! [*Crossing to R.H.*]

NED. [*L.*] Hush, Mary, be calm—they'll hear you in the hotel. For heaven's sake, be calm. [*Crossing to hotel*]

MARY. Calm! How can I be calm, with the knowledge that you have twice failed to keep your promise to me, that day by day—I am losing faith in your manhood, upon which I have built all my hopes of happiness here and hereafter. [*Scraggs appears at back on rock, R.U.E., listening*]

NED. You're mad! Out of your senses! Do you think I would betray you! You whom I love so dearly!—Listen, Mary, when the clergyman makes his next monthly visit to Siskiyou, I promise to make you my wife.

JOE. [*C. Coming forward excitedly and placing hand on revolver*] Swear it! [*Mary, R., and Ned, L.*]

MARY and NED. [*Startled*] Joe!

JOE. [*C.*] Swear it! [*About to draw revolver*]

MARY. [*Restraining Joe in terror*] What would you do? Would you kill your friend, your partner?

JOE. [*Firmly*] As I would a snake. Swear!

NED. [*L.*] I give you my word.

JOE. [*C.*] Your word! You've broken that already. Swear!

NED. Well, on my honor then—

JOE. Your honor! O Ned, swear by something purer than that—by the eternal stars that are looking down upon us now, by the memory of your mother. [*Business*] By all that is good and pure and holy. Swear!

NED. Partner! Take care, you go too far—there is no necessity—

MARY. No necessity—

JOE. No necessity! Look at that poor, trembling child standing there, who tells you she hasn't slept for days and nights; whose faith has slipped from her, whose head is bowed, whose heart is crushed. I mean that you shall do her right, that here in the moonlight, on the threshold of that home you have robbed of its purity and peace, you shall solemnly swear to do this poor, motherless child justice. [*Mary sobs through Joe's speech*]

NED. [*Earnestly*] Any oath you like, Joe. Dictate it!

JOE. [*Dictating*] Swear then, as sure as there's a God in Heaven—

NED. [*Repeating*] As sure as there's a God in Heaven—

JOE. Within three days—

NED. Within three days—

JOE. I will make this gal—my—my wife.

NED. Within three days, she shall be my wife.

JOE. His wife—his wife! Dead—dead to me forever. [*Business. Picture, quick drop. Music crescendo at end of Act*]

ACT II.

SCENE: *Shasta drop for backing. Interior of Joe and Ned's cabin (not log) in the mountains. Door in F.R.C. Large square window in F.L.C., through which can be seen Mount Shasta. Set door, R.2.E. Large fireplace and hearthstone, L.2.E. Picks and shovels in L.U. corner. Map of California over fireplace and specimens of quartz on mantel. Deer antlers hanging against flat, buffalo robe on floor. Table, L.C., chair on either side. Bottle and glass on table. Cupboard, L.3.E. Scene boxed in 3. The interior of this house or cabin should be clapboard or plaster. Quite plain. Time, afternoon of following day. Plaintive music at rise. Ned Singleton discovered seated, L. of table. Lights all up.*

NED. [*Sadly*] Not home yet! [*Sighs*] Perhaps he has gone, never to return. Curse the luck! I wouldn't for the world lose his good opinion. However, he was unreasonable and it wasn't any of his business particularly. Why, if he had loved the girl—[*Stops short*] Perhaps he did! Nonsense! I wish he'd come. He don't surely mean to go away, and leave all his gold to me. [*Goes up to window*] I hope he hasn't slept out on the mountain all night. Pshaw! I'm a regular old woman! No more grit in me than a baby. [*Leaning in recess of window. Music. Enter Wing Lee, D. in F.R.*]

WING. [*Looking around*] House empty. No bollee in! [*Advances to table*] Bellee bad—leave a bottlee—no corkee. [*Smells of bottle*] Loosee all strengthee. Bellee bad house-keep—[*Takes drink*] Me no let him go to wastee. [*Drinks again*] Him no lose him strengthee now.

NED. [*Coming down, L. of table*] Hello!

WING. [*Concealing bottle under blouse suddenly*] Hello! Hello!

NED. [*L. of table*] What do you want, Wing?

WING. Me gottee lettee—from young lady, sabee?

NED. You have written a letter to a young lady?

WING. No sabee! Wing Lee got a letter—young lady.

NED. What young lady would write a letter to you? Come—no lies now!

WING. Chinaman no tellee lie. [*Putting letter on table*]

NED. [*Searches for bottle, misses it*] There was a bottle here a few minutes ago. [*Still searches*]

WING. [*Affecting surprise*] Bottlee gone?

NED. It cannot have gone very far, in such a short time. [*Glances sus piciously at Wing*] Did you see it?

WING. [*Eyes fixed on ceiling*] Wing Lee can't see bottlee now.

NED. [*Crossing to Wing Lee*] Not as long as your eyes are on the rafters What's this in your breast? [*Touches his ribs*]

WING. [*Laughs and jumps*] Melican man, Wing Lee—muchee ticklee Me ticklee! No ticklee! [*Crossing, L.*]

NED. Steady! [*Takes bottle from beneath blouse*] What's this?

WING. [*Affecting innocence*] Looking vellee muchee likee a black bottlee [*Wonderingly*]

NED. I thought Chinaman didn't see it, and that you didn't tell lies.

WING. Chinaman no tell lies—couldn't see bottlee in a breastee.

NED. Now, what ought I to do to you? [*Putting bottle on table*]

WING. Givee me halfee dollee for lettee—blingee up top side mountain

NED. [*Threateningly*] What? What ought I to do with you? [*Holding up bottle*]

WING. [*Alarmed*] Ah, no hurtee—don't knock stuffee out poor China man—keep 'im and puttee in glass case.

NED. [*Going for poker*] I'll glass-case you.

WING. No can catchee. [*Exit hurriedly, D. in F.R. Ned returns from fire place, sees that Wing Lee has disappeared, laughs heartily, throws poker back to fireplace as Wing Lee looks in window from outside*] Ha, ha, ha! Melican man no can strike Wing Lee! [*Hastily closes window as Ned makes start towards him*]

NED. [*At table. Aside. Picks up letter*] Now, what's this? A letter from Mary to Joe! What does this mean? [*Sinks on chair, L. of table*] What can she have to say to him? [*Musingly*] Can it be possible—No! No! The idea is degrading! I'm made of meaner stuff than I thought, to give it a moment's consideration. Come what will, I'll do my duty, and trust Heaven with the rest. [*Knock outside*] Come in. [*Enter Major Britt, D. in F.*]

BRITT. Afternoon! Afternoon!

NED. Come in, major. Come in! Sit down!

BRITT. [*R. of table*] Have only a moment to stay. Middle of a canvass, you know! Make a speech tonight at Lame Man's Lodgings against Billings and the Capitol appropriation. Climbing the mountain takes the wind out of a fellow—whew! [*Sits*]

NED. Perhaps you'd better have a drop of something to steady you? [*Pointing to bottle*]

BRITT. Thank you. [*Starts to drink, then stops*] I'm not touching anything of late. My opponent Billings has been publishing in his infernal newspaper a lot of figures which he calls my bar bill during the last season. It looks like a Chinese puzzle. I'm refuting his figures by an almost total abstinence.

NED. Your bar bill is not calculated to hurt you in this district very much.

BRITT. [*Pursing up his lips*] No—not among the men—but the women.

NED. They have no votes.

BRITT. But their moral influence goes a great way. I tell you once a woman gets her moral influence on a man, he's a goner! Besides they've started a Baptist Church in the lower end of the district, and I'm afraid the canvass will drift on to a high moral plane, and I've got to join the Baptist Church.

NED. You are a Methodist, are you not?

BRITT. Yes, in Sacramento. But a fellow can't maintain his grip on Methodism against a clear majority of two hundred Baptists in the district. [*Looks longingly at bottle*] So, I've flopped.

NED. Politics are not what they were in California, when the longest knives and best shots won.

BRITT. [*In disgust*] Nothing like it! Those were the days when a man was as proud of the hue of his nose as of the color of his meerschaum, when a fellow could throw out a string of adjectives baited with patriotism and haul in enough votes to elect him every time.

NED. [*Turns to Britt*] You had better try a little. [*Offering liquor*] One drink won't hurt you! Just one. Oh, do! [*Persuades him*]

BRITT. [*After persuasion*] Well, I don't care, just a drop. [*Holding glass*]

NED. [*Pouring it out*] Say when you have enough.

BRITT. There! There! There! Why, my dear sir, you don't expect me to drink all that?

NED. It's first rate. I'll get you a cigar. [*Goes to cupboard, L.U.E.*]

BRITT. I wouldn't be able to speak for ten minutes if I were to drink all that. [*Pours out more and drinks hastily, then replenishes the glass, draining the bottle*] There, that's more like it. Ordinarily a little goes a long way with me.

NED. [*Returning to table*] Take a cigar. [*Offers cigar. Business*] What! No!

BRITT. [*Taking cigar*] Ah! Yes!

NED. Have a match. [*Offering match*]

BRITT. I've got a match. [*Produces and lights one, then lights cigar*] As you may suspect, I'm around stirring the boys up a little.

NED. [*Sitting, L.H.*] I hope you will make it hot for Billings.

BRITT. [*Still lighting cigar*] Hot! Hot! [*Burns fingers with match*] Red hot!

NED. He said some hard things about you in his paper.

BRITT. Hard things! He has called me everything. I sent him a challenge but he kicked my friend, Colonel Greene, downstairs, and poured a bottle of ink and mucilage all over him—red ink at that. Then he came out next day with a whole column in his paper shrieking for the freedom of the press. Not that I object to the freedom of the press, if it will only let someone else have a little liberty at the same time. If they call names, why shouldn't I? [*Goes to take another drink. Ned looking straight ahead*] It makes me mad. But I'll have a royal revenge, I'll sweep the district by a clear three hundred majority, if it takes every darned Baptist in it. [*Going to D. in F.*]

NED. That's the proper plan, major.

BRITT. [*Pausing on the threshold*] By the way—we want to draw up some resolutions, requesting me to run again for the legislature. Can we have the use of this room for the purpose during the course of the afternoon?

NED. Certainly! Joe and I are with you heart and soul, major, under any circumstances.

BRITT. [*Shaking hands*] Thanks! Thanks! As we sometimes say in the legislature, *Virtus incendit vires!*

NED. Meaning—

BRITT. Virtue kindles strength. [*Touching his heart*] See you later. [*Exit pompously, D. in F.*]

NED. There are worse men in the world than Britt, [*Taking up bottle*] but few better judges of whiskey. I can't imagine what keeps Joe. I think I'll go down and see Mary. [*Picks up hat*] Perhaps she may have seen him and there is that letter. [*Turns it over on table, biting his lip*] I'd like to know what is in it, but I wouldn't break the seal for a million. [*Seeing Mary, who enters D. in F.*]

MARY. Ned!

NED. Mary!

MARY. Yes, I sent a letter here to Joe, and Wing Lee, failing to find him, and returning somewhat under the influence of liquor, I came myself. Has he received it? Is he in? [*Eagerly*]

NED. [*Coldly*] He has neither received it, nor is he in.

MARY. And the letter?

NED. Is here. [*Handing letter*]

MARY. [*With a sigh of relief*] I feared it had fallen into other hands.

NED. And are its contents such that you dare not have them known? I had no thought [*Bitterly*] that you shared such fearful secrets with him.

MARY. [*Sorrowfully*] That is unkind to me, unjust to him, unworthy of you. How much so you shall judge for yourself. [*Opening letter*]

NED. You need not read it! I know that I am all you say—ungenerous, unkind, unjust—[*Drops in seat at R. of table*] I'm beginning to despise myself!

MARY. [*Placing her hand on his shoulder*] No, Ned, there is enough good in you to save you from that, and in the future let us lead such a life as will win our esteem, the world's regard. Now please let me read the letter. I don't want the shadow of a secret between us—please—please. [*Coaxingly*]

NED. As you will, go on. [*Music*]

MARY. [*Reads*] "Dear Joe: You've been such a good, good friend to me always, that I am sure you will grant me one more favor; please do not blame Ned any more, and for the pain my sin has caused you, forgive us both—[*Her voice trembles with emotion*] And we will try never to wound your dear good heart again"—[*Sinks on her knees beside Ned and places her head upon his knees. Sobs aloud*] O Ned! Ned! [*Music stops*]

NED. [*Places his hand caressingly on her bowed head, and after a long pause*] I'm not worthy of you, Mary, not fit to tie your shoe, and as for Joe, I'm ashamed to look him in the face; ashamed for the first time in my life.

MARY. [*Rising solemnly*] And for the last time, too, with Heaven's good help.

NED. [*Rising*] Yes! We are standing on the threshold of a new future—as man and wife, in a few short days, we will begin a new life, a purer and a better one.

MARY. O Ned, you don't know how happy I am. [*Kisses his hand, they embrace. Enter Britt, Sam and Miners, D.F. Business at door*]

BRITT. [*Turns, looks aside knowingly at Ned*] All right? [*Ned nods, Britt then turns to Miners and resumes*] Come in, boys, what the devil are you doing standing out there for? [*Miners all come in and range themselves on R.H.*] Ahem! Beg pardon! No intrusion, I trust!

NED. [*Taking up hat*] None at all.

BRITT. [*Coming L.C.*] Not driving the lady out? [*Bows politely*]

NED. Oh, no, we are just going down the mountain. Come, Mary! [*Mary takes his arm, they go to the door, Miners standing aside respectfully and bowing*] I will see you home.

BRITT. That's right, gentlemen, respect the ladies always! My dear Miss Brandon, [*Mary stops*] it delights me to see such unaffected chivalry encased in flannel shirts. That's the stuff out of which great states are made. The pioneers of California stand before you; every one of them a knight in courtesy and a king in honor, and what is more important, every one pledged to vote the straight Britt ticket. [*Ned and Mary exeunt, D.F. Britt goes L. of table*]

OMNES. Every time!

NED. [*Through window*] Just make yourselves at home, boys, I'll be back presently. [*Exit, L.H.*]

SAM. Never saw Singleton so agreeable.

BRITT. Gentlemen, are we ready to proceed? [*Using bottle as gavel and rapping on table*]

SAM. [*Back of table*] There is nothing to do but draw up the resolutions, eh, major?

BRITT. Excuse me! [*Drawing paper from pocket*] Everything cut and dried—a regular endorsement of my official course. All we have to do now is to affix the signatures of the committee. [*Gets pen and ink from cupboard*]

SAM. But hadn't they better be read, so as the gentlemen will know what they are signing?

OMNES. Yes! Yes! Read it!

BRITT. Not necessary, a mere formality. I have given hundreds of letters of introduction to men I never saw, vouched for the integrity of others whom I never heard of, recommended men to office whose names I didn't know. Have to do it, they all do it. It's public life! [*Holds up pen*]

OMNES. Sign the paper! Sign the paper! [*General business*]

BRITT. [*Passing pen*] Thanks! Everything regular, I can assure you. [*First and second Men sign their names, third Man makes a cross*] How are you, Mr. Cross? [*They all laugh. A fourth Man approaches, Britt stops him by wave of hand*] Three will do. I will fill in the other 297 names myself. Now, gentlemen, as we have been invited to make ourselves at home, as we sometimes say in the legislature, take a drink with me. [*Coming C.*]

OMNES. [*They all produce cups from cupboard and press around Major Britt*] Three cheers for Britt and the whole ticket. [*Wing Lee enters unobserved during the cheering and passes around to L.H. corner and sits on chair by fireplace. He is much intoxicated*]

BRITT. Before drinking, permit me to make a few remarks.

OMNES. [*Demur*] Oh! Oh!

BRITT. Concerning my career as your representative! To give, as it were, some account of my stewardship.

OMNES. Order! Order!

BRITT. [*Mounting chair, R. of table*] The opposition have opened the sluice gates of vituperation upon us; and for what? [*Pipe business, Wing Lee*] Simply because my opponent says I am not a moral man. [*Wing Lee nods head*] Bah! As if politics and morality had anything in common!

OMNES. Hurrah for Britt!

BRITT. They say I am opposed to immigration, and consequently to the growth of the state—why, gentlemen, I am in favor of every form of increase of population, and I have even gone so far as to draw up a bill furnishing free transportation to one class of immigrants, and nursing bottles to the other.

OMNES. Hurrah for Britt!

BRITT. And if that don't do, I would offer a prize of a new bonnet for every baby born in the state.

OMNES. Hurrah for Major Britt!

WING. [*Down L. Much under influence of liquor*] Hulla for Major Brittee—hulla, hulla, hulla!

BRITT. Gentlemen, I said I favored immigration. I believe in men changing their address at will. Now there is a man whose address should be changed to Hong Kong.

SAM. Chinese must go. Go back to Hong Kong.

WING. Me no go backee Hong Kong.

BRITT. [*Addressing crowd*] I can only add that I am grateful for this spectacle.

WING. Hulla for Major Brittee!

OMNES. Shut up!

BRITT. [*Contemplating Wing Lee in silence a moment*] What is more saddening than to see a fellow man addicted to the soul-destroying influence of rum?

OMNES. [*Holding up cups*] Eh! Major!

BRITT. I mean opium. Rum's all right. [*Taps breast pocket, which contains bottle*]

WING. Melican man talkee muchee allee timee—Chinaman want to talkee allee samee Melican man. [*Staggers from seat to front of table, much under influence of liquor, and falls on stage*]

OMNES. Ha, ha, ha!

BRITT. Order! Order! The gentleman from China has the floor. Pick him up. [*Sam and others carry Wing Lee off, R.2.E., and return*] The last motion having been carried—off—there is nothing more to be done. [*Gets down from chair, all laugh*]

SAM. How about treating, major?

BRITT. [*Coming down, C. Crowd closing up around him, with glasses and cups in hand*] Ah! Yes! Of course! Of course! Excuse me! I quite forgot! Glasses, gentlemen, glasses. [*They gather around*] The bottle is strikingly light. [*Attempts to pour some liquor, all holding up cups and glasses*]

OMNES. [*Disgusted*] Empty! [*Sam whispers into ear of Major Britt*]

BRITT. It would seem, boys, that as much as I dislike to even suggest it, I'm afraid we will have to levy a small—I said a small—assessment to defray the expenses of the campaign. [*Evident disfavor manifested, which Britt is quick to sense*] What! You won't have it?

SAM. As the candidate, I'm afraid you're in for it, major.

BRITT. Well, in that case there is nothing for me to do but throw myself once more upon the hospitality of my friend Brandon, so if there is no objection we will now adjourn to the bar of the Golden Gate.

OMNES. Bully for you, major! Hurrah for Britt! [*Boisterous jolly crowd jams the door to exit*]

BRITT. I've got 'em. I've got 'em, every mother's son of 'em. I've got 'em. [*All go through door, followed by Britt. Ned Singleton enters, D. in F.*]

NED. Not here yet? What's the matter with the man? [*Impatiently*] He can't be such a moralist as all this. If Mary is satisfied, why shouldn't he be? [*Sits, L. of table, with his back to door. Plaintive music. Joe Saunders enters, D.F. Ned, turning to table, sees Joe*] Hello—Joe! Home at last, eh!

JOE. Yes, at last, and for the last time, too.

NED. What do you mean?

JOE. That I'm going away.

NED. Going! Where?

JOE. I don't know where! Anywhere, so it be far enough to bring forgetfulness, and too far to let me ever get back.

NED. Why, Joe, you don't mean to say that you can't forgive me; that after all these years we are [*Dropping his voice*] going to part like this?

JOE. Yes, that's just what I mean.

NED. I can't understand this. I've not wronged you in any way, have I?

JOE. Not much. [*Business*] Only broken my heart—that's all—that's all

NED. [*Amazed*] Broken your heart?

JOE. Yes, does that surprise you? [*Business*] I'm only a rough, plain, blunt fellow, [*With scorn*] and don't know half as much as you. But, my boy, I— I—loved that gal—Mary Brandon—How well—I never guessed until I knew she was lost to me forever. Why, last night, I felt like a man standing at an open grave, helping to hide under the clay all his hopes of happiness. Can you understand that the pain was not easier to bear because the blow was struck by my partner?

NED. [*Rises, earnestly*] Joe, had I known you loved her, I would have seen my arm wither, my heart turn to ashes—[*Crosses to R.H. and sits on stool, R.C.*] O Joe! Joe!—

JOE. Pshaw! There's no use in regretting now. All I ask of you is that you'll do her justice, 'cordin' to your oath, and make her life as happy as you can.

NED. But you—you need not go away.

JOE. I must! Can't you see that you and me must part? The old confidence is gone. I could never trust you again—you see—I'm not angry—only sorry that things happened so. [*Walks to and fro, to R. and then to C.*]

NED. Pshaw! You've grown morbid over this, by brooding over it all night.

JOE. There you're wrong again. Why I didn't come home last night was 'cause I was too excited to trust myself where you were. 'Twasn't that I lost her—not that. For it's more than likely she wouldn't a had me, under any circumstances, but that you should have caused her to suffer so—you on whose honor I'd have staked my life—you—pshaw! There's no use talking. Come—come, sir—let's settle up and quit. [*Crossing back of table, L. Music*]

NED. [*With a sigh*] Oh! Very well! [*Goes to table, sits, R.*]

JOE. [*Goes to hearthstone, lifts stone, takes out pan of gold nuggets, brings it to table, pours out gold, etc.*] There's the gold, Ned, thar! Divide it.

NED. [*Quietly*] No! I would rather you would do that.

JOE. All right! Whar's the scales?

NED. No need to weigh it. Take what you like, and leave the rest.

JOE. [*L. of table, dividing gold, etc.*] Well, does that seem about right?

NED. Yes—but how about the claim, and the cabin?

JOE. [*Business of pocketing share of gold, etc.; leaving knife on table*] Well, as you are going to stay here, why, of course, the claim is yours, and as for my share in this house, I give it to Mary, that is, if you don't object.

NED. No—I would rather pay you for it.

JOE. It won't hurt her to take it, and it'll make me feel better.

NED. All right. [*With a shrug*] Have it your own way.

JOE. Now, we're square, ain't we? [*Ned nods, with his back to table, still seated, eyes bent upon floor*] Ten years together—[*Goes to door, long and particular business. Gold business*] Ten long years! [*Business. Aside*] I feel something choking me, I must get out of here. [*Aloud*] Good-bye—Ned Singleton—ye can't have more good luck than I wish you both! Good-bye!

NED. [*Rises and offers hand*] Good-bye, Joe—good-bye!

JOE. No! [*Business*] No need to shake hands now. If when ye've made her your wife—we should ever meet, I'll take the hand ye offer. But I can't now. [*Business*] Ye mustn't think hard of it, but I can't—I can't do it, and I won't. [*Exit hastily, D.F. Passes by window, pauses, looks in, closes window and disappears, L.U.E. Music stops, dim lights*]

NED. [*After pause*] Gone! [*Walks slowly over to table, sinks on seat, dejected*] Gone! It all seems like an ugly dream! [*As if dazed. Pause. Enter Scraggs, D.F. Aside, speaking as he enters*]

SCRAG. Quarrelling, eh? So much the better. At last I've got a chance to speak to him. [*Comes forward noiselessly to immediately behind Singleton and coughs to attract attention*]

NED. [*Looking up*] Well?

SCRAG. [*R.H. Meekly*] You don't seem to remember?

NED. Yes, I do—your name is Scraggs—a friend of Mr. Brandon's.

SCRAG. Correct! [*Crossing behind table*] I will just drop into a chair. [*Sees gold on table. Aside*] Gold! [*Aloud*] You are very careless of your wealth, young man. [*Drops into seat, L. of table*]

NED. [*Moodily*] It's safe enough.

SCRAG. You are doubtless astonished that I should make a formal call upon you.

NED. [*Shaking his head*] No, sir!

SCRAG. [*A trifle disconcerted*] Ah! [*Pause*] I thought you would be. Fact is, I came into possession of a secret of yours.

NED. [*Suddenly*] Of mine!

SCRAG. Yes, of yours! I witnessed that little affair last night between you and Miss Mary Brandon.

NED. [*Angrily*] You were playing the spy, were you? [*Grasping knife*]

SCRAG. [*Soothingly*] Not at all! Came across you quite accidentally.

NED. [*Dropping knife*] As the friend of her father you will feel in duty bound never to speak of this again—as a gentleman, sir, you cannot.

SCRAG. [*With deliberation*] As far as the outside world is concerned, certainly; but you forget that another knows of it—

NED. Oh, I'll answer for him.

SCRAG. You seem to have a great deal of faith in a man who, within twenty-four hours, has threatened your life.

NED. [*Bluntly*] May I ask what is the object of this visit?

SCRAG. Nothing but kindness to you, sir. May I speak plainly and without reserve?

NED. As plain as you wish.

SCRAG. You, of course, don't mean to be bound by that foolish oath, forced from you in such a manner.

NED. I don't feel called upon to answer that question.

SCRAG. [*After a pause*] Oh, you don't seem to appreciate my motive in coming here.

NED. [*Eyeing him closely*]   If I could once understand it, perhaps I might. [*Turns away*]

SCRAG.   Then to be plain: although a friend of her father—I was a clerk in her grandfather's countinghouse in London, many years ago—I cannot remain silent and witness the success of a scheme to entrap a young man in a disgraceful alliance. [*Music. Agitato*]

NED. [*Fiercely, rising*]   Stop, sir, I think you have said quite enough.

SCRAG. [*Rising*]   But suppose I should show you that this fellow Joe's work of last night was but a bit of bluster, to cover up his own crime; to force you, my dear young friend, to marry his wretched mistress.

NED.   What! What's that you say?

SCRAG.   I say Mary Brandon is the mistress of Joe Saunders.

NED. [*Wild with rage*]   And I say you lie like a dog!

SCRAG. [*In alarm*]   What are you going to do?

NED.   Force you to swallow that vile slander upon your knees, or take your worthless life! [*Seizing him by throat and forcing him across table*]

SCRAG. [*As if choking*]   Murder! Help! [*Picks up knife from table and plunges it in Ned's side. Ned utters a cry, falls in chair, rises, takes a step towards Scraggs, who stabs him a second time. Ned falls in chair, R. of table, with head on table, his arm resting on gold on table. Plaintive music*]   I had to do it! It was self-defense. [*Drops knife*]   It was self-defense. [*Goes to window*]   No one in sight! Dead! Dead! There's the gold! [*Pauses, looks cautiously around*]   If I take it, 'twill divert suspicion! They'll think 'twas robbery. [*Takes gold*]   I'm safe! I'm safe! No one need be the wiser. What was that? [*Starts*]   No marks! What's this? Blood on my cuff! [*Tears off cuff fiercely, goes to window, looks out, starts back, exclaiming in a fright*]   Joe! [*Shrinks back out of sight, R.H., as Joe appears at window*]

JOE. [*Looking in at window at Ned*]   There he is! My partner! And he hasn't stirred yit—say—Ned—Ned! [*Leaves window and starts for door; at the same time Scraggs crosses hurriedly from R.H. to window, and disappears through window, dropping cuff in his haste. As Scraggs disappears Joe Saunders enters, D.F. Business, pause*]   Well, you see I've come back. [*Business of hat in chair*]   I couldn't go away without a feeling that we parted friends—when I got down dar in the canyon—where we worked together, I sat down to take a last look at the old familiar spot. The dry leaves were a-dancin' in the wind, the birds singing in the branches, and the creek laughing among the boulders, as if there were no such thing as pain or parting— Everything came back to me. The days we worked together, the plans we used to lay for the time we had made our pile, and could afford to let the pick grow red and rusty in the mine. All your good acts came a-crowding around me, making me ashamed of myself, that I'd refused a hand I'd often been glad to grasp when I warn't able to help myself—and so—I'm here— here to offer ye my hand, and to ask yer pardon [*Business*] before I go away forever. [*Business. Pause. Extends hand*] What! Ye won't take it—[*Business*] All right—remember I offered it! That's all I can do. [*Business. Goes to door in flat with hat, stops*] Oh! darn it Ned—we mustn't part like this—[*Hat down. Business*] You arn't sick, are you, partner? Say, partner, what's the matter? [*Now takes hand and gets in front*] What's this? Ned! Cold and rigid. [*Business*] Dead. [*Sets him up*] No—No—Ned—Partner—look up! [*Business*] Don't sit staring there like that. Only speak to me once more— only say—say you forgive me—Oh—my God, he's dead—dead—dead. [*Business, very particular. A pause during which there is an utter silence save the plaintive music which continues for 12 bars after Joe speaks last word*]

Scrag. [*Outside*] I tell you it's true, they're quarrelling. [*Music changes. Enter Scraggs hurriedly, followed by Sam, Jim, Brandon, Miners and Britt, D. in F. Scraggs, as he enters*] I heard a cry of murder as I passed, and I feared someone had been hurt.

Bran. [*C., back of table*] What's this—dead?

Omnes. [*Shrinking back*] Dead!

Joe. [*Business. Rising*] Yes, gentlemen! My partner—dead—stone dead, right here!

Bran. [*Dazed*] What is to be done?

Joe. Done! Find the guilty one!

Omnes. Ay, and hang him.

Joe. Hang him! No—cut him into pieces.

Scrag. [*R. corner*] As you were alone with him, it seems to me you ought to be able to explain.

Joe. I explain! Why, Mr. Scraggs, you don't dare to suspect, that—[*Appealing to Miners*] Boys! Boys! Look here! If you think for a moment, that I took his—my partner's life—No, no, don't speak, but take me out and— take me out and strangle me without mercy—[*Business*] I don't know that I want to live any longer—Life to me has been a failure every way! Every way! [*Business*]

Britt. [*Gravely*] Gentlemen, Saunders has spoken the truth. Is there a man here doubts him?

Omnes. No! [*Sam picks up knife and hands it to Britt*]

Bran. The murderer cannot have escaped—search the premises. [*Sam and one Miner exeunt, R.2.E. Taking Joe's hand*] You don't know how sorry I am.

JOE. You! [*Aside*] Mary's father sorry. [*Aloud*] Ah! He has good cause
—he has good cause. [*Business. Noise of voices in altercation, R.2.E. Sam
and the Miner rush in with Wing Lee, R.2.E.*]

OMNES. [*Rushing at Wing Lee*]   Hang him! Hang him!

JOE. Stop! No you don't! He's a poor heathen but the God who made
him made us! He's a stranger in a strange land, and he don't neither understand our language or our laws. But I'll stake my life on his innocence, and
before you take his life—ye'll have to give him a fair square trial. [*Crowd
makes a rush for Wing Lee. Seizing chair, raising it over his head threateningly*] Stand back! [*Sam picks up knife and calls attention of Britt to
blood stains on blade. Wing Lee on knees in front of Joe, Brandon restraining Miners on L.H. Picture, quick curtain*]

In the manuscript of *My Partner* owned by Mrs. Abbott Graves, the
daughter of Louis Aldrich, the end of the second act as given above is followed by a note reading, "When wished to—end at times this way." Then
comes the text printed below. In several of the existing manuscripts of the
play this second ending is used and the first omitted. A discussion of these
two endings follows the text.

BRITT. Gentlemen, Saunders has spoken the truth. Is there a man here
who doubts him?

OMNES. No!

SCRAG. Indeed! Then what's that? [*Pointing to knife. Sam picks up knife
and hands it to Britt*]

BRITT. Joe's knife—and covered with blood?

SHERIFF. Joe Saunders, I arrest you, for the murder of Ned Singleton.

JOE. What! My partner? No! No! [*Picture. Curtain*]

BRAN. The murderer cannot have escaped—search the premises. [*Sam
and one Miner exeunt, R.2.E. Taking Joe's hand*] You do not know how
sorry I am.

JOE. You. [*Aside*] Mary's father sorry. [*Aloud*] Ah! He has good cause—
good cause. [*Business. Noise of voices in altercation, R.2.E. Sam and the Miner
rush in with Wing Lee, R.2.E.*]

OMNES. [*Rushing at Wing Lee*]   Hang him! Hang him!

JOE. Stop! No you don't. He's a poor heathen but the God who made
him made us. He's a stranger in a strange land, but he don't neither understand our language or our laws. But I'll stake my life on his innocence, and
before you take his life—ye'll have to give him a fair square trial. [*Crowd
makes a rush for Wing Lee. Joe seizes chair, raising it over his head threateningly*] Stand back! [*Sam picks up knife, calls attention of Britt to blood*

*stains on the blade. Wing Lee on knees in front of Joe, Brandon restraining
Miners on L.H. Picture. Curtain*]

In discussing the two versions of the ending of the second act of *My Partner,* the ending first given will be referred to as the "first ending" and second one printed, as the "second ending," without any reference to the actual date of composition of either.

In most of the existing manuscripts of *My Partner* the first ending is the only one given. The fact that in the manuscript once belonging to Louis Aldrich the first ending is given as a part of the text and the second ending as a variant which may be used "when wished to" indicates that the first ending was the preferred one. This is corroborated by Mrs. Abbott Graves who writes that the first ending is the "one I consider the most used." Mr. Robert Campbell, who was closely associated with his father and with his father's work, goes even further and says that the first ending was the only official one. He states that it was the ending written by Bartley Campbell, the one used in the first performance, and the one used by Louis Aldrich in all of his performances of *My Partner.*

Unfortunately, the reviewers do not support Mr. Campbell's contention that the first ending was the one used by Louis Aldrich in the first and all subsequent performances. A careful search was made of the reviews of the first New York, Boston, and Chicago performances of *My Partner* with the result that two reviews were found that categorically said Joe was arrested at the end of the second act. The *New York Herald* of September 17, 1879, stated, "Then comes the discovery of the murder and the despair of Joe, while the act closes with Joe's arrest." The *Chicago Tribune* of February 10, 1880, stated that "at the end of the second act Joe Saunders is arrested for the murder of his partner." While none of the other reviews stated positively that Joe was arrested at the end of the second act, none of them said anything which would contradict this. Moreover, none of the reviews made any mention of Joe's plea for Wing Lee. The first reference I have found to this plea is in an 1884 playbill on which there is a picture of the scene.

It seems to me there are three possible interpretations of the facts presented.

1. The first ending was used in the 1879 and 1880 performances, and the *New York Herald's* and *Chicago Tribune's* references to Joe's arrest in the second act were errors.

2. The second version was used in 1879 and 1880, but no reviewers referred to Joe's plea for Wing Lee or even mentioned Wing Lee in connection with the second act.

3. In the 1879 and 1880 performances *neither* the first nor the second ending was used but one in which the act actually ended with Joe's arrest; in which case either or both the first and second endings were written between 1880 and 1884.

At present I am inclined to accept the third possibility and I offer the following defense of my views. Not only do the definite statements of the reviewers that Joe was arrested in the second act make me reject the first ending, but the absence of any reference to Joe's plea for Wing Lee makes it seem improbable that the second was used. Therefore, the act must have ended at the first curtain fall of the second version, that is, with Joe's arrest, and before his plea for Wing Lee. While this ending met all the requirements of the subsequent action and dialogue, it was not a "strong curtain," especially coming after the "big scene" earlier in the act; and so it was rewritten. The "second ending" is then the actual second ending of Act II. This new ending was made simply by adding to the original version another scene, the scene of the mob's attack on Wing Lee and of Joe's defense of him. This new scene was not only a "strong curtain," leaving the hero in a noble attitude, but it had the virtue of bringing together for the first time the two stars, Aldrich as Joe and Parsloe as Wing Lee.

The first ending is, in my opinion, the third version of the ending of the second act of *My Partner*. In it Joe was no longer arrested, but merely made sufficiently the object of suspicion to keep the audience from being too surprised when it found Joe's trial going on at the beginning of the third act. Thus the unpleasantness of the hero's arrest was relegated to offstage and nothing detracted from the big scene.

It may be doubted that Joe's plea for Wing Lee fitted into the logic of the play as a whole as well as did his arrest for murder, but what dramatist of the period ever hesitated for a moment between a "strong" ending to an act and a logical one?

NOTE: While this material was in the process of publication my attention was called to a manuscript written by A. M. Palmer, and now in the Harvard Library. In this Palmer gives an account of his part in the production of *My Partner* at the Union Square Theatre, and although he does not settle the question of the ending of the second act, he does throw some light on the problem. He mentions Aldrich's "predilection for the center of the stage and the ends of acts" and refers to the "interjected part of a Chinaman." As has already been suggested the problematical "original" ending of the second act did not place Aldrich in an especially favorable position, while the "first" and "second" endings gave him the center of the stage. How should the word "interjected" in Palmer's manuscript be interpreted? Does it mean that the part of Wing Lee was added after Campbell had written the play, or, what seems more likely, that the part was not an essential one to the action of the play? Is it not possible that Parsloe, who played Wing Lee, after he bought an interest in the play, asked to

ACT III.

SCENE: *Parlor or general sitting room of the Golden Gate Hotel. Six months after. Room neatly furnished, but not elegantly. Door, R.C. in flat. Window, L.C. in 3. Set practical doors, R.2.E. and L.3.E. Windows look out on wintry landscape. Sofa against flat, R.H. Carpet down. Bunch light behind window, L.C., and behind doors, R. and L. Lights up full. Music.*

GRACE. [*Discovered in armchair by fire*] Do you hear anything, Posie?

POSIE. [*Discovered at window in flat, L.C.*] No! Not one thing.

GRACE. Nor see anything?

POSIE. No! Yes, now I see some men standing at the courtroom door, and shaking their heads solemn like.

GRACE. Poor Joe! Everything seems to go against him.

POSIE. [*Coming down C.*] I suppose they'll hang him. [*Sighs*]

GRACE. [*L.*] If found guilty.

POSIE. [*L.C.*] Somehow, Miss Grace, I can't get it into my head that Joe killed Ned. It don't seem natural.

GRACE. Nothing seems natural any more. Look at Mary's going and disappearing the same night that Ned was killed, and never showing her face again. And now it's six months ago.

POSIE. Well, didn't that Chinaman do the same thing?

GRACE. Yes! But everyone knows he ran away fearful of being arrested for Ned Singleton's murder; while Mary's going is a mystery no one can explain.

POSIE. I wish people didn't try to.

GRACE. [*Rises, crosses, C.*] Has anyone dared—

POSIE. Dared! The last time I was down at the Valley Church I heard one woman say to a lot of other women under the porch, just before service when you and yer father went by, "Ah, there goes Mr. Brandon now," and they all poked out their necks long like [*Stretches her neck*] and looked after ye. An' one freckled-faced thing, with big beau-catchers, turned up her nose like that [*Makes a grimace*] and said, "He don't carry his head so high as he used to before pretty Miss Mary ran away," and then they all giggled.

GRACE. Rejoicing in an old man's misery! A Christian act truly! Did you say nothing?

have his part made more important, and asked to have, not the center of the stage, but a spot near it at the end of the important second act?

Incidently, Palmer states that the part of Posie Pentland was originally that of a young girl, and that at his suggestion Campbell changed it to an old maid.

Posie. I tried to, miss, but I couldn't speak.

Grace. [*Bitterly*] You couldn't say a word for poor Mary, who was always so good to you?

Posie. Not a word! But I flew at them beau-catchers, and tore some of them out by the roots, and then they all rushed into church and sent out the preacher to tell me I was sinful, and needn't come to meetin' any more.

Grace. [*Running over to her*] Posie, you are just the sweetest creature ever lived. [*Embracing her*]

Posie. But I didn't let him off.

Grace. [*Amazed*] You didn't talk back to the preacher!

Posie. Didn't I though! I jist up and told him that if I war sinful, them was the kind of people that the good Lord died for, and if the Bible was true, the Church belonged to God, and wasn't none of his'n and it was his duty to coax people into church, not drive 'em out.

Grace. [*In wonder*] What did he say?

Posie. He got very red at first, as if he was a-going to bust all to pieces; but directly he simmered down, and said he was sorry for me, and axed me to come in and forgive my enemies.

Grace. But you didn't go?

Posie. Yes, I did! When anyone talks soft to me, I always cave right in; but I didn't forgive that freckled-faced thing! I sat close to the organ, and made faces at her all through the meetin'.

Grace. That was dreadful in church.

Posie. One of the deacons got awful mad 'cause he thought I was making faces at him, but when service was over, I axed his pardon, and kind o' explained, and then he said it was all right, and he was a-going to kiss me. [*Quickly*]

Grace. [*Amazed*] And did he?

Posie. [*R.*] Well, no, he didn't; but he wanted to awfully. Oh! some of them deacons are a hard crowd! [*Shakes her head solemnly*]

Grace. Oh, dear me. I do wish we could hear how the trial is going. [*Up to window*] It's a wonder someone don't run over and let us know. Here's Sam Bowler at last.

Sam. [*Enters, R.C.*] I never saw such a crowd in my life! It's almost over! He'll be convicted sure.

Grace. [*L.*] Then the jury must be a very stupid one!

Posie. [*R.*] Reg'lar born fools!

Sam. [*C.*] No, ladies, excuse me! The evidence, while entirely circumstantial, is very strong. Scraggs swears to a quarrel between Joe and Ned, which Joe foolishly admits, and there is Joe's knife covered with blood, and the gold of the firm missing, and found on Joe. It seems as if the chain was complete, and Scraggs's testimony is the rivet that holds it all together.

POSIE. [*R.H.*] But the shirt cuff found in the shed?

GRACE. [*L.H.*] Yes! That ought to be a clue.

SAM. The cuff is of fine linen, and don't seem to belong to any shirt yet found of Joe's, but still that's a mere thread, and won't weigh against the other facts.

GRACE. Why then, did Joe say what the quarrel with his partner was about?

SAM. Why, he wouldn't tell.

POSIE. What did Scraggs say the quarrel between Ned and Joe was about?

SAM. Major Britt was just trying to draw that from him by a clever bit of cross examination when I left.

POSIE. If anyone can get him clear, Major Britt kin! [*Crosses, L.*]

SAM. [*To Grace*] Get rid of Posie for a few minutes. I want to say something to you in private. [*Goes up L.C.*]

GRACE. Posie, you can get the table set now, papa will soon be home. [*Goes up to Sam on his L.*]

POSIE. Say, look here, you won't talk about the trial 'til I come back, will you? [*Going, L.3.E.*]

SAM. [*At door*] Not a word.

POSIE. I won't be long. [*Aside*] Nothin' curdles up the blood so comfortable-like as the particulars of a murder trial, or a hangin'. [*Exit, L.3.E.*]

GRACE. [*L.H.*] Now; what is it?

SAM. [*R.H.*] Haven't you noticed anything in my personal appearance?

GRACE. [*L.*] Nothing but your other clothes.

SAM. [*R.*] You haven't noticed a sort of a desperate resolve, have ye?

GRACE. No!

SAM. Not in the corners of my eyes?

GRACE. Nothing!

SAM. Well, it's there; I've been trying to screw up my courage for some time, but I flatter myself I've got it up at last.

GRACE. For goodness sake, what is it?

SAM. Grace! I am going away.

GRACE. You are not going away now?

SAM. Yes, I am. If Joe is convicted he will be taken across the mountains to Yreka tonight, and I will go with him that far, just to show him that he is not entirely forgotten.

GRACE. And after that?

SAM. I'll rejoin the big show at Marysville and again become "The Peerless Emperor of the Air." [*With a sigh*]

GRACE. What! Join the circus?

SAM. I always loved art!

GRACE. Art! In a circus?

SAM. [*Solemnly*] High art! There is no art half as high as a trapeze fifty feet from the sawdust. Ah, if you could only go with me! We would be so happy!

GRACE. On a trapeze!

SAM. There's no life like it! I've tried burrowing in the ground, but it's low, when compared to tumbling through the air. Grace, may I—[*Business*] may I—speak to your father?

GRACE. Speak to papa with all this trouble! I don't see how you can be so heartless.

SAM. I've waited six months for your sister to come back, and it's getting a trifle monotonous. Suppose she should never come back!

GRACE. [*Starting*] Never come back!

SAM. I don't mean that.

GRACE. If she should not—I will never leave poor papa all alone. I love him too dearly to see him utterly desolate.

SAM. But don't you think of my desolation?

GRACE. Your desolation! Young men's hearts are soon healed; not so, a man of his age. See how changed he is since Mary went away. His spirit seems utterly broken; there are days and days he never breaks the silence with a word, and he appears to have lost interest in everything.

SAM. Except Joe's trial.

GRACE. But if Joe is condemned I fear he will drop into his silent moody way again, that looks so much like despair. [*Crosses to R.H.*]

SAM. Why don't you try and cheer him up?

GRACE. I did try, but every word I spoke seemed a fresh blow, and when mentioned Mary's name he burst into tears, the first I ever saw him shed. *Goes to chair, R.H., and sits, crying with handkerchief to eyes. Sam tries to console her*]

POSIE. [*Enters, L.3.E., crossing to C.*] It's all ready now, Miss Grace, and —[*Stops suddenly, sees Grace crying. She bursts into tears, crosses back, .H., and leans against mantelpiece, sobbing, face to wall, back to audience*]

SAM. Well, if they don't let up soon, I'll blubber myself. [*Goes up C. Enter Major Britt, passing window in L. flat, through door and arch, R.C.; places is hat on sofa and down, L.C.*]

BRITT. Well, it's all over. The judge has summed up, the case has gone to the jury, so I thought I'd just run over and wet my lips.

SAM. [*Down to R.C.*] You made a splendid defense, major.

BRITT. I did my best; ever since my defeat for the legislature, by over nine hundred majority, three hundred of them Baptists at that, I have devoted my entire time to the practice of my profession. I am free to confess that I spread myself in this case, but as they had all the evidence, I fear poor Saunders must make up his mind to die as gracefully as possible. [*Sighs. Sam goes up to window*]

GRACE. [*Rises*] Won't we see him any more?

BRITT. [*C.*] Oh! Yes! He'll get his supper here. No use in locking him up until they take him to Yreka. Besides he has given the sheriff his parole of honor and that settles it. He will come over to supper with your father, I suppose. [*Goes up, C.*]

GRACE. He shall have no reason to complain of his last supper here. [*Crossing to door, R.2.E.*] For I'll get it ready myself. [*Exit, L.3.E.*]

SAM. [*At window*] And while you perform the great culinary act, I will assist. [*Exit, R.2.E.*]

BRITT. [*Coming to R.C.*] Hard heads and soft hearts is becoming a feminine characteristic. [*Posie, still at mantelpiece crying loudly*] Hello! Weeping! [*Turns and sees Posie*] A regular mountain Venus. A rear view hardly does her justice. [*Crosses to Posie, taps her gently on the shoulder, she turns round and blubbers out loudly in his face. They come forward, down C.*] Why surely you're not crying, Miss Posie.

POSIE. [*L.C. Snappishly*] Then I suppose I'm laughing.

BRITT. [*R.C.*] No occasion for losing your temper, Miss Pentland. Anger is rarely becoming in a man, and in a woman it's a positive deformity.

POSIE. [*Tartly*] I don't never lose my temper.

BRITT. [*Shocked*] "Don't never!" Your grammar is even worse than your temper. It actually sets my teeth on, edge.

POSIE. [*Crossing to R.H. and upstage*] If you don't like it, take less of it!

BRITT. I shall certainly take as little of it as possible. I have no disposition to lumber my mind with vagrant verbs and broken-backed adjectives.

POSIE. [*Advancing on Britt, who retreats to L.H. corner*] Who's a broken-backed—ad—ad—! Well, what you said.

BRITT. The remark did not apply to you.

POSIE. No!

BRITT. No!

POSIE. Oh! [*Curtsies and goes towards R.C.*]

BRITT. [*Following up*] What! Call you a broken-backed anything, you! A living expression of the primitive innocence and beauty of your sex. [*Posie curtsies*] A lovely type of God's first best gift to man! A fair oasis of femininity in a desert of homely masculinity. [*Business*]

POSIE. [*After a very low curtsy*] Oh! You are always such a comforting man, major!

BRITT. [*C. Bowing*] Thank you! There's nothing so gratifying to a public man as to possess the love and confidence of his constituents—and when said constituents are of the softer sex, the pleasure is doubly distilled.

POSIE. [*R.C. Leaning towards Major and softly*] Major, I'm an orphan.

BRITT. Most women are at your age.

POSIE. [*Sharply*] Eh?

BRITT. I said, it's a great pity at your age.

POSIE. It's awful for a woman to be alone in the world.

BRITT. Yes, I suppose so. [*Turns partly from her*]

POSIE. [*Reclining on Major's shoulder*] O major!

BRITT. [*Aside. Business*] I wonder if she means business. [*Gently disengages himself, aloud*] Yes, I've heard that you were an orphan.

POSIE. But I've a rich uncle in Santa Clara, who's goin' to put me in his will.

BRITT. Will he? For about how much?

POSIE. A good deal! More'n twenty thousand dollars. [*Business*]

BRITT. [*Aside*] Twenty thousand dollars! [*Aloud*] Come into camp. [*Embraces her*] Do you know, Posie, you are a well preserved—

POSIE. [*Indignantly*] Preserved! Major—preserved!

BRITT. [*Business. Aside*] That preserve has got me into a pickle. [*Aloud*] In the sense that preserved is offensive as suggesting ages, I withdraw the remark, [*Business*] but as it also suggests sweets, I refuse to lay it upon the table, and repeat, a very well preserved lady. [*Business*] But, this uncle of yours, does he enjoy health? [*Business*]

POSIE. [*R.C.*] Splendid.

BRITT. [*Seriously. L.C.*] Umph! That's bad!

POSIE. [*Astonished*] Bad!

BRITT. For you.

POSIE. No, it isn't! I'd rather work hard all my life, 'fore Uncle Jack should suffer one day, for he's been very good to me.

BRITT. With twenty thousand dollars, Miss Posie, that sentiment does credit to your heart, even if it does reflect somewhat severely upon your head. [*Contemplating her. Aside*] A good figure—fine eyes—a little ancient! But, that uncle! [*Crosses to her*] Miss Posie, if you and Lindley, Murray,

Webster and Worcester were on better terms, say a sort of speaking acquaintance, your beauty might one day illuminate the galleries of Congress.

Posie. But, I don't want to go to Congress.

Britt. [*Soothingly*] Oh, don't let that worry you. There's no immediate danger of your being sent there, at least, not against your will. But, by the way, I'm very anxious to wet my lips. Just see how parched they are. [*Puckers up lips*]

Posie. Are they? [*Posie looks at them. Major gradually gets his lips near her face and at last kisses her. Indignantly*] Well, I like that. [*Flounces out, R.3.E.*]

Britt. [*Nonchalantly*] They all do; but few women are frank enough to confess it. [*Going up, C. Gets hat*] That lady is not unattractive, and that uncle—twenty thousand times more so. Twenty thousand dollars would purchase a seat in the Senate—Major Henry Clay Britt, California's a capital state, but hardly large enough for your great genius and usefulness. [*Exit pompously, R.C. Music. Funny music, "Slur." Enter Wing Lee cautiously from R.C., looks around*]

Wing. No bodee homee, me lestee. [*Sits*] Me vellee tired, foot sickee. No can walkee, me sleepee, oh, me allee blokee up. [*Sits in chair by door, R.2., below it. Enter Posie, R.2.E., speaking as she enters and going towards whatnot, L.U. corner*]

Posie. Where is that almanac? If the moon is at its full, I'll know what's the matter with Major Britt. [*Turns and sees Wing Lee*] You back here?

Wing. [*Advancing, R.C.*] Keepee coolee! Keepee coolee!

Posie. Oh, you yellow rascal! To go and run off the same night as poor Miss Mary, and have everyone think she ran away with you.

Wing. No can help what evlybody thinkee—evlybody foolee.

Posie. Hold your tongue. [*Holds tongue. Business Wing Lee*] Don't speak a word! [*Business Wing Lee*] Now tell me where you have been. Speak.

Wing. Me holee tongue. If me dontee speak a wordee how can me tellee where I've been! Sabee?

Posie. Shut up! [*Business Wing Lee*] Where have you been, I say?

Wing. Closs top side mountain.

Posie. Did you see anything of Miss Mary?

Wing. [*Looking up at ceiling*] Me no tellee you! Tellee allee to Missie Gracee. [*Doggedly*]

Posie. Then you do know something!

Wing. Lillie bit! Lillie bit!

POSIE. Just as we all suspected. You've carried her off and killed her. Is that it, eh? [*Business of slapping Wing Lee*]

WING. [*R. Disgusted*] No can tellee! No can tellee! Melican woman all samee likee damee foolee.

POSIE. [*C.*] There's one thing certain, that you better not let Mr. Brandon lay his hands upon you. You'll have to find other lodgings until he forgets your treachery.

WING. Me sleepee anywhere. Up the tree, down the shaftee, top side clothesline. [*Strikes his breast*] Me toughee! Me toughee! All samee like Melican man. [*Business. Spells*] T-u-f-y—toughee.

POSIE. Oh, you rascal, I'd like to pull that pigtail out of you. [*Crosses to him threateningly*]

WING. [*Coiling up and holding pigtail tightly, and in a frightened manner*] Me no can spare pigee tailee. [*Business Posie and Wing Lee*] Chinaman's joss, no like pullee pig tailee. [*Enter Grace and Sam, R.2.E.*]

GRACE. Why, Posie. [*Sees Wing Lee*] Wing Lee at last! [*Crosses to C.*]

POSIE. [*R.C.*] Yes, Miss Grace, and he won't tell anything about Miss Mary except to you.

SAM. [*Eagerly*] Of Mary! What of her?

WING. [*R. corner*] Me no tellee anybody else Miss Gracee. No bolee else! No bolee else!

SAM. Yes, to me. [*Striking breast*]

WING. Him toughee, too. [*Business. Crossing hurriedly to L.H., behind Miss Grace*] To no bolee else! No bolee else. [*Sam makes a break for Wing, but is prevented by Grace*]

GRACE. [*C.*] Leave him alone with me, then. [*Music*]

WING. [*L.*] Yes, go takee walkee, longee walkee. [*Exit Sam and Posie, R.2.E.*]

GRACE. [*C. Turning to him*] Now, what have you got to say? [*Mary enters very slowly, R.C.F., unperceived by Grace, and down R.H.*]

WING. [*L.C.*] Polee Missis Maly wantee to comee velly muchee, sabee?

GRACE. [*Impatiently, with back towards Mary*] Yes! Yes! I understand! But where is she?

WING. [*Pointing to Mary*] There! [*Business and exit, R.C.*]

GRACE. [*Turns and surprised*] Mary!

MARY. [*R.C. Covering her face with her hands*] Yes, Mary.

GRACE. Mary! In heaven's name, what does all this mean?

MARY. [*With emotion*] That I am a sinful wretch.

GRACE. This is terrible. [*Turning away*]

MARY. Don't turn away from me. I know I am unworthy of your love any longer, but oh, I want to feel your arms about me once again and hear you say you forgive me.

GRACE. [*Turning back, coming to Mary*] I have nothing to forgive. You are still my sister. [*About to embrace her*] How pale you are! Have you been ill?

MARY. [*With faltering voice*] Almost unto death, the night the baby died I—

GRACE. [*Aghast*] A mother! [*Mary moans and bows her head in silence*] O Mary! Mary! Our poor father! It will break his heart! [*Turns back to audience*]

MARY. Yes, I know, and I wouldn't have come back, but that Joe, I heard, was to be tried for Ned's murder. He is an innocent man who has suffered much and he must not perish in this way!

GRACE. How do you know?

MARY. Because it is absurd to think that Joe Saunders could do this thing. It's madness to believe he could be guilty of the murder of his friend and partner.

GRACE. But do you know anything that would help him?

MARY. Yes! I know that he has a great good heart, [*Down*] a noble soul, a tender, patient, self-sacrificing nature. I also know that these are not the qualities out of which are made assassins. [*Crosses, L.*]

GRACE. This is faith, not proof. It can do no good.

MARY. [*Passionately*] Perhaps not. But to remain away when he was helpless, friendless, seemed cruel and cowardly, and I could not, and I would not do it. [*Sits in chair, L.*]

GRACE. But what is he to you?

MARY. [*As if dazed*] What is he to me? [*Shakes her head*] Nothing and everything.

GRACE. O Mary, sister, is it possible—

MARY. I don't know! There is in my heart such a mingling of pity, and gratitude and—Oh, [*Wringing her hands*] I don't know what it is—I have never dared to ask my heart.

GRACE. But, father—

MARY. [*In a low voice*] What does he say of me?

GRACE. Nothing! Your name has not crossed his lips for months. Oh, why did you go away at all?

MARY. What could I do? As soon as Ned died, I fled. I feared my father's anger, I could not look upon his misery; oh, what have I done! What have I done!

GRACE. You did not go alone?

MARY. No, I took Wing Lee with me. But for him I would have perished in the mountains. [*Music ceases*]

WING. [*Outside, R.C.F.*] O Missee Malee! [*Appears at C.*] Missie Malee! Bossee comee—me cutee stickee! [*Exit, R.2*]

MARY. [*L. Hopelessly*] What shall I do?

GRACE. [*R. Nervously*] I don't know. It is too late to do anything now, you must meet him.

MARY. Oh, no, I cannot, I cannot. [*Exit hurriedly, L.3.E., followed by Grace. Enter Brandon and Joe arm in arm, followed by Sheriff, through D., with gun*]

JOE. [*C.*] Thank you, sheriff; I won't forget this kindness.

SHERIFF. That's all right, Joe, everybody knows you're square, and your word is as good as your bond. I'll wait outside for you. [*Exit, C.F.*]

BRAN. [*R.C.*] Courage! Courage, man, the jury is sure to be out all night, and that's a good sign. Besides you have the sympathy of everyone, and that is something.

JOE. Yes, but to be accused, that's it—and of this thing—this dreadful thing—of which I am innocent. Oh, it's hard! Hard!

BRAN. Everyone realizes that, Joe, and even with the evidence in view, none of those who knew you both can believe you guilty of this crime.

JOE. Believe! Why, I loved him as dearly as a brother; better than myself— a thousand times better. It's not death I fear—I hope no one here thinks that— but the shame of such an end, the bitter, burning shame. [*Goes up, C.*]

BRAN. [*Down R.H. and in a low voice, aside*] I know what that is—no one better. [*Grace enters slowly, L.3.E.*] Grace, child, is supper ready?

GRACE. Yes, sir. [*Mary enters slowly, L.3.E.*]

BRAN. Why, what's the matter? Your eyes are red and—[*Sees Mary, starts back. Joe Saunders turns quickly and exclaims. Sam and Posie, R.2.E.; Britt enters from R.C. and down, R.H. Scraggs appears at back, C. Joe goes up, L.C.*] Mary! Mary!

MARY. [*L. Starts impulsively forward*] Father!

BRAN. [*R. Puts up his hand and waves her off*] No! No! Not yet!

MARY. [*Sinks on her knees before Brandon*] Mercy! Mercy! [*Music*]

BRAN. Stop! [*Solemnly*] Before you have a right to rest upon my breast, I must first know what you are, where you have been and with whom? [*Sam, Posie, Britt, Scraggs enter here, Mary drops her head*] Why don't you answer? Have you no defense?

MARY. [*L.C.*] Pity! Pity! [*Scraggs at back, gloating, rubbing his hands*]

BRAN. Where was your pity when you left my heart and home empty?

GRACE. [*L., near fireplace. Crossing towards Mary, appealingly*] Father!

BRAN. Don't go near her. She must first answer to me for the spotless name I gave her.

MARY. [*L. of C. Through her tears*] Oh! Father—father, what shall I say?

BRAN. [*L.*] The truth, the whole truth. In heaven's name, girl, don't be dumb—give me some hope—give me the right to look at these people in the face. You see I'm not angry. I don't demand justice, I only ask for pity.

MARY. Father, [*Rising*] I cannot speak. Let me go! Let me go! [*Going, L.H.B.*]

BRAN. Go! Where can you go? There is no refuge for such as you. Oh, my child—my heart is breaking. [*Crosses to R.C.*]

SCRAG. [*Coming forward to Mary*] You owe obedience to your father. 'Tis your duty to tell the truth. [*Retires up a little to R. at back*]

MARY. [*Desperately*] Yes—Father, I will speak.

JOE. [*Coming down, L.C., on Mary's R.*] Hush, Mary, not a word.

BRAN. [*R. Pausing, amazed*] Saunders, how dare you interfere; I command her to speak, she is my daughter.

JOE. And I forbid her to utter a word—she is my wife.

OMNES. His wife!

BRAN. [*After a pause, as if dazed*] Wife! Wife! [*Pause*] What does this mean? [*With severity*] When were you married—where? And by whom?

JOE. Why, sir, I—

BRAN. Is this the treatment I had a right to expect at your hands?

JOE. Mr. Brandon—

BRAN. Why your marriage should have been a matter of mystery, why my child should have been subjected to the suspicion of shame, I leave to your conscience, sir! But I demand that you shall go further and make her vindication complete.

JOE. What do you mean?

BRAN. I mean, that I demand you shall give me some proof.

JOE. Proof?

BRAN. Yes, proof so strong that it cannot be gainsaid. Proof strong enough to dispel every vestige of doubt.

JOE. Well, sir, I can prove—

SCRAG. [*To L. of Brandon who is R. corner. Approaching, insinuatingly and to Brandon*] Yes, their marriage certificate. [*Joe and Mary start, look at each other*]

JOE. [*Aside to Mary*] Our marriage certificate—what'll we do?

BRAN. Mr. Scraggs is right—your marriage certificate. [*Holding out his hands for it. Scraggs goes up again, R.*]

JoE. [*L.C. Despairingly*] There was no certificate given.

BRAN. And do you expect me, after what has taken place, to accept your unsupported word?

JoE. Do not ask impossibilities of me. I can give you no further proof.

BRITT. [*Advancing to C.*] Yes, you can. The best proof you can give of your truth, is a repetition of the marriage ceremony. I, as a magistrate, can perform it. [*To Brandon*] There certainly can be no objection to that?

BRAN. [*Pause*] Do you refuse?

JoE. [*Looking at Mary*] No. [*Britt retires, up R.H., with Sam and Posie, Brandon; crosses to C.*]

MARY. [*C. Aside to Joe*] Joe! Joe! Joe! Think, think what you are doing.

BRAN. [*R. Points to door, R.2.E.*] In that room her mother died; it is sacred to her memory. Major Britt, there the ceremony shall take place. [*Britt exit, R.2.E., followed by Posie, Sam and Grace, who goes round by back*] And these friends shall witness it. Come, my child, follow me. [*Crosses and exit, R.2.E.*]

MARY. [*Crossing to R., then returning to him, R.C.*] O Joe, this cannot be; you must not make this sacrifice for me.

JoE. [*Crossing to Mary*] There are others as well—Your poor old father, your sister. Besides, in a few hours I'll leave you forever, and in a few weeks my death will set you free again. Might I but give you my name—it isn't a glorious one—but poor as it is, it will serve as a shield against your enemies. [*Business*]

BRAN. [*Appears at door, R.2.E.*] We are waiting for you. [*Extends hand to Mary, who goes forward with eyes bent on ground and takes her father's hand. Brandon continues*] Well, Saunders? [*Exit Brandon and Mary, R.2.E.*]

JoE. [*L.H. corner*] Yes! Yes! I'm coming! [*Crosses as if towards door. Scraggs, who has been upstage, advances rapidly, grasps Joe by the arm after he has crossed to R.*]

SCRAG. Man, are you mad? Would you cover up that guilty girl with a marriage that to you is but a mockery? [*Joe hastily closes door, R.2.E.*]

JoE. [*Turning fiercely*] How dare you question me, you who have put the halter about my neck?

SCRAG. I had to swear the truth! But did I tell it all? No! I kept her secret! I won't do it again!

JoE. [*Advancing*] Bah! This that I am going to do renders words of yours powerless. As my wife she can defy you.

SCRAG. We shall see. [*Attempts to pass Joe*]

JoE. [*Intercepting him*] Stop! Where are you going?

SCRAG. To tear this gauzy veil in shreds, to show this old fool that his angel daughter is—

JOE. I don't know your motive for such an act, but don't yer do it on yer life!

SCRAG. [*Glaring at him*] What would you do?

JOE. My hands are yet free from the stain of murder, but if you attempt to mar the name of that poor trusting child, I'll fasten my fingers on your false throat and still its cruel work forever! [*Music forte. Picture. Quick curtain. No wait. Move chair down, C., chair, R.H., up R.H., then ring up Act IV*]

ACT IV.

SCENE: *Same as Act III. Music. Time, ten minutes after. Scraggs discovered seated, C., looking off, R.2.E.*

SCRAG. I'm a weak fool! A contemptible coward! I should have told her story to the court! What was I thinking about? Now, none will believe me. His last action is so remarkable, they wouldn't believe the recording angel against it! Ever since that night up there, I am no better than a child in courage. Even the gold I gained seems to have a terror for me. I can't go near it! It seems to be all eyes, yellow, glaring, staring up at me! I'm afraid to take a step, lest it may lead to discovery. Marriage! [*Chuckles*] A wedding and a winding sheet! Odd enough! Odd enough! [*Drops his voice into a whisper. Posie enters, R.2.E., looking back*]

POSIE. [*R.*] Dear me, I never did see such a wedding in all my born days.

SCRAG. [*C. Rising*] It's all over, I suppose.

POSIE. [*Turning*] Oh, you're there, are you, Mr. Scraggs?

SCRAG. You don't like me, do you?

POSIE. Well, I'm not in love with you.

SCRAG. You hate me, don't you?

POSIE. I don't express my private opinion.

SCRAG. Well! What then! Do you think I care! You're a mere worm in my path; not worth my while stepping upon. [*Going towards door, L.3.E.*]

POSIE. If I'm a worm, you're a great big snake. [*Following him up*]

SCRAG. [*At door, L.3.E.*] Take care! I'll have your master teach you better manners. [*Exit, L.3.E.*]

POSIE. [*Calling after him*] Well, he won't learn them of you—you old wretch! [*Alters tone*] Everybody's crying in there. More like a funeral than a wedding. [*Sits by fireplace. Britt enters, R.2.E. Crosses to L.H. and back to C., not seeing Posie*]

BRITT. Well, it's all over. In all my magisterial career, I never met anything like it. A marriage under such circumstances—it's like a dream, a page of unwritten romance. [*Starts to go to C.D.*]

POSIE. [*Rises, to C.*] I don't realize it myself, major.

BRITT. [*Stopping at C.D., turns, replaces his hat on sofa, L., and comes down, R.C., to Posie*] Well, it proves the old adage that "Truth is stranger than fiction." But, after all, you see how easily it is done, once a couple have made up their minds. [*Placing arm around Posie's waist*]

POSIE. Oh, it's easy enough done; but getting out of it, that's the thing. [*Gently disengaging herself and stepping back*]

BRITT. [*R.C.*] But, there need be no thought of that, when Cupid presides at the ceremony.

POSIE. [*L.*] Why, surely you don't call yourself Cupid, major?

BRITT. Hardly! Merely a deputy.

POSIE. Major, why do people always cry when they get married?

BRITT. You mean after marriage—a year or two, say.

POSIE. No, I don't, I mean just at the time.

BRITT. Well, I really can't tell, unless it be that the heart is so full it overflows at the eyes.

POSIE. I don't think I'd cry if I got married.

BRITT. No! I don't think you would.

POSIE. It would just please me so, I believe I'd laugh for a whole week. [*Britt laughs immoderately and ends by a choking cough. Posie hits him on the back*]

BRITT. Thank you! But you forget, my dear woman, the circumstances that surround these nuptials are very remarkable, and not without a very sad aspect.

POSIE. Do you really think they will take Joe away now?

BRITT. I'm sorry to say there is hardly a doubt! Indeed I may say that I regard the verdict as a foregone conclusion. [*Embraces Posie*]

SAM. [*Outside, R.2.E.*] Well, this is a genuine novelty. [*Posie and Britt separate, Posie going towards mantelpiece; Britt, up C. a little. Sam enters, R.2.E., to R.H.*] Never saw anything to excel it under canvas.

BRITT. [*C. Back to Sam*] Don't tell me, Miss Posie. I attribute it all to the sudden rise in the price of butter, and the recent tumble in lard. [*Turns and sees Sam*] Ah! Mr. Bowler! [*Crosses to him*] Let us go over to court and see if we can learn anything new. [*Shakes hands with Sam and goes up, C.*]

SAM. With all my heart! [*Following up Britt, and to Posie*] Posie, I'll be back soon.

BRITT. [*Turning sharply, C., and eyeing first Sam and then Posie*] I'll be back soon. [*Looks daggers at Sam as he exits, C., and off, L.H.*]

POSIE. There's no use talking, this is simply awful. [*Sits in chair R. of C. Wing Lee appears at C.*]

WING. [*Calling*] Missie Posie! Missie Posie!

POSIE. Well? Oh, it's you, eh?

WING. [*Advancing, L.H.*] Yes, Missie Posie, where Mister Blandon? Where im bossee?

POSIE. Oh! You are afraid of meeting him; that shows your good sense.

WING. Me no likee fightee. Me no likee kickee. Kickee hurtee Chinaman samee Melican man! No difflence. No difflence.

POSIE. What's that you've got there? [*Points to Wing Lee's bosom*]

WING. Where? [*Business*]

POSIE. There! [*Touching Wing Lee's breast*]

WING. No got here! No got here!

POSIE. There! There! [*Touching Wing Lee's breast, which appears extended*] Have you broken your breast bone?

WING. No gottee bloke blestie. Me gottee clothsee. See! [*Showing shirt from bosom*] Me washee—washee—

POSIE. Got some clothes, eh? Stole them, I suppose.

WING. Me no stealee, Wing Lee goodee Chinaman, findee clothsee in shaftee, where me sleepee. Me washee im in liber.

POSIE. Found them! Oh! A very likely story.

WING. Vellee likee! Vellee likee!

POSIE. Well, I'd advise you to leave Siskiyou County as soon as possible, for Major Britt will have you arrested as a nuisance.

WING. [*Puts shirt back*] All lightee, me go! Me sollee for Joey—me bellee good to Miss Mally—me good to evlybody—evlybody bad to poor Wing Lee.

POSIE. Poor wretch!

WING. Poor letch! Yes, me poor letch!

POSIE. Well, if you would only learn to keep your place.

WING. Keep place—all lightee—me no takee sackee—me keep place.

POSIE. But you Chinamen are such a precious pack.

WING. Pack! Pack! Me sabee. Me got packee. Chinaman always got packee. You playee. Pokee. Pee Nuckle. Slankee Pleadlee. Seven upee. Me playee all samee Melican man. [*Producing and shuffling cards. Gets R. of table, R.C.*]

POSIE. Well! I like you.

WING. You no likee packee—you likee me!

Posie. Oh, yes! I'm in love with you. [*Business. Sits, R.C., chair before table*]

Wing. Oh! She loves me. Me makee mashee. [*Gets chair and draws it up to Posie. Sits. She moves away, he follows her with chair*] Chinaman no likee Chinawoman. He likee Melican woman—me likee you.

Posie. [*Startled*] What!

Wing. Oh, you no givee bluffee! You lovee me—me lovee you! Me mally you! Me keepee housee, all same Melican man. [*Pokes her in ribs*]

Posie. [*Rises, screams*] Don't you dare. [*Business of gag*] Oh! Oh! Here comes Mr. Brandon.

Wing. [*Hurriedly*] Missee Blandon comee. He catchee me. [*Runs across to C., then up to door, L.C.*] Me catchee kickee. Me skippee. [*Exit quickly, L.3.E.*]

Posie. Well, I always knew that Chinaman was a fool. [*Crosses to L., up to door. Music. Enter Mary and Grace, R.2.E.*]

Grace. There! There! Be brave.

Mary. If I only knew what form of bravery would reach this case. [*Sinks into chair, C.*] I might try, but as it is, look which way I may, I see no light—no hope!

Posie. [*L. Aside*] Poor girl! What a wedding! [*Exit, L.3.E.*]

Grace. [*R.*] But you owe a duty to Joe; if he sees you suffer so, it will make his lot harder to bear.

Mary. If I could only help him to meet his fate; if I could only aid him in some way.

Grace. You can, by showing him that you are not hopeless yet.

Mary. [*Earnestly, after a pause*] Grace, I have something to tell you—a secret.

Grace. A secret! [*Joe appears, R.2.E.; Grace goes up, C.*]

Mary. [*Hesitatingly*] You once thought I—I loved Ned Singleton?

Grace. I certainly did—but now—

Mary. I thought so, too. He was young, handsome, my ideal! At one time his image filled my heart, and a romantic girl's imagination clothed him in such a garment of goodness and truth that he appeared to me little less than divinity.

Grace. [*Eagerly*] Yes! Well?

Mary. Since then I have seen with a purer, truer vision; the love of that man in his grave was a shallow stream, lovely to look upon in the sunlight of prosperity, but not deep enough to launch one's barque of life upon.

Grace. [*In half alarm*] I fear I don't know what you mean.

MARY. I mean that a great love has flooded my life, [*Going R.*] a sweeter, healing tide, with all the power of purification in it.

GRACE. I cannot understand you yet. Do you mean that Joe after all is not—

MARY. I mean to say that to save me—[*Turns and finds herself face to face with Joe. She drops her eyes and stands silently*]

JOE. [*C. Stops Mary, pause, then turns to Grace and speaks*] Grace, just see that we are left alone for a few minutes. I've got something very particular to say to Mary. [*Grace exit, R.2.E.*] Mary—I've heard all—I prefer you should not finish your story—promise you won't. It wouldn't make her happier to know the truth—besides, I want your breast and my—grave alone to hold our secret. Do you promise? [*Pause*]

MARY. [*L.C. In a low voice*] Yes! Yes!

JOE. When I claimed you for my wife, I had no hope of ever gaining anything, but just a tender thought. You kin understand that standing as I am on the edge of my grave, I couldn't have had any plans for the future. 'Twas just an accident—my claiming you—I saw you in tears, I saw your father's agony, I saw your sister's shame—and I did it. The thought that you could love me never crossed my mind. But now, if anything should come to spare my life—

MARY. [*L. Tearfully*] You will be free—don't fear, I will not ask you to sacrifice yourself for me. No—out of my love for you has faded every gleam of selfishness! Let mine be the burden of repentance.

JOE. [*C.*] I was going to say, that if I was spared, and was sure that you did love me—that it wasn't mere gratitude that's filling your heart now, I would give my life to make yours happier.

MARY. Oh, no, Joe. I am not worthy! Think what I've done, think what I am.

JOE. To me, you are his widow, that's all.

MARY. You forgive me then? [*Rising*] You forgive me?

JOE. Forgive you? Why, God bless you, Mary, I've forgotten it long ago! Why, I've forgotten everything but that you was a poor child raised out here in the wilderness, without the same chance as most wimmen, and little as I know about Scripter I feel sartain Heaven will not be too hard on a poor gal as had no mother to guide her.

MARY. But, the world—

JOE. The world of Him who made it; the world of right and marcy and forgiveness has but one law for both sexes, and here where civilization has not built its temples, above the green groves of God—where men live nearer him—wimmen have an equal claim with men to the charity that covers a great mistake.

MARY. [*Solemnly and earnestly*] Joe, I wish, oh, how I wish, that I could die with you. [*Falling on his breast*]

JOE. [*R.C.*] Hush—stop, Mary, don't wish that, [*Business*] for if the worst comes—

MARY. No! No! No! Something must be done.

JOE. Hush! We must be prepared to meet it. So, if the worst comes, and I've got to die—which is likely enough—I want you to go there to Fargo's and git all my gold. It's yourn now! [*Mary sobs*] There, there, gal—don't cry! There's no time for tears now. [*Goes up, C.*]

MARY. [*As if struck with an idea*] Joe, why not escape? Once in the woods—

JOE. No! No! I can't.

MARY. Why not?

JOE. Have you forgotten, gal, that it's owing to the sheriff's kindness, that I'm not in the log coop, up there now; besides, I've given my word of honor, and I'd rather die than break it.

MARY. [*Dropping into chair*] Then all hope is gone!

JOE. [*Coming down to back of chair, L.*] Yes! Yes! It's hard to say farewell forever. But I suppose it might as well be said now, for they'll want me soon, and when they come, both of us must be calm and brave.

MARY. [*Rising, calmly*] Yes, I will be brave. Good-bye.

Joe. Good-bye—and when—it's all—all over and I am dead—[*Mary sobs loudly*] No! No! I mean, when I am gone, forever, I want you to take and bring me up here where I first met you, and lay me out there, 'long side of "My Partner"!

MARY. [*With a wail and falling on Joe's breast*] O Joe! Joe!

JOE. [*Puts her in chair and leans over her*] And when—your own time comes—you can rest beside us both, us partners—And if there's any knowing after death what's going on in this here world of ours, it will make that long eternal sleep sweeter to all of us, I know. [*Enter Brandon with Sheriff. Music stops. Enter Scraggs from L.*]

SCRAG. [*Down, L.H.*] The verdict is in, and—Mr. Saunders, they are coming after you.

JOE. [*Calmly*] And I am ready. [*To Mary*] Remember! [*Grace, R.2.E.*]

BRAN. [*R. To Scraggs*] So the verdict has been reached?

SCRAG. [*L.*] Of course, the verdict is not declared yet, but—[*Enter Sam, C., from L., running*]

JOE. [*C.*] Well!

SAM. [*R.C. To Joe in a low voice*]   The deputy sheriff who had charge of the jury whispered to me there is no hope; it's guilty. [*Music. Grace, Sam and Sheriff go up, R.C.*]

JOE.   Farewell, gal. [*Kisses her, she sobs*] Here—Mr. Brandon, take her away. [*Brandon assists Mary towards door, R.2.E. Joe follows up, kissing her repeatedly, etc. Grace comes down, C. Sam goes to window, L.C.*]

BRAN. [*Leading her off, sobbing, R.2.E.*]   My child.

JOE. [*At door*]   Good-bye—Mary! Forever! Grace, gal, good-bye—and be good to your poor sister, for she has suffered more, ah! more than you can guess. [*Going up, C. Brandon reenters, R.2.E. Comes to R.C., turning boldly to all*] And now gentlemen! I'm ready, ready to hear the verdict that will send me to my death. I am an innocent man, still I've weak moments like others. You'll see now I'm square, for I'm not afraid to die. [*Three loud shouts are heard outside, L.U.E. Posie enters, from L.3.E., and crosses to window in flat*]

SAM. [*At window. With amazement*]   They're cheering.

GRACE. [*Up R.H.*]   Are they cheering at the verdict? [*Coming down, R.*]

SAM.   No! No man in these diggings will cheer at a verdict of guilty against Joe Saunders. What does it mean? [*Coming down to Grace, L. Three more loud cheers are heard outside, L.U.E. Major Britt rushes in, C. from L., excitedly, down C.*]

OMNES.   What does it mean, major?

BRITT.   It means that we've discovered new evidence, that we've got on the trail of the real murderer, and the natural enthusiasm of the boys is such, that they must have an escape valve or bust. [*All the Miners and Girls rush in from C.L. and down, R.H. Britt, C. Authoritatively*] Order! Order! Let us proceed regularly! That we may understand the new find, let me state the case! Circumstances pointed to Joe Saunders very strong, yet, notwithstanding all this, we believe the crime was committed by another.

OMNES.   Another!

SCRAG.   It's growing dark! [*Wipes forehead*]

BRITT. [*C.*]   The man who murdered Singleton had his shirt cuff smeared with the blood of his victim. [*Crossing to Sam, R.C.*]

BRAN. [*R.C.*]   Well, we all know that. [*Britt whispers to Sam, who exits R.2.E. Scraggs, L., starts to go, but is stopped by Joe*]

JOE. [*C.L.*]   Don't go, Mr. Scraggs, just hear this out, just hear this out!

BRITT. [*Crossing back to C.*]   Exactly! But while we had this cuff, the garment from which it was torn was missing. But a kind of Providence filled a poor wretch with fear and drove him into the black depths of a shaft fo safety and sleep, and placed that missing garment, minus the cuff, into the hands of an humble but competent and intelligent witness.

OMNES. A witness?

WING. [*R.C.*] No punchee! No kickee!

BRAN. [*R.*] No!

WING. Then me tellee allee. Me flaid of bossee, me go downe shaftee--me hidee, me sleepee, me findee shirtee!

SCRAG. [*L.*] Pshaw! Is this all?

BRITT. No, it is not all. Wing Lee put me in possession of this new find, and we soon discovered that the cuff in court belonged to the shir—[*Pause*] In view of the ladies present, we will say garment.

WING. You got 'em cuffee—me got'em shirtee. [*Produces it*]

BRITT. And we also made another discovery, more important than any others, and that is that the name of its owner was printed on the band in stencil.

OMNES. What name?

BRITT. Josiah Scraggs. [*General stir*]

BRAN. [*R.*] Mr. Scraggs—impossible!

SCRAG. [*L.*] It's not true! It's not true! [*Sam enters from R.2.E. with handful of gold, and down, R.H.*]

BRITT. Isn't it? We shall soon see. [*To Sam*] Find anything else?

SAM. [*Giving gold to Brandon. On Brandon's R.*] This in Scraggs' trunk. [*Goes up, R.H.*]

BRITT. [*C. Looking at gold*] More proof, more proof! [*Waves his hand-kerchief exultingly*]

WING. [*C., upstage, waving shirt*] More ploof! More ploof!

BRAN. [*R.C.*] I see no reason why this gold should not belong to Mr. Scraggs by right.

SCRAG. [*L.*] Yes, why not?

JOE. What proof is there in that, major?

BRAN. [*Gazing intently at gold, starts, aside*] What's this?

SCRAG. Who says the gold is not mine?

BRAN. [*R.*] I do! You all know, it was the habit of these partners to bury their gold under the hearthstone, and see, these nuggets are filled with ashes. *Miners come in on each side. All crowd around and look at gold. Joe crosses, Britt, Posie cross to R.*]

JOE. [*Looking at gold*] Boys, he speaks the truth; that is my partner's gold! And here stands the man who killed him. [*Rushes at Scraggs, but is stopped by Britt, who is now L.C. Brandon gives gold to Sheriff*]

SCRAG. It's a lie! He struck me first; he would have killed me; 'twas in self-defense.

OMNES. [*Rushing at Scraggs*] Hang him! Hang him! Lynch him! [*Joe and Britt stop them. Grace exit, R.2.E.*]

JOE. No! Let him live long enough to realize the doom that's waiting for him. Sudden death would be too much mercy to show to such a wretch as him. [*Sheriff gets to L., back of Scraggs. Britt goes up, L.C., to Sam*]

SAM. [*Advancing to L., at back*] All right, Joe! But he swings in one hour. [*Business of Wing Lee with clock, up C. All laugh*]

BRAN. [*Advancing to Scraggs*] And, has it come to this at last, Josiah, I'm sorry—very sorry.

SCRAG. [*L.C.*] I don't want your sorrow! I despise your pity! Besides, you have none to waste! Go to Lady Mary and hear her story, or will I tell it to you here, before all your friends?

JOE. [*Coming to his R. and drawing Brandon away over to R.*] No! No! You must not hear this. [*To Sheriff*] Take him away. [*Exit Scraggs in custody of Sheriff, L.3.E., followed by Miners shouting, "Lynch him! Lynch him!"*]

WING. Lunch him! Lunch him! [*Exit after others. Posie crosses to L.H., to Britt*]

JOE. They've got him now—it's all right, major.

BRITT. [*L.C.*] All we have to do now is to return to court and secure a legal acquittal, so come. [*Crossing to door, R.C.*]

JOE. [*C.*] But, I must see Mary first! [*Calls, R.2.E.*] Mary!

BRAN. [*At door, R.2.E. Calls*] Mary! Mary! [*Mary enters from R.2.E., followed by Grace. They face in front of Brandon, who drops down, R.*]

MARY. [*R.C.*] Is it true? Has the light come at last?

JOE. [*C.*] Yes, dear! The night has been long and dark. But on the heights of happiness, where we are standing now, our love will illuminate our lives forever. [*Music*]

CURTAIN

A TRIP TO CHINATOWN;
Or, AN IDYL OF SAN FRANCISCO

In Extenuation: The author begs to say that whatever
this play may be, it is all that is claimed for it.

By Charles H. Hoyt

CAST OF CHARACTERS

The cast of the New York opening of *A Trip to Chinatown* on November 9, 1891, was as follows:

WELLAND STRONG, *a man with one foot in the grave*	HARRY CONOR
BEN GAY, *a wealthy San Francisco bachelor, of the Union Club*	GEORGE A. BEANE
RASHLEIGH GAY, *his nephew*	LLOYD WILSON
TONY GAY, *his niece*	LILLIAN BARR
WILDER DALY	
WILLIE GROW, *proposed at the Bohemian Club*	BLANCHE ARKWRIGHT
NORMAN BLOOD, *chum of Rashleigh*	ARTHUR PACIE
NOAH HEAP, *waiter at the Riche*	HARRY GILFOIL
HOFFMAN PRICE, *landlord of the Cliff House*	FRANK E. MORSE
TURNER SWIFT	
SLAVIN PAYNE, *a servant to Ben Gay*	HARRY GILFOIL
WAITERS	
ISABELLE DAME, *a family friend*	GERALDINE MC CANN
CORA FAY	MAGGIE DALY
MAY WING	LUCY DALY
FLIRT	ALLIE ARCHMERE
MRS. GUYER, *a widow from Chicago, not too strenuous on culture but makes up for it with a "biff"*	ANNA BOYD

THE SCENE IS LAID IN THE CITY OF SAN FRANCISCO.

ACT I: RECEPTION ROOM IN THE HOUSE OF BEN GAY.

ACT II: "THE RICHE" RESTAURANT.

ACT III: BALCONY OF THE CLIFF HOUSE IN SAN FRANCISCO WITH A VIEW OF SEAL ROCKS AT BACK.

[NOTE: The first version of Act III here printed is from a prompt copy of the play; the second version of Act III is from the copy of the play in the New York Public Library.]

ACT I.

SCENE: *Reception room in Ben Gay's house.*
DISCOVERED: *Slavin Payne.*

SLA. [*Reads the superscription on an envelope in his hand*] "Mr. R. Gay!" I haven't a doubt that it's an "R," and it's meant for Mr. Rashleigh. Besides, it's from a lady. The shape, the perfume—[*Smells it*] the handwriting, all prove it to be from a lady, and the old gentleman never receives notes from ladies. There's no doubt in my mind it's for Rashleigh. Still, the "R" looks enough like a "B," I think, to warrant me in giving it to Uncle Ben. He'll open it and I hope find out from it how the young man is going on. I'll give it to the old man. [*Enter Wilder*]

WILD. Slavin, has Mr. Rashleigh come in?

SLA. [*R.*] No, Mr. Daly.

WILD. When do you expect him?

SLA. I don't expect him, sir. I would not dare take the liberty of expecting him, sir. I know my place, sir. [*Enter Rashleigh*]

RASH. Hullo, Wilder, old man! You here? I was over at your house looking for you.

SLA. Is anything required of me?

RASH. Yes. Get out! [*Exit Slavin*]

WILD. Now, Rash, you know the masquerade ball tonight. Well—

RASH. I know! I'm going to be there.

WILD. Yes. But the girls are going. Flirt is up in Tony's room now. The scheme's all fixed.

RASH. They going! Why, how? I can get out, but Uncle Ben'll hear of it —and your father'll never let Flirt go.

WILD. To the ball, no! But we're not supposed to be going there. We have got permission to go on a night tour of Chinatown. That will account for our being out late. Well, instead of going to Chinatown, we all meet at The Riche, have a jolly supper. Our masks will be sent there; we'll put them on and go to the ball. Being en masse, nobody'll know us, and when we get home, the old folks will never suspect we haven't been to Chinatown. See?

RASH. That's all very well, if it works. How did Flirt get your father to consent to her going through Chinatown?

WILD. Oh, he consented when Mrs. Guyer said she'd go as chaperone. Didn't you get a note from her telling you all about it?

RASH. No. Did she send me one?

WILD. Yes. She sent it by messenger from our house.

RASH. I never got it. Very strange!

WILD. Now, does it all go?

RASH. Why, yes. If Uncle Ben will consent to Tony's going through Chinatown.

WILD. Leave the girls to coax him.

RASH. But, say, if the widow's going along, we'll need a third fellow to balance the party. You bet she doesn't go without a fellow all to herself.

WILD. The widow! Well, hardly! She's the one who got up this whole scheme, my boy. The trip to Chinatown story and all! And you bet she's taken care the party isn't short on men. She's got Towne Painter to go as Flirt's escort, so you can devote yourself entirely to the widow.

RASH. Well, that suits me! The widow's more fun than any girl I know. Say, Wilder, I don't believe a woman is ever at her best till she becomes a widow.

WILD. The boys all seem to think she's in her prime anyway. That's a great song Billy Parker wrote and dedicated to her. [*Starts to sing. Duet, Rashleigh and Wilder: "The Widow"*]

Do you know her? Have you met her?
If so, you'll ne'er forget her—
The pretty little widow with the laughing eyes of brown.
Demure in her sobriety,
Severe in her propriety,
But the life of all society,
The jolliest thing in town.
No giddiness or giggle,
No shyness and no wriggle,
That makes the budding maiden such a nuisance and a bore.
So bright in conversation,
So free from affectation,
You can bear no hesitation,
And you hasten to adore!

CHORUS

But when you come to tell her how you love her,
As never was a woman loved before!
Do not think you can deceive,

Don't expect her to believe,
She has heard it in the days of yore!

Most likely she'll refuse you,
Most likely 'twill amuse you,
She's got so many clothes in black, to mourning she must cling;
But if your pray'r impresses,
And besides, she rather guesses,
But along with her addresses,
A husband is the thing;
She'll breathe hard for a minute,
But, my boy, there's nothing in it;
It's only strict propriety that makes her tremble so.
She long ago has brooded
On the question, and concluded,
Very likely before you did,
If you'd be the man or no?

CHORUS

But when you come to put your arms around her,
And squeeze her till you can't squeeze any more,
If you think she's going to faint,
She will fool you, for she ain't!
She has been there several times before! [*At end of song, voices heard outside*]

WILD. It's the girls and your uncle. [*Enter Ben, Flirt, and Tony*]

BEN. I don't care if night trips to Chinatown are the fashion! I say, no!

TONY. But, uncle, I've lived here in San Francisco all my life and have never been through the China quarter, and this is such a good chance. We'll have a whole party together, and of course a policeman. And we'll ask Mrs. Guyer to chaperone us.

BEN. I don't see that she'd make any difference.

FLIRT. Why, she's a widow.

BEN. Yes, and is always sniveling about it. Why doesn't she get married again? I suppose because no man's fool enough to yield to her blandishments. I know I wouldn't!

TONY. But if she goes—

BEN. She goes alone! I won't have you out all night chasing through Chinatown. That settles it!

TONY. [*Bursts into tears*] I think you're just as mean as you can be! [*Exits crying*]

FLIRT. [*Crying*] Poor Tony! [*Exits crying*]

RASH. Come, Wilder. [*They exit*]

BEN. Now I'm an infernal old beast, I suppose. Well, I can't help it. They're my sister's children, and I'll do my duty as their guardian, if I earn their everlasting hatred! [*Enter Slavin with letter*]

SLA. Letter left for you, sir, by messenger boy. [*Gives letter*]

BEN. [*Looks at it*] For me!

SLA. Yes, sir. Anything I can do for you, sir?

BEN. Yes. Go away! [*Exit Slavin*] Looks like a woman's letter. What woman would write to me? [*Opens letter and reads*] "My dear old boy!" [*Look*] "You must take me to the grand masquerade ball tonight! Even if I am in mourning, I'm bound to go on the strict Q.T., and you are the only man I dare to trust. You get the masks—it wouldn't do for me to order them —meet me at The Riche, don our masks and drive to the ball, and nobody'll know anything about it. Don't fail, for I'm dying for a good time. Yours — —. P.S. If you want to make it a party of four, I can bring Flirt." [*Speaks*] Well, I'll be—! Well, that letter's plain enough. These widows know what they want and are not afraid to declare themselves. But this to me! Why, I know she's been running to the house to see Tony, but I never suspected it was me she was after! Damn bright woman, that widow! I'll not disappoint her. But how can I stay out all night without the family knowing it? Change my mind. Let 'em go to Chinatown! By jove, how lucky it comes! [*Orchestra begins*] There's that cussed street band. Playing dance music, too. That's suggestive. I hope I haven't forgotten how to shake my feet. [*Dances. At close, enter four young people and catch him*]

TONY. Why! Uncle Ben!

BEN. I—was only thinking. I've turned matters over in my mind.

TONY. I should think you must have with such violent exercise.

BEN. I've decided to let you go to Chinatown. It's highly proper that you should see it thoroughly. Promise me you will go. Go early and stay late!

ALL FOUR. We will! [*Exit Ben, R.*] Well!

FLIRT. There's a change of mind for you. I wonder what did it.

TONY. I don't know nor care. We go to the ball! That's the point! [*All burst into chorus during which Widow enters and goes to C.*]

WID. And for it all, you can thank me!

TWO GIRLS. Our chaperone!

WID. That will do, young ladies! Rashleigh, why didn't you answer my note?

RASH. Because I didn't get it.

WID. Didn't get it? How stupid of you!

RASH. Oh, I know what it said. And it's all right. So you can dispense with those black looks.

WID. Not for twenty-nine days. You must remember I'm a widow.

WILD. Still mourning for poor Jack?

WID. Bitterly! I shall wear a black mask at the ball. Wilder, don't forget that in ordering the masks. [*Enter Slavin with a letter*]

SLA. [*To Rashleigh*] Note for you, sir. [*Gives letter*] Can I oblige you, sir?

RASH. Yes! Go and hide yourself! [*Exit Slavin*] It's a note from Painter. [*Reads*] "Dear Rash:—May be a little late, but will join you at The Riche. Will inquire for Mr. Gay's room. Wait for me. Yours, Towne Painter." That settles it! Our party of six is complete! Of course we'll wait for him. You wouldn't care to go with the party one man short?

WID. Care to? I just wouldn't! [*Enter Ben*]

BEN. Now, Tony—Why, Mrs. Guyer! Good morning! How do you do?

WID. [*Rather surprised*] Good morning, sir!

BEN. [*Aside*] I see! Discretion!

TONY. Uncle, she's going to chaperone us!

BEN. Is she? That's nice! But if she changes her mind—[*Winks at Widow*] you can go just the same. [*Aside*] She's throwing 'em off. Fly woman! I must speak to her. [*Aloud*] Tony, I want you four young people to get 'round the piano and sing me my favorite quartette.

TONY. Anything to oblige. [*The four gather around. Business at the piano*]

BEN. Mrs. Guyer, sit down. [*Seats her. Aside to her*] Of course, you mean to keep your appointment tonight?

WID. Most surely! Why?

BEN. Oh, I shouldn't let the young folks go out, only for that.

WID. You flatter me! [*Aside*] What ails the man?

TONY. We can't find the quartette, but here's a quintette. Come, Mrs. G., help us out. [*Widow goes to piano to sing*]

BEN. [*Aside*] Rats! I asked 'em to sing so I could talk to her. Well, I'll be— —! [*Quintette sings "Push Dem Clouds Away"*]

If you want to git to Heaven on de nickel-plated road,
Just push dem clouds away!
Bring along all yer baggage and check it to de Lord,
When you push dem clouds away!

If de train am a-speedin' an' you can't catch on,
When you push dem clouds away!
You're a coon dat's gone, and wuss dan none,
When you push dem clouds away!

CHORUS

Just push!
Don't shove!
Just push dem clouds away!
Keep a-pushin', an' a-shovin', an' a-pushin', an' a-shovin'
Till you push dem clouds away!

Oh, de chickens up dere don't have to scratch,
When you push dem clouds away!
All green and yaller is dat water-million patch,
When you push dem clouds away!
If de people am a-yellin' for pie and milk,
Just push dem clouds away!
De angels dere all dress in silk,
When you push dem clouds away!

There'll be no boys a-puffin' cigarettes,
When you push dem clouds away!
They'll all have wings, those mammy's little pets,
When you push dem clouds away!
Old Gabriel's horn will toot and roar,
When you push dem clouds away!
There'll be no dudes around the stage door,
When you push dem clouds away!

FLIRT. Does that satisfy your craving for music?
BEN. Entirely! I don't care if I never hear you sing again!
WID. That's nice! Now, I must run home and get rested for tonight
Good-by, all.
BEN. [*Opens portières. Aside to Widow*] Everything's O.K.?
WID. I hope so.
BEN. You and I are all right, but no Flirt!
WID. Certainly not! [*Exits*]
BEN. Young ladies, there's a woman whose example you ought to follow
TONY. You don't know how hard we try to, sir. [*Enter Slavin with
telegram*]

SLA. Telegram, sir! [*Hands it*] Any service I can perform, sir?

BEN. Yes. Leave the room! [*Exit Slavin. Ben reads telegram*] "You will probably see me before this reaches you, for I am at Oakland. Will reach your house in an hour. Welland Strong." Whew! I didn't expect him till tomorrow.

FLIRT. Who is he? A nice young fellow, or an old codger like—oh, lots of folks.

BEN. He is a dying man, an old and dear boyhood friend of mine on whom Death has fixed its clutch. He comes here as my guest in the hope that our glorious climate may prolong his existence. Poor fellow, he used to be the picture of health. I dread to see him, hollow-chested, cheeks hectic, flushed, and glassy-eyed. And he, my boyhood's dearest friend! Say, he's liable to be here any minute. We must—[*Rings*] make ready to receive him. Get a lounge ready. [*Girls obey. Enter Slavin*]

SLA. Did you ring?

BEN. Ring? I next thing to turned in a fire-alarm! Get a glass of wine ready on this table. Bring fans and smelling salts. Have a man help you bring him from the carriage. [*Everybody bustling and get everything fixed*] He'll probably faint after his long journey. Now, is everything ready? [*Enter Welland Strong with cat and parrot*]

STRONG. Ah, there! [*All turn to him*]

BEN. What? Welland Strong!

STRONG. Yes! Welland Strong!

BEN. Why, how do you do?

STRONG. I may die before night! [*Business*]

BEN. Sit down! Here, Slavin! Take the gentleman's wraps! Have a glass of wine? [*Exit Slavin with wraps*]

STRONG. I will! Wine is harmful to me. It shortens my life. But I'll take it! [*Drinks*]

BEN. You don't look badly, old man!

STRONG. No! That's the exasperating thing about it!

WILD. Which lung is affected, sir?

STRONG. Neither as yet. But the left one probably will be by Saturday night.

RASH. Do you cough much?

STRONG. Not at all! That's a very serious feature. My malady is so deep-seated that I can't bring the cough to the surface. But instead I feel a sensation which, in a well man, would be called a thirst for liquor.

TONY. And what do the doctors say?

STRONG. No two agree.

BEN. And who shall decide when doctors disagree?

STRONG. Usually the coroner. Why, I had seven of them. One fool said that nothing ailed me. Do you know, the only man who really understood my case was a horse doctor! He said if I stayed in Boston I'd die in sixty days. Out here I'd live two years if I obeyed certain rules. Here's the book of rules and it tells just how much I shorten my life each time I break one. That glass of wine shortened it nineteen hours. [*Enter Slavin*]

SLA. Shall I take the gentleman's game to his room, sir?

STRONG. He may as well.

SLA. Anything else I can do?

BEN. Yes! Keep out! [*Exit Slavin with pets*]

STRONG. By the way, can you give me the address of a good horse doctor?

BEN. Why, yes. But hadn't you better see our family physician?

STRONG. Oh, no! He's no good! None of these M.D.'s are! They're used to catering to their patients' whims. Giving them what they want to take. A horse doctor don't try to please his patients. He gives them what they need. I'll never trust any but a horse doctor.

BEN. Well! Well! I'll see you have one. I know a man who cured my mules of colic.

STRONG. That's the man I want. He'll keep me going along, if any one can.

TONY. What feature of our climate do you rely on to help you?

STRONG. The earthquakes!

ALL. Earthquakes?

STRONG. Yes. They're very invigorating.

BEN. Have you ever seen an earthquake?

STRONG. I was chased three miles by one once.

BEN. Now, old man, you've got two or three years anyhow and we'll try to make you comfortable. After dinner we'll sit down and talk over old times. [*Aside*] I forgot! I've got to be out tonight. What'll I do with him? [*Aloud*] We'll have the house all to ourselves, for the young people are going out to see Chinatown by night. You'd enjoy it if you were only able to go with them. [*The four young people look at each other, startled*]

TONY. But he isn't, uncle. It's a very fatiguing trip.

STRONG. I don't know! I have sworn to see Chinatown, and, fading daily as I am, I shall never again be so able as tonight. It will, of course, shorten my life, but I'll go if the young people will take me!

BEN. Why, of course! Just delighted to have you go! Aren't you?

QUARTETTE. Oh, yes.

STRONG. Then I'll sacrifice—[*Looks in book*] ten days of my life and go! [*Cats heard outside. Enter Slavin all scratched*]

SLA. Your cat's got at our cat, sir! You'd better come, sir! [*Exit Strong and Ben, excited. Brief cat fight outside. Four young people down C.*]

WILD. Damn!

FLIRT. M-m-m!

TONY. M-m-m!

FLIRT. This is a nice fix!

TONY. We're dished on going to the ball, and we've got to put in a night toting that old fool all over Chinatown!

FLIRT. It's bad enough to lose the ball.

TONY. But toting him around is such a cheerless task.

WILD. What's to be done?

OMNES. Ask the widow! [*Enter Widow*]

WID. What? How to get out of this new scrape?

GIRLS. You know—?

WID. Just met your uncle in the hall. He told me this Mr. Strong would go with us to Chinatown, so I need have no compunctions about not going. And then—then he winked most mysteriously.

TONY. Uncle winked at you! I can't understand what he meant!

WID. Neither can I, and I'm a widow!

FLIRT. But this dying creature that's tucked upon us! What are we going to do with him?

WID. Take him along!

ALL FOUR. To Chinatown?

WID. No! To the ball!

TONY. But if we tell him where we're going, he will go straight to uncle with the story.

WID. But don't tell him where he's going; just take him along.

TONY. But when he comes home he'll tell on us.

WID. Then he'll have to tell on himself, too! I don't know this Mr. Strong, but if he isn't as deep in this scrape as we are before we get home, then may I always remain a widow.

TONY. But he'll make four men to three ladies. Some girl will have to manage two beaux.

WID. I think somebody will prove equal to that emergency!

TONY. On the whole, I'm rather glad he's going. We'll have a lot of fun with him.

WID. He's got an exciting evening in store for him. [*Enter Strong*]

STRONG. The excitement of that cat fight has taken a week off my life.

TONY. Here he is. Oh, Mr. Strong, I want to introduce you to our charming young widow, Mrs. Guyer.

Wɪᴅ. [*Curtsies*] I am honored.

Stʀᴏɴɢ. [*Pathetically*] A widow and a woman!

Wɪᴅ. Those affiliations usually go together.

Stʀᴏɴɢ. How pathetic! In the flower of youth to be bereft of sweet companionship! To be doomed henceforth forever to tread life's pathway unaided and alone!

Wɪᴅ. Ye-yes. But, say—there's no law against her marrying again.

Wɪʟᴅ. Well, if I left a widow—

Wɪᴅ. You'd be pig enough to want her to stay one. That's a man. He thinks it's a slur on him for his widow to marry. Nothing of the sort. It's a compliment. Shows he made married life so happy that she wants more of it.

Rᴀsʜ. When I marry, I think I shall marry a widow.

Fʟɪʀt. Oh, Rashleigh! Why?

Rᴀsʜ. I'm too lazy to do any of the courting myself.

Wɪᴅ. We will change the subject. Mr. Strong, is your visit to San Francisco for pleasure?

Stʀᴏɴɢ. I came here to die.

Wɪᴅ. To die!

Stʀᴏɴɢ. Yes! It's a sure thing. The remedy I am taking for my lung trouble contains dynamite. If the disease conquers the remedy, why, I die of the disease. If the remedy conquers the disease, I shall be so full of dynamite eventually that I'll go off with a bang—[*Widow startled*] like a torpedo dropped from the roof on a policeman's head! Think, I may suddenly vanish with a loud report—[*Widow screams*] before your eyes! [*Widow screams again*] And it may happen any moment! Now!!! [*Widow shrieks wildly and faints in chair*] Great heavens! She's fainted! Send for the horse doctor!

Wɪᴅ. [*Springs up and glares at him*] What!

ACT II.

Scᴇɴᴇ: *"The Riche" Restaurant. The stage is divided into three compartments: C., private supper room; R., the office with desk, etc.; L., another private supper room.*

Dɪscᴏᴠᴇʀᴇᴅ: *Noah Heap in C. room.*

Nᴏᴀʜ. Mr. Rashleigh Gay's party of six. Well, that means up all night for me and plenty of wine on ice. But it also means five dollars for a tip. Mr. Gay may sometimes forget some of the commandments, but he always remembers the waiter. He'll go to Heaven. [*Voices outside*] Here they are.

[*Opens door C.*] Right this way, Mr. Gay. This is your room. [*Enter three ladies, Rashleigh, and Wilder*]

TONY. Number 10, with a piano. I'm glad we've got that!

FLIRT. But what's that orchestra?

WILDER. They have one that plays every night in this restaurant from eight to twelve.

NOAH. [*Points to R.U.E.*] The ladies' dressing room in there! [*Points L.U.E.*] The gentlemen's here. The dresses are in the room.

FLIRT. Let's go and get dressed at once while they're getting supper so we'll lose no time. Come on, Tony. [*Exit Tony and Flirt, R.U.E.*]

WILD. [*To Widow*] What shall we order for supper?

WID. Oh, some Pommery. [*Exits R.U.E.*]

RASH. Mr. Painter's not here yet?

NOAH. No, sir.

WILD. We'll have to wait for him; he's got our tickets to the ball.

RASH. Couldn't we buy others?

WILD. No, none are sold at the door. So we've got to wait for him. We'll go ahead with supper—though—sa-say! Where's our dying companion, Strong? [*Enter Strong*]

STRONG. Here I am!

RASH. What's happened?

STRONG. The hackman said five dollars. I said two!

WILD. What did you agree upon?

STRONG. Five! Tell me! Do we stop here long?

WILD. Our friend, Mr. Painter, who is to meet us here, hasn't arrived and he has the tickets.

STRONG. Tickets! For Chinatown?

WILD. Ye-yes. Of course.

RASH. Oh, you're not let into Chinatown without tickets. [*To Noah*] Isn't that so?

NOAH. Yes, sir. Fifty cents, please. [*Rashleigh gives Noah a coin*]

STRONG. Supper! [*Consults book*] Eating at night shortens my life ten days!

RASH. Well, you can sit and see us eat.

STRONG. You're very kind. But I'll not impose upon your courtesy. Lend me a pencil till I put down—[*Writes*] "Late supper, ten days off." What's ten days' life to me? Here, waiter, my coat and hat! [*Exit Noah with wraps*]

WILD. Now, Rash, we must be getting dressed. But, say, we haven't ordered supper.

RASH. That's so. Mr. Strong, what would you like? Won't you give the order?

STRONG. I fear the taste of a dying man may not exactly suit your fancies.

WILD. I don't know. I never tasted one. But you go ahead and order the supper. [*Rashleigh and Wilder go to L.U.E.*]

RASH. The wines we get out here are harmless. [*Exit both, L.U.E.*]

STRONG. I don't quite understand all this! [*Enter Noah, C.*] Oh, waiter! I hope you were careful of my coat. There was a large bottle of medicine in each pocket.

NOAH. Yes, sir.

STRONG. If the medicines got mixed, they would explode.

NOAH. Why didn't you say so before? [*Grabs carafe and drinks*]

STRONG. Waiter, I will order the supper. Give us—[*He pantomimes business of ordering the supper*] And, waiter, could you give me a glass of whale's milk?

NOAH. Whale's milk?

STRONG. Why, yes. My doctor recommends it.

NOAH. Well, you tell him to go milk a whale and get you some. It ain't on our bill of fare.

STRONG. Too bad! Say, waiter, will you do me a favor? There's a porous plaster between my shoulders that's drawing me crazy. Will you kindly reach down my back and pull it off?

NOAH. Certainly, sir. [*Puts hand down Strong's back*] How do you like your agony, sir?

STRONG. Take it slow. There's not a bit of hurry.

NOAH. I know, sir. A hair's breadth at a time. I won't hurt you, sir.

STRONG. Easy! Easy! [*A bell rings in outer office. Noah bolts for the door, R.L.E., taking porous plaster with him. He leaves Strong quivering with pain. Noah enters outer office and looks at annunciator*] He took skin and all! [*Reenter Noah in room C. with plaster stuck to his fingers*]

NOAH. I'll swear I heard a bell ring. Didn't you? [*Business with plaster*]

STRONG. No, sir! I wasn't listening for bells.

NOAH. [*Bothered by plaster*] Here's your plaster, sir! [*Gives plaster to Strong. It sticks to Strong's hands*]

STRONG. I don't want it. I never save these things as souvenirs. You throw it out.

NOAH. Excuse me! I've got to get supper. [*Exits C. and reenters room R., the office*]

STRONG. [*Business with porous plaster. Gets badly stuck up with it and in desperation exits C., calling*] Waiter! Waiter! [*Meantime Noah has gone behind office desk. Enter Ben, office, R.*]

BEN. Has a lady been here inquiring for Mr. Gay?

NOAH. No, sir.

BEN. I'm in time. Show me to a private supper room for two.

NOAH. Certainly, sir. This way. [*Exit both from office. Enter Widow wearing Hamlet dress into room C., from R.U.E.*]

WID. It seems I am to go to the ball in the guise of a man. I was forced to it. A man among the women! Well, that's what I always wanted to be! What sort of a young fellow shall I be to catch the girls? The very English young man: "Good morning, dear boy. Awfully pleased, awfully! Beastly weather this—in London, you know. Come 'round to the club, old chappie! Have a brandy and soda. We've new windows in our club now—special glass, magnificent fog effect! Brightest day makes you feel right at home in London, dear boy." And there's the young freshman in college: "We boys— ha! ha! ha!—have lots of—ha! ha!—fun. We've had a cow in the president's chair twice, and—ha! ha!—we've had a cane rush—ha! ha! ha!—and three men had bones broken, and it was lots of fun, and—ha! ha! ha!—Let's waltz! What! Engaged for the next? And all the rest? And here comes Mr. Winner. Yes, he's a senior, and I'll have to excuse you! Oh!" Or I might be one of those dear, delightful toughs: "Say, dere, sis, come and do a toin! What's dat? Engaged, be blowed! If he says a woid, I'll t'row him out, see?" but I guess I'll do best as just the average young man right up to date. [*Sings "The Chaperone"*]

> A crisp young chaperone,
> Who is always bright and gay;
> And when they dare not go alone
> They always take a chaperone
> To take the curse away,
> To take the curse away.
> Although it's far from pleasing
> To be severe and hurt,
> I'm chaperone this evening,
> That all of you may flirt.
> A crisp young chaperone,
> Who is always bright and gay;

And when they dare not go alone
They always take the chaperone,
To take the curse away,
To take the curse away.

A gay young chaperone,
Who is always bright and gay;
And captivating at a glance,
Will set your sluggish heart adance:
And eyes that fire and flash,
And eyes that fire and flash.
But still she's oft demurely,
Quite shy, reserved and plain;
Perhaps you think so surely,
Her heart and hand you'll gain.
A crisp young chaperone,
Who is always bright and gay;
And when they dare not go alone,
They always take the chaperone,
To take the curse away,
To take the curse away. [*After the song, a dance, and then Widow exits R.U.E. Enter Ben and Noah, room L.*]

BEN. This will do. When the lady calls, show her right in. And, say, you'd better have supper all ready. I shan't have to wait long for her.

NOAH. Yes, sir. Champagne, and what else, sir?

BEN. The best of everything. A corking supper, my boy! Nothing's too good!

NOAH. Yes, sir. Like to look at the evening paper, sir?

BEN. No. No paper for me! [*Exit Noah*] I'll just sit and think of what a lucky dog I am. I wonder how Strong's enjoying Chinatown. [*Sits and smokes. Enter Widow and the two girls in costume, R.U.E.*]

WID. I think you are very unkind, girls, to make any such remarks. You know I won't be out of mourning for twenty-nine days yet, and it's the only black dress of the lot. [*Strong enters C., sees Widow; exits C. and coughs outside*] Here comes Mr. Strong! I—I—Where's my mask? [*Dons mask*] Now to win him over to our frolic. I wonder if he's got a mask. [*Strong looks out C.*]

STRONG. May I come in?

WID. Certainly, Mr. Strong. I want to ask you a question. Are you stuck?

STRONG. Not now!

WID. But you have been!

STRONG. [*Aside*] That waiter told her. [*Aloud*] Yes.

WID. And you may be again some day.

STRONG. Not if I know it!

TONY. [*Exhibits costume*] Will these do? [*Sees Strong*] Oh!

STRONG. Bless my soul! What does all this mean?

WID. Girls, we may as well throw aside all attempts at concealment. [*Strong turns to go*] Mr. Strong [*Removes mask*], we are not going to China-town. We are going to the masquerade! We expect you to go with us, to join in the fun with us—and when we get home, we rely on your sense of honor to swear that we've been to Chinatown!

STRONG. But, my dear—

WID. Swear as an honest man that you will do this.

STRONG. But I don't think your uncle would deceive me! [*The girls offer him a glass of wine*]

BEN. [*In the other room*] I wonder what Strong would say if he knew I was here.

WID. Swear it!

STRONG. I do!

TONY. Ah, I knew he was a thoroughbred!

STRONG. Say! Come to think of it, it's a mighty good joke on the old fel-low! [*Laughs*] One moment. [*Produces book*] This means two weeks more off my life—but let her rip! [*Enter two boys, L.U.E.*]

FLIRT. Are you dressed at last?

RASH. We are! Now for the supper, and then we're ready to start.

WILD. Mr. Strong, perhaps we ought to explain.

STRONG. It might be as well, but if you've got a really good lie fixed up for me, I don't mind hearing it.

TONY. He knows, and he's with us.

TWO YOUNG MEN. He is? Good boy! [*One each side of him and sing, "We'll Show You 'Frisco!" Then they all sing, the girls between them, "Out for a Racket!"*]

> Out for a racket, racket up to here!
> Out for a racket, racket up to here!
> Out for a high old frolic,
> Strictly alcoholic,
> Wine or whiskey, ale or lager beer!
> Out for a racket, racket up to here!

Out for a racket, racket up to here!
Out for a high old frolic,
Strictly alcoholic,
Out for a racket up to here!

[*Widow sings*]

In me, a modest maid you see!
Of course you know I'm college bred!
I've learned to calm my ecstasy,
To worldly joys seem dead!
This air demure is all put on,
I love to romp and make a noise!
My mamma thinks I'm an angel, but—
You ought to see me with the boys!
I love to romp and make a noise,
And you should see me with the boys! Ah!

Although, you see, I'm scarce of age,
I love to have a high old time!
Just now this seems to be the rage,
To me it is divine!
A cigarette, a glass of wine,
With lots of fun and lots of noise!
I would not be an angel when
I have a night out with the boys!
I love to romp and make a noise,
And you should see me with the boys! Ah!

BEN. [*Looks at watch*] Ten minutes of ten! By jingo, she ought to be here. It's prolonging the agony. [*Rings. Enter Noah*] Waiter, are you sure that lady hasn't called?

NOAH. Sure, sir! Supper's ready to serve when you want it.

BEN. I don't want it till she gets here. She can't be long now.

NOAH. Patience is a great thing in these cases, sir. Don't you want the evening paper, sir?

BEN. No, no! I didn't come here to read the evening paper. Bring me a cocktail. [*Exit Noah*]

FLIRT. Say, let's not wait for Mr. Painter. I'm starved. [*Enter Noah, C., with tray*]

RASH. Waiter, you can bring the supper. [*Music begins*]

TONY. There's the orchestra. Say, we're losing time! What's the matter with dancing right here?

FLIRT. That's so! Come on! Mr. Strong, you'll dance?

STRONG. If you can bear the spectacle of a man with one foot in the grave trying to be merry with the other, I'll do my best. [*Minuet. To finish it, Noah, who has been setting table, drops tray. Strong falls in chair. Noah exits C.*] There goes that lung!

FLIRT. Why, no! The waiter dropped a tray of dishes.

STRONG. I thought that lung had busted, sure. It's likely to at any minute.

BEN. Some pack of hoodlums in that next room! By jove, this is getting monotonous. [*Enter to Ben, Noah with four cocktails*]

NOAH. You didn't say what kind of a cocktail, so I brought four.

BEN. You know your business.

NOAH. I can take three of them back.

BEN. Over my dead body! [*Takes tray*]

NOAH. Hadn't you better look at the evening paper, sir?

BEN. No, sir! I had not! [*Exit Noah. The three men gather about Widow, R.U.E. Tony and Flirt are left alone down L.*]

FLIRT. Will you look at that!

TONY. Excuse me! I'd rather not see it.

FLIRT. I don't know why men go crazy over widows! It's enough to drive one—

TONY. To marrying some man and then poisoning him. This man Strong's only going to live two years. I've a mind to make love to him. With what I'd keep him out nights, I think I could shorten his existence to six months.

FLIRT. And she—

TONY. She's doing her duty as chaperone. Taking care we don't get familiar with the gentlemen.

FLIRT. Yes, and taking great satisfaction in it. I can see she's laughing at us!

TONY. I vow I'll break it up. [*Aloud*] Mrs. Guyer, how long did Mr. Guyer last after you were married?

WID. Only six months. [*Men draw away*]

TONY. I—I heard he died from the effects of a blowing up!

WID. [*Unruffled*] Yes. Excursion boat. Dear boy! He was insured for fifty thousand dollars! [*Men right back around her*]

TONY. [*Aside to Flirt*] I wish I was a man or a parrot! I want to swear! Say, Flirt, sing a song. They'll have, in common decency, to listen.

FLIRT. I can't.

TONY. Then ask me to.

FLIRT. [*Aloud*] Say, everybody. Tony knows this song the orchestra's playing. I want you all to listen to it.

TONY. [*Sings song, "Never to Know." Business of weeping with the song*]

STRONG. Beautiful! So touching! How much we miss in this life by not daring to speak out. I went thirsty two days in a prohibition town because I didn't dare to ask the landlord for a drink. [*Weeps again*] Forgive these tears! But that song has turned all my thoughts to sadness. The separation of two fond beings makes me think of the fast approaching day when one of my lungs will be withered and vanished, leaving the other desolate, alone and overworked. I have often in the still watches of the night pondered on this and at last my sad musings took the form of a little poem.

TONY and WID. Oh, give it to us.

STRONG. [*Takes drink and makes memorandum in book*] It's called the "Lay of the Lingering Lung." I wish that band would play a soft, tuneful melody. [*Recitation with music by Strong. As they break up, Strong goes to Tony and Rashleigh to Flirt. Widow sizes up situation*]

WID. Ahem! Have you heard the latest scandal? [*Every man rushes up to her*]

THREE MEN. What is it?

TONY. What have you been doing today?

WID. That remark was contemptible! Now, you shan't hear the story. [*Tells story to men in dumb show*] It isn't long. [*To girls*] And I really am not trying to monopolize the gentlemen entirely. I shall probably insist, as a favor to me, that they devote themselves to you. [*Goes on with a cry. Makes gestures*]

TONY. There they are again! I vow I'll be a widow within a year.

FLIRT. I know what it is. It's the dress. [*Widow makes parenthetical gesture*]

TONY. Did you see that gesture? I'll bet I know what she said. A widow'll say anything. Come, Flirt. [*They rise*] Gentlemen, we wish to use your dressing room just a moment. [*Exit L.U.E. Ben rings*]

WID. I'll bet I know what they're up to. [*Rises*] Pray excuse me. [*Exit Widow R.U.E. Noah enters Ben's room*]

BEN. Fill 'em up again all 'round.

NOAH. [*Takes tray*] Yes, sir. I have the evening paper.

BEN. Keep it! [*Exit Noah*] By thunder, that widow takes her time! [*During the above, Rashleigh has filled glasses and passed them*]

STRONG. Gentlemen, you ought not to tempt me like this. [*Drinks and reaches for bottle*] Every glass of this stuff is a day off my life. [*Drinks*] You are aiding and abetting suicide. [*Produces book*] Has anybody kept tab on me?

WILD. That last one was seven, I think.

STRONG. A week gone! I've wasted five weeks of my life tonight, and I came here for my health. [*Enter Noah with note and four cocktails on tray, C.*]

WILD. What's that?

NOAH. Cocktails. The gentleman in the next room ordered them.

RASH. Very good of him. [*Passes glasses*]

STRONG. [*Takes glass*] That man's bent on my murder. [*All drink and replace glasses on tray*]

BEN. [*Rings*] I wonder what's become of my cocktails.

RASH. Tell the gentleman we're very much obliged.

NOAH. Yes, sir. A note, sir. [*Gives note and exits, C.*]

RASH. [*Reads note*] It's from Painter. "Unavoidably detained. See you very soon." [*Noah enters Ben's room*]

BEN. Where's my cocktails?

NOAH. Gentlemen in the next room drank them, sir, and sent in their compliments.

BEN. They did! Well, I like their nerve! You go back quick and get me four more. Stop! Make it eight! And, say! Are you sure that lady hasn't got here?

NOAH. Sure, sir. Only ladies here are with the party next room. I rather think, sir—

BEN. Think what?

NOAH. You're shook!

BEN. Shook?

NOAH. Hadn't you better eat your supper alone, sir?

BEN. No, sir. She'll be here, sir! You get those cocktails!

NOAH. The evening paper!

BEN. Damn the evening paper! [*Exit Noah*] Shook! Me shook!

WILD. Mr. Strong, this isn't the first time you've been out for a pleasant evening. I see by the way you handle that bottle.

STRONG. When I was on earth I was not obtuse to the redeeming features of wine, women, and song.

RASH. Well, be a boy again. We have the wine and the women. Give us the song.

STRONG. If you care to listen to a voice from the grave, I'll—let me see—give you a little story of the course of true love. [*Song, "2:15," by Strong. During this scene Strong and the two boys are drunk*]

BEN. I'm having a devil of a good time. This is what you get for trusting a widow. [*Enter Noah with cocktails*]

NOAH. Cocktails, sir! Shall I put them down? [*Strong, in other room, is getting a bit loaded*]

BEN. No, I'll do that. [*Takes tray*]

NOAH. The evening paper!

BEN. [*Somewhat jagged*] Give it to me! [*Takes paper. Tears it up*] Now, are you easy in your mind? I came here to have supper with a lady! Do you think I'll be satisfied with an evening paper?

NOAH. What about that supper, sir?

BEN. I'll eat it. Bring it up.

NOAH. The evening paper, sir, had a whole page about a scandal in high life.

BEN. [*Looks at fragments*] It did? Well, I'll be—! Have you got another copy?

NOAH. No, sir. [*Exits. Ben gets on floor and tries to piece paper together. Enter, into other room, the two girls in shape dresses*]

TONY. Now can we have a little attention? [*Enter Noah at C. Musical introduction. Tony and Flirt down C., and sing. Then the two boys join them. Then as they go up R. and L., Widow enters R.U.E. in white Chinese dress and does Chinese specialty. Then Strong, who is getting pretty drunk, down C., and sings with Widow, all joining in chorus and dance at finish*] The widow in white! Have the twenty-nine days gone by so soon?

WID. [*Bursts into tears*] Oh, Tony! How cruel of you! To think I'd forget the respect due poor Jack! Don't you see this is a Chinese dress, and the Chinese for mourning wear white. I know my business.

NOAH. Supper is served.

WID. Come on! Let's get it over before you boys get to making love to each other's girls and the quarrels begin. [*They sit at table, filling time while Ben speaks in the other room*]

BEN. I can't put it together. It's all mixed up with the market reports. [*Reads*] "The infuriated husband, revolver in hand, rushed madly after a drove of prime western hogs just arrived." Oh, rats! [*Rises, pretty drunk; kicks at paper. Falls in chair*] By jove, I'm drunk! [*Rises and tries himself*] Drunker'n a boiled owl! That's a good one! I'll just keep it up and get paralyzed. I'll have some fun out of this racket yet. [*Rings*]

WID. Please pass the salt.

RASH. With all my heart.

WID. Just the salt, please.

TONY. [*Rises*] Well, here's to all of us!

ALL. Drink hearty! [*Song: "Reuben and Cynthia"*]

> Reuben, Reuben, I've a notion
> If the men were sent away,
> Far beyond the stormy ocean,
> Female hearts would all be gay.
> Cynthia, Cynthia, I've been thinking,
> If the men should take that trip,
> All the women in creation,
> Right away would take that ship.
>
> Reuben, Reuben, I've been thinking,
> What a strange thing that would be,
> If the streams of drinking water,
> All turned salty as the sea.
> Cynthia, Cynthia, I've been thinking,
> You can safely take my word,
> More than half the population,
> Wouldn't know it had occurred.
>
> Reuben, Reuben, I've been thinking,
> Will you tell me where or when,
> Women will be forced to stop this,
> Doing things just like the men?
> Cynthia, Cynthia, I've been thinking,
> And can answer with dispatch;
> She must cease her mannish methods,
> When she comes to strike a match.
>
> Reuben, Reuben, I've been thinking,
> Why do people risk their gold,
> Betting on the wicked races,
> Knowing they are bought and sold?
> Cynthia, Cynthia, I've been thinking,
> That is where the laugh comes in;
> Each man thinks that he has fixed it,
> So the horse he backs will win.

STRONG. Anybody have some cold meat? Mutton or beef?

FLIRT. Which is the best?

STRONG. [*Smells each*] It appears to be a case of horse and horse! Waiter, this knife is very dull.

NOAH. Permit me, sir. [*Takes knife; gets behind Strong; imitates sharpening knife*] Try that, sir.

STRONG. [*Tries it*] Much better!

NOAH. Anything else you want, sir?

STRONG. What have you got?

NOAH. Anything on earth.

STRONG. If there's anything you have not got, I want it.

NOAH. I can give you anything from a train of cars to a dog fight.

ALL. Give us a dog fight! [*Noah's imitations. At start of dog fight, Ben in next room starts looking for it. Afterwards, exit Noah*]

STRONG. [*Rises*] Ladies and gentlemen—

WID. He's going to make an after-dinner speech! Stop him!

RASH. Head him off!

ALL. Come on! [*Medley. At end of medley, all off*]

BEN. [*Rings, after entering from hall where he has been looking for dog fight*] She's here! I've found this handkerchief in the hall and it's hers. [*Enter Noah*] You demented lizard, do you see that? It's her handkerchief! She's here! Now, trot her out!

NOAH. Was that the lady you were waiting for?

BEN. Yes! Well?

NOAH. Why, we thought it was your wife! We said you weren't here!

BEN. Well!

NOAH. And she went away!

BEN. [*Grabs him*] While I've waited, she's been here and you sent her away!

NOAH. I regret it, sir.

BEN. Regret it! Regret it! I'd kill you where you stand, only I don't want to become known as a foolkiller! But I'll make it cost you your job. I'll give you a character at the office! [*Bolts out. Noah exits after him. Strong enters L.U.E., and crosses to R.U.E.*]

STRONG. [*Bows*] Did any of you ladies bring a corn knife?

TONY. [*Looks out*] No. Will a curling iron do?

STRONG. No, thanks! I can't curl my corns. [*Exits R.U.E. Enter Ben at office, followed by Noah, who goes behind counter*]

NOAH. What is it, sir?

BEN. I want to see somebody in authority.

NOAH. Gaze right on me!

BEN. You! You're in authority! Well, I want to tell you that the waiter I've had is a blear-eyed tramp, a bandy-legged idiot, and a foul hedgehog!

NOAH. I'll make a note of it. Anything else, sir?

BEN. Yes. Your place is a dive, and I'll never set foot in it again. [*Starts to go*]

NOAH. [*Locks door*] Hadn't you better settle your bill first?

BEN. I forgot. How much is it?

NOAH. One hundred dollars.

BEN. One hundred dollars! What for?

NOAH. Well, there's sixty-five dollars for the supper.

BEN. But I haven't had supper.

NOAH. But you ordered it.

BEN. All right! I deserve it! I—I—[*Business of looking for pocketbook*] Why, I've—I've lost my pocketbook. I'll send you the money tomorrow.

NOAH. We don't do business that way.

BEN. But I'm perfectly good.

NOAH. What name?

BEN. Excuse me! But you shall have your money.

NOAH. I mean to—before you go.

BEN. But, my boy—

NOAH. Send home for it!

BEN. Send for the money to pay for a racket here! Impossible! Now, my dear boy—

NOAH. No! I'm a blear-eyed tramp, and I get that money, or you go to jail. See?

STRONG. [*Enters L.U.E.*] I'll see why they don't answer that bell! [*Exits C.*]

NOAH. Do I get it, or do I ring for the police?

BEN. My very dear boy, I'm a respectable citizen! Don't arrest me! The story'll be all over town.

NOAH. Yes, but you won't be all over to hear it. You'll be in the jail. [*Strong enters office*]

STRONG. You hyena, I want—[*Strong and Ben look at each other. Both yell. Strong turns to run*]

BEN. Here! I want you! [*Starts after Strong*]

NOAH. Here! Come back, you! [*Starts after them. Grand chase. As they rush through C. room, everybody on exclaiming: "What's the matter?," etc. Strong yells "Murder!" and "Help!" Ben and Noah ad lib. Everybody working up excitement. At finish Ben overtakes Strong in room C., and grabs him*]

BEN. Now, I've got you!

STRONG. I'm a dying man! Mercy!

BEN. Mercy! Not a damned bit! Lend me a hundred dollars!

ACT III.

SCENE: *Balcony of Cliff House, San Francisco, with a view of Seal Rocks at back.*

MUSIC: *Offstage at rise. Sounds of laughter off R.*

DISCOVERED: *Turner Swift running ice crusher; Landlord shoveling ice into glasses on tray, which Waiter, who is standing upstage C., is holding.*

LAND. [*Gives bowl with ice to Turner*] Keep it going, Turner. This dance they're doing now is the last but one on the list. This ball has been a corker. [*Goes down L.*]

TURN. [*Near ice crusher*] I never saw people want so much cracked ice.

LAND. It was lucky we brought the crusher up here on the piazza. The waiters never could have gone downstairs for it. [*Exit Turner L.3 with a bowl of ice. Enter Flirt R.U.E., laughing and throwing a flower off R. after kissing it. Then she runs down C.*]

FLIRT. [*To Landlord*] I must take off my mask and breathe for a moment. [*Removes mask*] Well, monsieur, have I earned a *douceur*?

LAND. [*L.C.*] You're a dandy. More men have tried to find out who you were than any other woman at a ball before. Haven't you enjoyed it?

FLIRT. In a way, yes. I have danced with all my mistress's beaux. That was fun, but it was stupid.

LAND. Stupid? Why?

FLIRT. If I spoke they would know me. So all ze time I had to hold my tongue—a very hard thing for a woman to do.

RASH. [*Off R.2.E.*] Come, let's have one drink.

FLIRT. They are coming. I fly. [*Exits L.3.E. very quickly*]

LAND. [*Crosses to R. to table*] She's been the life of the ball. Lucky thought of mine. [*Enter Rashleigh, Willie, and Norman R.3. They are laughing and fanning themselves*]

WILL. [*As he goes down L.*] It's out of sight, isn't it?

RASH. and NORM. Great!

LAND. [*R.*] You have enjoyed yourselves?

RASH. [*R.C.*] Indeed we have! We got here late but we've had fun enough in half an hour to pay us for coming. Say! [*Leads Landlord to R. Aside*]

Who's the girl that kicks so high? The one dressed as a magician, the one in yellow? [*Norman and Willie talking L.*]

LAND. How should I know? She's masked.

RASH. That's so. She came without an escort, didn't she?

LAND. I believe so.

RASH. She won't go home without one. That is, if I can get away from my party. I wonder where she went.

LAND. I think that way. [*Points R. Rashleigh goes up and looks off R.3.E.*]

NORM. [*Crosses to Landlord. Aside to him*] Say! [*Leads him to R.*] Who's the magician girl?

LAND. Everybody in a mask is a stranger to me.

NORM. Oh, I forgot that. Very appropriate dress for her—a magician. Any man she waves her hand at is gone.

LAND. I see. Very good.

NORM. Which way did she go?

LAND. [*Points L.*] I think that way. [*Norman goes up and exits L.3.E.*]

WILL. [*Crosses to C.*] Say, landlord—

LAND. [*Crosses to C.*] Yes, sir, the lady in yellow dressed as a magician is not known to me, but I think you'll find her on the beach. [*Landlord exits L.2.E. Willie goes up C. and looks over rail. Rashleigh and Norman back on, all three men waving handkerchiefs as if flirting with someone. Enter Tony, Widow, and Isabel, R.2. They see the three waving their handkerchiefs*]

WID. There they are. [*Each goes up to one of the men and takes him by the ear. Tony to Norman, L. Widow to Willie, C., and Isabel to Rashleigh, R. They bring them downstage*] What's all this waving of handkerchiefs?

RASH. Waving of handkerchiefs? Nothing of the sort. We had them out to wipe our fevered brows, and the sea breeze made them flutter. Don't you see how it sways the lights?

TONY. Oh! We thought you were flirting with somebody. Forgive us! [*All embrace. Willie goes upstage laughing*]

WID. [*Advances. Aside*] The innocence has not all gone out of the world yet. [*Aloud*] Oh, doesn't this sea air feel good after that hot ball room? [*Goes up C. Enter Landlord, L.3.E.*]

RASH. Let's not go in for the last dance, but have a cooling drink out here. Landlord, give us six lemonades and some of that cracked ice. And, Willie, you go order the carriages up. [*Exit Willie, R.U.E.*]

WID. And, landlord, the sea breeze is just a bit strong. Can't you give us a screen to break it?

LAND. I can. [*Exits L.3.E.*]

ISA. [*R.C.*] I should think you might feel the air.

Wid. [*C.*]　It was the only black costume in the lot. [*Laugh. Enter Willie, R.U.E.*]

Will. [*C.*]　Our carriages are gone!

All.　Gone!

Will.　Yes. The doorkeeper says it was my fault.

Rash.　I'll bet it was!

Will.　So we had to telephone to town, and we've got to wait till they get here.

Norm.　Did you telephone?

Will.　I didn't think to. But I will. [*Exit Willie, R.U.E., very quick*]

Isa. [*R.C.*]　We'll have to wait here an hour. [*Enter Landlord, L.3.E.*]

Wid. [*Aside*]　It will give Mr. Strong time to get here. [*Aloud*] Just time for breakfast. Landlord, breakfast for the party in a private room. [*Up C.*]

Norm. [*Goes up L.C. to Landlord*]　And say, landlord, have those professional dancers gone yet?

Land.　No, sir.

Norm.　Here's fifty for them, if they'll come here and dance for us.

Land.　I'll arrange it. [*Exits L.U.E.*]

Norm. [*Goes down L.C.*]　I wonder if Strong is still at The Riche. [*Enter Willie, R.U.E.*]

Isa.　Oh, what are we to tell uncle?

Rash. [*R.*]　Why, that we lost Strong at The Riche and had to go to Chinatown without him.

Isa.　He won't believe it. I'm afraid we're in for an awful scrape.

Will.　Here are the dancers! [*Exits L.U.E. All sit. Enter Dancers. Specialty and exit. Turner and Servant place a large screen C. Widow goes up to screen*]

Wid. [*C.*]　Oh, that's much better.

Rash. [*R.*]　How Strong would have enjoyed it! I'm almost sorry we shook him. [*Enter Strong, R.U.E., quick*]

Strong.　You didn't! [*All rise, greatly surprised and gather around Strong*]

Norm.　What! How did you get here?

Strong. [*C.*]　Ran! After I got away from The Riche, I rushed madly downstairs. Nothing but a nighthawk coupe stood there. I jumped in. "Drive to the Cliff House!" said I. "Drive like the devil!" He did so! As we turned into the park, the bottom of the rickety old vehicle dropped out. The driver didn't notice it. He kept on driving like the devil, and I had to run inside that hack all the way out here! [*All laugh*] I wouldn't have minded it though, if i

hadn't been such a chestnut. But, bless my soul, what does all this mean?
[*Girls a bit confused and hesitate. Then Widow blurts out*]

WID. [*R.C.*] Girls, we may as well throw aside all attempt at concealment.

STRONG. [*Looks at her*] Throw aside all attempt at concealment? Excuse
me! [*Rushes upstage. Norman and Isabel stop him; then all downstage as
before*]

WID. [*Business*] Mr. Strong, I might as well tell you my story. Instead of
going to Chinatown, we've been to the ball. Hence these dresses. How am I
as a harlequin?

STRONG. [*C.*] I appreciate the take-off—but—

WID. But if Uncle Ben knew of it, we'd be in an awful scrape; so we rely
on your generosity not to tell him.

STRONG. Me tell him? I'm in a worse scrape with him than you are. Say,
you've all had a narrow escape. Your uncle was in another room at The Riche!

ALL. [*Astonished*] How do you know?

STRONG. Met him. We had a fight and a foot-race. He won the foot-race
and I won the fight!

WID. Was he there looking for us?

STRONG. Not all of us. He was waiting for you, Mrs. Guyer.

WID. Waiting for me? What for?

STRONG. He somehow had the idea that you were to meet him there and
go to the ball with him.

ALL. [*Guying*] O—o—h!

RASH. [*R.*] What's all this? Now I understand his actions towards you
this morning.

WID. Absurd!

STRONG. Perhaps, but I've got his clothes on. [*Laughs*] And here's a letter
that I found in the pocket. [*Takes out letter and reads*] "My dear old boy—"

WID. [*Grabs letter and goes R.C.*] Why, that's the letter I wrote to Rashleigh!

RASH. [*Takes letter*] And the letter I didn't get! [*Looks at envelope*] Say,
was this meant for me?

WID. Why, of course.

RASH. Well that "R" looks a good deal like a "B."

WID. [*Takes letter*] Somebody has evidently changed it. [*Gives it to
Strong*]

RASH. Changed it? It does look so. And it was in Uncle Ben's clothes?
I'll bet Slavin did it and then gave it to Uncle Ben!

Wɪᴅ. That's just it. I understand now his behavior this morning. He thought that note was for him and went to The Riche to meet me! [*All laugh*]

Sᴛʀᴏɴɢ. Yes, and he'll be out here to meet you—[*Pause*] as soon as he gets some clothes. [*Laughs*]

Rᴀsʜ. [*Serious again*] Then we'll be caught after all.

Tᴏɴʏ. [*L.C. Serious*] Let's start for home, quick! [*All rush up to R.3.E.*]

Wɪᴅ. [*Turns to them*] Stop! Do nothing of the sort! Stay here and—

Aʟʟ. [*Turn to her*] Get caught?

Wɪᴅ. [*C.*] No! Catch him! [*All laugh*] We'll have it the talk of the town. [*Enter Landlord, R.2.E.*]

Lᴀɴᴅ. [*At door*] Breakfast is served.

Aʟʟ. Come on! [*Exit all but Strong, R.2.E., laughing*]

Sᴛʀᴏɴɢ. [*Looks at letter*] I wonder if she did mean that letter for Rashleigh or for Ben. That does look like a "B." Well, if she did mean it for old Ben, she's going to make him bear the consequences to save herself. She's going to disgrace that old man before his family. And these are the creatures we love and trust. [*Goes upstage to R.3.E. Looks at sign over door—"To the Aquarium." Then looks across stage to L.3.E. Sees sign over door—"To the Bar." Rushes off L.3.E.*]

Rᴀsʜ. [*Off. R.2.E.*] We must find Strong! [*Flirt screams outside L.3.E. Then she runs on to R.3., meets Norman, who enters L.3.E. She screams again, runs around back of screen to L.3.E. with Norman after her. Meets Strong entering L.3.E. She screams and runs to door R.2., with both Norman and Strong after her. Rashleigh enters from door R.2. Flirt screams and runs around screen, men after her, to door R.2. Enter Willie, R.2.E. He catches her. All grab her and take her downstage to C. Rashleigh, R.C.; Willie, R.; Norman, L.C.; Strong, L. The men form group around her*]

Aʟʟ. Our little kicker! [*The men all hold hats as high as they can. Flirt looks at the hats. She shakes her head*]

Rᴀsʜ. [*Suddenly*] I forgot to tell you. She can't talk! She's dumb! [*All lower hats. Widow sneaks on R., and goes behind screen*]

Nᴏʀᴍ. [*L.C.*] Too bad, isn't it? Won't you just try to speak? [*She shakes her head. Widow advances*]

Wɪʟʟ. [*R.*] And won't you sing and dance? [*She shakes her head*]

Nᴏʀᴍ. You won't open your mouth? [*She negatives*] And such a pretty mouth, too.

Sᴛʀᴏɴɢ. I know why she won't open her mouth. She's got no teeth.

Fʟɪʀᴛ. [*Angry*] It's nothing of the sort! [*Then sorry she spoke*]

Sᴛʀᴏɴɢ. [*Goes to L. corner*] I knew I'd make her speak.

Rᴀsʜ. That voice! I've heard it!

NORM. So have I!

WID. [*Advances to C. quickly*] So have I. I know who your charmer is—my maid, Flirt! [*Snatches off Flirt's mask. Flirt, R.C.*]

STRONG. Great Scott! [*Men astonished*]

WID. [*C.*] So, young lady, you are the high kicker who has captured all our beaux away from us. Who taught you to go to masquerade balls on the quiet?

FLIRT. [*Demurely curtsies*] My mistress.

FOUR MEN. Good!

WID. Then I forgive you. On the whole, I'm glad you're here. I want you to retie my shoes. Go in that room. [*Exit Flirt, R.2.E. Widow crosses to R., laughing*] Gentlemen, I congratulate you on your conquest of my maid. [*Exit Widow, R.2.E., laughing*]

STRONG. [*Crosses to C., laughing*] Gentlemen, we are in the same fix as the vigilance committee who hanged the wrong man by mistake.

ALL. How's that?

STRONG. The laugh's on us. Well, this is my first night in San Francisco, but it's a great one. [*Business*] It reminds me of the first night I struck New York.

RASH. What happened?

STRONG. I may say I have embalmed these facts in a little song.

ALL. Let's hear it.

STRONG. [*Sings. "The Bowery"*]

> Oh! the night that I struck New York,
> I went out for a quiet walk;
> Folks who are "on to" the city say,
> Better by far that I took Broadway;
> But I was out to enjoy the sights,
> There was the Bowery ablaze with lights;
> I had one of the devil's own nights!
> I'll never go there any more!

CHORUS

> The Bow'ry, the Bow'ry!
> They say such things and they do strange things
> On the Bow'ry! The Bow'ry!
> I'll never go there any more!

> 1 had walked but a block or two,
> When up came a fellow and me he knew;

Then a policeman came walking by,
Chased him away, and I asked him, "Why?"
"Wasn't he pulling your leg?" said he;
Said I, "He never laid hands on me!"
"Get off the Bow'ry, you yap!" said he;
I'll never go there any more!

I went into an auction store,
I never saw any thieves before;
First he sold me a pair of socks,
Then, said he, "How much for the box?"
Someone said, "Two dollars!" I said, "Three!"
He emptied the box and gave it to me;
"I sold you the box, not the socks," said he.
I'll never go there any more!

I went into a concert hall,
I didn't have a good time at all;
Just the minute that I sat down
Girls began singing, "New Coon in Town."
I got up mad and spoke out free,
"Somebody put that man out!" said she.
A man called a bouncer attended to me.
I'll never go there any more!

I went into a barber shop,
He talked till I thought he would never stop;
I said, "Cut it short." He misunderstood,
Clipped down my hair as close as he could;
He shaved with a razor that scratched like a pin,
Took off my whiskers and most of my chin;
That was the worst scrape I ever got in.
I'll never go there any more!

I struck a place that they called a "dive,"
I was in luck to get out alive;
When the policeman heard my woes,
Saw my black eyes and my battered nose,

"You've been held up!" said the "copper" fly!
"No, sir! But I've been knocked down!" said I.
Then he laughed, but I couldn't see why!
I'll never go there any more!

The Bow'ry, the Bow'ry!
They say such things, and they do strange things
On the Bow'ry! The Bow'ry!
I'll never go there any more! [*After the song, exit à la militaire, L.3.E. Widow enters R.2.E.*]

WID. They are taking Mr. Strong down to the bar. I don't understand it. They can't want to put him to sleep and leave him there. Well, there's no danger of their doing it, even if they try. [*Exit R.2.E. Enter Strong, L.3.E.*]

STRONG. [*Advances to C.*] Something's the matter. I don't feel like taking a drink. [*Goes to steamer chair, R.*] Must be at the point of death. In the excitement of this night I have forgotten that I am a sick man. Somehow, I always do forget it the moment my attention is called away from it. I don't know how much I have shortened my life. I only know I feel a draught. [*Picks up fur rug. Landlord crosses from R.3.E. to L.3.E. with a tray of beer*] What's that?

LAND. Draught beer.

STRONG. [*Slips into steamer chair*] Take it away! Take it away! [*Lies down, covering head with fur robe. Flirt enters R.2.E., and seeing men have gone, goes to steamer chair*]

FLIRT. If those four men will let me alone, I'll sit out here and watch for Mr. Gay. [*Sits down on Strong, who grabs her. She screams and runs off L.U.E. Strong sits up, looks around, puts thermometer at the back of his neck*]

STRONG. Well, this is simply devilish. [*Lies down again, covering face. Flirt on L.U.E., sneaks over to the chair and looks under the robe. Then hits Strong in the face hard. Jumps back. As Strong jumps up, she laughs*]

FLIRT. Oh, pardon, are you ill, monsieur?

STRONG. [*On chair*] My head! I must have eaten something that disagreed with me.

FLIRT. I cure madame's headaches with my hands. Perhaps I can cure yours.

STRONG. Try it. [*Flirt goes to back of Strong and begins to chafe his temples*] That's the idea. That's just what I want. [*Widow enters R.2.E., and crosses to C. upstage*]

FLIRT. My mistress taught me this.

STRONG. Your mistress is a very fine woman.

WID. [*Advances. She motions to Flirt to leave and resumes rubbing Strong's temples. Flirt exits R.2.E. Widow stands back of Strong and imitates Flirt's voice*] You think my mistress charming?

STRONG. You bet. [*Widow rubs harder*]

WID. You enjoy her society very much?

STRONG. More than any lady I ever met.

WID. You could devote yourself to her?

STRONG. With all my heart.

WID. And some day you might marry her?

STRONG. After last night? Not for gold and precious stones!

WID. [*Slaps his face, goes C. Strong springs up, sees who it is, turns and walks off R.U.E.*] That's what a woman gets for being a good fellow. It's all right for the time being, but they've no use for you afterwards. [*She sits on steamer chair and cries*]

STRONG. [*Reenters R.U.E. Sees her. Aside*] She's crying. I do believe she's in love with me. I don't see any reason why she shouldn't be. And if I thought —[*Aloud*] My dear Mrs. Guyer—why those tears?

WID. You cruel man! You've broken my heart!

STRONG. [*Sincere*] Say not so! Say not so!

WID. Am I so very bad?

STRONG. Why, I never hinted at such a thing.

WID. [*Crosses to Strong*] You said you wouldn't marry me for gold or precious stones.

STRONG. [*C.*] But I didn't say I wouldn't marry you for your own sweet self.

WID. [*R.C.*] Mr. Strong, is this airy persiflage, or do you mean business?

STRONG. [*Takes out thermometer. Business of taking his temperature*] It may shorten my life, but it's—

WID. What?

STRONG. Business. [*He kisses her*] This is business, isn't it?

TONY. [*Off R.*] Daisy! Daisy Guyer! Come to breakfast. [*Strong crosses to steamer chair*]

WID. [*C.*] Yes. [*To Strong*] That reminds me! I've got to get them out of their scrape, and old Mr. Gay may be here any moment! [*Calls*] Landlord! Landlord! [*Enter Landlord, L.3.E.*] Have you another private dining room?

LAND. [*Points L.2.E.*] Right here.

WID. [*C.*] It's mine. And I want you to prepare breakfast for two. And I want it served here on the piazza. And when the gentleman arrives, show him in there.

LAND. [*L.*] Yes'm. What name will he give?

WID. Perhaps not any. But he's a nice-looking old gentleman with grey side-whiskers.

LAND. How will he be dressed? [*Strong slips into steamer chair*]

WID. [*Looks at Strong's clothing*] Good heavens! [*Turns back to audience. Strong puts end of robe to his face*] I hadn't thought of that. If he isn't properly dressed, don't let him in. [*Exit Landlord, L.3.E. To Strong*] Now, I'll go and await the coming of Mr. Gay. And you must keep out of the way till it's all over. See? [*Exits L.2.E.*]

STRONG. [*Gets up and crosses to the ice crusher L.*] Engaged to me and going to breakfast with Ben Gay! And I'm to keep out of the way till it's all over. [*Leans against ice-box. Looks into the door*] I don't like it. [*Puts thermometer to back of his neck*] The thought chills me. [*Sees that he is leaning on the ice-box*] No, it's this ice-box. By jove, I've an idea. I'll hide in here and keep tabs on that breakfast. I have some little confidence in her but none in him. [*Gets into crusher. Three boys enter L.U.E.*]

NORM. What became of Strong? [*As they cross to R.*]

RASH. He's probably at breakfast. Come on. [*Exit R.2.E.*]

BEN. [*Enters R.U.E., running*] Landlord! Landlord! How am I to find her? Where's the landlord? [*Exits L.U.E.*]

SLA. [*Enters R.U.E., running*] Mr. Gay! Mr. Gay! Oh, where did he go? I knew when that boy came to the house for his clothes that something was wrong. Oh, what shall I do? [*Turns to go off L.3.E. Landlord enters L.U.E. and sees Slavin. Ben crosses behind screen from L.3.E. to R.3.*]

LAND. [*Looks at Slavin*] Grey side-whiskers. Peculiar dress. That's the man! [*Aloud to Slavin*] Are you looking for somebody?

SLA. [*R.C.*] Oh, yes, sir.

LAND. [*C.*] I know who it is. You just step in this room and you'll find the party.

SLA. Oh, thank you, sir. [*Crosses C. in front of Landlord and exits L.2.E. Widow screams from room L.*]

LAND. [*Goes upstage*] And he's seventy if he's a day! [*Exits R.U.E. Strong looks out of ice crusher*]

STRONG. I wish I could see into that room.

LAND. [*Outside R.3.E.*] A lady in black? [*Strong closes crusher. Enter Landlord and Ben, R.U.E., Landlord on first*] The lady you describe is here, but she is taking breakfast with another man.

BEN. [*C.*] Another man! Well, this takes the cake. Heavens, how fast she catches them! I know. It's the fellow who got her card by mistake at The Riche. I wonder if it's Strong. By thunder, I won't stand it! You go and tell that man I want to see him.

LAND. I hope there'll be no trouble.

BEN. No, no. Call him out.

LAND. [*L.C.*] Would you like to look at the evening paper, sir? [*Ben looks at Landlord and then takes paper. Exit Landlord, L.2.E. Ben throws the paper on the floor in disgust*]

BEN. I want to know who the fellow is that cut me out so easily. [*Crosses to R. Enter two Waiters, R.3.E. The first with two bottles, the second with tray, etc. They exit, L.2.E. Ben looks on in astonishment*] Two bottles of wine with the oysters. He's a money spender, anyhow. I wonder who this dude can be. [*Enter Slavin, L.2.E. He coughs. Ben turns and recognizes him.* PICTURE] Merciful heaven! What, you the dandy masher? You the prodigal son giving wine suppers at The Riche and breakfast to swell women! It can't be! It's preposterous! It's a joke or a nightmare! I'm crazy! That's it!

SLA. [*Advances to C.*] You are, sir. That's it. [*Widow looks out from window, L.3.E.*] Oh, Mr. Gay, forgive me, but you've been such a good friend to me for twenty years, I couldn't help it.

BEN. Help what?

SLA. Following you, sir. When you sent a messenger boy home at two in the morning for those clothes you've got on, I knew something was wrong. So I followed the boy to The Riche, and when you took a cab, I got on the seat with the driver. I remembered how many of our rich men have committed suicide. "If Mr. Gay tries it," I said, "I'll be there to save him!"

BEN. Is that what you came here for?

SLA. Yes, sir.

BEN. You dear, devoted, damned old fool! I'm not going to commit suicide. [*Goes toward him. Slavin crosses back of Ben to R.*] Go back to town. I don't want you here. [*Ben crosses to L.*]

SLA. [*R.C.*] That's what folks bent on suicide always say. I know my duty, sir.

BEN. [*L.C. Aside*] Great Scott! What am I to do? He mustn't know what I'm here for. [*Aloud*] See here. This has gone far enough. You go back to town or I'll discharge you!

SLA. Discharge me, sir, if you will, but while you're crazy, I'll stick to you!

BEN. While you stick to me, I'll be crazy! Slavin, what would you think if I told you the truth?

SLA. I'd know you were crazy, sir.

BEN. There is a lady in that room.

SLA. Yes, sir. Mrs. Guyer.

BEN. I'm out here to take breakfast with her.

SLA. You, Mr. Gay? And you're not crazy?

BEN. Crazy! No! You understand. One must have his little flirtations. [*Strong raises lid of ice crusher*]

SLA. You're just like me, sir. No fool like an old fool.

BEN. Now, if Strong isn't here, he will be soon. He mustn't see me, or her. Now, I'll forgive you for your cussed nonsense on one condition. Keep watch! If he comes around, drive him away.

SLA. How will I do it?

BEN. Threaten to shoot him with this. [*Takes revolver from his pocket. Strong slams down the lid. Slavin and Ben start suddenly*] Take this and keep your eyes open.

SLA. [*Goes up R.*] Will I shoot him?

BEN. No. Don't shoot him. Just make believe.

SLA. All right, sir. I'll make believe to shoot him, and maybe I will shoot him. [*Exits R.U.E.*]

BEN. [*Crosses to door, L.2.E.*] At last! [*Raps at door*]

WID. [*Off L.*] Come in. [*Exit Ben, L.2.E. Enter young folks, R.2.E. Rashleigh first, others following quickly*]

RASH. I saw him go in there. She said we were to hide behind this screen. [*All go behind screen. Sound of kissing heard off L.2.E.*]

WID. [*Outside L.2.E.*] Why, Mr. Gay!

BEN. [*Outside*] Now, Mrs. Guyer. [*Widow runs out of L.2.E. followed by Ben. Both go up front of screen C.*] My dear Mrs. Guyer!

WID. Mr. Gay, I'm astonished that you would do such a thing.

BEN. Didn't you ever hear of a gentleman's stealing a kiss?

WID. Not before the fish was served.

BEN. Now, don't be offended.

WID. Then swear you won't do it again.

BEN. Must I do that?

WID. Yes, or I'll go home this minute. Kneel! [*All look over screen at once. Rashleigh at L. and Norman at R. end. Ben kneels*] Now, look up! [*Ben looks up and sees the young folks laughing at him. He falls flat*]

ALL. Why, Uncle Ben! [*All come from behind screen and come down L. and R.*]

BEN. [*On knees again*] Mrs. Guyer, I can't tie that shoe. [*All laugh. Looks around and gets up*] Great Scott! My whole family! [*Down C.*] What does this mean? Why aren't you in Chinatown?

TONY. [*L.C.*] Because we're here. [*Crosses R.*]

BEN. [*L.C.*] I see you're here. I gave you permission to go to Chinatown and I catch you all at the Cliff House. [*Goes to L.*]

WID. You catch us? Pardon me, we catch you! [*Aside to others. Turns to Ben*] Mr. Gay, I may as well tell you the joke. I have won a bet. I wagered Tony a breakfast that any halfway pretty woman could get you out on a racket. Then I wrote you to meet me at The Riche. [*Aside*] Heaven forgive the story! [*Aloud*] Haven't you been at The Riche and all over town after me? [*All laugh*]

ALL. Own up! Etc. [*Ad lib*]

BEN. [*Goes to L.C.*] To win a breakfast, you've led me on to make a fool of myself before my whole family. This was a mean trick to play on an old man!

WID. [*C.*] Old men shouldn't run after young girls. [*Enter Landlord and Waiter, L.U.E.*]

BEN. Everybody likes a good time once in a while. [*All laugh*]

WID. That's just it. Hereafter, when the young folks want a little fun, don't oppose it.

BEN. No. I'll declare myself in on it. [*All hurrah*] And we'll begin right now. Landlord, some champagne! [*All hurrah and laugh*]

LAND. [*To Waiter*] You get the champagne and I'll crush the ice. [*Turns handles of the ice crusher. Exit Waiter, L.U.E. Strong torn up, comes out of the ice crusher. Girls scream. Then they laugh when they recognize Strong who goes down C. quick*]

BEN. It's Strong! Revenge! Revenge! Strong, you're a sight!

STRONG. [*C.*] I don't care! They're your clothes! [*Enter Slavin, R.3.E., pointing revolver at Strong. Ben rushes up and stops him. Girls all scream. Ben then down R. Landlord, Slavin, and Waiter upstage*]

RASH. [*L.*] Well, what's to be done?

WID. [*C.*] Have a bird and a bottle and go home! [CHORUS: "*Out For A Racket.*" *Ben and Strong dancing. Isabel, R.; Flirt, R.; Tony, L.; Willie, R.*]

CURTAIN

ACT III.

SCENE: *Private gymnasium in the house of Ben Gay.*
DISCOVERED: *Tony and Flirt in wrappers.*

FLIRT. I think we're the first ones up. And I had a good mind not to get up at all!

Tony. This settles the "out for a racket" business for me, Flirt. Do you realize that we're in an awful scrape? Of course uncle can't do anything worse to you than tell your father.

Flirt. That's so. He couldn't do anything worse. I'd rather he'd whip me. I guess it does settle the "out for a racket" business. Oh, Tony, isn't there anything to keep him from telling? I'll get killed.

Tony. I don't know of any. We'll all have to suffer except the widow. And she's the only one who had any fun. The way the men devoted themselves to her ruined my evening. Flirt, I've made up my mind. I'm going to be a widow!

Flirt. Oh, Tony! But you've got to be a wife first, and your husband may live forever.

Tony. No, he won't! I shall marry Mr. Strong! Heaven has sent him here, I feel, to my relief. [*Enter Wilder and Rashleigh*]

Flirt. Oh, Wilder, did you send word home that we were here?

Wild. I did. And, say, it's lucky we didn't go to the ball. It was closed by the police.

Rash. And Painter was arrested! That's why he didn't come to The Riche. [*Enter Widow*]

Wid. Good morning, everybody!

All. Good morning.

Tony. To what are we indebted for this early call?

Wid. I've come over, first, to have a little practice with the foils. [*Throws off cloak, disclosing fencing costume*] Second, to get you out of the scrape.

Flirt. Oh, can you?

Wid. Well, you know me! What do you think?

Wild. We'll bet on you every time.

Wid. Last night after I reached home, I began to think that you were in a fix. "They've got to tell some story to get out of it," said I. "And they're not good at telling stories," said I. "They may lay the blame on me," said I. "Then my reputation will be in the laundry, and a widow has to be careful of her reputation. I must go over there and tell a story that will get us all out of it," said I. And here I am!

Tony. One word for us, and two for yourself! You're very good!

Wid. Now, am I in time?

Rash. I think so. Neither uncle nor Mr. Strong are up yet.

Wild. That Strong's a thoroughbred, after all.

Wid. A delightful man! It's a pity he's got to die so soon!

Tony. Nothing of the sort! I—I mean—perhaps he hasn't. [*Aside*] But I'm sure he has!

FLIRT. Well, say, what story are we to tell uncle?

WID. I don't know yet. But there's a way out of this scrape, and I know how to find it. I've only got one favor to ask. Don't mix in and spoil things. How soon will they be up?

RASH. Nobody knows.

WID. I've got to be at my dressmaker's in an hour. Can't you call them?

TONY. Not for worlds!

WID. Then we must make a racket so they'll have to get up! Where are their rooms?

TONY. [*Points R. and L.*] There and there! Come, Flirt, let's get our gymnasium suits on. [*Exit two girls*]

WID. We may as well start the racket! Come on! [*Medley, during which the two girls return in gymnasium suits. At finish, all exit. Enter Strong from R., Ben from L. They look like wrecks. Neither knows what to say. Strong has a bowl of ice and offers some to Ben*]

STRONG. Have a piece?

BEN. [*Takes ice*] Thanks! Don't you think a little absinthe would do us good? [*Rings*]

STRONG. It can't shorten my life much! [*Noah[1] heard singing below. Comes up stairs still singing "Out For A Racket"*]

NOAH. [*Pretty drunk*] Here I am!

BEN. Noah! Sirrah! What does this mean?

NOAH. I've been right with you. Drunk as a boiled owl! I knew everybody else was on a toot, so I filled up! Three very pretty jags we three gentlemen had! [*Exits*]

STRONG. What a beastly fellow!

BEN. This is strictly between us! My catching you was an accident. I went to The Riche to have supper with a lady.

STRONG. You old rascal!

BEN. But if my family knew that, I'd lose their respect forever.

STRONG. Why, you didn't do anything wrong, did you?

BEN. No, damn it! The widow didn't—

STRONG. The widow didn't what?

BEN. Why—er—that's—that's something you didn't understand. What I was going to say is this: That loan of a hundred dollars squares you, but in order to save my own reputation I must make these youngsters believe that I followed them there, and I must punish them accordingly. It's rough on them, but—

[1] In this second version of Act III, that was found in the New York Public Library, the servant is called "Noah" throughout. Obviously he should be "Slavin."

STRONG. Don't make it too rough. Remember we used to enjoy a little racket in the days gone by when we were their age.

BEN. By thunder, we did! [*Duet, "Days Gone By," Strong and Ben. Enter Noah with three drinks*]

NOAH. Here we are, brother sufferers.

BEN. [*Takes drink*] If you don't stop your impudence, I'll discharge you! [*Ben and Strong drink*]

NOAH. That's what I want! I'm drunk and I'm glad of it! I'm a whale!

STRONG. A whale? No!

NOAH. This is the first time in forty years I've dared to open my head and now I'm going to let 'er go. I'm looking to get kicked out of the house!

BEN. You shall be! [*Exits downstairs, kicking Noah*]

STRONG. He'll just give it to those children to prove his own probity. I think I'll take to bed till the affair's over. [*Enter Tony*]

TONY. [*In gymnasium dress*] Oh, there he is! Oh, if I can get him to marry me! Black is so becoming to me. Ahem! Good morning! Mr. Strong, how do you feel this morning?

STRONG. I think I shall live until dinner time.

TONY. Oh, I hope so. We should miss your cheery "Yes, thanks," when the wine is served. Oh, Mr. Strong, do you know, everything about you interests me? Have you got a wife?

STRONG. A wife? No.

TONY. Then you're a jolly bachelor!

STRONG. No! Not a bachelor!

TONY. Not a bachelor! Oh, forgive me if I've touched a tender spot in your heart. You are a widower!

STRONG. No, not a widower!

TONY. Excuse me, Mr. Strong, you say you're not a single man?

STRONG. I am not.

TONY. Nor a married man nor a widower! Will you kindly tell me what you are?

STRONG. Well, if you must know, I'm a divorced man!

TONY. A divorced man! How romantic!

STRONG. Yes, and very expensive.

TONY. And when are you going to—try it again?

STRONG. Never!

TONY. Never? Oh, don't say that!

STRONG. Why, I'm a dying man!

Tony. That's it! With such a glorious opportunity to make a woman a widow, you have no right to remain single a minute. You ought to marry the first woman you can lay your hands on!

Strong. [*Puts his hands behind him and shies away*] But I don't want a wife!

Tony. You do! To wear mourning for you! Now, you must—

Strong. But the divorce forbade me to marry. It would be contempt of court.

Tony. Then contempt the court! Positively despise it!

Strong. And go to prison? Say, it's time to take my medicine! Excuse me! [*Exits L.*]

Tony. Well, I declare! [*Enter Wilder*]

Wild. Sweetheart, I want to—

Tony. Oh, go away!

Wild. What?

Tony. Go away! You weary me!

Wild. Weary you? Why, I thought you loved me!

Tony. I do, but you won't do! You're not going to die in two years!

Wild. I hope not!

Tony. Then that lets you out. You're not in it. So don't bother me! [*Rushes out*]

Wild. Well, I declare! [*Terrible crash below. Enter three ladies*]

Three Ladies. [*Ad lib*] What's that? Etc. [*Noah enters, coming upstairs, singing. Girls much alarmed*]

Noah. [*Has parrot and cat. To Wilder*] You're wanted below. [*Throws Wilder downstairs*] That's two! [*Girls scream*] I'm going to do 'em all! I've been discharged, and before I go I'm going to lick every man in the house! Then I'll kiss all the women! [*Women scream and exit; Widow into Ben's room*] I'm a whale! Where's that dying man? He's my pie! I'll make him eat his own game! [*Exiting*] I'll give you your medicine! [*Tremendous crash, R. Enter Tony, Flirt, and Rashleigh*]

Rash. What is it?

Flirt. Noah is in there killing Mr. Strong!

Tony. Go save him! [*Crash R.*]

Rash. Give me something to hit him with! [*Grabs Indian club*] That's too heavy! [*Drops it. Crash R.*]

Tony. [*Hands him the same club*] Here, try this!

Rash. That's too light! [*Crash R.*] Where's my ball bat?

Flirt. Locked up in the locker! The key's downstairs.

RASH. Go get it! [*Exit Flirt, downstairs. Tremendous crash R.*] Oh, wait till I get something to hit him with! [*Crash*]

TONY. Oh, he'll be killed! Take the Indian club!

RASH. No, I can't! I must have the bat! [*Crash*]

TONY. Oh, Rashleigh, save him! He'll surely be killed!

RASH. Then I'll avenge him! [*Enter Widow, L.*]

WID. What's the matter?

TONY. Noah is killing Mr. Strong! [*Grand crash. Widow and girls yell. Enter Strong, throwing Noah out, who is all torn up; handful of parrot feathers*]

STRONG. I have shortened my life one year!

NOAH. You've shortened mine fifty! I'll never be able to digest that parrot!

ALL. The parrot!

NOAH. He made me swallow it! [*All laugh*] That's right! And damn it! How I hate feathers! [*Spits some out*] Ladies and gentlemen, is there anything I can do for you?

ALL. Yes! Get out! [*Exit Noah*]

WID. Mr. Strong, you are a brave man!

STRONG. I know it!

WID. Hadn't somebody better go and see if the others are hurt?

STRONG. With pleasure! [*Exits C.*]

WID. Tell me, whose room was that I ran into?

TONY. Why, Uncle Ben's.

WID. [*Bursts out laughing*] I see it all. You're out of your scrape! Oh, this is funny! [*Laughs. Enter Wilder, C.*]

ALL. What *is* it?

WID. Only a letter I saw lying on his desk! [*Laughs*] But I shan't tell you a word more, only back me up in all I say to him, and I'll get you out of your scrape. But, listen, we must all seem very merry and when he comes in, all laugh at the good joke on him.

FLIRT. But what is the joke?

WID. You'll see! Come on. Start a chorus or something. What, must I start it? Very well! [*Specialty, Widow and quartette. Enter Strong, C.*]

STRONG. The servant has apologized to everyone but me. He says he hasn't done anything to me, and I agree. By the way, your uncle's coming. [*Enter Ben, C. All laugh at him*]

BEN. Oh, that's the way you feel, is it? I suppose you consider this affair of last night a laughing matter?

WID. Decidedly! With the laugh on you!

ALL. With the laugh on you!

BEN. On me? We'll see about that!

WID. Gently, now. Mr. Gay, we want you to settle a bet.

BEN. I never settle bets.

STRONG. How about loans? I have the check here as evidence.

WID. [*Grabs check*] Just what I wanted. Now, Mr. Gay, listen! Your niece here, poor innocent Tony, was telling us what a good man you were, and I laughed at her.

BEN. Very nice of you!

WID. I offered to bet her a supper at the Cliff House that if any decent-looking woman asked you to take her to the masquerade, you'd do it.

BEN. [*Aside*] I've been buncoed!

WID. She took the bet, and so I wrote this note which I have just picked up in your room—[*Shows note*] for you to meet me at The Riche. Then we all went to The Riche to see if you were there. And you were!

WILD. [*To Tony*] What a corking lie! She's a wonder!

TONY. Oh, uncle, I never thought it of you! [*Widow whispers to Tony, who exits L.*]

FLIRT. What will my father say when I tell him?

BEN. [*Yells*] Hold on! I—I—Why, that letter made me think that you had all gone to The Riche; so I went there to catch you, and I did! Ha! Ha!

WID. How did you happen to run up such a big bill? [*Looks at check*] What is this item for supper ordered for self and lady? [*All laugh. Enter Tony with masks*]

TONY. And what did you want of these two masks?

BEN. Why, I—you understand?

WID. Mr. Gay, don't you think I've won that bet?

BEN. Oh—I—don't think anything about it! Don't one of you dare to mention this affair again as long as you live! [*To Flirt*] Especially to your father!

WID. But about that supper at the Cliff House?

BEN. Oh, I'll pay for that and we'll all have a good time together. Eh, Strong?

STRONG. It will shorten my life a year, but I'm with you!

CHORUS—*"Out For A Racket"*

FINALE

CURTAIN

THE GREAT DIAMOND ROBBERY

By Colonel Edward M. Alfriend and A. C. Wheeler

CHARACTERS

DICK BRUMMAGE

FRANK KENNET

MR. CLINTON BULFORD

GRANDFATHER LAVELOT

MARIO MARINO

DR. LIVINGSTONE

SENATOR MCSORKER

THE COUNT GARBIADOFF

SHEENEY IKE

JIMMY MCCUNE

PHILIP

JACK CLANCY

MICKEY BRANNIGAN

POLICEMAN

MRS. MARY BULFORD

MARY LAVELOT

MOTHER ROSENBAUM (FRAU)

MRS. O'GEOGAN

PEGGY DALY

MME. MERVAINE

INCIDENTALS: HEELERS, CLUBMAN, SALVATION ARMY LASS, MESSENGER BOY, BAR-KEEPERS, WAITERS, STREET GAMIN, BLIND MUSICIAN, GUESTS.

ACT I.

SCENE: *Small cosy breakfast or supper room in Mr. Bulford's house on Lexington Avenue in New York set in 2. It is tastefully furnished with grate fire burning, and an easy chair and table in front of it. Room lit by gas or lamps, but not glaringly. There is a sofa R. with buffet in corner C. It is furnished with glass, silver, decanters, etc. There is an entrance R.2.E., another L. in back flat. Bitter storm outside—howling of wind heard with banging of shutter. See fire lighted and red medium for rise.* TIME: *Nine o'clock at night, late winter or early spring.* DISCOVERED: *Mrs. Bulford at half open door L. in flat. She is listening intently at door and is nervous. At the expiration of half a minute, she goes to a little table and strikes bell. Crosses R.C. and to R., then listens. Enter Philip L.*

MRS. B.   Philip, that shutter in the parlor is banging.

PHIL. [*L.C.*]   Yes'm. [*Is about to go*]

MRS. B.   Where is my brother, Marino.

PHIL.   In his room, ma'am. I smelt his cigar in the hall.

MRS. B.   Tell him to come here.

PHIL.   Yes'm. [*Is about to go*]

MRS. B.   What have you in your hand?

PHIL.   It's a letter, ma'am. It came by messenger a few minutes ago. It's for Mr. Bulford. I couldn't give it to him because he's got parties in the reception room. [*Puts letter on table*]

MRS. B.   Did you see the people in the reception room?

PHIL.   Yes'm. I let 'em in.

MRS. B.   What did they look like?

PHIL.   Like foreigners! [*Mrs. Bulford starts*]

MRS. B.   Did they bring anything?

PHIL.   Yes'm. One of them had a hand bag.

MRS. B.   Go and fasten that shutter and tell my brother to come here.

PHIL.   Yes'm. [*Exit leaving door ajar. Mrs. Bulford stands a minute in perplexed attitude looking at letter, then places it on table and going to buffet, takes a drink of water and composes her face in the glass. Enter Marino, ..., with book in hand*]

MAR.   Hello, dear!

MRS. B.   Are you going to the club tonight? [*Crosses to L.*]

MAR. [*Yawning*]   Heaven forbid! It is almost as dull there as it is here. I was reading Daudet and smoking.

MRS. B. [*Shutting the door*]   Did you see the men who are with Mr. Bulford in the reception room?

MAR.   See them? No, I didn't know there were men there. [*Crosses to sofa*]

MRS. B. [*Relieved*]   I was going to ask you to go out in the storm and execute a commission for me. You will object, of course?

MAR. [*Sitting on sofa R.*]   Santa Maria, my charming sister, why do you insist on making me uncomfortable?

MRS. B. [*Petulantly*]   You would be comfortable on the edge of Hades. As for me I wish we were in Rio tonight. Think of it! They are celebrating the feast of St. Catherine with flowers. [*Lights cigarette at buffet C., then crosses to fire L.*]

MAR.   Aye—and the streets are filled with black eyed señoritas, who have tropical faces all the year around. I detest this northern climate. But you, who have spent a winter in St. Petersburg, ought to be comfortable in New York.

MRS. B. [*Facing him*]   I should be more comfortable in New York if I had never been to St. Petersburg. I made the mistake of my life there.

MAR.   I only know of one.

MRS. B.   What's that?

MAR.   You got married. [*Rises, crosses to C. up to buffet*] Most adorable of sisters, you did not send for me to tell me this.

MRS. B. [*Sits by fire*]   Why not? I have been telling it to you for months. You think because I wear a calm face I am comfortable. My heart is like a volcano covered with snow, but wearing a core of fire! I can play at respectability, but the play must not be too long or too tedious.

MAR.   Well, if I were going to play the respectable thing, I'd get rid of that senator you keep hanging about. It makes me feel sorry for your generous old husband.

MRS. B.   Senator McSorker is the most powerful and influential politician in New York.

MAR. [*R. of table, L.*]   And one of the most disreputable, I fancy.

MRS. B.   Nobody is disreputable in New York, unless they are unsuccessful.

MAR.   Oh, but he dresses so damnably and smokes such rank cigars.

MRS. B. [*Seated at fire L.*]   Bah—you are a child. I shall never make a man of you. In Europe we have to fight brains, finesse and diplomacy to get on [*Rises, crosses to L.C.*] Here the canaille are the supreme rulers and we ought to be princes among them. Instead of going to St. Petersburg and marrying a respectable old gentleman because he was attached to the American Legation there, and who keeps you in cigarettes and pays your club bill to please me, we should have come direct to New York; for here every politician is a gold mine and every clever woman can defy the law. [*Crosses C. at back of sofa*]

MAR. By Heavens, if you were single, I believe you would marry that senator.

MRS. B. No. But I should like to have the chance for six months to make him think I would. [*Leans over back of sofa*]

MAR. Well, you have been scheming for six months. I hope you will not do anything to disturb our respectability and comfort. For my part, I rather like this sort of thing. [*Wind. Enter Mr. Bulford door L., evening paper sticking out of his pocket—jewel-case under his arm; looks at the pair on the sofa, shivers and places jewel-case on the table*]

MR. B. Boo-oo. I am chilled through. That reception room is like a vault. [*Wind*] Listen to that wind! Now, this is cosy. [*Warms his hands at grate fire L.*]

MRS. B. Your visitors must have had business of great importance to bring them out on such a night.

MR. B. Importance? Yes, I should say it was. It's the most extraordinary thing I ever heard of.

MAR. [*Seated on sofa; eagerly*] Why, what is it pray?

MR. B. [*Back to fire*] Do you remember the robbery of the Garbiadoff diamonds in Europe? It took place just before we left there, a year and a half ago. It was all in the papers, but I did not pay much attention to it, although I knew Garbiadoff well. We are friends in fact.

MAR. I remember it very well. They were stolen in Cracow by—

MR. B. [*Stands back to fire L.*] By the cleverest thief in Europe. They were said to be worth fifty thousand pounds. [*Mrs. Bulford C., standing*]

MAR. Fifty thousand pounds?

MR. B. The thief, who is known as Don Plon, has operated in both hemispheres. He was in this country once, I understand, but incurred the deadly enmity of a powerful criminal who is a woman, for he betrayed her son to the authorities, and she swore to be revenged. He accomplished this robbery in Cracow by introducing a handsome woman in the count's house, and while the count was carrying on an amour, the diamonds disappeared with the woman. After chasing the jewels through Europe, the Russian police got upon their track in this city and succeeded in negotiating with some of the conspirators and getting the jewels back, but so afraid were those agents of Don Plon or this woman that they came to me tonight with the property and wanted me to go to the bank with them and have the jewels deposited. There they are in that case.

Mar. [*Going to table*] Why, this beats Daudet! Fifty thousand pounds! [*Sits at head of table L.*]

Mr. B. I told them I wouldn't go out tonight for all the jewels in the Russian Empire, but they assured me that it was in their interest that they should get them out of their hands into the safe keeping of a responsible party. [*Mrs. Bulford crosses and leans on back of sofa R.*]

Mar. [*Seated at head of table L., looking at the case*] But do you really mean to say they are worth fifty thousand pounds!

Mr. B. [*Sitting L. of table by fire*] Yes—that is the estimate put upon them by England. There is said to be a ruby in that case worth five thousand pounds. It was known along the upper Ganges as the "heart of fire."

Mar. [*Rises*] You are assuming a great risk by accepting the property in this way.

Mr. B. The men appeared to think they were lessening the risk by getting the property into my hands.

Mrs. B. And none know they are here, but those men?

Mar. [*Turning to Mrs. Bulford*] Don't you wish to see them, Maria?

Mrs. B. [*On sofa R.*] No. It has given me quite a sensation. I can fancy the mysterious Don Plon hanging about our house tonight when we are asleep, and, if they should disappear—

Mr. B. [*Seated L. of table, interrupting*] Oh, nonsense! Don't say anything to the servants and I'll be responsible for them until morning. I've the count's order and I will see the jewels deposited carefully.

Mar. [*Seated at head of table, taking up case*] Can't we see them?

Mr. B. [*Seated by fire*] No. It is sealed. You see, there is some difficulty in identifying the diamonds, owing to the absence of the count. Nobody but Don Plon or that woman of his could identify them and it would be a very easy matter to change them. [*Marino returns to the lounge thoughtfully, stands at back of it. Mr. Bulford turns around in his chair again. Enter servant L., hands card to Mr. Bulford, then stands by door L., L. of it*]

Mr. B. [*Looking at card*] Kennet—Kennet—Frank Kennet? What does he want to see me for? It's no use.

Mrs. B. Who is Frank Kennet?

Mr. B. It's a young man I put in the bank six months ago. He's got into some kind of trouble with his accounts. I feel sorry for him but it's no use running after me here.

Mrs. B. [*Music for Kennet's entrance until well on*] Oh, you had better see him. Perhaps he wishes to confess.

Mar. I'll be in the way, please excuse me, I'll go back to Daudet. [*Exit L.*]

Mr. B.   Well, I am not going into that cold reception room again. Tell him to come here. [*Servant bows and exits*]

Mrs. B. [*Rises*]   Perhaps I had better retire. [*Crosses a little to C.*]

Mr. B. [*Rises*]   Nonsense—sit still. Confound it—why can't young men go straight.

Mrs. B. [*R.C.*]   What is the trouble?

Mr. B.   There's something crooked. I've got to lay it before the directors. A case of bad habits and worse companions, I suppose. [*Enter servant L., stands R. of door L., showing in Frank Kennet who wears a great coat with collar turned up and carries a soft hat in his hand. Servant exits L. Kennet stops at entrance, disturbed that Mr. Bulford is not alone*]

Frank. [*Up C.*]   I expected to see you alone, sir. [*Mr. Bulford doubles his newspaper and places it carefully over jewel-case on table*]

Mr. B.   If you come into my family this way, sir, you must expect to see some of the members of it. [*Points to Mrs. Bulford*] Whatever you have to say—you can say it here [*Mrs. Bulford goes to window, looks through*] but make it short. [*Sits L. of table*]

Frank. [*Goes slowly down to Mr. Bulford*]   I came to appeal to you, sir, not to make public the charges against me until they are investigated. I am innocent.

Mr. B. [*Seated L. of table*]   Hum-ph! I hope so, but the business of the bank must be carried on regularly. I must report the matter to the directors tomorrow.

Frank. [*L.C.*]   Tomorrow? A day or two cannot injure the bank, but it may give me time to vindicate myself. There are others who will suffer from haste.

Mr. B.   Ah, there are others—of course—your associates.

Frank. [*L.C.*]   No sir—I have no associates.

Mr. B.   Come—come—this is idle talk. What do you mean?

Frank. [*L.C.*]   I am engaged to be married. I thought that perhaps that act would incline you to listen to me kindly.

Mr. B.   Oh, there's a woman at the bottom of it, is there? I thought as much.

Frank.   Pardon me, sir, you are going too far. Some women cannot stand even the rumor of dishonesty and Mary Lavelot is that kind of a woman.

Mr. B. [*Impatiently*]   Well, this is all very fine, but as a bank officer, I've got to stick to the accounts. I am responsible to the stockholders.

Frank. [*R. of table L. above it*]   I did not come here as a culprit, sir. I only ask you to satisfy yourself of the injustice of these charges before making them public. Once that bank sets in to prosecute me, I have no means to fight it and no friends. I am not thinking of myself as much as others. [*Mrs. Bulford is listening from window, R.*]

MR. B.   If you are innocent, you need not fear an official examination—in fact, there is no other way whether you are innocent or not.

FRANK.   [*At head of table L.*]   But sir, what if some of the directors, in order to save the real culprit, should desire to make me appear guilty?

MR. B.   [*Rising*]   What's that? What's that? You have a warm temper young man. It is sheer folly to accuse me of unkindness. I have done a great deal for you.

FRANK.   It is that which hurts me, for you are undoing it all now.

MRS. B.   What's the matter? Is he faint? Let me offer him a glass of wine? [*She turns to buffet C., back to audience and pours glass of wine*] We can afford to be generous as well as just on such a night.

MR. B.   Nobody ever accused me of being either ungenerous or unjust.

FRANK.   But you intend to take this action tomorrow?

MR. B.   Young man, I shall do my duty tomorrow, if I live, as I have always done. [*Mrs. Bulford hands Frank the glass of wine, R. of him*] But you needn't go away with any hard feelings to me. Maria, you can give me a glass of sherry. [*Mrs. Bulford comes to table with glass of wine in a cut sherry glass, gives wine to Mr. Bulford, looks at them a moment and goes to window R.*] Drink that young man—it will warm you. [*Frank and Bulford drink*] Let us hope matters will not be as bad as they look. [*Frank drinks the wine, places glass on table, stares at Mr. Bulford a moment, goes to door L. where he stands irresolute*] Good night! [*Goes and sits L. by fire. Frank attempts to speak, breaks down and exits. Mr. Bulford sighs, takes newspaper from table L. and resettles himself in his chair. Fifteen seconds elapse. Mrs. Bulford tries to appear unconcerned. Business ad lib*]

MRS. B.   [*Coming from window R., crosses to table L.*]   Oh, there is a letter for you—did you get it?

MR. B.   No. Where is it?

MRS. B.   [*R. of table at head of it*]   Philip placed it here on the table. Here it is. [*Gives envelope. Mr. Bulford tears it open and takes out enclosed foreign letter*]

MR. B.   Why, this is a foreign letter sent to the care of the Russian Consul here, and by him delivered to me. It must have come by messenger. [*Opens letter and looks at signature*] It is from Count Garbiadoff himself.

MRS. B.   [*R. of table—eagerly*]   Garbiadoff! [*Goes back a step or two*]

MR. B.   [*Seated next to fire*]   Yes. There is his signature—Garbiadoff. It doesn't look like the signature on the order. What did I do with that order? [*Feels in his pockets*]

Mrs. B. [*Eagerly*]   Never mind about the signature. Read the letter.

Mr. B. [*Looking at the two names*]   Yes, the letter must be genuine. There is the count's coat of arms in the corner. I remember it very well—and there's the Imperial postmark on the envelope. Do you see Maria, do you see?

Mrs. B. [*R. of table, agitatedly*]   Certainly it must be genuine. Why do you not read it?

Mr. B. [*Seated L. of table, L.*]   But if the letter is genuine, the order cannot be. It must be a forgery! Why should any one forge an order to get the jewels into my hands? There is something wrong here.

Mrs. B.   Let me read the letter for you.

Mr. B. [*Holding letter open and reading*]   No! No! I will read it myself! "Dear Sir:

"Recalling our pleasant acquaintance while you were in St. Petersburg, I venture to address you. If in this communication I give you pain you must not blame me—necessity compels me to write as I do. You will remember that for a few weeks prior to your departure from Russia I was absent from home. I returned to find that you had married, resigned your position as Attache of the American Legation and departed for America. Curious to find whom my good friend had honored with his name, I made inquiries at the Embassy and elsewhere, but beyond the fact that you had married somewhat suddenly, a woman supposed to be French, I could learn nothing. In point of fact your old companions seemed somewhat reticent and so disinclined to impart any information upon the matter that I dropped it entirely. More than a year has passed, and today it has been brought back to me by an occurrence at once remarkable and painful. You know all about the theft of my diamonds, how I was tricked out of them by the wiles of a woman, at the time the mistress of that supreme scoundrel calling himself Don Plon. Happily for the world this villain never lived to enjoy his plunder, for he died in Paris eight months ago. I have employed the best detectives to find my property, and while I have been unable to recover it, so closely have I been on its track that a sale of the diamonds by the thieves in any of the markets of Europe has been made impossible. Today, however, a woman formerly a servant of Don Plon's mistress, was arrested by the Russian police on some petty charge, and sent for me in prison, saying if I would procure her release, she would give me information that might aid in the search for my lost property. The information she gave me was startling—even tragic. It was that the diamonds had been recently sent to America and that the wretch who had tricked me, Don Plon's partner in the theft, was"—My God!—"Marie Marino, the same woman who had married my American friend Bulford." [*Bulford starting up in great agitation—stop music*]   Is this the truth? Speak, or I shall kill you where you stand. You do not answer. You cannot. Ah, I see it all now. The men who brought those diamonds here tonight were not the police but your tools! The order was a forgery and you are—you are—Plon's woman! [*Mrs. Bulford stares at him for a moment or two, goes to buffet, puts poison in glass then pours in wine, with back to audience, turns, brings glass to Bulford, behind him on his R., pours it down his throat*]

MRS. B. Take this, my dear it will revive you. [*He drinks*] Oh! [*Steps a step back with look of triumph then looks frightened*]

MR. B. Oh! My God, my God, the shame of it! The shame of it! It will kill me! It will kill me! Oh—Oh!—[*Falls, struggles in chair, dies. Mrs. Bulford stands a moment horrified, then goes around to front of chair, presses his head back with her hand. It falls on his breast. She goes to his R. at back takes the letter out of his hand, puts it in her bosom. Taps bell on table. Enter Marino L.*]

MAR. What's the matter?

MRS. B. Quick, a doctor! He is dying! He says the young man who was here poisoned him, but I think it is apoplexy. [*Imperatively stamping her foot*] Why do you stand? Go! Go! [*Music till curtain is well down. Wind and rain outside. Exit Marino hurriedly L. Mrs. Bulford watches him off, clasps her head in her hands for a moment as if bewildered and listens. Then staggers and facing audience goes to table and gets sherry glass—quickly seizes it with left hand and with the right grasps jewel-case through the paper—staring wildly into space. Quick curtain*]

ACT II.

SCENE: *Old Lavelot's house and shop in Houston Street. Three days later. An old-fashioned apartment littered with old clothes and personal effects on pegs and tables. Stove rear, window L. and curtains showing street. Children's shouts. Doors L. in back flat, R.1. and R.3.* TIME: *Morning.* DISCOVERED: *Old Lavelot sitting at stove doubled up, with poker in his hand. Dr. Livingstone and Mrs. O'Geogan down front C.*

DR. L. I'll give you a powder to put in his tea at night to keep him quiet

MRS. O'G. Tay, is it? If I put tay in the medicine he wouldn't take it. He'd taste the water in a drink if it was a foggy mornin'. Sure tay is for the strong minded sex, like meself, doctor.

DR. L. [*R. at head of table*] I'm sorry to find the old man such a wreck It was lucky I happened to be in the neighborhood.

OLD L. [*At stove*] Oh, you come here too much, damme! Fire him out—fire him out! [*Strikes the stove viciously with the poker. They disregard him entirely*]

MRS. O'G. Don't mind him, don't mind him. It's very good of you, doctor. To think of the loikes of him, and you havin' so many rich people to attind.

DR. L. Don't mention it. I knew the old man when he was a political influence in his ward.

MRS. O'G. I mind it well. That was in the Fourteenth, and he ought to be goin' to Albany this blessed minute. I hear, doctor, that the women do be takin' the politics in their own hands, thank God!

DR. L. You always had your share of political influence in the Fourteenth I believe.

MRS. O'G. But nary a job did I ever get. If I'd had the scrubbin' of the City Hall and the Court House as long as Mrs. Dooley, I'd be a ridin' in me coach meself, this blessed minute. [*Goes to door L.*]

OLD L. [*Seated R. of stove*] Lay for'ed—lay for'ed. [*Strikes the stove with the poker*] How long is this thing going to last?

DR. L. [*Crosses to C.*] You had better give him two powders Mrs. O'-Geogan.

MRS. O'G. I'll give him half a dozen and choke him at wanst. It's yourself cud be doin' an honest widdy a good turn by spakin' to the senator.

DR. L. [*R.C.*] Oh, you have more influence with him than I have.

MRS. O'G. Influence, is it? May St. Peter fly away with him! He has a heart as big as his fist, but his tongue ought to melt in his mouth with his own blarney. Aha, is that you, Mrs. Dooley—you'll be comin' up to see me in my new house on the Avenoo, says he, and drink a glass of champagne with the boys, at election toime. The devil an invite do I get to the house on the Avenoo and me workin' like a nager with the gang on election day. I'm thinkin' I'll put on me trousseau at the next blow-out, and march into the house on the Avenoo. [*Imitating him with hands on her hips*] A-ha—is that you, sinator? You'll be givin' Biddy O'Geogan a mug of champagne I don't know, or divil another whack will you git of election day.

DR. L. Where is Pop Lavelot's granddaughter, Mary. I saw the girl once —in fact, I assisted at her début.

MRS. O'G. She never had it. A healthier baby I never saw.

DR. L. [*Smiling*] I mean, her first appearance. [*Music till Mary is well on*] She promised to become a very handsome girl.

MRS. O'G. She is a good girl and kept her promise. Didn't ye see her, doctor, she must have stepped out. I'll call her. [*Goes to door R.3. and calls*] Miss Mary—whist—here's the doctor.

MARY. [*Outside*] I'm coming in a moment.

MRS. O'G. [*Coming down*] It's no place for the loikes of her with her schoolin' and tinder sinsibilities. But the old pelican there has got a pot of money, and she's the only one who can manage him. [*Going up to door R.3. Enter Mary R.3. Coming C.*] This is Doctor Livingstone, miss. He knew your mother.

DR. L. [*Advancing to Mary*] It's no use my telling you we have met before. You wouldn't remember it. [*To Mrs. O'Geogan*] She has kept her promise indeed! A little pale, however—and—[*Regarding her closely*] I don't like the look of worry on your face.

MRS. O'G. Bedad she's breakin' her heart, doctor!

MARY. I need exercise, doctor.

MRS. O'G. [*Aside*] Exercise—listen to that. Does a cat need fur?

DR. L. Well, you will have to let me come over and look after you a little. It will never do, your eyes are red.

MARY. It is nothing, doctor. I took a little cold in them. [*Crosses L.*]

DR. L. [*Going toward door L.*] Mrs. O'Geogan, don't forget two powders at night and one in the morning. Miss Lavelot, let me advise you to take care of your health. Good-bye. [*Exits L.*]

MRS. O'G. Good-bye! He's the foinest doctor in New York. I'll speak to Senator McSorker about him. He ought to be on the health board—his medicines are so tasty.

MARY. You are very careless with your tongue and I am surprised at you.

MRS. O'G. When you have killed me with your trouble, I'll not be able to speak of it.

MARY. I don't want it spoken of to anybody.

MRS. O'G. You're killin' yourself entoirely and there isn't a man on earth that's worth it.

MARY. [*Going to window*] Oh, why does not Frank send me some word. I seem to be wandering about in a ghastly dream.

MRS. O'G. It's that young man Frank Kennet, that's wanderin' about with the police at his heels. [*Mary opens window and looks out; laughter; children's voices heard*] Listen to that, and our hearts are as heavy as a hod of bricks.

MARY. There is a girl dancing for them. She is a brazen thing. [*Speaks to some one outside*] Yes, this is Pop Lavelot's. You'd better come inside, I can't hear what you say. [*Opens door L. Enter Dick Brummage and Peggy Daly*

Door is left open. Brummage is roughly dressed as a longshoreman—pea jacket and cap, muffler, etc. Peggy wears a short coarse skirt, cheap waist tucked into it, coarse jacket, yarn stockings and heavy shoes. She is eating an apple with juicy exuberance]

BRUM. [*Laughing. To Mary*] I promised the girl to buy her a frock if she'd shake a horn pipe and blow me if she didn't kick it out on the flags like a boatswain's mate. She's got a foot like a ripple and a leg like the spar on the commodore's yacht. Shake them out a shuffle, old gal.

MRS. O'G. Oxcuse me. This is a respectable man's house!

BRUM. Well, she's respectable round the ankles. Wait till you see her.

MARY. [*L. at back of sofa*] Do you wish to buy something?

BRUM. Yes. I got to buy the girl some togs.

MARY. [*L.*] You had better go to a store. We've nothing but odds and ends.

PEG. Say, old man, will you buy me a sweater?

MRS. O'G. You had better hold your whist and get out of here. [*Mrs. O'-Geogan and Peggy scowl at each other*]

PEG. [*To Brummage*] Wait till I eat me apple and I'll take a rise out of the old woman. [*To Mrs. O'Geogan*] Say, old lady I'm the champion contor-tion-east.

MRS. O'G. [*R.C.*] You are, are you? Well you'd better take a tumble to yourself. I'm the Columbian terror from the Fourteenth when me rules and regulations is interfered with. [*Gets broom*]

BRUM. [*C.*] If you don't dance she'll lather you.

PEG. Lather me? Wait till I show you how I can dance? [*Wild dance ad lib; Arapahoe spasm*]

BRUM. Now, old woman—fetch her frock out.

MRS. O'G. You don't need no decent woman's frock. You'd better go over on Broadway and buy yourself a set of tights. [*Peggy goes up L.C.*]

MARY. [*Coming down from window*] Oh, get her what she wants, Mrs. O'Geogan and let her go. There's a lot of stuff in that back room. [*Crosses to R.*]

MRS. O'G. It doesn't become me to be waitin' on the loikes of her.

MARY. [*Going to door R.3.*] Very well. I will wait upon her myself. [*To Brummage*] Wait a moment, sir.

BRUM. All right. Take your time. [*Crossing to R. Peggy dancing up stage C. Mrs. O'Geogan follows Mary to the door*]

MRS. O'G. Oi wouldn't ruin me reputation by stayin' alone with them. [*Exit Mrs. O'Geogan and Mary R.3. Brummage immediately shuts door L. and returns to Peggy, who is dancing very quickly*]

BRUM. [*L.*] Now then, Peggy Daly, what are you doing in Houston Street when your beat is in Canal Street? Come, straight out with it. I'm looking at you. The old woman sent you up here—what for?

PEG. [*Frightened*] Who be you?

BRUM. You ought to know me pretty well. I'm Dick Brummage.

PEG. Dick Brummage. [*Takes a step or two towards R.*]

BRUM. I got you out of the Oak Street station, but I'll put you back there pretty quick if you don't give it to me straight—you were sent up here by Rosenbaum to watch this house.

PEG. [*R.C.*] I hope to die, if I've done anything. A gal can come to Houston Street, can't she?

BRUM. Yes, and she can go to Blackwell's Island when I've got a through ticket. The old woman sent you here to see who was hangin' about this house.

PEG. [*Beginning to cry. R.C.*] She'd broke my back if I hadn't come.

BRUM. That's all right. Keep your mouth still and I'll stand your friend yet. The old woman never bought you a frock since you've been with her. [*Peggy crosses to table R. Enter Mrs. O'Geogan and Mary R.3. Mrs. O'Geogan carries a bundle which she puts on table R. Group to table examining clothes. As Brummage speaks to Mary, she goes to window, leaving Mrs. O'Geogan and Peggy facing audience at table. While the conversation is going on between Mary and Brummage, Peggy picks up a lorgnette from table and hides it in the folds of her dress, going up R.C.*]

BRUM. [*To Mary*] I want to get some duds meself.

MARY. I don't think you'll find what you want here, sir.

BRUM. Oh, that room is full of odds and ends. I'll get the old lady to let me pick out what I want.

OLD L. Oh, take him down the cellar and give him some oats. [*Peggy looks sharply around*]

BRUM. Well, gal, you got your frock?

MRS. O'G. [*R. of table R.*] Yes, sir, there's the frock. It will cost you a dollar.

MARY. [*At window; to Mrs. O'Geogan*] The gentleman wishes to buy some things himself. You'd better show him what you've got.

MRS. O'G. [*Resignedly*] Oh, very well. Step this way, sir.

BRUM. Good-bye, Peggy. You can start a dancing school now.

PEG. [*By door L.*] So long—so long—I'm goin' to the Eyetalian Opera. [*Exit Peggy L. Mary comes down and sits L. of table R.*]

MRS. O'G. [*At door*] This way, sir.

Brum. [*To Mary*] I'll see you again, lass, before I go. I might have something to say to you. [*As Mrs. O'Geogan and Brummage exit R.3. Mary drops her head in her hands*]

Old L. Get over—get over. Stand round. What's the matter with you? Whoa! [*Strikes the stove with a poker as if it were a horse then rises and exits grumblingly and slowly R.3. Enter suddenly Frank Kennet street door L.; he turns, locks the door and comes C. quickly*]

Frank. Mary! [*Going to her*]

Mary. [*Seated L. of table R. Looking up*] Frank! [*Covers her face with her hands*]

Frank. [*L. of her*] Look me in the eyes. I'm hunted! Tell me if I am a murderer?

Mary. [*Staring at him*] Where have you been these three days?

Frank. Trying to get to see you to see if you believed in me, for that was the only thing worth living for. [*Puts hat on table R.*]

Mary. You were hiding.

Frank. Do you believe that?

Mary. [*Rises*] They were looking for you everywhere—why did you not face this terrible charge of murder and robbery if you are innocent?

Frank. [*Turning away aside*] My God! Even she suspects me. [*Goes up to window*]

Mary. You do not answer me. [*Crossing to L.C.*]

Frank. [*Comes down R.C.*] I will tell you. When I left Mr. Bulford's house on that fatal night, I started to come to you. My senses became bewildered. I was numb with cold. I must have fallen down somewhere. When I recovered my senses, I was on the deck of a South American ship, and was being carried out of the country. I waited till dark set in, cut loose one of the boats and escaped from the vessel. A strong ebb was running—no effort was made to pick me up. Almost dead with cold I succeeded in reaching the Jersey shore in the grey of the morning. When I saw the papers and saw the crime with which I was charged [*Mary sits on sofa L.*] one desire influenced me. It was to see you first and then give myself up and demand a trial. I have made my way to you to tell you I am innocent and to hear you say you believe me. The rest is fate. [*Crosses to table, takes up hat and steps up a little. Reenter Brummage dressed as Old Lavelot. Seats himself R. of stove*]

Mary. [*Rising*] What are you going to do now?

Frank. I am going to the nearest station.

Mary. [*L. back of sofa*] Can you prove your innocence?

Frank. [*R.*] Is that worth proving which no one will believe in?

MARY. [*L. back of sofa. Approaching him*] Frank, this is a terrible mystery. The blow has numbed me—my heart tells me that you are innocent, but the dreadful facts stare me in the face. If you are innocent, we must prove it. [*Crosses to C.*]

FRANK. [*R. at head of table*] Mary, I can fight adversity, and poverty and keep my spirit, but I cannot fight fate. [*Throws his hat on table, R.*] What cursed luck was it that sent me to that house that night and put me in these toils? [*Comes down R.*] I'll tell you what it was. [*Back to C.*] I was thinking of your happiness.

MARY. You can never make me unhappy if you are innocent.

FRANK. [*R.C. Turns Mary to his R.*] I am innocent and you are the only friend in the world that I thought would believe me. [*Crosses a step to L.C.*]

MARY. [*R.C.*] Oh, no! You must have a friend who can advise you and help you.

FRANK. [*L.C.*] I thought so before I came here.

MARY. [*R.C.*] Well, in Heaven's name think so yet.

FRANK. [*L.C.*] There is not a person on earth who will not believe me guilty after reading the newspapers. [*Goes, looks out of window*]

MARY. [*R.C.*] I don't want to believe the newspapers. I want to believe you.

FRANK. Mary!

MARY. [*Looking into each other's eyes*] Let me look at you—yes—you are the same Frank to me—no matter what happens. There is no murder in your eyes. [*Embrace, C.*]

FRANK. [*L.*] No, my darling, I could not put these arms around you again if they had committed a crime. All that I want you to do is to believe in me.

MARY. Oh, I must do more. I only wish that I knew how. [*Marino gives a loud knock at street door, L. They are both startled*] Go in there. [*Pointing to door R.1.*] You must not be taken yet, I have so much to say to you. Go! Go! [*Knock again. Exit Frank R.1. Mary goes to street door and, unlocking it, admits Marino*]

MAR. Are you Miss Lavelot?

MARY. Yes. What do you wish? [*Crosses L. to behind sofa*]

MAR. I am in search of Frank Kennet.

MARY. [*Aside*] He has followed him here. [*Direct*] What is it you wish to know?

MAR. [*Coming down L.C.*] I will be frank with you. I have learned that you are engaged to be married to Frank Kennet.

MARY. Well, sir—

MAR. He is suspected of murder and the theft of valuable jewels.

MARY. But he is innocent of both.

MAR. You think so?

MARY. I am convinced of it.

MAR. [*Quickly*] Ah, then you have seen him since the murder and he has convinced you.

MARY. [*Aside*] He does not know he is here. [*Direct*] He has not convinced me.

MAR. I assume that you know where he is.

MARY. But you must not assume that I would betray him if I did.

MAR. I came here to open negotiations with him through you for the recovery of the diamonds, and to discover the murderer.

MARY. I, too, am anxious to discover the murderer.

MAR. [*Eagerly*] Has the murderer wronged you? [*During the speech they are standing one each side of the table, facing each other*]

MARY. Yes, he has.

MAR. Then we ought to be able to act together.

MARY. [*R. of table R.*] To what end?

MAR. To the discovery of the murderer. If Frank Kennet is that murderer, you would like to know it, wouldn't you?

MARY. I am anxious, as I have told you, to discover the murderer.

MAR. Then we can be of some assistance to each other. Now put me in communication with him. It is much the best way. He will be caught in time and then it may be too late for us to recover the property. Think it over and I will come back and see you again. It is not my intention to annoy you. [*Goes to door, L. Politely*] I beg your pardon for this intrusion. [*Bows and exits L. Door left unlocked*]

BRUM. [*Getting up from stove, looks out of door L. Coming down C.*] Well, you got rid of him very nicely, my girl.

MARY. [*Astonished*] You? Who are you?

BRUM. An officer from Headquarters, and I am waiting to see Kennet.

MARY. [*Overcome*] Oh, Heaven! Then it's no use. I have betrayed him!

BRUM. Well, don't go to pieces. Frank Kennet is suspected of two crimes, you know that?

MARY. [*At head of table R. back to end of it*] Yes, I know it, but he never committed them.

BRUM. [*C. up a little*] He went to the Bulford's house full of revenge. He was left alone with the old gentleman. They had an angry conversation. They drank wine together, and Mrs. Bulford says that when she returned to the room, Mr. Bulford was dead and the diamonds had disappeared. Have you read the papers?

MARY. Oh, yes—everything is against him—but—he is innocent—I know it.

BRUM. It is one thing to know and another thing to prove.

MARY. Everything. [*Covers her face with her hands*]

BRUM. No, not everything. Sit down here, you are trembling. [*Mary sits on L. of sofa*] Now listen to me. The coroner said Mr. Bulford was poisoned. But the inquest could not tell with what. It might have been in the wine he drank and the belief is that Kennet slipped it in the sherry glass when Mrs. Bulford went out. He drank it out of a cut sherry glass. That is in evidence. Are you listening to me carefully?

MARY. Oh, yes.

BRUM. [*R. of sofa L.*]   Mrs. Bulford in her examination said that the two glasses were on the table when she returned to the room. But the police were in the house before twelve o'clock that night looking for the diamonds. Something had disappeared.

MARY. Yes, yes, the jewel-case.

BRUM. The cut sherry glass.

MARY. Let me think. Yes. Go on.

BRUM. Somebody had made away with it, and it could not have been Kennet. Don't you see that? [*Mary jumps up*] Don't excite yourself. Why was that glass made away with, and who made away with it?

MARY. I understand. What do you intend to do?

BRUM. I am going to save Frank Kennet if I can.

MARY. Who are you?

BRUM. I am Detective Brummage of the Central Office, the one friend that the newspapers haven't convinced. When I was a poor man and a friendless boy, Frank Kennet's father befriended me and helped me. What are you crying for? [*Goes up, opens door L., looks out*]

MARY. I suppose it is because he's got such a good friend.

BRUM. [*Comes down C.*]   I suspect there is some kind of deviltry at work in that house of the Bulfords. Do you know who that man was that just left here? It was Mrs. Bulford's brother. [*Mary rises, goes L. around sofa at back of it*] But he will not suspect that Kennet is in town when he discovers the mistake he has made.

MARY. [*Behind sofa L.*]   Oh, tell me what do you want me to do?

BRUM. It isn't much. [*Takes newspaper from pocket, points to paragraph*] Read that. [*Goes up, opens door L.*]

MARY. [*Taking paper and reading*] "Wanted—a neat maid to attend a lady—must not be over twenty-three; with good penmanship and a knowledge of hair dressing; apply in own handwriting to No. 400 Lexington Avenue." [*Speaking*] What does it mean?

BRUM. It means that Mrs. Bulford has discharged all her old servants and is hiring new ones. Can't you apply for that place?

MARY. I? In that house? [*Crosses to R., sits L. of table*]

BRUM. There are some things in that house I want to find out. Once inside of it you can help me.

MARY. [*Seated L. of table*] But you forget that Mrs. Bulford's brother who has seen me here will see me there and betray me.

BRUM. No. I don't forget. You must take the risk of meeting him in order to help me.

MARY. [*Gets up and approaches Brummage*] I will take all risks and encounter all perils.

BRUM. [*Going to her—placing his hand on her shoulder and speaking tenderly*] You must be guided by me. We must not let it be known that Kennet has returned. The conspirators think he is out of the country and that makes them careless. I will take care of him and be responsible for him. [*Door L. opens softly and Marino looks in and listens*] You must trust me. I don't want to be known. [*Marino beckons to someone outside*] If you betray me we may lose everything.

MAR. [*Aside*] The very man! Frank Kennet!

MARY. I will believe in you and trust you. [*Marino closes door and disappears L.*]

BRUM. Good! Keep your counsel. Frank shall not give himself up to anyone but me, until this is settled. Now I'll go and get these things off, or your grandfather will think his double is walking about. [*Goes to door R.3.*] Brave girl! Keep your spirits up. [*Exits R.3.*]

OLD L. [*Outside R.3.*] Mary! Mary! [*Enter Old Lavelot from door, growling; he reseats himself at stove and takes poker*]

MARY. Yes, grandpa, dear, I'm coming. I'm coming.

OLD L. I want my bran, damn it! Been chewing on my manger ever since sunrise.

MARY. Grandpa, dear, I'll get you something to eat right away. [*Enter from L. door Marino and officer. Marino advances and points to Lavelot*]

MAR. There's your man. Ah, Kennet!

MARY. Kennet!

MAR. [*With quiet triumph*] This is better than we expected. You're a pretty sly bird but your game is up.

OLD L. [*By stove*]   Throw 'em down the hay-loft stairs—I'm getting tired of this.

OFF.   It's no go. Will you come quietly or shall I put you out? Don't be a fool any longer.

MAR. [*Down to table; to Mary*]   It is not too late. Ask him where the diamonds are. [*Crosses to C. Mary indicates by her manner that she understands the mistake and to save Frank is willing to keep it up*]

MARY.   Frank—[*Breaks down; officer seizes Lavelot; business of absurd struggle in which officer succeeds in getting him out of L. door followed by Marino. The moment they are gone Mary runs to door and locks it; calls in suppressed voice*] Frank—[*Frank enters R.1.*] We have only a few moments. They have taken the old man by mistake and will be back as soon as they discover it. [*Enter Brummage R.3.*]

BRUM.   I'll be responsible for you. If they lock you up now, you can't help me. I've the superintendent with me, but the people we are going to fight have only the commissioners and politicians.

FRANK.   And I, God help me, have nobody. [*Brummage is between Mary and Frank*]

BRUM.   Nonsense! You've got two of the best friends that any man ever had on this earth and they are going to help you.

MARY.   Yes, we are going to help you.

FRANK.   *You?*

BRUM.   Yes, she! [*Puts their hands together*] We've got a big fight, but if you'll be steered by Dick Brummage, we will run the real culprit to earth. [*Quick curtain*]

ACT III.

SCENE: *Two days later. Dining room in Mrs. Bulford's house. Two entrances —one at portieres in rear wall L. with screen in two folds, the other a hall door well up R.3. Buffet back C. Table with cloth up C. with chair R. and L. of it. Large mirror L.* TIME: *Early morning.* DISCOVERED: *Mary at buffet with back to audience looking at glasses. She wears a white apron and is plainly but tastefully dressed as a maid.*

MRS. B. [*Outside L.*]   Susanne!

MARY. [*At buffet, startled*]   Yes, madam.

MRS. B. [*Outside L.*]   There is a man coming with flowers—let him in and see who they are from. I am not dressed yet.

MARY. Yes, madam. [*Mary goes to hall door R.3. Enter Dick Brummage disguised as an Irishman and carrying two bouquets—one large and the other small*]

BRUM. [*Coming to table and looking around*] Where's your mistress?

MARY. You can put the flowers on the table.

BRUM. How the divil then do Oi know I'm givin' them to the right person?

MARY. Mrs. Bulford is dressing. It's all right.

BRUM. Drissin', is she? Begorra it's yourself that needs no drissin'.

MARY. You may leave the room.

BRUM. Av course I'll lave the room. D'ye think I'd be takin' it wid me? Let me speak a word in your ear, my darlint. [*They go around the table; Mary goes to hall door and opens it*]

MARY. Leave the flowers and leave the room.

BRUM. There, me darlint. [*Puts flowers on the table, approaches her, changes voice*] Lass, don't you know me? [*Goes to door L.*]

MARY. [*Astonished*] You?

BRUM. Sh-sh-sh, not too loud. Where is she?

MARY. She is dressing.

BRUM. There's something going on here tonight. Keep your wits about you. Have you discovered anything?

MARY. Nothing.

BRUM. Well, you will tonight. Keep your eye on that portiere—if you see it move signal me at once and I'll stop. I've brought these flowers so as to keep you in sight. I am going to pretend that I have brought the wrong bouquets, so as to come back again with the right ones. Do you understand?

MARY. Yes; you frighten me.

BRUM. Keep your courage up, my little woman. If anything should happen to you tonight in this place and you want to communicate with me— write a line and put it in this small bouquet. I will leave it here and when I come back, I'll get it. Is it perfectly plain to you?

MARY. What can happen to me?

BRUM. Well, not much—if you keep me informed. You haven't found out who made away with that glass?

MARY. No, I have found out nothing, yet.

BRUM. Well, keep your ears open tonight. A girl's instinct is better than man's reason when she's got a man to save.

MARY. Yes—poor Frank. Has he given himself up yet?

BRUM. Yes—to me. I am responsible for him. [*Mary suddenly looks right him and starts. Crosses L. Portieres move; Brummage's voice and manner change*] Phat the divil, then, do I care for the trouble. I'd carry the blissed flowers forty toimes to git a look at a pretty gurrl loike yourself, so I would. [*Enter Mrs. Bulford through portiers*]

Mrs. B. [*C. up stage*]   What's the matter?

Brum. [*At table*]   The divil of anything's the matter save meself who's brought the wrong flowers. Axin' your pardon, I'll have the right ones here before a billy goat cud eat them.

Mrs. B.   Very well, you may leave the room.

Brum. [*Taking up large bouquet and leaving small one*]   I'll lave that to sweeten your room anyhow. [*Going at door*] But with two such beauties, it's too sweet already for an Oirishman. [*Exit through hall door R.3.*]

Mrs. B. [*Looking at flowers at head of table C.*]   Who sent the flowers?

Mary.   The man was so rude I could not find out and as you heard, he brought the wrong bouquets.

Mrs. B.   Never mind. Attend the door—I expect Dr. Livingstone. [*Turns down R.*]

Mary. [*Starting*]   Dr. Livingstone?

Mrs. B. [*Turning quickly*]   What's the matter—do you know him?

Mary.   No—o. But, are you ill?

Mrs. B.   No. He calls on business. [*Door bell rings*] There he is now Show him in here. [*Takes bouquet from table, smells it and places it on sid table L. Mary opens hall door R.3; timidly screening herself with it, and Dr Livingstone enters, walks straight in without perceiving her. He comes dow hat and cane in hand; Mary exits door L.*] I am glad you obeyed m summons, doctor. [*Doctor puts hat and cane on table. Mrs. Bulford at sofa L*

Dr. L. [*Taking off gloves*]   Yes, you have summoned me for what?

Mrs. B.   Will you be seated? [*Indicating chair*]

Dr. L. [*Still standing*]   Proceed, madam—why have you summoned me

Mrs. B. [*Crosses to sofa end of it L.*]   I have a woman's curiosity and wish to ask you some questions.

Dr. L. [*Gravely*]   I trust, madam, that you will not occupy my time gratifying your curiosity.

Mrs. B. [*Sits on sofa*]   I pray that you will be seated, doctor. [*Indicatin chair. Doctor sits easy chair close to Mrs. Bulford*] On the night that M Bulford died, you told me that he died of apoplexy and that you would gi me a certificate, but you changed your mind and notified the coroner.

Dr. L.   You are correct, madam. Proceed!

Mrs. B.   What I wish to know is, why you changed your mind af leaving my house. [*Dr. Livingstone gets up and walks toward door R.3. a does not immediately reply. Mrs. Bulford goes to the portiere L., loc through, and returns to sofa*] We are entirely alone so you may be confidential. Why did you change your mind after leaving my house? [*Mary appears at L. door listening; Dr. Livingstone sits on sofa L.*]

DR. L. [*Speaking deliberately*] Madam, I changed my mind because I saw you.

MRS. B. [*On sofa L.*] Not after you left the house, doctor.

DR. L. Yes.

MRS. B. I did not leave the house that night.

DR. L. [*Looking at her and speaking slowly*] No, but you came to an upper window. [*Mrs. Bulford starts but recovers herself*] You lifted the sash and threw something out. [*Mrs. Bulford clutches arm of sofa involuntarily but smiles and looks the doctor in the eyes*]

MRS. B. What a curious hallucination. You must have seen my ghost.

DR. L. Madam, that which you threw out of the window could not well be an hallucination, for I picked it up. It was a cut sherry glass with a monogram on it. It fell upon a heap of rubbish and was unbroken. [*The two look at each other for a moment. Mary, in her eagerness to hear, has pushed herself in at door*]

MRS. B. This is really interesting. What did you find in the phantom glass, doctor?

DR. L. A little of the wine adhered to the bottom of the glass.

MRS. B. And you sent it to the chemist?

DR. L. That was not necessary—I tested it myself.

MRS. B. And of course—in all such romances—you found—

DR. L. Poison.

MRS. B. [*Still seated on sofa*] But, doctor, of course you didn't know what kind of poison it was?

DR. L. Fortunately, I am one of the few who are familiar with it. It was the deadly Para poison made only in South America. It was that fact that defied the coroner. [*Mary closes the curtains and disappears*]

MRS. B. Capital! And what did you say when you made this charming discovery?

DR. L. I said to myself—a woman will undo the craft of months with the impulse of a moment. [*Rises*] Instead of washing the glass you threw it out the window. It is by such miscalculations that crime is detected.

MRS. B. [*Rises*] No, it is by such fairy stories that detection is misdirected.

DR. L. I scarcely understand you.

MRS. B. [*Taking a few steps to C. with assumed lightness of manner*] I mean—that a disinterested person hearing your story would say the doctor was a confederate of ghosts and that phantoms threw the glass out to him, especially when he acknowledges he is one of the few persons familiar with the poison. [*Goes and stands by sofa*] Besides, he went away the next day so as not to be present at the inquest. Then too he was, in all probability, on intimate terms with the phantom and may have made her visits extra professionally—just as you are visiting me tonight. [*Crosses to C.*] Doctor.

Dr. L. [*Bitterly*] Madam, you are not only a clever, but an unscrupulous woman.

Mrs. B. But not so clever as you are, doctor, at inventing stories. Let me ask you—have you told this to anyone? [*Dr. Livingstone walks up and down R.*] Try and compose yourself, doctor. Let me beg of you to be seated? [*Sits L. of table C.*]

Dr. L. I was called away early in the morning after Mr. Bulford's death by a professional appointment at Montreal, and have only returned this morning. I have had no opportunity to give it much thought.

Mrs. B. Well, now, doctor, don't you think that in view of your own peace of mind and your future success in New York (I understand you have an eye on the position of health officer of the Port, which is a political gift— I believe), don't you think, doctor, that for your own interests it would be well to abandon these ghost stories and thus save some estimable people from a great deal of annoyance? You are so eminent in your specialty of compounding medicines that it seems a pity to assume the risk of a romancer at your age.

Dr. L. [*Seated R. of table C. After pause—looking at her*] You are right, madam, I have compounded medicines for many years, but I never compounded a felony.

Mrs. B. Now you are angry, doctor; I beg your pardon.

Dr. L. If you had studied faces as long as I have, madam, you would know that what you call anger is only a man's pity.

Mrs. B. Not pity for me, doctor, I hope.

Dr. L. No, madam—pity for an innocent man somewhere who is accused of a crime he never committed.

Mrs. B. But who, if the papers are correct, ran away from the crime?

Dr. L. [*Turning*] But I am informed that he had a friend who has no run away.

Mrs. B. Are you referring to yourself, doctor?

Dr. L. No, I am referring to a woman. So far as I am concerned I hav been trained to the rigid performances of two duties—one to my patien [*Pause*] The other to the public.

Mrs. B. [*Rising*] Then, doctor, I hope that you will always permit me t be your patient. [*Mrs. Bulford goes L. Doctor R.C., watching her*] Docto would you mind telling me who is the woman in your fairy story so interested in this matter? [*Doctor is surprised, but does not answer. Mrs. Bulford calls through portiere*] Susanne! I have a morbid desire to meet her. [*The doctor has turned toward audience and does not see her*] You and this woman both know of the phantom glass I suppose?

DR. L. [*Annoyed*] Madam, I have already told you that I just returned to town and have as yet communicated with no one. She therefore could not know it—unless—unless she had been listening to our conversation. Madam, as I can be of no further service to you, I think it would be well for you to change your physician. [*Bows. Mary enters L. Doctor goes to table to take his hat and cane and comes face to face with Mary across table. Doctor starts as he recognizes her. Mary appealingly puts her finger to her lips and signals him not to betray her; all of which Mrs. Bulford sees in the mirror L. and turns quickly in blank dismay to watch them. Doctor hesitates a moment, looks from one to the other, takes his hat and cane and comes down C. With dignity*] Madam, I wish you good evening. [*Mrs. Bulford is speechless and only glares at him. Doctor exits hall door R.3. Mary glides quickly out at R.3. Mrs. Bulford comes down to table in great agitation*]

MRS. B. [*Leaning over table C.*] What does it all mean? Let me think— let me think? They know each other—what were his words? What were his very words? Unless she has heard our conversation. There are two of them who know. I have been spied upon in my own house. Where are my wits— where are my wits. What I do now must be done quickly. Who is this woman? [*Enter Mary R.3.*]

MARY. Madam, the senator.

MRS. B. Ah! [*Mary holds door R.3. Enter Senator McSorker dressed in Prince Albert coat; wears a large diamond; typical well-to-do New York politician*]

SEN. [*Heartily*] Ah—ha—there you are, lovelier than wax. Madam, yours obediently. You look like a four-year-old.

MRS. B. A four-year-old. Do I look childish, senator?

SEN. No, no, no—I mean a horse.

MRS. B. Look like a horse—Heavens, senator.

SEN. I beg your pardon—of course not—of course not. You know what mean—an angel.

MRS. B. [*Still L. on sofa*] I see, when you say a horse—you mean an angel.

SEN. [*Front of sofa*] What's the matter? You look as though you'd been ominated and withdrawn.

MRS. B. We all have our troubles.

SEN. [*Seating himself in chair*] I'll buy your troubles at your price and carry them around for a pocket piece. What's your price?

MRS. B. [*Coquetting with her foot*] Yes, I dare say a man with your influence could soon end my troubles—if you were sufficiently interested in me.

SEN. [*Seated R. of sofa L., looking at her foot*] Say, that's good. I like that —interested in you—do you want me to get down on my knees like they do in the play? Lock the doors—I'll do it.

MRS. B. No, no—if there is any appealing to be done, I must do it.

SEN. Ha—ha—that's good. Now I particularly like that. You appeal to me? Say—that's rich. What'll you have?

MRS. B. You're a generous man, but I want too much.

SEN. *Name it! Name it!*—put up your scale. If I haven't got it, I'll borrow it.

MRS. B. Ah, what would I have given to have met a man like you earlier in my career—how different my life would have been.

SEN. [*Slapping his knee*] Better late than never. Call off your wants.

MRS. B. You're like all men when you're in a generous mood and would play the lover.

SEN. By Heavens, I would do anything else but play the lover.

MRS. B. I am afraid I want something more than a lover.

SEN. Anything you like—how would slave do?

MRS. B. What I want is a protector.

SEN. All right—I'll protect you from other lovers and I'll begin now. [*Sit down on sofa beside her and puts his arm about her*]

MRS. B. I want protection from powerful enemies. The man that wins my favor must shield me from scandal if he has to stop the law and defy the machinery of justice. Are you able to do that?

SEN. [*Attempting to rise*] Ain't you drawin'—a—it a little strong?

MRS. B. [*Attempting to rise*] I see—your power and your devotion are no boundless!

SEN. [*Pulling her back*] Don't go off that way—I'm yours. Do you war me to start something—or stop something?

MRS. B. I want something stopped. That dreadful affair of Mr. Bulford'

SEN. But you didn't have anything to do with it.

MRS. B. [*Snatching his hands*] I don't want anything to do with it—that the point. I have enemies who hope to drag me into court.

SEN. Look here—I'm gone to pieces on you—see? I don't know wh you want me to do, but I'll do it if you don't play me.

MRS. B. I want you to stand between me and my personal enemies when the time comes, no matter who they may be, you will crush them with all the influence and power that your position gives you. Now do you know?

SEN. [*Fondling her*] It's a go. I'll show you how we handle these things in New York. [*Seizes her hand*]

MRS. B. You are hurting my hand, senator—I have a sharp ring on it.

SEN. [*Looking at ring*] Gee—willikens—where did you get that blazer? You must have been in politics yourself. I've carried the district attorney's office in one pocket and the Central Office in the other, but I never had a stone like that on my finger. [*Mrs. Bulford pulls her hand away quickly*]

MRS. B. Senator, I'm going away in the morning to a quiet place in the country.

SEN. [*Rising*] Going away! Oh, come now, you can't do that. Damn it—I beg your pardon. I've made all arrangements. [*Sits on sofa again*]

MRS. B. Arrangements for me?

SEN. Now see here, I told you tomorrow is election day and if things go right, I'm going to give the boys a blow-out at my house on Madison Avenue and I want you to be there.

MRS. B. Oh, but senator, I should dislike to appear in public at this time.

SEN. 'Tain't in public—it's my private house. I'm going to give a banner to the Fourteenth and I wanted you to give it away. I made all calculations.

MRS. B. Who will be there?

SEN. Only my friends, the politicians, and they're your friends. See? And you have to stand in with them. You needn't come till late. I'll take you away as soon as it's over.

MRS. B. You don't have to announce me by name?

SEN. No—we'll call you the glittering Goddess of Liberty—anything you like. I'll waltz you through and take care of you. That's the way to see whether I can protect you or not.

MRS. B. [*Rising*] I suppose I must earn my protection by obeying you. [*Enter Marino hurriedly from L.*]

MAR. How-de do, senator. [*To Mrs. Bulford*] Was Dr. Livingstone here half an hour ago?

MRS. B. Yes, yes. What's the matter? [*L.C. senator L.; goes round sofa to L. to C.*]

MAR. He is killed! A fire truck run into his carriage on the Avenue and threw him out on his head. I happened to pass at the time and the ambulance attendant, who had the doctor's book, said that his last call was here. [*Mrs. Bulford clasps her hands and shivers*]

MRS. B. Dead!

MAR. What's the matter?

MRS. B. [*Laughing hysterically*] Nothing—it is so sudden. Give me a glass of water—dead—then there is but one.

SEN. [*To Marino, coming down C.*] Young man, go and sit down. [*Takes Mrs. Bulford over to sofa*]

MRS. B. Gentlemen, I shall have to ask you to leave me. You have undone me for the moment. [*Sits on sofa L.*]

SEN. Don't forget tomorrow night, dear. Get yourself in your best—good-bye. [*Goes to door R.3.*] Young man, you're too damn sudden! [*Exit R.3.*]

MRS. B. Come here and sit down.

MAR. [*Sits on sofa*] What is agitating you so? You don't usually take on in this way.

MRS. B. Did you send the message to the old woman, that I gave you?

MAR. Yes, I did.

MRS. B. I must have some money and I have a few jewels that she will pay me a better price for than any one else. Is she coming?

MAR. Yes, but I don't want to see her.

MRS. B. No, I will spare you this humiliating business, but I must have some money. You know more about this woman than I do.

MAR. I know too much about her to have her name linked with yours.

MRS. B. Did you understand that she is the woman who hates Don Plon?

MAR. Yes, he is said to have betrayed her son who was executed. What are you asking me this for, now?

MRS. B. [*Sotto voce*] And she has threatened to be revenged?

MAR. Yes. What has got into your head?

MRS. B. That is all. I wanted to be sure I had not dreamed it.

MAR. [*Rises*] You look as if you had a fever and a bad dream. If I were you I'd go and lie down before she comes. [*Bell heard*] There she is now. I'm going to skip. [*Music. Enter Mary R.3.*]

MARY. Madam, a lady in black—she would not give her name.

MRS. B. Let her in. [*To Marino*] You must be at the senator's house tomorrow night, I may need you.

MAR. [*Going*] Yes, but I don't like the crowd—I'm not a politician. [*Exit Marino L. door. Enter Mother Rosenbaum R.3; she advances to C.*]

ROS. [*Down to C.*] Ah, madam, you will not come to see me in my little store, so I must come to you, when you have something to sell.

MRS. B. [*Fastening back the portiere*] Sit down, madam. I did think of selling my few family jewels, but I have changed my mind as I am going to remain in the city. [*Both seated on sofa*]

Ros. You have not many diamonds? Ah, madam, you are too modest. I think you have the finest jewels in America.

Mrs. B. [*Sits in chair next sofa*] What makes you think so? I am not a rich woman.

Ros. Ah, it is not the rich woman who has the most diamonds.

Mrs. B. I have a few jewels that were presents—

Ros. [*Interrupting*] They were presents to you—heh?

Mrs. B. I said—presents, but I have concluded to keep them.

Ros. Are they diamonds?

Mrs. B. Yes, but of no great value.

Ros. Have you not a ruby?

Mrs. B. [*Face to her in chair by sofa*] Now if we are to do any business, let me beg of you to be at least respectful.

Ros. Respectful, madam? I very much respect the woman who has a ruby and a large ruby—what you call—u-m. Mein Gott, woman, I could not, at my time of life, ask where people get things.

Mrs. B. You are affected with the same suspicion that besets other people, and that is that I have the Garbiadoff jewels. You and your friend Plon are both of one mind. I sent for you to get you to help me against his plot.

Ros. The dog! You say Plon is my friend and he and I are of the one mind? Oh, madam, do not say that again, or you will make me your enemy for life. Plon—the hound! It was he who made my poor and only boy suffer. The dog! I wish I had my fingers on his throat.

Mrs. B. The miscreant has a woman whom he employs to obtain his plunder.

Ros. Yes, yes—I know, I know.

Mrs. B. [*Seated R. of her*] She is here in my house. She obtained service as a maid. I caught her tonight telegraphing to a visitor. She has been eavesdropping here for a week.

Ros. [*Eagerly*] Where is she now?

Mrs. B. She is at the other end of that passage and she cannot approach without my seeing her. [*Rises and crosses to end of sofa L.*]

Ros. [*Going up and down. Hesitates, then eagerly*] How do you know that she is Plon's woman? [*Down by sofa R. of it*]

Mrs. B. [*Hesitating*] Because I discovered a letter from him in her room.

Ros. [*Viciously*] Ah—the sweet little creature—give her to me.

Mrs. B. How can you take her?

Ros. I will not take her—she will go herself—just as gently—you shall see. What is she here for? Is she not looking for the diamonds?

Mrs. B. Yes, yes—well?

Ros. Will she not know that I come to buy the diamonds—anybody can tell by my poor dress that I buy diamonds—I do not wear them. You shall tell her to go in my carriage and bring the diamonds here from my place. She will think they are the Garbiadoff's and to get them in her hands, she will be so eager she will go. [*Viciously*] But she will come away not again.

Mrs. B. But I cannot consent to any step that will imperil my character.

Ros. Gott in Himmel. If I did not respect your character, I would not be seen in your house. I have a character myself.

Mrs. B. But my friends—Senator McSorker.

Ros. If you did not have Senator McSorker for your friend then would I not do it? Of course you will marry the senator.

Mrs. B. Marry the senator?

Ros. Aye. Aye. You will marry the senator. You will go to his party to-morrow night. You will put on all your jewels and your fine dresses and when he sees you come down the staircase, he will think you came down from Heaven, like the angel you are. Now if you do not fix the senator to-morrow night, not even Rosenbaum can save you. Now let me see the jewels —the diamonds.

Mrs. B. Let you see the jewels? What for?

Ros. What for? Mein Gott! Woman, do you think I make a bargain with a cat in a bag?

Mrs. B. You are a queer creature. You are erratic.

Ros. Am I? Well, I see, I see, Rosenbaum cannot do any straight business with madam—so I'd better go. [*Starts to rise*]

Mrs. B. Stop! Sit down.

Ros. Well, I sit! Well?

Mrs. B. I cannot lay hands on the jewels at the present moment—

Ros. Yes, you can.

Mrs. B. How?

Ros. Because they are here.

Mrs. B. Here? Where?

Ros. On your person. Get them out. To save you I must see the jewels. [*Mrs. Bulford goes to portieres, pulls curtains together, then goes to chair L. of table, takes up cloth with back to audience at C. table in front of it, and pretends to take jewels out of her bosom—then goes down L. of Rosenbaum, who is on sofa. Mrs. Bulford sits, unwraps cloth. While Mrs. Bulford is at table*] I always thought she killed old Bulford, and now I know it. [*Mrs. Bulford goes down to Rosenbaum. Examining jewels*] Now shut them up. [*Mrs. Bulford rises, goes to C. table. Business*] And now let me see Plon's woman. You shall send her in my coach to my house on an errand.

Mrs. B. *Very well!* [*Goes to portiere and calls*] Susanne! Susanne! [*To sofa*] Be careful, or she will suspect. [*Enter Mary L.*]

Mary. [*Down C.*] Yes, madam.

Mrs. B. Susanne, pay attention. I have some jewels which this lady took to her house to sell for me, but as I have changed my mind, I want to get them back again. Can you get in this lady's coach—go to her house and bring me the jewels?

Mary. Yes, madam. [*Aside*] Heavens—the jewels! [*Direct*] Do you wish me to go now? [*Mrs. Bulford at back of sofa*]

Ros. [*Seated on sofa L.*] Right away, my dear. What a beautiful child you are. You must be careful and come right back—heh—while I wait here for you.

Mary. Yes, madam.

Ros. Come here, my child. [*Mary crosses to head of sofa, Mrs. Bulford crosses to C.*]

Ros. [*Taking her hand*] What a beautiful hand! [*To Mrs. Bulford*] Madam, it is not right to send a child on such an errand—I will go myself.

Mary. [*Nervously*] I can do it, madam.

Mrs. B. There is no danger that I can see. Give her a note—she will get the package and come straight back. I would not have her take any risks. [*To Mary*] Go bring paper and pencil, Susanne. [*Exit Mary at L.*]

Ros. [*Clutching Mrs. Bulford by the arm*] I will save you, but how will you save me?

Mrs. B. Save you—what do you mean?

Ros. Mein Gott! Woman, do you think I save people for the amusement?

Mrs. B. [*In chair next to sofa*] What do you want?

Ros. [*With her face close to Mrs. Bulford and with hissing intensity*] I want the "Heart of Fire."

Mrs. B. [*Rises and suddenly with dignity*] Why?

Ros. If we cannot understand each other, then what for do I come here? Do you think I have no heart? I have, my dear, I cannot take a young lady from such a nice home—it is too cruel. [*Sits again on sofa*]

Mrs. B. I must have my jewels to wear tomorrow night at the senator's. The day after I will talk to you. Can you trust me?

Ros. I do not have to trust you when I have the young woman. [*Enter Mary at portieres with paper; place it on side table front L.; crosses to C. table and takes bouquet from table and goes to buffet with it where she is seen by audience putting a folded paper into the bunch of flowers, which she places on table while Rosenbaum is writing on side table. Mrs. Bulford is watching Rosenbaum*]

MARY. [*At C. table, aside*] If anything happens to me he said he would get this.

Ros. Come here, my dear. [*Gives note to Mary who comes down*]

MRS. B. [*Behind Rosenbaum without turning around*] Do be careful of yourself, my child.

Ros. [*Rising and crossing to Mary*] I will tell my coachman to be very careful of her and bring her right back. [*Exit R.3. Rosenbaum and Mary. Mrs. Bulford watches them off nervously and the moment they disappear, she jumps up and walks stage to C. Enter Marino from L.—the two face each other*]

MRS. B. You! Why have you come back?

MAR. Did Susanne go out? [*Goes toward portiere*]

MRS. B. [*Quickly*] Yes, why?

MAR. I wish to speak to her.

MRS. B. [*Controlling herself*] Try and behave yourself in my room— what do you want of Susanne?

MAR. [*Going up a little*] Do you know who she is?

MRS. B. What do you mean?

MAR. I have been thinking of her a great deal. She may know something of the murderer of Mr. Bulford.

MRS. B. [*Sotto voce*] Yes, she may.

MAR. [*Catching Mrs. Bulford by the arm impressively*] Maria, are you sure that when you returned to the room that night the jewels were gone?

MRS. B. What are you talking about? Have you lost your wits?

MAR. Where is the girl? [*Enter Rosenbaum at R.3.*]

MRS. B. [*Hesitating and looking at Rosenbaum*] She is gone.

MAR. [*Astonished*] Gone where?

MRS. B. [*Impressively*] I do not know. [*Walks rapidly*]

MAR. [*Excitedly*] But I will know. [*Rosenbaum and Mrs. Bulford to front L. together*] I am going to find the murderer of Mr. Bulford. [*Marino takes bouquet from table and mechanically sniffs it as he walks. Enter Dick Brummage from R.3. with flowers*]

BRUM. Oi've brought ye the right flowers. [*Looks at bouquet in Marino's hand disconcertedly*] And Oi'd thank you to give me that one.

MAR. [*Walking, carelessly*] Oh, I'll keep this one—I like it. Leave the room.

BRUM. [*With comical distress*] Shure you wouldn't have a man lose his place, by lavin' the flowers wid ye that belonged to some one else.

Mrs. B.   Oh, give him the flowers and let him go. [*Marino throws bouquet to Brummage, who seizes it eagerly and goes to door behind screen, faces audience, looking into bouquet for paper. Marino continues walking*]

Ros. [*To Mrs. Bulford*]   You will bring me the "Heart of Fire" on Thursday.

Mrs. B. [*To Rosenbaum*]   You are sure that when she left this house, she could communicate with no one?

Ros.   Ah, when she go away from here, no one shall ever know one word from her. [*Brummage pulls Mary's note from bouquet deliberately, putting it in his pocket*]

ACT IV.

Scene: *Hoffman House Café. The set represents the room as if seen from Twenty-fourth Street. Square bar in C. with fixtures; barkeeper dealing liquors. Groups ad lib. Large frame of Bouguereau's Nymphs seen in profile L.C. lit from above. Statuary, plants, etc., and six tables arranged at equal distances in front and up R.* Time: *Eight o'clock in the evening. Brummage seated at table L. Enter countryman L.C., comes down slowly and stops in front of picture. His attention is fixed. He is amazed—looks intently, looks furtively away and looks back at the picture in the same way. Enter Mrs. O'Geogan looking at picture and then to Marino who is at the bar.*

Mrs. O'G.   Is Senator McSorker here? I came here to find him.

Mar.   No, I have not seen him.

Mrs. O'G. [*Looking at picture aghast, pointing to it*]   What's them?

Mar.   What do you mean, the picture?

Mrs. O'G.   *Yes.*

Mar.   The picture is called the Nymphs and the Satyr.

Mrs. O'G.   Please say that agin to me, I didn't catch it.

Mar.   The Nymphs and the Satyr.

Mrs. O'G.   That's a funny name for them women. Why they ain't got no clothes on. Why don't they put some dresses on them?

Mar.   They are painted natural.

Mrs. O'G.   Yes, they's mighty natural. There is no mistake about that. It ought not to be allowed. It is sinful. [*Pauses*] But they are daisies you bet.

Mar.   Why do you look at them, if it be sinful? [*Crosses down below*]

Mrs. O'G.   I can't help it, they fetches me so. Them gals is peaches, ain't they? Why, I can't just take my eyes off them. Natur is natur, and I'm just as natural. Air you still hungering for the flesh pots of Egypt? If you see the senator tell him his old friend Mrs. O.'G. is looking for him. Good-bye. [*She *and Marino exit L.2. Enter Count Garbiadoff R.; he comes down front. Dick Brummage, who has been seated at table L. since rise, sees count and approaches him*]

BRUM. Well, Count Garbiadoff, you are, I observe, taking in all the sights of the city.

COUNT. [*Surprised*] Who are you?

BRUM. [*Opening coat and showing badge*] Detective Brummage. We met at the Central Office today.

COUNT. Oh, yes. I remember now. Haf you tell me something?

BRUM. Yes. Sit down. [*They sit L.*]

COUNT. What is it, speak. I am anxious to hear.

BRUM. Could you identify your diamonds if you saw them?

COUNT. Every stone.

BRUM. Even if on the person of the woman we suspect and at night?

COUNT. Yes, under any circumstances.

BRUM. The politician under whose protection this woman is, gives a party at his home, No. 1360 Madison Avenue. You must be there.

COUNT. What for?

BRUM. The woman will be there, and I think will wear your diamonds.

COUNT. Wear my diamonds? The audacity—it is not possible!

BRUM. I think she will wear them. A woman's vanity is always greater than her caution. She does not believe that anybody can identify them, and as she does not know the Count Garbiadoff is here. Be careful, remember you are sent there only to see them.

COUNT. Oui. I came all the way from Cracow to see them and to see her. [*Aside*] I will tear them from her—the pitiless wretch.

BRUM. Let me warn you not to be rash. If you can identify your jewels on her it will be all we can do tonight. If you are not prudent you may ruin us both, and destroy all chances of recovering the property.

COUNT. Mon dieu! Do you tell me I shall take only ze look and go back to Cracow with vat you call ze tail between ze legs? Pah! You shall call the gendarmes.

BRUM. Everything will be gained for the courts if you can identify the woman and the jewels. That is enough. Everything else would be madness. You do not understand this politician's power.

COUNT. Canaille, I do not understand.

BRUM. Calm yourself and meet me at the senator's tonight. Any cabman will carry you there.

COUNT. The entrée? How will I get that?

BRUM. Walk boldly in. The company will be so mixed that the senator will not know his guests and you will not be recognized. Now we had better say good-bye for the present, as I have other work to do.

COUNT. Au revoir. [*Exit door off R. at back. Brummage waves his hand and sits L. reading paper. Enter senator L.2., followed by Marino, Clancy, Brannigan and others. He is greeted cordially by several as he comes on to front of bar*]

SEN. Well, well, boys, as I was telling you, I have always depended on the Fourteenth. She deserves the banner and tonight she gets it—see? The handsomest woman in New York, my friend Mrs. Bulford, will make the presentation. Gentlemen, Mr. Marino, her brother. He is going in politics. [*To bartender*] Set 'em up, councillor. [*The two heelers shake Marino's hand, boisterously*]

CLAN. There's nothing the matter wid the Fourteenth. She gits the banner, dat's all right; and I get me brudder out of Sing Sing, eh, senator?

SEN. You bet. Have some cigars. [*Business with cigars. First heeler takes a handful from the box and puts them in his coat pocket, conversation in dumb show*]

BRAN. Ah, what d'ye know about the Fourteenth? You was brought up in de Sixth.

CLAN. De men in de Sixth learned the trade of votin' before de Fourteenth was made.

BRAN. Ah, de Fourteenth don't depend on no votin' when dey can do de countin'. What's de Fourteenth care for voters when dey got de inspectors?

COUNT. I am very anxious to learn the political methods of New York, but I don't know at present what I am to do to help on the glorious cause.

BRAN. Well, you kin do the drinkin' can't yer, like the rest of us?

CLAN. Ah—what does the Sixth know about drinkin'? [*Sheeney Ike appears L. coming down R., stops at corner of bar L. and tries to catch the senator's eye. Brummage moves so as to see Sheeney Ike over his paper*]

SEN. [*Laughing*] You'll have to take my friend down in the Sixth and show him the ropes. [*Sees Sheeney Ike*] Excuse me a minute, gentlemen. [*Goes to corner of bar, conversation of heelers continues in dumb show*] Are you looking for me?

IKE. Yes, Mother Rosenbaum sent me up from Canal Street.

SEN. What's the matter with her now?

IKE. She says there's a special from the Central Office a workin' the Bulford lay.

SEN. Well, it's none of his business. I'm takin' care of that. Tell the old woman to brace up. What's she got to do with it anyhow?

IKE.   She says they're a tryin' to fix it on the widder—Mrs. Bulford.

SEN.   Oh, they are, are they? Well, it don't go, because I'm lookin' out for the widder, and he can't work no lay there for I'll call him down. I've got a party at my house tonight—going to have Mrs. Bulford present the banner to the Fourteenth. You tell the old woman to rest easy in her mind—I will see her tomorrow—they can't work no lay without me. You bet. [*Marino going. Senator and Ike's dialogue continues in dumb show. While this conversation has been going on, the two heelers have got into violent altercation in dumb show which Marino absurdly tries to prevent, and both rush to senator for a decision, coming to the corner of bar L. and opposite table where Brummage sits*]

BRAN.   [*With great excitement*]   Well, I'm bettin' me pile on it. [*Pulls an enormous roll of bills from his hip pocket and slaps the roll down violently on table. First heeler pulls a still larger roll from pocket and imitates defiantly*]

CLAN.   Say, your money was born deaf and dumb. Here's the money what talks. [*Brummage gets up, disgustedly holding paper. Business continues between heelers in dumb show, Marino showing absurd anxiety and astonishment, senator leaning against bar and laughing at them. Senator and Ike move away from heelers*]

SEN.   [*To Ike*]   Who's the officer that's meddlin' in this matter?

IKE.   She says it's Brummage.

SEN.   Well I'll break him tomorrow, see? Have a drink, have some wine? [*Heelers coming promptly to bar again. At this moment great shouting is heard in the office and a crowd of Princeton and Yale boys shouting college cries and waving flags, singing songs, come crowding into room. Everybody yells, scenes of confusion, students cluster around the bar or sit at tables and pound bells ordering drinks. Senator and his friends form a group at bottom of bar, drinking and looking amusedly at boys. Frank is seen coming on at back mingling with the crowd. The moment he is well on, Brummage spies him and rushing across to him, takes him well R. and in a low voice but excitedly, says*]

BRUM.   My God, what are you doing here? I told you not to leave the house.

FRANK.   I know, I know. But I couldn't stand the suspense any longer. So I came here hoping to see you, and hear something of Mary and my own fate.

BRUM.   Well, I have something to say to you, and not much time to say it in.

FRANK.   Where is Mary?

BRUM.   Don't look around—we may be watched. Mary's kidnapped.

FRANK. My God, then what are you doing here? [*Ike's attention is attracted by Frank's manner*]

BRUM. Do you want to tell everybody in the place what we are talking about?

FRANK. [*Dropping back in his chair*] Kidnapped on my account and I am helpless!

BRUM. I respect your feelings, but just now they are damned risky, for we've got work to do.

FRANK. Why don't you tell me—where have they taken her? Who are the miscreants?

BRUM. Well, don't shout—I'm trying to find out. I've got a letter from the girl. If you'll keep quiet I'll show it to you. [*Produces note that he took from bouquet. Subdued laughter in bar, rear. Brummage and Frank listen a moment. Brummage then hands Mary's note to Frank*]

FRANK. [*Reading with difficulty*] "I am going to Madam Rosenbaum's to fetch the diamonds to Mrs. Bulford—don't know where. I am suspicious and nervous. I depend on you if anything happens to me." [*Direct*] What Madam Rosenbaum, where has she gone?

BRUM. There's only one old woman in New York that's likely to be mixed up in this, and she's a desperate character protected by the politicians and rolling in ill-gotten wealth. She has never hesitated at murder when it served her ends, for she goes to that senator there for protection. There stands the senator and there's the old hag's man talking to him.

FRANK. [*With gesture of impatience*] My God! What iniquity!

BRUM. Well, don't telegraph it. It must occur to you that in any case they wouldn't send the girl to fetch the diamonds and if they made her believe it, it was to trap her.

FRANK. Go on—you've got the knife into me—turn it around. Is there no living show for innocence in this city?

BRUM. Well, there is if you've got patience, and if you've got your facts right. But there's something else on that paper I couldn't make out. [*Frank looks at paper*]

FRANK. Yes, there's something else, but it's rubbed. [*Holds paper to light*] Oh, yes. It says "I know all about the glass." What does that mean?

BRUM. [*Starting*] Does it say that? [*Snatches paper and looks at it*]

FRANK. What does it mean?

BRUM. It means that she knows something and they've tried to make way with her.

FRANK. For God's sake, tell me what you're going to do.

BRUM. I'm going to get the information tonight. Tomorrow it will be too late. They are celebrating that politician's power now. Tomorrow he will stand between us and justice.

FRANK. We are wasting time—it may be too late now.

BRUM. Try and be cool and listen to me. The only way to save her is to get that information. [*Ike leaves senator and comes slowly and guardedly toward picture back of table where Brummage and Frank are sitting. Senator goes up R. to other groups*]

FRANK. Very well, man, let's be quick about it.

BRUM. The old woman has two places—one in Rivington Street—that's her store. The other in Canal Street near the river. That's her den. We've got to get in those two places tonight. If we only see Mary for a moment and get that information. [*Brummage and Frank have their heads down intent on the subject and Ike goes past them trying to listen just as Brummage has uttered the last speech*]

FRANK. Yes, yes.

BRUM. I am going to one place and I want you to go to the other. You can do just what I tell you. I'll write the number of the place in Canal Street on this card. [*Writes on card*] And on this side of it—[*Turns card over*] I'll give you a line to the patrolman on the beat. He will know it and will keep his eye on you. [*Hands card*] I will go to the other place. If the girl isn't there, I will be in Canal Street almost as soon as you are. We may not save the girl, but we may get the information that will save you. [*Ike is approaching the table and trying to listen*]

FRANK. I will not be saved at such a sacrifice.

BRUM. Never mind the rescue. See the girl—[*Brummage stops suddenly and eyes Ike fixedly. The latter seemingly does not turn his head—cowed by Brummage's gaze slinks off hurriedly at back*]

FRANK. Well—well—why do you stop? You wanted me to go to Canal Street to this old woman—

BRUM. But I don't want you to tell it to that ruffian who has just passed us. [*Marino, who has been intently watching all this, goes to senator and points to Brummage and Frank. Senator starts and looks in their direction*]

BRUM. Wait a moment. Is that sheeney still there?

FRANK. No. He has gone, but the senator is watching us closely. Does he suspect?

BRUM. Yes, very likely. We have got to act quickly. The girl, if you can get to her, will tell you all, and if you can get away with the information we will hang the right person.

MAR. [*Motioning his head in direction of Brummage*] Senator, there's your friend the detective, I am sure.

SEN. [*Astonished*] Brummage?

MAR. Yes, and the young fellow with him is startlingly like that young fellow Kennet I saw that fatal night at Mr. Bulford's.

SEN. You don't mean it! He would never dare—

MAR. 'Tis he. I would swear it.

SEN. [*Amazed*] I'll make a bluff and have him taken and spoil Brummage's game whatever it is. [*Senator beckons to Clancy and Brannigan. They join him. Senator talks to them in dumb show. They shake their heads knowingly and affirmatively. Frank and Brummage rise—they start towards door L.2.*]

SEN. Hold on! Both of you! Don't be in a hurry. I want you, see?

BRUM. Are you talking to me, sir?

SEN. Well, I am talking straight at you. See. I am on to you!

BRUM. Sir?

SEN. Oh, "sir" don't go, I won't have any frills. You are meddlin' in something that's my business. [*Tapping his breast*] And I'm going to call you down right here.

BRUM. You are drunk, sir, and I have no time to waste with you. [*Senator gets squarely in front of him*]

SEN. You're a liar. What are you doing? Where are you going?

BRUM. I am going out of that door.

SEN. Not yet, you ain't. You are going to stay here where my eye is on you.

BRUM. I am going. [*Slowly*]

SEN. And I am going to stop you.

BRUM. Oh, no. Remember you can't stop me tonight. You may tomorrow. [*Music till curtain*]

SEN. I'll stop both of you now. That man there with you is a murderer. [*Frank shudders*] And I am going to have him taken in. [*Motioning head toward Brannigan and Clancy. Brummage looks over his shoulder cynically at them*]

BRUM. Touch him if you dare. He is in my charge, by order of the superintendent, and while there, no man can arrest him. I represent the law, and don't you dare to put your hands on him.

SEN. Not a step shall he move until I get an officer. Patsy, Shorty seize him. [*Patsy and Shorty start to seize Frank; Brummage puts himself between them and Frank, one hand behind him on his pistol, the other on Frank, making picture*]

BRUM. Stop! I'll make daylight shine through the man who puts a finger on him.

SEN. [*As if to draw pistol*] You dog, I'll make an end of you here, and now, and I'll take in that murderer.

BRUM. *Draw!* I dare you. I am prepared for that. I am doing my duty and I shall protect this man unless you kill me. [*Places himself between senator and his men, shielding Frank completely. Senator and his men make picture standing at bay*]

SEN. Damn you—if I didn't have a party on my hands tonight, I'd have the buttons pulled off of you—you infernal hound.

BRUM. [*With intensity and deliberation*] Your party will be over by midnight; I'll report to you at twelve o'clock. [*Goes to door L.2.*] You'll have your friends around you. That hour will be yours—till then the hours are mine. [*Arm about Frank, pistol in hand, forcing way through crowd L.C. They give way in fright*]

CURTAIN

ACT V.

SCENE: *Canal Street. Exterior of Mother Rosenbaum's house, front scene. Old fashioned house, brick with green blinds. Alley in drop with practicable door. One practical window. Music for rise until curtain is well up.* TIME: *Nine o'clock at night.* AT RISE: *Old man playing harmonica. Peggy Daly dancing to his music. Four boys looking on; they have shinny sticks; clapping hands and keeping time with their feet. Enter Jimmy McCune with girl on his arm. She is leading a dog. He wears a silk hat and the girl carries a satchel.*

PEG. [*L.*] Where are you goin', Jimmy McCune, with your consort? How's yer sore eyes?

McC. Don't you gull me, Peggy Daly. Here, take me dorg into the alley. I am going down to Lumpy Kidney's.

PEG. Dere ain't no free lunch at Lumpy's today. [*Exit L.1. with dog. While they are talking, one of the boys snatches the satchel; Jimmy makes a dash at him, his hat falls off. Immediately the boys begin playing shinny noisily with it, two on a side. Peggy reappears from the alley and finally rescues the hat and gives it to Jimmy*]

McC. I'll make the old woman pay for that. Tell her I'm down to Lumpy Kidney's. [*Exit L.1. with companion. As he goes off there is a sound of rushing wheels and a gong. Boys all strike listening attitude and boy No. 1 shouts*]

BOY No. 1. Hi, fellers, there's a fire!

Boys. Fire! Fire! [*Exit hurriedly L.1., followed by Peggy. At the same time Sheeney Ike comes on R.1., goes to entrance of brick house. The blinds of practicable window open cautiously and Mother Rosenbaum's head appears with shawl thrown around it. Noise stops here*]

IKE. Is that you?

Ros. Yes, what's the matter?

IKE. [*Looking guardedly around*] There's something up. I just came from the Hoffman House.

Ros. Is the senator all right?

IKE. He's all right. Where's the gal?

Ros. I've got her here—she's all safe.

IKE. They are coming for her.

Ros. Who's coming?

IKE. A young fellah's coming down here fer to get word from her. I got onto it straight in the Hoffman House by listenin'. He's to spot the cop on his beat who's a goin' to look out for him.

Ros. Who's the nice young gentleman who's a comin' to visit the old woman?

IKE. [*R. of window*] I think it was Brummage was puttin' him up. But I steered the senator onto Brummage, and he'll take care of him. What we've got to look after, is the other one.

Ros. And the other one is coming to the pleceman on this beat?

IKE. That's the way I heard it.

Ros. And if he don't see the pleceman and comes in—

IKE. Then they'll never know he come.

Ros. Quick—where's Peggy?

IKE. There she comes—she's been down to Lumpy Kidney's. [*Pointing to L.1. Enter Peggy L.1.*]

Ros. Come here to me and mind what I tell you. [*Peggy to window*] Where's Jimmy McCune?

PEG. He's down to Lumpy's now. [*Takes a dancing step and hums*]

Ros. Stop that! Go back there and tell him to put on the cop's dress and lay for the young man what's a comin' here. Be quick about it. He's to steer this young man in here and not let the regular cop see him. Do you understand? Here's the shield—the coat's in the saloon. [*Hands out shield*] Tell him to keep out of the patrolman's sight. Go on now and if you make a mistake I'll skin you! [*Exit Peggy L.1. dancing. To Ike*] Go up to Cahill's saloon and tell the boys to keep the regular patrolman there till this is over. Here's the money. [*Gives money*] Buy whiskey, will you—no wine. Go on and come back here—I want you. We will give my young friend a chance to see [*Music till she closes window*] the old woman at her best. [*Ike takes money and hurriedly exits R.1. Rosenbaum looks up and down and then closes the shutters. Enter Peggy L.1., crosses to R. and exits through door. Enter Frank Kennet, R.1., looks about him*]

FRANK. This must be the place. I wonder if Mary is in that dismal hole—and I am the cause of her misfortune. My God! She may be dead before this. [*Walks L. and looks about*] I wonder where I'll find the patrolman. [*Looks off L.*] Thank Heaven, here he comes. [*Music tremolo till change of scene. Enter McCune, L.1., disguised as policeman. He walks guardedly along drop. Frank advances*] Are you the officer on this beat? [*McCune assents inarticulately*] There's a card for you. [*Gives card*] I want to find Mother Rosenbaum's.

McC. [*Pointing to the house*] You are right on top of it, see!

FRANK. Do you understand this card? You are to keep your eye on the place if I get inside.

McC. All right, I won't let go o' you, see!

FRANK. If I do not come out in twenty minutes—

McC. I'll fetch you. See? This is the way. Here, and I'll introduce you meself. See. [*Exit McCune followed by Frank through door. Dark change*]

SCENE 2: *Mother Rosenbaum's den. A large stone room in a cellar with one exit up a practicable swinging steps, C. of rear wall, with practicable door at top cut across in C., about eight feet up. On L. of room is a door to closet or dark room. Room is lit by iron grating. Small pine table extreme L. front, on which is a butcher's knife. Two wooden chairs at table. At extreme R. is a trap in 2. closed.* DISCOVERED: *Mother Rosenbaum seated at table L. Sheeney Ike and Peggy Daly half way down steps. Lights down.*

PEG. [*On steps*] He's got the man—they're comin' in.

Ros. [*Seated at table, screaming*] Go back to the front window and keep your eye out. [*Girl stands irresolute a moment. Mother Rosenbaum throws knife at her viciously and crosses a little to C. Peggy runs up steps and exits. Sheeney Ike picks up knife*]

IKE. [*R.C. crosses to Mother Rosenbaum*] You'd better let me keep it. You'll have it into somebody while this fit's on.

Ros. [*Screaming*] I'll have it into you if you don't mind your business. Give it to me. [*She clutches the knife and goes to table L. Ike shrugs his shoulders and relinquishes it*] Open that door. [*Pointing to door, L.*] I put some ointment on me beauty's head, and I want to see her. [*Comes to C. Ike unlocks door and opens it, pulls Mary out roughly. She is poorly dressed, has her head bound up and is terrified*]

MARY. [*Crosses to C., shrinking*] Do not kill me.

Ros. [*Striking knife on table*] Kill you, eh? Yes, I kill you easy enough. But first tell me who made you play the spy—who is he, eh? [*Seated at table L.*]

MARY. [*C.*] Let me go. I do not wish to play the spy. I am a helpless girl. [*Looks about piteously*]

Ros. [*Seated at table L., contemptuously*] Yes, you are a helpless girl. You have some friends, eh? Mebbe they come here and help you. [*Laughs bitterly*] Who put you up to this? You tell me who it is or maybe I cut it out of you this time. [*Viciously. Business with knife*]

MARY. You are mistaken. I do not know you. You brought me here yourself.

Ros. You lie! You were looking for the diamonds. You play the maid, eh? You shall play the maid for me. [*Rises and crosses to Mary advancing upon her*] You shall dress my hair. [*Clutching fingers*] No, I will dress your beautiful hair. You have a friend who comes to see you. I will show you what I will do to your friend. [*Mary shrinks terrified, Ike coming down and throwing Mary to R.*]

IKE. Oh, don't tear the girl to pieces. We've got enough to attend to without this.

Ros. [*R.C., swinging Ike, L.*] Don't you interfere—maybe I tear you to pieces.

IKE. [*Stepping back*] Oh, well I ain't murdering girls. You'll have the whole Central Office swarming over us.

Ros. [*Defiantly*] What does Rosenbaum care for the Central Office, you sneaking coward? If it was not for Rosenbaum you would be hanged long ago. It is Rosenbaum who has defended and released you when they had the rope on your neck, because you did what I told you. When you change your mind—pif! away you go. [*Goes up and turns*] You think Rosenbaum has no heart. Yes, you are right because it was torn out of my bosom when they killed my beautiful boy. I have lived with no heart waiting for Plon and his woman. I have laughed at the police and have bought the judges with my stolen money. And now when at last there comes to me Plon's woman, you think I will get my heart back again. Ha—ha—! you shall tear to pieces what I like. You shall do what Rosenbaum tells you or go like Red Leary and Scotty Jack. When you do not what I want you shall hang. [*Goes up, music*]

IKE. [*Astonished*] Plon's woman! Here? Why didn't you say so before. [*Crosses and seizes Mary. Crosses with her to door L. Half door at head of stairs opens and Jimmy McCune in policeman's uniform puts his head in and looks down. All start*]

Ros. Put her back there. [*Pointing to L. Ike seizes Mary and crosses with her*]

MARY. [*Piteously*] Oh, no—no—anywhere but in there. [*Appealingly to McCune*] Are you an officer? [*Ike roughly thrusts her in the dark closet and closes it*]

Ros. [*To McCune*] What are you grinning there for, McCune?

McC. [*At head of stairs*] De bloke's comin' in—here's de card he gave me. [*Throws down card. Ike picks it up and gives it to Mother Rosenbaum*]

McC. [*Looking back*] Look out for the steps. [*Frank appears at door, looks down and then slowly descends the steps. McCune leans on the half door. Ike up L.*]

FRANK. [*Down R.C.*] Are you the woman they call Mother Rosenbaum?

Ros. [*Screaming*] Shut the door McCune and stay here.

McC. All right. [*McCune starts to shut the door, and gets behind it. Brummage, disguised as a policeman, substitutes for McCune. (NOTE: Brummage and McCune must be made up alike, and be of same size and height so as to successfully accomplish substitution) Brummage shuts the door and comes down steps as if drunk, goes to the extreme upper R. where he sits down sideways to the audience on a box. He is disregarded by Ike and Mother Rosenbaum who are occupied with Frank*]

Ros. [*L.C.*] Madam Rosenbaum, if you please.

FRANK. [*R.C.*] You or some of your friends have a girl that I wish to communicate with. I come to you because—

Ros. You come to me, eh? Mebbe I brought you and you don't get away so easy.

FRANK. It is useless to threaten me for I communicated with the police before I came in.

Ros. [*Spitefully*] Yes, you tried to. Well, I stopped you. There's the card you gave to my man. The piece don't know you're here [*Flips the card up to him, then up to Brummage. Frank picks it up with some astonishment*]

FRANK. [*Aside*] What does this mean? I am trapped. [*Goes down R.*]

Ros. [*Up by Brummage, L. of him. To Brummage*] Jimmy, he thought you was a reg'lar. I'll have to be payin' you reg'lar salary pretty soon. [*Down C.—Brummage simulates drunkenness*]

FRANK. [*Alarmed*] Madam, I come here with but one purpose—it was to see the girl. I only want to speak to her.

Ros. [*Striking knife on table. Sits*] Well, I'm going to let you see her. Ikey, bring her out. [*Ike goes to closet door, unlocks it, and brings Mary out She puts her hands to her eyes as if the light dazzled her. Sees Frank*]

MARY. Frank Kennet! You here?

Ros. and IKE.   Frank Kennet! [*Mother Rosenbaum starts to her feet*]

FRANK. [*Advancing to Mary*]   Mary, my poor girl. What have these miscreants done to you? [*Music*]

IKE. [*Interposing*]   Keep back!

Ros.   Frank—ha—ha. Quick, Ikey, the steps. [*Rises and goes down R.C. presses button, throws steps up, cuts off retreat by means of a spring in the wall; at the same time Mary and Frank come together and the girl clings to him terrified*] So—o—o, you are Frank. You've been hiding from everybody since you killed the old man. Nobody knows you are in New York and nobody will miss you—and you set out to ruin the old woman. Let me look at you. For thirty years they have been trying to ruin Rosenbaum. They killed my boy. They put spies in my house. They set the police on me, they dragged me into courts. Because I am Rosenbaum. [*Goes to table and down L.*]

FRANK.   You dastardly wretches—you are making a big mistake.

Ros.   Ha—ha—ha! Rosenbaum makes no mistakes.

FRANK.   Dick Brummage knows where I am. [*Music stops*]

Ros.   The copper will tell him he didn't see you. If I were to let you run, you'd be tryin' to prove you didn't kill Mr. Bulford and we couldn't have that. [*Advances upon Mary slowly R.*] And I ain't going to let you run loose. [*Seizes Mary suddenly by the arms, pulls her away from Frank violently and thrusts her into chair L. As Frank attempts to interfere Ike catches hold of him behind by arms back; struggle; Frank throws him off and the three glare at each other. To Mary*] Now, you set there and see what we do with men who try to ruin the old woman. If you move an inch I'll put this into you. [*Picks up knife. Mary drops her head into her hands piteously and shudders*]

FRANK.   Hellhounds! If you think you can murder me without a fight for it, you've made the mistake of your lives. [*Takes his coat off and throws it behind him. Music*]

MARY. [*Half rising*]   No, no, they will kill you.

Ros. [*Thrusting her back in chair*]   Set down or I'll settle you first. [*Ike goes to trap R. and lifts it up (be particular about carpenters attending to steps—they fall when button is pushed). Brummage appears to be in drunken sleep*]

FRANK.   Mary—tell me—have you anything to say to me—what about the glass?

MARY. [*L.*]   Mrs. Bulford threw it out of the window the night of the murder and Dr. Livingstone has it.

Ros. [*By Mary, L.*]   Ha, that settles you—when you're both dead, the madam will be free. Ikey, open the trap. Jimmy, you drunken dog, get up. [*To Mary*] Now you sit still. [*Men struggle up and down the stage and*

Frank gets the better of Ike. Ike calls on Mother Rosenbaum; women watch the fight intently. Mother Rosenbaum goes R. Mary also rises and goes L. and thence to steps. The action of the two women must be so timed that Mary arrives at the spring in the wall at the same time Mother Rosenbaum reaches steps a second after they fall. Mary touches the spring and they have come down with a bang. All three of the group turn sharply around and Mother Rosenbaum makes two impulsive steps toward Mary and stops undecidedly. Mary runs up the steps but the door at the top is locked and she pounds on it with her fists. The two men glare at each other] Can [*On foot of steps C., to Ike*] you get away with him?

IKE. [*Struggling with Frank*]   Can I? Give me the knife. You take care of the girl. [*Mother Rosenbaum tosses the knife to Ike. It falls on the floor. Ike instantly goes toward Brummage to pick it up*]

Ros.   Quick, finish him—you are man to man and even. [*Ike stoops to pick up the knife when Brummage leans forward, presenting pistol; stands up R.C. above Ike*]

BRUM.   But what are you going to do with the old man? [*Change music till curtain. Tableau*] How are you going to get away with Dick Brummage?

TABLEAU. CURTAIN. RING.

2ND CURTAIN: *Mary comes down the steps, stops at bottom. Frank jumps to her, they embrace.*

FRANK.   Mary!

ACT VI.

SCENE: *Senator McSorker's house on Madison Avenue. Music off R.2.E. for rise. Interior showing handsome corridor and grand staircase C. coming well down stage, with lamps at bottom on either side flanked by heavy tropical plants. Arcaded entrances to salon L.2.; smoking room and hall R.2. Guests in evening dress standing at salon entrance looking at guests and conversing. At rise soft chamber music heard. Burst of laughter from group.* TIME: *Eleven o'clock at night.*

CLANCY. [*L.*]   Yes, if it ain't Lumpy Kidney I hope to die.

BRANNIGAN.   Well, I never expected to see him in a dress coat. He wears it like an epileptic fit. Say, boys, there won't be any eating until twelve o'clock. Let's go over to the chophouse and get a welsh rarebit. [*All come down C.*]

CLAN.   Oh, you'll miss the show. He's going to trot out her royal highness.

BRAN.   That's what we're here for. We've got to throw our posies at her. It's a go-as-you-please. Grand entrance. Procession of maids. Burst of music

—lights up—shower of bouquets. Three cheers for the flag and the senator on top.

CLAN. Well, I like it. No invites. No airs—no introductions.

BRAN. Say, if you don't keep your mug shut, I'll shove this into it. You act as if you were on Eighth Avenue instead of Madison. De Sixth ain't celebratin' tonight. [*Music stops*]

CLAN. When I get me brudder out of Sing Sing and he's a sheriff, I'm agoin' to move on de Fifth meself.

BRAN. Yes, I hear the whole Sixth is goin' to move up. [*Both go to salon entrance L.2. Bursts of laughter from guests*]

CLAN. She's a rich widow, I hear, from South America.

BRAN. Well, what's the matter with havin' her over to the Chowder Club? Come, let's go in. [*Move toward salon entrance and group themselves. Enter Mrs. O'Geogan from R.2. She is fantastically dressed and has a feather fan*]

MRS. O'G. I wonder if the senator calls that a party. It's more like a soree. [*The male guests laugh and exit R.2.*]

BRAN. No, madam, it's a levée.

MRS. O'G. I thought a levee was something that kept the flood out. Where's the cook room? [*Going R.C. Enter second heeler*] It's yourself that's cuttin' a fine shine this evening, Mr. Brannigan, with your shwaller tail.

BRAN. Oh, I ain't cuttin' no shine. We wuz to hang around the edges for a call. But it's all guzzle and munch and no jumpin'.

MRS. O'G. I have a stick in my mind a soakin' for the senator.

BRAN. I heered you was on the school board Mrs. O'Geogan.

MRS. O'G. You did? The same to you Mr. Brannigan. I heard you was workin' a reform ticket on the Fourteenth. You'll be goin' to Albany wid your shwaller tail, I don't know. [*Enter first heeler from R.2. with his coat on his arm*]

BRAN. [*To second heeler*] Say, dere is one of the dry dock tarriers in the crowd. We don't want no dry dock tarriers among us gents, do we?

CLAN. Oh, put your coat on; why can't you act like a gent in a gent's crowd and stop for de word before you do any mussin'.

BRAN. [*Putting his coat on*] I ken tump him, if it wasn't fer de coat. What's the good of our bein' here. [*Two heelers cross toward R. When they reach R.2. they encounter Count Garbiadoff and Madame Mervaine who are entering R.2. Heelers exit R.2., Count and Madame Mervaine cross L.*]

MME. M. Thanks, count, it is so close in there that, but for your kind attention, I should have fainted.

COUNT. I am only too delighted to be of service to you, madam. You say Mr. Brummage asked you to guide me through this strange assemblage.

MME. M.   Yes—but take care how you mention that name here. [*Indicates that Mrs. O'Geogan might overhear them; then quickly to Mrs. O'Geogan*] The senator has all his friends here tonight?

MRS. O'G.   Yis, ma'am. Shure it would be a little more lively if some of his inimies were on deck.

MME. M.   Are you one of his friends?

MRS. O'G.   Of course I am—one of his best friends. I knew him when he tended bar in Tim O'Shaughnessy's and had to mix drinks in a buttoned up coat while I washed his shirt. He's got to be a great dude, has the senator.

MME. M.   Will the lady who is to make the presentation come down those stairs? [*Pointing to stairs C.*]

MRS. O'G.   Well, I'm thinkin' she wouldn't come down the fire escape, with her diamonds and starched skirts. I wonder if that door has a kitchen behind it. Sure it's starvin', I am. [*Exits R.2. Count and Madame Mervaine laugh heartily at Mrs. O'Geogan's remark and at her exit*]

COUNT.   Is zis ze sort of canaille which your mansions are filled with at evening parties?

MME. M.   Oh, count, when you are the guest of an American politician you must wonder in silence and endure silently. Fretting about your environment is quite out of order. Let's take another stroll and see if we can find Mr. Brummage.

COUNT.   Yes, I must find him. [*Aside*] And I must see zat woman. [*They exit L.2. Enter two heelers from R.2. and two college boys*]

2ND H.   Break away, here comes de drum corp. [*Enter senator L.2. He is fussy, anxious and exuberant, followed by several male and female guests*]

SEN.   Ah, ha, gents, enjoying yourselves, I hope. Don't forget to go to the saylong before the horns go off. I've arranged everything on schedule time and that's the signal that the lady's coming downstairs. I don't want you to miss it. Have you got your flowers? [*Looks around at them. The two heelers and two college boys raise their bouquets as if to throw them*] Stop! All right. Don't throw them until she gets at the bottom of the stairs. [*Looks at his watch*] Half past eleven. Great success, eh?

2ND GUEST.   Perfectly paralyzing. Beats the Wild West, senator.

1ST GUEST.   Regular coop—de-e-tat. [*Senator moves fussily toward smoking room R.2. looks in and calls*]

SEN.   Gentlemen—everybody in the saylong. The ceremony is about to begin. [*Looks at his watch again. To guests in front of stage*] Now then, gents—all in the saylong. [*Male guests move to entrance L.2. Senator crosses to L. and meets Marino, who comes from salon L.2.*] Is the lady all ready?

[*Looks at his watch*] I expect them horns to go off every minute. How does she look.

MAR. Like a goddess—she always does, senator.

SEN. [*Slapping Marino on back*] Damme! I'll make her the Goddess of Liberty. I'll have her walk in roses knee deep. It's going to be the proudest moment of her life, my boy. Just go up and see she is ready, will you? [*Marino goes up stairs and exits. Senator exits into salon L.2. followed by guests. Coutche-coutche polka. Enter Mrs. O'Geogan R.2. She is noticeably under the influence of wine. She carries a large fan and has an elaborate head-dress with two feathers*]

MRS. O'G. Oh, my! Oh, my! I've been havin' the greatest toime out there. Shure I don't know what's the matter with me. I wuz hungry just now, and —now—I'm loaded with everything good to eat and drink—ah! that pink stuff in a great glass christian bowl, with strawberries and pineapple all thrown in gratis. And they give it to you for nothin'. They kape fillin' your glass whenever it's empty, and just don't give you toime to get thirsty. [*Enter senator L.2., approaches her, and goes with great rush. Business, while senator is talking to Mrs. O'Geogan, of her leaning forward and bowing her head in acknowledgment of what he says, and the headdress feathers tickling his nose and face—he trying to escape*] It sounds like the Midway of Plaisance, I heard at the World's Fair. [*Business. Crosses to L and sits on sofa. Business*] Oh! my, oh, my. Oh, this is like the cable car, without the bumps.

SEN. [*To guests*] Mrs. O'Geogan—one of my constituents—what the devil brought her here?

MRS. O'G. Mister Conductor! Mister Conductor, please let me off at Forty-Second Street. [*Business. Senator coughs, comes down C. Mrs. O'Geo-gan turns on sofa; sees him, rises, crosses to C., bowing*] I'm here, senator, I'm here.

SEN. Yes, I see you are.

MRS. O'G. How do you like me get up?

SEN. Gorgeous! Gorgeous! I'm glad to see you on this glorious occasion. [*Crosses L.C. turns and faces her*] The Fourth of July ain't anywhere; music —fireworks—illuminations, beautiful women. And you, Mrs. O'Geogan, are queen of beauty and the jewel among women. The Kohinoor ain't in it with you.

MRS. O'G. [*R.C.*] Oh, thank you. I don't know Mrs. Kohinoor. But, senator, I'm wid you every toime.

SEN. [*Shaking hands*] I know you are, Mrs. O'Geogan. [*Aside*] How the devil am I to get rid of her. [*Goes up L.C.*]

Mrs. O'G. Oh, I'll always be wid ye, senator, you are the one man of my affeshuns. Come here, sinitor. [*Senator comes down to her, L.C.*] Mrs. O'-Dooley tould me that you are a great flirt.

Sen. Damn Mrs. O'Dooley. [*Goes up L.C.*]

Mrs. O'G. [*Sings*] "You're the only man in all the world for me," etc. [*Goes up R.C.; business; comes down*] Come here, senator. [*Senator comes down L.C.*] I can sing better than that if I like.

Sen. Well, I hope so.

Mrs. O'G. But, senator, I've always loved you. Senator, pardon my blushes.

Sen. [*L.C.*] Where did she get it? [*Turns away; steps up a little; turns facing her*] Mrs. O'Geogan have you had something to eat?

Mrs. O'G. Eat, is it? Shure, I've been down in the kitchen to see Mary the cook. Shure, Mary's an old friend of mine, and she had an elegant christian bowl full of punch, with strawberries, all floating on the top of it, and I helped myself—ah, shure I didn't have time to get thirsty. Senator—I'm loaded.

Sen. Eh?

Mrs. O'G. Wid the supper—wid the supper. Ah! Senator, you keep iligant liquors.

Sen. How d'ye know?

Mrs. O'G. Sure I imbibed—

Sen. What? [*Goes up L.*]

Mrs. O'G. I man, I inhaled—inhaled the aroma, and I intend to marry you—

Sen. [*Aside*] The devil you do.

Mrs. O'G. With your consent. You are—[*Business of patting him on the face*] my love's young dream. [*Business*] You are so beautiful, so fresh, so innocent. [*Putting her finger on his chin*] You're a daisy.

Sen. Oh, am I? [*She leans her head on his breast; business*]

Mrs. O'G. Sure, Mrs. O'Dooley told me. [*Putting her face close to his. He pushes it gently away. She puts her face to his again*] Senator, Mrs. O'Dooley tould me—[*Coutche-coutche polka*]

Sen. Damn Mrs. O'Dooley. [*Goes up, listens to music which plays off L.2.*] That's the way to get rid of her. Mrs. O'Geogan, I know you love music and dancing—

Mrs. O'G. Love music? The idea. Do you remember when we used to go speeling in Walla Walla Hall? Did you ever know an Irish lady that wasn't fond of music and dancing? Senator, will you dance a step wid me?

Sen. What? [*Looks off L.2. turns to her*] Not on your life.

Mrs. O'G. Oh, come here, that or nothin'. [*She takes him by left hand; they dance a few steps toward R., turn facing L.2., dance and exit L.2., laughing. Enter Count Garbiadoff and Madame Mervaine R.2.*]

Mme. M. Mr. Brummage has not come.

Count. Bah—the police Americans are what you call ze grande hoom-poog.

Mme. M. They are cautious, count. He probably did not want to witness this woman's triumph. Be careful, she is coming. If the earth does not open and swallow her before she gets to the bottom of the stairs, you will see the most magnificent victory of audacity. It was worth coming from Cracow to witness! [*Enter Marino from top of stairs, comes down past the sofa and speaks*]

Mar. The lady is coming. Will you not enter the salon? [*Exit Marino into salon L.2. Count rubs his glasses with his handkerchief, and leaving the sofa goes to stairs, standing off behind the plant. Mrs. Bulford appears at top of staircase in full evening dress, bejewelled and attended by maids of honor. She holds her head high and wears a triumphant look. Guests enter. The female guests are bending eagerly forward to see her, count is peering at her through his glass behind balustrade. When Mrs. Bulford has reached the middle of the stairway, Mary Lavelot suddenly steps out from behind the plants on L. of steps and stands like a statue under the lamps. At the same moment the trumpets are heard playing a fanfare. She is attired in the same dress she wore in Rosenbaum's den and her head is bound up in the same cloth. She is pale and distressed. Mrs. Bulford comes slowly and smilingly down steps, chatting and laughing to maids. When she reaches the bottom she is suddenly confronted by Mary. Fanfare stops. Mrs. Bulford starts, recovers herself and speaks, the maids forming a tableau of astonishment*]

Mrs. B. Who are you?

Mary. Susanne!

Mrs. B. [*Agitatedly*] What are you doing here?

Mary. Meeting you face to face for the last time.

Mrs. B. [*Imperiously*] Stand aside. I cannot waste words with my servants now.

Mary. I have come out of a living grave to confront you in your triumph and to tell you that the God of Justice reigns even in New York. I cannot stand aside even if I would. [*Mrs. Bulford exhibits great distress*]

Mrs. B. [*Almost at foot of stairs*] Who is this lunatic? Why is this outrage permitted? Where is the senator? Where are the police? [*Turns and looks R. Enter Brummage, R.2.*]

BRUM. Madam, the police are here and waiting. [*Mrs. Bulford turns her head and sees Garbiadoff standing a few paces down stage L.*]

MRS. B. Garbiadoff! [*Falls on steps, recovers, starts to go up steps and falls backward, falling in the arms of Garbiadoff, who is L. and Brummage who is R. Recovers again, goes up steps, struggling with Brummage who is holding her by the left wrist*] Don't touch me! Let me go! [*She is now on platform on top of steps*] My God! This is the end! [*Taking small vial from her bosom—puts it to her mouth—falls and dies. Brummage kneels by her a moment to see if she is dead. Takes the vial from her. (Brummage should carry a duplicate vial—she may lose hers.) Holds it in his right hand. Enter Marino quickly from L.2.; he looks about in wonder*]

MAR. What is the matter?

MME. M. The lady has fainted.

MAR. Fainted? Impossible! [*Rushes upstairs, looks at Mrs. Bulford in astonishment. Enter senator, L.2., followed by guests and Mrs. O'Geogan, L.2.*]

SEN. Well, what's the hitch? Where's the lady? Will somebody stop the music? [*Turning and looking off L.2.E., then turns to stairs again*] Where is she? [*Enter several other male and female guests R.2.*]

MAR. [*On top of stairs C.*] Dead!

OMNES. [*Solemnly*] Dead!

MAR. [*Kneeling by his sister*] Dead!—my God—dead!

BRUM. [*Holding up vial*] The Para poison! [*Senator takes a step or two towards stairs in rage*]

SEN. You damnable dog! [*Slight pause*] Here, Patsy, Shorty, where are you? [*Enter L.2., first and second heelers. They come left and right of senator. All the guests looking extremely anxious at stairs. Madame Mervaine at sofa looking at stairs, Garbiadoff a little above her, all looking to C. in suspense*]

BRUM. [*Who has come down a step or two holding up his hand authoritatively*] Stand back! The lady belongs to the law—her diamonds to the Count Garbiadoff! [*Pointing to the count*] Senator, it is twelve o'clock! [*Mary in Frank's arms L., a little above the senator*]

PICTURE

CURTAIN

THE HEART OF MARYLAND

A Drama in Four Acts

(1895)

By David Belasco

CAST OF CHARACTERS

GENERAL HUGH KENDRICK, *commanding Southern forces*
COLONEL ALAN KENDRICK, *his son, of the 9th Cavalry, Northern forces*
COLONEL FULTON THORPE, *a spy*
LIEUTENANT ROBERT TELFAIR, *Battery B., Southern artillery*
SERGEANT BLOUNT, *ex-jailer, now a Provost Sergeant in the Southern Army*
TOM BOONE, *of Boonesboro*
LLOYD CALVERT, *Maryland's brother*
THE SEXTON OF THE OLD CHURCH
UNCLE DAN'L
BLAIR
HAYNE
BRYCE } *Aides-de-camp of General Kendrick's staff*
LEIGHTON
CORPORAL DAY
BLUDSOE, *an orderly*
PRIVATE JOHNSON, *Southerner*
PRIVATE WILLIAMS, *Northerner*
LITTLE TRUE BLUE, *a bugler*
O'HARA
RUGGLES } *exchanged Northern prisoners*
FORBES
CORPORAL (ACT I)
PHIL, *a Northern prisoner*
SENTRY
SCOUT
OFFICER (ACT III)
MRS. CLAIBORNE GORDON, *nee Calvert*
MARYLAND CALVERT
PHOEBE YANCEY, *Lloyd's sweetheart*
NANNY MACNAIR, *Mrs. Gordon's ward*
SOLDIERS, SCOUTS, SENTRIES, EXCHANGED PRISONERS, ETC.

SYNOPSIS

ACT I: "THE LILACS," BOONSBORO. "GREEN-WALLED BY THE HILLS OF MARYLAND."
ACT II: SOUTHERN HEADQUARTERS AT "THE LILACS." THE NEXT MORNING.
ACT III, SCENE I: EXTERIOR OF THE OLD CHURCH. NIGHT. (CURTAIN DOWN THREE MINUTES)
    SCENE 2: COLONEL THORPE'S HEADQUARTERS IN THE VESTIBULE.
    SCENE 3: THE BELFRY. (DARK CHANGE)
ACT IV: AT "THE LILACS." A LITTLE AFTER DAYLIGHT.

ACT I.

PROPERTY PLOT: *Plenty of yellow ochre for dust, etc. 4 flour dredgers for same. 1 flour dredger filled with powdered charcoal. Letter in large envelope for Colonel Thorpe. Small bird (supposed to be wounded and unable to fly), a lark, for Nanny. A general's saddle and bridle for Bludsoe, off R.2.E. Transport order for Blount. Small salver with leg of chicken, for Uncle Dan'l, off L.U.E. Large piece of bread for Blount. For effects offstage, R.: 12 horseshoes; large stone slab, 6 by 2 ft.; 2 pieces of lumber, 6 ft. long, 2 in. thick, 12 in. wide, covered with carpet and rubber. Also two small trestles for same. 12 cavalry sabres tied together with chains. Wood crash and loose logs. 2 trucks with wooden cogwheels filled with heavy weights, chains, etc., for artillery effects. Heavy iron weight for rumble. Large loose chain for use in artillery effect. 2 long rolls of matting for men to stamp on. Marching effect. Large watermelon on stage, C. Hanging vines on lower L. corner of balcony and railing. One lilac tree, high enough for a person to stand under and one lilac bush, L.; some of the blossoms and petals have fallen to the ground. Table made out of stump of tree, between lilac tree and lilac bush. On table, workbasket, plenty of sewing materials in workbasket, also one very large blue woolen sock, and one partly knitted. 4 steel knitting needles with a ball of blue wool on table, L. Small bench 12 by 18 in., 18 in. high, above gate to orchard, R.2. Large stone for little True Blue to rest on, R. of gate above house, L. Carpet inside house on upper and lower platform, also on steps inside house. Picture on backing inside house, facing front door. Field glasses in case with straps to sling over shoulder for Telfair. War map on rollers, made out of tracing linen for Aide. Memorandum books and pencils for General Kendrick and Colonel Thorpe.*

CALCIUM PLOT: *Lens in flies on low stand, R.3.E., large focus, to cover balcony and lilac tree in front of house, L., and "run" upstage, L. Red all through act. Green on high stand, R., back of bridge to cover drop Amber at rise; at cue "Drunk or in love, or both," change to Red until end of act. Lens in flies, R.2.E., to cover steps and stage front of house, C. Amber, change to Red at cue. Lens in flies, R.3.E., to cover lilac tree and table, front of house. Both these lights Yellow at rise. At cue, "Drunk or in love, or both," change to Red until end of act.*

ELECTRIC LIGHT PLOT: *Red and Amber proscenium lights, L. Amber proscenium lights, R. Red and Amber strip lights, R.1.E. Red and Amber strip lights, R.3.E. Red and Amber strip lights, on wing of stage, R. 3 set rows on set pieces upstage, Red and Amber. White strip on set house, L. White strip over windows in house, L., light at cue. 1st, 2nd, 3rd, 4th and 5th borders, Red and White; back border, Red, White and Blue. Footlights, Red and White. Note: All these lights must be worked on resistance. The Act opens with a warm summer afternoon. Lights changing gradually to a deep sunset.*

"THE LILACS." BOONESBORO.

"GREEN-WALLED BY THE HILLS OF MARYLAND."

SCENE: *Old Colonial homestead with veranda facing road, R. The veranda is four or five feet from ground, and rests on corbels. Vines droop over lower corner. Flagstaff slants from upper corner. French window opens on veranda. Steps, facing audience, lead to door of house which opens into hall. A fanlight is over door. Large brass knocker on door. The view from veranda commands the old country road, which leads to off R.2.E. Gate with latch to orchard, R.1.E. A brook runs from R., nearly to C. and disappears among meadows at back. Water lilies grow in it and the bank is covered with grasses. An old moss-covered, low-pitched rustic bridge crosses stream, overhanging boughs bend over bridge. Nearly L.C. is a path leading to a military camp, tents are seen near-by and in the distance. Adjoining house is a hedge with gate opening into private grounds. By upper corner of veranda is a lilac bush in full bloom, high enough for a person to stand under. Some of the blossoms have fallen to the ground. An old stump, about the height of an ordinary table, covered with vines, is by lower corner of house. Shrubs and flowers grow under the veranda. Ancient lilac bushes in full bloom hug the sides of house, thereby giving name of "The Lilacs" to the place. The scene is "walled in by the green hills of Maryland." Effect of lowland lights comes from valley at back and sunlight bathes all in a tender glow. The odor of lilacs fills the air. A soft melody is played at rise of curtain. End of prelude.*

DISCOVERED: *Uncle Dan'l, a lovable old darky with shining bald pate, and snow-white wool. His skin a dark brown. Dressed in a rusty old-fashioned suit of black, frilled shirt and high white stock, is asleep on front steps. His hat has fallen on the ground, and a large watermelon lies near him. When the music ceases the stillness is broken only by the heavy breathing of Uncle Dan'l; he draws a long breath, sighs and snores, ending with a little soft whistling sound. Lieutenant Robert Telfair, a tall young fellow, with all the elegance of a Southern gentleman, and an ultra-military bearing, dressed in the uniform of Confederate artillery (a sort of "Jeb Stuart"), enters down road at back, L.*

TEL. [*By bridge, unslings field glasses, looks off, R.*] No signs yet of General Kendrick's advance along this side of the hills. [*Replaces glasses in case, comes down, R.C. Uncle Dan'l utters a prolonged snore, followed by a whistle*] Eh! what the devil's that? [*Faces L., sees Uncle Dan'l*] Oh, of course! Ripening in the sun—[*Crosses over by house. Uncle Dan'l brushes back of his ear as if annoyed by an insect*] and a bumblebee singing to him. [*The bee is supposed to come near him*] Sho! Sho! [*Strikes at it with his hand*] Sho! Here! [*Tapping Uncle Dan'l on shoulder*] Wake up! [*Gives double rap on his bald pate*] Attention! [*Uncle Dan'l gives a short grunt like snore, his head falls forward*] A cannon shot wouldn't rouse him. [*As he moves away sees melon*] Ah! Cooling suggestion! [*About to pick it up*]

UNCLE. [*Raising the lid of one eye*] Le' go—le' go dat million! [*Recognizing Telfair, rises, his manner is courteous, imitating the old school of colonial gentry*] L'ten'n Telfair, I ax yo' pa'din, sah. I t'ought some ob yo' boys wuz a' prankin' agin, sho', sah.

TEL. You weren't asleep at all, uncle! You were playing possum.

UNCLE. 'Deed I wuz in de lan' ob Beulah, but—[*Going L.R., with unctuous chuckle*] b-b-but I had one eye on de million! Won't you had sum, lootenen? [*Picking up melon which is very heavy; admiringly, insinuatingly*] A slice ob dis million'll slide down de troat like de grace ob Hebben. [*Starts to exit through orchard gate, R.1.E.*]

TEL. No—no—thank you. [*Turns up L., quickly. Whistle. Goes up and signals, off L., towards the Post*]

UNCLE. [*Sort of paralyzed*] 'Fusin' million! 'Fusin' million! [*Horse distant, H.E.S. Smacks his lips and exit into orchard, R.1.E., with melon*]

TEL. [*Up C., speaking to someone off L.U., a little distance away*] Sergeant! No signs of General Kendrick yet? I'll take a look from Flag Staff hill. [*Starts L., Bludsoe is heard outside, R., Telfair stops. Bludsoe is supposed to have halted his horse down road*]

BLUD. [*Offstage*] Hello-o-o, there! [*Horse coming and halt*]

TEL. [*Facing road*] Hello!

BLUD. Lieutenant!

TEL. Ah, the general's orderly.

BLUD. [*Running across bridge, R., salutes*] I'm from General Kendrick.

TEL. Ah!

BLUD. With a message to Colonel Thorpe. [*They go downstage. Takes paper from belt and shows same to Telfair*]

TEL. [*Pointing from R. to L.*] Ride along that road to the foot of the hill. [*Bludsoe starts R. Horse going*]

BLUD. [*As he gallops off, his sabre clanking*] Yesterday morning.

Tel. [*Calling after him*] All quiet—along—the—Potomac?

Blud. [*Distant*] All quiet—[*Voice gradually dies away*] except a stray bullet—[*Almost inaudible*] now—and—then. [*Sound of horse's hoofs and clank of sabre die away*]

Tel. [*C., looking R.*] Kendrick's advance! That's meat for the mess at our Post tonight. The second invasion of Maryland has begun in earnest. Hot days ahead! [*Nanny MacNair, a merry, little, bright-faced girl, about fifteen, frank and innocent, with a quaint brusque manner, dressed in a plain frock, and wearing a large gipsy palmetto hat, trimmed with long red, white and blue ribbons, comes through orchard, R.1.E. She has a bird snuggled in both hands up against her cheek. The gate is on the latch, and, without taking her hands down, she leans her elbow on the gate to push it open with her knee. Telfair salutes her with marked gallantry*] Miss MacNair. [*Nanny looks steadily at him, and with a manner equally marked, ignores his presence. She pushes the gate open and shuts it with a vicious little backward kick, passes him, and walks over to the corner of balcony, looking at hanging vines*]

Tel. [*Amused*] Little Northern nettle. She thinks her silence is stinging. So it is. I haven't deserved it—I won't stand it! [*As he watches her searching through the vines*] Miss MacNair, my services are at your command, if you're looking for anything in particular. [*Comes down*]

Nanny. [*Throws him a little disdainful glance, and continues her searching*] Where's that hummin' bird's nest? [*Giving up the search with a little disappointed cry*] Oh, shucks! It's gone!

Tel. Routed by a petticoat! [*Glances at her over his shoulder*] And such a short one, too. Never! [*Boldly and with lots of manner*] May I ask what you have there?

Nanny. [*Incisively*] A victim of war! [*Holding out bird*] Look there—what you've done!

Tel. [*Backing before her, astounded*] I—?

Nanny. Your men—choppin' down the trees for kindlin's murdered the parents and broke up the home. I found this—the only one alive, and they were all nearly ready to fly. Looters! Poor little shivery thing. [*Rummages in workbasket on porch*]

Tel. I'm sorry. Anything in the way of indemnity I can offer—

Nanny. [*Taking from basket a partly knitted blue woolen sock set on the needles. Without looking at him*] —will be refused! [*Drops on her knees to adjust sock in small bush. Cooingly*] Didums! There—this sock will do for a nest. You've lost your mother and I'll have to bring you up by hand. [*Puts bird tenderly in sock*] You shall have the sunshine!

TEL. Yes, but what a waste of good hosiery—and you knitted them! I'd love to wear them. I'd love to march in your socks—No, no, I mean—in those socks. [*Pointing to socks*]

NANNY. [*Facing him, still on her knees, taking very large sock out of basket*] What! A Southerner march in those! [*Saucy toss of her head*] H'm! [*With a contemptuous glance at his foot*] These are number twelves! I'm knitting them for a good, square-footed Northerner!

TEL. [*With a little extra interest*] Is that the measure of his foothold in your heart?

NANNY. [*Ignoring his interruption*] And when he comes down with both feet, [*Rising*] you 'uns better get out of his way.

TEL. [*To her*] Miss MacNair, am I to suppose then, that this young giant —is—your—sweetheart?

NANNY. If you want to.

TEL. I'm honored with this confidence, and I can certainly say [*With his most gallant manner*] the gentleman is to be congratulated. I can see you're devoted to him.

NANNY. Heart and soul.

TEL. And you've been engaged—?

NANNY. Since I was old enough to choose.

TEL. May I have the honor to know the name of your conqueror?

NANNY. Uncle Sam! [*Turns again to bird*]

TEL. [*Aside*] She's toasting me! [*To her, affecting great perplexity*] Uncle Sam, oh, that's the gentleman with whiskers on his chin, who dresses himself up in a white hat, with stars on his coat-tails.

NANNY. Never mind how he dresses himself up, he'll dress you down. [*Turns away*]

TEL. However does a rabid little abolitionist like you manage to get along under the same roof with Miss Maryland?

NANNY. Oh, she enjoys me, calls me her whetstone. It's the old lady I'm skeered on. [*At foot of steps, L., facing audience. Taking ribbons off hat, and cramming them into her pocket*] I reckon it's just as well not to rouse her secesh. [*About to go into house, L.*]

TEL. [*Tenderly, as she starts to go L.*] Don't go! You quaint little sprig of bittersweet.

NANNY. [*Looking back over her shoulder*] What's that, you Johnny?

TEL. Why do you hate us so, Yank?

NANNY. Oh! Never mind! [*Turning away*]

TEL. That warlike spirit of yours was never left you by your father, dear old Parson MacNair.

NANNY. [*Moving a little to him, facing him, with rising feelings*] No—it's my brother Ned's, who was shot by one of you. P'rhaps I don't know what it is to be an orphan like—[*Pointing to bird in bush*] that.

TEL. [*Starts to speak, with tender gravity*] I'm so sorry—I—I—it's awful for a country to divide, the North on one side, the South on the other. But we shouldn't be enemies.

NANNY. [*Suddenly realizing she is opening her heart, turns on him like a little fury*] Don't speak to me! Oh! Why wasn't I born a man?

TEL. For the delight of the fellow who was!

NANNY. I'll never forgive any of you! Never! Never! I hate you! You—you—[*Turns and runs up steps*]

TEL. Say it!

NANNY. I won't! [*Exit into house. Telfair crosses to R. Fulton Thorpe enters by road at back, R. His face is one not to be soon forgotten: sallow complexion, almost livid, and his hair, jet black. He has the look of a man addicted to very hard drinking, but never unsteady on his feet, nor in his speech. He wears the uniform of a colonel of Confederate infantry*]

THORPE. [*Speaks as he sees Telfair cross to R.*] Lieutenant!

TEL. [*Saluting*] Colonel Thorpe! [*Down R.*]

THORPE. [*L.*] General Kendrick will halt at One Tree Hill until the main force has crossed the river. By the way, do you know, is he related to Colonel Alan Kendrick of the Northern Army—let me see—colonel of the 9th Cavalry now holding Charlesville? [*Pointing, R.C., at back*]

TEL. Father and son.

THORPE. Too bad they should be fighting on opposite sides!

TEL. That's the pity of civil war, colonel.

THORPE. Of course, you know Alan Kendrick's not in command now, he's a prisoner at Danville.

TEL. That hole! You know Alan Kendrick, colonel?

THORPE. I've met him! [*Brusquely*] Keep a sharp lookout! [*Goes L., front of steps, looks off, L.*]

TEL. [*Salutes, aside*] Been drinking again—about time he sobered up. [*Thorpe turns, R. Exit down road, R.3.E. Lloyd Calvert, a pale-faced lad, with an earnest enthusiastic face and manner, dressed in a neat civilian's suit, enters by the road at back, L.3. Sees Thorpe and halts*]

THORPE [*Eyeing him closely*] What are you looking for? [*Lloyd, R.C., Thorpe, L.C., front steps*]

LLOYD. [*Pointing to house, L.*] This is my home, sir.

THORPE. You're Lloyd Calvert? [*Crossing to Lloyd*]

LLOYD. [*Looks at him searchingly*] Yes, sir.

THORPE. [*Lowering his voice*] When'd you leave headquarters at Washington? [*Lloyd starts*] Don't spasm, boy! [*Thorpe whispers a word*]

LLOYD. Oh! [*Saluting timidly*] You are Colonel Thorpe, of the Northern Secret Service?

THORPE. Sh-h! [*Low*] Yes, but don't say that again! Be careful! Remember, I am known here as a trusted officer in command of this Post. [*Glances about without moving his body. Lloyd salutes. The following dialogue is spoken in low guarded tones*] When'd you leave headquarters?

LLOYD. Yesterday.

THORPE. Detailed on secret service—to enlist in the Southern ranks and report to me. You've enlisted?

LLOYD. Just now! [*Pointing off, L.U.E.*]

THORPE. Your family is the first here; your sister Miss Maryland, one of the most loyal women in the South, and your local knowledge makes you invaluable. That's why you were sent to me.

LLOYD. [*Aghast*] In—my—own—home! [*Crosses to L.*]

THORPE. What's the matter with you? [*Putting hand on his shoulder, stopping him*]

LLOYD. [*L.C.*] Nothing—but, on my way here I saw a Union spy hanged. As he stood with the rope 'round his neck, his coffin at his feet, his eyes were fixed on *me*.

THORPE. [*R.C.*] Nervous, eh?

LLOYD. [*Turns strongly, with spirit*] No! When I entered the Military Academy at West Point, I took the oath of allegiance to the North, I swore to serve it, and I'm going where my duty calls me. I know I'm doing right. But if I'm caught—Oh! I'm not afraid to die—[*Turns to look at his house. His voice falters as he looks toward the house*] They—my people will learn I have not been fighting for them—I was a spy against them.

THORPE. My young friend, emotion's a very fine thing—but curb it, if you don't want to fill a pine box like that fellow you saw hanged at Middletown. Don't stand so close. [*Lloyd takes a step, L., pause*] What news from Washington?

LLOYD. [*Distinctly and impressively. Front face, soldierly, low, distinct*] They know that General Kendrick is advancing with 60,000 men—that he intends to take our strongest post, Charlesville, and cut off all communication with headquarters at Washington.

THORPE. Well?

LLOYD. [*Increase a little*] General Hooker has been sent with a large force of artillery to strengthen the garrison at Charlesville and check Kendrick's advance.

THORPE. Well? [*Until after Lloyd's exit, he has a preoccupied air, even when talking*]

LLOYD. The reinforcements should reach there by daylight. [*Make a climax*] Every energy is bent on holding Charlesville. I have here orders for you. [*Hand to bosom*]

THORPE. Careful. [*Lloyd drops hand. After both have looked cautiously around, Lloyd takes paper from bosom, Thorpe takes paper from Lloyd*] Seen your sister?

LLOYD. No! She thinks I'm in Pensacola.

THORPE. Say you've been sent here to await orders. Sleep home tonight. Report to me in the morning. [*Lloyd starts to move, L.*] Mind, [*Stops, then goes on*] trust nothing to writing and be careful about speaking to me. [*Thorpe goes up to bridge, R., reading paper Lloyd has given him. Lloyd salutes, approaches door, hesitates. Phoebe, a sweet, modest-looking girl of seventeen comes out of orchard, R.1.E., sees Lloyd*]

PHOEBE. Lloyd! [*R.E.*]

LLOYD. [*By steps*] Phoebe! [*Hoofs ready; he comes toward her; they meet, L.C.*]

PHOEBE. Lloyd! [*Recovering from her surprise, runs into his arms*] Oh, I'll have to pinch you to make sure you're real. [*Pinches him*] That's not hard enough. Oh, isn't this good! [*Throwing her arms around him again*] Where are your soldier clothes? You're too sure of me—you stayed away so long. When did you get back? Have you seen Aunt Elinor? No! We'll steal in quietly and surprise them. [*Tiptoes up, crosses and takes him by the hand*] Sh! Sh! Don't make a noise. [*Calls*] Aunt Elinor. [*Pushes him into house*] Come! O Lloyd, won't they be glad to see you! [*Both exeunt into house, L. Phoebe pushes him in*]

THORPE. [*On bridge. Has kept eye on Lloyd and Phoebe while reading. He has torn up one paper and now looks at another which was enclosed in his*] So Hooker's to check Kendrick's advance; one false move on either side— what a calamity! [*Pause, looking at paper*] Instructions for officer in command of the cavalry at Charlesville. [*Sound of an approaching horseman and clank of sabre heard coming from L. to R. Crosses to L.C.*] I don't know why I should warn that damn 9th Cavalry that drummed me out. [*Single horse. Pause*] This paper—with the information the boy gave me, placed in the hands of General Kendrick, should be worth a generalship to me. I'll give it [*Hearing horseman close by, calls out*] Hello there! Halt! Where to? [*Noise of horseman ceases*]

BLUD. [*Outside*] Back to General Kendrick, colonel.

THORPE. Here. Give my compliments to General Kendrick. Tell him that his plans are known at Washington and I must see him immediately. [*Clank of spurs and sabre heard. Bludsoe, an orderly, enters, R.2.E. Salutes. His boots and uniform are very dusty. Thorpe whispers a short, hurried message to him*] Now, ride like the devil! Tell him there's not a moment to lose. [*Bludsoe salutes and exit hurriedly, R.2.E. Horse. Bludsoe pats horse on neck and immediately starts off at a gallop*] I've struck my first blow at the United States today. [*Mrs. Claiborne Gordon appears at door. She is an aristocratic Southern lady. Her white hair is rolled in pompadour style. Her manner is stately, and she makes discreet use of Southern accent*]

MRS. G. Why! Colonel Thorpe! [*Wears glasses*]

THORPE. Mrs. Gordon. [*Lifting his hat. He makes a point of being exceedingly polite to the old lady*]

MRS. G. [*Coming down steps*] I want to thank you for allowing our mail to pass through your lines. Most co'teous of you! Just like a gentleman of our a'my. Always watching fo' occasions to se've a lady. [*C. Looks at letter. Calls*] Maryland! O Maryland!

MARYLAND. [*Inside*] Yes.

MRS. G. Run yeh! [*Holding up letter. Maryland comes, L., to door, bows to Thorpe, who returns salutation*] Fo' you, deah. From the front.

MARY. Colonel Thorpe—[*Takes letter, opening it; on steps*] your pardon. From Southern headquarters; from General Lee. [*Comes down steps, reading letter*] O auntie, read that! [*She gives Mrs. Gordon letter and joins Thorpe, carrying her delight into her greeting. Talk dumb show*]

MRS. G. [*Adjusts her glasses and scans ahead a little*] Oh, my deah! I must read this to Colonel Thorpe. [*Reads with pride. Maryland turns to lilac bushes, picks slip*]

"Headquarters, Southern Army.

My dear little Miss Patriot:

Your last contribution of tobacco, coffee and shirts, is hereby gratefully acknowledged. Were all hearts in Maryland as loyal as yours, she would stand with her sister states, ovo'hthrowin' her present shamblin' indecision.

Yours with most grateful regards,

Robert E. Lee."

THORPE. [*R.C.*] Ah!

MRS. G. [*C.*] What chivalrous dignity—and yet how co'dial! Our house is honoh'd. [*Maryland comes down*]

THORPE. [*To Maryland, jocularly, touching his hat*] Miss Calvert is known to be the fiercest Southerner of us all. [*Maryland returns salutation in same spirit. Laugh*]

Mrs. G.   I'm proud of it. [*Laughingly*] Why, she takes fire quicker than I—don't you, deah?

Mary.   I reckon!

Mrs. G. [*Puts letter in her reticule. Crossing Maryland, to L., by steps*] My niece—this letteh shall go in the frame with the one f'on Cha'les; the fi'st to our ancestor, the fi'st La'wd Baltimo', who melted down his family plate to se've his king.

Mary. [*Crosses to L.C., turns up*]   And for his devotion to his royal master he very nearly lost his head! [*Crosses to Mrs. Gordon*]

Mrs. G. [*L.*]   Colonel Tho'pe, it's a real pleasure to have you with us. We weren't in touch with Colonel Chan'ler, who had charge here befo' you came! We found out he took *pay* fo' his se'vices in the war.

Thorpe. [*In a shocked tone*]   Oh, my dear Mrs. Gordon!

Mrs. G.   After that, when the Boonesboro' ladies passed him, they drew aside their skirts.

Thorpe.   Do you know, I find a strong tide of sympathy for the North amongst the people here?

Mrs. G.   Ah, but there's an undercurrent of love for their native state. Were it not fo' those Northern soldiers at Cha'lesville—[*Points to C. at back*] stationed there to ove'awe the people—they would rally to our ranks. [*Enter Telfair hurriedly, R.2.E. Comes down, R.*]

Tel. [*Excitedly, saluting*]   Colonel Thorpe, General Kendrick has reversed his march, and is moving up rapidly. Something important must have happened.

Thorpe.   Turn out the men to receive the general. [*Aside, as Telfair crosses, L.R., up*] I thought my message would startle the old man. [*Distant cornet. Thorpe starts upstage and looks off, R. Telfair salutes, and exit by road, L., at back, touching his hat to the Ladies as he passes them. Distant bugle call heard, R., the echo resounds through the hills. Maryland runs on bridge, looking off, R. Two echos*]

Mrs. G. [*Speaks after echo of second bugle*]   Ah! That sound that rings through the hills, will find an echo in their hearts. [*Bugles. Roll of drums beat "The Assembly" and shouts heard from Post, L. Answering bugle call, off R. Voices of Men, Women and Children heard from Post, L., singing "The Bonnie Blue Flag," at first very low, getting louder as the crowd gathers, seeming as if the whole village is aroused and joining in the song, which is intermingled with shouts and hurrahs*]

Mrs. G.   They are awake at last! [*Phoebe runs from house waving her handkerchief excitedly and exit, L.U.E.*]

THORPE. [*Looking off, R., shading his eyes*] General Kendrick will be up before long.

MRS. G. A julep fo' the general. [*Goes briskly towards house; at steps, to Thorpe*] and fo' the colonel commandin'—[*Thorpe, taking off his hat in salute, goes off, R.2.E. Mrs. Gordon exit. Maryland stands waving her handkerchief. As the song is gradually dying away, her handkerchief wavering down with her own spirits, she stands a moment looking out into emptiness before her. Tom Boone, a well-to-do young Marylander, appears at gate, R. He wears a riding suit and carries a short, heavy whip*]

BOONE. Maryland!

MARY. [*Opening gate*] Why—why—Tom Boone! I declare! [*He enters. Holds out her hand cordially*] How d'ye do? [*She closes gate*] When did you come back to Boonesboro?

BOONE. [*Crosses, L.C., riding whip*] Just rode in.

MARY. [*Going, C., to him*] Well, I'm right glad to see you. Why, it's more than a year since you went away. Do you know, when you all left here, the place seemed like a deserted village. Ah! New neighbors may come, but the old ones are best, after all! Look heah, I certainly feel inclined to scold you for not coming over to see us before.

BOONE. It's a long way—and—

MARY. The road is never long to the house of a friend. Come in! Come in! [*Crosses him, to L. She moves towards house. Turns, Boone stands looking down. Noticing he is not following*] Aren't you coming?

BOONE. I didn't allow to stop at your door—but—as I turned down the road, something—drew me in here—[*Looking at her for the first time*] the old love—Maryland!

MARY. [*L.C.*] Tom!

BOONE. [*C.*] I haven't seen you since the day I asked you to be my wife. If I live to be a hundred, I shall never forget it!

MARY. You shouldn't have asked me, Tom! You knew I was engaged to Alan.

BOONE. [*Bitterly*] Alan Kendrick is out of your life—now.

MARY. [*Sadly*] Yes.

BOONE. Maryland, there's a chance for me?

MARY. Don't, Tom! Please don't! [*Lights amber; dark reds down*]

BOONE. [*Gradually getting enraged*] You love Alan Kendrick still! You love him with all your heart and soul! You can't—you won't forget him— though he is your enemy, and has taken up arms against your cause. This cursed Yankee!

MARY. [*Firing up*] At any rate, he has taken up arms! He is fighting— not staying at home, making love to women!

BOONE. I can't go away from you! I can't forget you! I can't! I can't! As long as you live I'll love you. [*Thorpe, backing on the bridge as if watching approaching cavalry, turns*] I wish to God you were dead! [*Thorpe comes slowly down, R. Maryland is about to reply, but pauses, and picking up the slip from table, passes into the house. Lashing his boots in fury*] Scorned! The second time! Shamed! Damn! Damn! [*Sees Thorpe*] I beg pardon, sir!

THORPE. [*C.*] Well?

BOONE. [*L.C.*] I want to enlist.

THORPE. [*Looks him over. Pointing to L., at back*] Report to the recruiting sergeant. [*Boone exit, L., at back*] Drunk, or in love, or both. [*To bridge. Start cavalry, not too loud. Bugle call near, cavalry heard in the distance, single tap of drum heard which continues until the infantry which is in the rear of cavalry, is ordered to halt. The dialogue goes on all through this. Re-enter Telfair, L.U.E., at back*]

TEL. [*To Thorpe, who still remains on bridge. Saluting*] The lines are drawn up, colonel. Any further orders? [*Bugle call and cavalry nearer*]

THORPE. [*On bridge. Telfair comes down, L.*] Wait here. [*Slight pause, looks off, R., and calls*] Send word they'd better halt to the right of that stream. [*Uncle Dan'l enters hurriedly through orchard gate, R.1.E., crosses to C.*]

UNCLE. More sojers am comin'. Lord help the million patch and strengthen them chickens' wings. [*Bugle forte. Uncle Dan'l is startled and rushes off through small gate above house, L.M.C. Stop march. Cavalry heard very near. Bugle sounds "Halt," drum taps heard a little nearer as cavalry stops*]

BLOUNT. [*Outside*] I'll tickle the commissary for some stuffin' for ye, boys! You fellers come on with me. Reckon this is the shortest cut. Oh, break down the fence. [*Breaking timber heard outside, R. Sergeant Blount, a big, picturesque, loud-voiced Missourian enters, R.2.R. His uniform is a study, ragged and dusty. He wears a broad sombrero. His boots, however, are brand new with red tops. Telfair crosses to front of balcony. After Blount is on, bring on another squad of horses for General's entrance, 6 Officers, 1 Scout*] I'd give my new boots—I got 'em off a Northern general—for a good ole Missouri toddy with a roasted apple in it. [*Exit, L.3.E. Bugle sounds "Dismount." General Kendrick, a soldierly man of about fifty-five, dignified but evidently terribly stern on occasion, with traces of grief on his face, enters R.2.E. followed by Captain Blair, Captain Leighton, Lieutenant Hayne Aides-de-camp and a Scout. Their uniforms bear signs of hard travel*]

TEL. [*Saluting. Advancing from L.*]   General.

KEN. [*Returning his salute in surprise*] Ah! Telfair! [*Laying his hand on his shoulder*] It's a long while since we've met. [*Abruptly breaking off*] Where's Colonel Thorpe?

THORPE. [*Who has come down, L., saluting*]   I'm Colonel Thorpe, general.

KEN. [*Dismisses Telfair with a gesture. Telfair salutes and joins the Officers at back. They study map, Telfair has map giving information. Bludsoe enters, R.2.E., carrying the General's saddle and bridle. Exit, L.U.E., saluting Officers as he passes them*] My orderly brought me your hurried message. [*Apart from the others, over L.*] My plan of operations known at Washington! Good God! Thorpe, do you know this endangers the success of the whole campaign?

THORPE. This is why I ventured to cut short your halt at One Tree Hill, general, and ask you to come here. This is the one post along the line with telegraphic communication.

KEN. Well—well! [*Snapping his fingers anxiously*] Your information!

THORPE. [*Has cast a furtive glance about*]   Your army is known to a man. Hooker is hurrying forward to Charlesville, to strengthen the garrison, and will meet you with a large force of artillery. Every energy is bent on holding Charlesville.

KEN. Ah! They'd force me to a battle before our armies can concentrate. You did right. So "Fighting Joe's" to check my advance? A defeat now means the fate of Richmond. [*Crosses, L.R., turns. To Thorpe*] Your source of information!

THORPE. [*For a moment staggered, glancing towards house, then calmly saluting*] Your pardon, general, private—I cannot give it. It's private.

KEN. Private!

THORPE. All I can say is I took desperate chances to get it.

KEN. The source—are you sure it's authentic?

THORPE. It has served me before. I intercepted these instructions to the commanding officer at Charlesville. [*Producing paper, giving same to Kendrick*]

KEN. [*Looking quickly over paper*] Good! Good! In the nick of time! Colonel Thorpe, I shall make known your valuable service. [*Thorpe salutes, the General snaps his fingers to attract attention of Aide*] Bring me the map. Crosses to C. Aide advances and hands map to General, who examines it. Thorpe destroys the page in book containing notes, unobserved. Telfair leaning on bridge*] By following back the Boonsboro road to the right, we can reach Charlesville.

THORPE. [*Looking at his watch*] By eleven o'clock! [*Artillery ready. Kendrick hands map to Aide, who salutes and returns it to Telfair. Bludsoe reenters and stands, L., by rustic table*]

KEN. What d'ye know about that Post?

THORPE. [*L.C.*] I know it is held by the 9th Cavalry, a set of bulldogs who will fight to the death.

KEN. [*R.C.*] Bulldogs, eh? A stroke of lightning will smash 'em, before they can open their jaws. I must occupy Charlesville tonight. [*Drily*] I want to have some fireworks ready to welcome General Joe Hooker. What's the quickest he can get up with his reinforcements?

THORPE. By daybreak. [*Lloyd Calvert appears at door, L., and is about to come down steps, but hearing the next sentence, pauses and stands in the shadow, listening*]

KEN. I will surprise Charlesville. [*A terrible, subtle look comes into his face*] They'll not be prepared for a night attack.

LLOYD. [*Aside*] Ah! [*Kendrick's Officers are attracted by his voice and manner and separate, facing him, ready for orders*]

KEN. [*Calling*] Captain Leighton! Blair! Hayne! [*They come forward, R., and salute*] Keep the men under arms, ready to move. [*The three Officers start to exeunt, R.2.*] Remember—[*Officers stop. Looks around as though counting men present. Aside*] How many know? [*Start artillery. Lloyd steps back into shadow as Kendrick, counting, looks in his direction. To Blair*] —these instructions are secret. [*Rumble artillery. Officers down R. Distant rumbling of approaching artillery is heard, R. They salute and exeunt, R.2.E.*] My artillery! Good! Lieutenant Telfair, see how many guns are across the river. [*Telfair comes C., salutes and exit, R.3., bridge*] Is that the Boonsboro road?

THORPE. Yes, general. [*Ready bugle*]

KEN. Halt the guns! [*Calls off. Bugle sounding "Halt," loud*] Bludsoe— [*Bludsoe comes well forward, C., salutes and stands at "Attention." Kendrick, to himself, all the soldier in him aroused. Thorpe drops up a little*] Check my advance! Will he? [*Bring in artillery. Takes notebook from pocket and hastily writes, tears out leaf. To an Aide, R., snapping fingers*] Take a fresh horse! General Longstreet! Point of Rocks! Quick! [*Aide takes paper, salutes and dashes off over bridge. To Thorpe*] You are sure of your wire to General Headquarters?

THORPE. I used it an hour ago.

KEN. [*To Bludsoe*] Listen!

BLUD. [*Crossing*] Yes, general. [*Lloyd appears at door of house*]

KEN. [*With dogged determination, showing the true character of the man*] Telegraph this: General Kendrick's compliments. He has changed his plans and will surprise Charlesville tonight, and cut that garrison to pieces. [*Bludsoe salutes, exit quickly, R.2.E. Horse and sabre effect. Kendrick turns, R., snaps fingers at Aide*]

THORPE. [*Aside*] That's Kendrick's way. [*Start to bring in infantry, drum taps gradually getting louder. Kendrick turns to two Aides, R., who step quickly forward, saluting*]

KEN. [*To one*] Don't let the men remove their saddles. [*Exit Officer, R. To the other*] Take your glasses! Keep a sharp lookout! [*Exit Officer, L. Telfair enters and meets General, L. Lower lights*]

TEL. Forty of our guns are across the river, general.

KEN. [*To Telfair*] Come with me! [*They exeunt, L.U.E., together. All done without halt, while the General continues to move rapidly off. The rumble of artillery has ceased*]

LLOYD. [*The instant Thorpe is alone, Lloyd steps out from shadow of door. Coming halfway down steps*] Colonel—

THORPE. [*Facing him, L.C.*] You were listening?

LLOYD. [*Steps*] Let me warn them!

THORPE. [*Aside, relieved, L.C.*] Oh! He only heard Kendrick's orders.

LLOYD. [*Steps*] It will soon be dark! It will be impossible for the general to reach Charlesville till midnight. I can get there in half that time—I know every inch of the ground. Let me warn them, colonel!

THORPE. [*Aside*] I must keep this boy here. [*Aloud*] You couldn't even reach the lines.

LLOYD. [*Steps*] I can try! [*Starts to come down*]

THORPE. [*With sudden idea, quickly*] Don't come forward! Look down the road cautiously, to your left. [*Lloyd, who has halted at Thorpe's warning, turns toward L.1.E.*] See that man—the picket—looking this way? [*Unseen by Lloyd, he beckons someone to L.1.E. Marked*] There is a rumor that spies are about. If you attempt to leave you're as good as dead.

LLOYD. [*Steps*] There are only six hundred men at the Post; if surprised with those thousands against them—[*Points, R., with determination*] I'll risk it! Unless they are warned, God help them! [*Facing him*] Let me go.

THORPE. [*L.C.*] It's madness!

LLOYD. [*Steps*] Let me go?

THORPE. You'll be hanged and your sister disgraced.

LLOYD. [*Involuntarily backs up steps*] Colonel, do you think *you* will be able to warn them?

THORPE. [*L.C.*] No. I'm suspected and watched.

LLOYD. [*In despair*] What can we do? They must be warned!

THORPE. Ah! The picket is coming this way. Get into the house. [*As Lloyd hesitates*] Quick! [*Goes R. Lloyd goes quickly into house. Enter a Picket with a strong, marked face, L.1.E. Bryce salutes and exit, L.1.E. Blount enters, L.U.E., eating. Thorpe motions picket back; he retires. It is now nearly sundown, and the tap of drums has gradually come nearer. At this moment the infantry is supposed to come up close, outside R. Bugle sounds "Halt"*]

VOICES. [*One after the other down the line*] Halt! [*Near*] Halt! [*Further off*] Halt! [*Distant*] Halt! [*Very distant*] Halt! [*Faintly. Drum taps cease. Soldiers and Prisoners halt at the word of command*]

THORPE. Ah! [*Looking off, R.3.E.*] The infantry has just come up. [*Going L.*]

BLOUNT. [*Up L.C.*] Colonel, I brought along with me a batch of exchanged Federal prisoners. We're to lay over here till morning.

THORPE. [*Crossing, L.1.*] All right! I'll just tell that picket yonder to keep his eyes on young Calvert. Sentry—[*Exit, L.1.E.*]

BLOUNT. [*Calling off, R.U.E.*] Hello, there! Bring them swapped-off Yanks forrud. [*A plaintive minor air, with reminiscence of "The Red, White, and Blue" is played*] I'll halt 'em yer, till I find a place to stable 'em. [*A batch of wretched, pale, prison-worn men, in tattered Federal uniform, come on, R.U.E., and trudge wearily in a struggling manner over the bridge, preceded by dusty, travel-stained guards*] Close up! Close up! You fellers! [*Knocking down Forbes, R. The Prisoners still marching slowly. Blount pushes his way to C. of group*] Durn ye, d'ye want to be shot in your guzzles? Close up! [*To Corporal*] Corporal—that paper! Break ranks. [*Takes paper and goes down, L., at steps of house, reading same. Corporal crosses to gate, R. Some of the Prisoners have dropped wearily to the road at back. Ruggles, a gray-haired old man, stands leaning against the rail at end of bridge. O'Hara, under balcony, lays down at the first "Halt." Corporal directing them, the first four Guards come to "a rest" facing prisoners. Slight pause. Then enter Alan carrying Little True Blue, who is asleep on his shoulder. Alan Kendrick, pallid and exhausted, wearing a Federal colonel's uniform, dusty and worn. Little True Blue, whose foot is bandaged, wears a ragged blue overcoat around his worn-out uniform and his battered bugle is slung over his L. shoulder. They are followed by other Prisoners, four Guards bringing up the rear. As Alan gets C., he prepares to lay True Blue on the ground; O'Hara notices this and quickly takes off his overcoat which he throws on ground for True Blue to rest on. He salutes Alan wearily and resumes his position. Alan,*] *after fixing True Blue, starts to entrance of house, L., but is gruffly stopped by Blount who says*] Halt! Who are you? [*Crosses, L.*]

ALAN.   An exchanged prisoner from the stockade at Danville.

BLOUNT.   Well! Git back where y' b'long. [*Telfair has reentered, L.U.E., at back and recognizes Alan*]

TEL. [*R.C.*]   Oh, that's all right, sergeant. [*Blount salutes and goes up to Corporal and refers to paper and then exit, R.2., reading the paper*] Alan!

ALAN. [*L.C.*]   Bob! [*They embrace, R. arm on Telfair's R. shoulder*]

TEL. [*R.C.*]   I only heard today you were a prisoner at Danville.

ALAN.   There's no hardship in a soldier's life, old fellow, till he's been a prisoner—down there! [*His hand on his side as if in pain*] Ah!

TEL.   Why, here—here—what's the matter?

ALAN.   Oh, nothing—an old wound—jogs my memory sometimes. [*Rallying up C., to True Blue, bending over him*] That youngster kept the horses from trampling me to death in our last fight, and was taken prisoner with me. We're chums. [*Pats boy, rises, hand to side*]

TEL.   Why, man, you're bleeding! I'll call our surgeon.

ALAN. [*L.C.*]   No, I'll get along till we reach our lines. [*Crosses over to Telfair*] I was glad enough when I heard we were to be passed through at Boonsboro, for I wanted a sight of the old place—maybe a glimpse of her! [*Crosses to L.C.*]

TEL. [*Following Alan*]   It'll all end right. [*Cheeringly*] Don't give up. You know, April weather, card luck, and a woman's mind changes every five minutes. There's hope yet. Rally, dear boy, rally! [*Both down C.*]

ALAN.   Ah, Bob! If I could have fought it all out at the head of my regiment. But to be penned up—to sit day after day, week after week, and see nothing ahead but four narrow, hopeless walls—a low, dreary, whitewashed ceiling—it was such hopeless agony! [*Crossing, R.*] Bob, my life was ebbing out from a deeper wound than this. [*Crosses, C. Breaking off, chaffingly, as he turns his face to L.1E. Starts. Recrosses, looks*] Thorpe! [*Crosses, L.*]

TEL. [*C. Following Alan's look*]   Yes, our colonel! Lately transferred here —he's rather fond of booze—can surround more liquor without showing it than any man I ever saw. By the way—he knows you.

ALAN. [*L.C.*]   He was in my cavalry before the war. I had him kicked out!

TEL. [*Close to Alan*]   The devil you did!

ALAN. [*L.C. R. arm on Telfair's R. shoulder*]   He ruined and then heartlessly deserted the daughter of a dear comrade—my old color-sergeant—a little girl who had been adopted and was idolized by the whole regiment. We found her poor little body among the weeds of a mountain stream. I had it brought to the barracks—forced Thorpe to look on the face of his victim, and flogged him in the presence of the regiment he had disgraced.

TEL. [*Looking off, R.C.*] I'm sorry the scoundrel is now hiding his dishonor under our Southern gray. He's seen you.

THORPE. [*Enters, L.1.E. As he enters, Corporal who is up C. crosses to L.U., looks off road, then returns to C. Stands on guard as if to prevent Prisoners escaping in that direction. Telfair, retiring a little up R., watching. Having seen Alan before he comes on, familiarly*] Ah, I thought it was you, Kendrick. [*Alan looks Thorpe straight in the face, and turns away*] Still keeping up that old grudge, eh? My memory's as good as yours. [*Coming close to him, under his breath, with intense feeling. Blount reenters*] You broke my career for a chit of a girl—you did that—you! [*Changing his manner*] Odd, I should turn up so near your old lady love's home, isn't it? [*Alan stands immovable, Corporal down R. Blount down L.*] She's bigger game than that little simpleton, Dolly Grey. I might have to marry her, you know. [*Alan with rage, starts forward with uplifted hand. Telfair comes down, restraining him. The Prisoners, thinking their Colonel is in danger, rise to their feet showing a spirit of fight. The Guards, R. and L., aim at them, but the "Boys in Blue" show no signs of fear, their eyes fixed on Alan. True Blue wakes up and hobbles down with other Prisoners to fight for Alan. Thorpe starts to draw sword*]

TEL. [*Quickly*] Alan! Remember your comrades! If there's any trouble they'll be shot down.

ALAN. [*Restraining his fury, his hand falls slowly to his side*] For their sakes! [*Turns away, up a little, taking True Blue with him. Telfair indicates to Men that it is all right. Corporal charges on Prisoners and drives them back to their positions, and then takes his position in front of Guards on bridge, R. The Men resume their former positions. The Guards recover arms*]

THORPE. [*Mumbling*] D—n his eyes! [*Reenter Blount, R.2.E.*]

BLOUNT. [*Saluting*] Colonel, will you sign this transport order so I can get these prisoners away early in the morning?

THORPE. [*Taking paper*] All right. [*His eyes resting on Alan, aside*] I'm to sign his passport to freedom—[*As a sudden thought strikes him*] Am I? Am I? Charlesville! The place General Kendrick surprises tonight! [*Marked*] I'll do it! Come along, sergeant! [*Crosses, R., they go off, R.2.E.*]

ALAN. [*Having quieted True Blue, C., passing Men, C.*] Well, boys, we shall soon be ordered out of Boonsboro, and then—hurrah for the old regiment! [*Northern Soldiers shout a weak "Hurrah!"*]

TEL. [*R., aside*] His regiment—those doomed men at Charlesville! Thank God, he won't be there! [*C.*] O Alan! Alan! [*Alan comes down, L.C. Hesitatingly*] General Kendrick has just arrived.

ALAN. [*L.C.*] My father!

TEL. Shall I tell him you are here?

ALAN. [*L.C.*] No.

TEL. [*R. of Alan*] Have you no message?

ALAN. None! [*As Telfair is about to speak*] Bob! Don't! His injustice to my mother—[*His voice grows sad*] You know what I mean—the separation —shadowed her life. She was a saint—God bless her! My father found that out too late. When she died, I made up my mind never to see him, or speak to him. No! No! I can't forget! I can't! Don't let him know I'm here. [*Crosses to R. Bugle sounds "Officers' March" pp. off R. Maryland appears at window. Seeing Maryland*] Maryland! [*The sun has gone down behind the hills in a glory of deep red. Maryland comes on the balcony and looks towards the immense body of Soldiers who are supposed to be encamped, R. The glow of sunset illumines her figure. Alan turns, R., to hide his face, leans on fence. Apart to Telfair*] Speak to her for me. [*As Telfair starts to turn, L.*] When I am gone—Bob—say you saw me—and—[*His L. hand hold of Telfair's R.*]

MARY. [*Coming on balcony, seeing prisoners, to Corporal on bridge*] Corporal, where are these men from? [*Corporal salutes, is about to answer when Telfair replies*]

TEL. From Danville, Miss Calvert. Exchanged prisoners going North.

MARY. Oh! [*Seeing the sleeping bugler Boy*] Why, there's a child! [*True Blue turns restlessly in his sleep*] Poor little fellow! [*Goes back into house and comes out down steps during next two speeches*]

ALAN. [*To Telfair. During this action, back to Telfair, facing R.*] For God's sake, get me away!

TEL. Can't do it, dear boy! but I'll do the next best thing—I'll get the others away. [*Speaks to Corporal on bridge, who gives orders to guards, L., and Prisoners, who start to exeunt slowly, L.U.*]

MARY. [*Pityingly, dropping on her knees beside True Blue*] Look at his poor foot! Oh! You little enemy! [*Touching his cheeks*] Hollow cheeks— hollow—and the biggest hollow—right here. [*Touching his stomach*] Well, it certainly must be filled—if you are a little Northern boy. [*Goes L., calling*] Uncle Dan'l! O Uncle Dan'l! [*Uncle Dan'l appears at door. She beckons him to bend down to listen, gives him directions in whisper and sends him off saying, "Now, hurry! hurry!"*]

UNCLE. Yes, Miss Maryland.

MARY. [*Alan staggers, R., by fence*] Now please hurry. [*Turns in time to see Alan stagger as if to faint*] What's the matter with that man?

TEL. He's badly wounded, Miss Calvert.

MARY. [*To Alan, whose face is averted; approaching him*] Are you in pain? [*Alan, without turning, shakes his head and sits on small bench, R., assisted by Telfair*]

CORP. [*Yanks little True Blue to his feet roughly*] Here! Here! Wake up, wake up! [*During the above speeches the Prisoners have been slowly going off leaving True Blue; Corporal sees him. Little True Blue exit with Corporal*]

MARY. O Corporal, don't be so rough! [*Corporal respectfully salutes her. True Blue, half awake, rubs his eyes with his fists. Uncle Dan'l comes through the gate, L.3., bringing a chicken's drumstick on a salver. Maryland laughingly holds out the drumstick. True Blue, his eyes as large as saucers, grabs it. As Corporal raises Little True Blue up on his shoulder, the little fellow's cap falls off. Maryland notices this, picks it up and says*] Corporal! Corporal! [*Corporal stops and Maryland hands him the cap, which he carries off in his hand. Telfair goes off, R.2.E. As Maryland turns to go into house, she sees Alan, who still remains, his back to her. Lights are lighted in upper rooms of house, shining through windows*] Your comrades are going.

ALAN. [*R., rising, back turned to Maryland*] Thank you—I—

MARY. [*Starts at the sound of his voice*] Why—

ALAN. I—

MARY. [*A pause, very low, C.*] Alan, is it you? [*Alan faces her, head bowed down. With a glad cry*] Alan! [*Controls herself*] A prisoner just outside my door and you never let me know!

ALAN. Would it have done any good?

MARY. [*C.*] Why, you are wounded—weak—

ALAN. [*R.C.*] Yes, but still a Northern soldier! [*Facing audience, R.*]

MARY. [*C.*] Ah, Alan! What of that? I have helped many a Northern soldier—for your sake!

ALAN. You sent me from you!

MARY. I had to, Alan! I had to. Oh, you don't know how we feel—we women of the South! How our hearts are torn by this divided duty. On one side, our country—oppressed, forlorn, desolate! We couldn't desert it, could we? On the other, our very own turned to foes—and so the long days pass with this awful, awful struggle here. [*Crosses to L.C. Throws herself sobbing against the lilac tree*]

ALAN. [*Deeply moved, follows Maryland. Standing above her*] Maryland! [*The light shows the gradual coming of night. A pale, bluish mist rises from the lowlands at back*] Do you remember the last time we were here together, before this war cloud burst upon us? It was just such a night as this. You sang an old German ballad, to which I had scribbled some words. We little thought then, the simple tune would be a war song, to stir other hearts. It went—[*Alan bending close to her. The air, "Maryland, my Maryland," is played very softly*]

"She stood beneath the lilac tree,
        Maryland, my Maryland!
The girl I love, and she loves me,
        Maryland, my Maryland!
For her I'd live, for her I'd die,
I'd breathe her name in my last sigh,
She's leal and true—"[*Choking with tears*]
                "and so—am I,
Ma—"[*Breaks down, his head dropping on Maryland's shoulder*]

BLOUNT. [*Outside, R.2.E.*]   All exchanged prisoners, get ready to march.

MARY. [*With a low, stifled cry*]   Ah!

ALAN.   They're going to send us on tonight. It is so hard to think that before the stars fade into dawn, I shall be far away. [*Maryland crosses, C. The Soldiers outside, L., are heard singing "Kathleen Mavourneen." One verse only. His voice rising to intensity. As Alan starts to speak, singing is pp. Maryland, with a sigh of despair, crosses to L.C., Alan following her*] Ah, Maryland! My love! My love! I cannot part from you like this! I love you! I love you! You love me! Why should this war break our hearts? You sent me away once and I obeyed. Now I will not go till you promise to be my wife.

MARY. [*C., facing him, pleadingly*]   Then cease to fight against my people!

ALAN. [*L.C. Turns away, L.*]   And forget my honor? No! No!

MARY.   I don't ask you to fight for us. I only ask you not to fight against us. [*Going to him imploringly*] Alan, you are wounded—ill—there is no reason to take the field again. Put down your sword and—take me.

ALAN. [*Taking her passionately in his arms*]   Take you—take you! Maryland, you *are* mine.

MARY.   Yes!

ALAN.   And I am yours—yours. No more quarrelling.

MARY.   No.

ALAN.   No more bitterness.

MARY.   No, no—

ALAN.   My wife! Say it—say it! Say it!

MARY.   Your wi—[*Alan presses his mouth to Maryland's lips, and the word is finished in the kiss*]

Corp. [*Heard off, L.*] Northern exchanges ready!

Alan. [*Still embracing*] Ready—no heartache—no wound—ready for the front again.

Mary. [*Drawing back*] Alan! You don't mean—you're not going *back?* [*Indicating R.U.*]

Alan. [*L.C.*] Of course.

Mary. No, no, no, don't. Say you won't! [*L.C. Alan returns to Maryland*] I have prayed for you—my enemy—[*Clings to him with abandon*] Think what we lose if we let our happiness slip away. Alan, answer me—*you will? You will!* Say you will stay!

Alan. No, no, I cannot.

Mary. Ah! [*She leaves his arms*] You humiliate me—you cheapen my love! Oh! To have thrown myself at you like that! If you go now, that is the end—and I hope to God our side wins, even though your life be the price.

Alan. Maryland!

Mary. I'm a Southern woman to the last drop of my blood! I mean it. [*Pause*]

Alan. Good-bye! [*Pause before going. Maryland stands like a statue, making no answer and Alan goes off, L.U.R. Lloyd appears on threshold of door, pallid and unstrung, glances cautiously towards L.1.E.*]

Lloyd. [*Starting back into shadow*] That picket never takes his eyes off me. [*Despairingly*] I'm powerless to warn them!

Blount. [*Reenters briskly, R.2.E., and up, C. Calls off, L.U.E.*] Fall in! Forward! March! [*Corporal and advance Guards enter, L.U.E., followed by Prisoners. They go towards the road, R.2.E. From the time the march of the Prisoners begins till the curtain falls, there must be no halt. The march must be carefully timed to the dialogue and action. Maryland stands immovable, well down, L. Blount hands the Corporal a paper*] Orders changed, corp'ral! Pris'ners don't stay here a'ter all. [*Corporal puts paper in his belt. Alan holding Little True Blue in his arms is the first in file. The Soldiers march slowly. When Alan enters with Little True Blue, he turns to large stone by gate of house, L., places True Blue on same and fixes bandage on his foot*] Take a flag o' truce and deliver 'em to the commandin' officer at Charlesville tonight.

Lloyd. [*Overhearing*] Charlesville! How can I warn them?

Alan. [*Up C. Gladly, looking up*] To our own regiment again.

Lloyd. [*Hearing him, starts*] Alan Kendrick! [*His eyes resting on Maryland*] She loves him! [*From behind column of house he speaks to her, in a low but distinct voice*] Maryland! If those prisoners go to Charlesville, they go to death!

MARY. [*Low*] To death! [*Lloyd glances L.1.E., and dropping on his knees brings his mouth close to her ear, speaking rapidly in a whisper. Enter Thorpe, R.2.E. Lloyd must not see or be seen by Thorpe*]

THORPE. [*To Blount, apart*] When should the prisoners reach their destination, sergeant?

BLOUNT. [*Saluting*] 'Bout five hours, colonel.

THORPE. That won't do. They must be there in four. Rush 'em through. D'ye understand—rush 'em through. [*Exit, R.2.E.*]

MARY. [*Who has listened intently to Lloyd's whispered words*] Ah! [*Breathlessly*] You heard General Kendrick give those orders?

LLOYD. Yes! [*Rapidly, pointing R.*] That whole force—[*Alan takes up True Blue in his arms and starts to fall in line and exit with other Prisoners. O'Hara close behind him ready to relieve him of True Blue, when Sergeant gives him permission to fall in the rear. Maryland instinctively turns her eyes towards R.*] now resting on its arms—only waiting for the order to start—will fall upon the garrison in the dead of night—a thousand to one—not a soul will escape! [*With his eyes fixed, L.1.E., withdraws into house*]

MARY. My God! [*Seeing Alan who is within a step or two of passing out of sight*] Alan!

ALAN. [*Hearing her, to Blount*] May I fall in at the rear, sergeant?

BLOUNT. [*Drawling*] Ya-as. [*Alan passes True Blue to O'Hara, who is next in file. Alan steps out of line and stands well down, R., facing her. The Prisoners have continued marching, Blount stands facing them, L.3. The following dialogue is carried on swiftly in undertones*]

MARY. Does General Kendrick know you're here?

ALAN. No!

MARY. Alan, let me tell your father you're here.

ALAN. No, no!

MARY. [*Entreatingly*] Alan! Do—do!

ALAN. You know I cannot.

MARY. Oh, don't refuse me everything! [*Alan, impressed by her agony of manner, implies consent by a gesture. With a glad cry, forward*] Ah! [*To Blount*] Sergeant, where can I find General Kendrick?

BLOUNT. He rode to the river crossing, half an hour ago.

MARY. [*Eagerly*] But he won't be long, will he? The prisoners could be overtaken?

BLOUNT. Orders are to rush 'em through.

MARY. [*In despair, aside*] Ah! [*Running L.1.E.*] Lloyd! [*Calling*] Lloyd! Lloyd! Lloyd!

BLOUNT. [*To Alan, as the last prisoner is in sight*] Fall in.

MARY. Wait!

BLOUNT. Can't do it! [*To* Alan *authoritatively*] Fall in! [*He turns to the rear Prisoners, hurrying them along; one or two being wounded, lag behind. Alan, backing to the rear, touches her by her waist, her back to him. At his touch, her struggle ends and with a cry she turns and clings to him, speaking in a low, hurried voice*]

MARY. You are going to certain death!

ALAN. I am going to Charlesville—to my own regiment.

MARY. [*Following him closely, in a whisper*] It's a death trap!

ALAN. What?

MARY. General Kendrick's words were, "I shall surprise Charlesville tonight, and cut that garrison to pieces!" O Alan, save yourself! [*The last of the Prisoners are about to go off. Blount turns impatiently to Alan again. Maryland quickly, with intention to divert suspicion, extends her hand*] Good-bye! [*Alan grasps Maryland's hand and presses it to his lips. The curtain descends as he falls in at the rear. Picture*]

ACT II.

PROPERTY PLOT: *Old Colonial furniture, 2 armchairs, 2 side chairs, round table, C. (3 ft. in diameter) On table: large square piece of pink blotting paper; quill pens, inkstand, stationery, brass candlestick and candle; pair of field glasses; 2 maps on very thin paper; small map on paper, 7 x 7 in.; decanter of water and tumbler, parallel rule, compass and drawing pen, saucer of India ink, small saucer with wax matches, small tinkle bell, documents, etc., also letter for Maryland. Wet knapsack at side of table, L. Old snare drum, L. of table (above knapsack), with the word "Mail" roughly painted on it, large slit in top for dropping in mail. Fireplace, L.C., furnished with clock, vases, fender, fire-irons, firedogs, logs, brass blower; large map of Virginia hung in front of mantel. Medallion, ground cloth, 7 rugs (not skin) Small square table, 12 x 18 in., with old books, maps, and papers on top; the drawers in same are bulging out with papers and documents. 2 small round tables about 12 in. in diameter, 1 low Turkish stand. Large vase, broken into several pieces. Loose flowers for same. 2 army blankets covered with old paper books, knapsacks, coats and hats. Musket and Confederate battle flag against flat, R.3. Bass drum, 4 camp stools and old coat, up C. Army overcoat on armchair, L. of C. opening. 4 large family pictures hung on walls. 4 sets of curtains on opening, C. Canopy and curtains, L.1. Flag hung on large pole behind balustrade, C. opening. 2 small cannons backstage. Letter fast ened with a rose stuck through C., for Phoebe. Duplicate rose for Lloyd. C.S.H. mail bag for Corporal Day. About 100 letters in bag (from soldiers). Dispatch for Telfair. Bandana handkerchief for blindfold, off R.1.E.* **Open report for Captain Blair to hand Telfair.** *Map made out of tracing paper with clot of blood for Blount. Hall seat under window, up L. Camp stool, coat and hat, L.1. Armchair, L. (by passage) is turned upside down; thrown loosely on same, a military overcoat and sword with belt. Revolver in holster on mantel. Soldier's coat thrown over wheel of cannon is up R.C. The floor is strewn with pieces of paper. Dispatch box with key for Telfair. Map on rollers, made out of tracing paper, for General Kendrick.*

CALCIUM PLOT: *Open White lights, R. and L. of backdrop.*

ELECTRIC LIGHT PLOT: *Everything up at rise (on stage). House lights down. White strip, R.1.E. White strip on doors, R. and L.2.E. One strip on window, R. and L.3.E. Amber strip on back of last wing, R. White bunches, R. and L. of back drop. Amber ground behind balustrade, up C. 1st border, White and Red, footlights, White and Red; both these lights are on together. No change in light after rise of curtain.*

SOUTHERN HEADQUARTERS AT "THE LILACS"

SCENE: *The great hall in the Calvert Mansion. Windows at back, opening on a veranda. Large door, opening from the ground, well down R. Door, leading to a room, L.3.E. Large fireplace and hearth with dogs, fire-irons and mantel, L., well upstage, L. On front of mantel is emblazoned the crest of the Calvert family. A passage separates the hall from a room built out, with a solid door in the rounded corner, over which is a fanlight. Note: The construction of this room is important, as one of the principal situations depends upon it. At end of passage is a small window; nearly between 1. and 2. is the door of Maryland's chamber, with a portière and canopy. Several family pictures are suspended from cornice. Rugs and medallions are on the floor. The hall is in confusion, being used as General Kendrick's military headquarters. A table, L.C. Writing materials, a large map and field glasses, etc., are on the table. A knapsack used for waste paper under it and pieces of paper scattered around it. A chair is behind table. An old snare drum with a slit in it, and the word "Mail" roughly painted on its front, stands L. corner of table. A flagstaff is ushed C. of veranda, with the Confederate flag hoisted and partly seen; the halyards are hitched to a column. Large guns are mounted on each side, pointing to the Federal camp, off R., a full view of which is seen through the open windows, with guns, earth works, and the Stars and Stripes floating to the breeze, about half a mile distant, across a stream. Beyond are seen the "Green Hills of Maryland."*

TIME: *Early morning, the day after. The act begins in bright sunlight. After a few bars of music, the curtain rises.*

DISCOVERED: *Lloyd Calvert, dressed as in Act I, is seated back of the table, L.C., busily drafting a paper from a copy. After curtain rises, a short pause, then sentry crosses below veranda from L. to R. Lloyd looks suspiciously around; noticing he is unobserved, hurriedly places a copy of military operations inside the waistband of his trousers and quickly continues with his drawing up of the plans. Telfair enters from room (General's) opening on passage with dispatch box, with the key in the lock, which he places on table, L.C.*

TEL. [*L. of table*]   Finished? [*Stop music*]

LLOYD. [*Not looking up*]   Almost. [*Telfair takes field glasses from table and looks off, R. Crosses, R., from veranda. Mrs. Gordon, attired in morning dress, comes down passage, L. Lloyd absorbed in his work, pays no attention to the others*]

MRS. G. [*From passage, crossing to C.*]   Good morning, Lieutenant Telfair.

TEL. [*Bows*]   Good morning, madam.

MRS. G. [*Crossing, R.*]   What a dreadful night we've passed. How far off are the Northern outposts?

TEL. [*Giving her glasses*]   About half a mile. [*She goes up to Telfair, takes field glasses from him, and looks in direction of Union camp, off R.*]

MRS. G.   Dea'h me! Why, they all seem to be resting undeh the apple trees. [*Comes down, R.C., giving glasses back*] I hope the fruit is nice and green. [*Telfair takes glasses from Mrs. Gordon and places them on table, C.*]

TEL. [*C.*]   I'll let the general know you're here. [*Crossing, R., to General's room*]

MRS. G. [*R.C.*]   One moment, pray. [*Telfair turns to her. She crosses to him*] Has General Kendrick heard of the engagement that once existed between his son and my niece?

TEL.   I think not.

MRS. G.   Then, may I beg that, while the general honahs us by his presence, nothing be said about it? [*Telfair bows in assent, then knocks*]

KEN. [*From inside room. Mrs. Gordon turns to Lloyd*]   Come! [*Telfair enters room*]

MRS. G.   Ah! Lloyd! [*Patting him on head. Crosses behind him to L.*] M' boy! Chosen as confidential secretary to General Kendrick! Well, I am proud

[*Enter General Kendrick, L., from room opening on passage. He is without his sword, has an anxious and much disturbed manner but assumes a calmness while speaking to Mrs. Gordon. Telfair follows him and places dispatch box on chair; looks over Lloyd's shoulder*]

KEN. [*Crosses Lloyd, below table, to Mrs. Gordon, R., bows, takes Mrs. Gordon's proffered hand*] I am glad, madam, to express my thanks for permission to establish my headquarters at "The Lilacs."

MRS. G. We are honah'd, general. Breakfast will be served in half an houah. [*Crosses, L.*] Military fa'ah, you know. [*At passage, with good humor, yet with a kind of pride*] We are all soldiers at "The Lilacs" now. [*Bows and exit up passage. Sentry crosses, R. to L. Lloyd ends writing and hands paper to Telfair, who gives it to General Kendrick*]

TEL. The new plan of operations, sir.

KEN. [*R., by window, glancing over paper*] Very cleverly done. You've had good military training, young man. [*To Telfair, back of Lloyd*] Where's the rough draft of this? [*Lloyd hands it to Telfair, who hands it to General, who tears it in half and is about to throw it in knapsack under table. Pauses*] Such things are better burned. [*Telfair gets a match from table and coming R., strikes it on his boot, holds the flame to the General, who burns the paper*]

TEL. [*As the paper burns*] If the enemy could get a copy of this, general, the stars would jump out of their flag with joy.

KEN. [*Crossing slowly to table with the burning paper*] Everything depends upon it now. [*Throwing the ashes into knapsack under table and stamping out the dying flame*] Master Calvert! [*Front of table. Lloyd comes forward, L., salutes*] Remember, it is a young soldier's duty to hear—see—and forget. [*Lloyd salutes, crosses up to window between Kendrick and table, and, taking his hat from camp stool, R.C., goes out on veranda, C. He gives a quick searching glance, off R. and L., and then goes off, L., as if still looking for someone. With grim humor, Kendrick to Telfair*] That was a rolled-up porcupine we attacked last night—all quills. [*Feeling it keenly*] If I were a swearing man—[*Ugly*] I'd say, "Damn those 9th Cavalry bulldogs for keeping us at bay till Hooker came up with reinforcements. Our defeat is serious. We must hold Boonsboro now, or go to Heaven. Joe Hooker and I are face to face at last. Any news of Thorpe?

TEL. None, since he left you.

KEN. [*L., impatiently*] What detains him? I don't want to make a move until I hear from him. [*Enter Blount from L.C.*]

BLOUNT. [*Comes down, R.C., saluting*] Gen'ral, a number of men have deserted. One feller had an old pass which car'd him through the pickets.

KEN. Send out an order that all passes are rescinded. [*Blount salutes and exit, R.2.*]

BLUD. [*Offstage, R.U., excitedly*] General! General! [*Enter, R.C., saluting*] General Hooker is massing all his strength to the right.

KEN. Tell Blair to look out for our left. [*Bludsoe salutes and exit, R.2.*] Foxy Joe! Well, I'm ready for him this time. Lieutenant!

TEL. [*R.C.*] Yes, general.

KEN. [*L.*] Let Hayne and Leighton make sure of that half-dried swamp at the foot of the hill. That's the spot, if it will bear our artillery. [*Kendrick finishes this speech at the door of his room, L.2.E., and exit to room, L. Telfair exit, R.2. Sentry crosses, L. to R., at Telfair's exit. Lloyd reenters, L.C., seeming anxious*]

LLOYD. [*Anxiously, on veranda, C., upstage*] Where can Thorpe be? [*Coming into room*] I should be on my way now. [*Very impatiently*] Why doesn't he come? [*Puts hat on table. With bitterness, leaning on chair, R.*] No picket watching me today—no suspicion—I'm even entrusted with the drafting of their plans—all because of my people—[*Down, starting back, R.C., as Phoebe speaks. Phoebe appears at end of passage and calls in a big whisper*]

PHOEBE. Lloyd! [*Lloyd starts, as he is turning up*] St!—Lloy—d!

LLOYD. [*With assumed cheerfulness*] Oh—Phoebe—come in.

PHOEBE. [*In passage*] 'Fraid to. Aunt Elinor says the general's headquarters are sacred, and I must wait till you come out. Can't—got something on my mind. Been there all night.

LLOYD. [*By table*] What is it?

PHOEBE. Put it in this letter—read it and please answer. [*Throws a note with a red rose stuck through it, into room at his feet*] Good-bye! [*Darts off, L.U.E. Lloyd takes it up, taking rose out, presses it to his lips and fastens it on his breast. Phoebe, who has almost instantly reappeared, is eagerly watching him at end of passageway*]

LLOYD. [*L.C., by R. side of passage, reads*] "Lloyd, dear, what is the matter with you? I've given up trying to think it out—it hurts so. Since you came back, you act as though you were sorry for me—as though you regretted that I loved you—and—the kissing's all been on my side. Is there another girl?"

PHOEBE. Is there? [*Lloyd, looking up, finds her standing before him. Taking her in his arms*]

LLOYD. No—no! [*Kissing her*] No!

PHOEBE. [*Much relieved*] That's what I wanted. If you love me like this, how could you treat me so coldly?

LLOYD. [*Earnestly, by L. chair*] I wish you didn't love me—for your sake.

PHOEBE. [*Starting back, frightened*] There's that look again! Lloyd, why for my sake?

LLOYD. [*Slight embrace, turning to her*] I am going on a dangerous mission, and if anything should happen to me—it would leave only sorrow for you. [*Breaks embrace*]

PHOEBE. [*Making a pathetic little effort to laugh*] Is that all? Don't you know I'm a soldier's sweetheart? [*Throwing her arms about him*] You'll never see a tear in my eye, Lloyd! [*Furtively wiping away tear*] Not one. Did you think I was going to make it hard for you to do your duty? O Lloyd—I could give you up to your country—but I couldn't give you up to another girl. [*Embrace. Lloyd holds her close to him and kisses her with grave tenderness*] You don't blame me, do you?

LLOYD. No!

PHOEBE. [*R., concealing tears, suddenly running to window*] Aunt Elinor!

LLOYD. [*Follows*] No, it isn't.

PHOEBE. [*She turns*] I must go.

LLOYD. [*Going to her, taking her hands*] Phoebe!

PHOEBE. Quite sure there's no other girl?

LLOYD. Quite sure! [*Phoebe kisses him and exit, C.R., running off to hide her feelings. Up R.*] I can't wait any longer for Thorpe. I must get this paper—[*Puts his hand on waistband of trousers*] into the hands of General Hooker. [*Alan Kendrick, wearing a Confederate overcoat and hat is seen to come down passage, L. As he comes into hall, Lloyd turns suddenly and sees him, but does not recognize him. Sharply*] What do you want? [*Alan, placing hat at side of his face for an instant, not recognizing Lloyd's voice, stands on guard. Aside*] Can he be following me? [*Aloud*] What do you want?

ALAN. [*Crosses to C. Seeing Lloyd's face*] Lloyd!

LLOYD. Alan Kendrick here?

ALAN. Yes, and deuced hard work I had to get here, too. I came through the grape arbor—by the little door leading from the orchard. [*Up to table, L.*]

LLOYD. [*R.*] What brought you—[*Alluding to his appearance in a Confederate overcoat*] like that?

ALAN. [*Places hat on table, crosses to C.*] The hope of seeing Maryland!

LLOYD. But you're in danger of your life!

ALAN. [*Sits on chair below table*] I took the risk—where is she? [*Sentry crosses, R. to L., looks into room for a second*]

LLOYD. Sh! [*Warningly*] You're in Southern headquarters. [*Crosses to L., behind Alan, listens at General's door*]

ALAN. [*Astounded, rising, crosses, R.C.*] Southern headquarters! "The Lilacs!" [*Noticing military accoutrements, calmly, yet impressively*]

LLOYD. [*L.*] Escape while you can.

ALAN. [*R.*] First—where's Maryland?

LLOYD. [*L.*] Yes—but the danger—

ALAN. [*Silencing Lloyd by a gesture*] I'm determined to see her. Oh—what's prison—what's death a thousand times over, to all I've gone through since I left her yesterday. In the battle last night, for the first time, fear took hold of me—a fear that I should never live to ask forgiveness for the bitter insult with which I flung back her sweet love—[*Crosses, L.*] and she—she laid down more than her life for me. Lloyd—Lloyd, where is Maryland? [*Turns*]

LLOYD. [*Crosses upstage. R.C. up, in fear*] I tell you, you must go!

ALAN. Well—I know a safe place. [*Crosses to table and sits as if about to write, L.*] I'll send for her to come to me at the old mill. You'll help me—[*In front of table, prepares to write*] for the sake of old times. [*Lloyd gives a furtive yet a searching look at Alan coming down*]

LLOYD. [*Over table*] I tell you straight, Alan—she'll never see you! My word for it. [*Crosses above table to door, L.2.*]

ALAN. [*With fierce desperation, throwing down pen, wheels, facing front*] I must see her! O Lloyd, can't you do this for me—use any strategy. All's fair in love, you know. Only get her to come to me. [*Crosses, R.C.*]

LLOYD. [*Crosses to Alan*] Well then, quick, how can we do it?

ALAN. [*Rises, crosses to R.C.*] I'll tell you. You say there's a poor devil who came here to see his sweetheart. A Northerner!

LLOYD. That'll ruin the whole plan. By Jove, I see! It'll explain why I can't bring you here. All right! That might work. [*Crosses to Alan. Note: This message sent to Maryland by Alan must be given in a distinct and earnest voice*]

ALAN. [*C., L. arm on Lloyd's shoulder*] Tell her he's hiding in the old mill, in the hope of seeing his sweetheart, before the battle. Perhaps it's his last chance—by sundown he may be dead—and God knows that's true enough, old fellow! You have promised to aid him—but are suddenly called away, and dare trust his life with no one but her—[*Cross a little, R.*]

LLOYD. [*L.C., on the lookout*] Leave the rest to me.

ALAN. [*Shaking hands with Lloyd*] Make it strong, old man—send her there, anyway—[*Goes up, R.C., a little. The door of room, L.1.E., is opened behind portière and Maryland calls*]

LLOYD. I will.

MARY. Lloyd!

LLOYD. Sh! [*In a whisper*] She's there—in her room. [*Points to door, L.1.E. Alan starts towards room. Lloyd checks him in a low voice*] Are you mad? A Northern soldier found under her roof! [*Up above table. L.*]

MARY. [*A little louder*] Lloyd!

LLOYD. [*Back of table, L.*] Yes, sis. [*Motions Alan to withdraw behind portière by passage, L. Alan quickly obeys*]

MARY. [*Opening portière slightly and speaking through it*] Are you working still?

LLOYD. [*Hesitating*] Yes, but I'm not alone.

MARY. [*Letting go portière*] Oh! Then I'll wait.

ALAN. If I could only hold her in my arms. [*Lloyd, struck by a sudden idea at seeing letter on table, snaps his fingers to attract Alan, who stands gazing in the direction of Maryland*]

LLOYD. O Sis!

MARY Yes?

LLOYD. A letter for you! [*Picks up a letter from table with R. hand*] It has been lying here since the last mail. [*Alan beckons to Lloyd to give him the letter, which Lloyd does; he goes on his tiptoes to portière, kisses the letter and places it lightly in Maryland's hand, which she has stretched through the portières, partly showing herself "en déshabillé"*]

MARY. Thank you, dear. [*Alan seizes a ribbon which is hanging from her sleeve and kisses it. As she draws in her hand and turns to go, Alan, still kissing the ribbon, keeps her a prisoner*] Oh, something's caught me! [*Alan quickly lets go the ribbon and drops back a step*] Lloyd! [*He impulsively puts his arms about her outside the portière*] Lloyd, when you're alone, I want you to call me, dear. [*Alan gives her a little squeeze. Lloyd moves, R.C.*] O Lloyd! [*Closes door*]

ALAN. [*Before Maryland's door, crosses to table*] I had to send my love message to her under false colors! [*Taking up his hat from table*] Lloyd, if she consents, show yourself on the balcony. I can see you from the old mill. [*Crosses to Lloyd*] Good-bye—and thank you, Lloyd. [*By passage. Pulls his hat over his eyes and exit by passage, L. A pause. Lloyd stands listening. The Sentry, coming from L. to R., is seen passing at back. As Lloyd sees him, he draws a breath of relief and going to door, L.1.E., knocks*]

LLOYD. [*After standing, listening breathlessly, a moment*] Maryland! [*He partly opens door*]

MARY. Yes. [*Lloyd leaves her door and crosses to L.C. Short pause. Enter Maryland from her room. She wears a pretty, simple morning gown, her hair is knotted carelessly behind*]

LLOYD. [*Embrace*] You want to see me? What is it, dear?

MARY. Were—were many lives lost?

LLOYD. [*L.*] The enemy—lost—

MARY. [*Crosses to C., quickly*] I mean of our own people?

LLOYD. No.

MARY. [*Crossing to R.C., with relief*] Ah! [*In despair again*] But the whole plan of invasion of the North is defeated, and our forces driven back. My fault, too! [*Covering her face with her hands in bitter remorse, crossing to R.C.*]

LLOYD. [*L.C.*] Maryland, I've a great favor to ask of you. A friend of mine—is hiding in the old mill!

MARY. Hiding!

LLOYD. A Northerner!

MARY. [*Indignant, R.C.*] Lloyd!

LLOYD. [*In front of table*] Sh! He has come here in the hope of seeing—[*Looking up full in her face*] his sweetheart before the battle. Perhaps for the last time—by sundown he may be dead. I have promised to aid him—but I'm suddenly called away. I dare trust his life to no one but—you!

MARY. [*Crosses to L., quickly*] No, Lloyd! No, no, no, no!

LLOYD. [*C.*] Listen

MARY. [*Carried away by her feelings, vindictively*] A Northerner!

LLOYD. [*Stopping her, his back to R.C.*] He is the best friend I have in the world.

MARY. [*L.*] He is our enemy!

LLOYD. Yes, I know, sis, but I've given my sacred word to aid him. [*Putting his arms about her, pleadingly*] Come—you'll go there for me, won't you? There's no harm—in this. Think! Just think! He wants to see the woman he loves! [*Stepping back*] And she doesn't even know he's risking his life for her.

MARY. [*Turning to him*] No! [*Crosses farther toward her room*]

LLOYD. But—

MARY. Oh, no, Lloyd, don't beg me any more!

LLOYD. Maryland! [*Still pleadingly*]

MARY. [*With determination*] I will not go! [*By curtain, L.C., in her room*]

LLOYD. [*With a sudden thought, aloud*] I'm sorry, because I not only wanted you to see my friend but to—to detain him—

MARY. Detain?

LLOYD. [*Answering her look*] Until after the battle. [*Maryland comes down, above Lloyd. R.*] It's like this! I've got myself into a bit of a scrape by advising him to hide in the old mill. Since then—[*Watching Maryland*] I've—I've been thinking he could hardly *help* getting information—[*Mary-*

land looks at him, startled, very marked] and some idea of the plans of attack.

MARY. [*Eagerly, crosses to Lloyd. R.C.*] You think that?—and if he goes back with it—O Lloyd, Lloyd, the fate of this impending battle may be resting upon us. [*Arm around Lloyd's shoulders*]

LLOYD. [*Marked*] You might serve the Southern cause.

MARY. [*Eagerly*] Yes, yes! I see! I'll go! [*Turns to L.*] I'll keep him there! What shall I say?

LLOYD. [*Holding her by the hand*] Trust to your woman's wit. See him first! The rest will follow. Only, be cautious! [*She nods her head. Embracing her*] You're a trump, sis! Good-bye!

MARY. Good-bye, dear heart, and God bring you safely back to us. [*Kisses him*]

LLOYD. [*Back turned to audience, aside*] Safely back!

MARY. Oh, I'm another woman! [*Aside, as she exit, L.1.E.*] I have a chance to redeem myself. [*Aloud*] Trust me! I'll keep him here—I'll keep him here—I'll keep him here! [*Crescendo; goes into her room*]

LLOYD. [*R.C.*] I wonder what she'll say when she sees Alan? Now to let him know she's coming. [*Taking hat from table, R.C., goes out on balcony, and looking off, R., puts hat on his head as if giving a signal, then comes into room*] Dangerous business, this secret service, whether for war—or love. [*Takes rose out of his buttonhole and kisses same*] I should reach the Northern camp in half an hour—and be back in time to report. [*Exit, R.1.E. Enter Telfair quickly, R.C., throws hat on table. Sentry crosses, R. to L.*]

TEL. That swamp would hold a fort. [*Enter Corporal Day, R.2.E., with an old mail bag slung over his shoulder. Salutes and hands a package of letters to Telfair*]

DAY. Letters, sir. [*Salutes, exit, R.2.E.*]

TEL. [*Facing the Union camp*] Ah! The enemy is bracing up the men! Good! I'll rouse our fellows' ginger, too!

SENTRY. [*Outside, L.C.*] Halt!

NANNY. [*Outside, L.C.*] Ooh! [*Telfair places letters on table*] Say, don't you be so pert with your bayonets.

TEL. That voice! [*Crosses below table. Hurries to window, calling off, L.C.*] Oh, Miss MacNair—oh, Miss MacNair! [*With an inviting smile*] Sentry, let the lady pass. [*Nanny appears at window, from L. Comes down arranging appearance*]

NANNY. [*Turns and faces L.*] Thank you, sentry. [*Ignoring Telfair and addressing Sentry with cutting emphasis*] Sentry, if there should be anyone inside, will you kindly tell him that I'm sent to say the officers' breakfast is waiting?

TEL. [*On stage, raising voice*] Sentry, if there should be anyone outside, will you tell her that the invitation, although welcome, is informal. Would the bearer deliver it in person? [*Nanny leans against window, looking at Telfair, her arms folded, humming with the distant music*] No? So good of you to remember me—What? What'd you say?—What's that? This is such a nice little chat, isn't it? What? [*"Dixie" is heard near-by*] I hope our boys' singing doesn't disturb you. We only know that one tune—"Dixie." [*"Yankee Doodle" heard in the distance with drum and fife*] Ah! Your boys in blue are heard from now.

NANNY. We'll teach you that tune yet! [*Sings, coming into room*]

"Yankee Doodle came to town,
A ridin' on a pony,
His coat-tails stuck out straight behind,
His legs were long and bony."

CHORUS

"Yankee Doodle doodle do
Yankee Doodle dandy—"

[*Goes to General's door and knocks, calling*] Breakfast, general! [*Sings*] "Yankee Doodle," etc. [*Going L., looking saucily at Telfair over her shoulder*]

TEL. Don't go! [*As she gets out of window, L. Running up to window*] O Miss MacNair, don't go! Oh, don't go! Please don't go! [*Calling after her. Coming into room impatiently*] Well, go then! What the devil do I care? A soldier hasn't any time to waste on women. Give him a good pipe, a deep canteen—and a jolly yarn, and who remembers there is such a thing as a woman! Woman! Ah! Some of us have written our last letter! [*Leaning in front of drum. Reading, as he drops letters into it*] Miss Mollie Clay—Miss Sallie Hoyt—Miss Cornelia—Briggs, Miss Jane—Miss Eva—Miss Lulu—Miss Bessie—Miss Mary Ann—Miss—Miss—Miss—Miss—Miss—Miss—Confound it—[*Ad libitum. Slamming remainder of letters into drum*] It seems as if every fellow in the regiment has his heart wrapped up in a petticoat. [*Distant music stops*]

SENTRY. [*Outside, L.C.*] Halt! Pass! [*Thorpe enters, L.C., in civilian's dress. His trousers tucked in his boots, his clothing in disorder and covered with dust. His boots give evidence of hard usage. Telfair salutes Thorpe*]

THORPE. [*R.C.*] General Kendrick here?

TEL. [*L.*] Yes, colonel. [*Aside*] I wonder what's happened. Thorpe's sober. [*Knocks on General's door, which he opens*] General, here's Colonel

Thorpe. [*Enter General Kendrick anxiously. Kendrick has on sword, hat, and gloves*]

KEN. Well! Well!

THORPE. I got into the enemy's lines, sketched a plan of the works, with important notes. A mile outside of our pickets, two Northern soldiers shot my horse under me. By breaking the wrist of the man that took my paper—

KEN. You lost the paper!

THORPE. Yes.

KEN. Ah!

THORPE. I got clear just as the rest of their party caught up—lay hid in the underbrush for three hours and with difficulty made my way back.

KEN. That paper is in Hooker's hands by this time. [*Walks up and down, crosses R. and turns, troubled*]

THORPE. [*L.C., aside*] In my own writing, worse luck!

KEN. [*Halting before Thorpe*] They'll be on their guard now. [*Enter Bludsoe, R.C., saluting and coming down, R.C.*]

BLUD. All ready, general.

KEN. [*To Telfair*] Let us take a good look at the guns. [*Exeunt Kendrick, Telfair and Bludsoe, R.C.*]

THORPE. Hooker grabbed at my false news—and sent me away with a pat on my back. Then who the devil suspected me and sent them after me? Fighting Joe's paw would make breathing difficult if I were within patting distance now. [*Two shots heard, off R.*] Hullo! What's up? Somebody trying to pass the pickets. [*Looking off, R.C.*] A man running this way! [*Pause, starts*] Ah! [*Retreats to front of table, L.C. A few seconds after, Lloyd without hat, coat, and waistcoat, dashes breathlessly into room through door, R.2.E., and staggering, falls into Thorpe's arms. His boots are muddy, his face is ghastly pale. He is bleeding from a wound in the breast and one arm hangs limply by his side. Rose is fastened in his shirt*] Calvert!

LLOYD. [*Panting*] Is that you, colonel! [*Speaks hurriedly and with effort*] Tried to get to Northern camp—reached river—shot struck me in the arm—couldn't—swim across—sentry halted me—showed pass—he said order just out, all passes rescinded. Then the picket who watched me yesterday, you know, came up. I broke away—he fired—[*Clutching at the wound in his breast. With difficulty*] New plan of operations—[*Points to waistband of trousers*] Here! Destroy it!

THORPE. [*Glancing over him, R.*] They're coming.

LLOYD. [*Stands erect, R.C.*] Let them come! [*With boyish pride*] I saved Charlesville for the North, after all!

THORPE. [*L.C.*] How?

LLOYD. I told my sister—Alan Kendrick was going to his death—she loves him—

THORPE. [*Quickly*] And warned him—a woman!

LLOYD. [*Pleadingly*] O colonel, don't let them—[*Pointing, L.*] know what I am. [*Enter two men hurriedly, one is Bryce, the picket, followed by Blount. Thorpe lifts up Lloyd and throws him into Soldiers' arms, who catch him under his arms, supporting him as he sinks to his knees, his head dropping forward*]

THORPE. [*L.C.*] Arrest that man! [*To Blount*] Who is he?

BLOUNT. [*R.*] A deserter.

THORPE. [*L.C. Crosses to Lloyd, throws up his head and looks into his face*] Dead! [*Lets the head drop limp again. Aside. Crossing to L.*] Served him right! He was too infernally zealous!

BLOUNT. [*Beckons to Men, who enter, R.2.E. Picks up blanket and throws same to Man nearest to him who has just entered*] Fetch him along, boys. He'll be a warning to others.

THORPE. [*Points to room, R.3.E.*] Put him in there, for the present. [*The two Men ground arms, and the other two, as they enter, do the same. The other Man, who has just entered, takes the place of Corporal who has hold of Lloyd's R. arm; the Man who has the blanket opens same and places it on stage in front of Lloyd. The Corporal takes the lower end nearest Lloyd. As the two men holding Lloyd lift him up, Corporal and the other men push blanket about one foot and a half under Lloyd's knees. The Men holding him let him fall face downward on to blanket. Corporal turns him roughly on his back into C. of blanket, throwing Lloyd's L. arm against his body. They lift blanket by the four corners and carry Lloyd off feet first. Blount opens door and exit after them. At cue "Fetch him along boys," Sentry crosses, L. to R., halts and watches dead body being taken off, and then resumes his march. Thorpe, L.*] Maryland Calvert warned Alan Kendrick. That's why Charlesville wasn't cut to pieces; that's a good bone to lay by in my cupboard. [*Tom Boone, in the uniform of a Confederate private, enters, R.2.E. His manner is stoical. Salutes Thorpe who eyes him sharply as he passes him to go to door leading from passage. Blount and the Men reenter, leaving door open; they then take up their guns. Blount signals them to exeunt, R.C., which they do, two by two. Blount exit, L.C. Thorpe to Boone*] Halt! [*L.C. Boone salutes and faces him*] Aren't you the recruit who spoke to me yesterday?

BOONE. [*Up L.*] Yes, colonel!

THORPE. Why were you insolent to Miss Calvert? [*Boone looks at him*] I heard you! Know her?

BOONE. [*Reluctantly*]   Yes.

THORPE.   Your words implied a grievance.

BOONE.   Pardon me, colonel—that's a private matter.

THORPE.   Not when you threaten her in my hearing. Why did you? Answer me! [*Boone maintains a sullen silence*] Answer me! If you *were* sober yesterday, you are either a coward or—

BOONE.   Well, then, I love her, and when she—I—I lost my head for a moment.

THORPE. [*Aside*]   I thought so. Surly cuss. [*Alan Kendrick, still wearing the Confederate overcoat, is brought on by two Men, R.U.E., blindfolded. The Man on his R. is guiding him by holding his arm. Thorpe to Men*] Who's this?

BOONE. [*L.C.*]   A prisoner, just taken, sir.

THORPE. [*To Alan*]   Your name?

ALAN. [*R.C. Takes one step forward, giving no sign he has recognized Thorpe's voice*]   Alan Kendrick, colonel of the 9th Cavalry, Northern Army.

THORPE. [*Starts, recovers himself; to Boone*]   Oh! You captured him? [*Aside, as if understanding*] Hm! [*To Men*] Guard outside! [*They salute him, and exeunt, R.C. To Boone*] Remove the blindfold! [*Boone crosses to Alan and takes off blindfold*] Be within call. [*Boone salutes and exit, R.U.E. Thorpe, without stirring, casts a hasty glance from L.C. at back to door, R.2.E., seated*] Kendrick, strange that apparently sane men will run such risks for the sake of a woman. A soldier found in the opposing lines, in the uniform of the enemy—no matter what his errand, is in a pretty bad fix. [*Alan taking no notice of Thorpe's words, quietly takes off his overcoat and letting it fall on the floor, stands revealed in the full uniform of a colonel of the Federal cavalry, without sword. Calmly. Throws coat, L.C., front*]

ALAN. [*R.C.*]   Send me before the commanding officer! [*Sentry crosses to L.*]

THORPE.   You did a good thing when you had me turned out of your regiment. I'm Colonel Thorpe now, and hold here a position of honor and trust.

ALAN. [*Facing Thorpe*]   So I found out today, when my men seized you with a copy of our works on you.

THORPE. [*Enraged*]   So it was you then, who rode up and nearly caught me!

ALAN.   I was dismounting outside Hooker's tent, just as you left. I asked what you were doing there, and found out you were a spy in our service. [*Thorpe glances about uneasily*] I told the general that you were in a position yesterday to have warned me of the intended surprise of Charlesville. But no! You meant to strike that garrison—Hooker has sworn if you ever fall into his hands, he'll waste no lead on you. [*Facing audience*]

THORPE. Hang me! Eh? Huh! Ha! Ha! Did they really think I'd warn them? I don't care which rag I serve under. I fight for my own hand.

ALAN. And stand self-confessed—a man without a country! [*Thorpe rises quickly, places chair about one foot in front of table*]

THORPE. [*Livid*] You drove me from my country.

ALAN. [*In front of table, R.C.*] Your own base actions showed you unfit to serve the States.

THORPE. Damn the States! [*Alan turns quickly and clutches Thorpe by the throat. Thorpe in the struggle is pressed backwards over chair in front of table. Alan still holding him by the throat with both hands. Thorpe makes an attempt to call out*]

ALAN. [*Choking the half-uttered word*] Take back those words! Take them back! Take them back, I tell you!

THORPE. [*After a second's pause, gasps out*] I—take—them—back. [*Alan in disgust throws Thorpe from him over the chair and stands erect*]

ALAN. Now send me before the commanding officer!

THORPE. [*Calling off, R.*] Sentry! [*General Kendrick enters, R.C., followed by Telfair; a second after, by Bludsoe. The General throws hat on the table, takes off his gauntlets, and picks up a document, his back turned to Alan. Lieutenant Hayne enters, L.C., and speaks to Telfair. When Telfair enters he throws his hat on small table by passage. Thorpe, saluting*] A prisoner, general.

KEN. [*Seeing Alan's uniform but not his face*] An officer.

ALAN. [*Aside*] My father! [*Enter Captain Blair quickly, R.2.E., with paper; he hands same to Telfair, saluting him. Telfair reads and countersigns it, then hands it to Blair*]

THORPE. Of that 9th Cavalry that garrisoned Charlesville last night, and is now facing us. [*Hayne, R.C.; as soon as Telfair hands paper to Blair, he whispers to Telfair who delivers him a message*]

KEN. [*Eagerly*] Ah! Who brought him in? [*Thorpe to R.2., and beckons. Boone enters from R.2., and pauses on threshold*]

THORPE. [*Pointing*] This man.

KEN. [*To Boone, who salutes*] Where'd you capture the prisoner?

BOONE. Going into the old mill, sir.

KEN. Where's that?

BOONE. Out there, sir. He wore that. [*Points to overcoat, which still lies on the floor. Thorpe picks it up to emphasize the significance of Boone's words, and puts it in chair, L.C. Crosses, L., to coat*] So our men paid no attention to him, but I know him.

KEN.   Why wasn't this man blindfolded?

THORPE.   He was. I ordered it to be removed, sir.

KEN.   Indiscreet—you shouldn't have done it. This room commands a full view of—[*To Boone*] Draw those curtains! [*Pointing, R.2. Boone closes curtains*]

TEL. [*By table, R., aside to Kendrick. Enter Blount, gives dispatch to Telfair*]   Our guns are being masked, general. He saw nothing. [*Telfair hands the General a dispatch brought on hurriedly*]

KEN. [*His eyes half-engaged, reading dispatch*]   Prisoner, you have placed yourself in a serious position. What brought you into our lines?

ALAN. [*Facing him*]   General Kendrick, if you—

KEN. [*Amazed*]   My so—[*The word "son" dies in his throat. Telfair is astonished at sight of Alan. Lieutenant Hayne, who is about to go off, L.C., halts on threshold. From now until the General dismisses everybody, the scene is perfectly quiet. Kendrick and Alan stand gazing at each other in silence. Their positions are so arranged that the gray uniform of the Father and the blue uniform of the Son, make a strong contrast. After a pause, the General recovers and is once more the soldier*] Well?

ALAN.   I pledge you my word, sir. I came here on private business and not on a soldier's errand.

KEN.   In the face of the enemy—a battle threatening, an officer's unsupported word is hardly sufficient. I must know why you are in our lines.

ALAN.   I can explain, sir, but I must beg the indulgence of a little time.

KEN. [*Points to overcoat on chair, L.C.*]   You wore that?

ALAN.   I did.

KEN.   And you can explain? I hope so. Your object? Why do you hesitate?

ALAN.   General Kendrick, the indulgence I asked for was in order to gain time; that I might obtain permission to mention a name—the name of a woman, sir.

KEN. [*To Boone*]   Has the prisoner been searched?

BOONE.   Yes, general.

KEN.   Nothing found on him?

BOONE.   Nothing.

THORPE. [*Aside to Blount whose attention has been attracted and who has entered the room, pausing on the threshold*]   Search that dead man in there. [*Points to room, R.3.E. Blount goes into room, R.3.E.*]

KEN. Colonel Kendrick, give me your parole that, until you can justify your position here, you will not attempt to escape.

ALAN. [*Saluting*] You have my word, general. [*Facing audience, hands behind his back. Reenter Blount from room, R.3.E., with a paper, a clot of blood on it*]

BLOUNT. [*Saluting*] General, one of your men shot, trying to desert to the enemy.

THORPE. The body's in there. [*Points, R.3.E.*]

BLOUNT. Had this paper on him. [*Salutes, retires upstage*]

KEN. [*Takes paper and looks at it, a serious expression comes over his face; aside*] Our new operations. [*Looks closely at paper*] It can't be possible that—[*Aloud*] Lieutenant Telfair! [*Telfair comes down, R. of him, no salute*] Do you know this writing?

TEL. [*Looks at paper, starts, apart to General*] Yes. It is young Calvert's.

KEN. See who the dead man is.

TEL. [*Crosses behind Kendrick, looks through the door, R.3.E. Starts back in horror, comes down R. of General, greatly agitated. As he leaves door, R.U., Corporal Day looks in; he steps aside, saluting, as Lieutenant Hayne passes in front of him. All the characters upstage turn and look towards the room where the dead body is. In a low voice to the General*] Lloyd Calvert! [*Crosses to L., behind table. The others, except Thorpe, while not hearing the latter words, watch with breathless interest*]

KEN. [*Aside*] A spy! [*Aloud to Thorpe who comes forward, L.C.*] Colonel Thorpe, how long has he been in Boonsboro?

THORPE. I never laid eyes on him till he staggered into this room a moment ago, dying.

KEN. [*To Telfair*] Do you know?

TEL. [*L.*] Since yesterday.

KEN. [*Only within hearing of Thorpe*] Yesterday! That accounts for the Charlesville disaster. [*Aloud, sternly*] Aha! There's treachery here! [*Alan faces him, surprised*] In drafting the plans, he kept a copy, and—[*His eyes rest on Alan*] Colonel Kendrick, an important paper has just been found on the body of a spy. Under the circumstances I must retract the parole and hold you till the matter be thoroughly sifted. [*Alan salutes with quiet dignity. To Thorpe*] Colonel Kendrick will remain in there. [*Points to room, L., General's room leading from passage*] Under a strict guard, until further orders.

THORPE. The prisoner is in your charge, Private Boone. [*Boone salutes and advances to Alan's side. Sentry crosses, R. to L.*]

KEN. [*To Alan as he starts to go L., with Boone*] Wait! [*To Boone*] I'l call you. [*All salute and exeunt in dead silence. Blount goes off, L.2., Captain*]

*Blair, R.2.E., Lieutenant Hayne, L.C., Bludsoe, R.2., Boone into room, L.,
leading from passage. Thorpe exit, R.2., after Captain Blair, taking up his
hat and gloves from camp stool, R.2. Telfair goes up to small table, picks up
his hat, crosses below table, starting for exit, C. Picking up coat]* Robert, stay!
[Telfair pauses, but turns away, back to audience, above table] Alan, you
have reason to think harshly of me—you did right to stand by your mother.
[Alan folding his arms, turns away from the General] My love made me un-
reasonably jealous, and, suspecting a rival, I drove her from me—hurt beyond
pardon. Ah, Alan! *[Turning away with a passionate cry of pain]* I had hoped
that one day my boy—a man—would know the love of a woman—would feel
just one such pang as mine—to make him—forgive, and understand.

ALAN. I know—I understand! *[Extending his hand]* Father! *[They clasp
hands]*

KEN. *[C. In a choking voice]* My boy! My boy! *[Takes him in his arms.
Pause. The two men recover and stand erect and soldierlike again]* Your
presence here and the capture of that spy—*[Pointing, R.]* is an unfortunate
coincidence. It makes your position difficult. My son, let me come to your aid,
if I can. Let me send for the woman.

ALAN. *[R.C.]* No. I am here unknown to her. An enemy secretly received
in your lines—you see what might be inferred. Father, you have said it—it
was just that one—great pang—that brought me here. I can say no more
without her permission. *[Turns away. Kendrick pauses, as if to embrace
Alan, then collects himself]*

KEN. *[Calling to Boone, off L. Then goes up, R., behind table]* Private
Boone! *[Goes upstage, R.C. Boone appears at door, L.C.]*

ALAN. *[Crosses to L.C. Telfair turns and meets him. To Telfair who is
about to question him, unseen by the General]* Don't question me now,
Bob—don't worry—I shall come out of it. *[Exit into General's room, L.2., followed by Boone. General comes down, R.C.]*

TEL. *[L. of General]* General! What though that paper were found on
the dead boy—*[Marked]* there is no proof that Alan spoke to him—or even
saw him. *[A knock is heard at door, L.1.E. The knock is repeated]*

KEN. Who's there? *[Telfair opens door and Maryland appears on threshold. She wears a pretty, out-of-door frock, and her hat hangs on her arm by
its ribbons]*

TEL. *[Starting back in nervous apprehension; to General in a low whisper]*
Miss Calvert!

MARY. Lieutenant Telfair! I am called away from the house, and I want
to see General Kendrick before I go. *[Looking behind him and seeing the
General, advances with her hand outstretched. Telfair closes curtains to Mary-*

land's L.] General Kendrick! I feared you might go to the front before my return. [*The General has been looking earnestly at Maryland*]

KEN. [*In grave surprise and taking her hand*] Miss Maryland Calvert!

MARY. Yes. [*Drops hat on chair*]

KEN. I am glad to see you.

MARY. [*In answer to his fixed look at her. Telfair up close, R.3.C.*] We've never met before, general, but I know you from your son's strong resemblance to you. [*Telfair retires upstage, and, with his eyes fixed on Maryland, closes door, R.3.E., behind which is the body of Lloyd, then comes down to R. of General*]

KEN. [*Surprised*] You know my son?

MARY. [*Hesitating, drops her eyes for an instant*] Yes. I—I was to have been his wife. Colonel Kendrick was quartered here a year before the war.

KEN. [*Thunderstruck at her first words, with much relief. Aside*] Thank God! Alan's story is straight.

TEL. [*R., aside to General, dryly*] And he said his was not a soldier's errand, general.

KEN. [*Slapping Telfair heartily on shoulders, who goes up on balcony. Telfair upstage, R.C. Aside*] My boy! My boy! [*Aloud*] Pardon me, Miss Calvert! Only this instant, an anxious thought for Alan was filling my heart, and you—well, it's one of those strange fatalities—that you should come to me at this particular moment. [*With tender reverence*] And so you clung to our cause, eh? [*Up to Maryland, taking her hand*]

MARY. I tried to, General.

KEN. [*Patting her on the shoulder*] Brave little woman, to give him up. [*Sentry crosses, R. to L. Boone appears from General's room, L., leading from passage. He closes door, faces Kendrick, salutes*]

BOONE. Prisoner asks to hold communication with Lieutenant Telfair.

TEL. [*Coming down, has come in from balcony, R.C., aside*] Alan has heard her voice.

KEN. Presently. [*Boone salutes and exit into the room, closing door*]

MARY. [*L. of Kendrick*] So you've turned my little morning room into a jail! Who's the prisoner?

KEN. [*C. Hesitates*] A young man, held on suspicion of complicity with a Northern spy—just shot.

MARY. [*Looking at door of Prisoner's room*] And he's involved?

KEN. [*Taking her hand, which she unconsciously holds out*] No, I am sure he can prove his innocence—now.

MARY. Oh! Then there's no danger? [*Turns to table*]

KEN. Yes, but the spy probably had accomplices. [*Maryland, unnoticed by others, starts*]

MARY. [*Aside*] Accomplices! [*A suspicion coming to her. Telfair comes slowly down, R.*]

KEN. If so much as a breath—as a breath—connect the prisoner with that dead man—nothing can save him. [*Markedly looking at her*] There would be no extenuating circumstances—nothing but death. [*A thought has suddenly come to the General. He stands aghast. Under his breath to Telfair*] Her brother—if by any chance they met—

MARY. Ah, general, I won't detain you any longer. [*Taking his hands and looking up into his face, earnestly*] God speed you, and give us this battle. [*Gets her hat from chair, L., and starts to go up, R.C.*]

KEN. Amen!

TEL. [*Aside to General, quickly, R.*] Let me tell her it's Alan—in there. [*Pointing, remains R.*]

KEN. [*Aside to him, glancing towards room where body of Lloyd is*] After she knows about—him. [*Calls*] Miss Calvert. [*Maryland turns to him*] Just one moment, please. [*She comes down*] You have shown such loyalty to our cause, that—[*Maryland, conscience-stricken, lets her hat slip out of her hand. The General, picking it up, misses the expression on her face. Telfair also starts to pick up hat*] Allow me—that—[*She quickly controls herself and takes the hat with a nod of thanks*]

MARY. O General, I'm a woman—and I have all a woman's weakness, too.

KEN. Yes—but grief may come to any of us—to me—to you. [*Maryland looks at him with vague apprehension, remains standing by chair, L., her hand resting on the back for a moment. Points to chair*] Call up all your courage to hear bad news.

MARY. Is Alan—? [*Calmly*] Have no fear for me, General Kendrick. Tell me—[*Sits, tremulously*] Tell me—do please tell me.

KEN. [*Close to Maryland*] Your brother—

MARY. [*Starts, looking at him intently*] Lloyd? What is it, general? What is it? What is it?

KEN. Why—shall I tell you the worst? [*Maryland nods*] He is dead.

MARY. Dead!

KEN. He was shot.

MARY. [*Rises, General supporting her*] Lloyd—dead! [*Starts to her feet, calling out. Almost beside herself in General's arms; General gets back a step*] Where is he? Take me to him, general—oh, take me to him! [*Crosses, R.*]

KEN. One moment—he was entrusted with the drawing of an important military paper. He made a second copy and was killed trying to carry it to the enemy.

MARY. My brother a traitor! Oh, it's a lie! I don't care if you are the general—it's a lie! Why, only yesterday he came back to us—a Southern soldier, ready to give his life for our cause. [*Crossing, L., her eyes filling with tears, and passing her hand across her forehead, hardly able to realize the truth*] Just now I saw him here—only a little half hour ago—he held me in his arms—kissed me good-bye—he was going away for you—for you—and now—dead! Murdered! O Lloyd! Lloyd! Lloyd! [*Falls into chair, head on table. She yields to a passion of tears and passing General Kendrick falls prone on table, L.C., in hysterical sobbing*]

KEN. My child!

MARY. [*Dashing away her tears*] No, no, no, no! I won't believe it! I won't believe it! Ah, general, if you had only known Lloyd—he was so loyal! Don't accuse him—don't! Don't disgrace his memory until you are sure! [*Throws herself into his arms*]

KEN. I am sure. The man we are detaining on suspicion in there—[*Pointing to room, L.*]

MARY. [*Has thrown herself on him, in her passion of pleading; at his last word and gesture, struck with a lightning flash of intuition, grasps at his extended hand and holds it, pointing to the door of the Prisoner's room*] That man! That man! [*She fastens his eye and compels him to follow her gaze. Hoarsely*] Ah, yes, the spy is—there! [*Still pointing, she crosses and in a voice almost hushed in a fearful whisper*] There! There! There!

TEL. [*Crossing to C., in agitation*] Miss Calvert! [*Telfair is stopped by a gesture from General Kendrick, draws back*]

MARY. His friend! Lloyd's friend! Lloyd's friend! He knew his miserable life was in danger, and has fastened his own guilt on that poor, murdered boy! [*Facing door of Alan's room, fiercely*] Coward! Coward! Coward! Why, he is the man Lloyd asked me to meet—

KEN. [*Breaking in*] To meet?

MARY. [*Continuing, without noticing interruption*] In the old mill—

KEN. [*With a strong effort to control his agitation*] The old mill—

TEL. My God!

KEN. [*Repressing Telfair's effort to stop Maryland, apart to him*] It was there he was arrested. [*Aloud*] A man in the old mill?

MARY. Yes, yes, yes! A Northern soldier! [*A look of despair comes into the General's face. Telfair makes another attempt to silence her. The General*

who has recovered, quiets him by a gesture] He had come here in the hope
of seeing his sweetheart, before the battle—

TEL. That proves nothing, general.

MARY. Proves nothing!

TEL. It's his own story to you.

MARY. [*Crosses to General. To Kendrick*] Why, don't you see—it was all
a trick—a subterfuge! Why, he made the boy lie to me—work upon my sympathy, to gain access here—your headquarters. Don't you see—don't you see!
Ah! You hesitate to fix his guilt, but you don't wait to stamp his crime on
the dead body of a hapless boy, who cannot defend himself! Brother, my
brother! Oh, what can I do to clear your name? That man—[*Recollecting*]
Oh, I haven't told you all. Lloyd broke down—confessed to me! Oh, what
were his words—his words—oh! [*With bewildering agony, trying to remember*]

TEL. [*Up L.*] Stop her! You are his father.

KEN. [*Stolidly and sternly, R.*] I am the general.

MARY. [*Remembering with a cry, C.*] General Kendrick! You told me—
if only a breath connected them—hear—hear—Lloyd's last words to me—"If
someone does not detain that man, he will get back into the Northern lines—
with information and our plans of attack." [*General in pained amazement
drops backward a step. Telfair, falling back in despair, his eyes fixed on the
open fanlight. Maryland with a gathering vindictiveness*] My brother is dead,
but you shall clear his name, and punish that spy in there. [*Telfair, in desperation, throws open the door of room, L., in which Alan is confined. Alan,
pale as death, steps out. Boone back of him. At sight of Alan, Maryland stands
aghast, staring wildly at him. Realizing what she has done, she gives an
hysterical shriek. Her eyes are still riveted on Alan's face*] Alan, I didn't
know! I didn't know—[*Falls prostrate at Alan's feet. Picture*]

ACT III.

PROPERTY PLOT, SCENE 1: *Breastwork of logs, débris, etc., R. (as if thrown up
in a great hurry). Flag of truce stuck in breastwork behind gatepost, up L.C.
(Pole 10 ft. long with old piece of muslin, 3 ft. x 4 ft.). Two large cannon facing breastworks, R. (The one upstage disabled). 3 small pieces of wood at
foot of cannon, downstage. Old pickaxe and spade for Sexton, off L.2.E. Old
straps for lowering coffins, for Sexton, off L.3.E. Small flag of truce for Telfair, off R.1.E. 1 large bolt and heavy chain inside door of chapel, L.2.E. 1
large bolt outside gateway, L.1.E. Large brass bar and striker for heavy bell*

effect in flies, L.2. Bass drum and snare drum under stage, L., for "Dead March" effect. 4 revolvers and plenty of cartridges. Letter for Maryland.
SCENE 2: *Camp table, R.C. Chair, R. of table. Camp stool, L. of table. On table, trick bayonet with candle, inkstand, quill pens, writing paper, blotting paper, documents, sack with torn papers fastened to downstage legs of table (used for waste paper). Sure-fire revolver and cartridge for property man, to be used in case of accident to Boone's gun. Army cot, 2 blankets and 2 pillows, R. 3 old lanterns with candles lighted (1 for Blount, 1 for Maryland, and 1 on upper landing leading to belfry). Red army sash for Alan. 2 rosin boards with rosin (1, R. of stage and 1 in belfry). Large lock and key in door, L.2.E.*
ELECTRIC LIGHT PLOT, SCENE 1: *House lights down. Red foots full up, White foots one quarter up. Red bunch and Red ground row in the ruins, R.E. Red and Amber ground row, 3rd R. 2 ground rows in front of backdrop, C., with Amber lamps and double rows of Blue lamps; turn down Amber at cue, "Ring like H---," and turn up extra row of Blue. Red reflector, 100 C.P., lamp on church window, L.1.E., turn on when the soldiers march offstage. Red borders full on, White one quarter on, turn down White at cue, "When I gather them in." Work footlights down at cues. When the curtain comes down, turn on Blue foots.*
SCENE 2: *Blue foots dark, turn up a little when Thorpe comes in with lighted match. Turn up full when Thorpe lights the candle. Turn down one half when Maryland puts out candle. Turn all lights out dark at cue.*
SCENE 3: *2 double rows of Blue strips at back of church tower, full up with rise of curtain.*

THE OLD CHURCH

SCENE: *Outside the church. A very old church occupies nearly one third of stage, L., the front facing R. Over entrance door, a pointed arch resting on corbels. A wicket is in the door. It slides open from the inside. The stained glass windows are shattered and have temporary iron bars outside. Glass in tower window facing audience is broken to pieces and also barred. Small door in L. side of church facing audience. The church tower reaches above the borders so as to give apparent height. A country road leads to the gate, R.U.E.; the gates are unhinged and lie R. and L. of gateposts. The gateposts are very high and broken. A breastwork of logs, débris, etc., as if thrown up in a great hurry, is R.; encircles church. Portion of the sides are blown out Stuck conspicuously in the débris is a pole on which a flag of truce is flying. A cannon is planted, R., pointed off, R., through an opening in breastwork. A gate leading to churchyard. Another cannon, R.2.E., is disabled. An old ambulance marked C.S.A. is standing at back, L., outside fence. Scene show effect of a recent battle near-by, the haze of which still hangs in the air. Afar off, R.U.E., is seen the faint glow of a conflagration. In the distance at back, the ruins of a partly burned village.*

TIME: *Towards evening of the next day. It is late in the afternoon and the last rays of the sun fall on the corner of the church. Before the curtain goes up, a descriptive battle piece is played, with far-away sound of booming cannon. The curtain rises to "The Bugles sans truce, for the night clouds had lowered," heard faintly in orchestra. When curtain is up, fife and drum heard, off R.H., sounding "Lights Out."*

DISCOVERED: *A Sentry, crossing L. to R., his clothes very dusty, is seen pacing slowly outside the fence at back. Thorpe, his face more colorless than usual, wearing an army overcoat, his back against the church door, shading his eyes with his hand and looking off, R.U.E. He has been drinking heavily and his manner is morose but anxious. As last notes of bugle die away, Sentry disappears and the sound of hurried footsteps is heard. Bludsoe, his uniform torn and battle-stained, his eyes almost blinded with smoke, enters gropingly, by upper road, from R., panting. Thorpe shows eagerness at sight of Bludsoe.*

BLUD. [*Calling offstage*] Colonel! Colonel! Colonel! [*Enters, R.U.E.*]

THORPE. Well, Bludsoe, what is it?

BLUD. [*Saluting and speaking brokenly*] Couldn't get here before—village afire—missed my way in the smoke—It's been an awful day! [*Comes down, C.*]

THORPE. What news? What news?

BLUD. Our reinforcements driven back!

THORPE. Ah!

BLUD. Both sides worn out—withdrawn till morning.

THORPE. Has word been sent to General Headquarters?

BLUD. All communication cut off.

THORPE. And Hooker?

BLUD. Between us and reinforcements. Most of our guns captured.

THORPE. No retreat?

BLUD. The river road blocked.

THORPE. That will do. [*Motioning him off. Bludsoe starts up and off, L.U.E.*] That will do! [*Thorpe crosses, R.*] We're in a pocket. [*Bludsoe salutes and exit, L.3.E. Officer comes in hurriedly from church*] Yes, we're hemmed in! Hemmed in! [*Crosses to R.3.E. Pointing*] Well, darkness'll give us a breathing spell. We're well entrenched; there's no danger before daylight. [*Pointing, R.U.E.*] I want that bridge destroyed. [*Exit Officer, R.U.E.*] I'm safe till morning—but after—[*Corporal entering, L.3.E.*]

BLOUNT. [*Saluting*]   They're waiting for you in the chapel, colonel.

THORPE. [*Still looking off*]   In a minute. [*Aside*] But after—

BLOUNT.   Beg pardon, colonel, they're waiting.

THORPE. [*Angrily*]   In a minute! [*Corporal salutes and starts to go. Collecting himself*] Here, say I'll be there directly. [*Corporal salutes and exit, L.3.E.*] What the devil's the matter with me? I mustn't lose my nerve. No! No! [*The old Sexton singing outside, L.1.E.*] Damn that old croaker and his graveyard ditty—Hooker's hand's reaching nearer and nearer to me. I tried to kill him today, once—twice—a dozen times—but not a bullet touched him, and now he's there—[*Pointing off, R.1.E.*] waiting—waiting for me, for me! [*Starts back*] What's that? [*Looking before him on ground*] A grave! A dead body! With a rope around its neck—Good God! My own face! Ah! [*Stamping face out*] What the devil's the matter with me? [*Against gun carriage*] I'm getting maudlin—childish! Curse that boy Calvert for telling me of that dangling wretch he saw hanged! This is commissary whiskey—I'm drinking too much—I'll knock off after this one—after this one—Ha, ha, ha! [*Exit door, L.2.E. Bracing up. Sentry reappears, L., and passes slowly off, R. The old Sexton is heard close by. He is a withered, deaf, white-haired man, wearing a faded jean waistcoat, no coat and a pair of worn corduroy pantaloons tucked into muddy, patched boots, an old felt hat that has lost its shape, and a red comforter around his neck; he enters through gate, L.1.E., carrying a pickaxe and spade over his shoulder. He shuts gate and puts pickaxe and spade inside door of church, downstage L., and closes door after he has done this*]

SEXTON

"From my plantin' and my hoein'
  Where the grass grows green,
Comes no reapin' nor no mowin',
  Where the grass grows green!
But by the pa'son's word accordin',
  On the t'other side of Jordan,
It will ripen in God's garden, [*With a long drone*]
  Where the grass grows green." [*Coughing*]

The smoke of that durn'd battle keeps gittin' in a feller's windlass. [*Coughs*] I wish't they'd do their fitten som'er's else. [*Looks at church window, L., shakes his head*] Jes' see them winders! All those pattern saints busted right in! Northerners is packed like herrin's in a bar'l, in that. Well, 'taint no fun'ral o' mine. I reckon I'll see if everythin's in apple-pie order in the chapel. [*Sentry crosses, R. to L.*] Then I'll drap in on Miss S'lindy! [*Chuckles.*

Crosses to tongue of gun carriage, R.C., and picks up a twig] Mebbe she'll say, "Ha' suthin', Uncle Jeff, now du," en' then—[*Chuckles*] I'll smile— [*Puts foot on tongue of gun carriage and scrapes mud off boots. Chuckles, perkily*] an' say—thank ye kindly, S'lindy—I'll take you. He, he, he! [*Crosses to C.*] People will go on a dyin' and a dyin' jes' to keep me busy. Life is a game o' nine pins, and when they're knocked over, I'm the old boy that gathers 'em in. [*Goes upstage singing, not loud*]

> "And from pa'son's word accordin',
>   On the t'other . . ." [*Exit above chapel, L. Pause. The

bolts of the church are withdrawn and Thorpe reenters, followed by Blount. Thorpe evidently has been drinking again. Door closes and bolts are heard to be shot]

THORPE. [*C.*]   You know the fellow that brought Kendrick in?

BLOUNT. [*L.C.*]   Oh, yes! Boone—the new recruit. They say he's in love with that Calvert gal and arrested him out of pure cussedness.

THORPE. [*C.*]   Put him on duty here.

BLOUNT. [*Saluting and crossing to R.C.*]   He's a dead shot, colonel, but dead shots cain't cover ev-rythin' in this old rattrap of a jail. The bluebirds us'ter fly outer this cage pretty freq'nt 'fore I took charge. What I ben aprojectin' to say to yer—is this! When I was jailer down to Pigwog, Mizzoura, we had a trick to clip the wings o' fly-by-nights that was a dead sure thing, an' I'd like to try it yer, if you'll gimme leave.

THORPE. [*Leans against house, L.*]   Well, what is it?

BLOUNT.   Well, you see, colonel, the pickets don't always hear the alarm guns. There's so much random firin' done by skirmishers. O'ny las' night two bluecoats got off that way. 'Taint safe to trust to no such oncertin signals. Now, colonel—I was a thinkin'—if we was to set that yer clangin' old bell up there—[*Pointing up at the tower*] a swingin' when a jailbird got loose— why—'twould give the alarm for miles 'round. I allow no one 'ud git by the pickets then, without a halt bein' called.

THORPE.   Not a bad idea.

BLOUNT. [*R.*]   Well, that's how I worked it when I was jailer down to Pigwog, Mizzoura. [*Takes chew of tobacco. The old Sexton reenters from above chapel. He has slung over his shoulders two long and very old straps used to lower coffins, comes slowly down and is met by Thorpe*]

THORPE. [*C.*]   Here, sexton! Here!

SEXTON. [*C. With his hand to his ear*]   Eh?

THORPE. [*L.C.*]   Oh! Here, pay attention, you deaf old bag o' bones!

SEXTON. [*Bridling up*]   I ain't no bag o' bones!

THORPE. Don't answer back! I saw you talking to the condemned prisoner in the tower. Don't do it again! You're not to know where that fellow is—you understand?—or anything about him—mind that—or I'll trim your tongue for you! Do you hear? [*Sexton bows slightly. To Blount*] Tell him what you want. [*Thorpe off, L.1.E. At exit of Colonel Thorpe, Sentry crosses, L. to R. Sexton looks at Blount and then looks off after Thorpe*]

BLOUNT. [*R.C.*] Hm! Colonel's in a beauty of a temper! Been a "Comin' through the rye" more'n usual. I wish I had his load. The old parson down at Pigwog, Mizzoura, used to say—"Make not thy nose blush for the sins of thine mouth." [*The old Sexton has crossed, L., mumbling*] Here!

SEXTON. [*C., turns and sees Blount*] Eh? [*Goes towards him, hand to ear*]

BLOUNT. [*C.*] I've got orders for you.

SEXTON. [*L.C., looking him over*] Don't keep no boarders—[*Going, L.*] Evenin'.

BLOUNT. [*C., louder*] Here!

SEXTON. [*Returning, L.C.*] Say, I ain't de'f.

BLOUNT. [*C.*] No?

SEXTON. [*L.C.*] No. Only just a little mite hard o' hearin'—that's all. Otherwise enj'yin' rugged health. Evenin'! [*Starts to exit again*]

BLOUNT. [*Roars in his ear*] Look here!

SEXTON. [*Returning*] Say, don't you holler so loud—it bothers my ears. I kin hear you fus' rate ef ye on'y talk soft like. I can always hear Miss S'lindy, speshally her—[*Imitating a woman*] "Hev suthin', Uncle Jeff, now do."

BLOUNT. [*C.*] Yes! [*The old Sexton puts hand to ear. Softly and sweetly*] Ye're to stay by the bell rope an', when ye're ordered, ring like fu-r-ry! See? [*Imitates pulling bell vigorously*]

SEXTON. [*L.C.*] Ring fer a fun'ral. [*Blount gives him a look that speaks volumes and turns away*] All right, sir! I'll ring for a fun'ral. Two dollars is my fee. Is't yer wife? [*Hand to ear*]

BLOUNT. [*Disgusted, C.*] No!

SEXTON. [*L.C.*] Oh!

BLOUNT. [*Speaking slowly and distinctly*] When you're ordered—[*He mouths words so that his meaning is clear from almost noiseless articulation*] Ring like—Hell! See?

SEXTON. Ring the bell! [*Blount, out of breath, is relieved; effective climax*] All right, sir! I'll ring the bell. Kin' o' signalizin', ain't it? Same as a fire, eh?

BLOUNT. Yes, jes' so. I'll notify the pickets. [*Going up*] I'll bet there won't be no more Yanks givin' us the slip. [*Blount exit, L.U.E.*]

SEXTON. My pris'ners don't never escape. I sods 'em down hard! They keeps quiet. But I don't like to kill folks, if I does bury 'em. [*Looking up at the belfry*] This is a new business, for you an' me, ole bell. Fer more'n sixty year, we've been a ringin' t'gether, ringin' fer weddins, ringin' fer christ'nins, an' fer fun'rals; but we didn't think we'd ever ring to catch a poor devil strikin' out fer freedom, did we? [*Coming down*] But duty's duty. [*Crossing, L.*] And I must take my place up there in the old belfry. [*Exit by side door of church facing audience. Sentry crosses platform, comes down steps, is relieved, and marches off with Relief Guard. The tramp of feet is heard, L.U.E. The Relief Guard, one of which is Tom Boone, come on from L.U.E., and enter through gate, R.U.E. The Men wear army overcoats. Boone relieves the Sentry on duty, who falls in with the Relief. They exeunt, R.1.E. After Men are on stage, they are halted by Corporal*]

CORP. Relief! Halt! Number one, take your post. [*Tom Boone and the Sentry being relieved go through the military tactics of "Sentry Relief"*] Forward! March! [*Corporal exit, R.1.E., at head of Men. Boone looks up at the tower. Not till now does the audience know that the Sentry is Boone. He paces at back from R. to L. Every time he passes out of sight there is a fixed interval until he reappears; directly after he goes off, L.U.E., Maryland, wearing a long cloak, dusty and battle-stained, her face pale and anxious, enters breathlessly from R.U.E.*]

MARY. The old church. Alan's prison—at last. Thank God! [*Goes towards church door*] Ah! [*Totters, but instantly recovers. Enter Telfair, R.2.E. His uniform shows the marks of battle. Signal "Dead March" under stage, L., ready*]

TEL. [*R.C., seeing Maryland*] Miss Calvert!

MARY. [*L.C., turning*] You! Oh, I'm so glad! You can take me to General Kendrick. Alan—Alan—how is he?

TEL. I haven't seen him. I've just come in. [*Places flag of truce on cannon and returns to Maryland*] A truce has been granted for two hours—time to pick up the wounded, and bury our dead.

MARY. I've just come from the Northern camp.

TEL. [*Surprised*] The Northern camp? Across that open field of death! For what—

MARY. For Alan! To beg the Northern general to intercede.

TEL. [*Touched*] You—saw Hooker? [*Anxiously*] Well?

MARY. This is his letter to General Kendrick, asking him to stay the—execution. He begs for a delay. Because Alan is not the man Lloyd came to meet, but one of our own officers whose treachery can be proved. Look, General Hooker's own writing—so you see there is hope. [*Watches Telfair's face, which has grown sad*] Faint you think—but still hope. His father cannot refuse the request. Alan will be saved! He shall be! Ah, you shall see! [*Muffled drums and fifes are heard, off L.U.E. under stage, playing softly the "Dead March"*] Quick! Quick! Take me to General Kendrick! [*Marked pause. Telfair looks up and meets Maryland's gaze, who, hearing the funeral march, stands still. Noticing his distress she looks at him apprehensively*] Who—is—dead?

TEL. General Kendrick!

MARY. [*With a stifled cry, stands paralyzed*] Ah!

TEL. We kept his death a secret—we didn't want Hooker to know we had lost him. [*The funeral procession is supposed to start on the march to the grave. The muffled drums and fifes growing fainter. Pause*]

MARY. General Kendrick—dead!

TEL. And now Colonel Thorpe is in absolute command here. [*Maryland in helpless despair; the hand that holds the letter falls hopelessly by her side. She totters weakly and grasps Telfair's arm, which he extends to her. The sun sinks behind the horizon, burning red and low, casting a weird light on the scene. Alan Kendrick, attracted by the sound of the "Dead March," appears behind the bars of the tower window, facing audience. He wears his uniform. Maryland has stood, stifling her sobs, and gazing in the direction of the churchyard. Telfair whispers a few words to her, which she does not seem to hear*]

MARY. What shall I do now? What shall I do now? [*Crosses, down R., to cannon*]

TEL. Courage! Courage! You can but try. Wait here. I'll ask Colonel Thorpe to see you. [*Exit, L.1.E. The sound of the muffled drums and fifes gradually ceases*]

MARY. "O Lord—Lord, hear my voice." [*She stands with uplifted face by cannon, R., back to audience. Several Prisoners appear, peering through grating of crypt, L.U.*]

ALAN. What was that? [*Alan slowly leaves the window, Maryland sees Boone, who has entered by the gate, R.U.; his attention has been attracted to Prisoners watching through grating of crypt and charges on them*]

BOONE. Get back! Get back there! [*Calling from behind, R.U.E., comes in. He is about to resume his march, off L., when Maryland calls to him*]

MARY. Sentry! [*Approaching and almost touching him*] Sentry, tell me— [*Boone halts and faces her*] Tom Boone! Tom—when—when is Alan—to—be—

BOONE. [*Stolidly*] The prisoner will be executed in half an hour.

MARY. Half an hour! O Tom, is there no hope? No hope?

BOONE. None! [*Resumes his march. Exit, L.3.E.*]

MARY. [*Fiercely*] I won't give up! I won't! [*Her eyes turn towards the churchyard*] When Colonel Thorpe comes from the grave of Alan's father —oh, he will show mercy! Yes, yes! Of course he will! [*Looking up at the barred window. The pale face of a Federal Prisoner appears at the grating of crypt. She sees him and calls Alan's name interrogatively, as though seeking some news of him. Another Face appears at the same grating, then another and another. Only half of their bodies are seen, she runs up, then glances over her shoulder towards R.3.E. Turns quickly and peers into each face, calling softly*] Alan! Alan!

BOONE. [*Passes again; he notices Maryland talking to Prisoners. To Maryland*] It's against rules to make any signs to the prisoners. [*Brutally*] Don't do it again! Don't do it again, I tell you! [*A long roll of drums is heard*]

MARY. [*By door, C.*] What's that?

VOICE. [*Outside, L.*] Prisoners escaped! [*Church bell rings an alarm. Boone exit hurriedly, L.3.E.*]

BLOUNT. [*Throwing open door facing front, pistol in hand and calling back*] Look to the others inside. [*Looks up at bell*] You bet that bell 'ull do it. [*Calling off, L.3.E.*] Here! You fellers! Come back! Come back! Them runaways can't pass the pickets while that bell's a ringin'. [*Enter Thorpe hurriedly, L.1.E.*]

THORPE. How many got away? [*Far-away shots are heard. The bell ceases ringing and a dead silence ensues*]

BLOUNT. [*Significantly*] Not one. [*Exit, L. It is now night. A faint moonlight falls on background of scene. The foreground and off R. is illuminated by the after-effects and glare from the battlefield and dying sunset effect. A low, impressive air suggesting intense suspense, is played by stringed instruments only. Boone has come from L. again and by this time nearly reached R.C.*]

THORPE. Sentry! [*Boone halts and faces him, saluting*] They tell me you're a dead shot!

BOONE. Yes, colonel!

THORPE. All right. [*Boone salutes and turns to go, but hearing Maryland's voice, pauses, then remains on guard at head of steps, up C. She stands before church door, facing R. As Thorpe turns he sees her. To Maryland*] You asked to see me?

MARY. [*Approaching him with letter in her hand*] I have a letter from General Hooker, to General Kendrick. He is not here to read it—[*Imploringly, offering letter*] Will you?

THORPE. [*Surprised, aside*] From Hooker! [*Looking at her fixedly, brusquely with a show of politeness, knocks at door, L., the bolts are withdrawn and door thrown open*] Please step inside. [*Maryland with apparent calmness approaches door. Boone has resumed his march and reached well over R.H. and glances up at the tower*]

SCENE 2: *After a moment the curtain rises, showing Colonel Thorpe's headquarters in the vestibule. The pale moon shines through the large window, R., partly lighting the vestibule, the rest of which is in shadow. Outside is a view of the corner of a high stone wall, with a pathway running down to window, R. At back, a door, reached by several steps, opens on a staircase supposed to lead to upper room in tower, L., at back. A conspicuous opening, L.2.E., through which is seen steps leading high up to belfry. The walls inside this opening are old and grim, and made effective by the arrangement of lights as though from above. A door, L.1.E., opens from a dark passage. A table is near R.C. An old knapsack is lying below it, used for papers, etc. A common ink bottle and pen on table. A high-backed chair is in front of R. corner of table. A camp stool behind L. corner of table. A bayonet with end of candle in socket is stuck into L.C. of table. Against the wall, R., is a cot. The cot has been recently occupied, the gray army blanket lying partly on the floor. The door is opened, showing Thorpe holding out a half-burned match. Maryland appears on threshold. She passes Thorpe to L.C., the light from the window falling on her white face. Thorpe closes door after her; crosses to table*]

THORPE. [*Slowly when at table*] Where the devil's that bayonet? [*Searches for candle in bayonet, finds same and lights with same match. Stop incidental music when lights are turned up. He then faces Maryland, his eyes fixed on the letter in her outstretched hand. Thorpe opens the letter, starts to read it close to the candlelight, his face is half-committal. She watches him intently, he turns slowly, sees her anxiously looking at letter; looks sullenly at her as much as to say, "What are you looking at." Maryland steps slowly back. Thorpe turns and reads the letter with intense anxiety. Aside*] Hooker knows young Calvert came to meet me. Had this paper reached Kendrick it would have saved his son—and—hanged me! Humph! General Kendrick is dead. [*Looks at his watch*] Ten minutes more. [*Crosses to R. front corner of table. Aloud, pointing to seat, L. corner of table*] Be seated, Miss Calvert. [*Throws his overcoat and hat on cot*]

MARY. [*She does not sit*] Don't! Oh, please don't keep me waiting! [*Thorpe, his back to her, pours liquor from bottle into tin cup; both bottle and cup are on table, R.*] Tell me—if you'd only tell me now—

THORPE. One moment.

MARY. [*With increasing anxiety*] But you see there's no time to be lost! If you—

THORPE. [*Not looking at her*] One moment! [*Drinks*]

MARY. [*Trying to curb her impatience and clutching her hands nervously*] Oh! [*Goes up, L. Thorpe seats himself in chair at R. of table and writes hurriedly. With a faint ray of hope on her face she sits noiselessly in seat, L. corner of table, her eyes fixed on his moving pen*]

THORPE. [*Signs*] "Fulton Thorpe, Colonel Commanding." [*He blots paper and crosses to door, L.I.E., reading it. Aside*] "At seven o'clock detail a party; take the prisoner Kendrick and execute the order of the Court." [*Opens door and calls*] Orderly! [*Bludsoe appears, saluting*] Give this to Provost Sergeant Blount. [*Bludsoe takes paper, salutes, and exit, closing door after him. Maryland has come forward and watches with signs of increased nervousness*]

MARY. [*As the door closes after Bludsoe*] You've granted the delay! [*She runs to Thorpe; as he is turning he crosses in front of her, takes his L. hand, falling on her knees, repeating in a low tone of joyful relief*] You've granted the delay! Ah, Colonel Thorpe, I thank you! I thank you!

THORPE. [*Quietly removing his hand; draws back*] I'm very sorry— [*Maryland draws back in alarm*] but this letter, coming from the commander of the enemy's forces, will not justify me in setting aside the sentence of the court-martial.

MARY. But General Hooker hasn't asked for a useless reprieve. He said there must be a delay. There was a reason for it. A reason! You saw—you read it—perhaps the meaning wasn't clear. Read the letter again. [*She gets letter from table and holds it out to him, eagerly yet appealingly*] We'll read it together.

THORPE. [*Snatching letter from her, very marked*] I quite understood— [*Crossing, R., to front of table, tears up letter and throws it in knapsack under table*] who passed the sentence.

MARY. [*R.C., growing more excited*] I know, I know; but how glad he would have been to show mercy—Think how brave he was to condemn his own son—he loved him so—what it must have cost him! O Colonel Thorpe, can you refuse? You can't—you can't! As you hope in God for mercy, you can't! Alan's life rests with you—Oh—and mine, mine, too! If you kill him, you kill me! [*Sobbing*] I don't ask for pardon—but for time—time—a night —an hour—I beg of you. [*Hysterically she puts her hands on Thorpe's arms, which are folded, and as he drops them to his sides, she slips down to her *knees, never letting go*] Time! Time! Time! [*Clings to his L. arm as he crosses, L.*]

THORPE. He was condemned as a spy—

MARY. He is innocent!

THORPE. [*L. of her by this time*] He shall hang as a spy! [*Thorpe crosses, L.*]

MARY. No, no, no, no!

THORPE. I cannot interfere.

MARY. [*Rises, her cloak falls from her shoulders*] You will not! You hate him, because he is a Northern soldier. This is war! This is the way men fight! I'm glad I'm a woman! You want his life—I know it—I feel it—[*Putting her hand on her heart*] here! How dare you take life? You can't give it back! [*She is reaching the climax of her despair and anger*] This is not punishment! It is murder! [*She crosses*] And you—you are—no—no—I didn't mean that! I don't know what I'm saying! I don't know what I am saying! Forgive me! Listen! Oh, when I think of him—dying such a cruel, shameful, ignominious death—and not guilty! [*She breaks down and sobs wearily. Throwing herself on seat, L., rests her head on table*]

THORPE. [*Still L., struck with an idea*] If I could get her to confess her part in that Charlesville affair—[*He glances at Maryland, then turns away, pleased with his plan. A solemn rolling of drums heard outside, R.U., also tramping of Men, off L.U., who stop when Blount shouts "Squad, halt"*]

MARY. [*Starts to her feet, choking back a cry*] They're coming for Alan! [*Runs and throws open window, R., and sees the rope. Shrieking*] Ah! The rope! [*Shrinking back in horror, hides her face and sways back and forward. Rope on window outside*]

THORPE. [*Back of her, crossing to R. of table, quietly but suggestively*] I'd come away from that window, Miss Calvert.

BLOUNT. [*Outside, L.1.E.*] Squad, halt! [*Maryland is terrified at the sound. Gunstocks are heard to rattle on floor. Blount enters hurriedly with Thorpe's paper in his belt and goes towards steps, R., at back leading to room in tower. Maryland divining he has come for Alan, backing to steps, bars his way*]

MARY. No, no, not yet—not yet—only a little while longer—only a little while longer—[*To Thorpe*] Please wait—please wait—[*To Blount*] Not yet! Not yet! [*Clutching each side of the baluster*] No! No! No! No! [*In front of door*] You shall not! [*Blount pauses*]

THORPE. [*R. of table, to Blount*] Well! What are you waiting for?

MARY. No! [*Blount tries to take her hand from baluster*] No! No! No!—[*Ending in her resisting cry as he succeeds in forcing it off*] No—n—no!

[*Blount thrusts her R. She goes to Thorpe. Blount goes up steps and exit, closing door behind him. Telfair, downcast, appears in doorway, L.I.E. Maryland rushing down to Thorpe*] Oh! Can I say nothing—do nothing—to make you human! [*Thorpe waves his hand to her, as much as to say, "I cannot interfere." He crosses to window, R., looks up at tree, watching Men making preparations for hanging Alan. Maryland to Telfair, who comes to her side, her last hope gone*] He won't listen!

THORPE. [*Back of table, to Telfair who has crossed to R. of table*] I regret I can do nothing for Miss Calvert!

MARY. [*Tearfully to Telfair*] You see?

THORPE. I have reason to believe the prisoner, Kendrick, had a meeting with the spy, Calvert, previous to the one proved at the court-martial. [*Telfair looks at him surprised. To Maryland, deliberately*] When he passed through Boonsboro an exchanged prisoner, your brother warned him of the intended attack on Charlesville.

MARY. [*With woman-like eagerness*] No! No! That isn't true! I told him! [*Telfair stands aghast. Before he can speak, Thorpe addresses him*]

THORPE. [*At back of table*] Lieutenant Telfair, I shall have to ask you to take a note of Miss Calvert's confession.

TEL. Surely, Colonel Thorpe—you can't believe—

THORPE. Use her own words!

MARY. Yes! Yes! It's true—I told him! [*Telfair, almost doubting his ears, reluctantly sits at R. corner of table and writes. To Thorpe*] So you see there was no other meeting between them. You will grant the delay now—won't you? Won't you? [*The door at back is opened by Blount and Alan enters. His face is pale and calm. He wears a white shirt, his arms are pinioned by his own red sash*] Alan! [*She starts to go to him, but Blount roughly pushes her to L. He gives a last tug at the sash that binds Alan, and crosses and places lantern, L., at foot of stairs leading to belfry. Maryland stands, L., with her back partly to audience. Alan stands C. They do not take their eyes from each other's face. Telfair has finished writing, drops the pen and rises. A moment of silence. Then Thorpe turns to Telfair, holds out his hand, Telfair gives him the paper*]

THORPE. Draw up guns outside the church. His 9th Cavalry bluecoats will try to get at us. Keep them back, sergeant! [*Blount crosses to him. Thorpe looks at paper, Telfair salutes and turns to go. As he passes Alan he lays his hand on his shoulder in silent sympathy. This is unseen by Thorpe, who is speaking to Blount at back. Telfair passes Maryland, and goes out at L.I.E., taking off his hat*]

MARY. [*Grief-stricken but tearless*] Alan, forgive me!

ALAN. [*C.*] Hush! Don't blame yourself! You couldn't help it.

MARY. [*L.C.*] I brought you—to this.

ALAN. [*C.*] You didn't know.

MARY. My heart should have told me—that message came from you.

ALAN. Maryland, send me away with courage in my breast—do, dear—don't—don't let your poor heart upbraid you.

MARY. It will! It will! While I live!

ALAN. If I could only comfort you.

THORPE. [*To Blount*] You understand! Send Bludsoe to me! You can have the prisoner in five minutes. [*Blount salutes and exit, L.1.E., closing door after him. A distant boom of cannon is heard*] Ha! [*At window, R.*] The truce is over! Come, Kendrick, steady your nerves! [*Pours liquor from canteen into cup*]

ALAN. [*Paying no heed to him. To Maryland, to whom he has been talking in a low voice*] And now my own sweet girl—good-bye!

MARY. No! No! Alan!

ALAN. There is no hope!

MARY. Yes, there is! [*To Thorpe*] Isn't there, Colonel Thorpe?

THORPE. Here, sign this. [*Taking paper from his breast with R. hand, placing tin cup on table with his L. hand, dipping pen in ink, holds it for her to sign paper*]

ALAN. [*Stepping between her and Thorpe, crowds her up L.*] No! Sign nothing! [*Faces Thorpe*] I don't know what you're trying to do, but don't torture this poor girl any longer. I beg of you—let an orderly take her home —and then—[*Maryland darts by Alan, seizes pen and signs the paper*]

MARY. There!

ALAN. What have you done? [*Bludsoe enters quickly, L.1.E., salutes, crosses to L. of table*]

THORPE. [*Folding paper*] When you can make your way through, get this to General Headquarters. [*Gives him paper*]

MARY. [*Following Bludsoe to door*] Yes, hurry—hurry—ride for your life! [*Exit Bludsoe. Calling after him*] Ride for your life!

ALAN. [*C.*] What have you done?

THORPE. [*R. of table*] Miss Calvert has made a confession that makes it necessary for me to detain her here, under arrest.

ALAN. Under arrest!

THORPE. For betraying the attack on Charlesville to you. [*Maryland faces the Men, the door closing; listening intently, she soon realizes she has been fooled but listens on*]

ALAN. You coward! You've taken advantage of the frantic words of a desperate girl! Weren't you satisfied without that? My poor girl, can't you see he has lied—cheated you! That man is my bitterest enemy—I drove him out of my regiment—a scoundrel! Why, it was he sent me to Charlesville!

THORPE. [*About to take a drink*] Eh!

ALAN. [*To Thorpe*] Oh! I know that! Thorpe, let us fight it out to the last—but, for God's sake, leave the woman out of the question! [*Thorpe is yielding to the influence of drink. His speech is thick. As Alan ends he gulps down the liquor in the cup and turns on him savagely, throwing the cup on floor, R.*]

THORPE. [*Crosses upstage, C.*] Ah, now I've touched you—close—close! Haven't I? Haven't I? This—is luck! Luck! Ha, ha! You're pale now, are you pale! I know by daybreak Hooker will be master here—but it'll be too late—for you. I'll never fall into his hands. No, by God! I'll blow my brains out first. No matter what happens to me—you and I—are quits. Tomorrow is Hooker's—but tonight is mine! You leave this woman you love in my hands—[*With awful meaning*] and you know I can take care of women.

ALAN. [*Horrified*] Horrible! Oh, my poor girl! [*Frantically struggling to release his bonds. Maryland gives a long, shuddering cry, realizing the horrible meaning of Thorpe's words, then meeting Alan's eyes and answering their look of agony*]

MARY. No, no, Alan—rather than stay here, under his control—I'd—

THORPE. My dear Miss Calvert—be calm. Let me comfort you. [*Puts his arms about her*]

MARY. Let me go! Alan! Alan!

ALAN. [*Struggling to untie his hands*] Oh! Oh—Ah! God! [*Looking at Thorpe in helpless fury*] Oh!

MARY. Alan!

THORPE. [*Releasing Maryland*] Go!

MARY. Ah! [*Running away from him*]

THORPE. [*As quick as a flash he has caught her wrist and drawn her to him*] My dear Miss Calvert, I hold you in my arms! Ha! Ha!

MARY. [*Struggling*] You drunken wretch! Let me go!

THORPE. Ha! Ha!

ALAN. [*With a maddening cry, rushes at Thorpe*] You dog! I'll—[*He forces himself between them, and is about to butt Thorpe with his head; Thorpe strikes Alan full in the face several times, causing him to stagger backwards, stunned for a moment*]

THORPE. I kiss you—kiss you—kiss you—[*Maryland averts her face as Thorpe tries to kiss her. As he overcomes her resistance she gives a cry of disgust, horror and rage, and seizing the bayonet from the table, stabs him in the shoulder. In seizing the bayonet, the candle has been extinguished and the room is lit only by the rays of the moon. Thorpe falls over back of table, his face upwards*]

MARY. [*Frenzied*] Devil! [*Stabs again*] Devil! [*Stabs*] Devil! [*Thorpe slips from table to floor. Maryland, carried away by the force of her feelings, has followed him down and plunges bayonet into his breast*] Devil!

ALAN. [*Recovering from effects of blow, comes down, L., starts back dumbfounded*] Maryland! [*Almost simultaneous with Boone's voice*]

BOONE. [*Outside, L., close by*] Post number one, and all's well! [*Maryland is held by the Voice; recovering herself, draws bayonet from Thorpe's breast and throws same on stage, clinging to Alan*]

SECOND GUARD. [*Further away*] Post number two and all's well!

THIRD GUARD. [*Almost inaudible*] Post number three and all's well! [*Maryland and Alan stand still, listening, until the sound dies away, then Maryland strives to untie the sash that pinions Alan*]

MARY. Quick! Quick! You must go! Get to your own lines!

ALAN. I won't leave you like this.

MARY. You may pass Tom Boone—the pickets—unnoticed. I cannot! [*Alan is now free, a quick embrace, rushes and gets Thorpe's coat and hat from cot, leaves hat on table and holds coat ready for Alan to put on*]

ALAN. No, I won't leave you! [*Crosses to door, L.1.E., as if to secure same, then returns to Maryland, C.*]

MARY. You must!

ALAN. I will not!

MARY. You can't help me if you stay—you may save me—if you go. It's our only chance. Quick! Quick! Before they come! For my sake! Save yourself—rescue me!

ALAN. Rescue you—yes—I will. [*Maryland helps him on with Thorpe's overcoat. Alan's uniform is completely hidden. He takes up Thorpe's hat, which Maryland has placed on lower end of table. Maryland quickly goes to window and peers out*]

MARY. [*Drawing back*] Sh! Get back—ah! [*She looks out again. They draw back. Tom Boone passes on sentry duty, R. to L. Pause*] Now!

ALAN. And now, good-bye, my own dear girl! I will soon be back, with my own 9th Cavalry boys! My darling! [*Takes her in his arms, kisses her, pulls hat over his eyes and exit nonchalantly through the window. As he disappears, Boone is seen coming down the path, L.C.*]

MARY. Tom Boone! [*She draws back into shadow of window, keeping her eyes fastened as if on the retreating figure of Alan. Thorpe has been reviving, rises to his feet, supporting himself by the table. He looks about him and cries out faintly*]

THORPE. Prisoner—escaped! [*By this time Boone has reached the window, and hearing Thorpe's voice, looks in. Thorpe, thrusting table aside, staggers to window and sinking on his knees by the sill points*] Fire! Kill him!

BOONE. [*With ferocious exultation*] Hah! [*Turns, R., raises his rifle. Maryland from the shadow, the light falling on her face only, puts her hand appealingly on his shoulder. Their eyes meet for a moment*]

MARY. You are aiming at my heart! Tom, it's my heart you're aiming at! [*He hesitates a moment, then fires in the air, bringing his rifle to attention*]

THORPE. [*With fury*] Ah, missed! Missed! [*Blount rushes in, L.1.E., followed by Corporal*]

BLOUNT. What's happened? Where's the prisoner?

THORPE. [*Huskily*] Escaped! Give the alarm! [*Falls into Blount's arms, who lets him drop softly to floor. Thorpe is partially unconscious*]

BLOUNT. [*With swaggering assurance*] We'll ring the bell!

MARY. The bell! [*Leaps to the belfry, L., taking lantern which Blount had deposited at foot of stairs. Thorpe is grovelling on the floor*]

BLOUNT. Look to the colonel! Look to the colonel! [*Corporal drops his rifle and tries to assist Thorpe. Lets Thorpe, who is now unconscious, sink into the arms of the Guard*] The prisoner will never pass the pickets, they'll shoot him down.

THORPE. [*Reviving slightly*] Don't let him get away—why don't they ring the bell—ring the bell!

BLOUNT. [*Shouting*] Ring the bell! [*By this time the scene is darkness; instantly changes*]

SCENE 3: *The belfry. The bell is C. A ladder comes up from below. The light of the moon falls on the bell. The music is pp. The voice of Blount and several others heard, R. and L. of stage, also several Voices under stage, shouting "Ring the bell." "Prisoner escaped," etc. Roll of drums heard, off R.*

BLOUNT. Ring—the bell! [*Maryland is seen as she climbs the ladder. She has a lighted lantern in her hand which she throws away when she reaches the second story of the belfry (from stage). With excited exclamation she rushes to the top story. As she is appearing through top opening, Blount is heard shouting from below, angrily but faintly*] Ring the bell! [*The ponderous tongue begins to move and strikes faintly the lip of the bell just as Maryland stands facing it*]

MARY. The bell shall not ring! [*Maryland leaps and clings with both hands to the tongue of the bell. The bell moves higher and higher; she is dragged backwards and forwards by the swing. Shouting, etc., kept up until the curtain falls]*

ACT IV.

PROPERTY PLOT: *Same furniture as Act II, without the military accessories; room is tidied up. Small table, chair, and hassock, R.C. Large round table, L.C. On table: pens, ink, private stationery; army medicine box with lint and bottles, several of the latter partly filled; parole on official paper in writing, portfolio for Telfair to sign on; bowl containing floating island, also silver tablespoon, pack of cards, glass for water, small inkstand and pen for Uncle Dan'l. Army litter, down L.C., covered with army blanket; army blanket rolled up for pillow, regular pillow in white pillowcase on top of same. Telfair's overcoat, sword and belt on floor in front of litter. High-backed chair behind litter, with basin and two folded towels, pitcher at lower end of litter. Old-fashioned stone jug for Phoebe. Brass blower in front of fireplace. Federal flag, battle-stained and torn, on pole 7 ft. long, for Color Sergeant. Large Japanese vases, R. and L. Small stand with vase, and chair, R.3. Small chair, R. and L.C. opening. Thunder drum and striker off R. Single horse galloping effect, off R.U. Bugler on stage, off R.U.E. Glass crash and heavy lumber, for breaking furniture and glass effect, off L.*

AT "THE LILACS"

SCENE: *Same as in Act II, without the military accessories. The place in the background where the Northern camp was pitched, is now vacant. The windows at back are shattered and one of the columns on veranda is partially destroyed. The room shows the wear and tear of war. Several of the pictures have fallen to the floor and others hang crooked on the wall. Table at back, R., holds pen, ink and paper, several liniment bottles and lint bandages.*

TIME: *A little after daylight. The cold, gray dawn of daybreak. Impressive music, indicative of a lull after severe fighting.*

DISCOVERED: *Phoebe, in a simple morning gown, at window behind curtains, looking anxiously off, R. Mrs. Gordon, her face hard and set, gazing steadily in front of her, is seated in chair, L. of a small table which is nearly R.C. Telfair is lying wounded on a litter, L.C. He is dozing. His gray coat, sword and belt, lie on the floor, also a loose piece of lint, C. A basin and two towels are on chair behind litter, L.C., a water pitcher beside it. Nanny, quietly watching at back of litter. She is in a simple frock. Uncle Dan'l stands listening at Maryland's door. Two Southern sentinels on guard outside, beyond balcony. A Sentinel (Tom Boone) in the hall, resting on his gun, his eyes fixed on Maryland's room. Music continues pp.*

MRS. G. [*In a cold, hard voice*] What time is it, Phoebe?

PHOEBE. [*Coming down, looking at clock on mantel*] A little after five. I thought day would never break.

MRS. G. [*Covering her face*] What an awful night of suspense!

PHOEBE. [*Going to window*] This lull in the fight, I wonder what it means! [*Cannon ready*]

MRS. G. It's the first time they've stopped firing since the attack began. [*Uncle Dan'l has come from passage carrying a pitcher of water which he places on floor near table at back. A single boom of distant cannon heard*]

UNCLE. Dar she rumbles agin. [*Goes to R. window*]

PHOEBE. [*Covering her ears as though to shut out the sound*] Ah! [*Goes to window, C.*] There'll be many a black dress in Boonsboro. [*By Mrs. Gordon*]

TEL. [*In his sleep*] The 9th—Alan Kendrick's 9th Cavalry. By God! Dear old fellow, it's your sweetheart you're coming down on us for, I know—I know—I hate to train my guns on you, but—I must! Fire—[*Half sitting up with an agonized expression, his eyes closed, he suddenly opens them and looks straight before him. A dazed look comes over his face as he sees nothing. Nanny, with a tender impulse, half kneels on litter and softly placing her hand over his eyes, draws his head gently down on her shoulder. Phoebe picks up the overcoat which has slipped on the floor, and lays it on chair up near mantel*]

NANNY. [*Leaning over litter, softly mouthing words*] Uncle Dan'l, some water.

UNCLE. [*From table, up L.C.*] I jes fetched some nice cold spring water. [*Phoebe taking glass of water from Uncle Dan'l. Nanny takes it, puts it to Telfair's lips*]

NANNY. So queer—I never thought I'd love to nurse. [*Telfair opens his eyes and looks into hers*]

TEL. [*Awakened by this*] What am I doing here? [*Nanny steps aside a little. Makes a movement to rise, puts his hand to his shoulder*] Ah! [*Sinks back*]

NANNY. Does it hurt so? Surgeon says it's a right bad slash.

TEL. [*Anxiously, sitting up on side of litter facing front*] Miss Calvert?

MRS. G. [*Sitting, R.C.*] A prisoner! [*Phoebe goes to her*]

TEL. [*Anxiously*] Where? The old church?

MRS. G. [*R.C.*] No. Colonel Thorpe had her brought over here about two hours ago, after the second attack on the church. [*Sentries ready*]

TEL. [*With much relief*] Thank God, she is out of that hole anyway.

PHOEBE. [*Pointing, L.*] She's in there. [*Uncle Dan'l goes listening at Maryland's door*]

MRS. G. One of our women under arrest—[*Seeing Sentinel pass at back. Super*] the house guarded.

TEL. [*To Phoebe*] Colonel Thorpe has held the church all night?

PHOEBE. Yes.

TEL. I didn't think he could do it. [*To Mrs. Gordon. Although he speaks glibly, he shows that his wound troubles him*] I tried to speak to Miss Maryland last night when they brought her down the belfry stairs, but Thorpe set a guard at the door with strict orders that no one could pass.

NANNY. The rhinocerous! [*Catches sight of Mrs. Gordon; holds her mouth. Phoebe crosses slowly to lower end of litter*]

TEL. [*Sitting up, passing his hand over his forehead*] By Jove—how that 9th Cavalry fought to rescue that girl—charged over its own dead—straight for the old church—Alan leading the way. That's the last I remember before I got this cut—

PHOEBE. Nanny saw them carrying you to the hospital; it was pouring rain and she asked Mrs. Gordon to beg permission to have you brought here. [*Nanny, who has been motioning Phoebe to silence, suddenly sees Telfair watching her and tries to look indifferent*]

TEL. [*Looking straight at Nanny*] Awfully good of you, Mrs. Gordon. [*Cannon ready*]

MRS. G. [*Absently*] Thank Nanny. The child pleaded so piteously to have you here, the surgeon couldn't refuse.

NANNY. [*In consternation, goes upstage, shakes fist at Mrs. Gordon, goes into passage. Aside*] I wish she'd held her hush!

TEL. [*Wincing*] Oh! [*Both girls rush to help him*] Don't trouble yourselves. [*Nanny draws back*] Yes, do trouble yourselves. [*Girls turn to make him comfortable. Two booms of cannon heard. Nanny and Phoebe run to window. Another boom*] Ah! About a mile away—Alan has been joined by artillery. Thorpe can't stand a day attack, unless our reinforcements push through. [*Another boom in the distance. Helplessly lifting his sword with his L. hand*] And I cannot join my men. [*Loud boom. Throwing down his sword. Aside*] Damn it! [*Nanny runs back to him*]

MRS. G. I never expected to see the day when I should shelter the enemy. Dan'l, tell the guard at the gate, not to send another Northern soldier into this house.

UNCLE. I don' tel' that guard at the gate not to let any more wounded soldiers in here, for the rooms am all filled up now by both sexes of the blue and the grey. [*By this time a tall, gaunt-looking Southern soldier with a bandage over his eyes appears at window, R.C., with a crippled Northern soldier on his back. One of his legs is hanging helpless*]

BLIND SOLDIER (Southern). Can ye give us any place to lie down? The guard said we could try.

MRS. G. [*Looking at them; to Speaker*] You can come in, not the man with you. I have enough Northern soldiers under my roof, already. You are welcome. Come in.

BLIND SOLD. Can't do it, mum—I made an agreement with this cuss here —You see, mum, it's like this: I'm blind and he can't walk. We fell about a mile off. I told him if he could do the seein', I could do the walkin' 'till we could sail into a place and get patched up—

TEL. [*Who has not fully recognized man owing to bandage*] Is that you, Johnson?

BLIND SOLD. [*Saluting*] Is that you, Lieutenant Telfair?

TEL. Yes, Johnson.

BLIND SOLD. Can you tell us a house where we can both get in?

MRS. G. Uncle Dan'l, take them into the library. The surgeon's there. [*Red, White and Blue, change to Northern*]

BOTH SOLDIERS. [*Saluting*] Thank ye, mum. [*Both together, sharp, soldierly and gratefully. Loud cannon ready, distant*]

UNCLE. [*To Northern Soldier*] Dis way. [*Pointing up passage*]

NORTH. SOLD. Forward! [*Ad lib. When they get to C. of room*] Right about! [*Etc. Phoebe crosses to L.C., near Telfair. They face hall. As they go towards passage, Northern Soldier reaches out his hands and holds aside curtains Southern Soldier is brushing against, guiding the way. Order given at end of hall to turn. Nanny speaks to Uncle Dan'l at foot of passage*]

UNCLE. Yes, Miss Nanny! [*Faint bugle call. He follows soldier off. A loud boom of cannon near-by*]

TEL. Our cannon! That's Thorpe from the old church. [*Several loud booms in rapid succession, answered by several distant ones, with occasional faint bugle calls*] They're saying "How d'ye do!" [*Provost Sergeant Blount appears on balcony, from R.1.E., with four Men with overcoats. At order from him, two Men exeunt, R. and L., and at intervals cross and recross on balcony. 4 supers. Exit with port arm. Stop music*]

BLOUNT. [*Coming into room with two Soldiers*] Halt! [*Men halt, C.*]

MRS. G. [*Rising from chair, R.*] What is this?

BLOUNT. Orders from Colonel Thorpe to double the guard. [*To two Men, pointing, R.*] Don't let anyone pass that gate. [*Exeunt two men, R.2.E.*] Say, lady, I'm drove to askin' ye for some grub. Anything but mule.

Mrs. G. Nanny!

Nanny. I'll see what I can do for this—gentleman. [*Nanny goes up passage*]

Blount. An' be durned quick about it, miss. Thank ye. [*Going towards Maryland's room, crossing, L.*]

Nanny. [*To Phoebe*] Better wait till he gets it, before he thanks me.

Mrs. G. That is my niece's room, sir. [*Blount's hand on doorknob*] Don't go in there.

Blount. Orders not to let the prisoner out o' my sight. [*Exit into room*]

Mrs. G. [*Sinking back into chair*] God help us.

Phoebe. [*Anxiously to Telfair*] If Colonel Thorpe could hold Boonsboro what would become of Maryland?

Nanny. I heard them say, she'd be sent on to headquarters at Richmond for helping Alan Kendrick to escape.

Phoebe. O Maryland!

Tel. Oh—any woman's liable to help her sweetheart. Don't bother your little heads. That won't count seriously against her.

Mrs. G. [*With intense bitterness*] Oh, I can see our name trailing in the dust—the wiping out of our proud record of loyalty! [*Burying her face in her hands*] I'm ashamed to look the neighbors in the face. Lloyd Calvert, lying in a dishonored grave, and—

Phoebe. [*C.*] Brave men have done what Lloyd did—and their names are honored.

Mrs. G. [*Rises*] Stop—before—curse him—[*Facing Maryland's room, fiercely*] and her, too. [*To the Girls*] I want to speak to Lieutenant Telfair, alone. [*The morning light has gradually come by this time. Phoebe takes bottles, and packages of lint, and goes into up hall room, L., closing portières. Nanny goes off, R.2.E.*] Helping a Northern prisoner under sentence of death to escape—is a serious thing, I know, Lieutenant Telfair, but that's not the worst—tell me the truth. My niece's position, if our side win today? Don't hesitate, tell me.

Tel. She has confessed to warning the Northern post at Charlesville—night before last! I need not tell you what that defeat cost us. The feeling at Richmond headquarters will be very strong against her.

Mrs. G. I know you took down the confession—she signed it. But the penalty—the penalty—

Tel. Imprisonment—until the war is over.

Mrs. G. No, no, they wouldn't do that! The vile prison pens! What would become of her—a woman? [*Crosses, L.*]

Tel. If she were not a woman—it would mean death.

Mrs. G. [*Almost in a whisper*] Yes, I know—[*Breaking down*] Ah, my poor child! All night long I've watched and waited—not daring to think of the worst. They will drag her away from me. [*Crosses, L.*] God forgive me, Lieutenant Telfair, for my disloyalty—may our side lose today. [*Exit passageway, L. The sun begins to come out. There is a "Halt!" outside*]

Nanny. [*Entering from R.2.E.*] Every place I go, they tell me to halt. I might as well have a wooden leg. I've been halting every other step. Uncle Dan'l went down to the hospital to get some fresh liniment, and they wouldn't give him any without an order.

Tel. Strange our surgeon let him go without one.

Nanny. I didn't ask the surgeon. I sent him myself.

Tel. Oh, that's different. What do you want it for?

Nanny. What does anyone want liniment for? I didn't want to drink it. I meant to give it to the Northern prisoners. There's too much partiality going on in this house.

Tel. Oh—I'll give you an order. Hand me a sheet of paper—pen. [*Nanny spreads paper on blotter, dips pen in ink and hands it to Telfair*] "Please give bearer—" [*Looking up*] Uncle Dan'l?

Nanny. [*Politely*] Yes, please.

Tel. [*Mumbling words, writes a line or two, pauses*] How much do you want?

Nanny. All we can get.

Tel. Modest! [*Finishes writing*] There! [*Hands paper to Nanny*]

Nanny. [*Looking at it*] You forgot to sign it.

Tel. Oh, my head! [*About to sign, pauses*] If those fellows get better, they'll try to wallop us again.

Nanny. Of course.

Tel. I don't think I shall sign it.

Nanny. If you don't sign it, I shan't feed you—and it's your breakfast time.

Tel. That alters the case. [*Drawing her to him with his well hand*] To have you feed me—

Nanny. [*Pushing his hand away*] Sir! Keep your place! Sign—[*Pointing*] on that spot! Or you shan't eat. [*Telfair putting his lips to her finger, kisses it. Putting her hand behind her*] I hate to see a man take a mean advantage. [*With her eye fixed on the place, indicating with her head*] On—that—spot.

Tel. [*Taking up pen and dropping it*] Ah! This hand has given out at last. I thought it would. [*Pointing to his wounded arm*]—in sympathy with this. I can't write, unless somebody guides my hand.

NANNY. I'll help you. [*Nanny, R. of Telfair, in front of litter, innocently kneels beside him and guides his R. hand*]

TEL. Not so fast! [*As she finishes and starts to take her hand away*] Cross my "T." [*She does so and starts to rise*] Dot my "I." [*She does so*] Oh, what a blot! [*Nanny blows on it. Telfair quietly removes his hand and puts his arm around her, she starts to rise again, but finds herself in his embrace*]

NANNY. [*Struggling to free herself*] Oh, shucks! You only pretended to be hurt in that hand! [*Freeing herself, making a face at him*] Umph! I hate you—you tricky Southerner! [*Standing at head of litter*]

TEL. [*Looking straight at her*] Did I wake up just now and find myself in tender Northern arms? Or was it the sweetest dream I ever had in my life? Miss Nanny—

NANNY. [*Takes pad from Telfair, quickly*] Doctor left strict orders you're not to talk! [*Goes to door and calls*] Uncle Dan'l! O Uncle Dan'l! Here's your order. [*Hands it to Uncle Dan'l, who appears bringing food and goes off passage. Brings down a small bowl and spoon*] Now, here's your breakfast. You were to have something nourishing. This is apple snow. People that can't swallow a morsel, often have apple snow set right well. [*Places bowl on stool in front of litter. Offers him a spoonful*] Taste!

TEL. This is really very charming of you. [*Takes it and instantly makes a wry face. Nanny stirs apple snow in basin and places it on stool in front of litter, not noticing expression on Telfair's face. Aside*] Merciful heavens! They have taken the sugar out of the salt box! [*Coughs*]

NANNY. [*Not noticing*] I'm glad you think it's so nice—[*Offering him another spoonful, he is about to protest*] I made it myself.

TEL. It's lovely. [*Opens his mouth quickly and swallows it at a gulp. Nanny punching pillow. Aside*] I'd eat it if it killed me—and by Jove—I think it will! [*Watches Nanny as she punches pillow*] Do you know you're a regular little Florence Nightingale!

NANNY. Who's she?

TEL. A sweet young lady who nursed wounded soldiers—like you.

NANNY. O, shucks! [*Throws pillow back*] Did they give you chloroform?

TEL. No, they didn't dare. My heart's affected.

NANNY. [*Administering another spoonful*] Eat! [*As he is about to speak*] Eat! [*Puts another spoonful in his mouth and turns to leave the room*]

TEL. Oh, don't go—please.

NANNY. [*Over his shoulder, kneeling*] Reckon you could keep from talking? [*Telfair nods*] Sure? [*Telfair nods*] Sure? [*Telfair nods*] Then

I'll stay for a while. [*Dives into pocket and produces a pack of cards, kneels by the litter, behind stool, facing audience*] I'll play solitare while you rest.

TEL. But that's such a lonely game.

NANNY. Say, do you want me to tell you how the war is going to end?

TEL. Oh, you can tell fortunes.

NANNY. You bet I can. I'm a perfect witch.

TEL. [*Admiringly*] You are indeed!

NANNY. No personal remarks, sir, if you please—I can tell the future.

TEL. You don't tell the past?

NANNY. Nope!

TEL. Let her go.

NANNY. [*Shuffles cards dexterously, and kneeling, lays them out on the floor in front of litter. Pointing oracularly to them*] Behold the cards! [*On stool*]

TEL. The gallant fifty-two.

NANNY. Now pick out your card.

TEL. [*Taking one and looking at her*] Here she is—the Queen of Hearts.

NANNY. Eat! [*Telfair makes an unhappy gulp of one more spoonful. Nanny gathers up cards and holds them out to Telfair*]

TEL. What am I to do with her?

NANNY. Oh, tuck her in anywhere.

TEL. [*Putting card in pack*] Goodnight!

NANNY. [*Shuffling cards energetically and laying them out in four packs. Touching each pack as she counts*] One—two—three—four! [*She examines packs until the King of Clubs turns up*] Ah! The King of Clubs! [*Holds up pack with King of Clubs face up on top*] The hero of the future.

TEL. Who's he?

NANNY. The man we're counting on up North, General Ulysses S. Grant. See how set he looks. He doesn't say much—but ump—hum! He'll fight it out on this line, if it takes all summer! [*Puts some of the cards on floor, examines pack*] Look how the cards follow him—royal flushes right along.

TEL. [*Looking*] Where's the King of Hearts?

NANNY. [*Looking up*] Who's he?

TEL. The man we're counting on down South, General Robert E. Lee. We'd all die for him!

NANNY. Well, yes, I'll allow he's a popular favorite, but hearts ain't trumps this deal. [*Picking up cards, elated*] See! My man's on top!

TEL. Oh, you've stacked the cards.

NANNY. The oracle never lies! [*Telfair gets close to her as if looking at the cards; moves away from him, on her knees, still examining*] Oh! There's that Knave of Hearts. So he thinks—he won't take a snub. [*Looking roguishly under her lashes at him*] 'Seems I can't get rid of him nohow!

TEL. [*Putting his arm quietly around Nanny*] A bee will buzz about a honeysuckle, you know!

NANNY. No! Is that so?

TEL. Yes—[*Bringing his mouth very close to hers*] that's so.

NANNY. [*Drawing her head back, pretty picture*] What are you doing? [*Pushing him away*]

TEL. Nothing. [*Buzzing. Just going to buzz*]

NANNY. Then s'pose you don't do it again! Eat!

TEL. [*Gulping down another spoonful and putting his hand on his chest, disgusted expression*] Oh, I'm a very ill man! [*Aside*] Thank heaven, there's not much left!

NANNY. [*With a cry of delight*] Ah!

TEL. What is it?

NANNY. A clear sky! Good for us. [*Shuffles cards rapidly and lays them out in six piles. Touching each pile, throwing one card accidentally away from the others*] To yourself—to your house—to what you don't expect—to what you do expect—[*Shuffles cards which are all loose on floor*]

TEL. [*Interrupting her*] What do I expect?

NANNY. Nothing! [*Spreading pack*] Sure to come true—your lover's thoughts!

TEL. Can't you guess?

NANNY. [*Business*] Eat! [*Telfair picks up basin and looks into it. Cannon business, 3 times*] Look—there's the battle!

TEL. [*Kneeling beside her*] Good! I'm in this one!

NANNY. Nine of Spades—disappointment! Ten of Spades—misfortune! [*With a wry face*]

TEL. [*Triumphantly*] We are getting the best of it.

NANNY. Ace of Spades! [*Ready to cry with vexation*] Oh, we're in an awful fix!

TEL. [*Forgets his wound and sinks on his knees beside her*] Victory for us!

NANNY. [*Examining the three lower packs in rapid succession*] Oh! Oh! Oh! Nothing but Spades! That's bad—bad!

TEL. [*With badinage*] Come—come, give it up!

NANNY. [*Looking over her shoulder, hopelessly*] Oh!

TEL. We're winning! [*Cannon booms 3 times. Distant*]

NANNY. [*Fiercely*] No, you're not! I'd rather die than have you win!

TEL. [*Dead earnest climax*] God forbid—I love you!

NANNY. [*Not hearing, joyously*] Ah! [*Suddenly spying card lying at a little distance, which previously she had accidentally flitted away*] There it is! What were you doing way off there? [*Reaching out for card on all fours*] Nine of Hearts and the wish card, too! Just in the nick of time! [*Waves it above her head*] With reinforcements! [*Imitates bugle*] What you didn't expect. We've won! [*Starts to gather cards*]

TEL. [*Sitting on floor*] Well, you've prophesied like a true woman—all your own way. I see there's only one thing for me to do.

NANNY. [*In a military voice*] Surrender unconditionally!

TEL. Let us have peace! [*Holds out his hand. Both on knees, shake hands*] No ill feeling, I hope?

NANNY. Nope. Quite the other way.

TEL. [*Offering spoonful of apple snow*] With me?

NANNY. Yes. [*Takes it, makes a wry face, catching his eye watching her, both laugh heartily*]

TEL. You don't hate me as much as you did? [*On litter*]

NANNY. No—n—no! [*Gathers up some cards and places them on stool; they rise*] Not so much. You're an object of pity, you see. [*Telfair sits on litter, Nanny goes to the back of it*]

TEL. Oh, well—but pity's akin to—

NANNY. [*Snapping him up*] No, it ain't.

TEL. Yes, it is. [*Battle effect ready. Drums. Uncle Dan'l enters, C.D. As Uncle Dan'l enters with large bottle of liniment; Nanny turns quickly, sees him, picks up towel from chair and with her back to him, folds it up, very much embarrassed. Telfair at the same moment buries his face in the pillow at the head of litter*] Uncle Dan'l. [*Nanny has drawn away from Telfair— he sits on litter. Laugh. The cannonading begins in earnest, with musketry sound*]

UNCLE. I don' tol' them fellows at the hospital that this here liniment was for some of them Northern prisoners, and they tol' me to take it, and go to H-ll, but I ain't goin' to do it just the same. [*Gun*]

TEL. [*Runs to window*] Jove! That's close by! [*Mrs. Gordon comes down passage followed by Phoebe. Mrs. Gordon immovable, stands, Phoebe starts to window. A pane of glass breaks in pieces as though hit by a bullet. Telfair assumes control, calling to women*] Keep away from the windows! [*To Uncle Dan'l pointing to doors, R.2.E.*] Close those doors. [*Uncle Dan'l does so. Enter Tom Boone with paper in his hand; seeing Telfair, salutes him*]

BOONE. Provost Sergeant Blount?

TEL. [*Calling in Maryland's room*] Blount! [*4 Men ready for Boone*]

BOONE. [*C., opening door*] Provost Sergeant Blount! [*Giving paper to Blount who appears at door and stands reading. To Telfair*] The old church is almost destroyed. [*To Mrs. Gordon*] Colonel Thorpe is going to make "The Lilacs" his last stand.

MRS. G. [*L.C., up*] My home! What good is this place? It would be shattered to pieces in a minute.

TEL. [*C.*] I see his idea! He wants to gain time and thinks Alan Kendrick will hesitate to fire upon "The Lilacs."

BLOUNT. [*L.1. Putting paper in his belt*] Where's your squad?

BOONE. [*L.1.*] Outside.

BLOUNT. Bring 'em in. [*Exit Boone, C.D., goes on balcony, gives orders*]

PHOEBE. [*Going to Mrs. Gordon; Nanny follows*] O auntie! I'm frightened! [*Tom Boone brings on squad of 4 Men*]

BOONE. Halt! [*Men halt at C.D.*]

BLOUNT. [*Goes to door, L., and calls*] Miss Calvert! [*Maryland comes from room with both hands bandaged, but not in a sling*]

NANNY and PHOEBE. [*Trying to go to her*] Maryland!

BLOUNT. Keep back! [*They draw back, up L.C. Orders Squad, L.*] Guard that door! [*To Maryland*] Colonel Thorpe will see you in a moment! [*Goes to balcony*]

TEL. Miss Calvert, I regret this with all my heart. [*Girls by Telfair's chair. Goes R.C., by table*]

MRS. G. Oh, this humiliation! This disgrace! You—you—to whom our cause was our religion—

MARY. [*Crosses, C.*] What's the use of arguing? War is not for women—we may feel—reason—and sacrifice like soldiers in our patriotism—but a glimpse of a loved one in peril—and we are women again—straight our hand goes out to save, no matter what the consequences.

MRS. G. But think of yourself.

MARY. [*Turns, L.*] If they want to punish me, I am here. [*Seeing Tom, who stands with bowed head*] Tom! [*He comes down, L.C.*]

BOONE. Miss Maryland, I acted like a brute to you—I'm sorry. Thorpe—knew I loved you—and—made use of me. [*Clinching his fists*] The traitor! I hated Alan so.

MARY. But you missed your aim last night.

BOONE. A man isn't always sure of his eye.

MARY. Yours never failed before.

BOONE. A tear blinded me!—I missed—that's all.

MARY. Dear old Tom! [*Kisses him on the forehead. Goes up by big chair, L.*]

BLOUNT. [*Comes from balcony*] Boone, you may go. [*Start cannonading*]

TEL. [*To Blount*] We must get the women to safety. [*Enter Thorpe, looking off, R.*]

THORPE. The artillery—close—closer—[*Bring on cannon, R.C. and R.2.E.*]

TEL. Colonel, the house is full of wounded and women.

BLUD. [*Entering from R.C.*] They're calling for ammunition for the artillery—we cannot hold out.

THORPE. [*Comes down, C.*] That's my affair.

TEL. [*Crosses, R., to women*] The women had better go upstairs, Mrs. Gordon.

MRS. G. We will stay where we are. [*Cease firing and all noise*]

BLOUNT. [*Comes down, R.C.*] A flag of truce, colonel, coming from the enemy.

THORPE. Aha!

BLOUNT. [*At R.W., calling off*] Hello! Hello there!

VOICE. [*Off R.*] Colonel Alan Kendrick's compliments to Colonel Thorpe. Will he surrender?

THORPE. [*To Blount*] Tell him to say to Colonel Alan Kendrick, with my compliments, I will make terms with him in person. [*Exit Blount, C., off R.*]

TEL. [*Coming R. of Thorpe*] Any sign of reinforcements, colonel?

THORPE. No.

TEL. Then it is best we surrender. It would be madness to resist.

THORPE. That's my affair!

TEL. You heard that we were out of ammunition. We must surrender.

THORPE. That's my affair. [*Telfair remains R.C.*] Miss Calvert, I was waiting for instructions concerning you from Richmond. Under the existing conditions, I am forced to take matters in my own hands.

TEL. [*R. of Thorpe*] What do you mean?

THORPE. In the face of an attack, I shall use my judgment in dealing summarily with any prisoner dangerous to the cause I serve. [*Upstage*]

MRS. G. [*Stands paralyzed with fear*] Ah!

PHOEBE. Maryland! [*Nanny goes to her*]

MRS. G. Colonel Thorpe—I beg you—I beg you.

TEL. [*R. of Thorpe. Advancing, half aside to Thorpe*] This is cowardly.

THORPE. Fall back! [*Before Telfair can speak again*] Fall back!

BLOUNT. [*On balcony*] Colonel Alan Kendrick! [*Maryland makes no movement, stands motionless*]

THORPE. [*Throwing aside R. curtain, stepping out on balcony*] Colonel Kendrick. [*Saluting*] My terms are these—I—

ALAN. [*Outside*] Colonel Thorpe, you are not in a position to dictate terms. Will you surrender?

THORPE. Impossible—as you know.

ALAN. [*Outside, R.*] If I give the order for attack—in your present condition—it will be a massacre.

THORPE. You hesitate, because you do not wish to fire on this house.

ALAN. Again—for the last time—I ask you to surrender.

THORPE. No! My terms—

ALAN. I will make no further concession—I shall give the order to attack! The women of the house will be permitted to pass through my lines.

THORPE. All but one—a prisoner! [*Sensation*]

ALAN. If any harm come to her, I shall not wait to give you into General Hooker's hands, but hang you myself.

THORPE. [*Livid*] Bring her here! [*Guards step forward, hesitate, she waves them back, down C. The red haze of battle rests on her. They stand facing R. "Oh—oh" from women*] At the first order you give to resume hostilities I shall have the prisoner fired upon—at the first order! [*Steps back. In room to Squad*] Ready! [*Not a man obeys. Mrs. Gordon covers her eyes with her hands*] Ready! [*Not a man stirs*] What's the matter with you fellows? Ready there, I tell you! [*Not a man stirs*]

TEL. Colonel, our men won't raise their guns at a woman.

THORPE. Obey me! [*Men let their guns fall to their feet in rage*] Ah! [*Whipping out his revolver*] I'll do it!

MARY. Well, Colonel Thorpe? [*Telfair, starting for Thorpe, wrenches gun from his hand; Maryland goes up*]

THORPE. [*To Men*] Hold him! [*At this moment there is no officer on the stage save Telfair*]

ALAN. [*Outside to Blount, who is still on balcony*] Ask Colonel Thorpe what his terms are?

THORPE. [*In room*] Time to vacate Boonsboro.

BLOUNT. [*On balcony. Repeating outside to Alan*] "Time to vacate Boonsboro—"

THORPE. Safe retreat to Flag Staff Rock!

BLOUNT. [*As before*] "Safe retreat to Flag Staff Rock—"

THORPE. [*Going nearer window, delivering the following to Alan Kendrick in person*] The prisoner to accompany me to Richmond, where she must stand trial. [*Silence outside, a very short pause*] Well! Well!

BLOUNT. An orderly has come up to Colonel Kendrick.

THORPE. What's his answer?

BLOUNT. What's your answer?

ALAN. I accept. [*Thorpe relieved, lowering pistol and coming into room*] Before you give the order to retreat, I must have a word with you in private.

THORPE. [*In room*] No! [*Changing his mind*] Pass in Colonel Kendrick!

BLOUNT. Pass in Colonel Kendrick! [*Blount stands between Maryland and the window. Enter Alan Kendrick, R.2.E. His appearance shows signs of hard fighting. Maryland turns and looks at him. Alan does not look at her. Saluting*] Colonel Kendrick! [*Blount orders Guards up to R.C. Alan does not return the salute but faces Thorpe sternly*]

THORPE. I understand why you wanted to come in here—to speak to Miss Calvert; there must be no private communication between you and the prisoner. Whatever you have to say, you can say before us.

ALAN. I did not come for that purpose.

THORPE. Well, what have you to say to me? I thought I had made myself clear.

ALAN. Perfectly clear. [*Ignoring him, turning to Telfair*] Lieutenant Telfair—

THORPE. I am in command here.

ALAN. [*Still ignoring him*] My men have just taken one of your couriers, Lieutenant Telfair. [*Calling, R.2.E. Crosses to C.*] Bring that man in. [*Bludsoe is brought in by two Northern Soldiers*]

THORPE. Bludsoe!—You've captured him—taken his dispatches addressed to me from Richmond—still I see no reason why I should change my plans. I shall have the retreat sounded.

ALAN. Wait! There was nothing on him addressed to you. Lieutenant Telfair. [*Alan takes paper from his belt*] A paper—brought by this man—

BLUD. [*Saluting Telfair*] I was to deliver it to you, lieutenant. [*Alan starts to hand Telfair paper*]

THORPE. *I* am in command here.

ALAN. From General Lee. [*Gives Telfair paper*]

THORPE. [*Under his breath*] General Lee!

ALAN. [*To Thorpe*] Colonel Thorpe, this retreat you forced from me—unsoldierly—cowardly—

THORPE. You're here under a flag of truce—

ALAN. —will not save you.

THORPE. I'll take my chances.

ALAN. You've been a traitor to both sides. They know it now at Richmond.

THORPE. General Lee sent no such orders.

TEL. [*Who has finished reading paper*] Arrest him! [*At order from Telfair, Men have come to attention. Reading*] "You will take command of

Thorpe's division. Give him a drumhead court-martial. The courier brings necessary evidence. (Signed) Gen'l Lee." [*To Men*] Boys—[*Thorpe leaps at Alan, who throws him off*]

ALAN. Take your prisoner. [*Men force Thorpe off, followed by Blount. Mrs. Gordon comes to L.U. Girls hug Maryland*]

TEL. Alan! [*Shake*]

ALAN. Bob! I will see you before your departure. [*Telfair exit, R.2.E. Uncle Dan'l, who has closed curtain, shouts and exit, off balcony. Mrs. Gordon going to Maryland, business and exit into room, L.1.E. The air, "Maryland, My Maryland" is played softly. Alan pauses, looking eagerly towards Maryland, who, feeling his presence, turns, and for a moment, they gaze silently into each other's eyes. The next instant Alan has gathered her in his arms. Softly*] Maryland!

MARY. Alan! [*Picture and curtain*]

THE MIGHTY DOLLAR

By Benjamin E. Woolf

CAST OF CHARACTERS

Lord Cairngorm

Charley Brood

Clara Dart

Mrs. Gilflory

Roland Vance

Judge Bardwell Slote

Colonel Tom Dart

Libby Ray

Pete

George

Servant

Blanche Thurston

Walter Saville

ACT I.

SCENE: *The home of the Darts. A mansion in suburbs of Washington, with lawn and trees, everything indicating wealth. House, L., with verandah up two steps; open door, L.2.E. Small table, down L., with chairs, R. and L. Rustic seat, down R., behind which is set tree and grassy mound. Set tree, up R. Trees, vines, foliage, etc., wherever appropriate. The backdrop shows Potomac River with fine scenery. At rise laughter heard, off L. Lord Cairngorm enters from house, going down L., lights cigarette and sits.*

LORD C. Upon my word, a merry party—what a whole-souled way of doing things these Americans have! Everybody seems to be making the most of life—at least all except that melancholy-faced young fellow who seems to have a failure of the heart when anyone wants to dance with that pretty girl—Libby—ah, yes, Libby Ray. The young man seems to be quite a sport in his juvenile way, but the supper and the wine and the pretty girls have been too much for his nerves. What an awkward fellow he is; bumped into me three times, and instead of apologizing gave me a look which carried a villainous desire to commit murder in it. [*Charley Brood enters from house and looks round*]

CHAR. I wonder where Libby has gone to? Her aunt called her away from me half an hour ago and I haven't been able to find her since. [*Sees Lord Cairngorm*] Oh—there is the English lord that wanted to dance with Libby and wouldn't give her up to me. What right has he got to come over here and monopolize the best girl in the house? He don't seem such a bad sort of fellow, but I'm desperate, and I'd quarrel with anyone that dances with Libby. [*Goes to Lord Cairngorm*] See here, Lord Cairngorm, I've got a bone to pick with you.

LORD C. [*Looks up, puts glass to eye*] By jove, it's the youthful sport—ah—where is your bone?

CHAR. You haven't got any right to come here and take my girl away—you have been dancing with her every chance you got, and I don't like it. I love the girl, and if any fellow thinks he can take her away from me, I'll make him sick of his job, and I don't care who he is, either.

LORD C. Oh, really! By jove, it's droll, but actually, I shouldn't have known it if you hadn't told me.

CHAR. Well, I wanted you to understand it.

Lord C. My dear fellow, you are not going to get jealous of me, are you?

Char. I am jealous of you. I'm jealous of everybody that she talks to, and smiles on.

Lord C. A desperate case for a young country.

Char. I have loved her ever since I have known her, but I never had the courage to tell her so.

Lord C. Faint heart never won fair lady, you know. It's easy enough, and the young lady evidently has not forgotten you.

Char. [*Anxiously*] Do you really think I have made an impression?

Lord C. Undoubtedly, and a lasting impression, I should say, considering that you danced on her dress and stepped on her toes, and tore about a yard of lace.

Char. The music was too quick—it confused me.

Lord C. I should have imagined it was the wine. But no doubt the music was at fault.

Char. It might have been a little of both. But the worst of it is that her aunt got angry about it.

Lord C. Her aunt?

Char. Yes, Libby is an orphan and lives with her aunt, who won't let me speak to her if she can help it.

Lord C. The charming widow who speaks French with such delightful persistency?

Char. Yes—Mrs. General Gilflory.

Lord C. Oh, yes—a most estimable lady, with such a droll manner of expression.

Char. Say, I don't believe you are such a bad fellow after all, and I'm sorry if I said anything out of line, but you see how it is, when a fellow is in love.

Lord C. Oh, yes, I have a brother who is continually making an ass of himself by falling in love.

Char. Suppose you were in my place, if you were trying to win a girl and you were running neck and neck right up to the wire, and something came in between you and the girl—how would you like it?

Lord C. I am afraid I should object very decidedly.

Char. Well, it just makes me feel as if I'd like to put the gloves on. [*Clara Dart, assisted by Mrs. Gilflory, enters from house*]

Mrs. Gil. Now Mrs. Dart, you must sit down and get a good breath of fresh air. [*Leads her to seat, R.*]

Lord C. There is our lovely hostess.

Char. How pale she is! She looks as if she had seen a ghost.

LORD C. She has no doubt exerted herself to entertain so large a party, and the excitement was too much for her.

CLARA. [*On seat, to Mrs. Gilflory*] Thank you so much. I feel better already since we came out into the cool evening air.

MRS. GIL. It is a beautiful evening, so clear and calm.

CLARA. Beautiful, indeed. How different is the peaceful calm out here from the excitement and heat of the dining room.

MRS. GIL. You and Mr. Dart have so many friends and your entertainments are on so lavish a scale. No wonder your strength is overtaxed.

CLARA. It is my only happiness to see my friends around me happy and enjoying themselves.

MRS. GIL. By the way, did you see Mr. Vance among the guests?

CLARA. Indeed? He has not spoken to me.

MRS. GIL. Hasn't he? Why, I thought he was an old admirer of yours, and would be glad to see you again.

CLARA. [*With apparent effort*] Oh, that was only a boy-and-girl affair, and forgotten long ago. But do not let me keep you out here. Indeed I would rather be alone.

MRS. GIL. I don't care to go inside.

CLARA. Yes, do—go and join the dancers. Lord Cairngorm will take you, won't you?

LORD C. With pleasure. [*Offers arm. Exit into house with Mrs. Gilflory*]

CLARA. [*Alone*] Ah, they do not know the battle I have been fighting with myself for the last hour in that scene of festivity. The dining room brilliantly lighted and the drawing room ringing with happy laughter and merry jests, my face bearing a smile, my heart dark and lonely. [*Vance appears at door of house*] Where is Mr. Vance now? Has he suffered, too? Perhaps I shall never know.

VANCE. [*Aside*] Why did I come here tonight? The sight of her has brought back all the painful memories of the days when my first bitter disappointment fell upon me. Clara Northwick's smile was then the sunshine of my life, and the sunshine was gone when she cast me off for a millionaire! How refreshing this cool evening breeze is. Ah—there she is now. She has gratified her ambition, she has married a man who is wealthy—but is she happy? She has everything that is dear to a woman's heart but love. Poor girl, how wan and pale she is—her face has not lost its beauty, but she is like the ghost of her former self, as she was when I told her of my love, and believed that I was loved in return. What a fool I am to tear open the old wounds. I will remain here no longer—I dare not trust myself: under the spell of her eyes I should be a traitor to Blanche Thurston and to myself. [*Clara has had face turned sideways, but now looks at him*]

CLARA. Mr. Vance?

VANCE. Ah, Mrs. Dart—pardon me, I did not wish to intrude. Good night.

CLARA. Stay one moment—I wish you to hear me.

VANCE. I am at your service.

CLARA. Why did you come here?

VANCE. Because your husband's invitation was so pressing—to decline would have been an insult.

CLARA. I would have avoided a meeting if I could—I feared my strength would be unequal to the strain—but it gives me the opportunity I have longed for, to speak to you of the past.

VANCE. The past is buried, and the wish to revive it comes with ill grace from the one who dug the grave.

CLARA. How cruel you are. If you could read my heart you would not say such bitter words.

VANCE. I thought once I could read your heart, but it was only a dream—and the awakening almost broke mine.

CLARA. Do not judge me so harshly, you know nothing of my motives—my reasons.

VANCE. They explained themselves. Mr. Dart is wealthy.

CLARA. O Roland, how can you be so cruel! Hate me if you will, but you shall not despise me, and that is why I have waited so long for a chance to clear myself in your eyes. Believe me, Roland, this marriage was not of my own seeking.

VANCE. But you are married to Mr. Dart.

CLARA. Yes, but my mother urged me to it; her fortune had been swept away—poverty, even starvation stared her in the face, and I sold myself that she might end her days in comfort.

VANCE. Poor girl.

SLOTE. [*Appears at door of house*] Will you join me in a stroll in the garden?

CHAR. [*With him*] With pleasure.

SLOTE. Well, well! If this isn't a pleasant change, from the hilarious scenes inside the house to the beauties of nature outside!

CHAR. This cool evening breeze is just what I wanted. I have been dancing till I am ready to melt. Does my face look flushed, judge?

SLOTE. Looks like the head of a torchlight procession. [*Both up C.*]

CLARA. [*To Vance*] Excuse me, Mr. Vance. I must return to my guests. [*Exit into house. Vance sits in deep thought, with averted face*]

CHAR. I say, judge, did you notice the young lady I was dancing with?

SLOTE. I should say so—you wouldn't let anyone else get near her.

CHAR. Devilish fine girl, isn't she—so high-spirited.

SLOTE. Yes, but you had better look out for her aunt.

CHAR. Mrs. General Gilflory? Oh, yes, she doesn't like me to dance with her niece. [*Mrs. Gilflory heard laughing in house*]

SLOTE. There she is now. You can tell Mrs. General Gilflory by her hearty laugh.

CHAR. I don't want her to see me, or else she will tell me I mustn't dance with Libby any more. Excuse me, judge. [*Exit, L.U.E.*]

SLOTE. That's right, you'd better step P.D.Q., pretty damn quick. 'Pon my soul, I consider the young lady's aunt is a more attractive specimen of irrational femininity than the young lady herself. Well, it's a good thing we don't all want the same woman. [*Sees Vance*] Why, bless my heart, if there isn't Mr. Vance. How do you do, Mr. Vance—delighted to see you! Resting yourself after the excitement of the dance?

VANCE. [*Coldly*] Thank you, I came out here for a moment's rest and the cool evening breeze.

SLOTE. Same case here, too much highfalutin' inside. Will you smoke a cigar? [*Offers one*]

VANCE. Thank you. I seldom smoke.

SLOTE. No? Well, I didn't know but you might like a little social chat.

VANCE. [*Turning away*] I prefer to be alone.

SLOTE. You'd rather be alone? Why, you ain't ill, are you? You look as if you'd just quarreled with your best girl.

VANCE. I have been overworked lately. You know we newspaper men have to get through a great deal of hard work.

SLOTE. Yes, that's right—and we statesmen are sometimes called upon to exhaust our vitality under the strain of immense responsibility. Now one of my committees—

VANCE. Pardon me if I decline to discuss professional affairs.

SLOTE. Oh, yes, certainly. I hate to talk shop at a garden party, but while we are here, it is so seldom a man of your prominence in the newspaper circle can be reached for a sociable ten minutes, I'd like to get the benefit of your vast experience and keen foresight.

VANCE. I am afraid you won't benefit much.

SLOTE. I just wanted to ask you for an opinion. Do you think, Mr. Vance, that there is a good chance for our railroad bill to go through?

VANCE. [*Interrupts*] Whatever information I may have on the subject is confidential, and I must decline to make any use of it.

SLOTE. But I don't want you to make any use of it. [*Aside*] I'll do that part of it. [*To him*] Merely asking your opinion—as man to man—what do you think about it, eh, my dear Mr. Vance?

VANCE. I cannot discuss the matter.

SLOTE. But you can tell me what you think.

VANCE. You must excuse me, Mr. Slote.

SLOTE. [*Following*] One minute, my dear Vance.

VANCE. Good night. [*Exit into house*]

SLOTE. [*Looking after him*] That's what I call the D.S., the dirty shake. No, sir, it's a D.D.S., a damn dirty shake, by a large majority. He doesn't like me, and that was one of his ways of showing it. I'd like to clip his wings a bit. I'd like to clip the wings of the whole brood of newspaper hawks. That's my sentiment, by a large majority. They come down here and parade about the legislative halls of the nation with more nerve than a duly elected member. They enjoy all the prerequisites of office without any of the responsibility; they stick their noses into people's private affairs, and when a patriotic Congressman tries to look after his own interests by a practical arrangement with some ambitious railroad, out comes the *Morning Clarion* or the *Daily Windbag* with a howl about bribes and corruption and rings. And they call that the freedom of the press! Freedom of humbug. I'd like to squelch the whole lot of them, that's my opinion, by a large majority. That fellow Vance don't like me. He called me a political dodo once in his weak-kneed journal. Yes, sir! He calls me, the Honorable Bardwell Slote, a dodo, and holds me up to the public ridicule. I don't know what a dodo is, but I'll bet it's something nasty. But every dog has his day, and I guess it's pretty much the same with dodos, and this dodo will have his day, and then Mr. Newspaper Vance will find that the dodo can sting. [*Colonel Tom Dart enters from house*]

DART. Ah, Slote! It's rather unusual to find you alone.

SLOTE. I had retired from the joyous scenes of festivity within those hospitable walls to enjoy the peaceful calm of the lawn.

DART. It is a beautiful evening and the air is pure and clear out here.

SLOTE. I wish you had come out here a few moments sooner. You would have seen something that might have made the atmosphere look cloudy.

DART. I was fully occupied in getting the guests comfortably settled down together, but what would I have seen that would raise a cloud?

SLOTE. You would have seen your friend Vance and your wife enjoying a little tête-à-tête in the friendly shadows of the trees, but when I say they were enjoying themselves, I am using the word in a parliamentary sense, for the expression on their faces indicated that there was a wagonload of trouble on their minds, and young Vance looked as though he was just getting over a hard stroke of fortune.

DART. Vance and my wife are old friends.

SLOTE. Yes, I guess they must have been. Maybe you're not very sensitive on those points, but I am, by a large majority, and if I had seen him talking to my wife with that look on his face, and bringing that look into her face, I'd create a vacancy among the newspaper men.

DART. I have heard Vance's name coupled with that of my wife, but I have the fullest confidence in her.

SLOTE. And she's worthy of it, too, but I can't say that much for Vance. Not by a large majority. Why did you invite him here?

DART. I did it more on my wife's account. She seemed averse to meeting him here for fear that malicious tongues might be set wagging, but I resolved to let her and the world see that I gave no heed whatever to the vagrant rumors, but trusted her implicitly.

SLOTE. And you can always trust her, but I'd keep an eye on the newspaper man. They will all bear watching, and they don't always make such fine distinctions in personal honor as a man would who wasn't eternally hunting for other people's secrets.

DART. O Slote, you are inclined to be severe on Mr. Vance, I think. You always were hard on them. A little too hard perhaps.

SLOTE. No, sir, not by a large majority. If I am hard on them, it's because they deserve it. What claim have they on my reverence? They never report a speech correctly. And how have they treated me? Sometimes with absolute silence, and at other times passed me by with half a dozen lines when my opponents are given a whole column. They have conspired to ignore me, sir, to ignore the Honorable Bardwell Slote! If I rise to address a few remarks to the members on a national subject, the next day the *Morning Bugle* says Mr. Slote amused the House for a few minutes, and if I make a speech bursting with eloquence, the *Daily Startler* says Mr. Slote took up the time of the members by some incoherent nonsense which was listened to with impatience. Do you call that freedom of the press? No, sir! Not by a large majority! Why, sir, if it was not for the *Congressional Record* the great and glorious name of Bardwell Slote would be handed down to posterity unwept, unhonored and unhung [*Dart laughs*] no, no—I meant unsung.

DART. Oh, but you said *unhung*.

SLOTE. But my time will come, sir! My time will come—and the whole world shall do homage to the name of Slote. Why, sir, our enemies will retract in terror all the vile calumnies they have uttered against our fair names, and from the highest pinnacle of fame to the utmost corners of the world I will in thunder tones proclaim that Bardwell Slote, though once crushed to earth, will rise again, and when that time comes, let the perfidious press look to itself!

DART. I have no doubt you would prove a formidable opponent.

SLOTE. Formidable, sir! Why, when I get after my friend Vance, I will make him look worse than he did when he was talking to your wife.

DART. Why do you couple their names so persistently? I understand that they have been friends since they were children, and it is only natural that a sort of familiarity should exist between them, but I am sure neither of them would forget honor and duty.

SLOTE. My dear Colonel Dart, I may be Johnny O.S., Johnny on the spot, but there is one thing I can lay to my heart; I am not so A.G., awful green. And I am neither wicked nor ungrateful, so when I think a friend's confidence is being abused I like to put him on his guard, even at the risk of giving offense.

DART. [*Good-natured*] O Slote, you can't make me jealous. Vance is not a bad fellow.

SLOTE. I'm glad you think so.

DART. But now to business. Have you any news regarding the Railroad Bill?

SLOTE. Nothing new, but we are pushing it along as fast as possible—I have done a heap of talking.

DART. Do you think there is any chance of getting it through our way?

SLOTE. Any chance, my dear sir! Of course, there is a chance, by a large majority. There are a great many people who want the road to run our way, but there are also a great many people who want it to go the other way.

DART. Of course—there is naturally some opposition.

SLOTE. My dear Colonel Dart, you know it is an F.F., a financial fact, that the concern must be run on a cash basis.

DART. Yes, of course, but the land out that way isn't fit for anything: it's all rock and stumps. I own a large tract in Chalkville and I can't sell it at any price.

SLOTE. Vance has got some land in Muggins Glen—one of his ancestors used to live out there and left him five hundred acres by will, and it's right on the line where our road wants to go.

DART. He knows nothing about the road?

SLOTE. Not a thing, and the political dodo won't tell him.

DART. If he should hear of it, of course he would work against the road running through my land in Chalkville, so why not purchase his Muggins Glen property and then he would have no interest in opposing us?

SLOTE. A good idea, and whichever way the road runs it will be a good speculation for you.

DART. Very well. I'll find a chance to get at Vance. He's in want of ready money and will be glad to sell, and then we will go in and rush the bill through. You see to that part of it—here's the money. [*Gives money*]

SLOTE. I will, by a large majority. The political dodo will wander across Mr. Vance's path and whichever way the road goes in the end, I will prepare him for an H.O.T., a high old time, by a large majority.

DART. In the meantime you sound the other members, and secure enough votes to carry our point.

SLOTE. I will send the flood of my eloquence to carry with it conviction of our ultimate success.

DART. And if we can get within a dozen or so votes of a majority, we can get those by buying them.

SLOTE. Buy a Congressman's vote? No, sir! P.T., perish the thought! But I know several honorable members who regard such matters in a strictly practical light.

DART. [*Laughing*] Of course, of course. Well, I will leave that to you. By the way, I have purchased a place up the river, and my wife has invited some of her friends to a sort of housewarming and picnic. Will you make one of the party? There will be several honorable gentlemen there whom you have met in political circles, and who may be of some service to us.

SLOTE. I accept with pleasure, my dear colonel. A good free lunch will go a long way toward opening a Congressman's heart.

DART. [*Laughing*] That's the idea exactly. One of the points of human nature—when you want a man to do you a favor, there's nothing like giving him a good dinner first, eh, Slote? [*Nudges him, exit into house, laughing*]

SLOTE. [*Has money in his hand*] Ha! There's a man after my own heart—am I in luck? Are things coming my way? Well, I should say so, by a large majority! That reminds me, I haven't seen the K. of his M., the color of his money, yet. The treasury department is running low, and I must vote a fresh supply. [*Puts money in pocket*] This is the best thing I have had since I was appointed chairman of the Buildings Committee. That Railroad Bill must go through. It shall go through, by a large majority. [*Takes money out and looks at it*] I have often caught a glimpse of the shadow, but never before had a squint at the substance. [*Laughter heard, off L., in house*] They seem to be enjoying themselves in there. That's what they call society! I'd like to have a contract to supply society with all the powder and paint it uses. It would beat a government contract, by a large majority.

Mrs. Gilflory. [*Enters from house*] Libby, dear! Libby, dear! Where are you? [*Libby Ray and Charley Brood enter, L.U.E.*]

Libby. Here I am, aunty.

Mrs. Gil. Come here at once. I want you.

Libby. O aunty, won't you allow me one more dance with Charley Brood?

Mrs. Gil. No, indeed.

Libby. O aunty—just one more—please.

Mrs. Gil. Not one—not a part of one. Lord Cairngorm is waiting to dance with you.

Libby. [*Aside*] Oh, shucks!

Mrs. Gil. Libby!

[*Enter Lord Cairngorm.*]

Lord C. [*Offers arm*] May I have the pleasure? [*Libby takes it. Charley, up C., looks angry*]

Mrs. Gil. Tell me frankly, Lord Cairngorm, what do you think of the American women?

Lord C. I think your American ladies are the prettiest in the world. By Jove, you are all beautiful. Really, it is wonderful for a new country, don't you know—you are all beautiful, and to think that only a hundred years ago you were all red savages! Wonderful, by Jove. And you American ladies have such a go-ahead sort of way—so independent and self-reliant. By Jove, I believe an American woman fears nothing.

Mrs. Gil. Quite *sans peur*. Excuse my French, Lord Cairngorm; we lived abroad so long. Libby, dear! Libby, dear! Don't do that—you annoy me. [*Libby is spatting with Charley Brood*] Excuse me, my lord.

Lord C. Don't call me my lord—it makes me feel as if I were out of place in a new country where there are no lords—call me colonel or major or judge. I would much rather you would call me plain judge.

Mrs. Gil. Oh, don't be embarrassed on account of a title, for the upper classes in America are not so much opposed to hereditary titles as they might seem to be, and I dare say you will think so yourself when you have had a further insight into our national characteristics.

Lord C. But how about the dignified simplicity of personal equality? I had always imagined that the glorious principles of Democracy were strongly opposed to the adoption of titles?

Mrs. Gil. Oh, dear, no—not so much as you might suppose. On the contrary, I assure you some of our very best families would not object to wearing titles, and forgetting the principles of equal birth.

LORD C. Ah, yes—after all it is only the lower classes who claim the equality.

SLOTE. [*Has been near*] Yes, and title or no title, I consider myself just as good as anyone, lords included.

LORD C. [*Carelessly*] No doubt—even a great deal better. [*Turns up L.*] One of the remarkable products of a new country. [*Exit, L.U.E*]

SLOTE. [*Looking after him*] He belongs to what they call the B.A., the bloated aristocracy, of Europe. I'd like to get him out West when the boys were looking for a little fun. They wouldn't do a thing with him—not a thing, by a large majority! [*Goes to Mrs. Gilflory, down L.*] My dear Mrs. General Gilflory, you are not wearing your usual air of serenity. You seem vexed.

MRS. GIL. I am vexed, very much vexed about Libby dear. That girl gives me no end of trouble. Really I cannot do anything with her.

SLOTE. I sympathize with you, my dear Mrs. General Gilflory.

MRS. GIL. You are *très aimable*. Excuse my French, won't you, judge—we lived abroad so long, you know.

SLOTE. Oh, *oui, oui*.

MRS. GIL. Oh, you speak French, too, do you not?

SLOTE. *Pas beaucoup.*

MRS. GIL. How delightful! Really you speak it beautifully, *très bien*.

SLOTE. Yes, but I prefer English.

MRS. GIL. It is such a beautiful language.

SLOTE. Oh, yes, it's a great language.

MRS. GIL. And so poetical compared to our plain English. Now when you see *pommes de terre au natural* on a bill of fare, who would think that it meant just common boiled potatoes?

SLOTE. But they taste the same in any language. [*Libby and Charley Brood appear at R.U.E., but seeing Mrs. Gilflory, they retreat*]

MRS. GIL. [*Seeing them*] Libby, dear! Libby, dear! O judge, that girl gives me no end of trouble and anxiety. I cannot make her obey me in anything, and she will persist in being unfashionable in spite of all I have done to make her a woman of *ton*. I took her all over Europe with us, and showed her the Coliseum at Naples, and the Bridge of Sighs at Berlin, and Mount Vesuvius in California.

SLOTE. That ought to have been a liberal education in itself.

MRS. GIL. Yes, indeed, the late General G. was always liberal; there wasn't a stingy hair in his head. [*Pause*] He was completely bald.

SLOTE. You must have traveled a great deal.

MRS. GIL. Oh, yes, Europe and Asia, and nearly all over the world.

SLOTE. When you were in Europe I suppose you visited the Dardanelles?

MRS. GIL. Oh, yes, we dined with them quite often. Oh, yes, Libby dear had every advantage, and now I can see a chance for her to settle down and make a *bon mariage*.

SLOTE. Lord Cairngorm?

MRS. GIL. Yes—he admires her very much. He is rich, comes from an old family, and it would be a splendid match for her. Well, I have set my heart on it.

SLOTE. She doesn't seem to care very much for his lordlets.

MRS. GIL. That's just it, she is so wilful and perverse, she is constantly running after young Charley Brood, to make a misalliance.

SLOTE. Come again?

MRS. GIL. A misalliance, if she married young Brood.

SLOTE. He's a pretty good boy.

MRS. GIL. Of course, I know a bird in the hand is worth two in the bush, but Lord Cairngorm is of a *grand famille*.

SLOTE. [*Aside*] Why the devil can't she speak straight United States!

MRS. GIL. And that is why I am looking for her now. I have *cherché* everywhere.

SLOTE. [*Aside*] There she goes again.

MRS. GIL. I want to speak to her about Lord Cairngorm, *entre nous*.

SLOTE. My dear Mrs. General Gilflory, would you oblige me by speaking English? My French is a little rusty.

MRS. GIL. Oh, *pardonnez-moi*—excuse me, judge—we lived abroad so long. I have tried to make Libby dear a woman of *ton*, but she always has so many *gaucheries*.

SLOTE. Then why don't you take the groceries away from her?

MRS. GIL. That's very good, judge—*Pas mal*.

SLOTE. [*Aside*] There she goes again.

MRS. GIL. So I have just made up my mind that Libby dear must give Lord Cairngorm a chance, and I'm going to do all I can to keep her away from Charley Brood. The idea of a girl like Libby dear throwing herself away on that young *bête noire*! When I have given her such a splendid education! She has always had the best of teachers and books, too—I bought her Macaulay's *Lies of Ancient Rome*, and Mr. Dickens' *History of David Copperplate*, and all those books, and we had the most expensive teachers for her music, and they taught her how to use the diagram of her throat, and after all my efforts to make her a lady of *ton*—to think that she should look no higher than that young monkey Charley Brood.

SLOTE. He is a P.A., a perfect ass, and I will tell him so.

MRS. GIL. I have done the best I could for Libby dear; our famliy is one of the oldest in the country. Our ancestors came over in the *Cauliflower*, and it is no more than natural I should want to see her married to someone who has blue blood, and now that she has got such a splendid chance, I have set my heart on seeing her Lady Cairngorm.

SLOTE. But isn't it rather hard on Libby?

MRS. GIL. She will soon forget all about Charley Brood—he is only a boy, though he is as rich as Creosote. He has got eight hundred thousand dollars.

SLOTE. [*Aside*] Eight hundred thousand dollars! When I called that young man a perfect ass I was using the expression in a parliamentary sense—and it don't go if he hears it. Eight hundred thousand dollars! I must make his acquaintance at once. [*Lord Cairngorm enters, L.U.E., and stands, up C., smoking cigarette. Slote goes close to Mrs. Gilflory*] Is that what you call blue blood?

MRS. GIL. Yes—that is Lord Cairngorm.

SLOTE. Lord Cleargone—and that is the man you want her to marry? That fellow there? Why, he's all collar and cuffs—blue blood you call it! It looks like green blood to me, and not Irish green either.

MRS. GIL. He is not green by any means, but *au contraire* he is very observing; besides he is very kindhearted, and quite a gentleman. [*Charley and Libby enter, L.U.E., laughing and playing*] Libby, dear! Come here to me! Directly. [*Libby goes to her*] You wicked girl! Why do you disobey me?

LIBBY. But, aunty, dear, can't I enjoy myself a little sometimes?

MRS. GIL. Certainly not, when you have to make a regular tomboy of yourself. For goodness' sake, let me straighten your necktie. You are a perfect fright. [*Down L., fixes her hat*] Don't you know it is highly improper to look as if you were enjoying yourself?

SLOTE. [*Down R.C., beckons to Charley, up C.*] Young man [*Charley goes to him*], let me have your ear for an hour—you want that gal, don't you?

CHAR. I would give the world for her.

SLOTE. Well, I guess you can get her for less than that, but you want to look out for that chap up there.

CHAR. Who? Lord Cairngorm?

SLOTE. Yes, Lord Cleangone—that lanky fellow with the eyeglass and two-story collar. He's after the girl, too.

CHAR. Yes, I know he is, but I think I can beat him out.

SLOTE. That's right, young man, let him come before the house, and after that we'll lay him on the table.

CHAR. I'm much obliged to you for the hint.

SLOTE. Don't mention it, my boy, I always like to help the young folks.

CHAR. If you help me, I won't forget it.

SLOTE. [*Aside*] I won't let you.

DART. [*Enters from house*] Lord Cairngorm—what do you think of that for natural scenery? [*Points R.*]

LORD C. It is magnificent! Magnificent—I am positively charmed with the natural scenery of this country. You know, in England the country is all cultivated. But here your scenery is like your women, naturally beautiful.

DART. And we hope they will ever remain so.

LORD C. [*Goes to Slote*] What a beautiful evening it is, Mr. Slote. Such a clear, pure atmosphere, and bright silvery moon—by Jove, there is nothing finer in the way of moonlight to be found in the old country. It is wonderful for a new country, really wonderful.

SLOTE. Why, this is the most wonderful country on the face of the earth, sir. We excel all the rest of creation in everything, sir, either natural or artificial. We have the longest nights and the brightest days, the highest mountains and the biggest rivers, the tallest trees and the greenest grass, the busiest cities and the highest buildings, the shortest pedigrees and the longest purses.

MRS. GIL. And the longest speeches.

SLOTE. You are K.K., quite correct, by a large majority.

DART. Now, my friends, that we are all here together, I hope you will thoroughly enjoy yourselves.

SLOTE. We are having a T.T.T., a tip top time.

LORD C. How royally you Americans manage your entertainments! You are as lavish as princes, and give dinners which surpass the best of our Old Country efforts, and you know we rather pride ourselves in the Old Country on having learned the art of dining.

DART. It is the pleasure of entertaining one's friends which compensates us for the hard work involved in our money-making lives.

LORD C. No wonder the American gentlemen are so popular in Europe.

MRS. GIL. You ought to see how they spend money in Paree.

DART. As it is such a lovely night, what do you say to a dance on the lawn by moonlight?

ALL. Oh, yes—won't it be lovely, etc.

SLOTE. My dear Mrs. General Gilflory—will you do me the D.O., the distinguished honor?

MRS. GIL. *Oui, oui—avec plaisir.*

CHAR. Libby—will you dance with me?

MRS. GIL. No, indeed—Libby dear has promised to dance with Lord Cairngorm. [*Takes her to Lord Cairngorm*]

LORD C. Mr. Slote—do you *dawnce?*

SLOTE. When I get a *chawnce.* [*They dance. Slote does comedy business*]

ACT II.

SCENE: *The picnic grounds. Lawn in front of country house. House is old-fashioned, with no sign of wealth. Surrounded by trees. At back is ravine crossed by small bridge (rustic). Backdrop shows country scenery, well wooded. The bridge and ravine are not used, but only to add to romantic effect. House, R., with practical door at R.2.E. Tree stumps for seats, down R. and L. At rise, Libby enters, L.U.E., leading Charley Brood by the hand, she running.*

LIBBY. Come along, Charley, come along. This must be the place.

CHAR. Oh, yes, this is the place, I suppose, but I can't say that I like it at all. [*Opens door and looks in*] Pooh! Smells just like a paint shop.

LIBBY. Yes, it does now, of course.

CHAR. Why? Does it belong to some artists' club?

LIBBY. No, you goose. It belongs to Colonel Dart—of course. He has just bought it from some old ruined family, and has had the rooms decorated and the whole place brushed up.

CHAR. It looks as if it wouldn't take much to brush it down.

LIBBY. Colonel Dart is giving a housewarming party, and is keeping open doors to all his friends. O Charley, how nice it must be to have a great big place like this and ask all your friends to come and have a jolly time!

CHAR. [*Absently*] Yes, awfully nice.

LIBBY. [*Looking off R. and L.*] What a romantic place it is! O Charley, see those nice trees down there. Wouldn't it be just lovely to go there and hide?

CHAR. Yes, lovely. But, Libby, if you only knew how my heart is twisted.

LIBBY. Your heart twisted, Charley?

CHAR. Yes, almost broken.

LIBBY. Oh, dear.

CHAR. With suspense.

LIBBY. With suspense? [*Aside*] There's no need of that. [*To him*] Why, what do you mean?

CHAR. My heart is all a flutter.

LIBBY. [*Expectant*] Why, what for?

CHAR. It's all on account of Kitty.

LIBBY. [*Disappointed*] Kitty?

CHAR. [*With memo book*] Yes—Kitty Bluestocking.

LIBBY. [*Aside*] The wretch!

CHAR. Yes, Libby. All my hopes are placed on her.

LIBBY. [*Weakening*] Your hopes?

CHAR. Yes, and five hundred dollars besides.

LIBBY. [*L., aside*] All his hopes are placed on her! Then he cares for her and I thought he liked me! [*Sits on stump and cries*]

CHAR. Do you think I shall win, Libby?

LIBBY. [*Angry*] I don't know, and I don't care, either. [*Aside*] Asking me if I think he can win her!

CHAR. Don't say that, Libby. For if I win it means a diamond necklace for you.

LIBBY. [*Aside*] With her money, I suppose! [*To him*] Thank you, but I would rather not have one.

CHAR. Oh, come now, Libby! How can you be so indifferent! By Jimminy, I ought to win. Kitty Bluestocking is a daisy.

LIBBY. Oh, indeed! Is she?

CHAR. Yes, and there's a fortune on the event for me.

LIBBY. [*Aside*] So she is rich, too! I suppose that is why he prefers her to me. Oh, the wretch!

CHAR. Though I am half sorry I risked so much, because she has a bad temper.

LIBBY. [*Spiteful*] I'm glad of that.

CHAR. What? Glad? Oh, but she can run! Whoo!

LIBBY. [*Aside*] She can't be very ladylike.

CHAR. But on the other hand she's a kicker.

LIBBY. A kicker! Some horrid skirt-dancer, I suppose?

CHAR. And she bites.

LIBBY. [*Aside*] Very charming! Ugh! I would like to bite her.

CHAR. But she has such grand action! Such a stepper!

LIBBY. Quite an attraction!

CHAR. Yes—but I am rather nervous. She is a little queer about the knees and I hear she pulled up lame yesterday.

LIBBY. Oh, the creature!

CHAR. And she has a cough.

LIBBY. I hope she will die.

CHAR. Oh, don't say that, Libby! It makes me nervous to think of it.

LIBBY. Then you must be very fond of her.

CHAR. I am! Fond of her? Why, who wouldn't be? You ought to see her! Her coat shines like satin.

LIBBY. [*Aside*] I'll get two satin coats tomorrow.

CHAR. Oh! I wish I could see her when she comes out this afternoon.

LIBBY. Then why don't you go to see her, if you are so anxious about her?

CHAR. I can't. It's too far.

LIBBY. I shouldn't think you would care how far it is if you want to see her so very much.

CHAR. But there isn't time. She runs at three o'clock and it's two now.

LIBBY. Oh, she runs today, does she? What a low creature! [*Cries*]

CHAR. [*Sees her*] Why, Libby? What is the matter? [*Goes to her*]

LIBBY. [*Shaking him off*] Don't touch me! Go back to your Kitty Bluestocking.

CHAR. Why, Libby! What have I said?

LIBBY. [*Sobbing*] You said you were fond of Kitty Bluestocking, and I thought you were fond of me.

CHAR. And so I am, of course, but that's nothing. Don't cry. Everybody is fond of Kitty.

LIBBY. Well, I'm not. I hate her, so there!

CHAR. What? Hate a horse? [*She rises with staring eyes and open mouth*]

LIBBY. A horse?

CHAR. Why, yes. Kitty Bluestocking is a horse.

LIBBY. O Charley. I thought she was a girl!

CHAR. [*Laughs*] No, Kitty Bluestocking is a horse, and the finest in America. She runs in the Great Brooklyn Handicap at 3 o'clock this afternoon, and I have bet five hundred dollars on her.

LIBBY. Only a horse? O Charley!

CHAR. Yes, only a horse, but such a horse! If she wins I shall get five thousand dollars, and I'm going to buy you a diamond necklace. You silly little goose. I believe you were getting jealous!

LIBBY. Jealous? No, indeed! I think I should like her very much, and I hope she will win. [*Aside*] But he did give me an awful scare for a while.

CHAR. I wish we could see the race.

LIBBY. So do I.

CHAR. How I should love to see her coming down the stretch!

LIBBY. [*Looking off, R. and L.*] I wonder where the rest of the people are?

CHAR. I heard their voices down there by the river. They seemed to be having a jolly time of it.

LIBBY. And where is my aunt? I suppose looking for me, as usual?

CHAR. Oh, I saw her go up that way to the flower garden.

LIBBY. [*Coaxing and trying to draw him on*] O Charley, isn't it a lovely day?

CHAR. Yes, lovely day. [*Anxious to make love, but afraid*]

LIBBY. [*Birds heard*] What a charming spot, so romantic, and O Charley, listen to the birds filling the air with their beautiful songs! That one in the tree there. How clear and sweet it sounds—just as if he were singing of his love.

CHAR. [*Aside*] This is a good chance for me to tell Libby. [*Goes toward her. Stops*] How dry my throat is! [*Tries again*] I say, Libby—in such a romantic spot as this, with that brave bird in the tree—[*Stops*] Don't you like birds, Libby?

LIBBY. Oh, yes, ever so much. How he does chatter! [*Awkward pause*] Say, Charley, were you ever deeply in love?

CHAR. [*Quickly*] Oh, yes—several times.

LIBBY. What?

CHAR. I mean, I don't know.

LIBBY. You don't know?

CHAR. No. Nobody ever asked me. Say, Libby, don't you think it would be the proper thing for a girl to make love to a fellow once in a while?

LIBBY. Why don't you try it instead of waiting for a girl to do it all?

CHAR. That's what I have been thinking of.

LIBBY. Well, why don't you do it? Why don't you tell her what you've been thinking.

CHAR. But she might refuse me.

LIBBY. [*Out of patience*] How are you going to know she would if you never give her a chance?

CHAR. But suppose she said "No"?

LIBBY. [*Eagerly*] Oh, but she wouldn't.

CHAR. If I thought she wouldn't—

LIBBY. [*Anxious*] Yes?

CHAR. If I thought that the girl I love loved me—I would—[*Pause*]

LIBBY. [*Coaxing*] You will never find out, Charley—if you don't ask her.

CHAR. Oh, but suppose she don't?

LIBBY. Oh, but she does.

CHAR. Does she always?

LIBBY. Of course she does. [*Turns away*] Isn't he stupid!

CHAR. If I thought so—

LIBBY. Yes—yes.

CHAR. If I were sure she wouldn't refuse me.

LIBBY. What would you do, Charley? What would you do?

CHAR. I would tell her all about it.

LIBBY. Then why don't you, Charley? Why don't you? Suppose it was me you were in love with, what would you say, Charley? What would you say to me?

CHAR. Are you sure you wouldn't say "No"?

LIBBY. You just try it, Charley—I'd be sure to say "Yes."

CHAR. Would you? [*Begins as if to propose*] O Libby—

LIBBY. Yes?

CHAR. O Libby! [*Pause*] O Libby! [*Pause*] Oh, pshaw! [*Turns up, C.*]

LIBBY. [*Disgusted*] Oh, shucks! I don't believe you'll ever say anything to anybody, and I don't half believe you want to. [*Goes down, L.*]

CHAR. [*Aside, Up R.C.*] I'm an ass.

LIBBY. [*Aside*] I thought it was coming then. But the silly fellow couldn't say a word, and what's more, I don't believe he ever will unless I make him. [*Lord Cairngorm enters, L.U.E.*]

LORD C. [*Seeing her*] Ah, there she is now. A charming girl—really a charming girl, by Jove. A little wild and unconventional, but after all it is better than the polite little deceits of the more fashionable dames. What I like about her most is that she is the only one I have met so far who does not think more of me because I am a lord. [*Looks at her with glass*] Really, a stunning girl, by Jove, a stunning girl, and unspoiled by the vanities of society. [*Goes to her*] Good afternoon, Miss Ray.

LIBBY. [*Turning quickly*] O Lord Cairngorm! You here again? And you are one of the party, too? I'm awfully glad.

LORD C. Oh, thanks, awfully. Kind of you to say so, don't you know.

LIBBY. I am sure you will enjoy an American picnic, and on such a lovely afternoon. You must confess, Lord Cairngorm, that our bright sunshine is preferable to the mists and fogs of your little Island.

LORD C. I confess it willingly, Miss Ray—but pray do not call me Lord Cairngorm. It is so awfully formal and insular, don't you know. Call me judge, or colonel, or something of that sort.

LIBBY. [*Laughs*] Call you judge? Or colonel?

LORD C. Yes, so much more sociable and jolly—don't you know, and besides, conforms to the customs of the country. [*They walk, R. and L., side by side, she seeming deeply interested, and Charley trying to attract her attention and call her away, pulling her dress from behind, she pushing him aside*] One feels so much more at ease when addressed familiarly as major, or even captain.

LIBBY. You are a close observer.

LORD C. I have always endeavored to be so, my dear Miss Ray, that I might adopt the peculiarities of expression which are so charmingly American.

LIBBY. I am so glad you like us. Lord Cairngorm.

LORD C. Judge, if you please, or professor if you prefer it. Of course, there are many little differences of speech and thought which are noticed by a visitor from the older countries, and sometimes I feel afraid of making myself conspicuous by failing to adopt them.

LIBBY. Oh, no. I am sure you do not.

LORD C. This is a young country, young and remarkably vigorous, I may say, and there are many new ideas presented to a stranger, but I hope to assimilate the best of them by persevering in the study of typical characteristics.

LIBBY. I think I shall have to call you professor.

LORD C. And I daresay I shall be able to drop into the American style sufficiently to perhaps pass for an American myself, and join the list of worshippers of the American girl.

LIBBY. I am afraid we American girls have fewer admirers than our English cousins.

LORD C. I would not think the men would show such wretched taste as to feel no heartbeats for such charming girls. I would venture that you have your devotees by the dozen.

LIBBY. I? Oh, dear, no. No one ever becomes devoted to me—or if they do they never say anything about it. [*Spoken to Charley, spitefully*]

LORD C. If I might be included among your devoted slaves, there would be one whose admiration would find expression in words—for during our brief acquaintance I have often told you—ah! [*Charley has been following them jealously, and as they reach R. and turn, they meet him, he putting his face close to theirs. Lord Cairngorm retreats, leaving sentence unfinished*] There is that extraordinary person again. I suppose he is another, though of remarkably well-developed nerve. [*Goes to Libby*] My dear Miss Ray, if I may have the pleasure of another half hour in your delightful society, I should propose a quiet stroll among the trees. [*Offers arm*]

LIBBY. With pleasure. [*Takes his arm*]

CHAR. Oh, yes, with pleasure. [*Starts up, L., beside her, she pushes him aside; she and Lord Cairngorm exeunt, L.U.E., leaving Charley staring blankly after them*]

LIBBY. [*In an aside when at L.U.E.*] There! I hope that will make Charley find his tongue.

CHAR. [*Alone*] How easily he did it! Why can't I do it, too? By Jove, I can, and I will, too. [*Up C., looking off, L.U.E.*] And as for him, I can see his finish. [*Pantomime of hitting and kicking. He exits, L.U.E. Slote enters, R.U.E. and comes down*]

SLOTE. No one here? That's good. B.B., bully boy, by a large majority. I knew I would be too late when I missed that B.B., blamed boat. Missed the boat by one brief minute, and missed the fun by a large majority. Had to come by train, found I had left my deadhead ticket at home, and I'm out 40 cents. The minions of a grinding monopoly demanded 40 cents! Of me! And they call this a free country. [*Looks himself over*] Well, I'm in a pretty plight to come to a high-toned party. [*Dusts himself with handkerchief*] Dust on my shoes, dust on my coat, in fact, dust everywhere except in my pocket. [*Turns empty pockets out*] I'm in a nice condition to make an impression on a susceptible female heart. The charming Mrs. General Gilflory is sure to be here, one of the party. It would not be a party if she were not a party. She is a charming woman! When I see her I almost feel like breaking the record and taking a second plunge into the matrimonial tide. No, no, Slote, my boy—you can't do it! You can't do it. The nation needs your services, by a large majority. But Mrs. General Gilflory might be a very useful friend. I might get her to do some lobbying for me when it would be most opportune, and I know she has some very influential friends in the House. If I can get a few more votes and put that Railroad Bill through, it will be ten thousand dollars in my pocket, and ten thousand dollars is a consideration not to be sneezed at in these hard times. No, sir, not by a large majority, and I'll get even with that scribbling fellow, Vance, for calling me a political dodo. Damn his newspaper skin. Come, come, judge, it's no use swearing—swearing won't do any good, least of all against those newspaper men—you might as well try to dam the Niagara River with the letters of the alphabet. [*Pete enters, L.2.E., with two other colored servants carrying lunch picnic baskets, which they put up C. Slote sees them*] Hello, here comes a small detachment of the civil rights. [*Watches them*] Well, I'll see if I can't get them to work on the rights and lefts of these shoes.

PETE. [*Standing down, L.C.*] Sure you have got everything there?

SERVANT. Yes, sah, sure.

SLOTE. [*Aside*] Dart's servants, evidently. [*To Pete*] O Pete, good morning.

PETE. Good morning, Mr. Slote, M.C. Good morning, sah.

SLOTE. Pete, have your boys got a brush among their baggage?

PETE. A brush, Mr. Slote, M.C., sah? Yes, sah, sure dey have got a brush. We always carry brushes with the rest of the picnic things, sah, so as to brush up de gentlemen when dey gets through with their sitting about in de woods, and make 'em look like dey has just stepped out of a barber shop, sah. You like to have a brush, Mr. Slote, M.C.?

SLOTE. Yes, Pete. If you will be good enough to let your boys remove some of this District of Columbia real estate from my shoes and coat.

PETE. Yes, sah. Sure, sah. Here, boys, come here and attend to Mr. Slote, M.C. Give him a good shine and a brush up. A good one, do you hear?

SERVANTS. Yes, sah—[*They come down. One has brush*]

SLOTE. Thank you, my good Peter, thanks for this great consideration.

PETE. All right, Mr. Slote, M.C., sah. Dem boys will attend to you, sah. [*They brush him and work on his shoes, each at one*]

SLOTE. How sweet and touching is this homage from a once oppressed race. [*Takes attitude of making speech, moves foot, the boy follows it on his knees*] Mr. Chairman! I mean fellow citizens and colored brethren. [*Bows to Pete, who bows in return*] When I gaze around me and behold the glories which are on every hand, my heart swells with pride of my native land. When I look up into the boundless expanse of azure sky with its uncounted stars—they don't come out in the afternoon—when I gaze upon these magnificent trees with their mighty limbs bending before the balmy breezes, I feel that I am breathing the glorious air of freedom, the air of freedom which is the heritage left to us by our brave forefathers. [*Boys are on their knees, looking up at him, staring and listening*] And Mr. Chairman, I am impelled to embrace the auspicious occasion, and in thunder tones remark—[*Whistle, steamboat, heard, off R. Slote waits till it stops*] There is something to be reported to the Committee on Nuisances.

PETE. [*To Boys*] What you doing there, you lazy niggers? Hurry up and shine them shoes, you hear? And you give Mr. Slote, M.C., a good shine.

SERVANTS. Yas, sah—[*They have small boxes like shoeblack box, which they try to get under his feet*]

SLOTE. Pete! Where shall I sit?

PETE. You want to sit down, sah? Just one moment, sah, I'll fix that for you—here, you George—go down on your hands and knees and make a seat for Judge Slote, M.C. [*One of the boys kneels and Slote sits on his back*]

SLOTE. Mr. Chairman, fellow citizens and colored brothers, I do not look upon this service which I am receiving at your hands as a favor, but as an acknowledgment of the true principles of universal freedom. [*Yells*] Hold on, there! That's a corn, a large and flourishing corn; please brush a little more gently on that particular spot. As I was saying, Mr. Chairman and colored brethren, this is an exposition of the true principles of universal freedom, principles which I have always upheld, in the military camp, in the halls of Justice and on the lecture platform. [*Swings his hat back and forward, hitting the head of boy he is sitting on*] Under the sheltering folds of our country's banner, no longer will the colored man be compelled to kneel at the feet of his master and lick the hand that holds the lash. [*Stands on boxes, boy gets up and goes up, C.*] Never again shall the colored race be crushed to the earth. No, Mr. Chairman, and my colored brothers, as the sun rises to perform his journey through the heavenly vault, so shall you rise to carry out the new destiny of your race, and before I sit down I will simply remark— [*Goes to sit, falls*] Damnation, where the devil is that black rascal? [*Darkies pick him up and brush him*]

PETE. You, George! What for you run away and let Mr. Slote, M.C., fall down like dat for?

GEORGE. 'Deed, I didn't go to do nothing, sah, deed I didn't.

PETE. Brush Mr. Slote off and see there ain't no specks of dust on him nowhere. [*The two boys brush him and stand before him holding out their hands. Slote feels in pockets*]

SLOTE. My colored friends, I will not insult you by offering you a mere bribe for the services rendered. That would be a stigma resting forever upon my life and upon yours, but as an evidence of my high appreciation of your efforts you shall receive—[*Pause*] my sincere thanks, by a large majority. [*Boys turn away disgusted. Mrs. Gilflory enters, R.U.E.*]

MRS. GIL. Am I the first to arrive again? Dear me, what a disagreeable sensation it is to be the only person on a picnic ground, and have the picnic all to yourself! Quite an *embarras de riches*. [*Voices heard, off L.*] Thank goodness, someone is coming. [*Clara Dart, Libby, Charley and Lord Cairngorm enter, L.U.E.*]

CLARA. Oh, here you are. I was afraid we had lost you.

LIBBY. O aunty, dear, where have you been, we have had such a lovely walk among the trees.

LORD C. What a charming spot for a picnic.

MRS. GIL. Lovely, and coming up here on the boat seemed just like taking another sail up the Rhine.

LORD C. Oh, you know the Rhine then?

MRS. GIL. Oh, yes, when we were abroad so much we had a delightful trip up the Rhine: we saw ever so many beautiful old ruins, there was the Drachenfels, and Heidelberg, and the ruins of Schwartz—Schwartz—oh, Schwartz something. Libby, dear [*Calls her, but she is talking with Charley, up R.C. and does not hear. Mrs. Gilflory calls again*] Libby, dear. Libby.

LIBBY. What is it, aunty?

MRS. GIL. [*Sitting on stump, down R.*] What was the name of that old place on the Rhine? Schwartz something—you know what I mean.

LIBBY. Schwartzbrod.

MRS. GIL. Schwartzbrod! The place I mean is a castle, not a bakery. That girl positively makes me ashamed, after all I have done to give her *ton*. [*Libby is with Charley*] If she isn't spooning with that young donkey, Charley Brood, again!

LORD C. You certainly have a beautiful river here, remarkably beautiful, especially for a new country. And the view is superb! I would doubt whether we could beat that in England, by Jove, and that is an old country, you know.

MRS. GIL. This is considered one of the finest bits of river scenery in this part of the country.

LORD C. You Americans certainly have some wonderful rivers, and will soon outdo us in natural scenery. I have never seen anything finer, by Jove, than this magnificent sweep of the historic Pótomac. [Póttomac]

SLOTE. [*Dart enters, L.2.E., quietly*] The What-o-mac?

LORD C. The Pótomac.

SLOTE. Oh, yes, it is great scenery, but you ought to see the Monon-gaily and the O-he-O. They would astonish you.

LORD C. What remarkable names are developed in a new country! The poor little wretches who go to school must suffer dreadfully during the geography lessons.

SLOTE. Geography comes natural to our American boys, Lord Cleangone.

LORD C. I beg your pardon; Cairngorm.

SLOTE. No, no; Cleangone.

LORD C. Cairngorm, my dear sir, Cairngorm.

SLOTE. That may be all right at home in England, but it's Cleangone here.

LORD C. Oh, very well—have your own way, have your own way. [*Aside*] Another remarkable product of a new country, I suppose.

SLOTE. [*Offers arm to Mrs. Gilflory*] My dear Mrs. General Gilflory, will you do me the D.O., the distinguished honor?

MRS. GIL. How very gallant you are, judge. [*Takes his arm*] *Merci*.

SLOTE. *We, we*. That is French, I believe.

DART. Now my dear friends, as this is the first moment that we have all come together, allow me to bid you welcome, with the hope that the day may be a happy one. There are still many beautiful spots to be explored, and if you will take a stroll down that way to the river, I will see that lunch is prepared. I am told that there are some splendid appetites to be found by walking as far as the river and back, so I trust each of my guests will bring one back.

LIBBY. [*To Charley*] I can find one easily enough—can't you, Charley?

CHAR. Yes, I can, and without going to the river to fish for one.

SLOTE. Lunch! What a welcome sound that word has. [*To Mrs. Gilflory*] My dear Mrs. General Gilflory, may I have the P.P., the particular pleasure, of accompanying you in the search for an appetite?

MRS. GIL. O judge, you are so attentive. I don't know what I should do without you.

SLOTE. My dear Mrs. General Gilflory, the pleasure of your society is my reward—shall we go this way? [*Leads her to R.1 E.*] The fairies' dell, the wishing well.

MRS. GIL. O judge—do you really mean it?

SLOTE. I do, by a large majority, my dear Mrs. General Gilflory, you have got the state of my heart down fine.

MRS. GIL. [*Sees Libby and Charley together*] Libby, dear Libby, come here. [*She leaves Charley unwillingly*] Lord Cairngorm will escort you, won't you, my lord?

LORD C. With pleasure, delighted to do so, I assure you.

MRS. GIL. [*Aside to Libby*] Don't let me catch you with that common young fellow again. You have a real lord to walk with now.

LIBBY. I don't care if he is two lords.

LORD C. [*Offers arm to Libby*] Shall we take the lead? [*Exit, L.U.E., with Libby*]

MRS. GIL. [*As they start*] Libby, dear, don't forget your *ton*. [*Aside*] There! That's what I have been trying to manage all the day. If that girl doesn't make the best of her chances I will disown her.

CHAR. [*Blankly*] I suppose I'll have to escort myself. [*Exit, L.U.E.*]

MRS. GIL. Now, judge.

SLOTE. [*Offering his arm*] It is my turn to be made happy. [*They exeunt, L.U.E. on the way he picks up campstool*] I *will* be chairman on this occasion.

DART. [*To Clara, sitting down L.*] Now, my dear Clara, this is to be your future home, and I hope you may spend many happy years beneath its sheltering roof. You will be mistress here, as you are in my heart, and you have only to express a wish and it shall be gratified.

CLARA. Dear kind husband, when you talk like that it makes me feel that I should be ungrateful indeed if I were not happy.

DART. I bought the place that we might have our little haven of rest together, as loving husband and wife, free from the bustle and turmoil of a busy city.

CLARA. It is more than I deserve. You have surrounded me with all the pleasures that wealth can bring. Who could not be happy with such a noble, generous husband?

DART. When I am weary and sick of political schemes and sordid speculations, how eagerly shall I turn to the quiet cheerful home, with loving wife to greet me at the threshold. O Clara, my darling, I know there are times when I appear hard and cold, but if I can only succeed in making you happy I shall be repaid for any sacrifice that I could make, and while I hold your love warm in my heart, the world can bring me no greater blessing. [*Exit into house*]

CLARA. [*Breaks down*] And I have no love to give him in return. [*Going to house*] Wealth, luxury, jewels, all that is dear to a woman, but a heart that is starving. Heaven help me! [*Exit into house*]

BLANCHE. [*Heard, off L.*] Yes, this is the way. [*Enters, followed by Vance, L.2.E.*] Come along, Roland, come along. Here we are at last. How familiar the dear old place looks—every tree and stone is the same. This was my dear old home, where I spent my happy childhood days, and now I see it as a visitor. O Roland, it makes me heavy at heart to see it thus, after all these years, in the hands of strangers. Home of my childhood, how happy were the bright golden days that I shall never see again—all the old faces have gone—other parents have the dear old rooms that mine had, and perhaps other children are here to play among the trees I loved so well. O Roland! It almost breaks my heart.

VANCE. [*Consoling her*] Do not cry, dear Blanche—perhaps we ought not to have come.

BLAN. I wanted to see the old place once more.

VANCE. There, there! Don't cry, don't cry. Let us set our faces to the future resolutely and with light hearts, think of the brightness that is in store for both of us, and so get even with capricious fate for the sorrow and pain that has been in each of our lives. Leave your future happiness to my care, and we will leave this scene, and in a new country build a home that shall be our own, with the foundations laid in love.

BLAN. O Roland, how nice it is to hear you talk like that. It rouses new hope. But are you sure that you will always love me?

VANCE. O Blanche, you know my heart is yours, for the years to come as much as for today. You are the star of my hopes, my ambitions, and here in sight of your dear old home I swear that I will devote my life to your happiness. We will journey through life as we have journeyed here, hand in hand, with love and trust in each other. Your love is more precious to me than all the world beside. Here, take this little flower, and wear it as a token that we have plighted our troth. [*Gives her a flower and kisses her. Clara has been standing in door of house listening, and groans loudly. Blanche is startled*]

BLAN. What was that? Did you hear no sound?

VANCE. No—I heard nothing—we are alone.

BLAN. It seemed like a groan—as if someone was in pain.

VANCE. I didn't hear it. It must have been the wind.

BLAN. Yes, that was it, of course—but it startled me so.

PETE. [*Heard, off L.*] Hurry up, you niggers, and get them things fixed up.

VANCE. Someone is coming. Some colored waiter, evidently.

BLAN. They must be the servants of the people who are living here now.

VANCE. Do you know who they are?

BLAN. I have not seen them, but I heard that the place had been bought by a wealthy family for a summer residence. Their name is Dart, I believe, Colonel Dart.

VANCE. Dart!

BLAN. Yes—do you know him?

VANCE. Yes, I know him, only slightly, I have met him once or twice.

BLAN. They say Mrs. Dart is a young and charming woman. How happy she must be with such a kind, indulgent husband, and so much money at her command.

VANCE. Yes, she must be very happy. [*Aside in thought*] Dart! Dart! [*To her*] And now, Blanche, I am afraid our happy half-hour must end, and thoughts of love give way to the sterner duties of life. I must go to work— you know we newspaper men have very little time for romance, and very little time for anything but hard work.

BLAN. Yes—and I must go meet my father. He will be expecting me.

VANCE. I will escort you as far as the lane, and leave you there. [*They start to R.1 E.*]

BLAN. Roland, do you know what they call that lane?

VANCE. No—what?

BLAN. Lovers' Lane.

VANCE. The name will be appropriate for this occasion anyway.

BLAN. [*Turns as they exeunt*] Good-bye, dear old home! Good-bye. [*They exeunt, R.1 E. Clara Dart enters from house*]

CLARA. Oh, will this pain in my heart never cease! How much longer can I bear it in silence! [*Sits down, L.*] Pah! Why am I so weak, so cowardly! Clara, Clara—be strong, be brave! Let the world see only the smiles, though your heart be breaking—breaking. [*Breaks down and weeps*]

BLAN. [*Enters, R.1 E.*] Roland! Roland! How happy you have made me! So happy that I had almost forgotten poor father. He will be waiting. [*Sees

Clara] Why, a lady, and she's crying. [*Goes to her*] What is the matter? You are suffering? Can I help you in any way? [*Clara looks up*] Why Clara, Clara!

CLARA. O Blanche! [*They embrace*]

BLAN. Is it you?

CLARA. Dear Blanche! What a pleasure to see you again.

BLAN. How glad I am to see you again! But how strange our meeting like this after all these years.

CLARA. Almost like fate.

BLAN. My dear old schoolfellow! Dear old chum. But you are in trouble—can I do anything?

CLARA. No, thank you, dear—you have the same kind heart. But it is nothing—only fatigue and the little excitement of the journey has upset me perhaps.

BLAN. Journey?

CLARA. Yes, we only arrived here this morning.

BLAN. Then you are—is it possible that you are Mrs. Dart?

CLARA. Yes, dear. I am Mrs. Dart.

BLAN. Then you are going to occupy this house, my dear old home. Oh, I am so glad, dear—you will love the old place as I do.

CLARA. I shall love it for your sake and for the sake of the old days at school.

BLAN. Tell me about yourself—are you well? Are you happy?

CLARA. I am well, and the world thinks I am happy.

BLAN. They tell me you have the dearest and best husband in the world, and his one thought is for your happiness.

CLARA. Colonel Dart is a generous husband and I know I should be very happy, but there are many crosses in life, dear, some which must be borne in silence and alone.

BLAN. Poor Clara!

CLARA. But tell me about yourself—are you happy? I need hardly ask that—your face shows that you are. Tell me about it.

BLAN. [*Kneels beside her*] I am so happy today, though I am ashamed to speak of my happiness while you are so sad.

CLARA. Let me share your joy, dear.

BLAN. Then you must know—I am in love.

CLARA. And loved?

BLAN. And loved by one of the noblest and truest of men.

CLARA. Who is he, dear? May I ask you such a question?

BLAN. Oh, yes—his name is Roland—Roland Vance.

CLARA. [*Starts*] Roland Vance! [*Stands up, excited*]

BLAN. Yes, isn't it a grand name? [*Notices her excitement*] Why, Clara dear! What is the matter? How changed your face is. You are ill.

CLARA. No, no, dear—don't mind me. It will soon pass off. There—I am better now. Go on, dear, tell me, dear, do you love this man so very much?

BLAN. O Clara, I love him truly, deeply, with my whole soul.

CLARA. And do you believe in him implicitly?

BLAN. [*Rising*] Of course I do, dear. One always does when one loves, you know.

CLARA. I wish you every success in life, dear, and pray that you and Mr. Vance may be very happy together.

BLAN. Thank you. I know we shall be happy together—Roland is so good, and we love each other so much.

CLARA. We are having a few friends to make a housewarming this afternoon. Won't you join us for a dance or a little lunch? I will take care of you and you may meet some old friends.

BLAN. Oh, yes, thank you. I should enjoy it very much. I must go now to meet my father, and will get back just as soon as I can.

CLARA. Yes, do, dear, and now that you know I am here, we must see a great deal of each other.

BLAN. We shall have so much to talk about, after so many years. Good-bye, dear. [*Going*]

CLARA. Come back as soon as you can, and in time for lunch.

BLAN. [*Up L.*] Yes, dear, and I will surprise you by bringing Mr. Vance with me and presenting him to you.

CLARA. Blanche! I beg of you—

BLAN. I can't stay another moment.

CLARA. [*In anxiety*] But let me explain.

BLAN. [*Gaily going to L.U.E.*] Not a word now. I will be back in a little while.

CLARA. Blanche! Stop! Do listen to me.

BLAN. You shall tell me by-and-by. I can't spare a moment. Good-bye. Good-bye. [*Exit, L.U.E., laughing*]

CLARA. She said she would bring him back with her. It must not be! I cannot meet him here. I cannot trust myself, and a look would betray me. What shall I do? Shall I go to my husband and tell him all? Alas—good as he is, I fear he would suspect and mistrust me forever afterward. Oh, for a friend, one good true friend to whom I could turn for aid!

MRS. GIL. [*Enters, R.U.E.*] Libby! Libby, dear! Oh, dear, where has that girl gone to now! It is enough to make me gray-headed watching that girl.

Libby! Where are you? [*Looking round, sees Clara*] O Mrs. Colonel Dart, is that you? How do you do. [*Clara returns salutation*] Lovely weather we're having aren't we? [*She is flurried*]

CLARA. [*Down R.*]   Yes, lovely.

MRS. GIL.   Quite *à propos* for a picnic, isn't it? Excuse my French, we lived so long abroad, you know.

CLARA.   So I have heard.

MRS. GIL.   O Mrs. Colonel Dart, do you know where my niece is, Libby? You know Libby dear? Yes—of course you do, everyone knows Libby dear. I have quite lost track of her, and I'm dreadfully worried about her. You haven't seen anything of her, have you?

CLARA.   No, I am very sorry.

MRS. GIL.   I can't imagine where she has gone to. [*Looks off, L.U.E.*] Well! As I live, if she isn't down there by the river and with that abominable little Charley Brood, and flirting with him just as hard as she can, and in spite of all I have said to her. Flirting with an empty-headed *garsong* like that, with a big cauliflower stuck in his buttonhole. After all I have tried to teach her about *ton* and *éclat*. [*Calls*] Libby! Libby! Libby, dear! [*Each time louder, waving handkerchief*]

CLARA. [*Aside*]   She has a kind heart in spite of her eccentricities. Shall I confide in her and ask her to help me? I will.

MRS. GIL. [*Calling*]   Libby, dear! Come here this instant.

CLARA.   I beg your pardon, Mrs. General Gilflory. [*Mrs. Gilflory does not hear*] Mrs. Gilflory.

MRS. GIL.   There! If she hasn't turned round and deliberately gone the other way. [*Calls frantically*] Libby, dear! Libby, dear! I suppose I might shout myself hoarse for all the young minx would care—I declare it is enough to drive one into hysterics. What's the good of trying to make her have some *ton* if she wastes all the advantages of her foreign education on a young scamp like that Charley Brood. [*Turns to Clara, who has been trying to get a word in*] Oh, excuse me, Mrs. Dart, were you speaking to me?

CLARA.   I should like to, at your convenience.

MRS. GIL. [*Going to her*]   Why, of course, my dear Mrs. Colonel Dart. I am ready—*à votrey service*, as we say in French.

CLARA.   I am in great distress, and in need of a friend. Would you be very angry if I were to ask you to help me?

MRS. GIL.   Why, certainly. I mean, of course I wouldn't. Now tell me what it is.

CLARA.   May I rely upon your generous nature to do me a great favor?

Mrs. Gil. [*Going to pocket*] With all my heart, my dear. How much would you like to have?

Clara. [*Smiling sadly*] Thank you—but it is not money that I want.

Mrs. Gil. Not money? Then what can I do?

Clara. I want you to prevent a gentleman from coming here this afternoon, whose presence would bring great pain to the hearts of two women if they should meet face to face. You can understand, I am sure your woman's heart will guide you.

Mrs. Gil. [*Nods knowingly*] Yes, my dear, I understand, and you can depend on me to help you, too. Oh, dear, I do love anything that has any romance in it, and this reminds me of a play that I saw when we were abroad, at the Theatre Française in Dublin. I can see it now: there were two romantic lovers, and they met in the mountains by moonlight, and they put their lips together in a long loving kiss, and a blustering blizzard came and blew them far away across the bounding billow, and they came to this country and were married, and lived happily ever after.

Clara. If I tell you the circumstances you will see the danger. A very dear friend of mine named Blanche Thurston is in love with a Mr. Vance. Vance, who is also a—who was a friend of mine before my marriage to Colonel Dart—. Blanche is coming here this afternoon, and is going to bring Mr. Vance with her. Can't you see how much pain it will cause me if we should meet? Go and meet him, detain him. Do not let him come till I am about to leave our guests and retire to my room. Detain him anyhow or anywhere, your woman's wit will supply an excuse—only do not let us meet, I beg of you.

Mrs. Gil. All right, my dear. I think I understand, and I know just what to do.

Clara. You will do this for me?

Mrs. Gil. You can make your mind perfectly easy on that score. I will find some excuse for meeting your *betey noir*, and I'll take care of him.

Clara. Oh, thank you, thank you from the bottom of my heart—you will not fail?

Mrs. Gil. My dear Mrs. Colonel Dart, when two women put their heads together, and one of them is Mrs. General Gilflory, there is no such word as fail.

Clara. You have taken a load from my heart, and I shall be very grateful.

Mrs. Gil. Not another word—now you go to your room and brighten yourself up a bit, and I'll go and head off the unwelcome young man.

Clara. [*Going into house, aside*] The blow is averted, but it must fall. *Exit into house*]

Mrs. Gil. [*Sitting down, R.*] Oh, these men, these men! Yes, and these women, too. Now let me think of all that I have got to do. Half a dozen important things on my mind—I declare, I am getting mixed up already. First of all, there is a young man coming here that Mrs. Dart doesn't want to come. That's all right, as plain as day. Mrs. Dart was in love with a young man before she was Mrs. Dart, and the young man was in love with Mrs. Dart and somebody else who wasn't Mrs. Dart—no that can't be the way. Now Mrs. Dart was in love with a young man before she was Mrs. Dart and the young man was in love with Mrs. Dart when he ought to have been in love with Mr. Dart before he married Mrs. Dart. Oh, dear—that's worse and worse. I must try it a little slower. Now Mrs. Dart is in love with a young man who isn't Mr. Dart before she became Mrs. Dart, and Mrs. Dart is afraid that Mr. Dart will find it out. No, that isn't right, there are two women mixed up in it somehow. Now Mrs. Dart was in love with a young man before she became Mrs. Dart who is not Mr. Dart but who ought to have been Mr. Dart, and the young man is in love with a young woman who is not Mrs. Dart, and Mrs. Dart wants me to keep the young man from meeting Mr. Dart—oh, well, that's near enough. Oh, dear, dear, my head is going round and round like a whirligig with all this young man and Mrs. Dart scramble. Shades of the late General G., look down upon me and help me to get the tangle straightened out! But there is one thing sure, I've got to prevent that young man from coming here this afternoon and meeting Mrs. Dart now that she has married Mr. Dart. Why will people persist in getting themselves into such ridiculous muddles? Now I never had any trouble with the late General G., never had the slightest difficulty. But he had a wooden leg, which he earned in the service of his country as quartermaster in the army, and when I went out I always kept that leg locked up. Consequently we were always happy, and when at last he died as a brave warrior should die, peacefully and at home in bed, he left me his blessing and his fortune. It was lucky that he was able to get himself appointed quartermaster in the army, for if he hadn't he would have left me his blessing without the fortune. Ah! He was a noble soul, full of military ardor, and he served his country well, and he had sense enough to see that his country rewarded him well for it. [*Rises*] Now I must see if I can find the young man who is to be headed off.

SLOTE. [*Enters, R.U.E.*] Oh, my dear Mrs. General Gilflory, all alone, admiring the transcendent beauties of nature?

MRS. GIL. Yes, Judge Slote, *toot de soole*, as we say in French—you will excuse my French, won't you?

SLOTE. Certainly, my dear Mrs. General Gilflory. I have been looking for you everywhere.

MRS. GIL. Looking for me, judge?

SLOTE. Searching earnestly, my dear Mrs. General Gilflory. I wanted to see you on a subject of some importance.

MRS. GIL. You do me honor, Judge Slote.

SLOTE. On the contrary, my dear madam, the honor is mine, and the pleasure, too, as I have found you.

MRS. GIL. You are trying to flatter me, judge, but what can I do for you?

SLOTE. My dear Mrs. General Gilflory, if I may be permitted to address you by such an endearing term, dear Mrs. General Gilflory, I want to ask you to do me a great favor.

MRS. GIL. Oh, dear, what great demand I am in today, to be sure! It seems as if everyone wanted me to do a favor.

SLOTE. It is because your magnanimous nature is so well known, and your kindness of heart is universally acknowledged, and that is why I have sought your assistance.

MRS. GIL. I will do anything I can, judge, you may be sure. It is always a pleasure to serve an old friend.

SLOTE. My dear Mrs. General Gilflory, you are generosity itself. I will annoy you with as few details as possible. There is a bill which is about to pass through the House, and I want to enlist your aid in getting it through.

MRS. GIL. [*Down L.*] Good gracious, you don't want me to go to Congress, do you?

SLOTE. No, my dear Mrs. General Gilflory. I do not want you to go to Congress, not by a large majority.

MRS. GIL. Then how can I help you?

SLOTE. By sending your magnetic individuality to Congress.

MRS. GIL. Send my what?

SLOTE. My dear Mrs. General Gilflory, Congress is composed of grindstones, and men who have axes to grind, and almost invariably the grinders and axes exceed the grindstones. Some enthusiastic writer has declared that an honest man is the noblest work of creation, but sometimes the noblest work is out of luck, probably because he is an honest man. Does the chair follow me?

MRS. GIL. [*Sitting down, L.*] I don't say that she does to any great extent.

SLOTE. Then I will speak more plainly and to the point.

MRS. GIL. Yes, for goodness' sake do.

SLOTE. Well, then, we are going to get a railroad through the House.

MRS. GIL. Won't it hurt the House?

SLOTE. If it hits the House hard enough it will hurt some part of it. On the other hand, some other part of the House, my part of it for instance, will be greatly benefited.

MRS. GIL. The chair is beginning to follow.

SLOTE. Now, my dear Mrs. General Gilflory, I know you have man influential friends in Congress, and if I can only have your assistance ou success will be assured, and I shall be your debtor for life, by a large majority

MRS. GIL. Then in plain English, you want me to lie for you?

SLOTE. Diplomatize, my dear Mrs. General Gilflory, diplomatize.

MRS. GIL. Oh!

SLOTE. Lying is a different matter altogether. A man who tells lies, eve: though they may be for the general good of the community, is a liar, and ca: never be considered a gentleman, but the man who diplomatizes in his ow: interest is a—

MRS. GIL. Liar?

SLOTE. A diplomat. Nobody would call him a liar.

MRS. GIL. Oh, yes—I see.

SLOTE. Now my dear Mrs. General Gilflory, if you will be good enough t use your influence in the direction of diplomacy, you will make me you E.D., everlasting debtor.

MRS. GIL. I am the soul of good nature, judge, tell me how I can be usefu

SLOTE. In our Railroad Bill there is a division of interests as to which wa the road shall be laid out. Now we want it to go through Chalkville, the other want it to go through Muggins Glen. If we can carry our point and send th road through Chalkville, my fortune is made; you shall have some shares i the enterprise, and I shall be your H.S., your humble servant, for life.

MRS. GIL. You say you want it to go through Chalkville?

SLOTE. Chalkville, my dear Mrs. General Gilflory, Chalkville, by a larg majority.

MRS. GIL. Then Chalkville it shall be.

SLOTE. [Elated] I can depend on you?

MRS. GIL. You can. There's old Major Wilson from Tennessee, and th bald-headed Congressman from Chicago, and half a dozen others that ar friends of mine, and I know they will do anything I ask them—there's . dozen votes that I know of now.

SLOTE. And we need only fourteen. My dear Mrs. General Gilflory, whe the proud bird of freedom soars aloft on pinions of victory to its everlastin home, and the nation is aglow with excitement, then in the highest niches o the temple of fame shall blaze in letters of fire the initials of Mrs. Genera Gilflory, O.B.I., our beauteous idol. [Kisses her hand]

MRS. GIL. Shades of the late General G., look down upon me and lend m some of your military enthusiasm! Chalkville versus Muggins Glen, up witl Chalkville and down with Muggins.

SLOTE. Chalkville down the Glen, by a large majority, hooray!

Mrs. Gil. Hooray!

Slote. I can depend upon you?

Mrs. Gil. You can, for all I can do.

Slote. I knew you would not refuse my ardent prayer. You are my G.A., my guardian angel. And now that my mission has been crowned with your consent, I will hurry with the good news to my waiting friends and tell them of our C.C., certain success. [*Going toward L.U.E.*] I will not say good-bye, my dear Mrs. General Gilflory, but as we say in French, O.R., *o-revoir*— over the river. [*Kisses hand to her and exit, L.U.E.*]

Mrs. Gil. Dear me, what great demand I am in today! That is the penalty of being popular. I wonder where my *protege* [pretty jay] is? [*Starts up L. but stops*] No, no—first I must go and meet the young man who ought to have been Mr. Dart, and prevent him from coming here and meeting Mrs. Dart. What a lovely romantic affair it is! And I do love anything that has romance in it. That makes me think of Libby dear and young Charley Brood again. [*Starts L., then R., and wavers*] Oh, dear. Between Mrs. Dart's young man and Libby's young Brood, and Mr. Slote and Chalkville and Muggins Glen, my brain is positively pulverizing. [*Libby enters, L.U.E., in condition of untidiness. Tries to retreat but Mrs. Gilflory sees her*] Libby! Come back here. Libby, dear. [*Libby meets her, C.*] Good gracious, what a condition for a girl with *ton* to be in! Your hair looks as if you had been dragged through a brush heap—what on earth have you been doing?

Libby. [*Demurely*] I have only been playing marbles with Charley Brood.

Mrs. Gil. What? On your head?

Libby. Of course not—we were playing on the grass.

Mrs. Gil. Playing marbles with Charley Brood! Nice intelligent occupation for a man and a full-grown girl. How dare you go romping about on the grass and out in the air when you have such disgustingly red cheeks! How often have I told you that red cheeks and sparkling eyes are positively vulgar this year. You ought to look pale and languid and interesting. I am surprised that you should allow yourself to become so healthy and robust.

Libby. You look pretty robust yourself, aunty.

Mrs. Gil. Never mind about me; we widows have no such restrictions placed around us as the social buds have.

Libby. But aunty, dear, I want to tell you what happened just now. Oh aunty—it's such news. I could hardly wait till I had a chance to tell you.

Mrs. Gil. Good gracious child—what was it? Has anything happened to that Charley Brood?

Libby. No.

Mrs. Gil. No, no such good luck.

LIBBY. Aunty, Lord Cairngorm was walking with me down by the river and—

MRS. GIL. Fell in?

LIBBY. No—he asked me to be his wife.

MRS. GIL. [*Delighted*] O Libby—how perfectly grand! Lord Cairngorm asked you to be his wife?

LIBBY. Yes.

MRS. GIL. To which of course you answered "Yes."

LIBBY. To which of course I answered "No."

MRS. GIL. [*Astounded*] Libby—you said "No"—you refused to marry Lord Cairngorm!

LIBBY. Of course I did.

MRS. GIL. What for?

LIBBY. Because I don't love him. And I asked him as a great favor never to mention the subject to me again.

MRS. GIL. O Libby—what have you done? And I had hoped and planned for him to propose. Libby—do you want to break my heart?

LIBBY. No, aunty, dear—but I didn't want you to break mine.

MRS. GIL. Break yours? Why, he would have been a splendid husband. He is so kind, besides, he is ever so rich, and you would have been a real aristocrat, and I had just set my heart on your marrying him.

LIBBY. But I don't want to marry him, aunty. I want Charley Brood.

MRS. GIL. Charley Brood. That young jackanapes again! Has he had the audacity to propose to you?

LIBBY. No. He hadn't got the courage, so I proposed to him.

MRS. GIL. [*Sarcastic*] Oh, indeed! Quite a creditable performance. *He hadn't the courage, so she proposed to him!*

LIBBY. Yes, I did.

MRS. GIL. Was there ever such a girl! She must be an idiot, a wild staring idiot. [*Talking to herself*] Refuse to marry a lord for the sake of a little monkey like that Charley Brood, and of course she has insulted Lord Cairngorm. He won't speak to any of us again. It's enough to drive a poor woman to the gates of a lunatic asylum. I must find Lord Cairngorm at once and apologize to him. It is too bad. It's too bad to have such a lovely romance spoilt just on account of a silly girl's notions. But I'll stop it. I'll bring it round again all right. [*Calls*] Libby, Libby—come here to me—come here to me—there, stand there, stand right there—don't turn your feet in like an Indian cigar sign. Now look at me. Don't squint like that—now smile. [*Libby makes a face*] Not so much—you look like a Chinese puzzle with the paint scraped off—. There—

that's better. Now don't you ever dare to speak to that wretch Charley Brood again—never—do you understand?

LIBBY.   Yes, aunty.

MRS. GIL. [*Excited*]   He is a first-class donkey, so are you, so am I, so is everybody. No, no—I don't mean that. [*Libby laughs*] Stop laughing, silly. Oh, that girl, she never did have sense enough to come in when it rains. Shades of the late General G., look down on me. [*Exit, R.U.E., all excited and flustered and rattled*]

LIBBY. [*Alone*]   And I am not permitted to choose my own husband! I think it's a shame. And all because Aunt Gilflory wants me to have some *ton*. The idea of not letting a girl have anything to say about who she marries! It's just awful to be a girl. I wish I was a boy. No, I don't, because I couldn't marry Charley Brood then. I guess it's better as it is. But I'm going to marry anyone I want to, just the same. [*Voices, off L. All enter, L.2. and 3. Mrs. Dart goes down, R., stands with air of sadness. Pete and the two colored boys are just finishing the spreading of meal on stage, up C., knives, forks, food as mentioned, etc. Dart stands, L.2.E.*]

DART.   Now, good friends, as lunch is ready it would be very poor tactics to delay the attack. Lord Cairngorm, gentlemen, will you lead the assault and see that the ladies have favorable positions? I have no doubt you all have good appetites after your stroll.

SLOTE.   Appetite? I am so hungry I could eat the plaster off an old wall. [*They all sit round the cloth. Pete stands at back, R.*] Before we take our places, where is our chief guest, Mrs. General Gilflory?

CHAR.   I saw her going down that way. [*Points, R.U.E.*]

LORD C.   Here she comes now. [*Mrs. Gilflory enters, R.U.E.*]

DART.   Come along Mrs. Gilflory. Just in time.

MRS. GIL. [*Looking at Clara, who is still standing, down R.*] There she is. How shall I tell her I missed him? [*Goes to her*] Oh, dear—I couldn't find your lover. [*Flustered*]

CLARA.   Oh—not a word. [*Goes to her place at lunch*]

MRS. GIL. [*Aside*]   She won't let me tell her I lost sight of him, and he went in another direction.

DART.   Come along, Mrs. Gilflory—the company awaits your grace. [*She takes her place, all sitting on stage*] Are we all seated now?

SLOTE.   All down.

DART.   Then let the attack be made, and carry out the old admonition, eat, drink, and be merry.

LORD C.   Quite a charming idea, lunch *al fresco*.

SLOTE.   *Al fresco*? Is that French for free lunch?

MRS. GIL. *À la for chetty*; excuse my French, judge. [*They pass each other food, etc.*] Libby, dear, remember your *ton*, and only eat just a little.

LIBBY. Yes, aunty. [*She takes leg of chicken and hiding behind Slote, eats ravenously*]

DART. Lord Cairngorm, may I help you to some chicken?

LORD C. No, thank you. I think I will stick to the roast beef of old England.

DART. Pete—some wine.

PETE. Yes, sir. [*Pours wine for each*]

DART. Gentlemen, will you see that the ladies are served? Fried chicken, quail, tongue.

LIBBY. Pass the tongue to aunty.

MRS. GIL. Libby! [*Slote takes chicken leg in his fingers*]

CHAR. A fork, judge? [*Passes him one*]

SLOTE. Not for fresh fried chicken, my boy. [*Eats with fingers*]

LORD C. Mr. Slote—will you kindly pass the tomato. [*Pronounces it toe-maw-to*]

SLOTE. I will if you will pass the po-taw-to.

MRS. GIL. Wouldn't it be lovely if we had some music?

LORD C. By Jove, it would—an orchestra.

DART. Or a song—Judge Slote—do you sing?

LIBBY. I'm sure he can.

SLOTE. My friends, who have heard me say that I do not—

DART. Now, good people, if you will fill your glasses we will drink to the health of the ladies, and Mr. Slote, with that charming eloquence which is his shining light, will respond to the toast. [*The men hold glasses up*] The ladies! [*They drink*]

SLOTE. [*Kneeling up and holding glass*] Fellow citizens—I mean, ladies and gentlemen and colored brethren. [*Bowing to Pete*] I have been honored by an invitation to address a few words to you upon this glorious occasion, where there is plenty to eat, and more to drink. I have been selected by our noble host to respond to the first toast, The Ladies. O woman, woman, lovely woman, the pride of our hearts, the sunshine of our lives, without you we would all be in—

DART. [*Passing soup*] The soup—

SLOTE. O woman—lovely, cheering, talkative woman. It is on record that woman started the first argument with man, for what did she say to Adam?

MRS. GIL. [*Business*] Apples.

SLOTE. O lovely woman, when weak man dares to oppose thee, what is the result?

CHAR. Pepper.

SLOTE. O woman, woman, lovely, consoling woman, what would man be without you?

DART. Lobster.

SLOTE. Woman, sweet woman, what is the dearest wish of thy woman's heart?

LIBBY. Pie. [*Reaches across tablecloth and grabs pie*]

MRS. GIL. Libby, dear!

SLOTE. O woman, gentle woman, always true and tender as—

LORD C. Chicken.

SLOTE. O woman, attractive woman, what is it draws us to you?

CHAR. Mustard.

SLOTE. O woman, adorable woman, with your charming qualities of heart and mind, you will always take—

MRS. GIL. The cake.

SLOTE. [*Bows to her*] My dear Mrs. General Gilflory, you are K.K., quite correct. [*Blanche enters, L.U.E., leading Vance by hand*]

BLAN. Come along, Roland, here we are—just in time. Come along. [*Leads him down R., where he turns to face the others, who all welcome them. Some rising, others making room for them. Clara has risen and when she and Vance meet face to face, she screams and falls into Charley Brood's arms, he standing near enough to catch her. All become confused*]

CHAR. Water—water! Get some water!

SLOTE. Whiskey, whiskey—[*Pulls out flask and goes to her*]

ACT III.

SCENE: *Room in Dart's house, handsomely furnished; chamber, boxed, with open entrance, arched, at back C., opening on to a balcony, and showing balustrade and view of country beyond. Balcony is two steps up from stage. Practical doors, R.3.E., and L.3.E. The door, R.3.E., has lock and key. Hatrack or hall tree, up R. A screen, up L., piano at L.2.E. Fireplace at R.2.E. Secretary [open] with writing materials and chair, down R. Covered table with books and album, down L.C. Circular ottoman, C. Other furniture and bric-a-brac to make it well furnished. At rise, Clara Dart discovered seated at writing desk, down R., and Blanche on settee, C.*

BLAN. Dear Clara, I am so unhappy when I think of my selfish vanity and the pain it has caused you. When I told you of my happiness you rejoiced with me, and in the pride of my heart I gave no thought of the ache that might be in yours, and when you and Roland met face to face and the shock was too great for you to bear, I knew then for the first time that you were not strangers, but had met before, and that there was more in your lives than a mere society acquaintance. It is but natural that I should wish to know more, and I have questioned Roland, but can learn nothing from him, so I have come to ask you to relieve my anxiety.

CLARA. Blanche, dear, why will you insist on worrying yourself over insignificant trifles which have probably passed out of Mr. Vance's memory long ago?

BLAN. No, no, Clara. It was no trifle which chilled your heart at the sight of one man, nor have they passed out of his memory. I cannot help worrying, for he is so changed since that afternoon; he is not the same these last few days, and I am sure there is some secret, some mystery which is clouding all our hearts, so I have come to you, as I always did in the past, for your advice and sympathy.

CLARA. What cloud can there be upon your heart, my dear child? Am I not married to Mr. Dart, and are you not engaged to Mr. Vance?

BLAN. Yes, but may he not have loved you once? And may you not have loved him?

CLARA. Blanche—Blanche—[*Libby enters, L.2.E., with card, which she takes to Clara*]

LIBBY. O Clara, dear—a friend of yours has just called to see you. Shall I show him up?

CLARA. [*Looking at card*] Roland Vance! [*To Libby*] No, no!

BLAN. I will go.

CLARA. Remain here.

LIBBY. [*Goes to L.2.E.*] O Clara—Mr. Vance is up here now.

CLARA. Detain him a moment, on any pretext—detain him till I send you word.

LIBBY. All right—I'll talk to him for you. [*Exit*]

BLAN. Clara, I must know what this all means, what is hidden behind this mystery.

CLARA. My dear Blanche, do not let yourself become disturbed by all the slight events which you do not clearly understand. Mr. Vance is nothing more to me than any other caller, I assure you; there is nothing between us, nothing.

BLAN. Then there can be no harm in your receiving Roland in the presence of his affianced wife.

CLARA. Blanche! Why will you insist on seeking to revive a dead and uninteresting past? My dear child, you must not let every little doubt or question worry you, if you would spend a life of happiness.

BLAN. It is those very doubts which would make my life miserable. If he has loved you once, has he ceased to care for you, and if you have loved him, may you not love him still?

CLARA. O Blanche, Blanche—why do you torture the hearts that love you! [*Pause*] Oh, well, the mystery must be cleared up sometime, perhaps it were better now than if doubt should become suspicion.

BLAN. Conceal me somewhere—where I may overhear what passes.

CLARA. What? You—Blanche Thurston, whom I have always thought the soul of honor, you ask as a favor permission to become a spy? an eavesdropper? You who have always been so frank and openhearted?

BLAN. I am a woman, and above all a woman who loves with all her soul, and I must learn at any cost whether the man I love is unworthy.

CLARA. You will not be satisfied when I tell you that he is in every way worthy of a good woman's love. But you shall do as you wish, but remember, if evil comes of it, it was of your own seeking.

BLAN. I will accept the consequences; let the cost be mine, but there must be no word of warning—no glance or sign to put him on his guard.

CLARA. Rest assured you shall know all. [*Places her behind screen, up L.*] Here concealed behind this screen you can see and hear everything. [*Returns, R. Aside*] So the blow has come at last, and the old sweetheart has in her hands the happiness of the new one! But he loves her, and I—

VANCE. [*Off L.2.E.*] Thank you, I will go to her now, if I may.

CLARA. [*Stiffens*] Now for the trial, and my agony. [*Vance enters, L.2.E., bows coldly. She is polite and frigid*]

VANCE. Mrs. Dart.

CLARA. Good morning, Mr. Vance.

VANCE. I should have called upon you some time ago to inquire after your health, but was suddenly called away from Washington and only returned last night.

CLARA. You are very kind—will you be seated?

VANCE. Thank you, it will hardly be worth while. I shall not detain you long.

CLARA. To what am I indebted for the honor of this visit? Some business, I presume?

VANCE. To be brief, I have called upon you to ask, to beg, that you will not tell Blanche anything of the past in our lives. I love Blanche Thurston, and if for one moment I have wavered in an unswerving loyalty to her pure and unselfish devotion, it was because the fascination of your society has bridged over the past few years and revived the scenes which made me forget that you had ever caused me to suffer. It is all over now, the past is dead. What joy and sorrows there were are only a memory; and to save a trusting, unsuspecting heart from such a sorrow I now ask you to keep our secret.

CLARA. Never fear. The past is dead—I shall say nothing of it to anyone. I promise to keep our secret.

VANCE. Thank you. I am grateful for the assurance.

CLARA. If you have nothing more to add, I presume we may consider this interview at an end. [*Speaks choking, and with difficulty*]

VANCE. I appreciate your frankness, Mrs. Dart, and hasten to withdraw. I had hoped to meet Col. Dart here to demand an explanation, but will call upon him some other time.

CLARA. Colonel Dart will be happy to receive your call. [*Vance takes his hat*] Permit me to congratulate you on securing the love of such a woman as I know Blanche to be. May you be very happy together.

VANCE. Thank you. It shall be the earnest hope of my life to become in every way worthy of her deep and true love. [*Clara has back turned to him*] Do not let us part as enemies. [*Goes to her*]

CLARA. No—not enemies—only strangers. [*Bows, exit, R.2.E.*]

VANCE. [*Crushed*] She despises me! She despises me. Oh, well—so be it. It is better so—better so. [*Turns, L.*]

BLANCHE. [*Comes from screen*] One moment!

VANCE. Blanche—you here?

BLAN. Yes—I have heard everything.

VANCE. You were concealed there—behind that screen! You have played the spy. And she was a party to it. Nay, it was her plot—she sought to ruin me, and she has accomplished it.

BLAN. No, Roland—it was all my fault, it was my doing.

VANCE. Yours? You in whom there was never a thought of deceit?

BLAN. Roland, dear—do not blame her. If evil came of it, it was of my own seeking, but the suspense was gnawing at my heart. I loved you so much, dear, and I was afraid.

VANCE. Afraid?

BLAN. O Roland, you do not know what suspense means to a loving woman's heart. But let us forget the past that is dead. Let us leave this house, with its luxury and wretchedness. Come, dear Roland, I will never question you, never reproach you.

VANCE. Blanche, you have shown that you have no trust in me. You, or whose faith I would have staked my life! O Blanche, you are cruel—unjust.

BLANCHE. And you reproach me with want of faith, you whom I loved and trusted—Heaven knows how I trusted you—you reproach me because feared the mystery that linked your life with hers? You were hiding it from me—a secret that was yours and hers—you were trying to hide from me that I was not your first love, but that you had once loved my dearest friend. I trusted you and you deceived me. I cannot trust you again. Farewell, Roland, a woman's heart can only love where it can trust—farewell. [*Exit, L.2.E.*]

VANCE. [*Sadly*] I will not call her back. She would only despise me the more. I will leave this place at once. Why did I ever enter it? It is accursed, this abode of gilded misery. [*Going to L.2.E., Dart enters*]

DART. O Vance—not going, are you?

VANCE. Yes—just going.

DART. Can you spare a few moments? I have been seeking you, and am lucky to find you where we can have a word or two in comfort. [*Motions him to sit*]

VANCE. [*Sits, L.*] I am at your service, Colonel Dart.

DART. I hear you have a few hundred acres of land in Muggins Glen which has very little prospect of ever commanding more than a nominal price.

VANCE. Yes—twelve hundred acres—a bequest from my father.

DART. Now you know I am always in some political speculation or other, and I want a few acres of clear land in that neighborhood. Would you be willing to part with it?

VANCE. [*Amused and surprised*] Willing to part with it? My dear sir, are you in earnest?

DART. Certainly—or I should not have asked you the question.

VANCE. Well—I only wished to warn you of the nature of the land, for fear you might repent of your bargain afterward. The land is clear out of the world—a wilderness of rocks and sand, and I didn't want to take an unfair advantage of you by selling to one who evidently knew nothing regarding its actual value.

DART. What does that matter to you as long as I can make it answer my purpose, and am willing to pay a good price for it?

VANCE. Oh, nothing, of course, except that I don't want to take you in with your eyes closed.

DART. Oh, that is my risk, of course; you newspaper men have really no idea of the risks involved in speculation. Now what do you consider a fair price for the tract as it stands, or to be more practical, what will you take for it?

VANCE. Well, the whole twelve hundred acres are taxed at twelve hundred dollars, which I suppose is its full value.

DART. It is taxed at twelve hundred dollars. I will give you fifteen hundred dollars for it—what do you say?

VANCE. [*Aside*] Fifteen hundred dollars! [*Elated*] With that sum I could leave this place and find a new and nobler field for my pen and brain. [*To Dart*] I will accept your offer.

DART. Very well. I will write my check for the amount at once and you can give me your receipt.

VANCE. Certainly. [*Goes up, C., while Dart sits at desk and writes, then Vance sits at desk and writes*]

DART. [*Aside while Vance writes*] If the railroad goes that way I shall have paid fifteen hundred dollars for fifty thousand. [*Vance rises*] Here is my check, Mr. Vance, fifteen hundred dollars. [*Gives him check*]

VANCE. Very well, Mr. Dart. Here is the receipt. The transfers can be made as soon as the papers are prepared. I wish you joy of your purchase.

DART. Oh, that is my lookout. I am greatly obliged to you. [*Taking hat*] You will excuse me for leaving you now. I have some rather important matters to attend to. So I will say "Au revoir."

VANCE. Certainly. Au revoir. [*Dart exits L.2.E.*]

MRS. GIL. [*Heard outside, L.U.E.*] Libby, dear. Libby, dear. [*Appears at back*] Where has that child got to? I hope she is not talking to that horrid little Charley Brood again. [*Enters, goes down C., and sits, L. Vance is down R. and she does not see him*] Oh, these dreadful stairs! I declare they make me all out of breath every time I climb them. By the number of steps and corners and turns I have taken since I left the sidewalk, I should certainly say I had reached the fifth story, and must be nearly up to the roof by this time. I can't understand why people that live in such houses can't have alleviators for visitors, instead of letting them climb so many stairs. I wonder where Libby dear can be? She ought to come when she hears my voice. [*Looks around, sees Vance*] Why, I believe there is the identical young man I have been seeking. Hum—hum. [*Coughs, he looks*] I beg your pardon, but are you Mr. Vance?

VANCE. [*Bowing*] Vance is my name, madam, but I am at a disadvantage.

MRS. GIL. I am Mrs. General Gilflory.

VANCE. Oh, yes—I have heard so much of you. I almost feel as if I had the pleasure of knowing you.

MRS. GIL. I'm glad of that, because you are just the gentleman I want to see.

VANCE. You flatter me. In what way can I serve you?

MRS. GIL. You are in Congress, aren't you?

VANCE. No, madam, I have not that honor.

MRS. GIL. Oh, well, it's very much one and the same thing—the voice o the press is just as powerful as the voice of Congress, and it very often reaches farther. Mr. Vance, I want you to do me a favor.

Vance.   I shall be pleased to, if it is in my power.

Mrs. Gil.   I thought you would. I have heard so often how kind Mr. Vance is, and I am sure you have great influence among the members of Congress. Now there is a Railroad Bill coming before the House, and I want some assistance from you in getting it passed.

Vance.   Well, that depends upon who are the promoters of the railroad, and who is behind the bill.

Mrs. Gil.   Oh, there are some of our best citizens interested in the railroad. There is Colonel Dart, and Judge Slote, and Mr. Watkins of Tennessee, and Major Wilson of Kentucky, and half a dozen others, all prominent men.

Vance. [Sarcastic]   A reputable party, truly.

Mrs. Gil. [Sarcasm is lost]   Oh, yes, they are quite a reputable party. There is no doubt about that. There is a question yet as to which way the road shall run; some want it to go through Chalkville, while the others say it must go through Muggins Glen.

Vance. [Aroused]   Muggins Glen, do you say?

Mrs. Gil.   Yes. Colonel Dart and his party want it to go through Muggins Glen, but Judge Slote and all the rest of us are in favor of Chalkville.

Vance. [Enraged]   Now I understand his eagerness to purchase my land, and I have sold a fortune for a song!

Mrs. Gil.   Why, what is the matter, Mr. Vance? You seem terribly angry about something. Has anything I said offended you?

Vance.   No, Mrs. Gilflory, there is nothing the matter, but you can depend upon me, the road shall not go through Muggins Glen if I can prevent it. [Goes to L.U.E.] Duped! Swindled! Tricked! But I'll beat him yet! I'll beat him yet! [Exit]

Mrs. Gil.   Well, upon my word, that young man seems to be in a towering rage about something. There's a friend for you! But it's just like the world —willing enough to ask for favors, but when anyone asks a friend for a favor in return, the friend takes himself off in a raging passion. But hold on— am I right? I wonder if I had it right, or have I got it twisted around. Was it Chalkville that Judge Slote wanted, or Muggins Glen? Let me see—yes— surely Judge Slote said Chalkville—of course he did. Yes, it was Chalkville— I remember distinctly. Now, I'm positive it was Chalkville.

Slote. [Enters, back C. from L.]   Oh, my dear Mrs. General Gilflory, I am delighted to see you.

Mrs. Gil.   Thank you, judge—I am very glad to see you.

Slote. You overwhelm me with joy, my dear Mrs. General Gilflory. I am indeed fortunate to find you alone—are you quite well?

Mrs. Gil. Quite well, thank you, and you? I hope you are well also?

Slote. Thank you, my dear Mrs. General Gilflory. I was not in the best of condition at the hour of rising this morning.

Mrs. Gil. O judge—nothing serious, I hope?

Slote. Nothing serious, my dear Mrs. General Gilflory. I presided at a committee meeting last night, and the cares of state weighed heavily upon my brow this morning, but a judiciously applied J.C., gin cocktail, repeated two or three times, has put me, if I may be pardoned for using the expression, upon my pins again, by a large majority.

Mrs. Gil. I am much relieved to know that you are entirely recovered from your *malade*—excuse my French, judge.

Slote. May I inquire, my dear Mrs. Gilflory, if you have executed the little favor I asked a short time ago?

Mrs. Gil. Oh, yes—I have seen Major Watkins and Colonel Wilson and several other members, and they have all consented to work for our side. They say we shall be too strong for any opposition, and the road will be sure to go through Chalkville.

Slote. [*In horror*] Chalkville!

Mrs. Gil. Oh, yes—I worked hard for two whole days, and got at least a dozen votes, and Chalkville will win.

Slote. Chalkville? Murder! G.I.C. Our goose is cooked!

Mrs. Gil. Why, what is the matter?

Slote. My dear madam, we must get those votes back. Where is Vance? He can help to put us right.

Mrs. Gil. Oh, Mr. Vance is on our side, too.

Slote. What? You haven't said anything to Vance, have you?

Mrs. Gil. Oh, yes—I saw him here only a few minutes ago, and he says we can depend upon him to do all he can for us.

Slote. Worse and more of it! We are G.U., gone up. My dear Mrs. Gilflory—gone up by a large majority. We must see Vance—he is a newspaper man.

Mrs. Gil. Oh, yes—I saw him.

Slote. What did he say?

Mrs. Gil. The young man was too much excited to say much, but he says the road shall not go through Muggins Glen if he can prevent it.

Slote. [*Wild*] Did he say that? Did he say that?

Mrs. Gil. Yes.

Slote. Why, he is a P.A., a perfect ass. He is whipping himself into the poorhouse. He owns land in Muggins Glen, and he must want the road to go that way. His case is ours. He will help us with his freedom of the press. Now go, my dear Mrs. Gilflory—go at once and see your friends. Retract what you have said under a mistaken impression, and secure the votes for Muggins Glen before it is too late, and I will be your E.F., your everlasting friend. If you succeed, the bill will go through swimmingly and we shall be A.H., all hunky. We only need those twelve votes, and they are in your hands.

Mrs. Gil. Did I understand you to say that Mr. Vance owned some land in Muggins Glen?

Slote. He does—a thousand acres or somewhere near it.

Mrs. Gil. [*Aside*] Now I begin to understand some of his remarks. [*To Slote*] Very well, judge, I will do what I can. I shall not forget Mr. Vance nor Muggins Glen. [*At back, C.*] However, I do not think I should make a good lobbyist. [*Going back, C.*] Shades of the late General Gilflory, look down upon me! [*Turns to Slote*] Gros bébé! [*Exit, back C. to L.*]

Slote. [*Alone*] Now she calls me a cross baby. Well, maybe she's right, I suppose I am a cross baby, by a large majority, but this railroad switching business is enough to make a wooden Indian take to drink. Now what is the matter with Vance? Why can't he work for the road to come our way? It's his way, too—has he no bowels for speculation? [*Dart's voice heard outside*]

Dart. The House stands within a dozen votes of a tie.

Slote. Here's Dart. I'll advise him to buy Vance's land at Muggins Glen, and when the road goes that way I will be even for that political dodo. [*Dart and Walter Saville enter, back C. from R.*]

Dart. I suppose you have heard that the road is to go through Muggins Glen?

Sav. Indeed I have heard nothing of the kind. In fact, I happen to know that it will not.

Slote. What do you mean?

Sav. I mean that we are going to send it round the other way, and have already got enough votes to do it.

Dart. But I only need half a dozen votes to carry it my way, and for those few votes I am prepared to make quite a sacrifice.

Sav. But not large enough to influence the result, as far as I am concerned.

Slote. What? Do you mean to say you are going to vote to send it round the other way?

Sav. I certainly am.

SLOTE. M.P., merciful powers! Is that the way you serve your friends in this free and enlightened country?

SAV. I propose to serve the best interests of the people I represent, and do my duty to my constituents.

SLOTE. Oh, damn your constituents! Think of your duty to yourself. If the road goes our way it will be a glorious victory for our pockets, and if it goes the other way, we shall all G.L., get left.

SAV. When I wish to barter my honor, sir, I will join you, sir, and not until then.

SLOTE. What do you mean by applying such language to me, sir? I will demand satisfaction at the bar of the House, sir, and have you read out of the party, sir, if you dare to insinuate that I barter my honor!

SAV. No, sir, for I have yet to discover that you have any honor to barter.

SLOTE. [*Raging*] H.M., Holy Moses! Listen to me!

SAV. No, sir, listen to me. It is such men as you that bring disgrace upon the government of this great country. You tricksters, the tools of rings and the creatures of grasping corporations, with your hands ever outstretched to receive the paltry bribes for which you are willing to betray every confidence reposed in you. You are the men who make politics a laughing stock and statesmanship a byword.

SLOTE. [*Emphatic, slaps hands*] I wish you to distinctly understand, sir, that in all the years I have been in Congress, I have never received one cent, sir, not one red cent.

SAV. [*Imitating*] No, sir, but you expect to, sir.

SLOTE. I do, sir, by a large majority, and in recognition of my great and valuable services I have been appointed one of the counsel for this corporation.

LORD C. [*Enters, back C. from L.*] The result will soon be known, they are counting the votes.

MESSENGER. [*Enters and goes to Saville*] The people are with us, Mr. Saville, and it looks very much like Chalkville.

SLOTE. Damnation! [*Cheers outside*]

LORD C. In passing along the street I observed a large number of bulletins which read "Chalkville versus Muggins Glen."

DART. [*Enters, back C.*] Muggins Glen is leading now, but only by two or three votes. [*Mrs. Gilflory enters at back, C., excited and out of breath*]

MRS. GIL. I've done it—I've done it! I have seen them all, and they are to a man for Chalkville. [*Slote collapses, Dart in a rage. Mrs. Gilflory dazed, Saville laughing. Libby enters with Charley to make picture. Vance appears, L.2.E., smiles*]

ACT IV.

SCENE: *Same as Act III. Clara Dart discovered seated at secretary, down R., reading a letter.*

CLARA. [*Reads*] "You will, I hope, forgive me for having dared to pass the barrier with which you have surrounded yourself, and regard me as one who seeks a friend in the time of need. You have within your hands the power to make two lives happy by reuniting the hearts which a moment of wounded pride has separated. I have no one else to whom this appeal could be made, and I throw myself upon your magnanimous and forgiving nature with the earnest prayer that your generous heart may be reached, for the sake of what has been in the days gone by. Yours, With respect. Roland Vance." [*Musing*] How strange that Roland should look to me again as the source of his happiness! Oh—what tricks time plays with us all! But if it is to reconcile him and Blanche I shall do as he asks, and try to give him the happiness which I can never know. [*Writes*] "Dear Roland, Come to me at once. I will do all I can to make you happy. We have been too much to each other in the past to live as strangers now. Yours in friendship, Clara Dart. [*Dart enters at back, C.*] My husband! He must not see the letter. [*Folds paper hastily and puts it in pigeonhole of desk*]

DART. [*Going to her*] O Clara dear, writing some letters?

CLARA. [*Confused*] Yes—one or two, that is, I was about to write a letter.

DART. Don't let me disturb you. [*She half rises*] No, no, I don't want to sit down. [*She sits*] The fact is I am very much annoyed at that fellow Slote, the blunderer—his stupidity has caused all my plans to fail, so I have at last decided to change my methods considerably, and I'm going to write him a few plain words telling him that I have resolved to sever my connection with him entirely. [*Reaches for paper, gets near her sheet*]

CLARA. No—no—don't take that—it's only half a sheet.

DART. [*Takes it*] Just a small piece I want.

CLARA. Here—take this, dear—here is some with your monogram on it.

DART. [*Going to table, L.*] Never mind—this will do very well. [*Writes*]

CLARA. My letter to Roland! If he sees what is written on the back of it I shall be lost! What shall I do?

DART. There—just a few short sharp words—but enough to make him understand what I think. [*Puts sheet in envelope*]

CLARA. [*Aside*] That letter must not go! How can I get it. [*Goes to him*]

DART. Just a few words canceling all arrangements for the future that I have made with him.

CLARA. [*Coaxing*] Don't send that letter, dear.

DART. [*Gentle*] Why not?

CLARA. Mr. Slote is very touchy, you know, and it would only make you more trouble, and you have enough already.

DART. Don't let that worry you, little woman. He won't try to make any trouble for his own sake—because no man wants to tell the world that he has been bribed. No, no, my dear—Slote is perfectly harmless.

CLARA. Then let me have it, and I will give it to one of the servants to deliver.

DART. No, no, my dear, I won't trouble you. The fact is I want him to get it at once, before he has time to do any more mischief. I will send it by special messenger. [*Going to L.2.E.*] I won't be gone long, dear, and when I return I shall have something to say to you about our plans for the new house. [*Exit, L.2.E.*]

CLARA. What shall I do! I must get that letter before it reaches its destination. When Judge Slote reads it he will be angry, and when he sees what I have written on the other side—my message to Roland—he will revenge himself on me. What shall I do?

MRS. GIL. [*Enters, back C.*] Why, my dear Mrs. Dart, what is the matter? You are so excited! Has anything happened?

CLARA. Mrs. Gilflory, I am in great trouble. [*Aside*] How can I tell her?

MRS. GIL. Oh, do tell me what it is! I love to hear about other people's troubles. They help me to forget my own.

CLARA. Come and sit here. [*Sits on settee, C.*]

MRS. GIL. Now for a real nice gossip. I have been trying for the last two hours to find someone to gossip with.

CLARA. Mrs. Gilflory—I am sorely in need of a friend who will help me, and if you will do me a very great favor I will not forget it as long as I live.

MRS. GIL. My dear child—I will not only do anything I can, but will ask you to forget it the very next minute.

CLARA. You are a great friend of Mr. Slote's, are you not?

MRS. GIL. If Mr. Slote will do as he says he would, that statesman would imperil his professional integrity for my sake. I really believe if I demanded it, he would lie for me.

CLARA. I want you to go to him at once and ask him to return unopened a letter which is on its way to him now.

MRS. GIL. A letter? Dear me! Is it as romantic as all that? I do love anything that has romance in it, and letters always have, especially when they are from a woman and she wants them returned to her.

CLARA. Oh, no, this is not a romantic letter. It is quite a plain business one.

MRS. GIL. A business letter—good gracious, I hope it is nothing about railroads, or Chalkville or Muggins Glen. I have just got my brain out of the muddle it was in about those dreadful votes, and I don't want another attack.

CLARA. Oh, no, there is nothing about railroads in it. It is just a plain everyday letter, but I must have it back. Get it, my dear Mrs. Gilflory. Get it any way you can, beg—borrow—or steal it—anything to get it. If that letter is opened and read, I am lost.

MRS. GIL. There, there, my dear Mrs. Dart, don't worry about it. I will do everything I can.

CLARA. I shall never be able to repay you.

MRS. GIL. Don't say a word about paying. A woman who would not stand by another in a case like this is not worthy of the name of woman, especially when it is all so romantic.

CLARA. I am so anxious—my heart is so full of dread!

MRS. GIL. My dear Mrs. Dart, make your mind perfectly easy—remember I am your friend, and Mrs. General Gilflory was never known to fail—never, never, never.

CLARA. [Both rising] I thank you with all my heart. You will excuse me if I leave you now. I am so unnerved, I must be alone—I go to watch and pray. [Exit, L.2.E.]

MRS. GIL. [At hatrack, up R.] Yes, that's right, my dear—a little prayer will do you good. [Alone, putting hat and wrap on hatrack] Oh, dear—what a week I have had of it! I never had so much excitement crowded into a week before, not even in all my travels through Europe, except that time when I got lost in the kittycombs in Berlin, or was it Constantinople? No, it was the Walhalla Hall we saw in Berlin, and the dried-up mummies in Constantinople, so it must have been Naples where the kittycombs were. Oh, they were just lovely—and so was the Dodges Palace in Rome and the Tragedians Arch in Venice, and the Campanilly at Nice. But those mummies just made the cold chills run all up and down my back. [Libby enters, L.2.E., running, with two tickets]

LIBBY. O aunty, such news! You could never guess!

MRS. GIL. You tomboy! You positively gave me a fright that will upset my nervous system for the rest of the day—why can't you have some ton, and be more dignitary and sedative.

LIBBY. But look, aunty. Two invitations to the President's Ball!

MRS. GIL. [Greatly interested] The President's Ball! O Libby! Tickets to the President's Ball and I haven't got a thing to be seen in, and Worth a thousand miles away! O Libby—what can I wear? Was there ever an unfortunate woman so blasé as I am. [Sits at desk, R.] Not a rag fit to be seen in.

Libby. Why can't you wear that white satin you brought from Paris?

Mrs. Gil. Oh, I hate white satin.

Libby. Well—wear the pink brocade with black velvet collar you bought in London.

Mrs. Gil. I always look like a fright in pink. You know it doesn't suit my complexion.

Libby. Then try old gold.

Mrs. Gil. Oh, pshaw, everybody buys old gold that can buy anything at all. Oh, dear—why can't you tell me what to wear? I must wear something, that's certain. [*Jumps up*] And I am forgetting all about that letter. Mrs. Dart will never forgive me if I don't get it. Well—I will go straight to Mr. Slote's hotel and get it now, if I have to break into his room and steal it, and then I'll think about the President's Ball when I get the letter off my mind. [*Putting on hat and wrap*] But suppose I should be arrested for burglary or highway robbery or something? Dear—if ever I do another favor for anybody I shall demand security against possible disaster. [*Going, up C.*] Oh, dear— if I don't come back in an hour, go to the police station for me. [*At back, C.*] Shades of the late General G., look down upon me and tell me what color to wear at the President's Ball! [*Exit, L.*]

Libby. Everything seems to be going crisscross with everybody today. Oh, well, I suppose we can't expect to have our own way always—and Aunty Gilflory is determined not to let me have mine—but I mean to have my way, and to have Charley Brood, too. It would have been all settled long ago if he had only had the courage to propose to me. I've made up my mind that if he doesn't propose to me I'm going to propose to him—somebody's got to do it, sure, and it's no use being so very goody-goody about a little thing like that, especially when I know he would do it himself if he could muster up the courage.

Char. [*Enters, back C. from R.*] Hello, Libby.

Libby. Well, Mr. Brood—and what are you doing here?

Char. Oh, I heard that you were in here, so I came, too.

Libby. But, Charley, don't you know you ought not to follow me around a strange house like this, unless [*Pointed*] you have some motive?

Char. Well, he does.

Libby. He does? Who's he?

Char. Why, that Lord Cairngorm.

Libby. But he has proposed for my hand, you know, and Aunt Gilflory approves of it.

Char. Well, ain't I as good as he is? You bet I am.

Libby. Yes, of course you are, but you can't do what he did.

CHAR. Oh, yes I can! [*Aside*] It's got to be done. It's no use putting it off any longer. [*To her*] Libby—Libby!

LIBBY. [*Aside*] It's coming at last.

CHAR. Libby—O Libby.

LIBBY. [*Encouraging*] Yes, Charley?

CHAR. Libby—O Libby—how is it done?

LIBBY. You silly goose! [*Charley kicks himself and she gets album from table, L. and sits C.*] Charley—see what lovely pictures these are.

CHAR. [*Sore*] Oh, damn the pictures—no, no, I mean—yes, they are very pretty of course.

LIBBY. See—those are views of all the places we visited when we were abroad—come and sit down here and I will tell you about them. [*He sits beside her, she trying to get him to put his arm around her, with business which accompanies her words*]

CHAR. Will you hold the book?

LIBBY. Yes, I'll hold it. [*Pause*] Oh, it's too heavy.

CHAR. Let me take it.

LIBBY. Yes—you hold it—there. [*He takes it*] That is the Cathedral at Milan—see the tall spire. [*Leans back on him so that her head is in front of his*]

CHAR. You'll have to hold it yourself. I can't see anything this way.

LIBBY. Oh, dear, how awkward you are! Here, you hold one side and I'll hold the other. [*Settles down to lean on him*] There—isn't that better?

CHAR. Yes, lots.

LIBBY. [*Pointing and turning*] That is the Chateau of Fontainebleau and that is the Leaning Tower of Pisa. Oh, dear—I can't do anything when you hold the book like that. You'll have to hold both sides. [*Tries to get him right*] Don't you know how to hold a book yet? [*Takes his R. hand and guides it to corner of book, leans back on him and looks under her L. arm for his other hand*] There, can't you see better now?

CHAR. [*Catching on*] Oh, I know how to hold it now. [*Puts his L. arm round her and holds book*]

LIBBY. At last! [*Sigh of relief, leans head on his shoulder*] Now I can turn the pages. That is the Bridge of Sighs—and, O Charley, you ought to see it by moonlight! It is just beautiful. That group of marble statuary on the other side is called Cupid and Psyche—isn't it lovely? [*He assents*] See what an expression of happiness Psyche has on her face? [*Coyly*] Cupid is about to kiss her.

CHAR. I suppose that is the reason she has the expression on her face?

LIBBY. I suppose so. I can't think what else it could be, can you, Charley?

CHAR. No.

LIBBY. [*As she lies back*]   See—she lays her head back on his shoulder—so. [*Lying back, looks up at him, he kisses her quickly and jumps up frightened*]

CHAR.   I couldn't help it, Libby. I couldn't help it, really I couldn't.

LIBBY.   Who said you could help it, booby?

CHAR.   I thought I was Cupid and you were Psyche. I beg your pardon, but honest I couldn't help it. You're not angry, are you, Libby?

LIBBY. [*Laughing*]   Do I look angry, Charley? [*Sits on settee, he behind her, with head over her shoulder*]

CHAR.   I love you, Libby—I love you devotedly, wretchedly.

LIBBY.   O Charley! Do you really?

CHAR.   Yes, and I have loved you for a long time, but I never had the courage to tell you so till now.

LIBBY.   Oh, I knew that six months ago, and have been trying to make you say so.

CHAR.   You wanted me to say so? And you don't love Lord Cairngorm?

LIBBY.   Of course I don't, and never did.

CHAR.   O Libby!

LIBBY.   O Charley! [*Embraces and kisses him. Slote appears at back, C., sees them, coughs and turns back, with comedy business, for few seconds. They separate*]

SLOTE.   Scat! Here comes Mrs. General Gilflory. [*They run away, she L.1.E., he to R.1.E. She puts head out*]

LIBBY. [*In low tone*]   O Charley.

CHAR. [*Head out*]   Yes?

LIBBY.   How much is five times five?

CHAR.   Twenty-five. O Libby.

LIBBY.   Yes?

CHAR.   How much is five times six?

LIBBY.   Thirty. Scoot! [*Both disappear. Slote comes down and sits on settee, looks through album*]

SLOTE.   Twelve times twelve are one hundred forty-four.

CHAR. [*Enters and goes to Slote*]   Judge Slote, are you alone? [*As he enters he looks about stealthily and tiptoes to Slote, and speaks in dramatic whisper*]

SLOTE.   I am in solitary magnificence, my boy—by a large majority.

CHAR.   I want to say a few words to you, and I hardly know how to begin.

SLOTE.   All men are born free and equal. Go ahead.

CHAR.   Well, in the first place—I—that is—we—in the first place, you see— I mean I want you to see—well, you perceive my emotion.

SLOTE.   I do, and I second it.

CHAR. Second what?

SLOTE. I second your emotion.

CHAR. That is just what I want you to do.

SLOTE. The question?

CHAR. I want you to act as my friend in a delicate and very important matter.

SLOTE. I am invaluable in such cases.

CHAR. Judge Slote, I am in love, awfully in love.

SLOTE. So I see.

CHAR. And with Miss Libby Ray—Mrs. General Gilflory's niece.

SLOTE. So I see.

CHAR. I have been in love for a long time and never had the courage to tell her so till today, but I did it, and my love is returned.

SLOTE. Didn't she want it?

CHAR. I mean my love is reciprocated.

SLOTE. Oh, yes—I thought she had adopted a rather unusual way of expressing dislike for you.

CHAR. She loves me as I love her, and we want to get married.

SLOTE. Of course.

CHAR. But her aunt objects.

SLOTE. Objection overruled.

CHAR. Mrs. Gilflory has set her face against our union, and wishes Libby to bestow her hand upon Lord Cairngorm, who has blue blood in his veins, and a pedigree, with barrels of *ton*. Of course, Libby could have hosts of offers from other fellows.

SLOTE. Yes—they all do.

CHAR. But I know it would break her heart if she was forced into a marriage with a man she hated.

SLOTE. Undoubtedly.

CHAR. Now you are always popular with the ladies and you are on excellent terms with Mrs. Gilflory; she would do a great deal for you. [*Slote swells up*] I want you to go to her, as my friend, plead with her, reason with her. Judge Slote—have you ever loved?

SLOTE. [*Looks blank*] What?

CHAR. Have you ever loved? [*Slote winks*]

SLOTE. By a large majority.

CHAR. Then you can feel for one who loves in vain. Go to Mrs. Gilflory, tell her how devotedly I love her niece, and that our future happiness is at stake, but you will know what to say far better than I could tell you—and if you succeed, you can have anything I have got.

SLOTE. [*Rises quickly*] I am retained?

CHAR. You are.

SLOTE. Then I will take the case. I will see Mrs. General Gilflory, and before you are forty-eight hours older, my boy, you shall have her consent.

CHAR. Good. Leave no word unspoken, no stone unturned, and if you succeed you may command my gratitude and my purse.

SLOTE. I will, by a large majority.

MRS. GIL. [*Heard, back L.*] Libby, dear—Libby, dear—where are you? Libby—O Libby. [*Enters, back C., Charley runs off through door, R.2.E.*] O Judge Slote, have you seen anything of Libby dear?

SLOTE. [*R.C.*] I regret that I have not, my dear Mrs. General Gilflory.

MRS. GIL. [*Down, L.C. Aside*] Now is my chance to get that letter for Mrs. Dart!

SLOTE. My dear Mrs. General Gilflory, I have a word to say to thee.

MRS. GIL. Why, Judge Slote, what makes you look so serious? [*Aside*] What can be the matter with the man? He looks like a disappointed pelican. [*Sitting, L.*] I am listening. [*He is standing, R. of settee, C., with one foot across the other, leaning on settee with L. hand, and R. hand in vest, making a pose*]

SLOTE. Madam, I am a queer old fish.

MRS. GIL. You certainly are a queer old fish.

SLOTE. Did you ever read *The Children of the Abbey?*

MRS. GIL. No—I never did.

SLOTE. Nor have I.

MRS. GIL. But I have read *All of a Twist*, and *Great Expectorators.*

SLOTE. I have not.

MRS. GIL. But why do you ask?

SLOTE. [*Solemnly*] My dear Mrs. General Gilflory, you have a young lady stopping with you, your niece, I believe—

MRS. GIL. Yes—Miss Libby Ray—I am her aunt.

SLOTE. Oh, my dear Mrs. General Gilflory. There is nothing so dear, nothing so dear to me, as Mrs. General Gilflory.

MRS. GIL. Why, Judge Slote—I declare you are quite a poet.

SLOTE. Yes, and while on the world's stage and playing my part I have frequently felt Cupid's keen little dart.

MRS. GIL. Well, you don't look it.

SLOTE. And I believe I can feel it now.

MRS. GIL. [*Aside, fluttering*] I wonder if he is going to propose? Shades of the late General Gil., look down upon me! [*Charley enters, R.2.E., and comes behind Slote*]

CHAR. [*Loud whisper*] Is it all right, judge? [*Slote is taken by surprise, kicks out behind and nearly falls, Charley escapes unseen by Mrs. Gilflory, who is frightened*]

MRS. GIL. [*Down L.*] What was that? [*Slote resumes pose and smiles blandly*]

SLOTE. Nothing, my dear Mrs. General Gilflory. Oh, you mustn't mind me. I have an impediment in my speech.

MRS. GIL. Then please don't have an impediment again. They make me nervous. Besides, I have heard they are catching.

SLOTE. My dear Mrs. General Gilflory—what book is that you are about to look at? [*She has the album*]

MRS. GIL. This is an album. It contains views of all the foreign places we visited while we were abroad. This one on the right is Brussels.

SLOTE. That's where the carpets come from.

MRS. GIL. [*Annoyed*] No. They make lace there. Carpets, indeed! That picture on the left is Venice. And there is the house where Othello lived.

SLOTE. Othello?

MRS. GIL. Yes. Othello was a Moor. Don't you remember him? He married Ophelia and was beheaded in the Tower of London.

SLOTE. No. I never met him. The only Moor I ever got acquainted with was in the 37th Congress, but he was Moore of Michigan.

MRS. GIL. [*Turning page*] This picture here is the Colossial of Roads, and that one over there is the Leaning Tower of Pisa.

SLOTE. That must be an awful ticklish job of building.

MRS. GIL. *Vous avez raison.*

SLOTE. [*Mystified*] Yes—I have got a razor. [*Aside*] What the deuce can she want with a razor?

MRS. GIL. And here is the Lake of Chromo where Claude Melnotty lived.

SLOTE. [*Shakes head*] Never met him.

MRS. GIL. Don't you know Claude Melnotty? He was one of Bolivar's heroes. He was originally a contractor, but like the late General Gilflory, he rose to be a quartermaster in the Army. Oh, I just adore Bolivar.

SLOTE. Do you?

MRS. GIL. Yes.

SLOTE. I wish I was Bolivar.

MRS. GIL. You do?

SLOTE. I do.

CHAR. [*Enters as before*] Say, judge, is it all right? [*Same business as before, but more so*]

MRS. GIL. [*After recovering*] Mr. Slote, excuse me, but the next time you are going to have a fit, if you will kindly let me know, I will leave you to enjoy it by yourself.

SLOTE. [*Meekly*] My dear Mrs. General Gilflory. P.D.G., please don't go. I have a favor to ask of you and I hope you will grant it before I ask it.

MRS. GIL. I will if I can. What is it? [*Aside*] I never saw him act so queerly. I believe he is really going to propose.

SLOTE. Oh, my dear Mrs. General Gilflory, you would not blight two loving hearts by a stern and unrelenting opposition to their united happiness, would you?

MRS. GIL. [*Aside*] It's coming now. [*To him*] Really, Mr. Slote, your question is rather sudden. I hadn't given it a thought.

SLOTE. Then I beg that you will now, and one of your own generous noble-hearted thoughts.

MRS. GIL. [*Aside*] It's coming.

SLOTE. Let Charley Brood have Libby.

MRS. GIL. [*In rage*] What? Let that young bump of conceit marry my niece! Most decidedly not. I have set my heart on her marrying Lord Cairngorm and I will never consent to her marriage with Charley Brood. He is a perfect donkey, so are you—so am I—no No! I don't mean that. But I have set my heart on a brilliant match for Libby dear, and Lord Cairngorm has proposed for her hand. I don't intend to let her become plain Mrs. Brood when I can have a real lord for a nephew. [*Suddenly recollects*] I shall never get that letter now. [*Changes to smile*] But you must not be angry. I did not mean to say as much as I did, and Libby dear is good enough for a lord's wife.

SLOTE. My dear Mrs. General Gilflory, you are a guardian angel. [*Standing, R. of settee. She sits near him*]

MRS. GIL. Mr. Slote—dear Mr. Slote.

SLOTE. [*Aside*] What is coming now?

MRS. GIL. My dear Mr. Slote, you received a letter this afternoon. [*Lays hand caressingly on his vest. He moves money from one pocket to another*] A very important letter.

SLOTE. Yes, I received a letter, but it was only a short note about the Railroad Bill—[*Aside*] or a bar bill.

MRS. GIL. But there is another letter. It was written to you this afternoon, and it must be at your hotel now.

SLOTE. Very likely, I guess it will be there by the time I get back.

MRS. GIL. Oh, yes, it will be sure to reach you. Now, my dear Mr. Slote, I want you to do me a very great favor. Won't you go to your hotel and get that letter for me? There was some mistake in sending it, it is very important, and if you will only get it and give it to me, I shall be under everlasting obligation to you, and you will make two miserable women happy. [*While speaking she has hand on his vest. He moves money to pants and turns vest pockets out*]

SLOTE. Then I will go to my hotel at once and get that letter without any more ado.

MRS. GIL. [*Pleased*] Go now, my dear Mr. Slote, and I will pray for your eternal happiness.

SLOTE. [*Going, up C.*] I go, my dear Mrs. General Gilflory. I go on the wings of devotion. [*At back, C., turns*] B.M., baby mine, by a large majority. [*Exit to L.*]

MRS. GIL. Now he's off my mind, so's the letter, and I can think about the President's Ball. I'm going to have a better dress than that detestable old Mrs. Moneybags over the way, or my name is not Mrs. General Gilflory. [*Libby heard singing, off R.U.E.*] There's my niece. I might as well put a stop to this Charley Brood nonsense, now and for all.

LIBBY. [*Enters, C. from R.*] O aunty. I am so glad I found you.

MRS. GIL. You are in disgustingly good spirits again, when you know you ought to be drooping and languid.

LIBBY. I can't help it, aunty. I am too happy to droop.

MRS. GIL. Excited over the President's Ball, I suppose?

LIBBY. No, aunty, it's ever so much better than that. I have proposed to Charley Brood.

MRS. GIL. What? Libby!

LIBBY. [*Calmly*] Yes. I have proposed, and been accepted.

MRS. GIL. [*Bewildered*] Libby! You—you proposed and have been accepted!

LIBBY. Yes, and all we want now is your consent.

MRS. GIL. [*Gasping*] Great Pyramid of Chops! Has the girl gone out of her seven senses, or have I? [*Sits on chair, L.*]

LIBBY. I haven't gone out of any of my senses. I promised Charley I would marry him as soon as he could get a flat ready, but we didn't want to go to housekeeping before we had your consent, and that's what we came to ask you for now. I expect Charley in every minute.

MRS. GIL. [*In rage*] And you want my consent to marry that young imbecile—oh, you—you—come here! [*Grabs her*] A pretty mess you've made of it! After all my teaching and example! I'm tired of this Charley Brood nonsense and I won't have any more of it. I'll put a stop to this silly little boy and little girl business. Do you see that room there? You just go in there and wait till I come back. Go on in—go on in, and stay in. [*Libby protests, but Mrs. Gilflory pushes her to R.2.E. and off. Locks door and takes key, then puts on hat and wrap*] Now I've done it. [*In triumph*] I'll have no love-making in my absence. Now I must go to Mr. Slote's hotel and get that letter. He has been gone so long I'm getting desperate. I must have that letter if I have to break open his door, or tear the hotel down. [*At back, C.*] Shades of the late General G., keep an eye on me! [*Exit to L. Clara and Blanche enter, L.2.E.*]

BLAN. O Clara, how can I ask you to forgive me. In the pride of my heart I would not listen to your words of friendship, but believe me, I have been well punished for my unreasoning curiosity. I have insulted Roland. He has resented it, for I have not seen him since he left me in righteous indignation. If the opportunity offers, will you not explain it all to him?

CLARA. With all my heart, dear. But I may not see him again forever, perhaps.

BLAN. I have started to write to him half a dozen times, but could not express my feelings as I would wish to. [*Vance enters, L.2.E.*]

CLARA. [*Facing L., sees him*] Mr. Vance!

VANCE. Pardon me. The servants told me I should find Mr. Dart here, or I should not have intruded.

CLARA. Mr. Dart may return at any moment. Won't you wait for him?

VANCE. Thank you. I wanted to make an explanation which I owe him before I go away.

BLAN. [*In dread*] Go away?

VANCE. Yes, Blanche. I have resolved to leave this place at once and forever, and in the busier scenes of a new country find a wider field for my pen, and forget what I have suffered here.

CLARA. Roland, do not let a moment's wounded pride bring a life's unhappiness to the two dearest friends I have. Young hearts are easily broken, and true love is too precious to be thrown aside for a single error.

VANCE. You are right. [*Offers hand to Blanche*] Blanche, let us forget and forgive.

BLAN. With all my heart. [*They embrace*]

CLARA. I am so happy to hear you say that. [*Turning away, aside*] If they only knew what those words cost me! [*Sad. Slote heard, off R.U.E., loud voice and angry*]

SLOTE. Where is he? Where is he? Show him to me! The W.T., the worthless traitor! Where is he? [*Enters, back C., with open letter*]

VANCE. What is the matter? Have you gone crazy, to come into a man's house like this? [*Blanche and Clara alarmed and mystified*]

SLOTE. No, sir, not by a large majority! Where is he?

CLARA. [*Sees letter*] My letter! [*Goes to him. All try to quiet him and find out what's the matter*]

VANCE. What's the matter with you now?

CLARA. Whom do you wish to see?

SLOTE. Let me see him—where is he? Where is the traitor—Dart? I want to see Dart—the villain! The traitor!

CLARA. Perhaps Mr. Dart can explain matters if you will give him an opportunity?

VANCE. What's he done to you now? You'd better wait and see if he can't explain it.

SLOTE. No, sir. He can't explain it. The Dart is not sharp enough, there's no explaining to it—this letter explains itself.

VANCE. But what has he done to you?

SLOTE. What has he done, sir? He has done everything, sir. Everything, sir. Does he think he can treat me like a peanut? Eat the rich kernel from the inside and then cast aside the empty shell? Cast aside into the gutter? But he can't do it, sir. No, sir, not by a large majority, sir! [*Waves letter*]

CLARA. [*Down R., aside*] He hasn't seen what is written on the other side yet. [*Goes to him*] Let me see the letter, Mr. Slote, perhaps I can explain something. [*Reaches for it, he snatches it away*]

SLOTE. No, madam. That letter shall never leave my hand.

CLARA. But perhaps there is some mistake?

SLOTE. No. madam! There is no mistake. It is all P.P., perfectly plain, madam, as plain as the nose on my face—this nose, madam, which has been likened to the corresponding organ of the great American eagle, that royal bird of freedom, the emblem of our country.

CLARA. But if I were to give you an explanation?

SLOTE. [*Interrupts*] If you were to explain it, madam, it would be T.T., too thin. This letter explains itself. It is an insult—a stab in the dark.

VANCE. But we could understand the matter more thoroughly if we knew what your complaint is all about.

SLOTE. My complaint, sir! It is my R.I., sir, my righteous indignation! To think that such words should be addressed to me!

VANCE. I'm sure I could explain them if I knew what they were.

SLOTE. You can explain, can you? Look at that! Look at that! You explain it if you can. [*Gives Vance letter*]

VANCE. [*Reads*] "Honorable Bardwell Slote, M.C. Dear Sir: In view of the serious and annoying misunderstandings which seem to be caused by our joint management, I wish to inform you that henceforth I shall dispense with your assistance and endeavor to conduct all my affairs unaided. Respectfully,

Alfred Dart!" [*To Slote*] All I can see is that Mr. Dart declines to associate himself with you in any further business, that's all.

SLOTE. And isn't that enough! The ungrateful wretch! After all I have done for him! [*Vance turns letter over, sees writing and reads it, wonderingly*]

VANCE. "Roland, come to me at once." [*Slote snatches letter*]

SLOTE. After I have been going about bribing honest people, and making them believe it was all legitimate business? After all the talking and lying that I have done for him! Cast me off! Throw me aside! Kick me out. It's B.I., base ingratitude, that's what it is.

VANCE. I can't see why you want to make such a fuss about a trifle like that.

CLARA. [*Tries to get letter*] Come into the library with me; we can talk it over with a glass of Mr. Dart's best sherry. Let me put the letter in my desk.

SLOTE. [*Gives it to her*] Lock it up! Lock it up. [*Snatches it*] Never mind, I'll take care of it. I will find the traitor—I will hunt the villain down, I will have his worthless life! I will track him like a Comanche Indian, and when I meet him I'll kill him! Kill him! By a large majority. [*Exit, back C. to L., raving*]

VANCE. There is not much to be feared from a man who talks like that.

BLAN. He would not kill a fly in cold blood. [*Mrs. Gilflory enters, back C. from R., and out of breath, hurries to Clara, down R., with six or seven letters*]

MRS. GIL. I've got it! I've got it! Mr. Slote wasn't at the hotel and I was bound to get it for you so I broke open the door of his room. There were a lot of letters lying around and I didn't know which was yours, so I took all I could get my hands on. Here they are, my dear—you know I would do anything for you.

CLARA. [*Coldly*] It is too late!

MRS. GIL. [*Disappointed*] Too late! Oh, pshaw! I'm always too late, or too soon, or something. [*Dart's voice heard, off L.U.E.*]

DART. [*Outside*] If anyone calls, show him in, Pete. [*Enters*]

CLARA. [*Hears Dart's voice*] Sh! [*Mrs. Gilflory retreats, up R. Dart enters*]

DART. [*Severe*] Mr. Vance, I am surprised to see you here after the hostile sentiments expressed so freely on our last meeting.

VANCE. In view of my intended departure for the West, I have made my just resentment subservient to my sense of duty. Mr. Dart, I have called to defend the good name of your wife, which has been coupled with mine by venomous tongues.

DART. [*Interrupts*] My wife's good name needs no defender, and if it ever should, there is only one man who has the right to champion her cause, and that man is her husband, who will be here to do it.

SLOTE. [*Heard, off L.U.E.*] Where is he! Where is he! Where is the traitor! [*Enters*] Oh—here you are! Read this, sir! Look at it! Look at it! [*Gives him letter*]

CLARA. [*Aside*] I am lost!

DART. [*Glancing at it*] I know what it is—it's my letter canceling all future dealings with you.

SLOTE. Read on, read on.

DART. [*Turns it over and reads*] "Roland—come to me at once. We have been too much to each other in the past. Clara." [*Looks at her. She has head bowed. Vance and Blanche silent, up L.C.*]

SLOTE. Are you all crazy? All crazy? By a large majority! Crazy! [*Raving, rages off L.U.E.*]

DART. [*To Vance*] How dare you remain beneath this roof, where your presence is an insult to me!

CLARA. [*Pleading*] Tom! Husband! Let me speak. Do not judge till you have heard all.

DART. Heard! I have seen. My eyes cannot deceive me. Did you write those lines? [*Clara silent*]

MRS. GIL. [*Near her. Aside*] Now for it! [*To him*] She did write them, but not for herself—she wrote them for me.

DART. For you?

MRS. GIL. Yes. You see, I wanted to go to the President's Ball, but I had no one to go with, so I thought I would ask Mr. Vance to take me, but I was so very busy I hadn't got time to write to him, so I asked Mrs. Dart to please write a few lines for me. "Roland, come to me at once," and so on, and that's what she wrote, only she signed her own name to it instead of mine. [*Winking and nodding to Vance*] Wasn't that it, Mr. Vance?

VANCE. Certainly.

CLARA. [*Aside*] Saved!

DART. [*Goes to her, down C.*] Clara! If this is so I must beg your forgiveness for my hasty and unjust suspicions.

MRS. GIL. That's right, old man. You ought to ask her pardon.

CLARA. [*To Mrs. Gilflory*] God bless you—you are a real friend.

MRS. GIL. Oh, I tell you we poor women have got to stand by each other when it comes to tight places. [*Lord Cairngorm enters, back C., followed by Slote*]

DART. Oh, there is Lord Cairngorm. Welcome, my lord. [*Others are pleased to see him*]

LORD C. Oh, dear friends! I have called to bid you all a reluctant farewell.

ALL. [*Regretfully*] What? Are you going away?

LORD C. Yes, I regret to say that family affairs demand my presence in England. My trunks are packed and my steamer sails from New York to-morrow.

MRS. GIL. We're awfully sorry to lose you.

LORD C. Thanks, my dear Mrs. General Gilflory, I assure you my recollections of your charming country will be most pleasant. The visit has benefited me immensely.

SLOTE. Allow me to congratulate you.

LORD C. [*Coldly*] Oh, thanks! [*Aside*] Presumably intended for a joke, or a sarcasm or something! Mr. Slote is one of the most remarkable products of a new country. I shall miss his cheerful imbecility. [*Goes to Mrs. Gilflory, down R.C.*] My dear Mrs. Gilflory, I am compelled to appear in the peculiar position of suitor for the hand of your charming niece.

MRS. GIL. [*Delighted, interrupts him*] O Lord Cairngorm!

LORD C. On behalf of my young friend Mr. Charley Brood, who has not the courage to speak for himself.

MRS. GIL. [*Angry*] What? Let Libby marry Charley Brood! No, sir. If she is fool enough to marry him, of course I can't help it, but I tell you once and for all I will never give my consent to it—so there!

CLARA. Where is Libby? I haven't seen her all the afternoon.

LORD C. Where is the young lady? [*Others join in*]

MRS. GIL. I have her safely locked up in this room here—I was determined to keep her away from that young monkey. [*Goes to door, R.2.E.*] I'll let her out now. [*Opens door*] Libby, dear—you may come out now. Come along, you will be a good child now, won't you? [*Brings Libby out with Charley holding onto her hand. Mrs. Gilflory staggers*] Shades of the late General Gil., look down on me! [*Turns on Charley*] You young scamp! [*To Libby*] Go home this minute. Go to your room and don't you dare to come out for a week, and then I'll take you to Europe with me.

LIBBY. Don't be angry, aunty dear, Charley and I love each other, and we want to get married.

SLOTE. My dear Mrs. General Gilflory, do not be so cruel as to cast the blight of separation upon two loving hearts. Love will not grow to order, and little Cupid shoots his arrows without consulting us more practical people. Let their young dreams of happiness be realized, my dear madam, and remember there are others.

MRS. GIL. O judge—your eloquence is irresistible! I surrender a discretion.

SLOTE. And you will give your consent?

MRS. GIL. Yes.

CHAR. Judge, you're all right. [*Takes out roll of bills and begins to count. Slote grabs the roll*]

SLOTE. Never mind about counting them. [*Goes down, L.*]

MRS. GIL. [*Down C.*] Libby, dear. [*With much ceremony*] Come here. Stand here. [*She obeys*] Young man come here. [*To Charley*] *Approchez, approchez.* [*He does. She gets them in front of her, Libby, R., Charley, L.*] Take her hand. Libby, dear— put your hand in his. That's right, Libby, dear. This is not quite what I had intended for you, but I want to see you happy, and I don't believe I could ever make you learn to have any *ton* or *noblesse oblige*. [*To Charley*] Take her, young man, take her, and make her happy. Heaven bless you, my children. *J'ai faim. J'ai faim.* [*Sinks back on settee, C., with resignation*]

DART. Clara, my wife, will you forgive me for my unjust suspicions? If I loved you less I should not be so jealous.

CLARA. My husband! The best and noblest of men! [*Embraces him*]

DART. [*Offers hand to Vance*] Roland, forgive me if I have seemed too anxious to secure financial gain. Let us be better friends in the future. I will give up political speculation and strive to earn the good will of my fellow men.

VANCE. You have always deserved it.

DART. [*To Slote*] Mr. Slote, I shall not forget you, nor that we have had many interests in common, and if I can aid you to climb the political ladder you may rely on my support, even to the presidential chair.

SLOTE. And there's where I am going to land, by a large majority.

LORD C. One of the remarkable conditions of a new country, that the road is open to him, and a man may be my employee today, and my president in the future.

SLOTE. My dear Mrs. General Gilflory, I am on the road—shall we travel together?

MRS. GIL. O judge—really?

SLOTE. Really—if you want me—grab me! [*She goes to him*] By a large majority!

CURTAIN

AMERICA'S LOST PLAYS

I. *Forbidden Fruit & Other Plays*, by DION BOUCICAULT. Forbidden Fruit. Louis XI. Dot. Flying Scud. Mercy Dodd. Robert Emmet. Edited by ALLARDYCE NICOLL and F. THEODORE CLOAK.

II. *False Shame and Thirty Years*, by WILLIAM DUNLAP. False Shame; or, The American Orphan in Germany. Thirty Years; or, The Gambler's Fate. Edited by ORAL SUMNER COAD.

III. *Glaucus & Other Plays*, by GEORGE HENRY BOKER. The World a Mask. The Bankrupt. Glaucus. Edited with introduction and notes by SCULLEY BRADLEY.

IV. *Davy Crockett & Other Plays*. Rosedale; or, The Rifle Ball, by LESTER WALLACK. Across the Continent; or, Scenes from New York Life and the Pacific Railroad, by JAMES J. McCLOSKEY. Davy Crockett; or, Be Sure You're Right, Then Go Ahead, by FRANK MURDOCH. Sam'l of Posen; or, The Commercial Drummer, by GEORGE H. JESSOP. Our Boarding House, by LEONARD GROVER. Edited by ISAAC GOLDBERG and HUBERT HEFFNER.

V. *Trial Without Jury & Other Plays*, by JOHN HOWARD PAYNE. Trial Without Jury; or, The Magpie and the Maid. Mount Savage. The Boarding Schools; or, Life Among the Little Folks. The Two Sons-in-Law. Mazeppa; or, The Wild Horse of Tartary. The Spanish Husband; or, First and Last Love. Edited by CODMAN HISLOP and W. R. RICHARDSON.

VI. *The Last Duel in Spain & Other Plays*, by JOHN HOWARD PAYNE. The Last Duel in Spain. Woman's Revenge. The Italian Bride. Romulus, the Shepherd King. The Black Man; or, The Spleen. Edited by CODMAN HISLOP and W. R. RICHARDSON.

VII. *The Early Plays of James A. Herne*. Within an Inch of His Life. "The Minute Men" of 1774-1775. Drifting Apart. The Reverend Griffith Davenport, Act IV. Edited with an introduction by ARTHUR HOBSON QUINN.

VIII. *The Great Diamond Robbery & Other Recent Melodramas*. A Royal Slave, by CLARENCE BENNETT. The Great Diamond Robbery, by EDWARD M. ALFRIEND and A. C. WHEELER. From Rags to Riches, by CHARLES A. TAYLOR. No Mother to Guide Her, by LILLIAN MORTIMER. Billy the Kid, by WALTER WOODS. Edited by GARRETT H. LEVERTON.

IX. *Five Plays* by CHARLES H. HOYT. A Bunch of Keys. A Midnight Bell. A Trip to Chinatown. A Temperance Town. A Milk White Flag. Edited by DOUGLAS L. HUNT.

X. *The Banker's Daughter & Other Plays*, by BRONSON HOWARD. Hurricanes. Old Love Letters. The Banker's Daughter. Baron Rudolph. Knave and Queen. One of Our Girls. Edited by ALLAN G. HALLINE.

XI. *An Arrant Knave & Other Plays*, by STEELE MACKAYE. Rose Michel. Won At Last. In Spite of All. An Arrant Knave. Edited, with introduction, by his son PERCY MACKAYE.

XII. *The Cowled Lover & Other Plays*, by ROBERT MONTGOMERY BIRD. The Cowled Lover. Caridorf; or, The Avenger. News of the Night; or, A Trip to Niagara. 'Twas All for the Best; or, 'Tis All a Notion. Edited by EDWARD H. O'NEILL.

XIII. *The Sentinels & Other Plays*, by RICHARD PENN SMITH. The Sentinels; or, The Two Sergeants. The Bombardment of Algiers. William Penn (Incomplete). Shakspeare in Love. A Wife at a Venture. The Last Man; or, The Cock of the Village. Edited by RALPH H. WARE and H. W. SCHOENBERGER.

XIV. *Metamora & Other Plays*. Metamora; or, The Last of the Wampanoags, by JOHN AUGUSTUS STONE. Tancred, King of Sicily; or, The Archives of Palermo (Fragment), by JOHN AUGUSTUS STONE. The Spy, a Tale of the Neutral Ground, by CHARLES POWELL CLINCH. The Battle of Stillwater; or, The Maniac, by H. J. CONWAY (?). The Usurper; or, Americans in Tripoli, by JOSEPH STEVENS JONES. The Crock of Gold; or, The Toiler's Trials, by SILAS S. STEELE. Job and His Children, by J. M. FIELD. Signor Marc, by JOHN H. WILKINS. The Duke's Motto; or, I Am Here! by JOHN BROUGHAM. Edited by EUGENE R. PAGE.

XV. *Four Plays* by ROYALL TYLER. The Island of Barrataria. The Origin of the Feast of Purim; or, The Destinies of Haman & Mordecai. Joseph and His Brethren. The Judgment of Solomon. Edited by ARTHUR WALLACE PEACH and GEORGE FLOYD NEWBROUGH.

XVI. *Monte Cristo & Other Plays*. Monte Cristo (JAMES O'NEILL's version), by CHARLES FECHTER. Hippolytus, by JULIA WARD HOWE. Mistress Nell, by GEORGE C. HAZELTON. Becky Sharp, by LANGDON MITCHELL. The Warrens of Virginia, by WILLIAM C. DE MILLE. Edited by J. B. RUSSAK.

XVII. *The Plays of Henry C. De Mille*, written in collaboration with DAVID BELASCO. The Main Line, by HENRY C. DE MILLE and CHARLES BARNARD. The Wife, by DAVID BELASCO and HENRY C. DE MILLE. Lord Chumley, by HENRY C. DE MILLE and DAVID BELASCO. The Charity Ball, by DAVID BELASCO and HENRY C. DE MILLE. Men and Women, by HENRY C. DE MILLE and DAVID BELASCO. Edited with an introductory essay by ROBERT HAMILTON BALL.

XVIII. *The Heart of Maryland & Other Plays*, by DAVID BELASCO. La Belle Russe. The Stranglers of Paris. The Girl I Left Behind Me, by DAVID BELASCO and FRANKLIN FYLES. The Heart of Maryland. Naughty Anthony. Edited with an introduction and notes by GLENN HUGHES and GEORGE SAVAGE.

XIX. *The White Slave & Other Plays*, by BARTLEY CAMPBELL. The Virginian. My Partner. The Galley Slave. Fairfax. The White Slave. Edited by NAPIER WILT.

XX. *Man and Wife & Other Plays*, by AUGUSTIN DALY. Man and Wife. Divorce. The Big Bonanza. Pique. Needles and Pins. Edited with Introductory Notes and a Play List by CATHERINE STURTEVANT.